The Franchise Handbook

A Guide to Companies Offering Franchises

Published by DMR Publications, Inc., Milwaukee

THE FRANCHISE HANDBOOK
Published May, 1981
Standard Book Number 0-89552-026-5

©1981
DMR Publications, Inc.
1410 E. Capitol Drive
Milwaukee, Wisconsin 53211

We acknowledge the aid of the U.S. Department of Commerce Domestic and International Business Administration and the Office of Minority Business Enterprises, whose research made this book possible. We further acknowledge the help of Mr. Collin Weschke, Secretary of the International Franchise Association.

TABLE OF CONTENTS

Introduction.................................... I
   What is Franchising I
   Investing in a Franchise...................... I
   Code of Ethics.............................. III
   Checklist for Evaluating a Franchise.......... IV
Franchise Companies 1
Index of Franchising Companies 106
   By Category 106
   Alphabetical 113

INTRODUCTION

Franchising is both an old and new concept. The term from the French originally meant to be free from servitude. Its meaning in the context of present-day promotions is the opportunity for one to own his own business even if inexperienced and lacking adequate capital. During recent years, franchising, as a type of business operation, has been expanding rapidly and entering into new areas of application. Statistical evidence of such expansion is contained in the study entitled *Franchising the Economy*, published annually by the Bureau of Industrial Economics. The latest study, covering the period 1978-80 reveals that franchised businesses accounted for $312 billion in annual sales in 1979 equal to 32% of all retail sales.

What Is Franchising?

Franchising is a form of licensing by which the owner (the franchisor) of a product, service or method obtains distribution through affiliated dealers (the franchisees). The holder of the right is often given exclusive access to a defined geographical area.

The product, method or service being marketed is identified by a brand name and the franchisor maintains control over the marketing methods employed.

In many cases the operation resembles that of a large chain with trademarkes, uniform symbols, equipment, storefronts, and standardized services or products, and maintains uniform practices as outlined in the franchise agreement.

The International Franchise Association, the major trade association in the field, defines franchising as "a continuing relationship in which the franchisor provides a licensed privilege to do business, plus assistance in organizing, training, merchandising, and management in return for a consideration from the franchise."

A former president of the International Franchise Association described franchising as "a convenient and economic means for the filling of a drive or desire (for independence) with a minimum of risk and investment and maximum opportunities for success through the utilization of a proven product or service and marketing method." However, the owner of a franchised business must give up some options and freedom of action in business decisions that would be open to the owner of a non-franchised business.

In a way, the franchisee is not his own boss because in order to maintain the distinctiveness and uniformity of the service and to insure that the operations of each outlet will reflect favorably on the organization as a whole—to protect and build its good will—the franchisor usually exercises some degree of continuing control over the operations of franchisees, and requires them to meet stipulated standards of quality. The extent of such control varies. In some cases franchisees are required to conduct every step of their operation in strict conformity with a manual furnished by the franchisor—and this may be desirable.

In return the individual franchisee can share in the good will built up by all other outlets which bear the same name.

A company which depends upon the successful operation of franchise outlets needs men who are willing to learn the business and have the energy for a considerable amount of effort; it can supply the other essentials for successful operation of the outlet. Among the services franchisors may provide to the franchise operators are the following: 1) location analysis and counsel; 2) store development aid, including lease negotiation; 3) store design and equipment purchasing; 4) initial employee and management training, and continuing management counseling; 5) advertising and merchandising counsel and assistance; 6) standardized procedures and operations; 7) centralized purchasing with consequent savings; and 8) financial assistance in the establishment of the business.

Investing in a Franchise

Be Aware of Risks

Everyone knows that there is some risk in investing money in the stock market. Investing in a franchise is not much different. In some ways the risks are even greater than the risks of buying stock. After all, if you buy a franchise you usually expect to invest not only your time, but a good part of your working life.

Some franchises carry a greater degree of risk than others. There are "blue chip" franchises which, like "blue chip" stocks, are offered by companies with a track record of successful operation. There are also high-risk franchises that are offered, like speculative stocks, by new companies without a proven track record, or by some fly-by-night operators.

The risk of buying a franchise is usually greater than the risk of buying a stock for another reason. When you buy stock, you are relying only on the business skills of the company that issued the stock. When you buy a franchise, you are relying not only on the business skills of the franchisor, but also on your own business aptitude and experience. If you give up a good job to purchase and operate a franchise, you will obviously have a lot more to lose than your financial investment if the franchise does not work out.

Protect Yourself By Self Evaluation

How can you protect yourself against making a mistake in buying a franchise? No answer to that question is 100 percent reliable. But there are some important steps you can take before you make a commitment to buy a franchise that may help to reduce the risk.

The first step, and often the most difficult, is to take a hard look at yourself. Ask yourself whether you are really willing to make the personal sacrifices—long hours at the franchise, hard work, financial uncertainty—that are often necessary for a successful business. Do you enjoy working with others? Are you a good supervisor? Are you an organized person? Or are you simply attracted by the potential profits?

Some franchisors will help you to take this careful look at yourself. A reputable franchisor, after all, is investing in you because the franchisor will profit from your continued success. Others may only check to be sure that you have the necessary money or credit to invest. In that case, you will have to do your best to ask these questions yourself. Your family and friends can make an important contribution to your self evaluation, and their answers will probably be more objective than the answers of a franchise salesman.

Protect Yourself By Investigating The Franchise

The second step is to investigate the franchisor and the franchise business as thoroughly as you can. The best way to proceed is to do what most people do when they buy a new car or a new home. Do some comparison shopping — look at more than one franchise, just as you would look at more than one car or house before deciding to buy.

If you have only talked with one franchisor about its franchise, the most important step you can take to protect yourself is to look at other similar franchises in the same line of business. This Franchise Opportunities Handbook will help you get started, since the first part of the index categorizes franchisors by the type of franchise they offer.

Look at the brief descriptions in this Handbook of the franchises offered of the type you are considering. But don't stop your investigation there. Call or write to at least a few of the franchisors listed in the same category for more detailed information. You may discover that some of them offer benefits not available with the franchise you have been considering.

Protect Yourself By Studying Disclosure Statements

If the initial information you receive from a franchisor does not include a disclosure statement (sometimes called an "offering circular" or "prospectus"), be sure to ask for one. It will be a great help in comparing one franchise with another, understanding the risks involved, and learning what to expect and what not to expect from the franchise in which you finally decide to invest. You should study the disclosure statement carefully before making an investment decision.

Franchisors are now required by law in 14 states to provide disclosure statements to prospective franchisees, and will soon be required to provide them to prospective franchisees in every state under federal law. A trade regulation rule issued by the Federal Trade Commission that will require the nationwide use of disclosure statements in the sale of franchises went into effect on October 21, 1979.

The disclosure statement will contain detailed information on some 20 different subjects that may influence your decision to invest or not to invest:

1. Information identifying the franchisor and its affiliates, and describing their business experience.

2. Information identifying and describing the business experience of each of the franchisor's officers, directors and management personnel responsible for franchise services, training and other aspects of the franchise program.

3. A description of the lawsuits in which the franchisor and its officers, directors and management personnel have been involved.

4. Information about any previous bankruptcies in which the franchisor and its officers, directors and management personnel have been involved.

5. Information about the initial franchise fee and other initial payments that are required to obtain the franchise.

6. A description of the continuing payments franchisees are required to make after the franchise opens.

7. Information about any restrictions on the quality of goods and services used in the franchise and where they may be purchased, including restrictions requiring purchases from the franchisor or its affiliates.

8. A description of any assistance available from the franchisor or its affiliates in financing the purchase of the franchise.

9. A description of restrictions on the goods or services franchisees are permitted to sell.

10. A description of any restrictions on the customers with whom franchisees may deal.

11. A description of any territorial protection that will be granted to the franchisee.

12. A description of the conditions under which the franchise may be repurchased or refused renewal by the franchisor, transferred to a third party by the franchisee, and terminated or modified by either party.

13. A description of the training programs provided to franchisees.

14. A description of the involvement of any celebrities or public figures in the franchise.

15. A description of any assistance in selecting a site for the franchise that will be provided by the franchisor.

16. Statistical information about the present number of franchises; the number of franchises projected for the future; and the number of franchises terminated, the number the franchisor has decided not to renew, and the number repurchased in the past.

17. The financial statements of the franchisors.

18. A description of the extent to which franchisees must personally participate in the operation of the franchise.

19. A complete statement of the basis for any earnings claims made to the franchisee, including the percentage of existing franchises that have actually achieved the results that are claimed.

20. A list of the names and address of other franchisees.

Protect Yourself By Checking Out The Disclosures

After you have read the disclosure statement carefully, and have compared it to other disclosure statements, you should check the accuracy of the information disclosed. A good way to start is to contact several of the franchisees listed in the disclosure statement, and ask them about their experience in the business. They can tell you whether the information provided, and any other claims that are made by the franchisor accurately reflect their experience in the business.

Be sure to talk to more than one franchisee. No single franchisee can ever be a very adequate representative of a franchise program. He is likely to be either better than the average franchisee or below average. If the franchise is worth considering at all, it should be worth your time to talk to three or more franchisees. While you may wish to talk to franchisees recommended by the franchisor, you should also make a point of talking to franchisees who have not been recommended.

Look for franchisees who have been in the business for at least a year. If none has been in business that long because the franchise is a new one, the risks you will run by investing in the franchise will obviously be higher than those you would face if you invested, instead, in a well established franchise with an established track record in your area.

You should also talk to franchisees who have been in business for only a few years. They are the ones who will be able to give you the best advice about what to expect during your first year of operation. That is important because the first year of operation is often the period during which the success or failure of a new franchise is determined.

Protect Yourself by Questioning Earnings Claims

If the franchisor or its representatives makes any claims about the sales, income, or profits you can expect from the franchise, you should examine these earnings claims carefully, and demand written substantiation for them. Remember: earnings claims are only estimates and there is absolutely no assurance that you will do as well.

Franchisors are now required by law in 14 states to provide detailed substantiation to prospective franchisees of any earnings claims they make. A trade regulation rule issued by the Federal Trade Commission is scheduled to extend that protection to prospective franchisees in every state after October 21, 1979.

This documentation of earnings claims, which will either appear in the disclosure statement or in a separate document, is required whenever an earnings claims is made — whether it is presented orally, in writing, or in advertising or other promotional materials. It is required regardless of whether the earnings claim is based on actual or projected results, or an average figures for all franchisees as opposed to arbitrary figures met by a small number of franchisees.

You should examine the documentation carefully and be certain you understand the basis for the earnings claim and the assumptions that were made in preparing it. Ask yourself what would happen if an assumption proved to be wrong. For example, what if the wages you must pay employees turn out to be higher than predicted or if you must pay a higher than usual rate of interest for any financing you need in order to obtain the franchise?

If you do nothing else, be sure to note what percentage of the franchisor's present franchisees have actually had sales, profits or income that equalled or exceeded the amount claimed. Then find out how many franchisees did that well during their first year of operation, when their operating results may not have been as good. Your own first year operating results are more likely to be like those of other first-year franchisees who have been in business for several years.

Protect Yourself By Obtaining Professional Advice

You would be well advised to obtain independent professional assistance in reviewing and evaluating any franchise you are considering. Such assistance is particularly important in reviewing the financial statements of the franchise and the franchise agreement to be signed.

The reason state and federal law requires franchisors to include their financial statements in the disclosure statement is to permit you to determine whether the franchisor has adequate financial resources to fulfill its commitments to you. The financial statements will reveal to a professional accountant, banker or other experienced business advisor whether a franchisor's financial condition is sound, or whether there is a risk that it will not be able to meet its financial and other obligations.

Unless you have had considerable business experience, you may need professional assistance in reviewing the franchisor's financial statements to determine whether special precautions should be taken to insure that you receive the services and assistance that have been promised in return for your investment. The cost of securing this advice before you invest will be a small price to pay if it saves you from getting involved with a franchisor that cannot meet its obligations.

The advice of a lawyer is unquestionably the most important professional assistance to obtain before investing in a franchise. Do not make the mistake of assuming that the disclosure statement tells all that you need to know about the consequences of signing franchise agreement and related contracts. The disclosure statement is not designed to serve that purpose.

A lawyer can advise fully about your legal rights if you enter a franchise agreement, and the obligations which will be legally binding on you as a result. In addition, a lawyer may be able to suggest important changes in the contracts you are asked to sign so that they will provide better protection for your interests.

A lawyer will also be able to advise you about any requirements of state and local law that will affect the franchised business, and to assist with the taxation and personal liability questions which must be considered in establishing any new business.

The cost of obtaining legal advice will be relatively small in comparison to the total initial investment for a franchise. Moreover, the cost of legal advice at the outset is invariably less than the cost of later representation to solve legal problems that could have been avoided in the first place.

At the very least, you should be certain that every promise you consider important made by the franchisor and its representative is stated clearly in writing in the franchise agreement. If such promises do not clearly appear in the contracts you sign, you may have no legal remedy if they are not kept, and you may be legally obligated to comply with your own continuing obligations under the franchise agreement.

Protect Yourself By Knowing Your Legal Rights

A trade regulation rule, issued by the Federal Trade Commission sheduled to take effect on October 21, 1979, will give you and other prospective franchisees a number of important legal rights under federal law:

1. The right to receive a disclosure statement at your first personal meeting with a representative of the franchisor to discuss the purchase of a franchise; but in no event less than 10 business days before you sign a franchise or related agreement, or pay any money in connection with the purchase of a franchise.

2. The right to receive documentation stating the basis and assumptions for any earnings claims that are made at the time the claims are made; but in no event less than 10 business days before you sign a franchise or related agreement, or pay any money in connection with the purchase of a franchise. If an earnings claim is made in advertising, you have the right to receive the required documentation at your first personal meeting with a representative of the franchisor.

3. The right to receive sample copies of the franchisor's standard franchise and related agreements at the same time as you receive the disclosure statement, and the right to receive the final agreements you are to sign at least 5 business days before you sign them.

4. The right to receive any refunds promised by the franchisor, subject to any conditions or limitations on that which have been disclosed by the franchisor.

5. The right not to be misled by oral or written representations made by the franchisor or its representatives that are inconsistent with the disclosure made in the disclosure statement.

No federal agency will have reviewed the disclosure statements and other documents you receive from franchisors before you obtain them. If you think they are inaccurate, or that you have been denied any of your other rights under federal law after October 21, 1979, you should send a letter describing the violation to John M. Tifford, Program Advisor, Franchise and Business Opportunities Program, Federal Trade Commission, Washington, D.C. 20580.

If a violation of federal law has occurred, the Federal Trade Commission is authorized to obtain civil penalties against the franchisor of up to $10,000 for each violation. If you and other prospective franchisees have been injured by a violation, the Commission may also be able to obtain a court order that will remedy the injury you suffered. Such remedies may include compensation for any money you lost, and relief from your future contractual obligations, where appropriate.

You should be aware that the Federal Trade Commission may not be able to act on your behalf in every case. In that event, you will need to consult a lawyer about your other legal rights, which may include the right to obtain relief in a private lawsuit for the violation of any of your rights under federal law.

You may have additional rights under state law if you are a resident of a state with a franchise disclosure law, or if the franchise you are considering is to be located in such a state. The 14 states which now have such laws are: California, Hawaii, Illinois, Indiana, Maryland, Michigan, Minnesota, North Dakota, Oregon, Rhode Island, South Dakota, Virginia, Washington and Wisconsin. You should contact the state agency, usually the state securities commission, which administers the applicable state law to obtain information about your rights and to report any violations.

The best protection, in the long run, is to know your legal rights, candidly evaluate your own abilities, and thoroughly investigate a franchise before you make a commitment to invest. To do this will take some time and effort at the outset, but you may save yourself a great deal of time and money later on — the time and money you could lose if the franchise does not work out.

One final word of caution is important. Do not make the mistake of thinking that an investment in a franchise is risk free, or virtually risk free, just because federal or state law may provide you with some protection. That protection is subject to a limitation, and may not be able to remedy every case.

As a result, investing in a franchise will always involve a certain degree of risk, which you can ignore only at your peril. It is always better to do everything you can to protect yourself than to be forced to rely on your legal rights and potential remedies.

In addition, you should investigate the territory you are considering and the market potential for the product or service you will handle.

For each of these factors there are questions to be asked, and many facts to be secured. A list of 25 questions was devised which should be helpful in evaluating a franchise opportunity. These questions are incorporated in this booklet under the heading "Evaluating a Franchise."

There are may local special business career counseling services which can help an individual determine his own qualifications by organizing the facts about himself and by surveying franchise opportunities in depth. Such counseling usually increases a franchisee's chances for success.

The obligations of a franchisor to the franchisee are in the Code of Ethics adopted by the International Franchise Association. A study of this code will help the franchisee evaluate the franchisor under consideration before making his final commitment.

Code of Ethics
(International Franchise Association)

Each member company pledges:

1. No member shall offer, sell or promote the sale of any franchise, product or service by means of any explicit or implied representation which is likely to have a tendency to deceive or mislead prospective purchasers of such franchise, product or service.

2. No member shall imitate the trademark, trade name, corporate name, slogan, or other mark of identification of another business in any manner or form that would have the tendency or capacity to mislead or deceive.

3. The pyramid or chain distribution system is inimical to prospective investors and to the franchise system of distribution, and no member shall engage in any form of pyramid or chain distribution.

4. An advertisement, considered in its totality, shall be free from ambiguity and, in whatever form presented, must be considered in its entirety and as it would be read and understood by those to whom directed.

5. All advertisements shall comply, in letter and spirit, with all applicable rules, regulations, directives, guides and laws promulgated by any governmental body or agency having jurisdiction.

6. An advertisement containing or making reference, directly or indirectly, to performance records, figures or data respecting income or earnings of franchisees shall be factual, and, if necessary to avoid deception, accurately qualified as to geographical area and time periods covered.

7. An advertisement containing information or making reference to the investment requirements of a franchise shall be as detailed as necessary to avoid being misleading any way and shall be specific with respect to whether the stated amount(s) is a partial or the full cost of the franchise, the items paid for by the stated amount(s), financing requirements and other related costs.

8. Full and accurate written disclosure of all information considered material to the franchise relationship shall be given to prospective franchisees a reasonable time prior to the execution of any binding document and members shall otherwise fully comply with Federal and state laws requiring advance disclosure of information to prospective franchisees.

9. All matters to the franchise relationship shall be contained in one or more written agreements, which shall clearly set forth the terms of the relationship and the respective rights and obligations of the parties.

10. A franchisor shall select and accept only those franchisees who, upon reasonable investigation, appear to posses the basic skills, education, personal qualities, and financial resources adequate to perform and fulfill the needs and requirements of the franchise. There shall be no discrimination based on race, color, religion, national origin or sex.

11. The franchisor shall encourage and/or provide training designed to help franchisees improve their abilities to conduct their franchises.

12. A franchisor shall provide reasonable guidance and supervision over the business activities of franchisees for the purpose of safeguarding the public interest and of maintaining the integrity of the entire franchise system for the benefit of all parties having an interest in it.

13. Fairness shall characterize all dealings between a franchisor and its franchisees. To the extent reasonably appropriate under the circumstances, a franchisor shall give notice to its franchisee of any contractual breach and grant reasonable time to remedy default.

14. Franchisor should be conveniently accessible and responsive to communications from franchisees, and provide a mechanism by which ideas may be exchanged and areas of concern discussed for the purpose of improving mutual understanding and reaffirming mutuality of interest.

15. A franchisor shall make every effort to resolve complaints, grievances and disputes with its franchisees with good faith and good will through fair and reasonable direct communication and negotiation. Failing this, consideration should be given to mediation or arbitration.

Checklist For Evaluating a Franchise

The Franchise

1. Did your lawyer approve the franchise contract you are considering after he studied it paragraph by paragraph?

2. Does the franchise call upon you to take any steps which are, according to your lawyer, unwise or illegal in your state, county or city?

3. Does the franchise give you an exclusive territory for the length of the franchise or can the franchisor sell a second or third franchise company handling similar merchandise or services?

5. If the answer to the last question is "yes" what is your protection against this second franchisor organization?

6. Under what circumstances can you terminate the franchise contract and at what cost to you, if you decide for any reason at all that you wish to cancel it?

7. If you sell your franchise, will you be compensated for your good will or will the good will you have built into the business be lost by you?

The Franchisor

8. How many years has the firm offering you a franchise been in operation?

9. Has it a reputation for honest and fair dealing among the local firms holding its franchise?

10. Has the franchisor shown you any certified figures indicating exact net profits of one or more going firms which you personally checked yourself with the franchisee?

11. Will the firm assist you with:
   (a) A management training program?
   (b) An employee training program?
   (c) A public relations program?
   (d) Capital?
   (e) Credit?
   (f) Merchandising Ideas?

12. Will the firm help you find a good location for your new business?

13. Is the franchising firm adequately financed so that it can carry out its stated plan of financial assistance and expansion?

14. Is the franchisor a one-man company or a corporation with an experienced management trained in depth (so that there would always be an experience man at its head)?

15. Exactly what can the franchisor do for you which you cannot do for yourself?

16. Has the franchisor investigated you carefully enough to assure itself that you can successfully operate one of their franchises at a profit both to them and to you?

17. Does your state have a law regulating the sale of franchises and has the franchisor complied with that law?

You - The Franchisee

18. How much equity capital will you have to have to purchase the franchise and operate it until your income equals your expenses? Where are you going to get it?

19. Are you prepared to give up some independence of action to secure the advantages offered by the franchise?

20. Do YOU really believe you have the innate ability, training, and experience to work smoothly and profitably with the franchisor, your employees and your customers?

21. Are you ready to spend much or all of the remainder of your business life with this franchisor, offering his product or service to your public?

Your Market

22. Have you made any study to determine whether the product or service which you propose to sell under franchise has a market in your territory at the prices you will have to charge?

23. Will the population in the territory give you increase, remain static, or decrease over the next 5 years?

24. Will the product or service you are considering be in greater demand, about the same, or less demand five years from now than today?

25. What competition exists in your territory already for the product or service you contemplate selling?
   (a) Nonfranchise firms?
   (b) Franchise firms?

FRANCHISING COMPANIES

AUTOMOTIVE PRODUCTS/SERVICES

AAMCO TRANSMISSIONS, INC.
408 East Fourth Street
Bridgeport, Pennsylvania 19405
Dave Levy, Director of Franchise Sales

Description of Operation: AAMCO centers repair, recondition and rebuild transmissions for all cars. This is done by specially trained mechanics. Franchisees do not need to have a technical background, but should have a strong business background.
Number of Franchisees: 834 in 50 States and across Canada.
In Business Since: 1958
Equity Capital Needed: $35,000.
Financial Assistance Available: A total investment of $85,000 required to open an AAMCO center in a major market. A total of $75,000 is required in a secondary market. Company can arrange financing for 1/2 of total requirement, if franchisee has good credit references. Franchisee has the option to arrange own outside financing.
Training Provided: A comprehensive 6 week training course is provided at the company headquarters. In addition field training is provided at the opening of the operation to see that franchisee is properly launched.
Managerial Assistance Available: A consulting and operation division continually works with each center on a weekly basis to insure proper day-by-day operation. Monthly area meetings are held.

ABC MOBILE BRAKE
181 Wells Avenue
Newton Centre, Massachusetts 02159
David B. Slater, President
Ron Kopack, Executive Vice President

Description of Operation: Franchisee operates customized Ford van outfitted with Ammco brake machining equipment, extensive parts inventory and radio/telephone communications equipment, providing wholesale brake repair services to service stations and automotive repair shops nationwide. Franchisees do not need a technical background, but should be strongly motivated to achieve success through owning their own business.
Number of Franchisees: 135 in 40 States.
In Business Since: 1962
Equity Capital Needed: $10,500
Financial Assistance Available: Total investment of $31,700. Company can provide financing up to $21,200 to qualified applicants, or applicant can secure own financing.
Training Provided: Comprehensive technical and sales training provided in Chicago followed by field training at opening of operation.
Managerial Assistance Available: Continuous managerial and technical assistance provided throughout term of franchise. Clinics, national conventions, national advertising and merchandising programs and technical bulletins, as well as a monthly news magazine, bookkeeping system and operations manual provide professional support to the business owner.

ABT SERVICE CENTERS
DIVISION OF ABT SERVICE CORPORATION
2339 South 2700 West
Salt Lake City, Utah 84119
William D. Platka, Director of Marketing & Real Estate

Description of Operation: Alignment - Brakes - Tune-up repair centers which specialize in the one day, high profit automobile and truck service needs. Guaranteed, fast, economical service performed in a "new" 8 bay facility, with the "right" equipment and the "right" training, is the backbone of this franchise. A strong managerial background is essential - training will provide the rest.
Number of Franchisees: 8 in 2 States.
In Business Since: 1977
Equity Capital Needed: $51,000 (includes $10,000 operating capital).
Financial Assistance Available: Franchise includes 8 bay facility, signs, equipment, training with no need for additional equipment. Should a franchisee want additional equipment, financing through leasing companies, banks and ABT is available to qualified applicants. Franchisee must be financially qualified to guarantee construction.
Training Provided: 2 weeks will be spent in an ABT Service Center and at the company headquarters in Salt Lake City, Utah. This schedule will be increased if necessary. ABT operational people will then shift to franchisee's center for the training of his manpower. A grand opening will be prepared and held during this period.
Managerial Assistance Available: On a regular basis ABT personnel visit the franchisee to provide consultation in day to day operations and to analyze monthly progress. ABT provides operation manuals, training manuals, bookkeeping systems, insurance programs, advertising assistance and other management tools.

ACC-U-TUNE
2510 Old Middle Field Way
Mountain View, California 94043
Stanley Shore, President

Description of Operation: ACC-U-TUNE centers specialize in automotive tune-ups, lubrication and oil changes, air condition service and other minor repair and auto maintenance services. Typical tune-up and complete lube, oil and filter change is less than $55, is done in about 1 hour, while customer waits and guaranteed in writing for 6,000 miles. Prices include both parts and labor.
Number of Franchisees: 3 in California
In Business Since: 1975
Equity Capital Needed: $30,000 and excellent credit.
Financial Assistance Available: Franchisee must have minimum of $30,000 in cash, financial assistance is available.
Training Provided: Extensive pre-opening home-study course, classroom training (about 2 weeks) and 2 weeks on-the-job training. Training includes technical aspects of doing a tune up, fundamentals of auto repair, bookkeeping, marketing, customer relations, shop maintenance.
Managerial Assistance Available: Complete technical manuals, advertising manuals, and operations manuals covering all day-to-day aspects of managing a profitable tune-up center.

AID AUTO STORES, INC.
1150 Metropolitan Avenue
Brooklyn, New York 11237
Alan Koller, National Sales Manager

Description of Operation: Retail sales of automotive parts, tools and accessories.
Number of Franchisees: 78 in New York, New Jersey, Connecticut and Florida.
In Business Since: 1954
Equity Capital Needed: $40,000
Financial Assistance Available: None
Training Provided: 30 day minimum. Continual assistance after initial training.
Managerial Assistance Available: All necessary to properly train franchisee to maintain a stable business.

AUTO OIL CHANGERS
525 East Pacific Coast Highway
Long Beach, Calfiornia 90806
L. Kennepohl, Vice President

Description of Operation: Auto Oil Changers specializes in changing oil and lubricating cars, motor homes and small trucks. The operation uses a unique drive thru building. The entire services takes about ten minutes and does not require an appointment.
Number of Franchisees: 3 in California
In Business Since: 1976
Equity Capital Needed: $30,000 minimum
Financial Assistance Available: A total investment of $62,000 to $112,000 is required to open. The minimum $30,000 equity capital pays for inventory, deposits, licenses, permits, working capital and a grand opening fund. Cash required varies greatly depending on whether a new building is constructed or a gas station is remodeled - total investment could reach $112,000 including the cost of construction. Auto Oil Changers will assist you in obtaining bank financing.
Training Provided: 2 weeks of mandatory training are conducted for the new franchisee at a company store. This covers all phases of company operations. A full time Auto Oil Changers employee will assist at the new outlet for one week after opening, one additional week of training and refresher courses are scheduled during the first year of operation.
Managerial Assistance Available: Franchisor will provide the continued services of a company representative who will periodically visit franchisee's outlet to inspect, offer advice and render assistance to promote the general business welfare of the franchisee. Franchisor will provide standard plans and engineering for the Auto Oil Changers outlet. Franchisor will provide initial inventory, tool and equipment lists. Franchisor will provide advice on site locations, financing packages, sign vendors and product vendors.

ATV, AUTO, TRUCK AND VAN, INC.
300 Bethpage-Spagnoli Road
Melville, New York 11746
Leonard Zuckerwise

Description of Operation: Franchisee retails major brand automotive parts, accessories, high performance, vans, 4 wheel-drive, and pick-up truck equipment.
Number of Franchisees: 7 in New York. Other states being opened in 1980.
In Business Since: 1974
Equity Capital Needed: $100,000 for inventory, equipment, signs, fixtures, working capital and fees.
Financial Assistance Available: Qualified prospects receive assistance in obtaining financial aid.
Training Provided: Complete training program covering all areas of the business.
Managerial Assistance Available: Franchisee receives constant assistance and guidance on a permanent basis. Includes executive, managerial, operating and sales assistance.

BERNARDI BROS., INC.
101 South 38th Street
Harrisburg, Pennsylvania 17111
C. G. Geiger, Director of Marketing

Description of Operation: Manufacturing of automatic conveyorized or drive-thru Turbo-Tunnel car wash, Turbo-Brush automatic brush car wash and Turbo-Spray automatic and self-service car washes. Customer remains in car while it is automatically washed or customer may use the equipment tow ash his car. May be operated by coin meter.
Number of Franchisees: Over 2,000 throughout the U.S.A. and abroad.
In Business Since: 1946
Equity Capital Needed: $10,000-$50,000. No franchise fee.
Financial Assistance Available: Some assistance available through individual distributors, Factory finance plan is available.
Training Provided: Service shcool held at the factory at no charge.
Managerial Assistance Available: None. Local distributor expertise available. Assistance of Bernardi Marketing personnel furnished as requested.

1

BOU-FARO COMPANY
274 Broadway
Pawtucket, Rhode Island 02860
Carmine DeCristoforo, Vice President

Description of Operation: Stop and Go transmissions - a transmission auto repair center.
Number of Franchisees: 40 in Rhode Island, Massachusetts, Pennsylvania, Connecticut and New York.
In Business Since: 1970
Equity Capital Needed: Total package $39,500
Financial Assistance Available: None
Training Provided: Approximately 4 weeks.
Managerial Assistance Available: Complete.

BRAKE & ALIGNMENT SUPPLY CORP., INC.
7700 Northwest 27 Avenue
Miami, Florida 33122
Murray Fischer, President

Description of Operation: Brake and wheel alignment center.
Number of Franchisees: 16 in Florida
In Business Since: 1970
Equity Capital Needed: $25,000 down, total price $50,000-$75,000
Financial Assistance Available: Franchisor will carry
Training Provided: Initial 30 day training at National Headquarters in Miami and then at location.
Managerial Assistance Available: Constant coordination. Mass advertising.

CAR DOCTOR INTERNATIONAL MARKETING, INC.
531 North Ann Arbor
Oklahoma City, Oklahoma 73127
Emmett Lunn

Description of Operation: Mobile Auto Repair System. A method of accomplishing vehicle repairs where they are most needed. At the customer's home, office, or on the road. The Car Doctor uses radio dispatched vans equipped with parts and necessary equipment. They provide a 24-hour service that has been very well accepted. Franchisees do not need to have a technical background, but should have some business experience.
Number of Franchisees: 8 in Arizona, Nevada and California
In Business Since: 1974 - Original Car Doctor - Marketing Franchises - 1977
Equity Capital Needed: Approximately $28,000 in addition, franchisee should have about $7,500 working capital.
Financial Assistance Available: A total investment of approximately $56,000 is necessary. However equity capital pays for all inventory and opening requirements. Balance is amount financed on vans and radio equipment. With good credit background and net worth, balance is easily financed through banks or other sources by franchisee.
Training Provided: Intensive 3 to 5 day training program at Company headquarters. In addition, field training is provided at the opening of the operation to see that the franchisee is properly launched.
Managerial Assistance Available: Managerial and technical assistance provided throughout length of franchise. Management aids, regional advertising, training manuals, seminars and periodic contact with Regional Directors. In addition, top management visitations made as considered necessary in furtherance of the business success.

CAR-MATIC SYSTEMS, INC.
P. O. Box 12466
Norfolk, Virginia 23502
W. W. Vail, President

Description of Operation: Car-Matic System operates a 2 level merchandising program. A distributor covers an entire marketing area. Retail profit centers handle the direct to consumer sales. A Car-Matic distributor supplies the retail profit centers in his marketing area with rebuilt automobile transmissions, engines, and other parts. He also operates a retail transmission and engine exchange center at the same location.
Number of Franchisees: 50 in 6 States.
In Business Since: 1919
Equity Capital Needed: Distributor—$29,974, Retail Outlets—$13,200.
Financial Assistance Available: Complete overall financing plans are available to qualified people.
Training Provided: 4 weeks, management and sales training, plus set-up and assistance in field operations.
Managerial Assistance Available: Initial training of 4 weeks, and continual consultation services available when and if needed.

CAR-X SERVICE SYSTEMS, INC.
444 N. Michigan Avenue, Suite 800
Chicago, Illinois 60611
Bernard J. Rowe, National Manager Corporate Development

Description of Operation: Car-X Service Systems, Inc., offers franchises for automotive specialty shops which engage in the retail and wholesale sale and installation of automotive exhaust systems and shock absorbers.
Number of Franchisees: 74 in 10 States.
In Business Since: 1973
Equity Capital Needed: $95,000
Financial Assistance Available: We assist in obtaining financing.
Training Provided: Our training program consists of a comprehensive 5 week program, expandable to suit the needs of the individual franchisee. The core syllabus encompasses operations, finance, accounting, marketing and human resource management in its broadest classification.
Managerial Assistance Available: We provide managerial assistance and have on-going field supervision in both the business management and technical area.

COOK MACHINERY COMPANY, DIV. ALD, INC.
4301 South Fitzhugh Avenue
Dallas, Texas 75226

Description of Operation: Sofspra car wash locations.
Number of Franchisees: 775 in all States and Canada.
In Business Since: 1946 Sofspra started 1961.
Equity Capital Needed: $5,000 to $10,000
Financial Assistance Available: Financing and leasing available for qualified applicants.
Training Provided: On-the-job training by local distributors.
Managerial Assistance Available: Managerial and technical assistance provided by local distributors.

COTTMAN TRANSMISSION SYSTEMS, INC.
575 Virginia Drive
Fort Washington, Pennsylvania 19034
G. Ellard McCarthy, Vice President, Marketing

Description of Operation: Cottman Transmission Centers repair, service and remanufacture automatic transmissions for wholesale and retail trade. Operator does not need previous automotive experience.
Number of Franchisees: 135 throughout the United States and Canada.
In Business Since: 1962
Equity Capital Needed: $36,000 to $59,900.
Financial Assistance Available: None
Training Provided: 3 weeks training at the home office and additional training at operator's location. We also assist in the training of proven procedures.
Managerial Assistance Available: The home office continually works with each operator on all phases of operation, advertising, sales, management, employee relations, remanufacturing techniques, etc.

DELK TRANSMISSION FRANCHISE, INC.
505 Northern Boulevard
Great Neck, New York 11021
Arthur Bernstein, Franchise Director

Description of Operation: The Delk Transmissions Center offers complete transmission service. You need any previous automotive experience. Upon being accepted to Delk, you will receive two weeks of complete training at our headquarters in New York City. A Delk Field Representative will be on hand during your first week of operation to guarantee that you do business immediately. Afterwards, the Delk Field Department, with more than three hundred years of accumulated experience, will be at your disposal with continuous guidance and assistance.
Number of Franchisees: 12 in New York
In Business Since: 1964
Equity Capital Needed: $43,000 ($7,500 initial service and license fee, inventory $5,500, equipment $20,000 working capital).
Financial Assistance Available: None
Training Provided: 2 weeks training at the home office and additional training at operator's location upon opening at which time technicians are assisted in proper techniques of rebuilding of the transmissions.
Managerial Assistance Available: Delk offers complete parent company assistance, bookkeeping and operational. Belk will portect your specific market area. Delk gives you complete training in every aspect of your business operation. We will provide on location assistance and supervisory aid for your first week in business to guarantee your doing business the first day. We also assist you in procuring proper inventory at far below market. In addition we provide a complete advertising assistance program, supplying all mats, ads, etc. A Delk Transmission Franchise offers the prestige of association with a highly respected and well-known organization, putting you in the wonderful position of pre-built acceptance from the very first day you are in business.

DIAMOND QUALITY TRANSMISSIONS CENTERS OF AMERICA, INC.
P.O. Box 6147
Philadelphia, Pennsylvania 19115
Alfred Gold, President

Description of Operation: Diamond Quality Transmissions Centers adjust, repair, service, recondition, and remanufacture automatic transmissions and three and four speed "stick" transmissions for cars and light trucks. Franchisee needs no previous automotive experience to be trained to manage a transmission center, no matter what occupation or profession previously held.
Number of Franchisees: 4 in Pennsylvania and New Jersey.
In Business Since: 1949
Equity Capital Needed: $10,000 to $35,000
Financial Assistance Available: Financing up to $20,000 to franchisees with good credit rating.
Training Provided: 4 weeks training in salesmanship, management, and technical operations, which includes on the location training and promotion to assure a successful operation, will be provided.
Managerial Assistance Available: Simplified bookkeeping system available on a daily, weekly or monthly basis. Service manuals and technical manuals are available. Seminars in operating technique and management salesmanship are available. On the location help available when requested to increase promotion and sales on a retail or wholesale basis.

DRIVE LINE SERVICE, INC.
P. O. Box 782
1309 Tradewind Circle
West Sacramento, California 95691
L. D. Wilson, President

Description of Operation: Franchising specialized automotive service shops that perform complete drive shaft service, repair, remanufacture, modification, and balancing. Service Centers are based upon use of equipment and methods specifically designed to precisely work on all sizes and types of drive shafts.
Number of Franchisees: 39 (plus 3 company-owned) in 17 States.
In Business Since: 1971

Equity Capital Needed: Approximately $50,000 for equipment and franchise, plus $30,000 for operation capital.
Financial Assistance Available: No financial assistance is currently offered.
Training Provided: The franchise includes 2 weeks training for the franchisee and one other person. All expenses except living and travel are born by franchisor. Training is conducted at the West Sacramento, California shop location or in one of several midwestern locations.
Managerial Assistance Available: Franchisor maintains a staff qualified to provide assistance over the duration of the franchise agreement in all matters of management, technical, and promotional. Unusual problems and solutions are passed throughout the organization by regularly scheduled communications, monthly newsletters, and unscheduled conferences.

NICK'S SYSTEMS INC.
DBA DR. NICK'S TRANSMISSIONS INC.
150 Broad Hollow Road - Suite 300
Melville, New York 11747
Russ Bartolotta, Marketing Director

Description of Operation: Transmission Service Centers providing quality repairs to all types of auto and light duty commercial vehicles in both the retail and wholesale trade.
Number of Franchisees: 9 in New York
In Business Since: 1972 - Franchising since 1977.
Equity Capital Needed: Up to $54,000. $10,500 franchise fee, $5,000 working capital required-remainder depending on inventory, lease equipment available, leasehold improvements necessary and personal credit rating.
Financial Assistance Available: Financial advice and counseling is available when necessary and upon request. The prospective franchisee is responsible for an investment to cover initial licensing fees and operating capital.
Training Provided: A comprehensive home office training program into all phases necessary to successfully operate your transmissions center. Also continuous field support and counseling.
Managerial Assistance Available: Prospective franchisee need not have any automotive technical experience. We provide on-going training and assistance in all phases of center operations, including but not restricted to Center Management - Personnel selection and financial management. A professional Co-Op Advertising Program. Site selection assistance. Regular monthly meetings.

EAST COAST RADIATOR FRANCHISES, INC.
125 Lincoln Highway
Fairless Hills, Pennsylvania 19030
Richard D. Barton, Secretary Treasurer

Description of Operation: Sales and service of complete radiator, heating, air conditioning, and cooling systems in automobiles and trucks.
Number of Franchisees: 6 units in Pennsylvania
In Business Since: 1974
Financial Assistance Available: $29,975 (lus leasehold improvements and working capital).
Financial Assistance Available: If prospect has adequate down payment and enough equity, ECRF, Inc., will help prospect secure loan by going to lending institution with him.
Training Provided: 3 weeks training course with complete technical, sales, and management covered. Training at company facility in Philadelphia, Pennsylvania. Travel and lodging not paid by ECRF, Inc.
Managerial Assistance Available: ECRF, Inc., provides on-going assistance through 2 week open period, and then weekly visits, periodic company meetings with other franchisees. Complete operations manual, continued advertising, and on-going business evaluation are also provided.

ECONO LUBE N'TUNE, INC.
18092 Skypark South
Suite A
Irvine, California 92714
Al Savage

Description of Operation: A complete "turn-key" lubrication and tune-up shop.
Number of Franchisees: 41 in California
In Business Since: 1973
Equity Capital Needed: Approximately $58,000.
Financial Assistance Available: Total package approximately $78,000.
Training Provided: 1 month training in all phases of operation. We hire and train all employees.
Managerial Assistance Available: Day to day managerial and technical assistance is provided.

ENDRUST
1725 Washington Road
Suite 202
Pittsburgh, Pennsylvania 15241
William A. Griser, President

Description of Operation: Engaged in establishing dealerships for automotive rustproofing. Dealers being owners and operators of body shops, new and used car dealers, tire dealers, gasoline service stations and separate rustproofing centers.
Number of Franchisees: 55 in 8 States
In Business Since: 1969
Equity Capital Needed: $25,000
Financial Assistance Available: None
Training Provided: Company training in all phases of operation.
Managerial Assistance Available: All that is required by dealer.

E.P.I. INC.
P. O. Box 702
Summit, New Jersey 07901
W. C. Koppel, President

Description of Operation: Manufacturers of world famous "Sparky, Washmobile" car wash equipment. *Sparky*, portable self-service coin-operated "50 cents, 75 cents and $.00" car wash and wax systems. Also washes trucks, vans, campers, boats, etc. Washes with cold water. *Washmobile* "countdown" has a functional stainless steel housing, completely automatic, and consists of motors, gear boxes, air cylinders, industrial brushes, electric controls to run machine automatically, all copper piping, with automatic detergent system and detergent and wax tanks and gauges. Optional: window brushes, 20 H.P. high velocity dryer, wheel washer, spray wax system, truck and guide, hose and trolley assembly, power pump, hot water heater, coin meter, vacuum cleaner, signs, towel dispenser and waste receptacles.
Number of Franchisees: 141 in 11 States and throughout the world.
In Business Since: 1948
Equity Capital Needed: $35,900
Financial Assistance Available: Depending upon personal statements of applicants.
Training Provided: Company training in all phases of operation including merchandising and marketing programs and direction.
Managerial Assistance Available: As above plus marketing Sales Manager and factory engineers available for sales and technical experience as requested. This is available for as long as owner or franchisee has equipment and is without default.

THE FIRESTONE TIRE & RUBBER COMPANY
1200 Firestone Parkway
Akron, Ohio 44317
W. F. Tierney, Wholesale Sales Manager

Description of Operation: Complete business franchise includes all phases for selling tires, auto and home supplies, and automotive services, backed up with national and local television, radio and newspaper advertising, periodic retail sales plans, display material, and many other sales and merchandising plans for increased sales and profits.
Number of Franchisees: Over 14,000 direct including many more associate dealers operating throughout the USA and Canada.
In Business Since: 1900
Equity Capital Needed: $50,000 or more; varies as to locations, business, equipment and inventory.
Financial Assistance Available: Sales and credit personnel counsel and assist franchisee to obtain necessary assistance through local sources or through company's assistance programs.
Training Provided: Home office and field personnel are available at all times to train the dealer and his employees in all phases of sales and business management. This continuous program helps to insure an efficient and successful operation. Films, self-training programs, on-the-job training programs, etc., are constantly being revised and up-dated to keep dealer informed on all aspects of his business.
Managerial Assistance Available: Home office and local sales personnel are available to give assistance on any matter requested, including all phases of retail selling.

5 MINUTE OIL CHANGE, INC.
6 Watson Place
Utica, New York 13502
Raymond Seakan, President

Description of Operation: The 5 Minute Oil Change is a patent pending unit that will visually pump the oil out of a customer's car into a glass cylinder showing the customer that his oil is very dirty and needs changing. The customer is asked whether he wants his oil put back in or whether he wants it changed. If he wants it changed, then the center cylinder is full of a clean fresh oil and this by pressing a button is pumped into his engine. If the customer should want the synthetic oils, then the third cylinder is there and that can be pumped into the automobile. We find there is a great need since most of the people today are adding oil or buying their oil from department stores or super drug stores at reduced prices. We also have found the need is because most gas stations are using their bays for mechanical repairs only. This 5 Minute Oil Change unit can be placed in shopping centers, gas stations, car washes, muffler shops, self service coin operated car washes, and anywhere there is an abundance of automobiles. It is a service that people need, want, and desire and brings back a very healthy profit.
Number of Franchisees: 11 in New York, Texas and California
In Business Since: 1979
Equity Capital Needed: $4,975
Financial Assistance Available: The total investment of this unit is $4,975 and with good credit and $2,000 down we can finance $3,000.
Training Provided: The distributor that we appointed to sell this unit will actually demonstrate the use of this unit at a gas station and run a two-hour class to show the operator and his designated employees the true operation of this unit. There will be a service prevention maintenance program, and a sales program that will go with the purchase of this unit.
Managerial Assistance Available: With the purchase of this unit, the owner operator will be shown how to promote this unit with big signs on location, hand out pamphlets, radio, newspaper, and television coverage. All of these sales aids will be available on a rental basis or on a purchase basis.

FRANK'S MUFFLER SHOP'S
Division of FRANK'S HOME & AUTO SUPPLY CO., INC.
P. O. Box 409
Delavan, Wisconsin 53115
Robert Hoppa, General Manager

Description of Operation: Privately owned, fully integrated shops for installation of guaranteed automobile mufflers and shock absorbers on the most efficient, cost competitive basis.
Number of Franchisees: 11 shops in Wisconsin
In Business Since: Franchising - 1978, Muffler Shops - 1969
Equity Capital Needed: $22,250
Financial Assistance Available: $40,000 needed to open average shop. Existing, operating shops up to $65,000. Franchisee will be counselled and assisted in setting up a plan and securing needed financing and leads. This is subject to credit rating of candidate.
Training Provided: A complete training program on the technical aspects of operations is provided for the owner and the initial employees at the company master shop in Delavan, Wisconsin. This program will be supplemented by scheduled visits from technically oriented management personnel, and updating correspondence to individual shops.

Managerial Assistance Available: A qualified staff person will be available to train and assist in general business matters. This will cover all operational business affairs including, customer contact, sales promotion, financial ratios, employee recruiting, wage structure, inventory levels, etc. Standardized bookkeeping procedures, forms policies will be given under the overall franchising plan.

GENERAL RUST PROOFING INC.
P. O. Box 6238
Canton, Ohio 44706
George Janevski

Description of Operation: General Rustproofing is not just undercoating, it's a complete rustproofing two-steps process. We apply our exclusive penetrating compound that kills and stops rust that is already in your vehicle. Then we go over the vehicle a second time with our unique sealant that prevents new rust from forming. Life time guarantee.
Number of Franchisees: 3 in Ohio and West Virginia.
In Business Since: 1975
Equity Capital Needed: $10,000
Financial Assistance Available: Direct credit not available. Financial planning available.
Training Provided: Complete training available till franchisee is expertly qualified - usually 1-2 weeks.
Managerial Assistance Available: Personal help and management assistance provided at franchisees place of business.

GIBRALTAR TRANSMISSIONS
60 Cutter Mill Road
Great Neck, New York 11021
Dennis Ballen, President

Description of Operation: Automotive transmission centers, servicing, repair and rebuilding of automotive transmissions.
Number of Franchisees: 21 in 3 States.
In Business Since: 1974 - franchising since 1977.
Equity Capital Needed: $65,000 total.
Financial Assistance Available: None, assist franchisee in equipment leasing.
Training Provided: We have a 6 week training program; 3 weeks of classroom, 3 weeks on-the-job.
Managerial Assistance Available: Continuous management and technical assistance.

B. F. GOODRICH COMPANY
Tire Group
500 South Main Street
Akron, Ohio 44318
John T. Lanshe, General Manager, Dealer Sales

Description of Operation: Establishes a total franchise to sell and service B. F. Goodrich tires and related automotive service merchandise. Franchise is supported by effective national advertising coupled with all necessary marketing support.
Number of Franchisees: Thousands of direct dealers and associate dealers throughout the United States.
In Business Since: 1870
Equity Capital Needed: Varies as to market, style of business, projected volume, etc.
Financial Assistance Available: Assistance is provided to help franchisee obtain required financing through local sources and/or franchisor's assistance programs. Required financing is dependent upon market potential, requirements and projected profitability.
Training Provided: Training on a continuous basis is provided by the company covering product knowledge, servicing techniques and business management.
Managerial Assistance Available: Same as "Training" above.

THE GOODYEAR TIRE & RUBBER COMPANY
1144 E. Market Street
Akron, Ohio 44316
A. Piquette, Manager, Tire Centers Division

Description of Operation: Retail and wholesale sale of tires, tire and automotive service and other car and home related merchandise. These are marketed through a long-established independent dealer organization and a more recently developed chain of franchised Tire Centers.
Number of Franchisees: Approximately 6,000 independent Goodyear dealers including 356 tire center franchisees in most States.
In Business Since: 1898. Tire Center franchise program has operated since 1968.
Equity Capital Needed: Varies for regular Goodyear dealership. $35,000 minimum required for Tire Center.
Financial Assistance Available: Lease real estate; equipment and fixtures, long-term note line as needed and justified; and open account credit as needed and justified.
Training Provided: Formal 3 month training plus continued on-the-job training.
Managerial Assistance Available: Business counsel and data processing provided on a continuing and permanent basis. Program also includes local, cooperative advertising to tie-in with national advertising; display and point-of-sale advertising; identification and fixture assistance; monthly and quarterly marketing and merchandising programs; complete sales training programs.

GREASE LIGHTING, INC.
832 Pennsylvania Avenue
Brooklyn, New York 11207

Description of Operation: 10 minute lubrication and wash. Turn-key operation.
Number of Franchisees: 12 in Illinois, Florida and New York.
In Business Since: 1977
Equity Capital Needed: Total package approximately $175,000.
Financial Assistance Available: Financial assistance available to qualified applicant with good credit rating.
Training Provided: We hire and train all technical and management personnel for 4 weeks in all phases of the operation.
Managerial Assistance Available: Continuous management and technical assistance is provided in cost controls, personnel management, quality control, individual guidance. A operations manual is also provided.

GREASE MONKEY INTERNATIONAL, INC.
811 Lincoln Street
Suite 500
Denver, Colorado 80203
Robert Palmer, Jr., Executive Vice President

Description of Operation: Franchisor is in the business of providing convenient quick-service lubrication and oil changes for automobiles and trucks and of licensing franchisees to use the mark GREASE MONKEY, THE 10 MINUTE LUBE PROS, and other trademarks, service marks, copyrights and concepts regarding the establishment and operation of automotive lubrication centers.
Number of Franchisees: 5 in Colorado, Wyoming, Nebraska, Missouri, and Iowa plus 60 under contract.
In Business Since: 1978
Equity Capital Needed: $55,000, excluding land and building. Building may be leased or purchased.
Financial Assistance Available: Franchisor does not offer financing to franchisees in any respect, however, it has been arranged subject to credit worthiness, that some equipment and inventory suppliers will provide financing. Generally $20,000 to $25,000 financing can be arranged.
Training Provided: The franchisor will provide basic indoctrination and instruction to franchisee and its employees in the operation and management of each center.
Managerial Assistance Available: Franchisor provides a recommended system of accounting and internal accounting control, grand opening and promotional advertising package, technical advice and assistance re. installation of equipment, construction of building, technical service, marketing and accounting manuals are provided, national and regional advertising programs, provide a system of quality control over all franchisees to maintain uniform quality of the products, services and inventory control. Franchisor also protects its trade and service marks.

GREAT BEAR AUTOMOTIVE CENTERS, INC.
827 Remsen Avenue
Brooklyn, New York 11236
Jack Kaplan, Vice President

Description of Operation: Great Bear Auto Centers, specializing in automotive aftermarket sales and installation of parts for front end, brakes, shocks, alignment, mufflers, springs and tune-ups. All work performed by specially trained mechanics. Franchisees do not require an automotive background but must have managerial experience.
Number of Franchisees: 82 in New York, Connecticut, New Jersey and Florida.
In Business Since: 1934
Equity Capital Needed: $35,000
Financial Assistance Available: A total investment of $65,000 is necessary to open a Great Bear Auto Center in a major marketing area. Company will assist in obtaining financing for Franchisees with good credit references.
Training Provided: Basic training at Company Headquarters followed by field training at the Franchisee's own location to guarantee a well-planned operation and an organized opening.
Managerial Assistance Available: Continued managerial, technical and advertising assistance at all times during the time of the Franchise.

HERCULES CAR/TRUCK RUSTPROOFING
Hercules Building, 231 Hay Avenue
Johnstown, Pennsylvania 15902
Norman Fellman - Marketing

Description of Operation: Rustproofing cars and trucks.
Number of Franchisees: 45
In Business Since: 1974. Member International Franchise Association.
Equity Capital Needed: $30,000 total funds needed, the majority of which may be borrowed.
Financial Assistance Available: We assist in securing financing and will joint-venture, we also lease all equipment needed through a subsidiary.
Training Provided: 2 weeks in special company shcool covering all aspects of technical and management requirements. Sales training in field when center is opened plus corporate personnel in attendance opening week.
Managerial Assistance Available: Causes of rust, its history and prevention. Product and application information and training. Equipment care and use. Telephone and personal selling. Bookkeeping training. Personnel and management training. Management and technical manuals furnished and constantly updated.

INSTA-TUNE, INC.
17995 Sky Park Circle
Irvine, California 92714
Ray Williams

Description of Operation: Insta-Tune centers perform automotive tune-ups using dynamometers, oscilloscopes, engine analyzers and infrared emissions testers. Tune-ups are typically performed in under 30 minutes for $38 to $42.
Number of Franchisees: 100 Coast ot Coast.
In Business Since: 1974
Equity Capital Needed: $20,000 and good credit
Financial Assistance Available: Minimum cash investment $20,000, financial assistance is available.
Training Provided: Technical training on equipment and on-the-job training are initially provided, followed by continuous field training and counseling.
Managerial Assistance Available: Operations manuals are provided, licensee receives constant assistance and periodic dealer meetings are held to discuss all aspects of operations of a center.

INTERSTATE AUTOMATIC TRANSMISSION CO., INC.
29200 Vassar Avenue, Suite 501
Livonia, Michigan 48152
Bradford D. George, Director of Marketing

Description of Operation: Interstate Transmissions Centers service, repair and replace all types of standard and automatic transmissions for automobiles, small truck and RV's. They are usually in a building large enough to service 5 or 6 vehicles with outside parking for up to 20 cars. Each center is completely equipped with new and unique labor saving and parts reconditioning equipment.

Number of Franchisees: 121 in 20 States
In Business Since: 1973
Equity Capital Needed: Subject to franchisees' financial status.
Financial Assistance Available: A total investment of $63,500, excluding working capital, is required. Because of the amount of equipment involved in an Interstate Transmission Center, and depending upon the individual licensee's credit standing, financing can usually be arranged.
Training Provided: 2 weeks of intensive management training is provided at the home office and then additional on-site training is given during the opening period.
Managerial Assistance Available: Interstate Transmission provides constant operational support in both management and technical services. Field operation managers visit each center on a periodic basis and each week licensee submits a report on his individual Interstate Transmissions Centers' operation which is reviewed by the home office.

JIFFIWASH, INC.
1177 California Street
Suite 308
San Francisco, California 98108
Merle Akers, President

Description of Operation: Service institutional clients at their locations, washing, brushing and cleaning their fleet of vehicles from a Jiffiwash mobile unit equipped with patented pressure washing equipment. Work is done mostly in the evenings and on weekends when rolling stock is parked in their respective yards.
Number of Franchisees: 30 now - exclusive franchises in 10 States.
In Business Since: 1959
Equity Capital Needed: $25,000
Financial Assistance Available: Franchisee is to arrange own financing for the purchase price. $20,000 is needed to purchase a Jiffiwash Franchise. The additional $5,000 is necessary to defray initial operating expenses for the first six months the franchisee is in business, or until such time sufficient revenue is generated for the franchisee to be self-sufficient with positive cash flow.
Training Provided: 2 weeks of on-site training with established Jiffiwash Dealer washing vehicles and making sales calls. Optional: a visit to the home office in San Francisco for additional sales training and a training period at the Jiffiwash machine shop to acquaint franchise with Jiffiwash patented equipment. Franchisee to pay all expenses incurred during training period.
Managerial Assistance Available: Jiffiwash will do all accounting functions on behalf of franchisee until the franchise is terminated. Jiffiwash will conduct periodic sales campaign in and around the area serviced by franchisee. Franchisee is to follow up leads thus generated, calling on interested parties selling the Jiffiwash Mobile Washing Serivce in and around his service area. Jiffiwash machine shop is available for technical assistance during normal shop hours. All equipment received by the franchisee is covered by a 9)-days warranty. After the warranty period, replacements will be shipped, at cost, to franchisee to keep the equipment working on the job.

JIFFY LUBE INTERNATIONAL, INC.
6666 Security Boulevard, Suite D
Baltimore, Maryland 21207
Edward F. Kelley, III, Executive Vice President

Description of Operation: Jiffy Lube International, Inc., offers a unique quick lubrication system for all motor vehicles including recreational vehicles. Each service center is approximately 2,000 square feet and open 10 hours daily 6 days a week. Jiffy Lube products as well as selected brand name merchandise is maintained.
Number of Franchisees: 10 in Colorado, Utah, Wyoming and Nevada.
In Business Since: 1979
Equity Capital Needed: $35,000 minimum.
Financial Assistance Available: Jiffy Lube International, Inc., does not provide any financing to franchisees. Franchisor may, however, assist franchisees in locating sources of financing.
Training Provided: Jiffy Lube International, Inc., provides an intensive mandatory course to franchisee or approved manager for a minimum of 5 days at an operating Jiffy Lube Service Center. Training is provided at franchisee's initial location of all other initial employees for a 3 to 5 day period and is given by a representative of franchisor.
Managerial Assistance Available: Jiffy Lube International, Inc., provides continual management service for the life of the franchise in such areas as accounting, advertising, policies and procedures, and operations. Complete manuals are provided. Regional managers are available to work closely with franchisees and visit service centers regularly to assist in solving problems. Jiffy Lube International, Inc., sponsors an annual meeting with seminars for franchisees.

KINETIC ENERGY MANUFACTURING COMPANY
P. O. Box 1334
2015 South Calhoun Street
Fort Wayne, Indiana 46801

Description of Operation: Kinetic Energy Manufacturing Co., Div. of Kemco Corporation, offers a unique and very lucrative product that can be used by every motor vehicle including farm and heavy earth-moving equipment. The auto and truck after-market product shows a drastic operation improvement immediately after installation and helps to reduce emission pollutions, plus increasing performance and efficiency.
Number of Franchisees: 10 in Michigan, Indiana, Ohio, Kentucky and Florida.
In Business Since: 1974
Equity Capital Needed: $5,000 minimum.
Financial Assistance Available: A total investment of $10,000 is required for inventory of equipment with Kemco Corporation financing one-half of the needed amount to any person with a good credit rating, and the ability to produce.
Training Provided: A 2 week school is provided for all new franchisees, with a refresher course following at 12 month intervals. Constant field supervision will be provided, and needed literature, brochures and selling aids furnished free of charge.
Managerial Assistance Available: Our testing laboratory will be able to assist if and when an unusual probelm occurs that cannot be corrected in the field. All of our products carry a 30-day written money-back guarantee, with a life-time replacement warranty. A complete turn key operation is available if desired by the franchisee, whereas the company furnishes the complete operation ready for the franchisee to open for business.

KING BEAR ENTERPRISES, INC.
40 New York Avenue
Westbury, New York 11590
A. Blaker

Description of Operation: Automotive repairs, brake, front end, shock, mufflers and under car repairs. All parts are sold to franchisees at jobber prices, or less.
Number of Franchisees: 42 in New York, Calfornia and Florida.
In Business Since: 1973
Equity Capital Needed: $30,000
Financial Assistance Available: Limited financing available.
Training Provided: In shop training for 2 weeks, plus full management training in our home office. Additional training provided in franchisee's shop.
Managerial Assistance Available: Same as above.

LEE MYLES ASSOCIATES CORPORATION
325 Sylvan Avenue
Englewood Cliffs, New Jersey 07632
Sam Eisner, President

Description of Operation: Lee Myles Franchised Transmission Centers offer complete one-stop transmission service. These centers perform complete quality automatic transmission service, from minor adjustments through and including major repairs and recondition. It is not necessary for franchisees to have a technical background; Lee Myles provides a comprehensive training course and shop set-up assistance by a training staff equipped with experience, knowledge & developments of 30 years in the automotive field. Territories of all Centers are defined and protected by franchise agreement.
Number of Franchisees: 135 in 8 States and Puerto Rico.
In Business Since: 1948
Equity Capital Needed: $29,500 cash
Financial Assistance Available: Assistance in obtaining partial financing to qualified individuals.
Training Provided: 4-week training course, consisting of 3 weeks at parent company classroom and actual shopwork, plus 1 week in franchisee's own operation. Staff of experienced field consultants provides continuing guidance and assistance at all times thereafter.
Managerial Assistance Available: A divisional field consultant works with each franchise dealer to promote success with updated marketing formulas, technical information, and sales training.

MAACO ENTERPRISES, INC.
381 Brooks Road
King of Prussia, Pennsylvania 19406
George E. Gardner, License Director

Description of Operation: MAACO Auto Painting and Body Centers are complete production auto paint centers that also perform bodywork. Knowledge of the auto paint business is not necessary as MAACO provides a thorough training course and shop opening assistance by a staff fully experienced in the field.
Number of Franchisees: 304 open and 103 others sold.
In Business Since: 1972
Equity Capital Needed: $119,500
Financial Assistance Available: MAACO will consider applicants with $40,000 investment capital and will assist franchisee in applying for balance required. MAACO, however, does not in any way guarantee financing.
Training Provided: Complete 4 week training program in company's home office as well as initial training in franchisees own shop.
Managerial Assistance Available: Continuous as long as the franchise is in operation.

AQUA SYSTEMS
dba MACCLEEN'S CAR WASH
P.O. Box 4905
Fairview Park, Ohio 44126
David Butz, President

Description of Operation: Automatic car wash two-bay operation—each having 5 brushes with individual blower dry systems and wax dispenser. 2 employees desired., peak periods up to 5 employees.
Number of Franchisees: 50 in 10 States
In Business Since: 1966
Equity Capital Needed: $20,000 - cost of complete franchise $59,000.
Financial Assistance Available: Thru commercial banking and American Leasing, Inc.—SBA.
Training Provided: On location and at existing operations if desired.
Managerial Assistance Available: Assistance by store manager and company engineer.

MAD HATTER MUFFLERS, INC.
7110 North 35th Avenue
Phoenix, Arizona 85021
Jay McKinley

Description of Operation: Mad Hatter Mufflers of Florida, Inc., has devised a unique and uniform method for the sale and installation of automotive mufflers and exhaust system parts, in a free standing muffler service center.
Number of Franchisees: 40 in 20 States
In Business Since: 1976
Equity Capital Needed: Total package price $38,000.
Financial Assistance Available: A total investment of $38,000 is necessary to open a Mad Hatter Muffler Center franchise. The down payment of $9,500 is needed, the balance plus $7,000 working capital.
Training Provided: Intensive 7-day training course at the National Training Center in Largo, Florida. A minimum of 3 days at the franchisee's outlet under the supervision of a full-time Mad Hatter Trainer.

Managerial Assistance Available: Mad Hatter Mufflers of Florida, Inc., provides continual management and training services for the life of the franchise in such areas as advertising, new products, complete product and operational manuals, all forms, letterheads, envelopes and point of sale material. Regional Training Directors are available in all areas to work closely with franchisees and visit the Mad Hatter Muffler Centers regularly to assist in solving problems and updating installation procedures, introducing new products and training on same. Mad Hatter Mufflers sponsors meetings of franchisees and conducts marketing and product research to maintain high continued consumer acceptance.

MALCO PRODUCTS, INC.
361 Fairview Avenue
P.O. Box 892
Barberton, Ohio 44203
J. Ginley

Description of Operation: Distributorship to sell complete line of automotive chemical specialities including cleaners, oil additives, brake fluid, etc., to service stations, garages, new and used car dealers, and industrial outlets. He is assigned a territory that can support him. The distributor and his men travel the area using step vans, selling to the above accounts.
Number of Franchisees: 435 throughout the United States
In Business Since: 1953
Equity Capital Needed: $3,000 for inventory investment only.
Financial Assistance Available: None
Training Provided: Thorough field and product training in the distributor's area by regional sales manager. Periodically during the year the regional sales manager spends time with the distributor and salesmen for training both in product knowledge and field training.
Managerial Assistance Available: Distributor sales meetings are held twice a year for further training. Complete managerial assistance provided through company personnel and field representatives.

MECHANICAL MAN CAR WASH FACTORY, INC.
6 Watson Place
Utica, New York 13502
Raymond Seakan, President

Description of Operation: Manufacturing of self-service units, roll-over brush units with or without blowers, conveyors all sizes, self-contained mobile truck wash units, tractor tailer brush units, subway and train brush units, and any custom designed car wash unit.
Number of Franchisees: 1,076 in 47 States
In Business Since: 1964
Equity Capital Needed: $16,500 to $62,000
Financial Assistance Available: 25 percent down payment, balance on bank loan or lease arrangement. Franchisee must have good credit references. No experience necessary. Franchisee has the option to arrange his own financing.
Training Provided: A comprehensive training course at our factory on hiring labor, business management, operating car wash equipment, preventative maintenance, service, advertising and promotion. Also 1 week of assistance and training at the installation when it opens.
Managerial Assistance Available: We offer assistance in advertising, promotion, retraining of new personnel at our factory, telephone assistance daily, if necessary, along with meetings setup for new programs and expansion. Bi-monthly letters sent with new ideas and promotions to help franchisee increase success.

MEINEKE DISCOUNT MUFFLER SHOPS, INC.
6330 West Loop South
Suite 103
Bellaire, Texas 77401
Harold Nedell, President

Description of Operation: Meineke Discount Muffler Shops, Inc., offer fast, courteous service in the merchandising of automotive exhaust systems and shock absorbers. Unique inventory control and group purchasing power enable Meineke Dealers to adhere to a "Discount Concept." No mechanical skills required.
Number of Franchisees: 189 in 24 States
In Business Since: 1972
Equity Capital Needed: $58,337.40 investment for inventory, equipment, signs, furniture, fixtures, estimated lease, utility deposits, start up costs and working capital.
Financial Assistance Available: 3 weeks schooling and on-the-job training at Houston headquarters. In addition, Meineke provides continuous field supervision and group operational meetings.
Managerial Assistance Available: Meineke Discount Muffler Operations Manual provides clear and concise reference for every phase of the business. Home office staff analysis of weekly reports is provided on a continuous basis.

MIDAS-INTERNATIONAL CORP.
222 South Riverside Plaza
Chicago, Illinois 60606
William Strahan, Vice President

Description of Operation: Automotive exhaust system, brake, shock absorbers, and front end alignment. Shops offer fast service "while you watch" in clean, pleasant, modern surroundings.
Number of Franchisees: 1,200 in 50 States, Canada and Puerto Rico
In Business Since: 1956
Equity Capital Needed: $125,000 investment for inventory, equipment, sign, furniture, fixtures, fees and working capital.
Financial Assistance Available: Franchisee receives complete assistance in obtaining necessary financing from appropriate lending agencies with which Midas has working arrangements.
Training Provided: Both a dealer orientation program and on-the-job training programs are initially provided, followed by continuous in-the-shop field counseling and periodic dealer seminar-type meetings on all aspects of shop operations. Provide formal training program at National Training Center, Palatine, Illinois.
Managerial Assistance Available: A shop operator's manual is provided along with record keeping and accounting manual. Training received from regional directors covers all aspects of management, marketing, and sales.

MINIT-LUBE
140 West 2100 South
Suite 254
Salt Lake City, Utah 84115
Robert F. Teed, Vice President

Description of Operation: Minit-Lube centers provide automotive preventative maintenance in ten minutes without appointments. They change oil and filter, lubricate, check and fill battery, brake fluid, differential, transmission, power steering, windshield washer, air filter, wiper blades, vacuum inside and wash windows.
Number of Franchisees: 18 in 26 centers in Washington, Oregon, Montana, Idaho, Utah and Nevada.
In Business Since: 1977
Equity Capital Needed: $40,000
Financial Assistance Available: None
Training Provided: 2 weeks at company training center in Salt Lake City, Utah. Complete training for operating a Minit-Lube Center including actual operation of a center by franchisee.
Managerial Assistance Available: A center operations manual is provided on-going operational assistance by monthly center visits by company operational staff along with periodic franchisee seminars.

MIRACLE AUTO PAINTING
Division of MULTIPLE ALLIED SERVICES, INC.
P.O. Box 5026
San Mateo, California 94402
James L. Fowler, Vice President

Description of Operation: Miracle Auto Painting offers quality body repair work and baked enamel auto painting with a written guarantee at a volume-producing low price. Miracle provides high quality, rapid service and lowest cost through the production line process. Assistance is provided to the franchisee in site selection, equipment installation, and sales promotion. Supplies and materials are available through Miracle's volume purchasing.
Number of Franchisees: 55 in California, Oregon, Washington, Nevada and Texas
In Business Since: 1953
Equity Capital Needed: $25,000 minimum
Financial Assistance Available: The franchisee usually needs a minimum of $73,000 cash to establish the business on a profitable basis. Financing assistance is available.
Training Provided: A 4 week training course is schedule for new franchisees. Two weeks of the training is at a "Miracle" location and 2 weeks at the franchisee's location. Training covers systems and procedures for production painting and body-work as well as sales and business procedures. Miracle operates full-time training center in South San Francisco.
Managerial Assistance Available: Miracle provides continuing consultation not only for production techniques and procedures, but also for sales and business management, accounting and record keeping and employee recruiting and training.

MR. TRANSMISSION, INC.
P.O. Box 111060
Nashville, Tennessee 37211
John Astles, Vice President, Marketing

Description of Operation: Transmission repair shops.
Number of Franchisees: 67 in 14 states
In Business Since: Incorporated in 1968
Equity Capital Needed: Approximately $60,000 ($14,000 franchise fee and $46,745 inventory and capital).
Financial Assistance Available: Will assist the franchisee in obtaining an SBA loan.
Training Provided: A 3-week in-office training school is required on franchisee. A period of approximately 1 week is then spent with franchisee at his service center by a member of the Company staff.
Managerial Assistance Available: A review of the franchisee's business is made monthly by the Home Office, a member of the Office staff periodically visits the franchisee to offer assistance; the franchise shop is periodically audited; and if the franchisee needs any type assistance, (technical, service, etc.), a mechanic or supervisor is provided.

NAGCOGLASS
Division of NATIONAL AUTO GLASS COMPANY, INC.
3434 West 6th Street
Los Angeles, California 90020
Arnold Hurwitz, Vice President

Description of Operation: Retail auto, commercial and residential glass replacement service centers. Facilities provide a broad spectrum of glass products and installation expertise.
Number of Franchisees: 55 in Western States
In Business Since: 1956
Equity Capital Needed: $15,000 to $25,000
Financial Assistance Available: Will assist franchisee in obtaining SBA or more conventional financing.
Training Provided: Operational, administrative, sales and business development programs; manuals detail complete procedures and standards. Field programs provide supplemental technical, administrative, sales training and advertising material. Training centers offer installation courses.
Managerial Assistance Available: Corporate, managerial and administrative assistance. Field representatives provide continuous technical aid and supervision. Employee referral systems and strong inter-company communication.

NATIONAL AUTOMOTIVE SERVICES ASSOCIATES
2721 Lemel Circle
Suite A
Salt Lake City, Utah 84115
Michael T. Coleman, President

Description of Operation: Automotive after market. A mobile wholesale operation to service automobile dealers throughout the United States. Franchisee does not need automotive after market business experience.

Number of Franchisees: 50 in 8 States
In Business Since: 1976
Equity Capital Needed: $8,000
Financial Assistance Available: The franchisee must arrange his own financing but we will assist in presentation.
Training Provided: New franchisees are required to attend a 1 week training course at our corporate headquarters in Salt Lake City. Training includes business methods, bookkeeping, salesmanship, marketing and the installation of after market products.
Managerial Assistance Available: Continuing managerial assistance is provided. Corporate headquarters is always anxious to assist you in any way. Our experienced staff is available to answer any of your everyday questions, or to assist you concerning your franchise operation.

NATIONAL AUTO SERVICE CENTERS
Division of NATIONAL AUTOMOTIVE INDUSTRIES, INC.
1751 Ensley Avenue
Clearwater, Florida 33516

Leonard D. Levin, Secretary

Description of Operation: Eight-bay automotive service centers. Full service repair, including air conditioning, tune-up, brakes, alignment, tires, electronic analysis, etc. Also, charging system, shock absorbers, and mufflers.
Number of Franchisees: 9 in Florida
In Business Since: 1972
Equity Capital Needed: $45,000
Financial Assistance Available: Will arrange financing for $47,500 which represents 54 percent of selling price of the franchise.
Training Provided: Minimum of 2 week classroom training and practical application of skills with equipment. Minimum of 2 weeks on-the-job training under supervision. Training includes business methods, bookkeeping, purchasing, salesmanship, marketing service and repair procedures and equipment operation. A 400 page operations manual is provided.
Managerial Assistance Available: Franchisor handles advertising, holds field seminars, refresher courses, updating in new operation and is constantly available to cover trouble areas in operation.

NTW, INC.
Division of NATIONAL TIRE WHOLESALE, INC.
6320 Augusta Drive
Springfield, Virginia 22150

Bryant Hinnant

Description of Operation: Major brand imported and domestic wholesale tires to the public.
Number of Franchisees: 35 including company-owned.
In Business Since: 1971 (franchise division since 1973)
Equity Capital Needed: Minimum requirement $150,000.
Financial Assistance Available: Assistance available on an individual basis from the parent company.
Training Provided: New franchises and employees are required to attend a 2 week training seminar. One part spent at corporate headquarters in Springfield, Virginia. On-going training at the franchise store on in Springfield for the duration of contract.
Managerial Assistance Available: NTW provides continuous management services for the life of the contract period. Areas such as advertising, salesmanship, inventory control are carefully managed. Regional managers are available on a full-time basis to trouble shoot all aspects of franchise. Routine franchise wide meetings are held in various parts of the country to address new trends.

OTASCO
11333 East Pine
P.O. Box 885
Tulsa, Oklahoma 74102

Robert E. Shireman, Vice President Dealer Division

Description of Operation: Retailing of home and auto supplies, sporting goods, major appliances, private label and major brands.
Number of Franchisees: 409 in 13 States
In Business Since: 1918 (established first franchise store 1934)
Equity Capital Needed: $45,000 minimum plus $5,000 operating capital.
Financial Assistance Available: Financing of fixtures and floor planning of major appliances through OTASCO Credit Corporation. Also financing of retail paper.
Training Provided: 2 weeks in company operated store initially.
Managerial Assistance Available: Field representatives in store average 1 day per month. Merchandise shows and sales seminars twice yearly. Regional sales meeting conducted two to three times per year. Operating Manual, forms, advertising assistance (co-op), bookkeeping system.

PARTS, INC.
Subsidiary of PARTS INDUSTRIES CORP.
601 South Dudley Street
P.O. Box 429
Memphis, Tennessee 38101

John J. Tucker, Executive Vice President

Description of Operation: Franchise is a jobber (auto parts store) operation wholesaling and/or retailing automotive parts, supplies, equipment and accessories. Retail sales are increasing in importance and may amount to as much as 50 percent or better of sales. Franchise has been reviewed and accepted by Small Business Administration and is fully known to the Federal Trade Commission. Inventory selection is from over 200 brand names and nationally advertised product lines.
Number of Franchisees: 1,200 in 39 States
In Business Since: 1911, franchising since 1958
Equity Capital Needed: Varies on basis of inventory investment but generally speaking, as low as $15,000.
Financial Assistance Available: Arranged if franchisee has outside collateral or will operate in a State where Uniform Commercial Code is applicable.
Training Provided: General management, to include bookkeeping and accounting system, operations manual, advertising and merchandising programs, market surveys, product and technical clinics; company retains field representatives as well as specialty sales representatives.
Managerial Assistance Available: Maintain daily contact through field representative and/or through WATS telephone calls to assist jobber in any phase of his business and to supplement written operating manuals, bookkeeping and accounting system manuals, cost books, catalog services. Financial ratios, expense control and inventory control are designed to improve the jobber's sales, profits and return on investment. Franchise owners have the option of utilizing in-store computer terminal which accomplishes the following: inventory management, accounts receivable, sales analysis, profit analysis and general ledger.

PENN JERSEY AUTO STORES, INC.
9901 Blue Grass Road
Philadelphia, Pennsylvania 19114

J. L. Rounds, Vice President, Agency Division

Description of Operation: Auto parts, Goodyear tires, national brand chemicals, accessory retail store. In operation since 1920, started in Easton, Pennsylvania. Operates 36 company stores; is now in its new executive offices and distribution center covering 4 acres in Northeast Philadelphia. Penn Jersey offers their Agency owners over 11,500 items, permitting the Agency owners to buy one of a kind at case lot prices. Available to its Agency owners are numerous business services, computer ordering, return of defective goods, advertises in 28 newspapers, some radio and some TV. Also, weekly computer price change service. Regularly scheduled visits by District Sales Managers.
Number of Franchisees: 110 (in 5 States - Pennsylvania, New Jersey, Delaware, Maryland and Virginia).
In Business Since: Company since 1920; Agency since 1947.
Equity Capital Needed: Total approximate price - turn-key $65,000.
Financial Assistance Available: SBA financing available with required up-front investment, supported by bank in the vicinity of store.
Training Provided: Extensive on-job type; continuing bulletins, etc.
Managerial Assistance Available: Accounting guidance, District Sales Managers' visitation on regularly scheduled basis, training to keep owners abreast of market changes and merchandising techniques and availability of other modern business practices.

PERMA-SHINE INC.
1425 Bishop Street
Cambridge, Ontario
Canada N1R 6J9

David J. Berta, President

Description of Operation: It is an International franchising organization specializing in the preservation of automotive paint for the motoring public and the trucking and yachting industry.
Number of Franchisees: 18 in 6 States, 64 Coast to Coast in Canada, 3 in the United Kingdom and 12 in Europe.
In Business Since: 1976
Equity Capital Needed: $35,000
Financial Assistance Available: Minimal
Training Provided: 2 weeks on-job and classroom training. One week at their site.
Managerial Assistance Available: Constant supervision with reference to product application, assistance in marketing program, and financial advice so long as one owns a franchise. Complete training manual provided to each franchise owner.

POLY-OLEUM CORPORATION
16135 Harper Avenue
Detroit, Michigan 48224

William McKay, President

Description of Operation: Poly-Oleum Corporation offers dealership in the expanding auto-truck rustproofing market. Tooling, sealant compounds, technical data, marketing are provided by Poly-Oleum for purchase by these dealerships.
Number of Franchisees: 52 in 4 States and Canada.
In Business Since: 1963
Equity Capital Needed: $15,000 to $20,000 plus operating capital.
Financial Assistance Available: Assistance programs, including preparation of bank documentation available.
Training Provided: 1 week technical training of application at Company Home Office or regional center, plus minimum of 1 week on location set up at time of opening. Technical data and quality control information and personnel follow-up as necessary.
Managerial Assistance Available: Company representative will assist during opening in developing a localized marketing program. Assist in fleet and wholesale account contact, plus variety of phone, mail and seminars to constantly upgrade efficiency of operations.

POWER VAC INCORPORATED
P.O. Box 771
500 Graves Boulevard
Salina, Kansas 67401

Description of Operation: Professional power wash business engaged in the cleaning of truck fleets, buildings, boats, heavy equipment, service stations and etc.
Number of Franchisees: 21 in 13 States and Canada
In Business Since: 1963
Equity Capital Needed: $10,000 to $15,000 plus operating capital.
Financial Assistance Available: Assistance is given in helping obtain local bank or other financing.
Training Provided: A representative from Power Vac Inc., spends the necessary time to train and guide him on the building of his new business. Repeat follow ups as needed. Newsletters and correspondence by mail and phone.
Managerial Assistance Available: Personal help and guidance provided by company representative at franchisee's place of business plus correspondence.

POWER WASH, INC.
47 Lincoln Highway
South Kearny, New Jersey 07032
Archie B. Joyner, President

Description of Operation: Franchisee washes trucks, trailers, cars, etc., with mobile equipment at customer's locations.
Number of Franchisees: 8 in New York, New Jersey, Pennsylvania and Florida.
In Business Since: 1968
Equity Capital Needed: $2,000
Financial Assistance Available: Financing of equipment up to $12,000 and account financing.
Training Provided: 2 to 6 weeks on-the-job training.
Managerial Assistance Available: Continuous management and sales assistance.

PRECISION TRANSMISSION, INC.
2040 State Road 109 South
Anderson, Indiana 46013
David E. Schwartz, President

Description of Operation: Service, installation and repair of automobile transmissions.
Number of Franchisees: 25 franchise locations and 5 company operations in Indiana, Ohio, Kentucky, Michigan and Florida.
In Business Since: 1974
Equity Capital Needed: Operating capital of $2,000 per bay and the ability to obtain loan to pay for franchise.
Financial Assistance Available: Precision Transmission, Inc., works closely with franchisee in attempting to locate outside financing sources.
Training Provided: Initial training of from 2 to 4 weeks is provided for each new franchisee.
Managerial Assistance Available: 2 to 4 weeks of training is provided for up to two managers per year per each franchise location. The company will provide up to 12 hours of consultation and technical services per year without charge to the franchisee and that additional consulting services will be provided when a suitable fee has been agreed upon. The company will sponsor at least one seminar each year for franchise managers.

PRECISION TUNE, INC.
P.O. Box 6065
755 South 11th
Beaumont, Texas 77705
Ric Figurell, President

Description of Operation: Precision Tune, Inc. licenses persons to operate tune-up centers. A Precision Tune shop usually consists of 2 or 3 bay centers which specializes in quick electronic tune-ups. Franchisee may convert existing gasoline station locations into a Precision Tune shop. However, free standing buildings may also be erected.
Number of Franchisees: 120 in 28 States
In Business Since: 1975
Equity Capital Needed: At least $30,000 in cash and the ability to finance an additional $30,000.
Financial Assistance Available: Precision Tune works closely with franchisees in attempting to locate outside financing sources. However, the company does not guarantee that it would be able to find financing for a particular franchisee.
Training Provided: Class room and practical shop training - 2-4 weeks at company headquarters and at training centers owned by sub-franchisors. Seminars are occasionally conducted to up-date both sub-franchisors and franchisees.
Managerial Assistance Available: The company will not provide management assistance to a franchisee, except that additional on-site training and on-site assistance is available through the company or one of its sub-franchisors.

ROCHEMCO
2330 Burlington
North Kansas City, Missouri 64116
Braxton P. Jones, President

Description of Operation: A two minute, fully automatic, high pressure carwash unit. A license is granted to franchisee in exchange for a nominal license fee and percentage of amount charged for each car washed. Protects licensee within prescribed territorial boundaries.
Number of Franchisees: Over 800 locations in the United States plus units in Canada, Europe and the Far East.
In Business Since: 1978
Equity Capital Needed: Minimum of $20,000 and up-dependent upon building, location and equipment requirements.
Financial Assistance Available: None
Training Provided: 2 to 5 days on-site technical training at time of initial hook-up. Semi annual service schools.
Managerial Assistance Available: National and regional parts inventory. Standard operating manuals and procedures (technical, promotional and business management). Continuous research and development. Periodic regional seminars (technical, management and promotional). Standard bookkeeping system. Frequent technical and management bulletins. Dealer oriented company magazine.

SEASONALL AUTOMOTIVE, INC.
100 White Spruce Boulevard
Rochester, New York 14623
William Waugh, President

Description of Operation: All Seasonall Automotive Centers repair and replace automotive heating and cooling systems. Some Centers also have facilities and equipment to perform exhaust, alignment and brake repairs. Centers may be opened as free standing unit or as conversions of or additions to existing facilities.
Number of Franchisees: 35 outlets in 11 States.
In Business Since: 1976
Equity Capital Needed: $15,000
Financial Assistance Available: A total investment of $41,821 is required to open a free standing Seasonall Automotive Center in a major market. Company can assist in qualifying for financing for 23 percent of total requirement if franchisee has good credit. Franchisee has option to obtaining financing elsewhere.
Training Provided: A minimum 1 week training program is provided. Longer period may be necessary depending on franchisee's background and the services to be offered by a given franchisee. Field training is also available to assist in the opening of the Center.
Managerial Assistance Available: Where necessary or requested by franchisee, a technical and managerial team is available to provide assistance to franchisee's in all areas to get properly underway. Regional advertising is also provided. The company wants every Seasonall Automotive Center to succeed.

SCOTTI MUFFLER CENTERS, INC.
c/o BEND-O-MATIC SERVICE COMPANY
P.O. Box 8032
Fort Worth, Texas 76112
Robert Cricchio

Description of Operation: Franchise is a muffler shop which involves the installation of exhaust parts. Franchisor provides assistance in advertising. Scotti Muffler Centers have a national warranty program and will provide sales aids and have available all exhaust products.
Number of Franchisees: Over 200 nationwide.
In Business Since: 1977 (parent company Bend-O-Matic has been in business for over 30 years)
Equity Capital Needed: The minimum package is approximately $12,000 and at least $800 cash is required.
Financial Assistance Available: Financial assistance is available to individuals with good credit background.
Training Provided: Up to 2 weeks training provided at company headquarters in Fort Worth, Texas plus follow-up training in franchisee's location.
Managerial Assistance Available: Continuous managerial and technical assistance is available at all times.

SERVICE CENTER
High Performance Auto Parts
11034 South La Cienega Boulevard
Inglewood, California 90403
Sheldon Konblett

Description of Operation: A complete "turn key" retail store specializing in high performance auto parts, accessories, marine and off road, etc.
Number of Franchisees: 34 in Hawaii, Washington, California and Nevada plus 7 company-owned stores.
In Business Since: 1963
Equity Capital Needed: $30,000
Financial Assistance Available: None
Training Provided: Complete 2 weeks of training period which will take place at our warehouse, offices and retail stores.
Managerial Assistance Available: We assist our franchise stores in inventory control and offer 'at our cost' W. D. prices on all merchandise. Assistance is offered in merchandising and how to profitably run a small business.

SIR WAXER AUTOMOTIVE GROOMING CENTERS
105 West Michigan Street
Milwaukee, Wisconsin 53202
Douglas M. Garber, President

Description of Operation: Sir Waxer offers complete Automotive Grooming Services, waxing and polishing using natural hard waxes, interior steam cleaning, scotchgard brand fabric protector, vinyl top cleaning and sealing, upholstery and carpet redyeing, vinyl top re-dyeing, engine nd trunk compartment cleaning, color coordinated body side moldings. Services are offered to the retail trade on a while-you-wait basis using completely automated equipment.
Number of Franchisees: 16 plus 3 company-owned in Wisconsin, Minnesota, Texas, Florida, and Illinois.
In Business Since: 1975
Equity Capital Needed: $15,000 - $20,000
Financial Assistance Available: Sir Waxer will provide a lease for entire franchise, including but not limited to equipment, installation, start up supplies, dependent upon franchisee's qualifications.
Training Provided: 2 weeks in Sir Waxer National Training Center, plus unlimited on-site training as required. Franchisee may also attend, or send his employees to the training center for training at any time with no charge. Franchisee pays only for his personal expenses.
Managerial Assistance Available: Regional Franchise Director is available for managerial assistance in franchisee's center. Technical assistance available on 24 hours notice. Operations Manager is available to assist in all areas of center operation on request. Advertising Department assists franchisee with local advertising and provides artwork, radio tapes and television commercials at no charge to franchisee.

SPEEDI-LUBE, INC.
2500 N.E. 49th
Seattle, Washington 98105
Clayton N. Loges, Vice President

Description of Operation: 10 minute oil change, lubrication and filter replacement performed by professional technicians in conveniently located and comfortable facilities.
Number of Franchisees: 11 in Washington
In Business Since: 1977
Equity Capital Needed: $40,000
Financial Assistance Available: No direct financing provided, however, assistance will be rendered with franchisee's application for outside sources of capital.
Training Provided: Formal classroom and on-site training provided over 3 week period. Additional training available at franchisee's request.
Managerial Assistance Available: Speedi-Lube provides technical and operational manuals with regular updates, construction support, business forms, operational control systems, accounting programs, sales, advertising and marketing programs.

SPEEDY TRANSMISSION CENTERS, INC.
50 Don Park Road, Unit 1
Markham, Ontario
CANADA L3R 1J3
William A. Gibson

Description of Operation: Speedy Transmission Centers repair, rebuild, and recondition automatic and standard transmission for automobiles and trucks. Franchisees do not require a mechanical background. Trained mechanics are used for the technical aspect of the operation. A franchisee should have some business management experience.
Number of Franchisees: 30 in California, Texas, Florida, New York and West Virginia. Canadian associated - 90.
In Business Since: Established in Canada as a franchisor in 1963, in the United States in 1973.
Equity Capital Needed: Total investment $50,000
Financial Assistance Available: Financial packages are available to qualified franchisees through various suppliers of the franchisor. Both financing and leasing is available in most areas. Franchisor will assist applicant in preparing and the presenting of a financial plan to secure financing.
Training Provided: Prior to opening the franchisor provides a 2 week course covering sales, management systems, advertising, accounting and operations management in addition to 2 weeks on-the-job training.
Managerial Assistance Available: The franchisor assists in securing a location, building design and layout, initial equipment and stock ordering, pre-opening and post opening operations and management supervision by the operations department. Continued periodical operations support, advertising promotions and technical support is supplied on an "on-going basis."

STOP A FLAT - CHALFONT INDUSTRIES
608 Masons Mill Business Park
Huntingdon Valley, Pennsylvania 19006
M. L. Stein

Description of Operation: Auto after market chemicals to be applied to automobiles for consumer protection and safety. Also sells other car-care chemicals to be used on all new and used cars.
Number of Franchisees: 65 in 41 States and world wide.
In Business Since: 1976
Equity Capital Needed: $12,500 and $100,000
Financial Assistance Available: Some financing available.
Training Provided: Initial 2 week training plus constant field training.
Managerial Assistance Available: Constant field and telephone contact.

THRIFT-WAY AUTO CENTERS INC.
396 Union Boulevard
Totowa, New Jersey 07512
Robert Bozzagtra, President

Description of Operation: Four bay and up automotive centers which specialize in brake, front-end, shocks, alignments, muffler, tune-up and oil change. All work performed by specially trained mechanics. Operator does not need previous automotive experience.
Number of Franchisees: 20 in New Jersey and New York
In Business Since: 1977
Equity Capital Needed: $18,000 plus building lease securities.
Financial Assistance Available: A total investment is $49,900, which, excluding working capital, is required. We assist in securing financing on the balance of investment, which is $31,000.
Training Provided: 6 weeks of intensive training in company shop is provided. In addition, Thrift-Way provides continuous field supervision.
Managerial Assistance Available: Company representative will assist during opening of new shop. There is continued managerial, technical and advertising assistance at all times during the time of the franchise.

TIDY CAR INC.
3918 Broadway
Cheektowaga, New York 14227
Gary Goranson, President

Description of Operation: Tidy Car Inc., offers a unique 'mobile appearance maintenance service' which is performed by Independent Operators (franchisees) for the owners of cars, vans, marinecraft, aircraft, RV's and other vehicles. Weather permitting, the service can be performed almost anywhere the customer's vehicle is parked, at his home or office, days, evenings or weekends. Services include exterior, long-term protective shine on painted surfaces; vinyl roof reconditioning; interior detailing; and a fabric protection process to prevent permanent staining from spots and spills.
Number of Franchisees: More than 2,000 in all 50 States, Canada, Puerto Rico, Trinidad, Curacao, Philippines, Malaysia, Australia, Guam, Tahiti, Thailand, Hong Kong, Germany, Holland, Belgium, Norway, England, Japan, Kuwait, Israel, Virgin Islands, and other countries around the globe.
In Business Since: 1976
Equity Capital Needed: Approximately $1,500
Financial Assistance Available: A total investment of approximately $1,500 is necessary to commence business on a part-time basis. This investment is for inventory of equipment, materials, supplies and advertising material. There is no initial franchisee fee as such; however an on-going royalty payment of $2 per job (minimum: $20 per month) is payable. No financing arrangements are offered due to the small required investment.
Training Provided: No formal training program is required. Franchisee is furnished with a comprehensive 115 page Operator's Manual and can gain required experience doing his/her family car(s). Further, it is recommended that a new franchisee gain experience doing friends' and relatives' vehicles before commencing to solicit the public. Any questions which the franchisee may have relating to any information not contained in the Operator's Manual and handled via mail and/or telephone from the head office.
Managerial Assistance Available: Tidy Car Inc., provides continuing assistance and information to its franchisees through its monthly publication 'TIDYings From Tidy Car.' In addition, Tidy Car Inc., sponsors Regional Meetings throughout the United States and Canada from time to time which include 'workshop sessions' to answer technical and administrative areas of the business. Tidy Car Inc., also provides franchisees with advertising materials and suggestions including newspaper repros, display kit (car dealer showrooms, mail displays, car shows, etc.), advertising brochures and other promotional aids and guidelines. Tidy Car Inc., also provides assistance and consultation by telephone and letter when requested. Complete guidelines are presented in all phases of the operation including application, recruiting workers, advertising and promotion, record keeping, etc.

TUFF-KOTE DINOL, INC.
P.O. Box 306
Warren, Michigan 48090
William F. Widger, President

Description of Operation: World's largest automotive rustproofing company. Rustproofing done through both licensed franchisees and company-owned outlets. Only major professional rustproofing company that guarantees its applications with a full repair-warranty for as long as the original purchaser owns the car. Only company with exclusive two-step system proven effective on used vehicles, as well as new. First, a penetrant is used that stops existing rust and thoroughly penetrates welded seams. Second, a sealant is applied that seals out air and moisture and prevents new rust from forming.
Number of Franchisees: Approximately 3,500 worldwide.
In Business Since: 1967
Equity Capital Needed: $45,000 to $65,000
Financial Assistance Available: Not available.
Training Provided: Comprehensive training is required at company's highly professional international training center in Warren, Michigan. Training consists of technical background, both theory and practical, as well as business management and sales training.
Managerial Assistance Available: Beyond classroom training, technical and management manuals are issued at graduation. Continually updated. Supported by field service and quality control personnel regularly helping franchisee in his own territory. Advertising representatives also aid dealers.

TUFFY SERVICE CENTERS, INC.
300 St. Andrews
Suite 402
Saginaw, Michigan 48603

Description of Operation: Tuffy Service Centers, Inc., offers a franchise to sell and install at retail mufflers, exhaust pipes, tail pipes, exhaust installation hardware, shock absorbers and brake parts. The franchise will also perform exhaust system services, brake adjustment and other brake system services.
Number of Franchisees: 75 in 11 States
In Business Since: 1970
Equity Capital Needed: A total of $90,000 is necessary to open a Tuffy Service Center franchise. This includes inventory, equipment, sign, fees, working capital and start-up costs.
Financial Assistance Available: The franchisee receives complete assistance in obtaining equipment financing from lending agencies with which Tuffy has working arrangements.
Training Provided: 10 days of training are provided at home office and at Detroit, Michigan area Tuffy Service Centers for franchisees/managers. An additional 10 days of training is provided at the franchise location when the shop opens.
Managerial Assistance Available: Tuffy Service Centers, Inc., provides the management and technical assistance of a field manager as requested and manages the advertising function.

TUNE-UP CLINIC, INC.
2675 Cumberland Parkway
Suite 240
Atlanta, Georgia 30339
Al Massey, President

Description of Operation: Tune-Up Clinic offers a franchise to perform automotive tune-ups and quick, low priced oil change and lubrication service using dynomometers, engine analyzers and infrared emissions testers. Knowledge of the tune-up business is not necessary as Tune-Up Clinic provides a thorough training course and shop opening assistance by a staff fully experienced in the field.
Number of Franchisees: 33 in Southeast United States.
In Business Since: 1975
Equity Capital Needed: A total investment of $56,000 is needed. Majority can be financed.
Financial Assistance Available: Tune-Up Clinic will consider applicants with $25,000 investment capital and will assist franchisee in applying for balance. Tune-Up Clinic will not finance remainder or guarantee financing.
Training Provided: Complete 2 weeks training program in Company's training center and franchisee's own shop.
Managerial Assistance Available: Tune-Up Clinic, Inc., provides continual management and training services for the life of the franchise in all areas.

THE TUNE-UP MAN, INC.
P.O. Box 204
Orange Vale, California 95662
Cary M. Tower, President

Description of Operation: The Tune-Up Man tune-up centers diagnose and repair of ignition, carburetion and electrical systems of passenger vehicles and light trucks, using the latest electronic test equipment. Franchisee need not have automotive background, nor a business background, as we will train using our proven systems.
Number of Franchisees: 15 in California
In Business Since: 1974
Equity Capital Needed: $25,000

Financial Assistance Available: None, but we will assist in securing financing from bank or SBA, or through our leasing company.
Training Provided: Sufficient training is provided.
Managerial Assistance Available: Technical and managerial support provided on a continuing basis.

TUNEX, INC.
556 East 2100 South
Salt Lake City, Utah 84106
Rudy Zitzmann, Vice President - Franchise Sales

Description of Operation: Attractive six-bay Tunex Centers offer a complete one-stop tune-up service. From low-priced maintenance tune-up to full analysis and repair of ignition, carburetion and emission control systems, plus full service of the automotive air conditioning system, using the latest test equipment and skilled technicians. Franchisee does not need special automotive skills. Strong business management abilities are essential.
Number of Franchisees: 26 operating in Colorado, Idaho, Montana, Nevada and Utah. 10 additional are under development.
In Business Since: 1972
Equity Capital Needed: $55,000 plus adequate credit to lease facility.
Financial Assistance Available: $25,000 unencumbered cash is needed, plus ability to finance equipment, inventory and $10,000 working capital. Direct financial assistance is not available, however, guidance in preparing application for SBA guaranteed or commercial loans can be provided.
Training Provided: 3 weeks training is provided at company headquarters and the service centers, which includes opening week training in the franchisee's center.
Managerial Assistance Available: Technical and managerial support provided on a continuing basis.

ULTRA TUNE, INC.
3305 West Spring Mountain Road
Suite 60
Las Vegas, Nevada 89102
James Scribner

Description of Operation: Fast automotive tune-up and lubrication service. Sales office located at 8350 North Central, Suite 660, Dallas, Texas 75206.
Number of Franchisees: 9 in 6 States and 20 in Australia and Tazmania.
In Business Since: 1979
Equity Capital Needed: $28,000
Financial Assistance Available: Complete financial assistance guaranteed.
Training Provided: 2 weeks, classroom and practical application. Must graduate to qualify.
Managerial Assistance Available: On-going supervision, TV training and update programs on each site.

VALLEY FORGE PRODUCTS COMPANY
150 Roger Avenue
Inwood, New York 11696
Raymond Pasternack, Vice President - Special Market Sales

Description of Operation: As manufacturers of electrical and electronic auto replacement parts, we establish mobile distributors to sell to service stations, repair shops, garages and fleets. The product line includes ignition, spark plugs, filters, wire products and chemicals.
Number of Franchisees: 275 in 49 States
In Business Since: 1969
Equity Capital Needed: $40,000
Financial Assistance Available: Open account offered on all re-orders of merchandise.
Training Provided: Initial training is 1 week with a Valley Forge field representative.
Managerial Assistance Available: Technical bulletins, hints, tips, marketing assistance are a permanent part of the program. Facilities of Quality Control Department are offered.

WESTERN AUTO
2107 Grand Avenue
Kansas City, Missouri 64108
Regional Vice President

Description of Operation: Retailing of hard lines and other home items—principal lines are automotive, hardware, sporting goods, tools and wheel goods, appliances, televisions, radios, other electronics, housewares, paint, toys and furniture.
Number of Franchisees: Over 3,400 in all States except North Dakota. Dealer stores in Bahama Islands, Virgin Islands, Saipan, British West Indies and Bermuda.
In Business Since: 1909; began Dealership in 1935.
Equity Capital Needed: $50,000 minimum

Financial Assistance Available: Financing available on store fixtures. Floor planning of major items and deferred terms on some seasonal merchandise offered. Financing of retail customer installment sales also offered. Other financial assistance extended depending on personal financial statements of prospects including partial loans to open.
Training Provided: 2 week training course in modern electronically equipped training facility prior to opening store provides instruction in store operation, display, bookkeeping, product information, advertising and credit management. Company personnel continue to offer training, counselling and sales meetings after formalized training school is completed.
Managerial Assistance Available: Dealer contacted periodically in store by company personnel, such as Territory Sales Manager and Territory Credit Manager, offering counselling on sales, credit, and store operation.

WHITES HOME AND AUTO STORES
(WHITE STORES, INC.)
3910 Call Field Road
Wichita Falls, Texas 76308
Weldon Herring, Director, Franchise Development

Description of Operation: Retail hardline merchandise for the home, auto, lawn and garden.
Number of Franchisees: 462 in 17 States plus 103 company-owned.
In Business Since: 1930
Equity Capital Needed: $100,000 and up depending on location selected. A minimum of $50,000 in personal funds required.
Financial Assistance Available: Floor planning of major appliances and datings on seasonal merchandise is available to franchisee. Amounts will vary depending on the size of operation and the franchisee's financial statement.
Training Provided: 1 week training school in home office (Wichita Falls, Texas) with continuous call-back program for the purpose of training and advising dealer. Periodic sales clinics.
Managerial Assistance Available: Continuous in-store training by field representative.

XPERT TUNE FRANCHISE GROUP INC.
1362 Union Avenue
Memphis, Tennessee 38104
Donald H. Hogan, President

Description of Operation: Xpert Tune Centers perform automotive tune-ups in a clean, modern and efficient manner while you wait, for under $35. The business may be operated from an existing building converted to certain standards or a specifically designed building plan may be used. Principal equipment used is the sun 2001 diagnostic computer.
Number of Franchisees: 8 plus 8 company-owned in Tennessee, Mississippi, Arkansas and Louisiana.
In Business Since: 1978
Equity Capital Needed: $28,000 cash, ability to finance an additional $25,000.
Financial Assistance Available: Occasionally, depending on circumstances.
Training Provided: 3 week school at company headquarters and franchisee site, on-going technical updates.
Managerial Assistance Available: Operations manuals provided. Staff assistance in all fields related to the proper operation of a unit including advertising, inventory control, bookkeeping, and purchasing.

ZIEBART RUSTPROOFING COMPANY
1290 East Maple Road
Troy, Michigan 48099
Bill Beaver, Manager Domestic Licensing

Description of Operation: Automotive appearance and protection services specializing in: rustproofing auto and truck bodies via special tooling and sealant, Zee-Glaze exterior paint protection, fabric protection, installation of quality sunroofs and more.
Number of Franchisees: 700 plus in 34 States and 33 countries.
In Business Since: 1963
Equity Capital Needed: Total project including operating capital averages $45,000 - $55,000.
Training Provided: The initial license fee is only $10,000 plus tooling, equipment and opening inventories totaling $14,000 and is so modest that we do not feel it necessary to invest in any financial assistance at this time.
Managerial Assistance Available: Ziebart provides 13 days of intensive technical and marketing training at the home office in Troy, Michigan. This is followed with technical assistance in setting up the dealership and marketing assistance in preparing proper ads and announcements. The dealer is called upon frequently by a district sales manager to assist in every way possible.

AUTO TRAILER/RENTALS

AJAX RENT A CAR COMPANY
8816 West Olympic Boulevard
Beverly Hills, California 90211
Jerry Kenney, Director, Ajax System

Description of Operation: Automobile and truck rental.
Number of Franchisees: Over 100 Coast to Coast
In Business Since: 1969
Equity Capital Needed: From $25,000 to $100,000 depending on size of territory.
Financial Assistance Available: None
Training Provided: 2 weeks at the System's headquarters. Complete procedure manual provided which is updated at all times by the head office.
Managerial Assistance Available: Accounting assistance available as well as continuous guidance regarding the acquisition and disposition of fleets. Periodic visits from District Manager to keep franchisee aware of new developments in the industry. National advertising and free reservation system.

AMERICAN INTERNATIONAL RENT-A-CAR
4241 Sigma Road
Dallas, Texas 75240
William E. Lobeck, Jr., General Manager

Description of Operation: Franchisor of daily car rental throughout the United States. All outlets franchisee owned, no corporate operations. The franchising company is completely owned by franchisees, all officers and directors are franchisees.
Number of Franchisees: 124 franchisees operating 267 locations in 41 States and the District of Columbia.
In Business Since: 1968
Equity Capital Needed: Minimum $15,000, additional needed depends on potential of licensed area.
Financial Assistance Available: Advertising support, national advertising program, national credit card programs, assistance in obtaining financing from lending institutions.

Training Provided: Initial on-site training and continuing training through regularly scheduled meetings, seminars and periodic business analysis.
Managerial Assistance Available: Managerial and technical assistance provided through comprehensive manuals and continuing updating and modification. Traveling representatives provide periodic business analysis and the franchisor has available a computerized accounting system. Centralized international travel agency commission payment program and central billing is furnished.

BUDGET RENT A CAR CORPORATION
35 East Wacker Drive
Chicago, Illinois 60601
Attention: Franchise Department

Description of Operation: Franchise of car and truck rental.
Number of Franchisees: 1,700 locations: in all States, Canada and worldwide.
In Business Since: 1960
Equity Capital Needed: Varies with size of operation.
Financial Assistance Available: Occasionally, depending on circumstances.
Training Provided: Management and operational training at the Budget training center, at selected locations and on-the-job.
Managerial Assistance Available: During the term of the franchise, budget has full management team available to include legal, financial, franchise, operations, promotion, advertising and insurance staffs.

COMPACTS ONLY RENT A CAR SYSTEM INC.
4785 Kipling
Wheatridge, Colorado 80033
James J. Scherer

Description of Operation: Compacts Only Rent A Car System Inc., offers an opportunity in the daily automobile rental business. By taking a position in only the company and sub-compacts rental field a loyal following can be developed by people looking only for "reliable transportation at economical prices."
Number of Franchisees: 12 in Nevada, California, Wyoming, Texas, Utah, and Arizona.
In Business Since: 1969
Equity Capital Needed: $35,000
Financial Assistance Available: Financing can be arranged on automobiles through local banks or automobile credit companies.
Training Provided: Extension 3 weeks of training plus ongoing help as needed.
Managerial Assistance Available: Aid in surveying the market, setting rates. Continuing advertising in regional media. Toll free reservation system. Toll free access for continuing management advice.

DOLLAR RENT A CAR SYSTEMS, INC.
6141 West Century Boulevard
Los Angeles, California 90045
E. Woody Francis

Description of Operation: Automobile and truck rental. Heavy concentration in airport operations.
Number of Franchisees: Over 400 in the U.S. and Canada. Over 1,250 Inter-Rent locations in Europe, Mexico, Mideast and Africa.
In Business Since: 1966
Equity Capital Needed: Approximately $100,000
Financial Assistance Available: Occasionally assist in financing.
Training Provided: Standardized accounting system set up. Operational training by franchisor's representative at site.
Managerial Assistance Available: Assistance in-site selection. Standardized free-standing building. Consultant on-site during construction. Guidance in selection and balance of fleet. Continuing guidance in accounting and operations. Nationwide advertising campaign, co-op program available, and nationwide reservations service.

ECONO-CAR INTERNATIONAL, INC.
4930 West 77th Street
Suite 260
Edina, Minnesota 55435

Description of Operation: Nationwide vehicle rental system utilizing cash or major credit cards for rental of current model, standard and compact; fully equipped vehicles at economy rates. Franchises available for local areas, cities and counties. Applicable franchise fee varies with size of area desired by licensee. Franchise inquires to: Vice President - Marketing/Franchises, Econo-Car International, Inc., 4930 West 77th Street, Suite 260, Edina, Minnesota 55435.
Number of Franchisees: 100 operating over 150 offices throughout the U.S. and Virgin Islands.
In Business Since: 1961
Equity Capital Needed: Dependent upon size of franchised area, with minimum of $10,000 and good credit rating.
Financial Assistance Available: None
Training Provided: Actual "on-the-scene" training by qualified personnel and updated training on an on-going basis. Pertinent manuals and guides are issued.
Managerial Assistance Available: Opening kit of all necessary materials and initial operating supplies. National advertising and sales, reservation system, home office personnel available at all times.

HERTZ SYSTEM, INC.
660 Madison Avenue
New York, New York 10021

Description of Operation: Hertz System, Inc., offers franchises for the conduct of car and truck rental and leasing businesses in the United States under the "Hertz" name.
Number of Franchisees: Over 1,100 car and truck rental locations in all States except Florida and Hawaii.
In Business Since: 1918
Equity Capital Needed: Varies according to franchise-operating capital as required by location.
Financial Assistance Available: None

Training Provided: Zone System Manager trains new franchisee before operation opens with Hertz Starter Kit (Kit includes all forms needed to run a location). Visits by System Manager on a periodic basis. Manager rental representative training classes. Manuals and guides for running a location issued. Corporate training class available to franchisees. Annual business meeting.
Managerial Assistance Available: Accounting and operational guides are provided to run the location. Visits by Corporate Zone System Manager to act as a liaison between the corporate and licensee locations. All forms and training classes provided as needed. Training and business meetings. Contact provided directly to corporate management for all areas of rental business (e.g., insurance, advertising, accounting, etc.).

HOLIDAY RENT-A-CAR SYSTEM
1400 - 66th Street, North
Suite 425
St. Petersburg, Florida 33710
George V. Durnin, General Manager

Description of Operation: Automobile renting and leasing.
Number of Franchisees: 72 in 24 States
In Business Since: 1975
Equity Capital Needed: $30,000
Financial Assistance Available: Assistance in establishing necessary lines of credit with which to acquire vehicles. Assistance in procuring fleet insurance.
Training Provided: Theory complete with procedure manual, 1 day. On-the-job training, 5 days. Opening assistance and review, 5 days. Follow-up visit and review, 2-3 days.
Managerial Assistance Available: As much time as necessary in vehicle procurement, insurance procurement, office and counter procedures, customer qualification, hiring and training personnel, business development, advertising, accounting, vehicle disposal, and fleet maintenance procedures.

NATIONAL CAR RENTAL SYSTEM, INC.
5501 Green Valley Drive
Minneapolis, Minnesota 55437
Tom Bonner, Director of Operations Licensee Division

Description of Operation: Automobile renting and leasing.
Number of Franchisees: 349 owning a total 948 franchises in all 50 States.
In Business Since: 1947
Equity Capital Needed: Varies according to franchise operating capital required by location.
Financial Assistance Available: Will accept promissory note for franchise fee.
Training Provided: Initial training by Field Representative utilizing complete start-up kit. Comprehensive accounting program tailored to the car rental business.
Managerial Assistance Available: Periodic visits and phone contact by Field Representatives. Maintain regional offices to service and assist licensees in areas of fleet and revenue planning, marketing, accounting, and all phases of the business.

PAYLESS CAR RENTAL SYSTEM, INC.
1505 West 4th Street
Spokane, Washington 99204
L. E. Netterstrom, President

Description of Operation: Payless Car Rental System, Inc., franchises companies or individuals to rent vehicles to the general public under the U.S. Registered Servicemark "Payless Car Rental System." Payless specializes in the rental of small economy cars at low rates with free mileage.
Number of Franchisees: 107 franchise operations in 33 States, Canada and Martinique, F.W.I.
In Business Since: 1971
Equity Capital Needed: Franchisee will require a credit line to finance rental fleet plus $5,000 investment for a franchise in a city with a population of 200,000. Financing of receivables, deposits, various start-up costs varies.
Financial Assistance Available: The $5,000 investment pays for the franchise fee, training, all supplies and forms during first year of operation, signs (interior and exterior) and accounting system. Payless will assist the franchisee in obtaining a credit line from local banks, GMAC, Ford Motor Credit, etc.
Training Provided: Payless agrees to furnish guidance to the franchisee in establishing, operating and promoting the business of renting automobiles, with respect to: the institution and maintenance of office management systems and business operating procedures; the institution of a continuing sales campaign and securing a vehicle rental location and office.
Managerial Assistance Available: Payless provides a continuing relationship with its franchisees in the following ways: Franchisees are allowed to call the Payless National Headquarters collect as regards technical problems, reservation handling, insurance questions, and supply or advertising needs; Payless will make calls to franchisees' office to help franchisee improve and promote his rent-a-car business. A monthly newsletter and Operation Manual changes are mailed on a regular basis to franchisee.

THRIFTY RENT-A-CAR SYSTEM
P.O. Box 35250
2400 North Sheridan Road
Tulsa, Oklahoma 74151
Cecil R. Davis, Franchise Director

Description of Operation: Daily car rental business. Thrifty rents new, full size, midsize, compact, and sub-compact automobiles to the general public at Thrifty rates.
Number of Franchisees: Better than 400 locations in all 50 States, Puerto Rico, Canada, Scotland, England, Central America, Mexico and Israel.
In Business Since: 1958
Equity Capital Needed: $25,000-$50,000
Financial Assistance Available: Franchisor assists licensee in setting up lines of credit for purchase of vehicles.
Training Provided: On-the-job training 1 week in company-owned operation, 1 week with licensee at opening and periodically thereafter.
Managerial Assistance Available: Franchisor furnishes continuing management and technical assistance to franchisee. Management assistance is under supervision of experienced, knowledgeable supervisors who are full time employees of Thrifty Rent-A-Car System, Inc.

BEAUTY SALON/SUPPLIES

EDIE ADAMS CUT & CURL
125 South Service Road
Long Island Expressway
Jericho, New York 11753
Don vonLiebermann, Vice President
Description of Operation: Operating of beauty salons with 12 to 20 stations under the Edie Adams Cut & Curl/Haircrafters.
Number of Franchisees: 350 to 40 States
In Business Since: 1955
Equity Capital Needed: $40,000
Financial Assistance Available: Up to $25,000 financing to qualified applicants.
Training Provided: In salon training about 10 days. Pre-opening training in franchisee's salon and complete supply of manuals.
Managerial Assistance Available: Home office, technical, seminars, new techniques, and management techniques.

THE BARBERS, HAIRSTYLING FOR MEN AND WOMEN, INC.
300 Industrial Boulevard
Minneapolis, Minnesota 55413
Description of Operation: A completely systemized men's and women's hairstyling shop with inventory controls, accounting systems, advertising, public relations, business management programs, and turn-key built locations.
Number of Franchisees: 80 in 17 States plus 35 company-owned.
In Business Since: 1963
Equity Capital Needed: $20,000 to $35,000
Financial Assistance Available: Available to qualified applicants. Investor partners welcomed.
Training Provided: Mangement and technical, 1 week, then quarterly seminars.
Managerial Assistance Available: Business management, including advertising, public relations, accounting and record keeping, training in hairstyling and all related services.

COMMAND PERFORMANCE
First International Services Corporation
Westbank Boardwalk
Westport, Connecticut 06880
Steve Schimpff, Director of Marketing
Description of Operation: Precision haircutting and styling salons for men and women. By employing a manager, most franchisees devote only 10-14 hours per week to the business.
Number of Franchisees: 278 franchisees own 840 franchises in 42 States
In Business Since: 1976
Equity Capital Needed: Total cost to purchase, construct and open salon: $75,000 to $100,000.
Financial Assistance Available: Up to $25,000 of financing is available to qualified individuals.
Training Provided: In addition to recruiting and training the shop's manager and staff, the franchisor conducts a comprehensive week-long training course for its franchisees in all phases of operations, advertising, promotion, legal and financial considerations.
Managerial Assistance Available: In addition to initial site selection, lease negotiations, hiring and training of staff, construction counsel, the franchisor furnishes continuing management, marketing, operational and technical assistance to franchisee and his employees.

GREAT EXPECTATIONS PRECISION HAIRCUTTERS
125 South Service Road
Long Island Expressway
Jericho, New York 11753
Don vonLiebermann, Vice President
Description of Operation: Great Expectations is a distinctive haircutting establishment primarily servicing men and women aged 18-34, appealing to the contemporary hair care customer. The franchise package offers: a thoroughly modern, attractively designed shop, streamlined equipment, operational support, training and personal recruitment.
Number of Franchisees: 117 in 33 States
In Business Since: 1955
Equity Capital Needed: Total initial investment $72,500 - $145,000.
Financial Assistance Available: Financial assistance available up to $35,000 to qualified applicants.
Training Provided: In salon training about 10 days. Pre-opening training in franchisee's salon and complete supply of manuals.
Managerial Assistance Available: Home office, technical seminars, new techniques, and management training. Advertising materials and promotions.

HAIR PERFORMERS
c/o John F. Amico & Co., Inc.
7327 West 90th Street
Bridgeview, Illinois 60455
Ronald Austin, Director of Sales
Description of Operation: Family hair care center which provides styling and hair cutting for the entire family. Most franchisees operate store on limited hours (8 to 10) all business and management aids provided. Regional offices and training facilities throughout the U.S. Two basic schools in Chicago.
Number of Franchisees: 50 franchised units in 10 States, plus 20 company-owned.
In Business Since: 1962
Equity Capital Needed: $25,000 to $50,000
Financial Assistance Available: Up to $25,000 to qualified applicants.
Training Provided: Staffing, recruiting, management selection and training provided for franchisee. Training conducted at home office, regional offices, company-owned college and in-store programs.
Managerial Assistance Available: Complete site selection, lease negotiations, salon design, full staffing and continual management assistance and full training at Hair Performers college.

KENNETH OF LONDON, LTD.
International Headquarters
1130 Burnett Avenue, Suite D
Concord, California 94520
Description of Operation: Complete hairstyling studios from men, women and children. Franchisor offers site selection and construction criteria. Interior design is standardized for all studios. Hairstylist and management recruiting and training is provided. Continuing education is provided through and audio/video program. Advertising is supported through a planned advertising program.
Number of Franchisees: 11 in California
In Business Since: 1976
Equity Capital Needed: $60,000 to $95,000
Financial Assistance Available: None
Training Provided: 1 week orientation and operations manual studies at Corporate Headquarters for franchisee.
Managerial Assistance Available: 2 to 3 weeks manager and stylist recruiting and system training at franchisee's location. Continuing provisions of audio/video tapes in studio operation and hairstyling techniques in each studio.

MAGIC MIRROR INC.
11337 Ventura Boulevard
Studio City, California 91604
Dale Scott, President
Description of Operation: Beauty salon-cosmetics sold at retail (private brand).
Number of Franchisees: 9 in California, New Jersey and Florida.
In Business Since: 1949
Equity Capital Needed: $40,000 - $50,000
Financial Assistance Available: Helps find financing.
Training Provided: 2 weeks at headquarters, 1 week at franchisee's shop covering management, and operation.
Managerial Assistance Available: Continuous training, counselor visits every 3 months providing assistance in accounting, operations, advertising brand name merchandise. Franchisee may buy from other suppliers.

ROFFLER INDUSTRIES, INC.
400 Chess Street
Coraopolis, Pennsylvania 15108
Dr. Larry Casterline, Executive Director, Franchise Operations
Description of Operation: Roffler Industries, Inc., formulates, manufactures and sells Roffler men's cosmetics and hair styling and hair care preparations for use throughout the U.S. by barbers trained in the Roffler Sculptur-Kut System of cutting and styling men's hair. Sales are made to 47 area distributors who in turn sell to approximately 8,000 barbers franchised as of January 31, 1978 by the company to use Roffler's name, hairstyling system and products and to sell Roffler products to the public. Roffler also manufactures and sells "Nu-Vita" and "Capilo" hair styling, hair care and cosmetic products, and in addition sells barber equipment and supplies purchased from others, to its area distributors as well as to barber and beauty supply dealers generally.
Number of Franchisees: Over 8,000 in all States
In Business Since: 1968
Equity Capital Needed: $495 to cover franchise fee, equipment and inventory.
Financial Assistance Available: None
Training Provided: Hairstyling fashions can change from month to month and Roffler takes great pride in not only keeping up-to-date in hairstyling trends, but anticipating them months in advance. Local and national seminars, part of a franchise, provide the personalized education that each Roffler Pro needs to assure continuing success. Refresher clinics are an integral part of the seminars. Seminars include education in additional services as hairpiece fitting, cleaning, and coloring; hair and scalp treatments; facials, hair coloring, and hair straightening. These techniques are mastered by the Roffler Pros since they provided significant increases in income.
Managerial Assistance Available: The franchisor has no obligation during the operation of the business to give assistance to the franchisee in the operation of his business since, in almost every case, the franchisee is operating a barber shop already in operation. Franchisor and its area dealers do from time to time conduct training seminars.

S.M.R. ENTERPRISES, INC.
5703 Quince
Memphis, Tennessee 38117
Sam M. Ross, President
Description of Operation: The company sells licenses for Fantastic Sam's Family Haircutters, a unique retail hair care establishment oriented to the demands, pocketbooks and convenience of the typical American family.
Number of Franchisees: 61 licensees are located in 22 states and operate 125 locations.
In Business Since: 1974
Equity Capital Needed: Approximately $48,000.
Financial Assistance Available: A total investment of $48,000 is necessary to open a Fantastic Sam's license. The $15,000 license fee pays for market research, media planning, site location, lease negotiation, and extensive training. $18,000 is the recommended allocation for advertising and working capital. The remaining $15,000 is for furniture and fixtures, for which leasing arrangements are available.
Training Provided: An intensive headquarters training course is supplemented by an additional week or more of pre-opening, start-up and reinforcement training.
Managerial Assistance Available: Regional and in-shop seminars are provided on at least a quarterly basis. Regularly-scheduled advance training programs for owners, managers and cutters are offered at corporate headquarters. Consulting services are provided upon request by licensee or on an as-needed basis.

BUSINESS AIDS/SERVICES

AMERICAN ADVERTISING DISTRIBUTORS, INC.
1424 East Broadway
Mesa, Arizona 85204
Richard Elliott, President

Description of Operation: American Advertising Distributors, Inc., has established techniques, methods, experience and know-how in establishing a cooperative direct mail business. Franchisee shall have the exclusive marketing license for a territory. The Company has facilities for the printing and production of coupons and other mailing pieces.
Number of Franchisees: 50 in 19 States
In Business Since: 1976
Equity Capital Needed: $25,000 to $50,000 depending on population territory.
Financial Assistance Available: None
Training Provided: 1 week of formal training school at the Company's home office, 2 weeks of training at either a similar operation, or in the Licensee's territory by a Company representative.
Managerial Assistance Available: Provided for in training school.

AMERICAN DYNAMICS CORP.
Box 11, Cathedral Station
New York, New York 10025
Frank Forrester, General Manager

Description of Operation: Financial Counsellors educate clients and promote seminars to demonstrate benefits of (a) Compounding savings at 12 percent tax-free in 12 percent Savings Club, (b) Deducting $1,750 off taxable income via IRS-approved IRA Master Pension Plan, (c) Saving state sales tax on cars, machinery, and farm equipment, (d) Avoiding probate court and estate and inheritance taxes with "Double Trusts," (e) Avoiding capital gains tax on investments via a U.S.-based, leased Tax-Haven, (f) Converting income to tax-free capital gains on all invoiced products, professional services, and future payments receivable including paychecks, and (g) providing 9 to 1 tax shelters.
Number of Franchisees: 103 in 37 States
In Business Since: 1959
Equity Capital Needed: $150 for counsellors; $500 for dealers
Financial Assistance Available: Franchisor has eliminated all normal licensing costs for the investment, tax shelter and tax haven business.
Training Provided: 70 page training manual plus cassette tapes. Further help by mail is free.
Managerial Assistance Available: The training manual solves all normal problems and answers typical questions. Also, it describes all services offered. New services and future improvements are covered in periodic newsletters, by correspondance, and by local seminars.

AMERICAN FACILITIES INSPECTION, INC.
300 Burntwood
North Little Rock, Arkansas 72116
Royce A. Flynn, Secretary

Description of Operation: An inspection provided for prepurchase and a facility condition evaluation pertaining to home, business and industry. An Associate License is granted for a secured area for a nominal fee, for a period of 5 years, and renewable for $100. A percentage of amount charged for each inspection is paid as a royalty fee. Tool box, tools, business cards, invoices, price guides, and some advertisements are furnished.
Number of Franchisees: 22 in 13 States
In Business Since: 1977
Equity Capital Needed: $2,000 to $5,000, plus $3,000 working capital.
Financial Assistance Available: None
Training Provided: A 3 day intensified training course provided to qualified personnel, with lodging paid at national headquarters, North Little Rock, Arkansas. Associates are carefully screened for character, and technical background with experience required in building maintenance, general knowledge of construction, quality control.
Managerial Assistance Available: Technical and manpower assistance available, standard bookkeeping system used. Periodic bulletins provided to improve both technical managerial operations.

ASSOCIATED TAX CONSULTANTS OF AMERICA, INC.
18552 MacArthur Boulevard, Suite 400
Irvine, California 92715
Paul A. Sax, Franchise Manager

Description of Operation: Preparation of computerized income tax returns, bookkeeping, and financial planning — company provides a complete marketing program for all three functions in addition to continuous training.
Number of Franchisees: 52 in California, Nevada, Colorado, Utah, Minnesota and Ohio.
In Business Since: 1966
Equity Capital Needed: $17,000
Financial Assistance Available: Company will finance two-thirds upon approved credit.
Training Provided: ATC will thoroughly train its franchisees in both Federal and State personal income tax returns, along with basic bookkeeping knowledge and financial planning. ATC will aid in helping individuals obtain their NASD and Life & Disability Insurance Licenses. Typically, the new franchisees will receive in excess of three weeks training during their first year.
Managerial Assistance Available: Associated Tax Consultants provides continual management services for the life of the franchisee including but not limited to bookkeeping, advertising, training, procuring new clients, forms and procedures, location, training new consultants computer updating, and sales.

AUDIT CONTROLS, INC.
87 Northeast 44th Street
Fort Lauderdale, Florida 33334
Arieh Douer, President

Description of Operation: Nationwide collection service. No collection fees. Nominal service charge. Trademark registered by the U.S. Patent Office #880,919. Audit Controls, Inc., representatives are supplied with mailers (a direct advertising brochure) and a complete set-up for Direct Mail, Magazine Advertising, Telephone Soliciting and Direct Sales.
Number of Franchisees: 490 in 50 States
In Business Since: 1960
Equity Capital Needed: $100 for supplies
Financial Assistance Available: No financial assistance provided.
Training Provided: No training required. Detailed instructions mailed to each Representative.
Managerial Assistance Available: Free advisory assistance is available to Representatives.

BEST RESUME SERVICE
The Penthouse
625 Stanwix Street
Pittsburgh, Pennsylvania 15222
Richard D. Hindman, President

Description of Operation: Best Resume Service provides a broad range of professional business communication services for the educational, commercial and individual client markets. These services include professional resume writing and printing, marketing proposals and brochures, direct mail processing, automatic typing and word processing.
Number of Franchisees: 26 in 16 States and Washington, D.C.
In Business Since: 1962
Equity Capital Needed: $5,000 to $25,000 depending on territory.
Financial Assistance Available: Franchisor will finance, or arrange financing, of up to 50 percent of required capital for qualified franchisee's with good credit rating.
Training Provided: Franchisor conducts a formal, intensive 2 week training program for all new franchisees in the corporate offices. Franchisee's managers may attend any scheduled training program at no charge. Update training seminars conducted periodically.
Managerial Assistance Available: Best Resume Service provides a continuous program of assistance to all franchisees in all phases of their business operations and management, finances and record keeping, marketing and personnel. Visits to the franchisee's office are made regularly by home office staff and all franchisee's participate in periodic refresher training seminars, Market research and testing of new products and services is done continuously by the franchisor's home office.

BINEX-AUTOMATED BUSINESS SYSTEMS, INC.
1787 Tribute Road, Suite M
Sacramento, California 95815
Walter G. Heidig, President

Description of Operation: Binex franchises offer a broad range of computerized services to small and medium sized businesses. Services include financial reports, general ledgers, accounts receivable, accounts payable, job cost, payroll, and specialized computer services are also available, and you can develop your own. You may operate your business in various ways from a bookkeeping office to a full computer service.
Number of Franchisees: 60 in 21 States and Canada.
In Business Since: 1966
Equity Capital Needed: $7,500. The fee covers training, manuals, and startup supplies. No expensive equipment is required.
Financial Assistance Available: None
Training Provided: Home study course, 2 week home office and 1 week on-the-job. Franchisees may return for further training as needed. Complete operations manuals, technical manuals, and promotion manuals are provided.
Managerial Assistance Available: Support is provided on a continuous basis. Frequent newsletters are sent out covering a variety of subjects including business operation, marketing, technical, taxes, etc. New programs and services are developed, documented, and made available regularly to all franchisees. Periodic regional meetings provide upgrading and review.

H & R BLOCK, INC.
4410 Main Street
Kansas City, Missouri 64111
William T. Ross, Vice President; Director, Administrative Operations

Description of Operation: The exclusive function of H & R Block, Inc., is to prepare individual income tax returns. The franchisee is operated in a city by an individual or partnership. The only warranty made by the franchisee is to respect and uphold a specific code of ethics and to abide by the policy and procedures of the company.
Number of Franchisees: Over 8,000 offices throughout the United States, Canada and 13 Foreign Countries. Over 4,000 offices are franchised with the balance operated by the parent company.
In Business Since: 1946
Equity Capital Needed: $1,000 to $2,000
Financial Assistance Available: None
Training Provided: Each year a training program is held in November for all new managers. Prior to tax season each year, a training program for all employees is conducted in major centers. Each summer a meeting is held for all managers for 3 days to discuss all phases of the operation and new developments and ideas.
Managerial Assistance Available: We work very closely with our franchisees and provide any and all assistance required or needed.

13

BUSINESS BROKERAGE INVESTMENT GROUP
42 Weybosset Street
Providence, Rhode Island 02903

Description of Operation: Business Brokerage Group offices are licensees of The Business Brokerage Investment Group, Inc., each office has an owner/manager which specializes exclusively in business sales, mergers and acquisitions of proprietorships, partnerships and corporations with gross annual sales of $2 million dollars or less. The total number of small businesses sold each year creates a strong market and is the basis of BBG's activity.
Number of Franchisees: 25 in 7 States with offices scheduled to be opened throughout the country.
In Business Since: 1977
Equity Capital Needed: $20,000 plus $5,000 operating capital.
Financial Assistance Available: Yes, to qualified individuals.
Training Provided: On-the-job training which includes all phases of operation, 2 week courses at home office, plus training for duration necessary after opening as deemed required by individual.
Managerial Assistance Available: Training is on-going. Initial managerial and technical assistance provided for continuous period after office opening. Continuous telephone contact, site visits and management assistance designed to support each licensee as needed. Periodic home-office conducted training seminars with required attendance by licensees.

BUSINESS CONSULTANTS OF AMERICA
Affiliate of: HORIZONS OF AMERICA
P. O. Box 4098
Waterbury, Connecticut 06714
Gregg Nolan, Franchise Director

Description of Operation: Franchisor offers time tested practice, dealing with advisory services for small and medium sized business operations. Training in services to include: management, marketing, sales tax advisory and financial advisory services. Additional training to include programs for mergers/acquisition, business brokerage, and estate planning.
Number of Franchisees: 14 in 9 States and Canada
In Business Since: 1973
Equity Capital Needed: $8,500 plus $5,000 working capital.
Financial Assistance Available: Assistance with bank/government financing.
Training Provided: 2 weeks intensive training at franchise headquarters, followed by 2 months cassette courses packaged by franchisor and other professional organizations. Continuing franchisor advisory newsletters and tapes.
Managerial Assistance Available: First year, non-fee technical and advisory services at discretion of franchisee. Continued services on an as needed fee basis from franchisor. Additional memberships arranged in professional associations.

BUSINESS DATA SERVICES, INC.
1867 Crane Ridge Drive
Jackson, Mississippi 39216
W. D. Whigham, President

Description of Operation: BDS Licensees provide a complete computerized accounting and financial advisory service to a wide spectrum of small to medium sized businesses. Services which the Licensees provide include bookkeeping, tax preparation, and related financial planning and analysis.
Number of Franchisees: 30 in 11 States
In Business Since: 1972, franchising since 1979
Equity Capital Needed: $14,500
Training Provided: All required first year training expenses, including transportation and accommodations, are bourne by the Licensor. Completion of a prerequisite home study course is required before the new Licensee attends a three week central office initial training seminar. Additionally, BDS provides field training in licensee's area, together with in-field follow-up for the first year at licensor's expense. Licensee must attend a 4 day post graduate training course after the first year covering operations and marketing management.
Managerial Assistance Available: Complete and continuous support is provided to licensee. Central office maintains regular communications with licensee in the form of newsletters, seminars, and periodic personal visits at licensee's office. BDS staff is constantly available for telephone inquiry on technical and tax questions. A toll free number is used by licensees to communicate with Marketing Director and Staff CPA concerning client acquisition and technical areas.

BUSINESS EXCHANGE, INC.
4716 Vineland Avenue
North Hollywood, California 91602
Marvin J. McConnell, President

Description of Operation: Company offers a barter service plan for business owners that allows the business owners in all franchised areas to trade their products (at retail) for the things that they need from the other participating dealers rather than paying cash. Company provides an exclusive TRADE ✓ CHEK book that allows one member to make purchases and pay for his purchases with TRADE ✓ CHEKS, not cash. Member pays for his TRADE ✓ CHEK purchases with offsetting TRADE ✓ CHEK sales to other members. As a result, members receive new sales from other members and as they pay for their purchases with offsetting retail sales, not cash, their actual cost is the cost of their own inventory.
Number of Franchisees: 40 in 20 States and Canada.
In Business Since: 1961
Equity Capital Needed: $19,900
Financial Assistance Available: All of the accounting is computerized and this detail and expense is borne by company. Company further finances all sales commission advances made to sales representatives in licensee's area to permit continued expansion by licensee without requiring additional investment by licensee.
Training Provided: Complete training program at home office with actual field works as well as theory. If requested by licensee, training and actual development of the program in licensee's area is also provided by company.

Managerial Assistance Available: Company provides accounting service for members and mangement assistance for franchisee on a continuous basis. Company provides Member Directories, to all members for all franchisees in all areas, BX Magazines, BX Hotlines and BX Newsletters.

COMMERCIAL SERVICES COMPANY
2699 Lee Road, Suite 150
Winter Park, Florida 32789
James G. Sherwood, Partner

Description of Operation: Commercial Services Company offices offer a continuing and complete bookkeeping, accounting and tax service to small and medium sized businesses.
Number of Franchisees: 14 in 7 States
In Business Since: 1959
Equity Capital Needed: $18,000 includes training, cost of starting inventory (double entry systems), supply of sales materials, continuing direct mail program.
Financial Assistance Available: Will finance $9,000 paid as a percent of earnings.
Training Provided: Training in all phases of operation is conducted by the home office in Orlando, Florida. Sessions are 1 week or longer as required. A Procedures Manual is provided containing operating instructions. General guidance will continue indefinitely.
Managerial Assistance Available: The home office provides immediate back-up assistance on all business matters, technical or managerial. Licensee will receive a response almost always within the same day to any specific or general question.

COMPREHENSIVE ACCOUNTING CORPORATION
2111 Comprehensive Drive
Aurora, Illinois 60507
John J. Keefer, President

Description of Operation: Comprehensive licenses independent degreed accountants to provide a monthly computerized bookkeeping, accounting and tax service to small and medium-sized businesses of all types. Services include complete computerized preparation of monthly balance sheets, operating statements, general ledgers, accounts receivable and job cost statements. Through its marketing force, Comprehensive furnishes its licensees with clients; licensees also develop referral accounts on their own through the use of marketing aids and sales methods furnished to licensees. In 1978, licensees with over 100 accounts averaged an accrual profit of $85,591 and a cash flow of $49,097.
Number of Franchisees: 100 in 11 States
In Business Since: 1949, Licensing since 1966
Equity Capital Needed: $12,000
Financial Assistance Available: Partial or full financing consisting of notes collateralized by the licensee's practice. Credit extended to licensee may exceed $300,000 in certain cases.
Training Provided: Each new licensee is required to complete a 6 week training course, both in the classroom at Corporate Headquarters and on-the-job training in the office of a experienced licensee with training experience.
Managerial Assistance Available: Comprehensive provides on an on-going basis a production consultant and a data processing consultant to aid success. Each consultant is available by phone or in person, for each licensee. Also provided are detailed production procedures and methods, client reporting forms, plus sales aids for use in obtaining accounts; audio-visual projector, two professionally prepared filmstrips portraying Comprehensive's service to prospective clients, a prospective client licensee the benefit of its experience gained through its current licensees who are providing services for over 19,000 monthly bookkeeping, accounting and tax service clients. A management information system provides statistics monthly and annually on the growth, production status, and other success criteria of all licensees for an interchange of ideas. Other seminars are conducted for licensees' staff. Annual seminar is conducted for licensees' clients.

COMPREHENSIVE BUSINESS CORPORATION
2111 Comprehensive Drive
Aurora, Illinois 60507
John J. Keefer, President

Description of Operation: Comprehensive franchises independent degreed accountants to provide a monthly computerized bookkeeping, accounting and tax service to small and medium-sized businesses of all types as Affiliates of Comprehensive. Services include complete computerized preparation of monthly balance sheets, operating statements, general ledger and payroll ledgers, accounts receivable, and job cost statements. Comprehensive trains its Affiliates to use the Comprehensive Client Acquisition System. The Affiliate can build his practice as fast as he is able to grow and maintain quality service.
Number of Franchisees: 80 in 30 States and Puerto Rico
In Business Since: 1975
Equity Capital Needed: $12,000
Financial Assistance Available: The appointment fee must be paid in cash. The franchise fee may be financed over a ten-year period.
Training Provided: The Affiliate is required to complete a 3 week course at the Corporate Headquarters after sufficient home study preparation in Comprehensive's production methods. Training at Corporate Headquarters is divided equally between Administration and Marketing. An experienced Comprehensive Marketing Manager will spend 1 week in the franchisee's market training him in Comprehensive's Client Acquisition System. In addition, a post graduate course lasting 1 week is given in the Home office approximately six months after the trainee has started his practice.
Managerial Assistance Available: Comprehensive provides on an on-going basis a production consultant, a marketing consultant and data processing consultant. Each consultant is available by phone or in person for each Affiliate. Also provided are detailed production procedures and methods, client reporting forms, plus sales aids for use in obtaining accounts, audio-visual projector, two professional film strips portraying Comprehensive's service to prospective clients, a prospective client presentation manual, sample computer financial statements and various sales brochures. Comprehensive gives the Affiliate the benefit of Comprehensive's experience gained through current licensees who are providing service for over 19,000 monthly bookkeeping, accounting and tax service clients. Comprehensive provides a list of approximately 2,000 prospects in the Affiliate's area. A management information

system provides statistics monthly and annually of all growth, production status, and other success criteria of all Affiliates for comparison. Seminars for Affiliates provide continuing education and interchange of ideas. Other seminars are conducted for Affiliates' staff. An annual seminar is conducted for Affiliates' clients.

COMPUTER SERVICECENTERS, INC.
714 North State Street
Jackson, Mississippi 39202
Julian Rish

Description of Operation: The franchisor offers computerized billing, management information and control systems to the medical, dental and veterinary professions through franchised representatives.
Number of Franchisees: 20 in 13 States
In Business Since: 1964
Equity Capital Needed: $12,000 minimum
Financial Assistance Available: None
Training Provided: 4½ days intensive training at company offices in how systems are sold, installed and serviced. Training is mandatory and all costs associated therewith are included in the franchise fee.
Managerial Assistance Available: Managerial and technical assistance is available thereafter from company employees and/or Area Directors. In some instances charges are made for technical assistance if it becomes excessively requested.

CONTACTS INFLUENTIAL
516 S.E. Morrison, 10th Floor
Portland, Oregon 97214
Matt J. Dutton

Description of Operation: Publishers of computerized business directories, special select business oriented mailing lists and a monthly updating service. Used by business firms to make contacts with other businesses - and for making more effective sales through personal calls and by using our direct mail lists to efficiently generate responses. We have over 300 national accounts - people such as Xerox, Metropolitan Life, American Cancer, Snelling & Snelling etc. Basically a non competitive service.
Number of Franchisees: 16 in 10 States and Canada.
In Business Since: 1961
Equity Capital Needed: Approximately $20,000 for operating capital only.
Financial Assistance Available: Negotiable
Training Provided: Approximately 4 months in the field, plus any back-up that is needed or requested.
Managerial Assistance Available: Constant contact is kept with franchisees. This is not a technical franchise. More of a marketing background is needed. All technical or computer assistance is taken care of by franchisor.

CORPORATE FINANCE ASSOCIATES
22 Perimeter Park Drive
Suite 104
Atlanta, Georgia 30341
Michael Rothberg

Description of Operation: Financial consultants on loans, mergers - acquisition brokers. For executives only.
Number of Franchisees: 35 in 18 States plus international offices.
In Business Since: 1956
Equity Capital Needed: $25,000 for operating capital.
Financial Assistance Available: No financial assistance except to sources for loan and venture funds.
Training Provided: For executives - one on one. Operating manuals are provided. Annual seminars. Regional meetings.
Managerial Assistance Available: Ongoing - case by case training.

CREATIVE PROSPECTS, INC.
222 Panorama Plaza
Rochester, New York 14625
Robert Thompson, Market Manager

Description of Operation: A unique advertising program that is easily adaptable to all cities dealing with retailers and national companies. High renewal rates and low overhead makes this a successful full or part-time business which can be operated from home. Major distributorships and part-time territories available to qualified applicants.
Number of Franchisees: 4 in New York and 1 in Texas.
In Business Since: 1970
Equity Capital Needed: $3,500 to $7,500
Financial Assistance Available: Financing to promising prospects is possible.
Training Provided: Up to 2 weeks in the field. Regular seminars and training meetings after franchisee is established.
Managerial Assistance Available: Assistance in bookkeeping, advertising, inventory control and tax advice. District and field managers render assistance. Continuous research in marketing, products and services.

CREDIT SERVICE COMPANY
101 Miles Building
2025 Canal Street
New Orleans, Louisiana 70112
E. G. Edwards, President

Description of Operation: Credit Service Company offers a unique medical-dental-hospital collection service. The methods used insure the collection of more than twice the number of accounts that can be currently achieved through other such services, 73 percent as against the national average of 34 percent. The franchise can be operated full or part time, and can be started in the home.
Number of Franchisees: 64 in 27 States
In Business Since: 1949, Franchising since 1962
Equity Capital Needed: $2,350
Financial Assistance Available: The $2,350 required covers everything except the initial supply of stationery, and this can be obtained by the franchisee in his own locality at an additional cost of about $200. The franchisee pays 3 percent royalty, based on gross profit before taxes, during the first 3 years of operation, and this is reduced to 1½ percent thereafter.
Training Provided: A comprehensive 2 week training course in New Orleans with round trip rail or air transportation (continental U.S.) meals and first class accommodations included in the cost. A procedures manual is supplied, with copies of all forms, letters and operational details. Further assistance is provided on a continuing basis at no added cost. There is no inventory to purchase and a typewriter is the only equipment needed.
Managerial Assistance Available: Credit Service Company requires monthly reports in order to determine areas in which the franchisee may require assistance. Newsletters are issued bi-monthly in order to keep franchisees informed on matters of mutual interest.

CRITICAL FACTOR SYSTEMS, INCORPORATED
10 Buch Avenue
Lancaster, Pennsylvania 17601
James D. Olson, President

Description of Operation: Small business, management services, i.e., management consulting, financial and tax planning, business brokerage, venture capital assistance, etc.
Number of Franchisees: 12 in Pennsylvania, Virginia, Georgia and Alabama
In Business Since: 1970
Equity Capital Needed: $10,500 for area directorship/$5,250 for associate directorship
Financial Assistance Available: Will finance half on standard note.
Training Provided: 1 week in field, as needed thereafter.
Managerial Assistance Available: Total continuous assistance. There is no limit in this area.

DIXON COMMERCIAL INVESTIGATORS, INC.
736 Center Street
Lewiston, New York 14092
E. L. Dixon, President

Description of Operation: Complete range of credit and collection services. Territories available by city or state/province (U.S. and Canada locations available).
Number of Franchisees: 6 in New York, Pennsylvania, Ohio, California and Canada.
In Business Since: 1956
Equity Capital Needed: $5,000
Financial Assistance Available: None
Training Provided: 2 to 4 weeks head office training. Continuous supervision and aid afterwards.
Managerial Assistance Available: Franchisee is trained in all areas of credit collection. Franchisee is in continuous contact with head office.

J.P. DOLAN ASSOCIATES AND COMPANY
7 North McDade Boulevard, P.O. Box 125
Glenolden, Pennsylvania 19036
Joseph P. Dolan, President

Description of Operation: Franchisee will represent leading Telecommunications Consulting firm in his/her own exclusive area of operations. Our service is sold on a performance basis (contingency). We share with our clients the refunds and savings we are able to gain for them. Our licensee must be able to deal effectively with entreprenuers and corporate executives. No technical experience is required.
Number of Franchisees: 3 in Massachusetts, Pennsylvania, Delaware and New Jersey.
In Business Since: 1966
Equity Capital Needed: Franchise fees are $15 to $20,000. Up to one-third of this will be deferred for qualified prospects.
Training Provided: 1 week of intensive training at corporate headquarters and 1 week in field. A very close and highly supportive association with headquarters personnel continues for the life of the franchise agreement.
Managerial Assistance Available: Franchisee represents J. P. Dolan Associates services in an exclusive marketing area. His clients are served by J. P. Dolan Associates trained consultants and engineers. Franchisee serves as the marketing arm of a highly competent Telecommunications consulting firm. He is trained to manage this marketing function, the technical support is provided by J. P. Dolan Associates consultants.

ECONOTAX, INC.
1211 Ellis Avenue
Jackson, Mississippi 39209
James T. Marsh, Vice President or
Keith J. Douglas, Secretary-Treasurer

Description of Operation: EconoTax, provides the public with a professional, full-service tax office. In addition to income tax preparation, EconoTax offers audit representation, accounting, tax planning, and tax-oriented paralegal services. EconoTax began and continues to operate in the spirit of a cooperative of tax professionals with low franchise fees and a maximum of local independent decision-making.
Number of Franchisees: 24 with 53 units in Alabama, Florida, Mississippi and Louisiana. Expanding throughout Southeast.
In Business Since: 1965
Equity Capital Needed: $3,000 minimum
Financial Assistance Available: EconoTax shares the cost of advertising and will arrange installment payments for the initial fee.
Training Provided: EconoTax provides a 12 week technical training program for franchisees and their employees. Technical backup normally provides a response within 30 minutes during tax season.
Managerial Assistance Available: Managerial assistance is provided as needed. EconoTax offers turn-key operation with support in site selection; recruiting, hiring, and training; work scheduling; internal controls and procedures; and financial controls.

THE EPICUREAN DINNER CLUB
317 Plaza Building
Pensacola, Florida 32505
William F. Johns, President

Description of Operation: The Epicurean Club is a dinner club that provides for dues paying members to dine out, any day or everyday, and save money through a buy one, get one free arrangement with Epicurean sponsored restaurants.
Number of Franchisees: 3 in Florida
In Business Since: 1977
Equity Capital Needed: Approximately $8,000
Financial Assistance Available: Some financial assistance is available to qualified applicants with good credit.
Training Provided: 1 week training at home office and then 1 week training setting up in the franchisee's territory.
Managerial Assistance Available: Continual management assistance for the life of the franchise in such areas as bookkeeping, advertising, operations manual forms, service to members, restaurant dealer relations and member relations.

GENERAL BUSINESS SERVICES, INC.
The GBS Building
51 Monroe Street
Rockville, Maryland 20850
Bernard S. Browning, President

Description of Operation: Business counseling, financial management, and tax services for the small independent business.
Number of Franchisees: Over 1,000 in all States.
In Business Since: 1962
Equity Capital Needed: $18,000 for Area Directors.
Financial Assistance Available: None
Training Provided: Approximately 30 d·'s training provided during the first year and approximately 15 days training each year thereafter. All selected franchisees are appointed Area Directors and receive without additional expense: (1) a 5-volume Operations Manual containing all operating instructions, company policies, and procedures; (2) Basic Training Institute and Advanced Training Institute in Washington, D.C.; (3) individual field training, periodic training development; (4) training and individual guidance continue indefinitely through permanently assigned Regional Directors.
Managerial Assistance Available: A complete and detailed program based on 17 years successful experience is provided to develop a professional practice; an experienced Regional Director is available for each State to provide local assistance on a continuing basis; a staff of over 300 in the National Office provides managerial assistance and technical support as required; 20 continuing support services are provided to franchisees and their clients.

GETTING TO KNOW YOU INTERNATIONAL, LTD.
9 Chelsea Place
Great Neck, New York 11022
Richard F. Wynn, Vice President

Description of Operation: Getting To Know You is a newcomer welcome service for retail merchants, professionals, and homeowner services. The franchisee sends a personal phone book and collateral materials to new families and invites them to patronize the recommended merchants. The franchisee contracts with sponsoring merchants to distribute the books. The home office prepares all standardized materials to franchisee's local specifications. No direct calls are made on new families. No hostesses are required.
Number of Franchisees: 34 in 12 states
In Business Since: 1962
Equity Capital Needed: $22,000 minimum
Financial Assistance Available: The franchise fee of $15,000 covers presentation materials, home office, and field training, basic area marketing survey and procedures. In addition, at least $7,000 operating capital plus a car is required for the first several months of operation, or until cash receipts are sufficiently established to defray expenses. The franchisor will assist the franchisee in making inventory purchases after six months.
Training Provided: Initially, 1 week of orientation procedures and sales techniques at the home office and 1 week of sales and marketing procedures in the franchisee's territory. Later, the franchisee receives additional training in renewal procedures prior to renewal sales.
Managerial Assistance Available: Franchisee receives total and constant assistance from franchisor in many forms, including marketing, production and distribution. Complete operations manuals are provided, plus regular supplements. Home office maintains a market research program, advertising program, and maintains regular and frequent contact with all franchisees.

HOUSEMASTER OF AMERICA, INC.
18 Hamilton Street
Bound Brook, New Jersey 08805
Robert J. Hardy, President

Description of Operation: HouseMaster of America is an organization of home inspection professionals. Qualified technical people conduct the inspections, while marketing-oriented people run the business end. Home buyers who want to know the condition of perhaps the largest investment of their lifetimes are the primary users. There are no inventory requirements and office space can be located within the person's home, initially.
Number of Franchisees: 4 in New York, New Jersey and Benelux
In Business Since: 1979
Equity Capital Needed: $9,000 to $16,000, depending upon the number of owner-occupied homes in area.
Financial Assistance Available: It is advised that an additional $10,000 to $15,000 is needed to get started. No financial assistance is provided by the franchisor.
Training Provided: 5-day orientation training for one; this is for the person who will run the business. 5-day technical training course for one; this is for the designated technical director. Also provided are (1) Sales and Promotion Guidebook, (2) Operations Guidebook and (3) Technical Training Manual.
Managerial Assistance Available: On-going counseling in all aspects of the business. Administration of referral system (WATS Line), advertising, publicity and promotion programs; regular newsletters, both technical and sales, as well as bulletins, trade digests. Periodic Seminars. Both technical and marketing research and development. A warranty program, backed by insurance. On-going availability of errors and omissions insurance.

INCOTAX SYSTEMS, INC.
223 Datura Street
West Palm Beach, Florida 33401
Richard Vondrak, President

Description of Operation: Incotax Systems is a volume tax service system. It has developed an outstanding method of providing high quality, accurate tax returns to the public at a minimum cost and also a truly modern method of management services for small and medium businesses.
Number of Franchisees: 14 in Florida
In Business Since: 1967
Equity Capital Needed: $14,500
Financial Assistance Available: None
Training Provided: Complete management and tax preparation training for both owners and manager is conducted by the Home Office. All previous owners and managers must receive refresher training once a year. Both training sessions are for 2 weeks conducted by Home Office personnel.
Managerial Assistance Available: Continuous Home Office inspection and management training is conducted. Home Office consultation and management suggestions are made to all franchisees. Complete procedural manuals and forms are furnished franchisees as well as monthly news bulletins.

MARCOIN, INC.
1924 Cliff Valley Way, N.E.
Atlanta, Georgia 30329

Description of Operation: Marcoin, Inc., is a nationwide service company providing accounting, management, counseling and other business and computer services to independently owned businesses. The Company also specially designs and tailors systems and services for several major industries, manufacturers, and associations who endorse the Company's services. Marcoin has designed and developed a package of computer software systems and programs which are used in its company-operated offices and are available to its licensees located in over 40 states in providing training and operations manuals to its new and existing licensees which cover basic and new programs, services, systems and operating techniques used in selling and providing services to clients.
Number of Franchisees: The Company has approximately 170 franchised territories plus 20 company-owned and operated territories located in 43 states and the District of Columbia.
In Business Since: The Company and its predecessor have been in business since 1952.
Equity Capital Needed: Initial franchise and training fees vary according to need and potential. Total capital needs including working capital will normally vary from $20,000 to $50,000.
Financial Assistance Available: None
Training Provided: 4 to 5 weeks training in an existing Marcoin Training Center plus installation and follow-up. Formal, required classroom training program consists of 1 week Advanced Financial Management Seminar, plus other training courses as developed or offered by the Company.
Managerial Assistance Available: In addition to providing complete management and operations manuals to all licensees. Marcoin supervises and operates offices on a direct basis and management information and guidelines obtained as a result of these operations are made available and provided to licensees for their information and guidance.

MEDI-FAX, INC.
35 East 7th Street
Suite 700
Cincinnati, Ohio 45202
Sylvan Reisenfeld

Description of Operation: Computerized accounts receivable management service for medical and retail professions.
Number of Franchisees: 3 in 3 States
In Business Since: 1968
Equity Capital Needed: Minimum $5,500
Financial Assistance Available: Yes
Training Provided: 4 day training session by psychologist and member of staff. Management people always available for consultation and to render varied types of assistance.
Managerial Assistance Available: Training manual provided, detail of program available in book form with proper indexing available to clients, small cost for program detail to clients.

MUZAK CORPORATION
888 - 7th Avenue
New York, New York 10019
Kirk G. Anderson, Vice President

Description of Operation: Lease of special work and public area music programs to businesses of all kinds. Sound systems and related communication systems included as lease or sale to customers. Available franchises limited in U.S.; wide opportunities overseas.
Number of Franchisees: Approximately 300 in all fifty States plus 25 countries.
In Business Since: 1934
Equity Capital Needed: Varies—information from Muzak Corporation.
Financial Assistance Available: None
Training Provided: Orientation sessions held regularly in New York City. Continuing sales training sessions at various sites around U.S.
Managerial Assistance Available: Field visits by Muzak corporate staff provided evaluations, assistance, progress reports also on continuing basis. National advertising, sales brochures, equipment specification sheets, etc., provided at all times.

NADW MARKETING, INC.
2701 Houma Boulevard
Metairie, Louisiana 70002
Jack Wood, President

Description of Operation: NADW Marketing, Inc., offers a complete line of Consumer Relations programs to buyers of new cars through franchised dealerships, and to those who purchase previously owned vehicles through independent dealers throughout the U.S. and in Canada. Additionally, NADW offers two versions of extended service contracts available through franchised dealerships, on new cars and trucks, and some select used vehicles. This phase of the business is known as VIP. Customers of the consumer relations programs are afforded travel information, discounts on repairing and maintaining their vehicles and a clear channel of communication with dealers for airing grievances concerning product and service. This phase of the business is known as NADW for the franchised dealership customers and AIADS for the customers of the independents. There are other services offered customers who purchase or are given more deluxe versions of the NADW and AIADS programs - these including vacation message center, credit card hotline and group travel. Like many auto clubs, NADW's consumer programs also offer a theft reward, and in some cases a household theft reward, too.

A recently formulated service contract agreement with the Mutual of Omaha Indemnity and NADW/VIP will constitute a widely-marketed extended service contract (kind of a mechanical breakdown insurance) which takes care of the major expenses for repairing a well-maintained vehicle for a minimum of 1 year and a maximum of 3 years after expiration of the factory warranty. It acts like major medical for motor vehicles. Customer services are managed by the home office, principally through customer access to 4 toll-free incoming WATS lines nationally, and toll-free long distance telephoning in the local Louisiana home state, and in Canada.

Number of Franchisees: 31 in 37 States and Canada.
In Business Since: 1972
Equity Capital Needed: Distributorships for separate aspects of the total package may be purchased separately from about $7,500, which includes point-of-sale materials, business forms, and an initial supply of merchandise. A package to market the whole system of programs costs about $17,500, and would also include same as above. Contracts include quotas to be met both for sales and servicing of accounts. Distributorships are based on a combination of geographic space plus population of new car dealerships and used car independent dealers doing business within that space.
Financial Assistance Available: Governmental grants and loans do not apply. NADW's experience shows that the more successful distributors are those with a wealth of experience as automobile dealers, top dealership management people, and those with many contacts in the aftersale market, or in finance or insurance. Distributorship purchases are on an all cash basis. No formal offices are required, nor expensive equipment. Distributorships are not designed to be successfully operated as a one-man business.
Training Provided: Sales and marketing experts, with heavy experience in training and implementation will provide, at no additional cost, on-site training to new distributors as needed, usually consisting of 3-7 days, initially, and will pay round-trip air fare to the home office for one visit upon purchase. Or, at the distributor's option, the home office will train at their location in New Orleans, and pay the new distributor's round-trip air fare and accommodations while there in training. The home office provides periodic seminars for training and retraining, publishes a monthly distributor newsletter, and holds an annual convention for distributors which includes intensive seminar/workshop and group meetings, as well as personal one-to-one consultation.
Managerial Assistance Available: NADW provides continuing management service for the life of the distributorship, including distributor toll-free access by telephone, without limitation. Some advertising support is offered, along with complete sets of operations manuals, forms and the benefit of constant marketing and product research to maintain and expand acceptance of their programs.

NATIONAL COMPUTERIZED CONTROL, INC.
4751 North First Avenue
P. O. Box 36150
Tucson, Arizona 85740
George C. Clapp

Description of Operation: Computer service for attorneys.
Number of Franchisees: 3 in Illinois, Texas and Arizona
In Business Since: 1979
Equity Capital Needed: $76,000
Financial Assistance Available: None
Training Provided: Actual operation on computer, 1 week in Tucson, and 1 week in franchisee location.
Managerial Assistance Available: Continuous

NATIONAL DIVERSIFIED BROKERS
P. O. Box 6924
Fort Myers, Florida 33901
O. Lee Owens, President

Description of Operation: Building a national network of business brokers with interlocking national listings and interchange of clients.
Number of Franchisees: 6 in Colorado, Ohio and Florida
In Business Since: 1975
Equity Capital Needed: $10,000
Financial Assistance Available: Franchisor will carry $5,000 with terms.
Training Provided: On-site instruction, classroom and actual experience. At least 7 days.
Managerial Assistance Available: Periodic training sessions at our offices in Florida, with 5 day telephone counseling.

NATIONAL FIRE REPAIR, INC.
855 Tod Avenue
Youngstown, Ohio 44502
Marc B. Rubin, Vice President

Description of Operation: Building damage estimating and repairing, primarily in residential market, insurance damage claims repaired and estimated.
Number of Franchisees: 8 in Ohio and Michigan
In Business Since: 1976
Equity Capital Needed: $5,000
Training Provided: Payment in full upon contract agreement.
Training Provided: 1 week training session at home office. Additional training at franchisee's office as needed.
Managerial Assistance Available: Operations manuals and forms are provided by the franchisor. Periodic visits to franchisee and two days of sales calls in franchisee's area are provided by franchisor.

NATIONAL HOMEOWNERS SERVICE ASSOCIATION, INC.
317 Plaza Building
Pensacola, Florida 32505
W. F. Johns, President

Description of Operation: A National Homeowners Service Association Franchise is a chapter in a growing network of homeowner and consumer clubs. It includes complete assistance and guidance in forming a readily excepted service club that is based on fair practices and better treatment of consumers. Income is from membership dues also all types of services for home and appliance maintenance and repair.
Number of Franchisees: 6 in Florida, Massachusetts and Alabama.
In Business Since: 1974
Equity Capital Needed: $15,000
Financial Assistance Available: Minimum investment is $15,000 which is necessary to open a chapter office, this includes cost of personnel and their expenses required for training and opening in home territory of chapter also all printing of literature, forms, manuals, etc. The balance of $4,000 may be financed by National Homeowners Service Association.
Training Provided: Training will consist of a closely regulated 21 days of office and field training, 1 week to be in home office with 2 additional weeks to be provided in the franchisee's chapter office. All training under supervision of well trained full time National Homeowner Service Association employees.
Managerial Assistance Available: National Homeowners Service Association, Inc., will provide continual management assistance for the life of the franchise chapter in such areas as bookkeeping, advertising, operations manuals forms, service to members, service dealer relations, and member relations, NHSA will provide refresher training when need indicates. NHSA sponsors meetings of franchisees and exchange newest developments and ideas in regards to better member service.

NATIONAL HOUSING INSPECTIONS
1817 North Hills Boulevard
Suite 3000
Knoxville, Tennessee 37917

Description of Operation: National Housing Inspections provides a complete inspection service for would-be purchasers of homes. Since most home buyers are not fully conversant with pit-falls, traps and repairs, it is usually necessary they "take a chance" or rely on impartial inspection from an independent inspector who has nothing to sell but his service. NHI inspectors make NO appraisals, nor do they suggest values of any kind, but they do show prospective buyers who want more for their money, how to get it, or how to buy for little or no money down. NHI is based solely on the English "purveyer" system which has been in operation in the British Isles for fifteen years.
Number of Franchisees: 69 in 46 States
In Business Since: 1970
Equity Capital Needed: $750 down payment, $150 30-day rental or longer. All rent applies to purchase.
Financial Assistance Available: Franchisor carries all paper between the $750 cash down payment and the $7,500 total exclusive area cost, with payments of $99 per month for 24 months. Or, prospective franchisee can rent the NHI on non-exclusive basis.
Training Provided: Complete instruction manual is included in both rental and sale of franchise. Also, franchisees can write free at any time for answers to any question on housing, available in the library of 10,000 facts at NHI home office. No charge for this free service.
Managerial Assistance Available: Instruction manual includes much promotional material, office handling procedure and full break-down on handling of leads generated by advertising. The Home Office Library of Home Facts—over 10,000—is available for use by any franchisee who cares to write. Regular newsletters apprise all franchisees of leading developments in the housing field. Since no real estate license is required. NHI franchisees usually follow company suggestions and learn by doing with NHI "dry-run" inspections of their own and neighbors homes. But the Home Office of NHI stands ready to help at any time.

NATIONWIDE INCOME TAX SERVICE COMPANY
14507 West Warren
Dearborn, Michigan 48125
Carl Gilbert, President

Description of Operation: Preparation of State and Federal income tax returns for individuals.
Number of Franchisees: 5 in 2 States
In Business Since: 1966
Equity Capital Needed: Dependent upon number of offices to be opened.
Financial Assistance Available: Assistance is available
Training Provided: 2 day training period in home office in all phases of income tax preparation and in the systems and procedures developed by Continental Tax Service.
Managerial Assistance Available: The company (franchisor) will: perform a market analysis that assists franchisee in selecting sites most suitable for business; provide personal guidance for personnel recruitment, selection & training of employees; office layout and design counseling; franchisor designs advertising and promotional materials, determining media & ad schedules; will maintain continuous liaison with franchisees through mail, telephone.

NEWCOMERS SERVICE INTERNATIONAL, INC.
5319 S.W. Westgate Drive
Suite 240
Portland, Oregon 97221
Harold Gramley, President

Description of Operation: Newcomers Service is a greeting service for newly arriving families in the areas which they operate, purpose of the service is to introduce new arrivals to places of business (retail) as well as products and services. Also, helpful community information is provided such as maps, directories and an area information book. Sponsors to the service are provided names of the families contacted. Additional services to be offered by franchisees will include direct mail and printing.
Number of Franchisees: 15 in Oregon, Washington and California.
In Business Since: 1935
Equity Capital Needed: Minimum $5,000 plus living expenses for 3 month start-up period.

17

Equity Capital Needed: Following minimal $2,000 down payment on area, generous extended pay plan. All sales brochures, stationery and office supplies are furnished during set up period and for the initial six to nine months operations.
Training Provided: Franchisee will spend a minimum of 4 days observing and working with greeters, sales staff and office staff in Portland, Oregon. Franchisor will spend a minimum of 1 week (depending on size of area) with franchisee on location, working with and advising on matters of setting up and operating.
Managerial Assistance Available: Newcomers Service International management and staff assist franchisee in training sales personnel and greeters. They also work with franchisee to obtain lead sources for newly arriving families, and to obtain a reliable printing source in the area. Supplies are available to franchisee on a cost plus 5 percent basis but are not mandatory. A minimum of one franchisee meeting per year is called at the company headquarters office in Portland, Oregon. During the first year of operation frequent visits are made into the area to assist in matters of sales and operation.

ONTOP DIVISION
SEAMAN NUCLEAR CORPORATION
7315 South First Street
Oak Creek, Wisconsin 53154
David C. Smart, Vice President, Marketing

Description of Operation: Provide roof moisture surveys including amount and location of water in flat built-up roofs, leak detection, and recommendation for repair and rehabilitation. Inspection and consultation services.
Number of Franchisees: 7 in 7 States
In Business Since: Manufacturing since 1962, franchising since 1979.
Equity Capital Needed: $15,000
Financial Assistance Available: None
Training Provided: Factory training seminars and field training after franchise is operational.
Managerial Assistance Available: Technical assistance available in the field at cost. Continuing management monitoring of franchisee operations.

PROFITPOWER INTERNATIONAL
185 Devonshire Street
Boston, Massachusetts 02110
Leo F. Meady, President

Description of Operation: Profitpower International is a professional sales organization. It is a Business Broker. It is a Franchise Sale Agency. It locates business sites, helps with financing small businesses, etc. In most States the franchisee will need a real estate broker's license.
Number of Franchisees: 8 in Massachusetts, New York, Connecticut and Florida.
In Business Since: 1969, started to franchise in 1977
Equity Capital Needed: $10,000 plus working capital for 6 months.
Financial Assistance Available: Will finance one-half franchise fee.
Training Provided: Mandatory training for minimum of 2 weeks in a company office, learning how to secure business listings, buyers and sites. How to interview buyers and sellers, help with negotiations, closing the deal, etc. On-site training during first few weeks of new office opening.
Managerial Assistance Available: The success of a Profitpower office depends to a great extent on the management ability, initiative, good business ethics and sales tactics of the manager. Therefore the company is constantly striving to upgrade its franchisees, through such means as periodic sales meetings, seminars with outside speakers, advisory bulletins and on-site working visits by headquarters personnel.

RELIABLE BUSINESS SYSTEMS, INC.
19 Ransom Road
Newton, Massachusetts 02159
M. Michael Licker, President

Description of Operation: Firm publishes the Reliable Business and Tax Service System, a service designed to meet the needs of all business, offering them a bookkeeping system that complies with all Federal and State tax laws, together with an advisory service and end of year Federal and State tax return preparation.
Number of Franchisees: 7 in 8 states.
In Business Since: 1955
Equity Capital Needed: $7,950
Financial Assistance Available: None. However, we will in particular situations where franchisee is above average, finance $2,000 of capital.
Training Provided: 1 week in the field training by another experienced distributor and further training at the home office if needed, continuous upgrading of distributor's knowledge.
Managerial Assistance Available: Continuous flow of new material, home office consultation available on an unlimited and continuous basis. Close contact with distributor maintained. Additional help regarding tax matters for client when called upon through home office accounting tax staff.

RFG, INC.
729 East Arrow Highway
Azusa, California 91702
Richard F. Greene, President

Description of Operation: A unique service offered to all three parties (buyer, seller, agent), involved in the selling of a home. Gives a full written disclosure to evaluate and reveal any hidden conditions of the home. Certificates are available on the five major areas of the home - plumbing, heating and air conditioning, electrical, roofing and termites. A one year guarantee is equivalent of the inspection and certification.
Number of Franchisees: 3 in California and Nevada
In Business Since: 1977
Equity Capital Needed: $25,000 minimum
Financial Assistance Available: A total investment of $50,000 is necessary to open RFG be able to financially support himself independently during the first year of his program. equipment, and initial cost of advertising and printed material. RFG, Inc., will finance the balance at the rate of 8 percent of gross sales per month.

Training Provided: 2 weeks of training at RFG, Inc., office and 2 weeks managerial assistance at franchisee office. The first 2 inspectors will be trained by RFG, Inc., at no cost. Any other inspectors employed by franchisee will be trained by RFG, Inc., for a fee of $600 per inspector for 2 weeks training period.
Managerial Assistance Available: RFG, Inc., provides continual management service for the life of the franchisee in areas of bookkeeping, advertising and area representation. RFG, Inc., has monthly meetings for all franchisees to continually update procedures and techniques.

SAFEGUARD BUSINESS SYSTEMS
470 Maryland Drive
Fort Washington, Pennsylvania 19034
John Benson

Description of Operation: Safeguard Business Systems offers a complete basic accounting function. In addition to standard systems, Safeguard has many special systems designed for specific industries and data processing services for the accounting profession. Distributor is under contract with protected accounts, commission structure, and salable equity.
Number of Franchisees: 800 nationwide, Canada and Puerto Rico
In Business Since: 1912
Equity Capital Needed: No franchise fee required.
Financial Assistance Available: Safeguard carries the accounts receivable and inventory, thus reducing working capital requirements.
Training Provided: Safeguard provides 80 hours of initial training. Provision is also made for continual field follow-up.
Managerial Assistance Available: Operation and sales manuals provided. Company provides advertising and promotional material on a national basis, together with both a cooperative and a corporate direct mail program.

SANDY HOOK SCIENTIFIC INC.
Sandy Hook, Connecticut 06482
D. N. Sneed, CDP

Description of Operation: An opportunity exists to aid owner-operated small business to plan, develop and control quantified goals for improvement of service to its market and consequently to increase profits. Using proven techniques and (in most cases) a small computer, the results can be most dramatic and far-reaching.
Number of Franchisees: 3 in Connecticut, New York, and Massachusetts.
In Business Since: 1976
Equity Capital Needed: $5,000 plus ability to live on reduced income for first few months of operation.
Financial Assistance Available: 5 day training course at the home office school with visits to local clients. Assistance is given to franchisee at his location to find clients, install initial phases of system and to follow-up progress. On a continuing basis there is constant monitoring of progress and results.
Managerial Assistance Available: New business leads to supplement franchisees effort. Project and program products constantly being developed/refined. Assistance with monitoring and controlling projects. Additional training as required. Manuals and other training aids for clients.

SIMPLIFIED BUSINESS SERVICES, INC.
100 Presidential Boulevard
Bala Cynwyd, Pennsylvania 19004
Martin B. Miller, President

Description of Operation: Simplified Business Services, Inc., offers bookkeeping systems and services which have been refined and developed over 44 years. These systems are designed for the small businessman, who must keep records, and who cannot afford a full-time CPA. The licensee can sell the system with or without monthly bookkeeping service and with or without tax preparation services.
Number of Franchisees: 30 in 8 States and Washington, D.C.
In Business Since: 1934
Equity Capital Needed: No franchise fee.
Financial Assistance Available: No inventory purchase limit is required.
Training Provided: Sales training available from various licensees. Bookkeeping training available at home office.
Managerial Assistance Available: Business and tax advisory bulletins on regular basis. Licensee may call or write home office for advice at any time.

SMI INTERNATIONAL, INC.
(SUCCESS MOTIVATION INSTITUTE, INC.)
5000 Lakewood Drive
Waco, Texas 76710
Charles G. Williams

Description of Operation: The Company's international distributorship organization markets specialized management, sales, and personal development programs to individuals, companies, governments, and other organizations. Materials are printed and recorded, using modern learning methods, personal goal setting, and management by objective techniques.
Number of Franchisees: 1,898 in 50 States and 23 foreign countries.
In Business Since: 1960
Equity Capital Needed: $12,950
Financial Assistance Available: Financial assistance provided.
Training Provided: Complete distributorship training program in printed and recorded form furnished with initial investment; continuous home office sales training and sales management seminars available monthly. Field sales training also available in many areas without cost to distributors.
Managerial Assistance Available: Continuous sales consultant assistance provided by home office to distribute through use of monthly mailings, company-owned WATS lines and prompt response to mail communications.

SOUTHWEST PROMOTIONAL CORPORATION
P.O. Box 81023
San Diego, California 92138
Jerry Nesler, President

Description of Operation: SouthWest Promotional Corporation offers a specialized

18

Advertising Proofs of Purchase Program for its franchisees to sell to prospective advertisers. Only one franchise offered each city or market area. The Program attracts such advertisers as banks, savings and loans, super markets, national food products, women's apparel and a variety of retail businesses. Some advertisers now in the Program over 10 years. Numerous major national accounts.
Number of Franchisees: 7 in California
In Business Since: 1970 - Franchised since 1975
Equity Capital Needed: $12,000
Financial Assistance Available: No other cash investment is necessary to obtain and start a Program in specified city or market area. However, it is essential that a franchisee be able to financially support himself independently during the first year of his Program
Training Provided: Total of 2 weeks training in Program and sales techniques and use of sales materials. Helpful if franchisee has a background in advertising sales but not essential, ideal for qualified woman franchisee. SouthWest provides all materials, visual aid and/or audio visual for the franchisee to sell the Program to advertisers effectively.
Managerial Assistance Available: SouthWest provides continual Program assistance for the life of the franchise in areas of print, billing, bookkeeping, sales advice and advertiser categories. Format of operation and program provided.

SYSTEMEDICS, INC.
Princeton Air Research Park
P.O. Box 2000
Princeton, New Jersey 08540
William P. Krause, President

Description of Operation: Computerized accounts receivable management system and related systems for the medical and health care delivery fields.
Number of Franchisees: 42 in 40 States
In Business Since: 1964 - Acquired by Equifax, Inc., Atlanta, Georgia, May 1978
Equity Capital Needed: $5,000-$10,000
Training Provided: Possible to finance part of purchase through company. No other form of financial assistance.
Training Provided: Approximately 5 day course at home or regional office provided in franchisee fee.
Managerial Assistance Available: Company provides continuing assistance and field support to all franchisees who desire this assistance.

TAX MAN, INC.
639 Massachusetts Avenue
Cambridge, Massachusetts 02139
Robert G. Murray, President

Description of Operation: Preparation of individual income tax returns. Interested in franchisees in New England.
Number of Franchisees: 7 in Connecticut and Massachusetts.
In Business Since: 1967
Equity Capital Needed: $2,500 minimum.
Financial Assistance Available: Advertising support. Bookkeeping Income Opportunity for rest of year.
Training Provided: Tax preparation training (8 weeks). Tax office management training (3 days).
Managerial Assistance Available: Complete tax advice, management assistance, site selection, advertising and marketing.

TAX OFFICES OF AMERICA
Box 4098
Waterville, Connecticut 06714
Gregg Nolan, Franchise Director

Description of Operation: Income tax preparation for individuals and small businesses. Thorough training program, exclusive territories. Estate planning and business consulting services.
Number of Franchisees: 10
In Business Since: 1966
Equity Capital Needed: Approximately $8,500 plus $5,000 working capital.
Financial Assistance Available: Financing arranged through Horizons of America, Inc., parent company.
Training Provided: About 2 weeks training provided at Waterbury headquarters, 2 weeks at franchisee's location plus a mail order course. If available in franchisee's area the company pays all expenses to a special training course set up by a nationally known organization.
Managerial Assistance Available: Company always available for counseling, plus on site office organization.

TELECHECK SERVICES, INC.
190 South King Street #1610
Honolulu, Hawaii 96813
Robert J. Baer, President

Description of Operation: In 1964, TeleCheck's personal check verification system met with instant acceptance by merchants and banks. Today, TeleCheck is the largest immediate information system of its type with offices in over 50 cities throughout the United States and Canada. TeleCheck's check verification provides immediate warranted response to inquires on personal checks written on any bank in the USA and Canada. This allows retailers to increase sales with the same worry-free acceptance of personal checks as they do credit cards. 40,000 merchants now build sales volume through friendlier, efficient TeleCheck service without the cost of processing, collecting and writing off returned checks, etc. TeleCheck buys all returned checks that are cleared through the system. No special card is required. Retailers pay all fees. Subscribers include every retail area, including markets, food service, clothing, hotels/motels, banks, credit unions, automotive, entertainment and product services. Territories are exclusive and TeleCheck provides national account support. TeleCheck's operations office is as follows: TeleCheck Services, Inc., 1611 South Federal Boulevard, #200, Denver, Colorado 80210, Operations Office.
Number of Franchisees: 34 franchisees in 25 States, District of Columbia.
In Business Since: 1971
Equity Capital Needed: $195,000
Financial Assistance Available: Limited

Training Provided: Franchisor provides comprehensive indoctrination at TeleCheck Minneapolis' operation. Franchisees are provided with comprehensive training at their locations. It includes every area of operation, including marketing.
Managerial Assistance Available: Regular visits are made to all franchises. The TeleCheck System has unique incentive for cooperation among franchises. Territories are exclusive and each new location adds to the marketing operations and collections efficiency. A management information system provides statistics monthly in addition to intermittent educational seminars which aid franchisees, measure their success and identify weak areas when they compare their operation to all other franchisees. An advertising agency and a public relations firm provide the system with necessary expertise in their respective fields. The Franchisor participates in advertising. The Franchisor monitors activities of certain Federal regulatory agencies which may have an effect on the franchise. Solicitation of national accounts is provided by Franchisor. Space and equipment requirements are very small. Nine of the 34 franchisees have purchased one or more additional franchises.

TEL-LIFE STATIONS OF AMERICA
A TCN, INC. Affiliate
23011 Moulton Parkway, Suite D-2
Laguna Hills, California 92653
Mark A. Wood, President

Description of Operation: A telecommunications system that provides better living information over the telephone from sponsoring organizations and businesses who pay a monthly fee to have a Tel-it-All audio library of recorded messages played FREE to the public about: Health & Hospitals, Leisure & Travel, Education & Self Improvement, Consummerism & Law, Home & Money Management.
Number of Franchisees: 7 in California, Nevada and Utah
In Business Since: 1977
Equity Capital Needed: From $15,000 to $60,000 deposit and territory reservation fee depending on territory and level of involvement.
Financial Assistance Available: The system and library valued at $250,000 is leased to the licensee in lieu of purchasing. Example: $330 per month, plus 15 percent of the gross revenue.
Training Provided: Intensive 5-day training course, in class and in the field about the system and techniques on how to obtain and maintain paying sponsors for the Tel-it-All Audio Library. Continual sales supervision and assistance is maintained.
Managerial Assistance Available: All accounting, billing and service of the system is provided by TCN, Inc., for its share of the monthly revenue. The sales responsibility of the licensee is to sell sponsorship of the library and manage the system.

TV FACTS
1638 New Highway
Farmingdale, New York 11735

Description of Operation: TV Facts offers readers a localized weekly television guide with seven days of national and local TV programming, cable TV, local news and advertising. Individually owned publications are operated by local associate publishers.
Number of Franchisees: Almost 300 in 32 States and Canada.
In Business Since: 1971
Equity Capital Needed: $9,500
Financial Assistance Available: None
Training Provided: 1 week home office training in sales, advertising and circulation.
Managerial Assistance Available: Continuous assistance is provided by home office and area supervisors.

T.V. TEMPO, INC.
387 Old Commerce Road
Athens, Georgia 30607
Paul M. King, President

Description of Operation: T.V. Tempo, Inc., offers a unique system of "free" weekly television scheduling, shopping and home entertainment guides. Each Associate Publisher (Franchisee) owns and operates his/her local edition of T.V. Tempo magazine which is distributed "free" in high traffic retail areas. Individual Associate Publishers place advertising around Saturday through Friday television scheduling listings and standard features such as crossword puzzle, horoscope and movie descriptions. No need for expensive equipment, fixtures or offices.
Number of Franchisees: 66 in 12 States
In Business Since: 1975
Equity Capital Needed: $8,900
Financial Assistance Available: None
Training Provided: 3 days of intensive classroom learning fundamentals of business operation. Follow-up field training at the actual site assisting the Associate Publisher put into operation the techniques of successful operation. Classroom training available to Associate Publisher on repeated basis for Associate Publisher, if needed. Periodic seminars conducted by home office.
Managerial Assistance Available: T.V. Tempo, Inc., offers guidance and assistance to franchisee on a continuing basis to enhance franchisee's ability and skills. Basic managerial control is always within the control of the Associate Publisher but T.V. Tempo, Inc., offers technical advice and assistance for improving and increasing Associate Publisher's business operations.

VR BUSINESS BROKERS, INC.
197 First Avenue
Needham, Massachusetts 02194
Daniel Verrico, Director of Marketing

Description of Operation: Network of business brokerage offices specializing in the marketing of small businesses. Proven techniques and consistent methods used to insure satisfaction of both buyer & seller. Regional and national advertising plus instant exchange of available business listings lead to cooperative success of all offices. Local offices normally open 6 days, staffed by 4 or more professionally trained sales associates. Franchise offered primarily to those with real estate licenses.
Number of Franchisees: 16 in Massachusetts, Pennsylvania and Georgia.
In Business Since: 1979
Equity Capital Needed: $7,500
Financial Assistance Available: None

Training Provided: 1 week class room training at headquarters or regional centers, supplemented by continuing training of franchisee and sales associates.
Managerial Assistance Available: Permanent operational department staffed by experienced business brokers will assist franchisees in all aspects of their business: recruiting, training, advertising, marketing, sales, closing, etc. In addition, full mangement support available by telephone, newsletter, bulletins, and regular office visitations.

WHITEHILL SYSTEMS
Division of SMALL BUSINESS ADVISORS, INC.
12 Franklin Place
Woodmere, New York 11598
Larry Speizman, President

Description of Operation: A nationwide organization devoted to counseling small and medium sized businesses with emphasis on recordkeeping systems, computerized programs, and tax service. The programs include complete, easy to maintain, preprinted manual, one-write or computerized recordkeeping system, custom designed to provide a monthly profit and loss statement and proof of accuracy, meeting requirements of the Internal Revenue Service. Locally authorized business counselors review and analyze recordkeeping requirements; furnish a complete set of records; provide personal instructions on use and maintenance of records; analyze records and financial statements; provide guidance through 't the year. Federal and State income tax returns are prepared with a guarantee of accuracy by professional staff at the national office. Tax specialists in national office provide tax advisory service and answer income tax questions, publish a monthly tax and business bulletin including up-to-date tax information and money-saving ideas.
Number of Franchisees: Franchises in 48 States.
In Business Since: 1974
Financial Assistance Available: $15,000, includes training, cost of starting inventory, supply of sales and promotional literature, initial direct mail campaign. A $10,000 life insurance policy premium (paid for the first year).
Financial Assistance Available: Limited

Training Provided: 6 days training at home office at company expense—in all phases of the system and selling methods. Five days field training in distributor's own territory, with experienced representative, at company expense.
Managerial Assistance Available: Re-training program and continuous assistance as needed.

EDWIN K. WILLIAMS & CO.
5324 Ekwill Street
P. O. Box 6406
Santa Barbara, California 93111
Gene H. Loeppke, Vice President, Field Operations

Description of Operation: Edwin K. Williams & Company provides business management counseling and computerized bookkeeping services to small business through a franchised licensee program which combines two systems in one franchise: (1) Edwin K. Williams & Company offers these services exclusively for service station retailers and petroleum wholesalers (jobbers). Edwin K. Williams & Company specialized recordkeeping systems are recommended by over 30 oil companies, and (2) E-Z Keep Systems, a division of Edwin K. Williams & Company serves all other types of small business.
Number of Franchisees: 260 Licensee offices in the United States
In Business Since: 1935
Equity Capital Needed: $8,000 to $25,000 & up (depending on size of territory being purchased).
Financial Assistance Available: Limited
Training Provided: New Licensees are provided initial training, including training in existing licensee offices, plus training and guidance by the Company's Regional Managers after installation. A Continuing program of training seminars is offered to all licensees. Subjects include internal procedures, taxes, business management counseling, E.D.P. and more.
Managerial Assistance Available: Regional Managers provide continued follow-up counseling in all phases of licensee operation. The Home Office Field Operations Staff provides technical support and other assistance. ■

CAMPGROUNDS

JELLYSTONE CAMPGROUNDS
Division of LEISURE SYSTEMS INC.
30 North 18th Avenue, Unit #9
Sturgeon Bay, Wisconsin 54235
J. E. Webb, Executive Vice President

Description of Operation: Franchising of rental and proprietary interst camp-resort developments, franchising of economy family motor inns, franchising of miniature golf courses and snak-shoppes.
Number of Franchisees: 68 in 26 States and Canada.
In Business Since: 1969
Equity Capital Needed: $75,000-$150,000 - Campgrounds and motels 20-75,000 miniature golf courses.
Financial Assistance Available: Assistance in preparing financial package and identifying loan sources.
Training Provided: Manager training.
Managerial Assistance Available: Engineering and construction planning; perpetual management service and advice.

KAMP DAKOTA, INC.
220 Bartling Building
Brookings, South Dakota 57006
M. L. Thorne, President

Description of Operation: Franchising of campgrounds to be used by camping and trailering vacationers.
Number of Franchisees: 36 nationwide.
In Business Since: 1964
Equity Capital Needed: $50,000 and up.
Financial Assistance Available: Other than assistance in preparation and presentation of loan requests to potential financiers, Kamp Dakota, Inc., offers no financial assistance.
Training Provided: Training is provided at each campground as required and as may be necessary.
Managerial Assistance Available: Managerial assistance offered franchisees on a continuous basis. Kamp Dakota, Inc., also provides franchisee with complete engineering and construction planning for their particular campground.

KAMPGROUNDS OF AMERICA, INC.
P. O. Box 30558
Billings, Montana 59114
Dave Collins, Assistant Vice President

Description of Operation: Kampgrounds of America, Inc. (KOA) is America's largest sytem of campgrounds for recreational vehicles. The average campground contains 100 sites equipped with water and electrical hookups; many sites have sewer hookups. Each campground features clean restrooms with hot showers, a convenience store, laundry equipment and playground equipment. Many have swimming pools.
Number of Franchisees: 840 in the United States and Canada.
In Business Since: 1964

Equity Capital Needed: $65,000 minimum
Financial Assistance Available: KOA does not provide direct financing to franchisees for campground construction. However, it does provide assistance in obtaining financing such as, assisting the franchisee in preparing his prospectus, developing operating projections, and meeting with potential lenders.
Training Provided: KOA provides formal classroom training in campground development and campground operations for franchisees and their personnel. Each school (development and operations) last three days and several sessions are conducted throughout the year.
Managerial Assistance Available: KOA provides formal classroom training and continual management services for the life of the franchise in such areas as development, general operations, advertising and merchandising. In addition, complete manuals of development, operations and supply catalogs are provided. Regional consultants are available in all regions to work closely with franchisees. Each campground is visited regularly to insure conformance with standards and to assist franchisees in solving problems. KOA publishes a Kampground Directory annually and sponsors an annual meeting of franchisees.

SAFARI CAMPGROUNDS
UNITED SAFARI INTERNATIONAL, INC.
5401 Kingston Pike - Suite 610
P. O. Box 11528
Knoxville, Tennessee 37919
John F. Burton, President

Description of Operation: United Safari has designed and standardized methods of constructing, advertising and operating unique, luxury camping and recreational facilities for campers under a nationwide system known as Safari Campgrounds. Safari has granted and desires to grant licenses for exclusive territories in which to operate Safari Campgrounds. Safari also will accept certain existing independent campgrounds which might wish to join their system.
Number of Franchisees: 150, with 100 operating campgrounds in 32 states and Canada.
In Business Since: 1966
Equity Capital Needed: $50,000-$100,000. Depends upon location and other considerations. In some cases cash needs could be less or more than above.
Financial Assistance Available: A comprehensive feasibility study, engineering drawing and financial plan are prepared and packaged by Safari for presentation to a lender. Safari is able to assist in obtaining financial arrangements or the franchisee may select a lender of his choice.
Training Provided: Real estate, zoning and financial planning school 1-2 day duration. Seminar covering construction, advertising, operating and accounting procedures involved in campground management, lasting approximately one week.
Managerial Assistance Available: Consultation regarding acceptable site criteria and selection. On-site construction assistance, including custom campground layout and building plans. On-going consultation on all facets of campground operations. Frequent inspection visits to insure chain wide adherence to quality standards. Maintenance of 800 number for toll-free reservations and national directory; published annually. National advertising in all industry media. Regional campowner association for cooperative advertising, and National Annual Convention. ■

CHILDREN'S STORES/FURNITURE/PRODUCTS

BABY-TENDA CORPORATION
909 State Line Avenue
Kansas City, Missouri 64101
David Jungerman, President

Description of Operation: The Baby-Tenda is a safety feeding table that converts into 11 different uses. A complete line of accessories are available including a crib that converts into a youth bed. Successful distributors are customarily hardworking self-starters who enjoy putting on a show in front of groups of people. The actual selling is done evenings and week-ends. Earning potential is tremendous for the right individuals. Non-sales

orientated individuals are not successful.
Number of Franchisees: 34 throughout the United States.
In Business Since: 1937
Equity Capital Needed: $9,000
Financial Assistance Available: None
Training Provided: Training is accomplished at an existing distributor's location. It is an on-going process, the length being determined by the sales ability of the trainee.
Managerial Assistance Available: Experienced and successful distributors of Baby-Tenda are available to answer questions plus factory sales manager's help is available. ■

CLOTHING/SHOES

ATHLETE'S FOOT MARKETING ASSOCIATES, INC.
601 Grant Street
Pittsburgh, Pennsylvania 15219
Ross Glickman, Vice President of Sales

Description of Operation: Company franchises its name and services, on a national basis, to individually-owned stores that specialize in leisure and athletic shoes, offering top-quality and higher priced lines of shoes. Major lines include shoes by Adidas, Puma, Converse, Uniroyal, Dunham, Tiger, Nike, Tretorn, Pony, Pro-Ked, Etonic, etc., plus related soft goods items such as T-shirts, tube socks, gym bags, warm-up suits, etc.
Number of Franchisees: 319 in 46 States
In Business Since: 1971
Equity Capital Needed: $7,500 for franchise fee plus approximately $70,000 inventory investment.
Financial Assistance Available: No financing provided by headquarters company. They do provide a package to present to bankers.
Training Provided: Short intensive training program provided by headquarters prepares franchisee for complete operation of store. Written manual also provided.
Managerial Assistance Available: Assistance in lease negotiations and site selections. Complete merchandise selection. On-going advertising and promotion suggestions.

FORMAL WEAR SERVICE
639 V.F.W. Parkway
Chestnut Hill, Massachusetts 02167
Murray and Jay Kuritsky

Description of Operation: Formal specialists in the sale and rental of men's formal clothes. Dealers receive stock plus photo album of every fashion and color we stock plus rental and sales catalog.
Number of Franchisees: 34 in Massachusetts, New Hampshire, New York and Connecticut.
In Business Since: 1940
Equity Capital Needed: $50,000 minimum for stock and fixtures.
Financial Assistance Available: Formal Wear Service will finance if franchisee has good credit rating.
Training Provided: 2 weeks at store. Complete training course in all aspects of formal rental business to all franchisees plus a 60 page book "Can A Nice Guy Succeed in Formals."
Managerial Assistance Available: The home office provides bookkeeping, inventory control and national and local cooperative advertising.

FLEET FEET
2412 J Street
Sacramento, California 96816
Sally Edwards

Description of Operation: Retail active footwear/sportswear with an emphasis on a sporting lifestyle. Brand names only - owners must be involved in physical fitness.
Number of Franchisees: 7 in California
In Business Since: Retail business 1975, franchise since 1978.
Equity Capital Needed: $5,000
Financial Assistance Available: Financial advice and preparation of papers for financial institutions. The total capitalization costs range from $28,000 to $55,000 including inventory, fixtures, fees, working capital. Bank financing is available but the franchisees responsibility. We will help with the preparation of forms.
Training Provided: Strenuous training program and franchise manual which involves all aspects of business operations and management. Course is 1 week long, mandatory attendance in Sacramento, California. Following course, franchisor-Fleet Feet spends 1 week with the new store owner during the first week in business.
Managerial Assistance Available: On-going weekly bulletin "Fleet Feet Flash" to announce the immediate. Monthly visit at no charge from franchisor "to help." Weekly phone calls to each franchise to offer assistance. Warehouse facilities which offer franchises inventory goods. Semi-annual franchisee/franchisor meetings to improve managerial, technical, and other business skills.

FORTY LOVE TENNIS SHOPPE, INC.
110 Newport Center Drive
Suite 200
Newport Beach, California 92660
Kay Dance, President

Description of Operation: The Forty Love active sports apparel store is a retail merchandise business devoted primarily to tennis and other active sports apparel and related services.
Number of Franchisees: 12 in 6 States.
In Business Since: 1971; offering franchises since March 1973.
Equity Capital Needed: Total initial investment varies from $85,000 - $130,000. Cash required depends upon franchisee's ability to arrange financing.
Financial Assistance Available: None
Training Provided: The franchisee will attend an intial training course held at a Forty Love store in Newport Beach and at Forty Love's headquarters in Newport Beach, California. The franchisee will be instructed in all aspects of operation of the franchise business, including merchandising, quality control, public relations, personnel management, bookkeeping, operations, inventories, and products. The training program will take place over a period of 1 week. Forty Love will provide additional training when necessary to maintain high quality and uniform operation.
Managerial Assistance Available: Forty Love provides franchisees with plans and specifications for construction of leasehold improvements, store layout, etc. Forty Love will, whenever possible, provide site selection assistance. Forty Love also provides advisory personnel who visit franchisee's employees. Forty Love also maintains regular communications with franchisees, particularly in the initial months of operation, to discuss operational or other problems, and provides each franchisee a complete operations manual.

GINGISS INTERNATIONAL, INC.
180 North LaSalle Street
Chicago, Illinois 60601
Joe Gingiss, President

Description of Operation: Specialists in the sale and rental of men's formal clothes.
Number of Franchisees: 140 in 32 States
In Business Since: 1936 franchising since 1968
Equity Capital Needed: $40,000-$60,000
Financial Assistance Available: Through external sources franchisor arranges and guarantees $50,000 financing for inventory and equipment.
Training Provided: 2 week comprehensive training at Gingiss International Training Center in Chicago approximately 1 month before center's opening. One week on-site training during initial opening week. Regular visits by training directors and various department heads on a continuing basis.
Managerial Assistance Available: Franchisor provides regular visits by field training directors, a comprehensive instructional manual, periodic bulletins and constant telephone assistance as required.

HEEL 'N TOE, INC.
5225 Monroe Place
Hyattsville, Maryland 20781
Michael C. Passas, Franchise Developer

Description of Operation: Heel 'N Toe is a retail women's shoe chain which specializes in preponderantly name brand shoes sold on consignment at discount prices. The stores are semi-self service, which minimizes salary cost. The Franchisee is also encouraged to carry handbags and shoe accessories.
Number of Franchisees: 24 in Maryland, Virginia, New Jersey, Massachusetts, Pennsylvania and North Carolina.
In Business Since: 1967
Equity Capital Needed: $20,000 - consists of ($3,000) for franchise fee. Security deposit for merchandise, which is returnable ($5,000). The balance of equity capital provides for the fixturing of the store, signs, cash register, carpeting, display materials, and includes working capital of $3,000-$4,000). The inventory is on consignment, and payment is made by franchisee as the shoes are sold on a weekly basis.
Financial Assistance Available: Heel 'N Toe pays 1/3 of all freight, 50 percent of any advertising, and provides assistance in finding a location.
Training Provided: Minimum of 3 days training at the home office consists of bookkeeping, procedures and sales training in a local store; plus additional assistance and training during grand opening at the franchisee's store.
Managerial Assistance Available: All stores are visited by a District Sales Manager on a continuous basis. Heel 'N Toe also provides management services in such areas as bookkeeping, merchandising, inventory control, and advertising.

JILENE, INC.
800 Miramonte Drive
Santa Barbara, California 93109
Jim Klobucher, President

Description of Operation: Jilene offers two different opportunities in the retail clothing business. One store is called "Kimo's Polynesian Shop," which specializes in colorful clothing for women and men. The other store is called "Shandar," which specializes in quality women's fashions. Jilene provides expert site selection, complete retail training program, professional buying service, merchandise control system, and advertising and sales promotion assistance.
Number of Franchisees: 13 in California and Florida.
In Business Since: 1969
Equity Capital Needed: $35,000 and up depending on size of store.
Financial Assistance Available: None
Training Provided: 2 weeks training provided in franchisee's store. Training covers all general aspects of a retail clothing store operation. A complete operations manual is provided to each store owner.
Managerial Assistance Available: After initial 2 week training period Jilene is always available for assistance for the duration of the franchise contract. Jilene also functions as a buying service for the franchisee.

JUST PANTS
310 South Michigan Avenue
Suite 400
Chicago, Illinois 60604
John Grey Davis, Director of Franchise Development

Description of Operation: Just Pants stores average 2,000 feet with expansion geared to regional shopping malls of 500,000 square feet GLA. Street or strip center locations can be considered if there are existing units in the market. Just Pants stores sell quality branded jeans, slacks, tops and accessories primarily to teenagers, college aged people and young men and women.
Number of Franchisees: 46 (136 units) in 27 States, with 22 more committed thru 1980, 16 to existing franchisees, 6 to new franchisees plus the addition of one new state. Areas available in all states except Florida and a few areas currently adequately covered by present licensees.
In Business Since: 1969
Equity Capital Needed: Regional mall ($80,000-$105,000). No initial franchise fee. Investment covers: site development, inventory, fixtures and working capital.
Financial Assistance Available: None
Training Provided: Just Pants will furnish a training program consisting of 2 weeks or more of "on-the-job-training" in 2 or more actual operating Just Pants stores plus much additional instruction to the manager with respect to other aspects of the business. The Licensee will be responsible for the travel and living expenses and the compensation of the manager while enrolled in the training program.
Managerial Assistance Available: Operating assistance will include advice and guidance with respect to: (1) buying pants and other merchandise; (2) additional products authorized for sale by Just Pants stores; (3) hiring and training of employees;

(4) formulating and implementing advertising and promotional programs; (5) pricing and special sales; (6) the establishment and maintenance of administrative, bookkeeping, accounting, inventory control and general operating procedures. Further, Just Pants will advise the licensee from time to time of operating problems of the store disclosed by financial statements submitted to or inspections made by Just Pants. Just Pants will make no separate charge to the licensee for such operating assistance.

KNAPP SHOE COMPANY
One Knapp Centre
Brockton, Massachusetts 02401
Walter E. Cullen, Manager, Franchise Division

Description of Operation: Retail shoe store selling Knapp Shoes and accessories.
Number of Franchisees: 30 in 14 States
In Business Since: 1919
Equity Capital Needed: $38,000
Financial Assistance Available: None
Training Provided: Direct selling - training as needed - retail selling - 2 weeks at a company-owned store.
Managerial Assistance Available: Continual ongoing supervision and advice in such areas as merchandising, inventory control, and store operations for the life of the franchise by field managers. Manuals for store operations.

LADY MADONNA MANAGEMENT COPR.
36 East 31st Street
New York, New York 10016
Ronald Sommers, Vice President

Description of Operation: Manufacture, wholesale and retail women's maternity apparel.
Number of Franchisees: 85 in 32 States
In Business Since: 1970
Equity Capital Needed: $35,000 to $50,000
Financial Assistance Available: Normal inventory terms (8/10 E.O.M.). No financing available; however, company provides a business package to present to bankers to qualified applicants. Licensee arranges own outside financing.
Training Provided: Intensified training program beginning with 1 week period in New York and continuing with in-store training by supervisor commencing with the store opening (up to 2 weeks). Continuous field supervision.
Managerial Assistance Available: Continuous merchandising guidance, buying service, all advertising material, forms and systems and continuous field supervision of retail operations.

MODE O'DAY COMPANY
2130 North Hollywood Way
Burbank, California 91505
Mills Whitney, Vice President of Store Operations

Description of Operation: Ladies' apparel specialty stores. Merchandise is placed in franchise stores on a consignment basis. The firm pays freight for merchandise shipments, provides display material and ad mats.
Number of Franchisees: 658 in 32 States
In Business Since: 1936
Equity Capital Needed: Capital is required for store fixtures and leasehold improvements. Average store ranges from $9,000 to $10,000.
Financial Assistance Available: Limited
Training Provided: Training is provided by competent personnel.
Managerial Assistance Available: Field supervisors work very closely with store owners to develop maximum sales.

MODERN BRIDAL SHOPPES, INC.
600 Route 130 North
Cinnaminson, New Jersey 08077
Jack Fine

Description of Operation: Retail sales of bridal apparel and cocktail formal wear. Locations can be free standing, shopping centers, enclosed malls, or operating from the home. Modern Bridal offers complete systemized operations procedures, continuous buying service, and national advertising program.
Number of Franchisees: 64 in 31 States
In Business Since: 1958
Equity Capital Needed: $12,000 - $35,000
Financial Assistance Available: Guidance offered regarding obtaining loan through SBA and other sources.
Training Provided: 2 weeks total training. One week training at home office company-owned operation. One week training in field.
Managerial Assistance Available: Complete manual of operations, field supervisor assistance, national seminar, continuous buying service.

PAULINE'S SPORTSWEAR, INC.
3525 Eastham Drive
Culver City, California 90230

Description of Operation: Pauline's Sportswear, Inc., Ladies Sportswear Stores featuring moderately priced Misses and Queen size garments of high quality. The price range is from $7 to $20. The line is sold exclusively through Pauline's Stores and consists of blouses, pants, suits, sweaters, shorts, skirts, and related items. Pauline's does all its own manufacturing and styling in California. New styles are offered to the stores each week. This eliminates the necessity of going to the market and stocking a large inventory. The stores range in size from 1,000 to 2,000 square feet and are easily managed by one or two people.
Number of Franchisees: 150
In Business Since: 1961
Equity Capital Needed: $25,000 to $40,000 depending on the size of the store.
Financial Assistance Available: None

Training Provided: Training is informal.
Managerial Assistance Available: Training on merchandising, inventory control, display and general sales techniques.

SALLY WALLACE BRIDES SHOP, INC.
232 Amherst Street
East Orange, New Jersey 07018
John Van Drill, President

Description of Operation: Sally Wallace Brides Shops offer a complete Bride Shop and bridal service. Wedding gowns, bridesmaids, mothers, party, cocktail, dance and formals plus all accessories. Inventory consists of all the leading designers and manufacturers. Heavily advertised in Brides and Modern Bride Magazines.
Number of Franchisees: 15 in 10 States
In Business Since: 1955
Equity Capital Needed: $30,000
Financial Assistance Available: A total investment of $30,000 is needed for a complete turn-key operation including inventory and $5,000 operating fund back-up. We will finance 30 percent if franchisee has good credit reference.
Training Provided: 3 week mandatory training course in one of our shops. Trainer spends 1 week with franchisee to open new shop. Six months follow thru by trainer with close supervision via written reports and telephone.
Managerial Assistance Available: Continuous. Consultant buyer and merchandise manager supervision on a weekly basis, checking sales, money, inventory and cost controls. Field personnel available as needed, to visit shops and assist in solving problems. Buying service supplied as part of franchise agreement.

SHIRT TALES, LTD.
2306 West Main Street
Evanston, Illinois 60202
Leonard B. Bolnick, President

Description of Operation: Shirt Tales stores sell mens shirts, ties, sweaters and accessories and outerwear. Stores average 1,600 square feet and are geared for regional shopping malls and high traffic areas.
Number of Franchisees: 5 (14 stores) in Massachusetts, New Hampshire, New Jersey and Illinois.
In Business Since: 1972
Equity Capital Needed: $30,000 to $75,000 depending on location.
Financial Assistance Available: While the franchisor offers no financing, they will assist where a qualified party needs assistance.
Training Provided: Shirt Tales will furnish a training program consisting of 3 weeks intensive training in our stores as well as 1 week in the franchisees store during his/her first week of operation. The Licensee will be responsible for travel and living expenses and the compensation of the manager during this training period.
Managerial Assistance Available: Shirt Tales will do the buying centrally for all units as well as setup for the store and its advertising. Monthly sales clinics will be held as well as seasonal merchandise meetings and the director of franchising will keep in touch with each franchisee either through memos, phone calls, or by periodically visiting the store to handle any problems. Merchandising will be done based on needs of the market area and if a store needs special merchandise Shirt Tales merchandisers will see that it is made available to that store.

WILD TOPS FRANCHISING, INC.
30 Main Street
Ashland, Massachusetts 01721
Richard Gold, President
Michell Gold, Vice President

Description of Operation: Wild Tops 'T'-Shirts Stores are contemporary in design. Stores are located in malls and range from 400-1,000 square feet. All 'T'-shirts are American made first quality. An extensive selection of over 1,000 decals will be stocked by the store. Other products merchandises in a Wild Tops Store are: golf, hockey, baseball, sweat shirts and a line of fashion tops.
Number of Franchisees: 17 in 6 States
In Business Since: 1973
Equity Capital Needed: $30,000
Financial Assistance Available: The total investment of $30,000 includes all equipment and fixtures as: heat press, cash register, press table, cash and wrap table counter, glass shelving, decal display books, promotional advertising, location assistance, lease negotiation, home office training and inventory. Wild Tops would consider financing a portion of the investment depending on the individuals credit worthiness.
Training Provided: Intensive on-the-job training at one of Wild Tops will last 1 week and cover the following topics: store opening and closing, transfer application, purchasing, store set-up, advertising, hiring procedures, customer relations and silk screening.
Managerial Assistance Available: Wild Tops' representative will be present for all franchisee's grand opening, and home office personnel are available on a daily basis to assist franchisee on a consultancy basis. A manual is also provided that outlines all policies, forms and procedures each store must adhere to.

WRANGLER WRANCH FRANCHISING SYSTEMS, INC.
335 Church Court
Greensboro, North Carolina 27401
Brad Helvenston, Director, Franchise Development

Description of Operation: Wrangler Wranch stores are franchised family sportswear specialty stores featuring Wrangler brand apparel in shopping center locations (or other high-traffic locations) of 2,000-3,000 square feet.
Number of Franchisees: 16 with 63 stores in 16 States and Puerto Rico.
In Business Since: 1971
Training Provided: Approximately 1 week sales training with periodic subsequent sessions as appropriate.
Managerial Assistance Available: Assistance in market analysis, site selection, store design. Assistance in beginning inventory plans, merchandise layout, and advertising/promotion. Training of sales personnel and training on operations manual systems and procedures.

CONSTRUCTION/REMODELING/MATERIALS/SERVICES

DAVIS CAVES, INC.
P. O. Box 102
Armington, Illinois 61721

Description of Operation: Davis Caves Franchise system offers Earth-Sheltered structures that are energy-efficient, requiring little or no maintenance. Structures include residential, industrial, commercial and agricultural. Davis Caves provides franchisee with leads, plans, advertising and promotional material.
Number of Franchisees: 97 in 31 States
In Business Since: 1978
Equity Capital Needed: $2,000 minimum
Financial Assistance Available: Financial counseling, advertising and credit available excluding Franchise fee.
Training Provided: Initial training school mandatory. Training updated through duration of contract.
Managerial Assistance Available: Management and technical assistance provided in areas of marketing, advertising, sales, construction and bookkeeping. Davis Caves provides initial bookkeeping system, forms and construction manual. Architectural and artist's services available.

DICKER STACK-SACK INTERNATIONAL
4313 Paredes Line Road
Brownsville, Texas 78521
Edward T. Dicker

Description of Operation: Process for construction.
Number of Franchisees: 10 in New Mexico, Arkansas, Texas and Idaho
In Business Since: 1967
Equity Capital Needed: $20,000 for equipment. Franchisee fee based on population of area desired.
Financial Assistance Available: Will finance franchise fee to suit franchisor.
Training Provided: On-the-site training, length determined according to structure(s) being constructed. Average 10 days to 2 weeks.
Managerial Assistance Available: Through duration of franchise agreement.

DURADEK PERMANENT SUNDECKS
14931 Northeast 40th Street
Redmond, Washington 98052
Ronald E. Sanders, President

Description of Operation: Duradek is a new concept in outdoor floor covering. This waterproof vinyl flooring provides beauty and durability to sundecks, pool areas, etc.
Number of Franchisees: 44 in Washington, Oregon and Canada.
In Business Since: 1975
Equity Capital Needed: $12,000 includes dealership fee and initial inventory.
Financial Assistance Available: None
Training Provided: Duradek managerial personnel provides on-the-job training, installation and sales tips.
Managerial Assistance Available: Complete and comprehensive assistance is provided continuously as well as an advertising program, technical manuals and brochures.

EASI-SET INDUSTRIES
Midland, Virginia 22728
Moffette Tharpe, President

Description of Operation: ESI provides a service to concrete products producers who are seeking diversification and to persons interested in establishing a precast concrete business. Our approach is to supply them fully developed standard products which have been proven successful and profitable and to provide them an on-going comprehensive program of service.
Number of Franchisees: 14 in 8 States, Canada and Belgium.
In Business Since: 1978
Equity Capital Needed: Varies with product selected and franchisee's manufacturing capabilities range $45,000 - $215,000.
Financial Assistance Available: None
Training Provided: Production training - 1-2 weeks. Sales training - 1-2 weeks.
Managerial Assistance Available: Marketing consultation, production consultation, provide co-op regional advertising, and periodic field visits - quarterly.

ELDORADO STONE CORPORATION
P. O. Box 125
Kirkland, Washington 98033
John E. Bennett, President

Description of Operation: Franchisee will manufacture and sell Eldorado Stone, simulated stone and brick building products. No technical background is necessary.
Number of Franchisees: 19 in 13 States and Canada
In Business Since: 1969
Equity Capital Needed: $35,000
Financial Assistance Available: None
Training Provided: Company provides 1 week of training in an established manufacturing plant, 1 week in franchisee's plant, and continuous supervision thereafter.
Managerial Assistance Available: Company provides continuous managerial assistance and sponsors annual meetings of franchisees.

GENERAL ENERGY DEVICES, INC.
1753 Ensley Avenue
Clearwater, Florida 33516
Leonard D. Levin, President

Description of Operation: Original equipment manufacturer of solar hot water systems, space heating systems, and pool heating systems sold through local distributors. Distributor is licensed to sell the full line of the company's solar energy systems and is given a qualified territory.
Number of Franchisees: 160 (distributors)
In Business Since: 1975
Equity Capital Needed: $18,750 for inventory materials, and training.
Financial Assistance Available: None
Training Provided: Distributors are carefully schooled for 3 days in product knowledge and background; installation and selling techniques at company manufacturing and office facilities. Continuing program of assistance is provided from home office by company personnel.
Managerial Assistance Available: Engineering assistance; merchandising and sales seminars, plus both regional and national meetings. Operations manuals, forms, research and development; Co-op advertising locally for local ads.

K-KRETE, INC.
7711 Computer Avenue
Minneapolis, Minnesota 55435
Dick Dahlstrom

Description of Operation: K-Krete, controlled density fill, is a patented formulation of cement, fillers and pozzolanic materials used in place of compacted earth. It is delivered and placed by standard ready mix concrete trucks.
Number of Franchisees: 29 in 9 States
In Business Since: 1972
Equity Capital Needed: $3,000 minimum plus plant capability of mixing and delivering concrete.
Financial Assistance Available: None
Training Provided: Training course covering manufacturing quality control, and marketing of K-Krete products - 1 day duration.
Managerial Assistance Available: Technical manuals, brochures and marketing aids are made available to franchisees. Engineering personnel are available to assist in technical response.

LAVASTONE INTERNATIONAL, INC.
P. O. Box 270523
Dallas, Texas 75227
Jack G. Busby, President

Description of Operation: Manufacture and sale of Lavastone and Lithos Architectural Pavers.
Number of Franchisees: 10 covering 26 States
In Business Since: 1969
Equity Capital Needed: $47,500
Financial Assistance Available: None
Training Provided: Company provides 2 weeks in franchisees plant.
Managerial Assistance Available: Company provides continuous managerial and sales assistance and sponsors annual meetings for franchisees.

MARBLE-CRETE PRODUCTS, INC.
3439 - 3441 Northwest 19th Street
Lauderdale Lakes, Florida 33311

Description of Operation: The manufacturing of marble at its finest, duplicated with a man-made process to improve the imperfection of real marble. We manufacture intergal shell vanity tops, all sizes, coffee tables, bathroom surrounds, elegant bathtubs, wall panels, desk tops, various novelties, and etc. This is a casting process, using molds, such as fiberglass and formica. Approximately 2,000 square feet of space needed to start operation. GREAT PROFIT POTENTIAL!
Number of Franchisees: 53 in 25 States and Mexico
In Business Since: 1964
Equity Capital Needed: Approximately $25,000.
Financial Assistance Available: An investment of approximately $25,000 establishes you in business, with a down payment of $5,000 on application. If accepted balance is to be paid before your training begins.
Training Provided: 2 weeks of extensive training in all aspects of manufacturing at our main plant. After which franchisee receives all materials and tools, we visit his place of business and help him for 1 week to get organized.
Managerial Assistance Available: We have a number of trained executives who make up the personnel of Marble-Crete Products, Inc., each representing many years of experience in promotion, advertising, and direct selling. We stand ready to assist Marble-Crete licensed dealers in developing the best and most profitable methods of merchandising and supplying the huge potential market for Marble-Crete Products, Inc.

MARBLE-FLOW INDUSTRIES, INC.
3439-41 Northwest 19th Street
Lauderdale Lakes, Florida 33311

Description of Operation: Our monolithic marble floor offers a new concept in the seamless floor field. This floor has much beauty and quality, containing the realism of natural marble. We have cultivated this field for about five years, and through extensive testing in our research department we have developed the marble floor, which we are now offering you. It is more durable than any floor of its type, including tile, asphalt, and vinyl floors.
Number of Franchisees: 52 in the States of Florida, Michigan and New York.
In Business Since: 1964
Equity Capital Needed: Over $9,500 which is returned in inventory.
Financial Assistance Available: An investment of over $9,500 establishes you in business, with a down payment of approximately $3,500 on application if accepted. Balance is due and payable to Marble-Flow Industries, Inc., then training and shipping of materials will be scheduled.
Training Provided: On-the-job training approximately 3 or 4 days, or on floor jobs franchisee may choose to do.
Managerial Assistance Available: We have a number of trained executives who make up the personnel of Marble-Flow Industries, Inc., each representing many years of experience in promotion, advertising, and direct selling. We stand ready to assist Marble-Flow licensed dealers in developing the best and most profitable methods of merchandising and supplying the huge potential market for Marble-Flow Industries, Inc.

MASONRY SYSTEMS INTERNATIONAL, INC.
600 South Cherry
Denver, Colorado 80222
Paul W. Powers

Description of Operation: Company franchises system of manufacturing and marketing virtually all types and shapes of masonry panels using semi-automated patented machinery and special mortars. Any type of brick, block or tile can be used.
Number of Franchisees: 6 in 6 States
In Business Since: 1970
Equity Capital Needed: $150,000 to $300,000 depending on size of start-up plant.
Financial Assistance Available: None
Training Provided: Intensive, 20 man days provided with purchase of franchise. Then further manufacturing and marketing assistance and training available on billable basis.
Managerial Assistance Available: Comprehensive assistance in all aspects of business.

MILL-CRAFT HOUSING CORPORATION
P. O. Box 327
Waupaca, Wisconsin 54981
Leon A. Church, Vice President and Marketing Manager

Description of Operation: Modular home manufacturer.
Number of Franchisees: 46 in Wisconsin, Michigan, Minnesota, Iowa, and Illinois.
In Business Since: 1969
Equity Capital Needed: Depending on size of business and franchise.
Financial Assistance Available: None
Training Provided: Training available at company headquarters for all phases of construction.
Managerial Assistance Available: Continuous assistance and updating of all building and energy codes and problem solving advice.

NEW ENGLAND LOG HOMES, INC.
2301 State Street
P. O. Box 5056
Hamden, Connecticut 06518
Vito Vizziello, President

Description of Operation: New England Log Homes, Inc. (NELHI), manufacturers precut, hand-peeled log homes from pine timber. Over 30 models are available from two-story models, ranch style, garages, etc. Franchise dealers are established from Maine to Florida and as far west as California. The dealer is required to erect a model home which serves as his office. This is provided at dealers cost.
Number of Franchisees: 77 nationwide
In Business Since: 1970
Equity Capital Needed: $100,000-$125,000 (this includes the log home cost, land, furnishings, etc., which are then the franchisees personal property.
Financial Assistance Available: None
Training Provided: Variable, depending on the individuals background. A yearly sales meeting is designed to upgrade the dealers in the latest changes in the log homes, sales methods, etc.
Managerial Assistance Available: Variable, depending on the individuals background.

PAUL W. DAVIS SYSTEMS, INC.
3515 St. Augustine Road
Jacksonville, Florida 32207
Paul W. Davis, President

Description of Operation: Paul W. Davis Systems, Inc., is a General Contracting Company with approximately 80 percent of its business obtained from Insurance Adjusters for the repair of fire, water and windstorm damage; the other 20 percent come from home and commercial improvements. A unique system of pricing and cost control enables our franchisees to, experience early success with no previous experience in this field. A good personality and a willingness to work is required. Franchising in Southeastern United States.
Number of Franchisees: 16 in Florida, North Carolina and Tennessee.
In Business Since: 1968
Equity Capital Needed: The franchise fee is $15,000. One half of this can be financed. The franchisee needs $15,000 to $20,000 operating capital.
Financial Assistance Available: Franchisor assists in obtaining bank financing for accounts receivable.
Training Provided: Before the selection of an area an initial survey is made by the franchisor with the franchisee. Franchisee trains in an existing franchise for 4 weeks. Franchisor then works with franchisee as required. Franchisor assists in all recruiting, hiring and training.
Managerial Assistance Available: Managerial and technical assistance continues throughout the life of the franchise for accounting, sales, management, cost controls, labor supply and expansion.

PERMA-JACK CO.
9127 Pardee Spur
St. Louis, Missouri 63126
George Langenbach, President

Description of Operation: A fast inexpensive building foundation stabilizing system. Hydraulically driven steel pipe columns support the building foundation on rock.
Number of Franchisees: 6 in Missouri, Texas and California.
In Business Since: 1974, incorporated 1975
Equity Capital Needed: Inventory and working capital $12,500. Franchise fee $20,000. A van in good condition.
Financial Assistance Available: None
Training Provided: Field training and complete instructions are given at the St. Louis, Missouri home office. Further training at the Franchisee's location and job sites. Continuing informational assistance and training is given. Art work, layouts, and outlines for advertising and suggested business forms and brochures are included.
Managerial Assistance Available: Managerial and technical assistance provided throughout length of franchise. Top management makes field visits as deemed necessary.

PERMA-STONE COMPANY
2495 Bancroft Street
Columbus, Ohio 43211
Aaron Chase, President

Description of Operation: Sales and application of Perma-Stone to owners' property.
Number of Franchisees: 32 in 10 States.
In Business Since: 1929
Equity Capital Needed: $10,000 minimum
Financial Assistance Available: None
Training Provided: Initial technical training provided to applicating employees, and sales school available to franchisee and sales force.
Managerial Assistance Available: See above.

THE PERMENTRY COMPANY
37 Water Street
Post Office Box 347
West Haven, Connecticut 06516
John K. Newton, Vice President & Manager

Description of Operation: Leases steel molds which will precast in one piece, concrete outside basement stairwell entrances. No royalties. Franchisor's financial interest is in furnishing all-steel doors-covers used with each stairwell. Direct assistance is provided.
Number of Franchisees: 60 in 18 States
In Business Since: 1960
Equity Capital Needed: Under $10,000.
Financial Assistance Available: None-Investment is nominal.
Training Provided: On the job training is made available. A complete "How to" manual is supplied.
Managerial Assistance Available: See above.

PORAFLOR
65 Davids Drive
Hauppauge, New York 11787
Arthur Noskin, President

Description of Operation: Parent company manufacturers resin coating systems. Sells and installs seamless flooring via franchised dealers. Sales are both residential and commercial, renovation and new construction.
Number of Franchisees: 136 in over 25 states
In Business Since: 1965. Poraflor is wholly owned subsidiary of Vitricon.
Equity Capital Needed: $4,950 and up depending on territory, most of which is returned in inventory and rebates.
Financial Assistance Available: Partial financing available depending on franchisee's background and other pertinent factors.
Training Provided: Thorough factory schooling in all phases including technical and sales aspects.
Managerial Assistance Available: Complete company support including field engineers calling periodically on franchisees to assist in sale and technical problems. Extensive sales aids including exhibit for shows are available.

PORCELAIN PATCH & GLAZE COMPANY OF AMERICA
140 Watertown Street
Watertown, Massachusetts 02172
Philip J. Gleason

Description of Operation: Refinishing, spraying, glazing, spot-blending and patching of porcelain and enamel finishes of all kinds, spray painting of lacquer and lacquer blending work of all kinds. Performed for appliance stores, home owners, movers, apartment house owners, plumbers, distributors of major appliances, dentists. A shop is not necessary.
Number of Franchisees: 21 in 17 states.
In Business Since: 1938
Equity Capital Needed: $3,500
Financial Assistance Available: 50% down to good credit risks.
Training Provided: 10 days at main office.
Managerial Assistance Available: Periodic visits, direct mail advertising.

PORCELITE INTERNATIONAL, INC.
14650 Southlawn Lane
Rockville, Mayrland 20850
H. D. Berardi, President
Lee Gilbert, National Marketing Director

Description of Operation: The Porcelite franchise offers a process for the repair and refinishing of procelain plumbing fixtures such as bathtubs and sinks for both commercial and residential use. Chips are repaired and complete fixtures refinished and restored. Used in homes, motels, apartment houses, etc. In white or choice of any color.
Number of Franchisees: 72 in 26 States
In Business Since: 1963
Equity Capital Needed: $7,500 minimum
Financial Assistance Available: None
Training Provided: 5 day training session from 9 am to 5 pm covering all aspects of porcelain repair, refinishing, and restoration.
Managerial Assistance Available: Advertising and sales promotional materials, continuing guidance and assistance as required. Operations manual provided.

POUR MAN SYSTEMS, Division of FREEWAY LUMBER COMPANY
Box 2395
Santa Cruz, California 95062
Paul E. Dunmire, General Manager

Description of Operation: The Pour Man System has been developed to serve the requirements for small quantities of concrete. With the Pour Man System the franchisee sells the ready-mix concrete in small quantities to the customer who drives the Pour Man mixer truck. Pour Man yards will also stock and sell building materials as required by the respective markets - featuring quality products, at convenient hours and locations.

Number of Franchisees: 3 in California
In Business Since: 1973
Equity Capital Needed: $50,000 minimum
Financial Assistance Available: A total investment of $88,500 is required including $7,000 franchise fee and $81,500 for equipment.
Managerial Assistance Available: Pour Man provides site selection and market analysis assistance. Franchise manual includes bookkeeping system, advertising program, operational budget guidelines and operating procedures check lists.

RAPID ECONOMICAL CONSTRUCTION SYSTEMS CORP. (R.E.C.S.)
3510 Biscayne Boulevard, Suite 203
Miami, Florida 33137
William Mann, Vice President—Marketing

Description of Operation: Rapid Economical Construction Systems will set up a turn-key combined home building and real estate company for the franchisee. R.E.C.S. will, in addition, provide a unique home building system that substantially reduces costs, time and labor in housing. R.E.C.S. will also supply complete engineering service, training and supervision and offers sales and marketing assistance.
Number of Franchisees: 14 in Florida, Texas and Louisiana
In Business Since: 1976
Equity Capital Needed: $12,500
Financial Assistance Available: An investment of $25,000 is necessary to open a R.E.C.S. franchise. The down payment of $12,500 pays for model home component materials, sales literature, security deposits, cash fund, licenses, permits, and training. R.E.C.S. will finance the balance if franchisee has good credit references (1 year, 12 payment basis). Franchise has option to arrange own outside financing.
Training Provided: A 7 day training course is scheduled for all new franchisees and their personnel. Three days are conducted at the home office school and on-site at company training facility; 4 days at franchisee's outlet under the supervision of full time R.E.C.S. employee.
Managerial Assistance Available: R.E.C.S. provides continual management service for the life of the franchise in such areas as engineering, bookkeeping, advertising, cost and quality control. Complete manuals of operations, forms, and directions are provided. Field managers are available to work closely with franchisees and regularly visit to assist solving problems. R.E.C.S. sponsors meetings of franchisees and conducts marketing and product research to maintain high consumer acceptance.

REDI-STRIP CO., INC.
11007 Forest Place
Santa Fe Springs, California 90670
J. Paul Deringer, President

Description of Operation: The Redi-Strip system offers a unique nondestructive paint and coating removal by a simple immersion system. The electrolytic deruster immersion "floats" the rust off of steel parts with no metal loss. Redi-Strip provides the tanks, chemical and some other equipment to start your business.
Number of Franchisees: 23 in 16 States and Canada.
In Business Since: 1951
Equity Capital Needed: $40,000 to $80,000. No franchise fees or royalties are involved.
Financial Assistance Available: This would be answered by J. Paul Deringer.
Training Provided: Intensive, 2 week mandatory work and training program at one of our plants. One week at the franchise location.
Managerial Assistance Available: Redi-Strip is available at all times to answer any and all questions.

SPEED FAB-CRETE CORPORATION INTERNATIONAL
1150 East Mansfield Highway
P. O. Box 15580
Fort Worth, Texas 75119
Ladd Holton, National Franchise Manager

Description of Operation: Speed Fab-Crete is a patented precast concrete building system utilizing lightweight loadbearing concrete wall panels as its core component. Each franchise acts as a manufacturer, general contractor, and sub-contractor. The franchisor provides complete training program and technical back-up support services.
Number of Franchisees: 15 in 10 States
In Business Since: 1968
Equity Capital Needed: $30,000-$50,000
Financial Assistance Available: None
Training Provided: Minimum 1 week training provided by franchisor at National Headquarters for franchisee and key personnel.
Managerial Assistance Available: On-site managerial assistance periodically provided at expense of franchisor. On-site technical assistance on request of franchisee. Complete manuals of operations, forms, and directions as provided.

ZELL-AIRE CORPORATION
410 Orrton Avenue
Reading, Pennsylvania 19603
M. W. Zellers

Description of Operation: Introduce-promote Electric Heating by working along with the Local Electrical Utility of the area into newly built and existing buildings. These may be residential, such as single residence or apartments, commercial and professional constructions.
Number of Franchisees: 20 in 15 States
In Business Since: 1966
Equity Capital Needed: $10,000 with $5,000 prompt payment for merchandise.
Financial Assistance Available: Investment is for inventory only. In all instances Franchisee had suitable business location with telephone.
Training Provided: 3 days training at home office, Reading, PA or other designated location when applicable for franchisees. Five days training at their location. Periodic supervision by Company representative at Franchisees location.
Managerial Assistance Available: Periodic supervision to assist franchisee promote business volume. Generally supervisor spends 2 to 3 days monthly with each franchisee.

COSMETICS/TOILETRIES

CHRISTINE VALMY, INC.
767 Fifth Avenue
New York, New York 10022
Henry D. Sterian, Chairman of Board
Judith O'Connell, Franchise Sales Director

Description of Operation: Christine Valmy, Inc., offers a totally vertical skin care salon franchise package. Manufacture our own skin care machines, apparatus, bulk and retail products for a retail salon operation. Each salon is approximately 1,200 square feet and is open about eight hours daily, six days a week. An extensive inventory of Christine Valmy products and skin care equipment is maintained in each salon.
Number of Franchisees: 20 in 9 States
In Business Since: 1964
Equity Capital Needed: Approximately $75,000
Financial Assistance Available: A 50 percent deposit of franchise fee ($10,000) is required upon commitment, and balance of fee due upon signing license agreement. Balance due on total investment upon salon opening.
Training Provided: Intensive 4-5 week mandatory skin care and makeup course for salon/owner manager and two skin care specialists (estheticians) given at the Christine Valmy International School for Esthetics Skin Care & Makeup (licensed by the New York State Board of Education).
Managerial Assistance Available: Managerial assistance provided in-site selection, salon design/layout, public relations, grand opening promotions, textbook and operational manuals, monthly newsletters. Manager/owner can observe daily activities of flagship Fifth Avenue Salon and work closely with salon director. Technical and managerial training plus yearly refresher and update training course.

COLOR ME BEAUTIFUL COSMETICS
P. O. Box 52
North Hackensack Station
River Edge, New Jersey 07661
Irving Davidoff

Description of Operation: The investment includes 20 sales locations, 20 merchandise showcase units and an opening inventory (retail value - $12,800). Licensees are selected to service retail outlets who display and sell Color Me Beautiful cosmetics.
Number of Franchisees: 10 in Connecticut, New York and New Jersey
In Business Since: 1960
Equity Capital Needed: $11,900
Financial Assistance Available: None
Training Provided: Complete indoctrination in the product and merchandising promotions on an ongoing basis. Continuous field supervision to insure optimum sales and profits to the Licensee.
Managerial Assistance Available: Company assists in set up of show case units and merchandise and provides advertising and publicity promotions.

FASHION TWO TWENTY, INC.
1263 South Chilicothe Road
Aurora, Ohio 44202
Ray A. Curtiss, Vice President, Sales

Description of Operation: Fashion Two Twenty, Inc., has a prestige line of cosmetics that are introduced to the customer through the party plan. They offer a wholesale training and distribution center operation to those people who have a direct sales background and have the ability to motivate people and form a sales force.
Number of Franchisees: Approximately 800 throughout the entire United States.
In Business Since: 1962
Financial Assistance Available: $1,300 for initial inventory package.
Financial Assistance Available: Cash basis
Training Provided: 3 days of concentrated schooling plus workshops and sales seminars twice a year.
Managerial Assistance Available: In addition to expert guidance, the Home Office provides recordkeeping support, effective sales aids, brochures, recruiting and training films and weekly and monthly publications recognizing organizations, national advertising, contests, promotions, car program for qualified managers, and sales meetings.

I-NATURAL COSTMETICS
NUTRIENT COSMETIC LTD.
820 Shames Drive
Westbury, New York 11590
Robert B. Greenberg, Executive Vice President

Description of Operation: Unique retail operation of a cosmetic boutique specializing in customer service and education primarily located in regional, fashion malls, shopping centers and downtown areas. Products based on natural ingredients and merchandizing includes out-of-shop demonstrations, classes and shows. Only products offered are i Natural cosmetics.
Number of Franchisees: 60 in 21 States
In Business Since: 1970
Equity Capital Needed: Total capital required $40,000 to $50,000 depending on location.
Financial Assistance Available: No financial assistance provided.
Training Provided: Formal classroom program held at site of retail location for staff, manager and owner. Minimum of 1 week.
Managerial Assistance Available: Training includes operations, selling techniques, promotional programs, and shop administrators. Our training staff visits each franchised shop generally once each calendar quarter for training in new products, refresher courses and problem solving.

JUDITH SANS INTERNATIONALE, INC.
3867 Roswell Road Northeast
Atlanta, Georgia 30342
Judith Sans, President

Description of Operation: Skin care and cosmetic centers.
Number of Franchisees: 6 in 6 States
In Business Since: $70,000
Equity Capital Needed: None
Financial Assistance Available: 14 days intensive training provided by franchisor at training headquarters in Atlanta, Georgia.
Managerial Assistance Available: Continuous

LADY BURD EXCLUSIVE COSMETICS, INC.
158-01 Crossbay Boulevard
Howard Beach, New York 11414

Description of Operation: Wholesale and retail cosmetics featuring services as facials, manicures, pedicures, body waxing. (Electrolyses and depilation hair removal) also haircutting. (Private Label Cosmetics.)
Number of Franchisees: 3 in New York
In Business Since: 1960
Equity Capital Needed: $5,000-$10,000 depending on location. Many start in home and when established, move to store.
Financial Assistance Available: None

SYD SIMONS COSMETICS, INC.
2 East Oak Street
Chicago, Illinois 60611
Jerome Weitzel, President

Description of Operation: Syd Simons Cosmetics offers a unique completely equipped makeup and skin care studio for the sale of a complete line of cosmetic products and accessories as well as related services. The package includes all furniture, fixtures, studio supplies, opening inventory, decorating, brochures and advertising and promotional materials.
Number of Franchisees: 6 in Illinois, Kansas, and California
In Business Since: Retailing 1940. Franchising - 1972
Equity Capital Needed: Approximately $30,000.
Financial Assistance Available: Franchisor will assist franchisee in obtaining business loan from appropriate lending institution.
Training Provided: Syd Simons Cosmetics provides basic 60 day training period in makeup and skin care as well as studio operations and business procedures at the franchisors home office. Additional on site training conducted periodically.
Managerial Assistance Available: Syd Simons provides continual managerial, legal, financial and promotional guidance in accordance with the needs of the franchisee, as well as assistance in sales areas.

Training Provided: We train completely. Can take 1 to 3 days of basic training.
Managerial Assistance Available: All help needed in guidance on how to run your operation.

DRUG STORES

LE$-ON RETAIL SYSTEMS, INC.
dba LE$-ON DRUGS
5301 West Dempster Street
Skokie, Illinois 60077
Leslie B. Masover, President

Description of Operation: Retail drug stores.
Number of Franchisees: 28 in Illinois
In Business Since: 1968
Equity Capital Needed: $10,000 to $50,000 depending on size of store and type.
Financial Assistance Available: Counsel and introduction to banking sources.
Training Provided: Minimum 2 weeks of training.
Managerial Assistance Available: Managerial assistance provided for duration of license agreement.

MEDICINE SHOPPES INTERNATIONAL, INC.
10121 Paget Drive
St. Louis, Missouri 63132
Edwin F. Prizer, President

Description of Operation: Retail sales of pharmaceuticals and medicines, emphasing ethics, professionalism, and profits.
Number of Franchisees: 320 in 44 States
In Business Since: 1971
Equity Capital Needed: Investment $40,000 which includes fee, fixtures, opening inventory and opening promotion.
Financial Assistance Available: Lease package for fixtures etc.
Training Provided: 5 day training seminar at corporate headquarters. Two days or longer store opening assistance.
Managerial Assistance Available: Continuous in-training program for marketing and store operations. We furnish computerized bookkeeping and marketing services and financial and operational analysis on a monthly basis. Assistance in-site selection, lease negotiation, store layout, fixturing, personnel selection and purchasing procedures.

EDUCATIONAL PRODUCTS/SERVICES

ALLSTATE CONTRACTORS SCHOOLS TRAINING CENTERS
16661 Ventura Boulevard
Suite 120
Encino, California 91436
Don Van Kempen, President

Description of Operation: Allstate Contractor Schools are in the private Adult Education Field, whereby we assist individuals in passing the State Contractors License examination. Our method for instruction is by closed circuit television. Each student is provided a program to follow for his particular category of contracting.
Number of Franchisees: 17 in California only.
In Business Since: 1976
Equity Capital Needed: $8,500
Financial Assistance Available: First year license fee is $19,500. Paid $8,500 for set up with equipment, films and training, these monies are placed in impound until licensor performs. The balance is paid in 11 equal monthly payments of $1,000 per month, licensee may terminate at anytime, 30 days written notice.
Training Provided: 2 weeks home office stay for familiarization training in all facets of operation.
Managerial Assistance Available: Continuing guidance for the length of the license agreement, upgrading of curriculum as needed, etc.

ALLSTATE REAL ESTATE LICENSE SCHOOL
16661 Ventura Boulevard
Suite 120
Encino, California 91436
Don Van Kempen, President

Description of Operation: Allstate Real Estate License School is in the private Adult Education Field where we assist individuals in passing the State Real Estate Sales exam. We use closed circuit television as a method of instruction.
Number of Franchisees: 9 in California only.
In Business Since: 1977
Equity Capital Needed: $2,500
Financial Assistance Available: First year license fee is $4,900. Paid $2,500 for set up with equipment, films and training, these monies are placed in impound until licensor performs. The balance is paid in installments of $200 a month for 11 months. Licensee may terminate within 30 days written notice.
Training Provided: 2 weeks home office stay for familiarization training in all facets of operation.
Managerial Assistance Available: Continuing guidance for the length of the license agreement, upgrading of curriculum as needed, etc.

ANTHONY SCHOOLS
4401 Birch Street
P.O. Box 2960
Newport Beach, California 92663

Description of Operation: The men and women who own and operate Anthony Schools franchises are involved in one of the most satisfying, personally rewarding fields of private education preparing adults for licenses and new career opportunities in real estate, contracting, insurance and securities. Schools, which vary in size from 2,000 to 6,000 square feet and larger, are located in high quality shopping centers offering both day and evening classes. Franchisor writes, publishes and prints the full educational product line of Anthony Schools courses, and updates them continuously for the franchisees students. Anthony Schools does not franchise outside of California.
Number of Franchisees: 5 in California. These are master franchises operating 35 of the 50 California locations.
In Business Since: 1945
Equity Capital Needed: Varies widely with number of schools franchisee wishes to operate and size/location of marketing area. Complete financial statements and excellent credit rating required.
Financial Assistance Available: None
Training Provided: In-depth training provided as long as required in all business and education phases, from initial marketing survey and site location studies to school operations, advertising, management, personnel selection and training, accounting, and instructional resources.
Managerial Assistance Available: Continuous management advice and assistance is provided for the duration of the franchise, covers functions of all school operations, all Anthony educational products, industry trends and data/information/guidance in education, administration, marketing, state and federal regulatory agencies. Franchise meetings, field consultations and headquarters visits provide continuing management guidance and operating assistance.

AUDIO VISUAL EDUCATIONAL SYSTEMS
6116 Skyline Drive
P. O. Box 22768
Houston, Texas 77027
Leonard J. Blumenthal, Vice President/Franchise Development

Description of Operation: Sales of audio visual equipment and supplies and video equipment and supplies to specific territory. All markets within such territory. Inventory, shipments, accounting, credit management to be maintained by national headquarters - monthly reports sent to franchisee.
Number of Franchisees: 3 in 3 States
In Business Since: 1963
Equity Capital Needed: $25,000
Financial Assistance Available: Up to 40 percent of equity capital required.

Training Provided: 1 week training at Houston franchise headquarters. One week training in franchisee territory. Daily communication by telephone to Houston headquarters.
Managerial Assistance Available: Once a quarter review in franchisee's territory for 1 or 2 days. More frequently if circumstances require.

BARBIZON SCHOOLS OF MODELING
3 East 54th Street
New York, New York 10022
B. Wolff, Executive Vice President

Description of Operation: Barbizon operates modeling and personal development schools for teen-age girls, homemakers, and career girls. The schools also offer a male modeling program, fashion merchandising course, acting course, and sell Barbizon cosmetics. We are the largest organization in this field.
Number of Franchisees: 66 in 28 States
In Business Since: 1939
Equity Capital Needed: $25,000-$50,000
Financial Assistance Available: Franchisee can finance 50 percent of franchise fee with franchisor. Total franchise fee is $19,500 to $35,000.
Training Provided: Intensive three week training program for franchisee and his director at corporate office. Extensive on-site field visits at franchisee's location by home office staff during first 6 months. Periodic staff visits and conferences at home office thereafter on a continuing basis.
Managerial Assistance Available: In addition to initial training indicated above. Barbizon makes available continuing staff programs, sales aids, new programs, brochures, direct mail pieces. etc.

BUTLER LEARNING SYSTEMS
1325 West Dorothy Lane
Dayton, Ohio 45409
Don Butler, President

Description of Operation: Audio-visual training program for salespeople, supervisors, and all workers. Sales to business, industry, banks, hospitals and government. Conduct open and closed seminars.
Number of Franchisees: 35 in 21 States and Canada.
In Business Since: 1959
Equity Capital Needed: No fees. $5,000 working capital.
Financial Assistance Available: None
Training Provided: Training in using and selling training packages and holding seminars.
Managerial Assistance Available: Continual management assistance.

CHILD ENRICHMENT CENTERS
6 Passaic Street
Hackensack, New Jersey 07601
Russell J. Rupon, General Manager

Description of Operation: A prestige pre school, kindergarten, and summer camp, 3,600 square foot building together with outdoor playground. Can be operated by owner or as absentee management. You don't have to be an educator. Alphabetland assist franchisee in obtaining land and building.
Number of Franchisees: 15 in New York, New Jersey, and Florida.
In Business Since: 1967
Equity Capital Needed: $20,000 plus operating capital
Financial Assistance Available: A total of $60,000 is required to own an Alphabetland franchise. A down payment of $20,000 is made on contract, balance can be financed both short-term and over 5 years, if qualified. An additional $15,000-$20,000 is needed for operating capital.
Training Provided: 10 days pre-training is offered to franchisee at home office. Minimum of 21 days post-training at franchisee's school.
Managerial Assistance Available: Advertising, bookkeeping, operations and curriculum manuals. Seminars to maintain consumer acceptance of our curriculum and methodology.

DOOTSON DRIVING SCHOOLS
9417 Las Tunas
Temple City, California 91780
Richard F. Dootson

Description of Operation: Driver education.
Number of Franchisees: 7 in California.
In Business Since: 1952
Equity Capital Needed: $20,000
Financial Assistance Available: 100 percent automobile financing and co-signature on equipment financing.
Training Provided: 2 weeks, 80 hour course given in the home office.
Managerial Assistance Available: Continuous

EVELYN WOOD READING DYNAMICS, INC.
155 Bovet Road
San Mateo, California 94402
Harris C. Smith, Director of Franchising

Description of Operation: Offer a reading enhancement course in the United States and abroad through franchisee and company-owned institutes. Course is designed to teach students to substantially increase their reading rate with equal or better comprehension.
Number of Franchisees: 10 plus 14 company-owned throughout the United States.
In Business Since: 1964
Equity Capital Needed: Dependent on area available for franchising.
Financial Assistance Available: Note pay-out plans for purchase price of franchise locations are usually mutually worked out as needed at initial stages.
Training Provided: Initial assistance to franchisee as provided for in the Franchise and License Agreement.
Managerial Assistance Available: Assistance in selection of location for institutes/physical layout of classroom facilities, etc., advertising and public relations/office techniques/business management and teaching. Assistance in developing teacher-training course; texts and materials for course and price lists covering same/certification of qualified instructors after completion

IMAGE IMPROVEMENT, INC.
1223 Edgewater Street, N.W.
Salem, Oregon 97304
Joanne Wallace, President
Jim Wallace, Executive Director

Description of Operation: Image Improvement, Inc., has developed self-image and grooming (personal improvement) courses for men and women which is unique in that it bases its instruction on Biblical principles. The women's course is called Image of Loveliness and the men's program is called His Image. The course is taught to a class of 15-30 men or women of all ages. The classes meet once a week in 3-hour sessions. The men's course is six weeks in length and the women's course eight weeks.
Number of Franchisees: 75 throughout the U.S., also in Canada, New Zealand and West Germany.
In Business Since: 1972
Equity Capital Needed: The franchise fee is variable depending upon population of exclusive area and option elected. Initial starting costs approximately $3,500.
Financial Assistance Available: The initial franchise fee must be paid upon the signing of the contract. The franchisor does not carry any contract. Student Handbooks and supplies are on a cash basis.
Training Provided: At the present time training is varied dependent on previous training and the availability of the franchisee to an existing franchise, the franchise fee includes a week of training at the home office. A manual which includes all lectures and tapes (cassette) of the founder of the course teaching her classes are provided each franchisee to assist them in their training.
Managerial Assistance Available: 2 mandatory training seminars are held each year for the franchise owner and their employees. Monthly newsletters are sent to all franchisees. The course material is continually being reviewed and updated to provide current information which is available to all franchises.

INSTITUTE OF READING DEVELOPMENT
4630 Geary Boulevard
Suite 303
San Francisco, California 94118
Paul Cooperman, President

Description of Operation: The Institute of Reading Development (IRD) offers several programs of speed reading and comprehension training for college students, professional persons, and junior high and senior high school students. The programs are marketed directly to individual students, parents, colleges, schools, businesses, and government agencies. They are endorsed by a number of major California universities, and were developed by IRD's founder and president, Paul Cooperman, who is the author of the widely acclaimed book on the decline of academic achievement of American students, The Literacy Hoax, (Fall 1978, William Morrow and Company).
Number of Franchisees: 6 in California
In Business Since: 1971
Equity Capital Needed: Between $10,000 and $50,000, depending on size of the exclusive territory granted franchisee.
Financial Assistance Available: None
Training Provided: IRD will supply extensive and continuous training in two areas; marketing, and reading instruction. The initial training consists of a 10 day session for franchisee at IRD's home office.
Managerial Assistance Available: IRD will supply franchisee with all marketing and instructional materials (including training manuals for all jobs), bookkeeping forms, and a cost accounting/sales analysis system. IRD will also supply continuous training and supervision in all phases of marketing and reading instruction, including training in new marketing and instructional programs as they are developed. This is an extraordinary opportunity for someone with a strong marketing/sales background who wants to work in private education.

INTERNATIONAL TRAVEL TRAINING COURSES, INC.
303 East Ohio Street
Time Life Building
Chicago, Illinois 60611
Evelyn Echols, President

Description of Operation: International Travel Training Courses, Inc., established in 1962, is the oldest and most prestigious travel training school in the United States, the only one recognized by the American Society of Travel Agents. The purpose of the school is to train students to be travel agents. The teaching staff of International Travel Training Courses, Inc., is comprised of executives and training personnel of major airlines, steamship companies, and travel agents, such as United Airlines, Pan-American Airlines, Trans-World Airlines, Holland American Cruises, and American Express.
Number of Franchisees: 4 in the District of Columbia and California.
In Business Since: 1962
Equity Capital Needed: $75,000. This capital is required for operating costs, including advertising, rent, furniture, etc., for first year of operations. Cost of an INTTCO franchise is $50,000, which is paid to INTTCO from gross receipts over a 2-year period. Franchisees also pays INTTCO 10 percent of the gross for the first 5 years and 5 percent of the gross thereafter. Contract renewable at option of either party every 5 years.
Financial Assistance Available: Franchisee must be able to handle their own financing.
Training Provided: Intensive 6-week mandatory training is scheduled for all new franchisees at Headquarters in Chicago. During this time franchisee is trained in sales and marketing and also audits classes in session. New personnel are also offered the opportunity for this type training.
Managerial Assistance Available: International Travel Training Courses, Inc., provides continual management service for the life of the franchise in the areas of marketing, advertising, and sales. All training materials are purchased through International Travel Training Courses at a very low cost. Executive personnel from International Travel Training Courses spend a minimum of 3 weeks in their area prior to the opening of the first class. They then visit each franchisee 10 days per year to assist in interviewing, selling and marketing. There is one meeting each year in the Chicago office for reorientation for the franchisee.

JOHN ROBERT POWERS FINISHING & MODELING SCHOOL
9 Newbury Street
Boston, Massachusetts 02116
Barbara J. Tyler, Executive Vice President

Description of Operation: John Robert Powers School offers finishing, self-improvement, drama, modeling, executive grooming, fashion merchandising, interior design, make-up arts and flight attendant to women and men of all ages. Classes are held year 'round - day and evening.
Number of Franchisees: 60 in 26 States, Guam and Greece
In Business Since: 1920
Equity Capital Needed: $25,000
Financial Assistance Available: None
Training Provided: 3 weeks of teaching and administrative training plus semi-annual seminars.
Managerial Assistance Available: We provide managerial and technical assistance during the life of the franchise by visiting field personnel. Accounting assistance is provided by home office personnel. Conferences are held during the year.

LEISURE LEARNING CENTERS, INC.
50 Greenwich Avenue
Greenwich, Connecticut 06830
Richard Bendett

Description of Operation: Leisure Learning sells over 23 different courses for adults and children within a store that offers the largest variety of educational products for every age and interest. The unique ultramodern stores average between 1,500 - 3,000 square feet. A section of glass enclosed booths (carrels) contain a variety of audio-visual teaching machines and programmed materials used to teach people such subjects as touch typing, foreign languages, shorthand, speed reading, flying, art, plus a whole variety of math and reading courses for children. The individualized format permits people to attend the centers at their own convenience since there are no formal classes or teachers. Within each store, attractively arranged sections of merchandise contain educational toys, books, records, tapes, adult mental games, puzzles, memorizing aids, science kits and craft items. Leisure Products, a subsidiary of Leisure Learning Centers also distributes children's games and activities through other retail outlets including toy stores, department stores, book stores, catalog stores etc. Distributors are available for these materials. Minimum investment $10,000.
Number of Franchisees: 4 in Connecticut, North Carolina, and Maryland.
In Business Since: 1972
Equity Capital Needed: Minimum total investment $80,000 plus leasehold improvement cost and working capital.
Financial Assistance Available: Will assist in securing equipment lease - average $21,000-$35,000.
Training Provided: Thorough training program includes: all aspects of retail management; complete introdoctrination in courses and teaching equipment; bookkeeping and controls; promotion planning; merchandising; purchasing procedures. Up to 4 weeks of training or until full proficiency is indicated.
Managerial Assistance Available: Full range of services include: new merchandise and course acquisition, advertising and publicity, sales forecasting, account management, store layout and design for special promotions, inter-store relations program, cooperative buying benefits.

MANAGEMENT INSTITUTE
P. O. Box 564
1523 Decatur Highway
Fultondale, Alabama 35068
Marene P. Fassina, President

Description of Operation: An educational institute promoting management training, personnel, testing, job evaluation and company internal consultation.
Number of Franchisees: 4 in Alabama and Pennsylvania
In Business Since: 1969
Equity Capital Needed: $2,500 minimum
Financial Assistance Available: Financial assistance available to qualified applicants.
Training Provided: Comprehensive management training, and sales dynamics.
Managerial Assistance Available: Close supervision for three months.

MARY MOPPET'S DAY CARE SCHOOLS, INC.
2404 West Huntington Drive
Tempe, Arizona 85282
Gerald J. Spresser, President

Description of Operation: Mary Moppet's Day Care Schools, Inc., provides complete plans for a building of approximately 3,400 Sq. Ft. which is designed to offer quality day care to children. Each school is equipped with playground equipment, interior school equipment and signs. Hours of operation range from 6:30 a.m. to 6:30 p.m. 5 days a week. Mary Moppet's aides in long term lease arrangements between franchisee and the owner of the building.
Number of Franchisees: 73 Franchise Schools and 13 company-owned schools in 14 States.
In Business Since: 1967
Equity Capital Needed: $30,000
Equity Capital Needed: A total investment of $45,000 is required to open a Mary Moppet's Day Care School. $15,000 down payment, $15,000 when building is 50 percent completed and $15,000 upon occupancy. The $15,000 down payment pays for expenses incurred in selection of sites, arranging leases, equipment, etc. Mary Moppet's will carry back a portion of the franchising cost, if the franchisee has good credit references. It is preferred that franchise obtains his own financing.
Training Provided: An intensive training program is held for 1 week at the home office. Other training is done periodically during the year at the franchisee operation.
Managerial Assistance Available: Mary Moppet's provides continued management counsel for the life of the franchise in the areas of bookkeeping, staff training, operational manuals, forms and directions for their use. Seminars are held during the year to answer questions and give qualified help in areas needing strength. It also holds an annual convention in Scottsdale, Arizona.

MASTERS' DRIVING ACADEMY, INC.
10381 Decatur Road
Philadelphia, Pennsylvania 19154
Barbara S. Griffith, Executive Vice President

Description of Operation: National franchisor of automobile driving schools.
Number of Franchisees: 18 in Pennsylvania and New Jersey
In Business Since: 1979
Equity Capital Needed: $15,000
Financial Assistance Available: Assistance in gaining necessary financing.
Training Provided: 2 weeks intensive classroom and behind-the-wheel training at home office and subsequently in-the-field training by field supervisors.
Managerial Assistance Available: 4 weeks intensive training and indoctrination at home office.

MIND POWER, INC.
P. O. Box 1464
Bethlehem, Pennsylvania 18018
Barkley Wyckoff, President

Description of Operation: Franchised speed reading and memory operation. Franchisee recruits students, responsible for teaching classes and the overall management of the business end of the franchise.
Number of Franchisees: 175 in 18 States
In Business Since: 1969
Equity Capital Needed: $3,000
Financial Assistance Available: Franchisor does not finance any part of franchise fee, however, firm will offer assistance in obtaining financing.
Training Provided: 2 day initial training program, all training sessions are open for retraining. All employees are also trained at any subsequent session.
Managerial Assistance Available: Continual assistance is provided by the franchisor both by telephone and personal contact.

MUSIC DYNAMICS
Fine Arts Building
Suite 922
410 South Michigan Avenue
Chicago, Illinois 60605
Paul S. Renard, President

Description of Operation: Music Dynamics franchises music sight reading teaching systems to music dealers throughout the world. It is also available to music school or individuals seeking to own a franchise.
Number of Franchisees: 12 in 6 States
In Business Since: 1974
Equity Capital Needed: $1,200 - company also takes 20 percent of teaching monies. Franchisee must supply his own studios and equipment.
Financial Assistance Available: None
Training Provided: 18 hours of training required to teach Music Dynamics sytem. Training is also provided to show franchisee how to operate a Music Dynamics studio.
Managerial Assistance Available: Continuous operating assistance given to franchisee by entire staff of Music Dynamics. An operations and procedures manual is available for all franchisees.

NADEAU LOOMS, INC.
725 Branch Avenue
Providence, Rhode Island 02904
Elphege Nadeau, President

Description of Operation: New therapeutic concept-patent protected-using audio visual teaching unit and revolutionary cloth making equipment.
Number of Franchisees: 22 in New York, New Jersey, Florida, Illinois and Pennsylvania.
In Business Since: 1959
Equity Capital Needed: $4,980
Financial Assistance Available: Financing available to qualified applicants.
Training Provided: 100 hours of training
Managerial Assistance Available: Continuous assistance and direction.

PATRICIA STEVENS INTERNATIONAL, INC.
P. O. Box 31818
Omaha, Nebraska 68131
Leonard Theise

Description of Operation: The Patricia Stevens Career Colleges and Finishing Schools are educational residence schools that operate throughout the United States and Canada. Subjects taught are merchandising, public relations, executive secretarial, professional modeling and finishing.
Number of Franchisees: 20 throughout the United States.
In Business Since: 1950
Equity Capital Needed: $25,000 minimum
Financial Assistance Available: No financial assistance is provided by the franchisor to the franchisee.
Training Provided: 3 weeks intensive training is provided at our educational headquarters, where we hold seminars for teachers quarterly, both beginning and advanced. Also franchisees are taught to operate schools from an administrative standpoint in our headquarters and at other locations. Personal attention is provided on the side after school is open.
Managerial Assistance Available: National headquarters maintains experts in the field of school operation under the training supervisor and educational director. National and local advertising aids are provided together with visual aids, etc.

R.E.A.D.S., INC.
10100 Santa Monica
Suite 750
Los Angeles, California 90067
Stephen F. Danz, President

Description of Operation: University, high school and professional rapid reading and

comprehension workshops. Company owns and operates its own programs throughout U.S.; now starting franchise operations. Also has "Scholarship Bank" for licensing.
Number of Franchisees: 3 in Washington and Texas
Equity Capital Needed: 1967
Financial Assistance Available: $7,500 plus additional amount depending on area.
Financial Assistance Available: None as to franchise fee but extensive as to operating assistance after programs in operations.
Training Provided: Training in all aspects of sales, teaching and business management. Most training takes place during July in one of several regional training centers. Lasts approximately 2 weeks with follow-up training and opening assistance in each location.
Managerial Assistance Available: Continuing assistance in all areas. National Student Enrollment Center supplies all sales materials, sends out information, forwards local student leads to franchisee. Continuous research in developmental reading areas, curriculum updates, test revisions, etc. New program materials for new audiences continuously being developed. On-site assistance in organizing sales outlets, selecting teaching locations.

ROBERT FIANCE SYSTEMS, INC.
Business Schools (Hair Design Institute)
404 Fifth Avenue
New York, New York 10018
Rocco Ferrara, President Corporate Development

Description of Operation: Robert Fiance's Beauty Culture Schools are designed by experts to retain the image of professiona' sm, warmth, invitation, and reliability. The pleasant, sophisticated atmosphere and the modern equipment and decor sell prospective students on sight. The curriculum and art of instruction provide the finest training available. Space requirements vary from 4,000 square feet and up - depending on location, number of students, etc.
Number of Franchisees: 4 in New York
In Business Since: 1936
Equity Capital Needed: Minimum of $75,000
Financial Assistance Available: Investment of $75,000 to $150,000 is suggested. License fee is $35,000 - balance to be used for school space, security, building alterations etc., equipment, promotion and advertising. RFS will provide financing for qualified individuals especially to those who devote full time to the school - people who are eager to build the business.
Training Provided: Robert Fiance Systems, Inc., provides continual management service for the life of the franchise agreement (15 years) and help train management personnel in all functions for a successful operation and to assure continued quality of service and a sound and profitable school business.
Managerial Assistance Available: A mandatory training and orientation course at Robert Fiance's headquarters in New York City for the executive director and other teaching and management personnel is part of the requirements set forth (2 weeks) - Continual supervision and training (as required) will be given at the home school, etc.

TELLER TRAINING INSTITUTES, INC.
Seaboard Building, Suite 700
Fourth Avenue at Pike Street
Seattle, Washington 98101
David Lonay, President

Description of Operation: Teller Training Institutes, Inc., offers the franchisee an opportunity to have a successfully proven concept set-up for the franchisee in metropolitan areas larger than one million population. All necessary information, instruction, and financial arrangements are included.
Number of Franchisees: 11 in Washington, Colorado, California, Missouri, Illinois and Minnesota.
In Business Since: 1971
Equity Capital Needed: Up to $50,000 depending on territory.
Financial Assistance Available: None needed
Training Provided: 1 month in home office for thorough instruction in teaching the course, and administration including marketing, financing, hiring, recruiting, and placement.
Managerial Assistance Available: See above; plus assistance continues in the field to insure the franchisee has working knowledge of successful techniques. Home office assists in site selection, equipment selection and provides advertising and accounting services.

UP-GRADE EDUCATIONAL SERVICES, INC.
2745 Carley Court
North Bellmore, New York 11710
Victoria Levy, President

Description of Operation: Private and institutional tutoring and teaching. Provides teachers for all subjects and all levels. Specializing in individualized programs for children with "Learning Disabilities." Work is done in cooperation with hospitals, mental institutions, drug rehabilitation programs, pediatricians, psychologists and psychiatrists, in institutions or privacy of individuals own home. All teachers that are recommended are certified or licensed in specialized areas. Can be fully operated from franchisee's home by professional and business oriented individuals.
Number of Franchisees: 17 in metropolitan New York area, franchises limited.
In Business Since: 1964 - Incorporated in 1969.
Equity Capital Needed: $7,500 and up according to size of geographic area.
Financial Assistance Available: 60 percent on closing - balance to be paid within 1 year.
Training Provided: Training initially in home office - concentrated in less than 1 week time. Operational manual - training unlimited.
Managerial Assistance Available: Continuous assistance as necessary—no time limit. Each franchisee is required to attend at least 1 group meeting a year. Newsletters are sent out at least 6 times a year, suggesting new business ideas and programs experimented with that proved successful in an area. Franchisee's are responsible for most of the material in Newsletter so there is a continuous exchange of ideas to develop and expand his business.

EMPLOYMENT SERVICES

AAA EMPLOYMENT FRANCHISE, INC.
400 - 83rd Avenue North
St. Petersburg, Florida 33702
Thelma Ramey, Executive Vice President

Description of Operation: AAA Employment Franchise, Inc., offers a highly ethical and professional service to both applicants and employers. AAA offices do not limit themselves to specialized areas of employment - full service is available - executive to domestic placement - both temporary and permanent employment. The low placement fee of only 2 weeks salary has proven to be in great demand for the past 20 years. Coast to coast, border to border territories available on a first to qualify basis.
Number of Franchisees: 7 in Arizona, Pennsylvania, Tennessee, and South Carolina.
In Business Since: AAA Employment, Inc. - 1957; AAA Employment Franchise, Inc. - 1977
Equity Capital Needed: Down payment depends on size of territory selected (minimum $2,000 - maximum $10,000) and approximately $3,000 (includes office space, furnishings, office supplies, and licensing).
Financial Assistance Available: Once down payment is made, the balance of the fee is paid $100 per month until paid off - no finance charge.
Training Provided: The franchisor's staff will provide the franchisee with an intensive 2 week training program at the corporate headquarters in St. Petersburg, Florida. Additional on-the-job training will be conducted in the field for the franchisee and employees. A representative from the home office will spend the first week of operation in the franchisees office to offer assistance. Seminars are held semi-annually to keep franchisees updated on new ideas and techniques.
Managerial Assistance Available: The staff of the franchisor will provide the franchisee with continual support and assistance. Some of the services provided by the franchisor are: 1) aid in selecting a prime location, 2) aid in negotiating a lease, 3) providing information and research requirements for city, county and state licenses, 4) selection of office furniture and supplies, 5) establishing an advertising schedule, 6) establishing a budget schedule, 7) hiring and training employees, and 8) record keeping. In addition to the continual communication between the franchisee and franchisor by phone, and the continued furnishing of information through the mail, visits will be made periodically into the field by a representative of the corporation. The franchisee will also be provided with a detailed operations manual as well as other reference guides. Every effort will be made by AAA Employment Franchise, Inc.

ACME PERSONNEL SERVICE
P. O. Box 14466
Opportunity, Washington 99214
D. Scott MacDonald, Franchise Director

Description of Operation: We have company-owned and franchised offices, operating to serve both applicant and employer clients in the placement of permanent personnel in all fields, from minimum wage up to upper level recruiting at income levels of $15,000- $50,000 or more. For permanent placements from minimum wage to $15,000 annual income, business is handled through "Acme Personnel Service." For employer-paid recruiting of permanent personnel in the salary range of $15,000 annual income on up, business is handled through "The Executive Suite." Territories are protected, and need not be renewed.
Number of Franchisees: 83 in 17 States
In Business Since: 1946
Equity Capital Needed: Franchise fee is from $9,500 to $19,500 depending on the size of the market territory. We recommend from 50-100 percent for support capital.
Financial Assistance Available: We may be able to recommend a prospective franchisee to suitable financing sources, if they should be needed. We also participate in national co-op advertising in franchisee's market on a 50-50 basis, up to a maximum.
Training Provided: Before opening the office, franchisee receives a unique, concentrated, 1 week training course. Franchisee is given and taught how to use our 400 page company Guide, which contains the essence of over 30 years of experience. Franchisee is also trained to use our system of personnel placement, as well as all internal procedures necessary to the successful running of the business. Within 90 days after opening, franchisee receives a personal visit from the franchise director and/or corporate district manager. Annual conventions are full of training sessions. Franchisee returns to 1-week training course every 3 years.
Managerial Assistance Available: Continual assistance is available from the franchise director, and/or corporate district managers in franchisee's area, in advertising, applicant recruitment, job-order promotion, internal staffing and training, bookkeeping and other internal operations, etc. All new forms, procedures, ideas, and aids of any sort whatever are sent to franchisee on a regular basis, usually weekly. Franchisees receive free national advertising exposure, free job-order promotion materials sent into their markets quarterly, and other assistance if requested.

ADIA TEMPORARY SERVICES, INC.
64 Willow Place
Menlo Park, California 94025
Leonard N. Swartz, Vice President, Finance and Treasurer

Description of Operation: Furnishing skilled office, technical, sales, and marketing personnel and industrial workers to clients on temporary, as needed, basis.
Number of Franchisees: 39 in 17 States and South America.
In Business Since: 1957
Equity Capital Needed: $25,000 plus, depending on market size.
Financial Assistance Available: Franchisor finances entire temporary help payroll.
Training Provided: 1 full week of formal, centralized manager and staff training with additional field training provided immediately after office opening. Provides complete operating manuals on ADIA Temporary Help System.
Managerial Assistance Available: Continued headquarters guidance through weekly newsletter and bi-monthly, monthly, and quarterly reports. Constant field training

follow-up visits; national and regional seminars. Advice and assistance in such areas as advertising, marketing, insurance, financing and sales.

BAILEY EMPLOYMENT SYSTEM, INC.
51 Shelton Road
Monroe, Connecticut 06468
Sheldon Leighton, President

Description of Operation: Profitable, nationally scoped, placementship techniques augmented with a centralized, electronically computerized, data retrieval system. Centrally filed applicants and centrally filed job specifications, registered by individual Bailey Employment System offices, allows all franchisees a constant pool of qualified applicants and employers with which to work with at all times.
Number of Franchisees: 20 in 5 States
In Business Since: 1960
Equity Capital Needed: $25,000
Financial Assistance Available: If desired, purchase price may be financed at going bank rates.
Training Provided: Complete training in the profitable operation of a Bailey Employment Service office is given to each franchise operator before a new office is opened for business. Our training courses may be audited again and again by the franchise operator and his or her staff at their convenience. Additional training in advanced techniques of professional placementship is offered 52 weeks a year. All such additional training is offered during nonworking hours and is free of charge to all franchise operators and personnel. Conventions are held at least four weekends a year to insure continued interoffice cooperation, comradery and profits.
Managerial Assistance Available: Every conceivable service to insure the owner a profitable return on his or her investment is offered. Experts in site selection, advertising and public relations, business procedures and placementship techniques, accounting and bookkeeping, teaching and instructional services, as well as on-site field representatives are maintained on the payroll of the parent company for the benefit of the franchise operators.

BAKER & BAKER EMPLOYMENT SERVICE, INC.
P.O. Box 364, 114-1/2 Washington Avenue
Athens, Tennessee 37303
Kathleen Baker, President

Description of Operation: Franchising of employment service agencies for small towns of 20,000 population and city suburbs.
Number of Franchisees: 20 offices open in 8 States
In Business Since: 1967
Equity Capital Needed: $8,000 to $10,000 dependent on location, plus $1,500 working capital.
Training Provided: Comprehensive training course before opening and additional periodical on-the-job training at the franchise location.
Managerial Assistance Available: Selection of suitable locations, a nationally aimed public-relations program and instructions and materials for obtaining maximum publicity in local advertising media, all forms required for the first 12 months of operation, an established accounting system, national placement Tele-System operating between offices, assistance in interpreting State laws and complying with license regulations. Trained assistance on call at all hours on any agency problem.

BRYANT BUREAU
A Division of SNELLING AND SNELLING, INC.
Executive Offices
4000 South Tamiami Trail
Sarasota, Florida 33581
William G. Allin, Group Vice President

Description of Operation: Offers professional placement and recruiting services in technical, managerial, sales and executive levels to qualified candidates.
Number of Franchisees: 49 in 27 States
In Business Since: 1976 (Parent Company since 1951)
Equity Capital Needed: $25,000 to $100,000 plus
Financial Assistance Available: None
Training Provided: 2 weeks training at home office in Sarasota, Florida, plus additional training in the field for franchisee and franchisee's employees. Franchisee's employees may be sent at any time free of charge to training classes given in Sarasota and throughout the country. Training includes the use of copyrighted training manuals for the Director, Staffing Specialists and the Registrar; and a Video Systems Training Center which gives each licensee a powerful additional tool for reinforcing the skill of each Staffing Specialist.
Managerial Assistance Available: Assistance in all facets of pre-opening site selection, survey, phone installation, office layout and design plus continued communication through various media along with periodic field visits.

BUSINESS & PROFESSIONAL CONSULTANTS, INC.
3807 Wilshire Boulevard
Los Angeles, California 90010
W. J. LaPerch, President

Description of Operation: Operates in the executive search, recruitment and placement of managerial and executive talent at the professional level. Covers engineering, banking, insurance, accounting, finance, data processing, sales, marketing, and management personnel. All recruiting fees are derived from client company. Where state law permits, does not operate as an employment agency but as executive recruiters. The ideal franchise owner will come from industry at the middle to senior management level, will be degreed or equivalent (an advanced degree is desirable), will be people-oriented, will work well as part of a national team, and yet be capable of individual accomplishment and leadership. An additional facet of this franchise is the inclusion of a professional level temporary service to serve the same customer base and thus be able to satisfy all of the customer's needs. The company finances and handles all details of payroll and billing for the franchisee, so no large amount of payroll capital is required.
Number of Franchisees: 8 in California
In Business Since: 1961

Equity Capital Needed: $10,000 Franchise fee
Financial Assistance Available: Will finance portion of franchise fee at no interest.
Training Provided: An initial 2 week program at the home office to cover the basics of executive search, hiring and training of staff personnel, operational and accounting procedures and market penetration. This is followed by an on-site training program of 1 full week at the franchisee's location, and by further field visits by home office training personnel.
Managerial Assistance Available: Continuous on an as-needed basis and may consist of seminars, field visits, refresher training at franchisor's home office, and constant communication.

CAREER CONCEPTS, INC.
Career Concepts Tower
136 East South Temple
Salt Lake City, Utah 84111
Ed Eynon, Director of Operations

Description of Operation: Career Concepts, Inc., is one of the fastest-growing franchisors in the employment service industry. Each franchise is independently owned and operated. Career Concepts provides extensive monthly training for each of its managers to insure that professionalism and quality of service remain high.
Number of Franchisees: 82 in 13 States
In Business Since: 1975
Equity Capital Needed: $15,000 purchase price plus approximately $5,000 working capital to cover 2-3 months operating expenses.
Financial Assistance Available: Career Concepts expends the $15,000 in providing assistance to the franchisee in setting up his new office. This assistance includes helping the franchisee to; lease office space, install phones, order furniture and supplies, obtain licensing, hire staff personnel, open accounts, and all other items concerned with opening the new franchise. This also includes training sessions both in the franchisee's area and at the corporate office.
Training Provided: Career Concepts provides an on the spot 2 day training session during the opening of the new franchise, and in addition, provides week-long sessions (monthly) at the corporate office in Salt Lake City for old and new managers alike.
Managerial Assistance Available: Career Concepts provides continual training services for the life of the franchise. Complete manuals of operations, forms, and directions are provided. District and field managers are available in all regions to work closely with franchisees to assist in solving problems. Career Concepts sponsors meetings of franchisees and conducts marketing research to provide the best possible information for our franchisees and their client applicants alike.

DELTA GROUP, INC.
Two Hopkins Plaza, Suite 1104
Baltimore, Maryland 21201
Harold E. Klee

Description of Operation: Specialized recruiting, consulting, and computer services within disciplinary fields.
Number of Franchisees: 7 in Maryland
In Business Since: 1971
Equity Capital Needed: $10,000 total cost
Financial Assistance Available: None
Training Provided: 1 month training.
Managerial Assistance Available: Computer services, client documentation, communications; direct mail, printing office management.

DR. PERSONNEL, INC.
1111 South Colorado Boulevard
Denver, Colorado 80222
George M. Fornnarino, President

Description of Operation: Dr. Personnel is a highly professionalized employment system providing paramedical and paradental personnel to physicians, dentists, laboratories, hospitals and other health care related entities.
Number of Franchisees: 30 in 14 States
In Business Since: 1970—Franchising 1975
Equity Capital Needed: $19,000 to $32,000
Financial Assistance Available: 10 percent of equity capital.
Training Provided: Phase I: Locate and assist in setting up each location. 1 week training in office. Phase II: Provide approximately 2-3 weeks training in franchisee's office by experienced medical personnel managers.
Managerial Assistance Available: Franchisees are required to submit a weekly operations report. Through continued analysis of these reports, management is generally able to define problem areas and recommend solutions in the early stages of development. Continuous follow-up and support.

DUNHILL PERSONNEL SYSTEM, INC.
1 Old Country Road
Carle Place, New York 11514

Description of Operation: A national personnel service with offices in over 275 cities throughout the United States, Canada, and Puerto Rico. Main areas of job activity; sales, administrative and technical as well as skilled clerical.
Number of Franchisees: 290 in 46 States, District of Columbia and Puerto Rico.
In Business Since: 1952
Equity Capital Needed: Based on a franchise price $25,000: 40 percent of franchise price ($10,000) setting up expenses of $4,000-$5,000 and 3 month's operating expenses of $9,000. Approximately $25,000 plus personal and relocation expenses.
Financial Assistance Available: Franchisor will accept balance of franchise price in promissory notes at 8 percent interest rates. When necessary, offer assistance in obtaining loan thru the SBA.
Training Provided: 2 weeks intensive training in Carle Place, New York operations and training center, covering managing, marketing, marketing research, financial planning, applicant interviewing, selling, recruiting, advertising and publicity. Pre-training for setting up- and post-training visits by experienced staff. Complete manuals and forms are provided together with current promotional material.

Managerial Assistance Available: Continuous followup and support. Field trips to franchisee's office and constant telephone contact by Vice President of Field Operations and field representative as well as all new systems and procedures inaugerated by home office, regional meeting of all offices. Established Franchise Advisory Council in 1972. Council members represent a cross-section of the country and members are franchise owners, Council acts in behalf of all franchise owners in conjunction with headquarters. New members are voted on by franchise owners once a year.

ELLS PERSONNEL SYSTEMS, INC.
1129 Plymouth Building
Minneapolis, Minnesota 55402
Richard E. Peterson, President

Description of Operation: Private employment agency - sales, office, technical placements.
Number of Franchisees: 2 in Minnesota
In Business Since: 1912
Equity Capital Needed: About $10,000.
Financial Assistance Available: None
Training Provided: Formal training varies up to 1 month and continuing during franchise whenever needed.
Managerial Assistance Available: Continuous managerial assistance. Frequent exchange of job orders and applicants. Mutual advertising program.

EMPLOYERS OVERLOAD COMPANY
EO Building
8040 Cedar Avenue South
Minneapolis, Minnesota 55420
Robert B. Miller, President

Description of Operation: Temporary help and business services, Employers Overload has the original ruling issued by the United States Treasury Department, February 9, 1951, which *established* Employers Overload as the legal employer of the people they hire and make available to industry. EO offers a complete range of business and temporary help service, including but not limited to, Office - Industrial - Marketing - Technical - and Payrolling services. EO's 30 years of professional experience qualifies and provides for a successful *EO Agency Program* in the booming multi-billion dollar temporary help industry.
Number of Franchisees: 25 in 12 States
In Business Since: 1947
Equity Capital Needed: There is no initial license or franchise fee. Licensee finances only his own start-up costs, which will vary, depending upon the marketing area.
Financial Assistance Available: EO will assist in financial arrangements, including but not limited to, the option of financing of accounts receivable, payroll for the temporary workers, as well as the applicable payroll taxes and insurance.
Training Provided: Training is available at headquarters and/or the specific location involved. The various manuals of operation are available, plus a continuous, ongoing training program.
Managerial Assistance Available: EO provides continuous management programs. This includes field trips to agent's office, all the facilities at the Home Office, which includes the latest innovations and developments in various techniques covering data processing applications, advertising, both local and national, as well as sales promotion, analyses of the agent's records, and general assistance in the operation of the EO agent's office.

ENGINEERING CORPORATION OF AMERICA
600 First Avenue
Seattle, Washington 98104
Carl J. Muia, President

Description of Operation: Engineering Corporation of America (ECA) is in the business of supplying temporary technical personnel. This is a service type business where the franchise operates the local office supported by ECA's national organization, payroll including providing all the money, taxes, etc.; a complete computer center also providing direct mail advertising and recruiting of personnel.
Number of Franchisees: 4 in 4 States
In Business Since: 1951
Equity Capital Needed: $10,000
Financial Assistance Available: Franchisor provides financing for all payroll.
Training Provided: 30 hours training plus operating manual.
Managerial Assistance Available: Assistance in all phases of the operation at any time.

F-O-R-T-U-N-E FRANCHISE CORPORATION
505 Fifth Avenue
New York, New York 10017
Roy S. Sanders, Vice President

Description of Operation: F-O-R-T-U-N-E Personnel Agency offers a quality Middle Management/Executive personnel service, utilizing unique, proven methods of operation to achieve its present status of industry leadership. F-O-R-T-U-N-E's reputation is highlighted by its professional service, innovative marketing concepts and sophisticated system of exchange of applicants and job orders, together with an excellent program of support for its franchise offices.
Number of Franchisees: 45 in 18 States
In Business Since: Founding company, F-O-R-T-U-N-E Personnel Agency started in business, 1959, 1967 as F-O-R-T-U-N-E Personnel System and 1973 as F-O-R-T-U-N-E Franchise Corporation.
Equity Capital Needed: $15,000-$40,000
Financial Assistance Available: The $15,000-$40,000 is cost of Franchise, part of which F-O-R-T-U-N-E may elect to finance. Additional funds are required to meet pre-opening expenses and working capital, which in aggregate should be $15,000-$20,000. This amount may vary by the size of office and number of personnel employed.
Training Provided: Intensive, 20 day training program is required. Fifteen days of which are conducted for the owner at F-O-R-T-U-N-E home office on business fundamentals and management controls, 5 days are spent on location by F-O-R-T-U-N-E executives training franchise owner and staff. Additional training is also available at the home office or on field visits.

Managerial Assistance Available: F-O-R-T-U-N-E provides ongoing management assistance in the areas of franchise controls, exchange programs for applicants and companies and daily operational support. Communication is maintained by regular telephone contact, workshop and periodic on-site visits. Innovative techniques to improve quality and profitability of the F-O-R-T-U-N-E offices are continual. Special attention is paid and as much time as required given to the support of each newly opened office until they are well-established.

GEROTOGA INDUSTRIES, INC.
219 Park Avenue
Scotch Plains, New Jersey 07076
Joseph A. Gerber, Franchise Director

Description of Operation: A permanent professional, technical and clerical employment service under the names "Gerotoga" and "Plusmates.".
Number of Franchisees: 12 in New Jersey and Pennsylvania.
In Business Since: 1960
Equity Capital Needed: $16,000 (includes franchise fee and office setup), plus approximately $10,000 operating capital for first 3 months.
Financial Assistance Available: None
Training Provided: Prior to opening of business, company will provide 3 weeks training at corporate headquarters, training and assistance is also provided the licensee and his personnel at the licensee's office. Operations and training manuals and training aids provided.
Managerial Assistance Available: Company provides printing and operating forms sufficient to do business for 90 days, continuous follow-up and support and field trips to licensee's office. Company will asssit and/or advise in complete set-up of office, advertising, accounts, hiring and training of initial personnel. Meetings and seminars are conducted to improve expertise and efficiency.

GILBERT LANE PERSONNEL SERVICE
750 Main Street
Hartford, Connecticut 06103
Howard Specter, President

Description of Operation: Gilbert Lane Personnel Service offers a broad based employment agency franchise which specializes in middle-management and professional level job placements, as well as office management placement.
Number of Franchisees: 11 in 6 States
In Business Since: 1957
Equity Capital Needed: Franchise vary in cost of $7,000 to $10,000 depending upon the particular market area.
Financial Assistance Available: Total investment would include franchise fee and approximately $2,500 for pre-opening expenses to include-rent deposit, utility deposit, advertising, legal fees, etc. Additionally, $10,000 - $15,000 recommended for use as operating capital. Company will give consideration to making financial arrangements.
Training Provided: The owner/manager is required to attend an intensive 2 week pre-opening training session at the company's home office. Additional training is conducted at franchisee's office for both himself and his staff at the time of opening. The operation is then closely monitored, including staff visits, until effectively operating.
Managerial Assistance Available: Gilbert Lane provides continuous guidance and assistance in all areas of agency management. Interchange job openings and applicants through-out the Gilbert Lane network. Annual franchise manager's meetings, issuance of training tapes and operating manuals are part of ongoing program.

HARPER ASSOCIATES, INC.
Division of SANFORD ROSE ASSOCIATES
265 South Main Street
Akron, Ohio 44308
George L. Mild, Director of Franchise Sales

Description of Operation: Harper Associates, a division of Sanford Rose Associates, specializes in personnel placement and recruiting of professionals for the Health Care and Food Service fields. Recruiting ranges from physicians to a variety of types of paramedical specialities. Included are technicians, therapists, dieticians, and various in-office assistants. Management personnel positions filled include those concerned with financial, data processing and administrative services. Key employees for the pharmaceutical, medical equipment, and other related industries are encompossed in Harper's recruiting activities. Ownership and staffing for a Harper Office is equally suited to men and women.
Number of Franchisees: 70 in 20 States and Canada (SRA/Harper)
In Business Since: 1959
Equity Capital Needed: $35,000 minimum
Financial Assistance Available: $35,000 includes the portion of the license payment due prior to opening, as well as usual start-up costs. Financing is available for the balance of the license fee. Normal operating capital is also included, the amount varying according to the site and type of office selected.
Training Provided: Current program is 3 weeks of intensive 8 hour days. This includes classroom as well as "hands-on" work. Extensive training manuals and tapes are furnished to each licensee... Regular 5 day personnel consultant training courses are also furnished on a no charge basis to the licensee's employees.
Managerial Assistance Available: Sanford Rose Associates, as the parent company to Harper Associates, provides a complete time tested system for personnel recruiting and placement. All forms, routines and procedures are included. National and State laws are taught as a part of training. Complete computerized financial statements are rendered monthly, to each office. Field operations personnel visit offices on a routine and request basis. Sales contests, seminars, and other counselor incentives are regularly used.

HARTMAN TEMPORARY PERSONNEL
3550 Biscayne Boulevard
Suite 401
Miami, Florida 33137
Helen L. Porter, Vice President - Marketing

Description of Operation: Hartman Services offers a proven method for the successful operation of a temporary personnel service. The Hartman license offers complete

31

training, constant supervision, total payrolling and billing services, industry insurance, advertising and marketing support, a national network of offices and, of course, a nationally recognized name and reputation.
Number of Franchisees: 3 in Florida and Texas
In Business Since: 1966
Equity Capital Needed: Minimum $25,000 for license fee, plus $10,000-$15,000 in equity capital.
Financial Assistance Available: Payroll
Training Provided: The initial training is done at the Miami headquarters and requires at least 10 working days. This is followed-up by no less than 2 weeks of additional training and assistance in franchisee's own office. During the training, the franchisee is counseled and instructed on every step from office set-up to getting clients and hiring temps. They will be taught how to go after a market in which 9 out of 10 businesses are potential clients.
Managerial Assistance Available: All forms and manuals necessary to start a successful Hartman Temporary Personnel Franchise are supplied and periodically updated by Hartman Services, Inc. A Hartman franchisee has consistent back-up support. Communication between the Hartman home office and a Hartman Temporary Personnel Franchise offers complete interfacing at all times. Through our regional licensing coordinator, a franchisee will be in constant contact with our entire staff to assure success. Our complete program of interoffice Management Information provides the most up-to-date data on all aspects of our business 365 days a year. Regularly scheduled visits by members of our staff are augmented with regional and national seminars.

HAZEL & JARVIS
P. O. Box 403
Pluckemin, New Jersey 07093
Barbara Swan, President

Description of Operation: Domestic employment agencies.
Number of Franchisees: 4 (including company-owned) in New Jersey
In Business Since: 1972
Equity Capital Needed: $10,000 to $15,000
Financial Assistance Available: None
Training Provided: 2 weeks of training provided.
Managerial Assistance Available: Ongoing managerial and technical assistance.

HERITAGE PERSONNEL SYSTEMS, INC.
2920 Highwoods Boulevard
P. O. Box 95025
Raleigh, North Carolina 27625
Robert A. Hounsell, Director of Franchising

Description of Operation: Full service, "across the board" personnel employment agencies, serving all job-seekers from minimum wage to top executives in all job categories, on both a "company-paid fee" and "applicant-paid fee" basis, with marketing emphasis throughout the Southeast. Heritage's applicant interchange provides a continuous service to those franchisees desiring exposure of their specialized positions throughout the system.
Number of Franchisees: 6 in North Carolina and Tennessee.
In Business Since: 1974; began franchising in 1977
Equity Capital Needed: $7,500-$30,000 initial franchise fee, plus approximately $3,000 start-up costs.
Financial Assistance Available: Possibility of company-financing of up to 50 percent of franchise fee, and advice and consultation in obtaining other sources of financial assistance.
Training Provided: 2 weeks at company headquarters; 1 week in franchisee's office; continuous consultancy and assistance thereafter.
Managerial Assistance Available: Continuous assistance to franchisee in advertising, marketing, hiring and training of staff, accounting, legal, office expansion and new job market development. Close cooperation in the system's "management by objectives" procedures is maintained by phone, mail and personal visits.

KOGEN PERSONNEL INC.
202 Whitemarsh Plaza
Conshohocken, Pennsylvania 19428
S. David Davis, President

Description of Operation: Franchise provides full service through placement of one or more of the following levels: placement of permanent and temporary clerical and staff support applicants; placement of entry level sales, administrative and technical applicants; placement of middle-management, engineering and professional applicants; and searches for executive and key personnel for $40,000 to $200,000 positions.
Number of Franchisees: 25 in 12 States
In Business Since: 1966
Equity Capital Needed: $20,000 minimum, depending upon location and personal objectives.
Financial Assistance Available: Franchise charge may be financed in part.
Training Provided: Franchisee receives extensive pre-opening instruction in basic business mangement, followed by detailed and hands-on instruction and training in all levels of the business. Instruction and training is provided over a period of several months for maximum effectiveness. Training courses are continuously available throughout the year.
Managerial Assistance Available: Assistance in any area of agency operation and at every level is readily available. New ideas and procedures are discussed and distributed monthly through two house organs (one for management; one for consultants). Resumes and job orders are distributed throughout the system through its unique intra-system alert.

MANAGEMENT RECRUITERS INTERNATIONAL, INC.
1015 Euclid Avenue
Cleveland, Ohio 44115
Alan R. Schonberg, President

Description of Operation: Search and recruiting service business under the names of "Management Recruiters," "Sales Consultants," "OfficeMates/5," and "CompuSearch."
Number of Franchisees: 314 Offices in 42 States, the District of Columbia and Canada.

In Business Since: 1957
Equity Capital Needed: Minimum $20,000 - Maximum $50,000, depending on location.
Financial Assistance Available: None
Training Provided: The franchisor's staff will provide the licensee with an intensive initial training program of approximately 3 weeks conducted at the franchisor's corporate headquarters in Cleveland, Ohio plus an initial on-the-job training program of approximately 3 additional weeks is conducted in the licensee's first office.
In addition to the above, the franchisor's staff will assist and advice the licensee in (a) securing suitable office space and the negotiation of the lease for same, (b) the design and layout of the office, (c) the selection of office furniture and equipment and the negotiation of the purchase or lease agreement for same, and (d) the establishment of a suitable telephone system for the licensee's office.
Managerial Assistance Available: The licensee is provided with a detailed operations manual containing information, procedures and know how for operating the business and the franchisor will furnish the licensee with continuing advice, guidance and assistance through national and regional meetings, seminars, correspondence, telephone and personal instruction with respect to the licensee's personnel placement service operations and procedures and their improvement and revision.

MANAGEMENT SEARCH, INC.
233 Peachtree Street, N.E.
1550 Harris Tower
Atlanta, Georgia 30303
Eric J. Lindberg, President

Description of Operation: Personnel Agency - Professional and clerical placement
Number of Franchisees: 5 in North Carolina, Texas and Georgia
In Business Since: 1968
Equity Capital Needed: $10,000 to $40,000
Financial Assistance Available: Up to 25 percent can be financed.
Training Provided: 3 weeks home office. One week on-site opening. Continuous field visitations, written reports and telephone consultation.
Managerial Assistance Available: We provide training films, tapes and manuals. Field trips by home office personnel, continuous telephone consultation and written reports.

MANPOWER, INC.
5301 North Ironwood Road
P. O. Box 2053
Milwaukee, Wisconsin 53201
William J. Gallagher, Senior Vice President, Franchise Relations

Description of Operation: Offers a complete line of temporary help services which include office, industrial, technical, marketing, data processing and medical-dental. Office and industrial services account for approximately 80 percent of total sales in the U.S.
Number of Franchisees: 250 worldwide
In Business Since: 1948
Equity Capital Needed: $50,000 minimum
Financial Assistance Available: Financial advice and counsel is available upon request. The prospective franchisee is responsible for an investment to cover initial costs and operating capital.
Training Provided: A comprehensive 1 week training program is offered. In addition, there are periodic meetings and seminars designed to maintain proficiency in operations.
Managerial Assistance Available: Manpower provides continuing advice, counsel and assistance. Operating manuals, forms and procedures are provided. Management personnel conduct periodic visits, and meetings and seminars are conducted to improve expertise and efficiency.

MARSETTA LANE TEMP-SERVICES
MARSETTA LANE SYSTEMS, INC.
1104 Park Building - 355 Fifth Avenue
Pittsburgh, Pennsylvania 15222
Richard L. Schweiger, CEC, President

Description of Operation: Marsetta Lane Systems offers a unique Temporary Help Service operation. Each Temp Service Center is equipped with a Small Business Computer for Payroll and Invoicing. A Complete Marketing System and a System for the Recruitment of Temporary Workers. The unique Software for the Computer is provided and constantly updated by Marsetta Lane.
Number of Franchisees: 4 in Pennsylvania and Florida
In Business Since: 1977 (franchising since 1979).
Equity Capital Needed: $25,000-$30,000
Financial Assistance Available: A total investment of $55,000 is necessary to open a Marsetta Lane Temp Service Center. $25,000 of this amount may be financed against Accounts Receivable using traditional Bank financing as the Business warrants. Marsetta Lane will assist in preparation of Loan applications and Bank presentations.
Training Provided: Initial site selection in Franchises Territory includes office location, phone service, Bank, Accounting and Legal arrangements. Franchisee then must attend a 9 day Home Office Training Course. Within 3 months of opening Franchisor will send a Field Service Representative to the Franchisees office for 3 days of on-site post opening Training.
Managerial Assistance Available: Marsetta Lane provides continual assistance to the franchisee for the life of the Franchise. Complete Manuals covering all phases of the Operation, initial supply of Stationery and Forms are provided by Marsetta Lane. Field Service Reps are assigned to each Franchisee and are responsible for on-site and Phone Consultation as necessary. Marsetta Lane sponsors National and Regional Franchisee Meetings to update Training in such areas as Sales/Marketing, Accounting/Bookkeeping, Advertising/Public Relations and General Operations. Marsetta Lane pays annual dues for each Franchisees membership in the National Association of Temporary Services.

NORRELL TEMPORARY SERVICES, INC.
3092 Piedmont Road, N.E.
Atlanta, Georgia 30305
Lawrence (Bud) Stumbaugh, Vice President and General Manager

Description of Operation: A national corporation with company-owned and franchised offices in 25 states, providing temporary help services to large and small companies. Emphasis is on providing skilled office, clerical and data processing personnel whose skills have been tested and references thoroughly checked.
Number of Franchisees: 40 in 24 States
In Business Since: 1963
Equity Capital Needed: $25,000 to $40,000 Operating Capital but no franchise fee.
Financial Assistance Available: Payroll financing and accounts receivable financing.
Training Provided: Initially, both field training and a 2 week classroom course are provided. Continuing seminars in the franchisees' area are provided semi-annually. Cassette tapes, manuals and other written programs are available for each individual franchise office.
Managerial Assistance Available: A full-time Director of Training serves franchise offices only. Additionally, Regional Managers and District Managers serve only 10 franchised offices each, i.e., making sales calls with the franchisee, teaching proper pricing, assisting in recruiting, etc. Also, Norrell supplies computer payrolling, customer billing, operations manauals, forms, brochures, national advertising and direct mail promotion.

THE OLSTEN CORPORATION
1 Merrick Avenue
Westbury, L.I., New York 11590
Joel B. Miller, Vice President

Description of Operation: A national, public company operating both branch and franchise offices. Provides temporary office and industrial personnel for as long as needed by businesses, government, industry and institutions. Olsten Health Care provides nurses, home health aids, homemakers and companions to hospitals, nursing homes as well as private patients who require temporary care. Franchises and licenses are available in temporary services and health care.
Number of Franchisees: 112 in 23 States and Canada
In Business Since: 1950
Equity Capital Needed: $15,000 minimum, plus working capital.
Financial Assistance Available: Will finance accounts receivable.
Training Provided: Comprehensive 1 week classroom training and additional 1 week field training as well as periodic visits to assist franchisee in every phase of business operations.
Managerial Assistance Available: Franchisor supplies full operating manuals to all franchisees. In addition, provides continuous, on-going assistance in all facets of the business including technical assistance, legal, insurance, marketing, sales, advertising and other areas of temporary help. Franchisor will also furnish sales leads in franchisees area whenever possible.

PARKER PAGE ASSOCIATES, INC.
910 Tower Building
1809 - 7th Avenue
Seattle, Washington 98101
Glenn D. Lindley

Description of Operation: Executive recruiting in the specialized fields of chemicals, plastic, paint, ink, adhesives, pulp and paper, food, computers and insurance. Office work together with an interchange system.
Number of Franchisees: 4 in New Jersey, Oregon, Georgia and Texas.
In Business Since: 1972
Equity Capital Needed: $12,000 working capital with reserve to support owner for three months.
Financial Assistance Available: Require 20 percent down on franchise cost ($12,500) with remainder paid in 36 installments commencing one year after start. Will aid in establishing credit at local bank to obtain loans on receivables.
Training Provided: Complete on-the-job training for 1 week. Daily consultation with toll free call to home office. Will aid in staffing and training all staff members.
Managerial Assistance Available: Continued program to develop new specialty categories and training of each office as developed.

PERSONNEL POOL OF AMERICA, INC.
303 S.E. 17th Street
Fort Lauderdale, Florida 33316
A. C. Sorensen, President

Description of Operation: Supplemental personnel service with the following divisions: Medical Personnel Pool furnishing medical and nursing services in private homes and health care institutions; Personnel Pool furnishing a complete range of supplemental personnel from highly skilled clerical individuals to unskilled and semi-skilled industrial workers. Franchises include one or both of the services depending upon market size and availability.
Number of Franchisees: Medical Personnel Pool - 155, Personnel Pool -100
In Business Since: 1946
Equity Capital Needed: $50,000 to $70,000
Financial Assistance Available: Growth capital financing for franchisees whose growth is greater than anticipated—normally loans of 12 months or less duration with monthly amortization at current interest rates.
Training Provided: 2 weeks' training at company's home office, including on-the-job training, plus 2 weeks' on-the-job training at franchisee's office after opening.
Managerial Assistance Available: Advice, assistance and preparation of advertising, marketing, recruiting and screening procedures; national account data and assistance; comparative sales and operating statistics; help with financial and accounting procedures; review and analysis of operating problems and procedures.

PLACE MART FRANCHISING CORP.
20 Evergreen Place
East Orange, New Jersey 07018
M. B. Kushma, President

Description of Operation: Employment agency.
Number of Franchisees: 15 in New Jersey
In Business Since: 1962
Equity Capital Needed: $15,000-$20,000
Financial Assistance Available: Yes, to qualified applicants.
Training Provided: Intensive training at corporate office from 3 to 6 weeks, then follow-up training at franchisee's location.
Managerial Assistance Available: Continuous training and supervision from field personnel, seminars, training sessions, newsletters, new ideas and systems constantly introduced. Periodic franchise meeting discussing policies and administrative problems and exchange of ideas for mutual help.

REMEDY TEMPORARY SERVICES, INC.
P. O. Box 699
32112 Camino Capistrano
San Juan Capistrano, California 92675
Paul W. Mikos, Vice President

Description of Operation: Provides a complete line of temporary help services to all types of businesses.
Number of Franchisees: 18 in California (including company-owned).
In Business Since: 1968
Equity Capital Needed: $10,000 to $20,000 depending upon market size.
Financial Assistance Available: Temp will finance the franchisee's payroll with its related taxes and insurance and accounts receivable.
Training Provided: Comprehensive training program which will be adjusted to the needs of the franchisee, and which includes a 5 day office training course, followed by on-the-job training and periodic seminars.
Managerial Assistance Available: On-going assistance and advice is provided. Operating manuals, forms, computerized payroll and billing, and marketing development.

RETAIL RECRUITERS INTERNATIONAL, INC.
188 Benefit Street
Providence, Rhode Island 02903
Jacques J. Lapointe

Description of Operation: Personnel Placement Service Business under the names of "Retail Recruiters," "Office Careers," "Spectrum." Specializing in middle to upper level management placement, and executive search primarily in the retail, hospitality, and data processing field.
Number of Franchisees: 14 in 13 States and Washington, D.C.
In Business Since: 1969
Equity Capital Needed: $20,000-$50,000 which includes working capital.
Financial Assistance Available: Up to 30 percent of franchise fee.
Training Provided: Complete training in all aspects of operation. Intensive 4 weeks training of new franchisee and new employes of initial franchise. Training at home office and at new franchisees first office. Continuous and follow-up training as needed. Assist in securing suitable office space, help negotiate lease, design layout of office, selection of proper office furniture and equipment, and proper telephone system.
Managerial Assistance Available: Company provides detail training manual and tapes that contain detailed information and know-how for operating personnel business. We will provide continuing advice, guidance and assistance through meetings, continuous basis to insure proper operation of business.

RITTA PERSONNEL SYSTEM OF NORTH AMERICA
One Weybosset Hill
Providence, Rhode Island 02903

Description of Operation: Complete personnel serivces including all professional and executive placement, clerical/secretarial placement and temporary office personnel placement.
Number of Franchisees: 23 in 9 States
In Business Since: 1956
Equity Capital Needed: $15,000 to $50,000 (depending on market area).
Financial Assistance Available: Company will aid in the securing of financing.
Training Provided: Complete training in selling, administrative and managerial aspects of the business. Initial training conducted at corporate headquarters in Providence (several weeks) followed by on-the-job training at the selected office site during the initial opening of the office. Then, training by selected staff personnel at the office of the franchisee on an as-needed basis, plus seminars and training sessions at the corporate office on an on-going scheduled basis.
Managerial Assistance Available: Franchisor will support and assist franchisee in all phases of the operation including visitations from the top executives in the parent organization, seminars at corporate headquarters, newsletters, research studies, training manuals for managers and employees, programs in financial, legal, advertising, sales and management, and continued access by phone and personal visits as required.

ROMAC AND ASSOCIATES, INC.
125 High Street
Boston, Massachusetts 02110
William I. Kelly

Description of Operation: Romac and Associates is a network of offices committed to providing quality placement services to clients, in need of professional level talent in the accounting, EDP, financial, and banking areas. It is staffed by business executives who, by background, are thoroughly familiar with the fields they serve. The cornerstone of its reputation for success has been confidentiality and interaction of the offices within the network as an organization.
Number of Franchisees: 14 in 11 States
In Business Since: 1966
Equity Capital Needed: $25,000 to $35,000

33

Financial Assistance Available: Financial stability is an indication of success in the business career of an individual. The need for assistance should be minimal. Romac will assist a franchisee in the preparation and presentation of a financial plan to finance institutions. In addition, as much as two-thirds of the initial financial fee, amy be deferred allowing it to be paid out of the first year cash flow.
Training Provided: Initially all franchisees participate in an intensive 1 week training program in Boston during which time all phases of the business operation will be covered. A follow-up session, 2-3 days, during the second month of operation is also required. At this time, highlights of the pre-opening program are reviewed and the operations to-date analyzed.
Managerial Assistance Available: Assistance is a constant process with on-going programs as well as management service. In programs, the inter-office job and candidate referral system is fostered and maintained, group plans for insurance and employee benefits, sample contracts, fee schedules are updated and maintained. The services provided include monthly foster better relations between offices and people.

ROTH YOUNG PERSONNEL SERVICE, INC.
43 West 42nd Street
37th Tower Floor
New York, New York 10036
Ralph Young, Chairman of the Board

Description of Operation: Employment agency and executive search service.
Number of Franchisees: 30 in 21 States
In Business Since: 1964
Equity Capital Needed: Approximately $70,000
Financial Assistance Available: Negotiable
Training Provided: Initial training of 2 weeks at home office, 1 week at licensees office. Further training as determined by licensor.
Managerial Assistance Available: Office visits, seminars, conventions, bulletins, manuals, etc., all at licensor's discretion.

SALES CONSULTANTS INTERNATIONAL
A Division of MANAGEMENT RECRUITERS INTERNATIONAL, INC.
1015 Euclid Avenue
Cleveland, Ohio 44115
Alan R. Schonberg, President

Description of Operation: An opportunity to join an organization involved solely in searching and recruiting of sales managers, salesmen, saleswomen, sales engineers, and marketing people.
Number of Franchisees: 85 in 32 States and the District of Columbia
In Business Since: 1957
Equity Capital Needed: $20,000 to $40,000, depending on location.
Financial Assistance Available: None
Training Provided: The franchisor's staff will provide the licensee with an intensive initial training program of approximately 3 weeks conducted at the franchisor's corporate headquarters in Cleveland, Ohio plus an initial on-the-job training program of approximately 3 additional weeks which is conducted in the licensee's first office. In addition to the above, the franchisor's staff will assist and advise the licensee in (a) securing suitable office space and the negotiation of the lease for same, (b) the design and layout of the office, (c) the selection of office furniture and equipment and the negotiation of the purchase or lease agreement for same, and (d) the establishment of a suitable telephone system for the licensee's office.
Managerial Assistance Available: The licensee is provided with a detailed operations manual containing information, procedures and know how for operating the business and the franchisor will furnish the licensee with continuing advice, guidance and assistance through national and regional meetings, seminars, correspondence, telephone and personal instruction with respect to the licensee's personnel placement service operations and procedures and their improvement and revision.

SANFORD ROSE ASSOCIATES, INC.
265 South Main Street
Akron, Ohio 44308
George L. Mild, Vice President

Description of Operation: "Professionals for Professionals." Activities center on a recruitment and placement of college graduates for Industry and Business with emphasis on companies having high technology products or processes. SRA Offices, while autonomous, share the resources of the parent company's Opportunity Center Division, the largest operators of career centers, world wide. All offices participate in Weekly Job Order and Resume Exchange. All offices receive hundreds of professional openings weekly from headquarters national marketing program. Ownership of an SRA Office is limited to college graudates with significant business or industrial experience.
Number of Franchisees: 70 in 20 States and Canada
In Business Since: 1959
Equity Capital Needed: $35,000 minimum
Equity Capital Needed: $35,000 includes the portion of the license payment due prior to opening, as well as usual start-up costs. Financing is available for the balance of the license fee. Normal operating capital is also included, the amount varying according to the size and type of office selected.
Training Provided: Current program is 3 weeks of intensive 8 hour days. This includes classroom as well as "hands-on" work. Extensive training manuals and tapes are furnished to each licensee. Regular 5 day personnel consultant training courses are also furnished on a no charge basis to the licensee's employees.
Managerial Assistance Available: Sanford Rose Associates provides a complete time tested system for Personnel Recruitment and Placement. All forms, routines and procedures are included. National and State laws are taught as a part of training. Complete computerized financial statements are rendered monthly, to each office. Field operations personnel visit offices on a routine and request basis. Sales contests, seminars, and other counselor incentives are regularly used by Sanford Rose Associates.

SARCO INC.
619 Rosedale Towers
1700 West Highway 36
Roseville, Minnesota 55113
Ralph E. Tarvin, President

Description of Operation: Employment placement and recruiting.
Number of Franchisees: 4 in Minnesota
In Business Since: 1977
Equity Capital Needed: $2,000
Financial Assistance Available: None
Training Provided: 48 hours of classroom training.
Managerial Assistance Available: Continuous over the period of the franchise for 5 years, including computer for interchange of data.

S-H-S INTERNATIONAL
Western Saving Bank Building
Broad & Chestnut, Suite 701
Philadelphia, Pennsylvania 19107

Description of Operation: S-H-S International franchises professional/executive recruiting firms on a national scale, assisting professionals and client companies in the Accounting, EDP, Sale, Marketing, Technical and Engineering, disciplines with their recruiting needs in the salaried areas of $16,000 to $60,000 plus market.
Number of Franchisees: 19 in 6 States
In Business Since: 1956
Equity Capital Needed: $35,000 plus
Financial Assistance Available: Presently not available.
Training Provided: A comprehensive 2 week program is held in Philadelphia that is mandatory. First week is Account Executive training, the second week is devoted to management. An additional week is spent training all staff upon opening. Further training and visitations is provided during the first 6 months of operation and thereafter on regularly scheduled basis. A full set of training tapes, tests and aids are also available. There are regional seminars conducted for all Account Executives.
Managerial Assistance Available: S-H-S provides continual assistance in the form of visitations, seminars, national conventions, the management newsletter "Focus," the Account Executive newsletter "The People Placers," updated Manager, Account Executive and Receptionists' manuals, research, national surveys, financial, legal and advertising assistance in addition to sales and advertising incentive programs.

SNELLING AND SNELLING, INC.
Executive Offices
Snelling Plaza
4000 South Tamiami Trail
Sarasota, Florida 33581
William G. Allin, Group Vice President

Description of Operation: Employment service offering full range of employment activity, specializing in all types of positions - secretarial, typing, bookkeeping, administrative, sales, and technical positions from draftsmen to research chemists. Average operation has three to five employees. Offices can be opened in cities normally 30,000 population or higher depending upon makeup of area.
Number of Franchisees: 670 in 46 States and South America
In Business Since: 1951
Equity Capital Needed: $20,000 to $60,000 plus, depending on location selected.
Financial Assistance Available: None
Training Provided: 2 weeks at home office in Sarasota, Florida. Additional training in the field for franchisee and employees. Franchise employees may be sent at any time free of charge to training classes given in Sarasota and throughout the country. Training includes the use of copyrighted training manuals - one for the manager, two for employment counselors and one for the receptionist. Company is constantly available for counseling and 16 Regional Directors travel throughout the U.S. meeting and helping offices to operate.
Managerial Assistance Available: Continued headquarters guidance through communication systems and periodic field training visits and national and field seminars.

STAFF BUILDERS INTERNATIONAL, INC.
122 East 42nd Street
New York, New York 10017
Walter E. Ritter, Vice President

Description of Operation: Temporary personnel services. Provides temporary help for office, medical, industrial, technical, data processing, and marketing operations.
Number of Franchisees: 16 in 12 States and the District of Columbia.
In Business Since: 1961
Equity Capital Needed: $25,000.
Financial Assistance Available: Staff Builders may finance temporary payroll for franchisee up to 80 percent of his weekly sales.
Training Provided: 2 weeks at headquarters in New York City for initial training. Manuals, procedures and systems are all provided as part of course.
Managerial Assistance Available: Continuous communication with franchisee via telephone, mail (bulletins, supplies, materials, etc.) and visits. Promotional aids, sales programs, recruiting assistance and financial advice are all part of on going programs.

TEMPORARIES, INCORPORATED
1015 - 18th Street, N.W.
Washington, D.C. 20036
Barry B. Wright, President

Description of Operation: Temporaries, Inc., supplies temporary office and medical help to business firms, governments, and medical Institutions. The franchise program started in November 1973 and will continue in medium to large size markets. Currently have 28 offices in 18 markets.
Number of Franchisees: 4 in 4 States
In Business Since: 1969
Equity Capital Needed: $75,000 to $100,000 which includes an initial licensing fee of $20,000 to $25,000, depending on the market. The remaining capital is needed for operating and receivables expense.
Financial Assistance Available: Yes

Training Provided: A home office training school offers initial management training for 2 weeks. Then intensive on-site, on-the-job training by franchisor sales and counselor trainers are continued for 2 weeks. Initial training is 4 weeks and then consistent field training by franchisor to assure profitability quickly.

Managerial Assistance Available: Continuous management service for the life of the franchise in all phases of an operation, i.e., sales, management, training of employees, accounting, advertising, recruiting, etc. Home office staff works closely via telephone and mail with all franchisees and makes periodic visits to assist in these areas.

TEMPORARILY YOURS OF AMERICA
681 Market Street
Suite 309
San Francisco, California 94105
Frank Baker, Director, Franchise Marketing

Description of Operation: Temporarily Yours of America specializes in the placement of temporary help, primarily office staff. Permanent staff is placed under the trademark "Tristed Personnel Consultants," which is part of the same franchise. The company has offices across Canada and opened its first franchise in California in 1979.

Number of Franchisees: 8 with 13 offices in California and Canada.
In Business Since: 1967
Equity Capital Needed: $9,500 minimum
Financial Assistance Available: A minimum of $15,000 is required to open a Temporarily Yours Franchise. The company finances the temporary payroll on an on-going basis. Working capital is available if franchisee has good credit references.
Training Provided: Initial 2 week training program given at head office. Additional 2 weeks of training at franchised location after opening.
Managerial Assistance Available: Operations, sales and management manuals provided to franchise. On-going management, sales, operations and accounting assistance provided for life of franchise. Field managers work closely with franchisees and visit offices regularly.

UNIFORCE TEMPORARY PERSONNEL, INC.
1335 Jericho Turnpike
New Hyde Park, New York 11040
John Fanning, President

Description of Operation: A national temporary personnel service which offers a complete line of services, including office, medical home health care, light industrial and professional. Services are provided to industry, business and government agencies. In addition to supplying basic temporary personnel services, Uniforce specializes in project temporaries, providing large groups of temporaries for long-term special assignment.

Number of Franchisees: 34 in 19 States
In Business Since: 1962
Equity Capital Needed: $25,000 to $35,000 which includes an initial licensing fee of $12,000. The remaining capital is needed for general operating expenses.

Financial Assistance Available: Payroll financing and financing of accounts receivable. Fifty percent of the licensing fee may be financed through promissory notes at current interest rates.

Training Provided: No prior experience is required. Owner and staff will spend 1 week of training at the company's home office training center. Utilizing the latest audio-visual training techniques, including video tape, Uniforce will provide training in all phases of temporary help operations, including specialized training for owner-managers, counselor instruction and sales representative training. On-the-job follow-up training is conducted by a home office branch service representative assigned to the franchisee's office to provide continuing training and guidance through a program of phone calls and periodic visits. In addition, Uniforce conducts a series of regional conferences and seminars for owners and their staffs, as well as an annual training seminar and conference.

Managerial Assistance Available: Assistance in initial selection of site and lay-out of office, negotiation of lease, selection of furniture and equipment and telephone systems. A continuous supply of all forms and materials necessary for the operation of the Uniforce business. Manuals, guides, monthly up-dates, unlimited phone consultation and periodic management visits. In addition, Uniforce business. Manuals, guides, monthly up-dates, unlimited phone consultation and periodic management visits. In addition, Uniforce prepares and finances the temporary help payroll, billing and accounts receivable and provides detailed computer analysis to each office on all phases of the temporary help operation. Monthly newsletters and management guidance tapes are provided in addition to the support provided by the home office staff. Video player and full training tapes provided at no charge.

VIP PERSONNEL SYSTEMS
485 Fifth Avenue
New York, New York 10017
Joseph Schupler, President

Description of Operation: VIP is a highly ethical, full service executive and professional level employment service catering to the $18,000 - $60,000 dollar salary range individuals. Areas specialized in are Marketing, EDP, Finance, Law, Engineering, Scientific, Cosmetics, Technical. All services are in the permanent placement areas of personnel operations.

Number of Franchisees: 5 in New York and New Jersey
In Business Since: 1969
Equity Capital Needed: Franchise fee ranges from $9,800 to $15,000. Start up and 90 day expenses are $8,500 additional and up.
Financial Assistance Available: VIP will accept a portion of the franchise fee upon signing and carry the balance of the debt on a prime interest plus balance of debt basis.
Training Provided: Minimum 3-4 weeks initial in-house training. Field training is continual. All training is done by divisional managers and full service staff located in New York home office. All training of future counselors and managers are trained in New York headquarters.
Managerial Assistance Available: Extensive initial training provided as owner/manager and as operating counselor. Length of training is ongoing and continuous and extends to office operations, finance, marketing of services, advertising, administrative etc.

EQUIPMENT/RENTALS

APPARELMASTER, INC.
10385 Spartan Drive
P. O. Box 15128
Cincinnati, Ohio 45215
James R. Wahl, President

Description of Operation: Offers unique business service recommended as a diversification possibility for drycleaning, laundry and/or linen supply establishments. Includes detailed instruction and on-site training of how to utilize existing equipment and personnel to sell, service and process industrial uniform, dust control, and career apparel rental. Other services and benefits inlcude optional data processing invoicing, accounting and inventory control, supplier discounts, seminars, workshops and training schools.

Number of Franchisees: 263 in 48 States, District of Columbia, Canada, United Kingdom, and New Zealand.
In Business Since: 1971
Equity Capital Needed: License of $14,600 or $10,900 if paid in lump sum.
Financial Assistance Available: None
Training Provided: Ongoing
Managerial Assistance Available: Operation and other manuals provided. Managerial and technical assistance provided on every aspect of the industry for life of franchise.

NATION-WIDE GENERAL RENTAL CENTERS, INC.
1408-B Miamisburg-Centerville Road
Dayton, Ohio 45459
I.N. Goodvin, President

Description of Operation: A Nation-Wide General Rental Center operates a full line consumer-oriented rental center including items for the contractor, do it yourself home owner - items as Baby Equipment; Camping Supplies, Contractor's Equipment and Tools; Concrete Tools; Carpenter Tools; Invalid Needs; Lawn and Yard Tools; Mechanics Tools; Painters Equipment; Moving Needs; Party and Banquet Needs; Plumbers Tools; Sanding Machines; Trailer Hitches; Household Equipment and Local Trucks and Trailers. Building required is 1,800 to 3,000 square feet with outside fenced storage area, good traffic flow and parking for 6 to 10 cars.

Number of Franchisees: 39 in 14 States
In Business Since: 1976
Equity Capital Needed: $14,000 plus $5,000 - $7,500 working capital. No Franchise Fees or Royalty.

Financial Assistance Available: With the down payment of $14,000, franchisee will get $58,000 worth of equipment and opening supplies. The balance can be financed over 5 years with local banks - company assistance to qualified applicants. No franchise or royalty fees, down payment goes toward equipment cost. All Risk liability, conversion, group health, accident and life insurance coverage available to franchisee. We also have a buy back agreement and exclusive area agreement.

Training Provided: On-the-job training for 5 full days at no charge to the franchisee. Training covers everything you need from familiarization and maintenance of equipment; accounting computerized system; advertising and promotion; purchasing add on equipment; rental rates; insurance; inventory control and operation manual covering much more.

Managerial Assistance Available: Consultation on location and market feasibility studies; assistance in securing and negotiation building lease; a monthly computerized financial report giving balance sheet - income statement and a list of all equipment in inventory with a month rental income per item. A rate guide book giving rental rates for each item and for your area. One hundred percent financing for growth inventory or new equipment. Franchisee can buy all their equipment at 10 percent over cost which offers great purchasing power and discounts to each store owner. Buy back agreement gives you full credit on equipment. At the grand opening we will be there to help establish the franchise in the community. We also mail 9,000 promotions to every home around a new center at grand opening time.

SHOWERTEL SYSTEMS CORPORATION, INC.
504 Fairmount Avenue
Jamestown, New York 14701

Description of Operation: Roadside placement of luxury shower and selfcleaning bathrooms for inexpensive motorist and traveler hourly rental use. Placements anywhere, and in motels, laundromats, carwashes, service stations, truckstops and campgrounds. Licensed manufacturing and sale of modules, molded units. Single Serve Sinkbowls with bracket and holders; $4.50 each by mailorder; $3.50 in quantity; $2.50 in lots of 5-10,000.

Number of Franchisees: 5 in Wisconsin, Texas, Michigan and New York
In Business Since: 1968
Equity Capital Needed: Service charce or $400 (up to 8 units) for on-site consultation by representative. For installation in your building(s), or otherwise; sufficient investment for installing a minimum of 2 bathrooms. All financing and contracting you and your local contractor. For area distributor; $1,500-$3,500. For manufacturing licenses (modules and molded parts and units); related manufacturing capacity and financial ability to lease-place same.

Financial Assistance Available: Lease plans available for prebuilt modules, FOB Elkhart, Indiana.
Training Provided: Two days on-site consultation regarding all construction details, and methods of operation.
Managerial Assistance Available: Installation operator is in complete control. Local distributor expertise available. Assistance of ShowerTel marketing personnel furnished as required.

TAYLOR RENTAL CORPORATION
P. O. Box 2618
570 Cottage Street
Springfield, Massachusetts 01101

Description of Operation: A franchised Taylor Rental Center operates a general purpose rental business carrying a complete selection of rental items including commercial and industrial equipment as well as houseware items. Building required is minimum 3,200 square feet with parking for 8-10 cars. Outside fenced in area is also required for equipment storage.
Number of Franchisees: 620 in 48 States
In Business Since: 1945
Equity Capital Needed: $30,000 to $35,000 (including down payment).
Financial Assistance Available: Down payments to franchisor ranges from $20,000 to $25,000 depending on recommended opening equipment and supplies shipment of $80,000 to $100,000. The balance can be financed through an installment load (5 year - 60 payments). Financing for growth inventory is normally offered with no down payment requirement. Franchisee has option to arrange own outside financing. There is a one time start-up fee of $6,000. Down payments are applied directly to equipment and supply purchases.
Training Provided: Comprehensive training at a company-owned training and operating center for 10 days at no charge to franchisee. Advanced on-the-job training for a minimum of one week in another established center.
Managerial Assistance Available: Assistance is offered in locating proper site. Taylor provides regional and main office dealer service representatives to assist both new and established dealers in all phases of operations. Various qualified staff people are available in each of the nine districts or at the main office to assist dealers in any activity requiring immediate action. A computerized monthly status report to franchisees provides current income and inventory data on every piece of rental equipment on a percentage return against original cost basis. A computerized management analyses accounting system is available to all franchisees. Taylor provides all franchisees with a descriptive product book including a suggested rental rate guide which is updated continuously to reflect current equipment and rate changes. Budgets, cash flow and projection assistance are provided to increase current and long range profitability. Complete operational, health and life insurance are included in the program.

TYPING TIGERS
P. O. Box 613
Bellaire, Texas 77401
Floyd MacKenzie

Description of Operation: Computer services to the business community. Rental of office equipment.
Number of Franchisees: 3 in Texas.
In Business Since: 1969
Equity Capital Needed: None-no franchisee fee; no minimum inventory required.
Financial Assistance Available: On approved credit, 30 day open account.
Training Provided: Continuous training in sales and location if retail outlet is desired.
Managerial Assistance Available: Continuous assistance in all phases of operations.

UNITED RENT-ALL, INC.
10131 National Boulevard
Los Angeles, California 90034

Description of Operation: General Equipment Rental Stores. The full line of equipment offered includes automotive, hand and power tools, contractors equipment, floor care, party, household and guest, medical, exercise, painting and plumbing, lawn and garden, sporting and camping, moving and towing. The "Total Rental Department Store" concept of rental equipment service finds its customers among homeowners as well as commercial accounts in the contracting, party and in-home patient care categories. Stores have an attractive image and are located in growing metropolitan communities throughout the country. Franchisor surveys market, selects site and prepares store for opening.
Number of Franchisees: Approximately 125 in 30 States.
In Business Since: 1948
Equity Capital Needed: Approximately $35,000 to $40,000 plus working capital.
Financial Assistance Available: A portion of the franchise fee can normally be financed. Financing available for rental equipment purchased through the franchisor. Store location may be sub-leased from franchisor for the term of the franchise. All risk replacement cost property insurance and comprehensive general liability and products liability insurance through a unique cooperative program are available as well as group health, accident and life insurance coverage.
Training Provided: A six week training program, both classroom style and practical on-the-job implementation at the store location is provided. Included is discussion of rental concepts, equipment familiarization and maintenance, counter systems, cash and accounting methods, inventory control and management, advertising, promotion, customer relations, store security, employee management, telephone techniques, insurance, purchasing, cooperative and commission renting. Subsequent training is also given by Regional Directors on an on-going basis.
Managerial Assistance Available: Company provides regularly scheduled in-store business development consultations. Development topics include budgets and forecasts, inventory management, equipment and merchandise sales, prospective customer business calls, marketing, employee training procedures, and overall business building techniques. Home office support services include equipment purchasing, insurance, advertising and operations.

━━━ FOOD-DONUTS ━━━

BITE SIZE MEALS, INC.
103 College Road East
Princeton, New Jersey 08540
Philip B. Seaton, President

Description of Operation: Wee Donuts is a food concept which offers miniature, crisp, bite-size donuts produced by an automated machine, on the spot for immediate consumption. Wee Donuts are intended to be eaten as a snack food within a short period of time after purchase.
Number of Franchisees: 6 in Pennsylvania, New Jersey, New York, California, Puerto Rico, and Florida.
In Business Since: 1977
Equity Capital Needed: Approximately $30,000
Financial Assistance Available: None
Training Provided: On-site training provided, updates when necessary.
Managerial Assistance Available: Unlimited

COUNTRY STYLE DONUTS INCORPORATED
2200 Erie County Savings Bank Building
Buffalo, New York 14202

Description of Operation: Franchised and company-owned coffee and donut shops featuring our "special" blend of coffee and over 56 varieties of donuts. Outside of Canada, Country Style sells master franchising rights to qualified groups or individuals. Master franchises are sold for specific geographic areas. (City, county, State, etc.)
Number of Franchisees: 68 stores in Canada and 4 stores in the U.S.A. Five of these stores are company operated. Also, the master franchise rights have recently been sold for Puerto Rico.
In Business Since: 1962
Equity Capital Needed: This is proportionate to the size and potential of the exclusive area granted to the Master Franchise.
Financial Assistance Available: None
Training Provided: A 4 week training program is provided at our training centre in Toronto, Ontario, Canada. The course includes intensive training in the art of making donuts, store operations, employee management, accounting and financial management, etc.
Managerial Assistance Available: Initial site selection is done with consultation, and requires our approval. Construction plans and specifications, operations manuals, training manuals, are all supplied to assist the franchisee. A quarterly newsletter plus information bulletins, keep our franchisee up to date on current developments. Our head office is continually testing and developing new formulae and products before introducing them at store level. Promotional material is available to all franchisees through our head office and advertising agency.

DONUTLAND, INC.
P. O. Box 409
Marion, Iowa 52302
Michael R. Nicholis, President
Dennis A. Wyatt, Vice President, Franchise Sales

Description of Operation: Retail coffee and donuts with dine in or drive up service.
Number of Franchisees: 40 in Illinois, Iowa, and Wisconsin.
In Business Since: 1965
Equity Capital Needed: $35,000
Financial Assistance Available: We will assist franchisee in obtaining a $35,000 equipment loan.
Training Provided: Franchisee is trained in the making of our product and in the operation of the shop.
Managerial Assistance Available: Continual training and supervision. Constant inspection of physical plant for the life of franchise.

DUNKIN' DONUTS OF AMERICA, INC.
P. O. Box 317
Randolph, Massachusetts 02368
Robert Rosenberg, President
Thomas Schwarz, Executive Vice President

Description of Operation: Franchised and company-owned coffee and donut shops with drive-in and walk-in units. Sale of over 52 varieties of donuts, munchkin donut hole treats and muffins at retail along with soup, coffee and other beverages. Franchises are sold for individual shops and, in selected markets, multiple license agreements may be available. Franchisor encourages development of real estate and building by the franchisee, subject to approval of Dunkin' Donuts of America, Inc. Franchisor also develops locations for franchising and for company operations.
Number of Franchisees: 1,007 (99 company) in 42 States and Puerto Rico.
In Business Since: 1950
Equity Capital Needed: Franchise fee, $16,000 to $32,000 depending on geographical area and whether franchisee owns or controls the real estate. Lower fee structure where franchisee owns or leases real estate directly. Working capital, approximately $17,000.
Financial Assistance Available: Financing assistance for real estate acquisition and development. Equipment and sign financing assistance is available to qualified franchisees.
Training Provided: 5 week training course for franchisees at Dunkin' Donuts University in Braintree, Massachusetts consisting of production and shop management training. Initial training of donutmen and managers for franchisees and retraining is carried out at Dunkin' Donuts University without additional charge.

Managerial Assistance Available: Continuous managerial assistance is available from the District Sales Manager assigned to the individual shop. The company maintains quality assurance, research and development and new products programs. The franchisee-funded marketing department provides marketing programs for all shops. The marketing programs are administered by an Area Marketing Manager who develops plans on a market basis.

MISTER DONUT OF AMERICA, INC.
Subsidiary of INTERNATIONAL MULTIFOODS CORPORATION
1200 Multifoods Building
Minneapolis, Minnesota 55402
Richard A. Niglio, President

Description of Operation: Franchised doughnut and coffee shops-drive-ins and walk-in units. Retail selling of more than 55 varieties of doughnuts and nonalcoholic beverages, primarily coffee. Located on well traveled streets, near schools, churches, shopping centers, amusements and entertainment. Each shop produces its own doughnuts in its own kitchen.
Number of Franchisees: 774 in 37 States, Puerto Rico, Canada, Japan, and Thailand.
In Business Since: 1955
Equity Capital Needed: Equipment package $35,000; franchise fee $10,000, working capital $5,000. Costs of real estate and building is responsibility of franchisee, but location is subject to Mister Donut's approval.
Financial Assistance Available: Equipment can be financed by company with 25 percent down payment. Financing over 60 months at current interest rates.
Training Provided: Continuous professional 4 weeks training program, consisting of practical as well as classroom training at company school in St. Paul, Minnesota.
Managerial Assistance Available: An area representative is permanently located at company expense in each area of the United States and Canada for managerial assistance to franchise operators. The company maintains a quality control service as well as a research and development department, marketing and advertising services, to assist franchise owners. Location analysis, lease negotiations and assistance with building design and construction is also provided by MISTER DONUT personnel.

SOUTHERN MAID DONUT FLOUR COMPANY, INC.
3615 Cavalier Drive
Garland, Texas 75042
Doris Franklin, Vice President

Description of Operation: Southern Maid offers a tailored to order operation for each prospect. We have available all technical, managerial, and business information. Southern Maid sells most major brands of donut equipment. We consider our flour blends of the finest quality for the price. We can service any investor from $22,000 to $50,000. Franchises are available nationwide.
Number of Franchisees: 70 in Texas, Kansas, Louisiana, Mississippi, Arkansas and Nevada.
In Business Since: 1937
Equity Capital Needed: A small operation can cost as little as $22,000. A large volume wholesale and retail operation can cost up to $50,000. A 40 percent down payment is required before equipment is ordered. Franchise fee is $5,000 with no royalties involved.
Financial Assistance Available: Bank financing.
Training Provided: In shop technical training for period necessary (time varies with each operation).
Managerial Assistance Available: Continuous advisory information is available. New recipes are added on a monthly basis.

SPUDNUTS, INC.
450 West 1700 South
Salt Lake City, Utah 84115
Frank D. Knowles, Vice President

Description of Operation: Spudnuts, Inc., offers franchisees a unique and established product for a retail donut shop. The store is approximately 1,600 square feet and includes drive-thru service whenever possible. The exterior image of the building has a brand new look that blends in any area. The interior includes both counter and table service.
Under the direction of a new aggressive ownership, Spudnuts, Inc., now projects to open 45 new Spudnuts shops over the next 18 months.
Number of Franchisees: 76 in 23 States
In Business Since: 1937
Equity Capital Needed: $15,000 Franchise Fee - $15,000 minimum start-up costs.
Financial Assistance Available: Franchisees to arrange their own financing.
Training Provided: 3 weeks of in-depth training is provided plus additional training in the new franchised shop at the time of opening and Grand Opening. This additional training is to give the franchisee confidence in working with the new equipment in his shop and to become familiar with the procedures learned while in training before the shop was completed. Training includes: making Spudnuts unique products; hiring of personnel; record keeping; promotional and advertising concepts; production control; quality control; marketing ideas and concepts.
Along with the in-depth training, Spudnuts, Inc., provides a Grand Opening package for each new franchisee.
Managerial Assistance Available: Spudnuts, Inc., assistance continues for the length of the franchise agreement. Spudnuts, Inc., know-how manual will be reviewed on a continual basis. Field support will visit shops and assist franchisee with complete operation of shops and introduce new products developed from the research and development department.

TASTEE DONUTS, INC.
P. O. Box 2708
Rocky Mount, North Carolina 27801
J. Robert Simpson, Business Development Director

Description of Operation: Tastee Donuts, Inc., offers investment and career opportunities to both multiple unit and single unit licensees. Our primary area of emphasis is the Southeastern United States, but licensing nationwide is available for licenses capable of developing entire market areas. Our concept is to provide a large variety of fresh, high quality donuts with excellent coffee and other beverages to take-out, sit-down, and drive-thru customers in both free-standing and shopping center locations.
Number of Franchisees: 41 in 5 States; 3 company-owned shops.
In Business Since: 1965
Equity Capital Needed: $35,000 cash; including $18,000 license fee. $40,000 financed. $75,000 total not including real estate.
Financial Assistance Available: Tastee Donuts, Inc., assist licensee candidates in arranging financing from major credit institutions on both an SBA and conventional loan basis. Real estate assistance is available for qualitative approval of site selection, but licensees are responsible for lease negotiations.
Training Provided: Intensive 4 week training course covering all aspects of production and shop management. The course is taught at the Tastee Donuts training school in Rocky Mount, North Carolina.
Managerial Assistance Available: Continuous managerial assistance is available from regional supervisors. Advertising and marketing assistance is provided through licensee supported programs.

FOOD-GROCERY/SPECIALTY STORES

AUGIE'S INC.
1900 West County Road C
St. Paul, Minnesota 55113
Ray Augustine, President

Description of Operation: Industrial catering. Special equipped trucks to serve hot foods to workers on-the-job.
Number of Franchisees: 60 in Minnesota
In Business Since: 1958
Equity Capital Needed: $1,000, some instances less.
Financial Assistance Available: Weekly payment on amount due.
Training Provided: Approximately 1 week training in driving and sales.
Managerial Assistance Available: Same as above.

THE BIG CHEESE, INC.
P. O. Box 33456
Phoenix, Arizona 85067
Arthur L. Thruston, Director of Marketing

Description of Operation: We develop complete turn-key cheese and wine stores as a Management Consultant Company, which allows a prospective buyer most advantages of a franchise without on-going costs of royalties, overrides, percentages, etc.
Number of Franchisees: 23 in Arizona, California, Texas and Montana
In Business Since: 1968
Equity Capital Needed: Approximately $30,000
Financial Assistance Available: It takes approximately $60,000 to $65,000 to open a Big Cheese operation. $30,000 or approximately one half cash required as a down payment and the balance financed through equipment lease purchase.
Training Provided: We have a minimum period of full-time training for 2 weeks in an owners store - however the average training time is 4 to 6 weeks with intensive, one on one training both prior to during and after the store opens with continued assistance available on an indefinite basis.
Managerial Assistance Available: We have a complete Management Consultant Program that includes financing, site location, leasehold improvements, equipment installation, and complete training in ones own store. The training covers product knowledge, handling, buying, advertising, marketing, ordering, merchandising, pricing, accounting systems, etc., and is available to a buyer on an indefinite basis.

CHEESE SHOP INTERNATIONAL, INC.
25 Amogerone Crossway
Greenwich, Connecticut 06830
Fred D. Walker, Jr., Franchise Administrator

Description of Operation: Retail sale of the fine cheese, gourmet foods, related gift items and wines where permissible. Typically located in a Shopping Center or on Main street of better suburban communities.
Number of Franchisees: 95 in 25 States
In Business Since: 1965
Equity Capital Needed: Variable $50,000-$75,000
Equity Capital Needed: None
Financial Assistance Available: 4 weeks; 5 days per week actually working in an existing Cheese Shop under the direction of a company expert.
Managerial Assistance Available: In addition to the training we provide an expert to help during the Grand Opening week. On a continuous basis we accept collect phone calls to plan and advise on all purchases necessary to run the business. This service includes discussing the following as applies to various suppliers; availability of product, freshness, specials, quality, next arrivals, trucking routes, air freight, costs, etc. It also includes recommending where to place a given order for a certain product at that particular time. This service is optional and typically done on a weekly basis. We also organize promotions, designed to increase sales. Continuous supervision and advice in all phases of retail operations is provided.

CHIPPER COOKIE SHOPS, INC.
3757C East Thomas Road
Phoenix, Arizona 85018
Ted Capen, President

Description of Operation: Chipper Cookie Shops offers a unique concept in franchising operations. Individual stores where cookies are scratch-baked on premises range in size from 350 to 600 square feet. They are typically located in malls or other high foot traffic areas. These shops offer fresh baked cookies in several different types, made from natural ingredients and contain no preservatives. Chipper Cookie Shops are a high margin, impulse purchase type of store. One of the primary assets is the permeating aroma of fresh baking cookies.

37

Number of Franchisees: 4 in Arizona
In Business Since: 1977
Equity Capital Needed: $20,000 to $40,000
Financial Assistance Available: None, however, the franchisor may direct franchisee to sources of funding for the equipment package.
Financial Assistance Available: 1 week of complete on-the-job training at franchisor's parent store in Phoenix, Arizona. Training consists of accounting, advertising, baking, business management, purchasing, inventory control, and public relations. Also provided is one week training by corporate personnel at franchisee's location.
Managerial Assistance Available: Location evaluation, lease evaluation, custom layouts for each store, full training, grand opening and continuing promotional assistance. Reduced cost on several equipment items and discounts on paper items from major suppliers. Continuing promotion, home office inspections, financial and administration consultation, and protected operating territory. Complete operations manual provided as part of the franchise fee.

THE CIRCLE K CORPORATION
Contract Operations
P. O. Box 20203
Phoenix, Arizona 85036

Description of Operation: Circle K has devised a unique system for the operation of convenience-type food stores, which system is identified by a trademark consisting of the letter "K" enclosed in a circle. Through the expenditure of time, effort and money, Circle K has established public acceptance, goodwill, and demand for such food stores operated under said system. Each store has approximately 2,600 square feet with ample store-front parking and is open as a minimum from 7:00 a.m. to 11:00 p.m. Circle K maintains an extensive inventory of Circle K products as well as other products and brands that are readily recognizable to the consuming public and for which the consuming public has a substantial demand. Circle K will *lease* to the Contract Operator (Franchisee) the real estate, building, and improvements, together with fixtures and equipment. The Contract Operator (Franchisee) is only buying the merchandise inventory. The term of the agreement shall be for an initial two year period with subsequent one year renewals.
Number of Franchisees: 212 in 6 States
In Business Since: 1957
Equity Capital Needed: $6,000 ($1,600 security deposit, $4,400 inventory deposit).
Financial Assistance Available: Circle K provides the complete merchandise inventory (approximately $20,000 at cost). The inventory less the down payment is financed by Circle K at an interest rate not to exceed 10 percent per annum, (see promissory note). The loan may be paid in full at any time.
Training Provided: 8 weeks of on-the-job training in all phases of the Circle K system conducted in a Circle K store that is owned and operated by Circle K. Circle K shall pay the operator (Franchisee) $200 per week while in training.
Managerial Assistance Available: Circle K provides continual management service for the life of the Contract Operation (Franchise) in all areas of operation, such as accounting, advertising, merchandising, inventory control. All forms and directions are provided. Zone, Division, and Area Managers are available in all areas to work closely with the operators and regularly visit stores to assist solving problems.

CONVENIENT FOOD MART, INC.
International Licensor
John Hancock Center
875 North Michigan Avenue, Suite 1401
Chicago, Illinois 60611
Anthony J. Conti, Chairman and President

Description of Operation: Grocery stores are 2,000 to 3,000 square feet in size with ample parking. Stores are open 365 days a year from 7 am 'til midnight. Stores stock complete lines of top name national brand merchandise normally stocked in a chain supermarket (except fresh red meat requiring cutting at store level). In the greater metropolitan Chicago area stores are franchised directly by parent company named, Convenient Food Mart, Inc., Regional Franchise Office #8, 418 North York Road, Elmhurst, Illinois 60126, Jack Roach, Sales Manager. In other areas CFM franchises regional territories to a franchisor under a licensing agreement who, as an independent contractor, in turn, franchises stores to individuals. The regional franchisor selects locations, negotiates with investors to build the stores, and takes a long term lease, subleasing same to CFM owner-operators. There are 53 licensed franchisors (some with multiple franchises) operating in parts of or all of 40 states and Canada. For information about open areas and licensing opportunities (investment $25,000-$55,000) write to national office listed above. Addresses of licensed area franchisors for any state may be obtained from national office.
Number of Franchisees: 900 throughout the USA
In Business Since: 1958
Equity Capital Needed: $22,000-$35,000
Financial Assistance Available: Financing of five to seven years up to $50,000 for fixtures, equipment and signs, interest at available rates. Chicago area, short term financing is available up to $15,000 for grocery inventory to qualified parties. Address inquiries to Jack Roach, Elmhurst, Illinois above.
Training Provided: Pre-store opening training of 288 hours given to owner-operator in classroom and an operating store. Continuous training throughout life of business provided by up-to-date manuals, bulletins, and on-the-spot counseling usually once a week by qualified, competent personnel to include, but not limited to, merchandising, advertising, promotion, inventory control and store management. Equity capital and financing assistance as listed applies to regional franchise office #8 only. Similar information for other areas must be obtained from licensees.
Managerial Assistance Available: Continuous in-field counseling, quality control, and annual area educational meetings and seminars.

COOKIE FACTORY OF AMERICA
600 Woodfield Drive
Schaumburg, Illinois 60195
Joel Rifken, President

Description of Operation: Retail selling of cookies and other specialty baked foods. Locations are in Regional Shopping Centers.
Number of Franchisees: 61 in 21 States
In Business Since: 1974
Equity Capital Needed: Total package approximately $80,000.
Financial Assistance Available: Assist franchisee in obtaining financing.
Training Provided: Training classes at home office. Program includes, planning, hiring, purchasing, merchandising, advertising, and business management. Easily implemented cash and inventory controls are also taught. Additional training at franchisee's store at time of opening.
Managerial Assistance Available: Continuous communication by bulletins correspondence, direct phone, in-store visits by qualified home office personnel, and ongoing training sessions are conducted.

EDGEMAR FARMS
346 Rose Avenue
Venice, California 90291
Charles F. Moore, Manager

Description of Operation: Retail home delivery routes.
Number of Franchisees: 17 in California
In Business Since: 1880
Equity Capital Needed: $1,000
Financial Assistance Available: Credit of accounts.
Training Provided: Accompanied by experienced person until trainee is able to handle the route.
Managerial Assistance Available: Records and materials.

EUROBAKE CIE, INC.
233 East Lancaster Avenue
Ardmore, Pennsylvania 19003
Jack Perlman, President

Description of Operation: Eurobake operates authentic French bakeries under the name "Elysee Boulangerie par Excellence" in major regional malls and urban high-traffic areas. Units produce from scratch a superb line of French breads, croissants and Continental pastries. Some stores have "cafe" seating, and serve beverages and snacks. Average store size is 1,100 square feet. Stores operate 2 shifts, employing about 8 persons, only one of whom is an experienced baker.
Number of Franchisees: 9 in 6 States
In Business Since: 1978
Equity Capital Needed: Determined by franchisee's net worth. Total costs of unit vary between $150,000 and $200,000.
Financial Assistance Available: Franchisor does not provide any financing.
Training Provided: Franchisor provides full training to bakers for as long as necessary prior to store opening, as well as to replacement bakers. Manager and sales crew are trained on premises prior to store opening.
Managerial Assistance Available: Franchisor provides 2 weeks of help during opening, as well as a continuous total support system during the term of the franchise, including on-going research and development, operations manuals, marketing and production advice, advertising guidance and continuous visitation and consultation.

THE GLASS OVEN BAKING COMPANY INC.
114 Old Country Road
Mineola, New York 11501
Sheldon J. Sanders, Vice President

Description of Operation: Retail bakery where all baked goods are baked directly in front of the customers. Each store is approximately 1,000 square feet and located in major enclosed malls or shopping centers. A complete line of baked goods is offered for sale.
Number of Franchisees: 11 in New York, North Carolina and Georgia
In Business Since: 1977
Equity Capital Needed: $30,000 minimum
Financial Assistance Available: A franchise fee is $15,000-cost of equipment is $40,000-cost of construction $25,000 to $45,000 depending on site location. Financing may be available through lending institutions and leasing companies.
Training Provided: Training is 2 weeks at company school consisting of on-job training plus classroom instruction. We can teach you how to bake and operate the franchise in two weeks.
Managerial Assistance Available: The Glass Oven provides continual management operations, technical merchandising advertising services for the period of the franchise. Manuals, forms and directions are provided. District Supervisor work closely with franchisees and visits stores regularly. On-going advertising is provided.

FOR GOODNESS SAKE FRANCHISE SYSTEMS, INC.
1608 East Algonquin Road
Schaumburg, Illinois 60195
Sunny Pagni

Description of Operation: For Goodness Sake Natural Foods is a health food store with a special emphasis on vitamins & food supplements. Stores are approximately 1,200 square feet. Inventories are selected name brand as well as extensive variety of private label items. Discount prices are our most outstanding feature.
Number of Franchisees: 3 in Illinois
In Business Since: 1976
Equity Capital Needed: $35,000
Financial Assistance Available: Franchisor will assist franchisee in arranging for financing of $20,000 of the equipment package, which financing is generally for a period of 5 to 7 years at prevailing interest rates.
Managerial Assistance Available: Prior to the opening of the franchise, the franchisor will instruct the franchisee as to the total management of the business. This will be accomplished during the 2 week training program. During the first week of operation, one of the franchisors representatives will be on hand to assist in establishing and standardizing procedures and techniques, as well as in training personnel.
Managerial Assistance Available: For Goodness Sake Natural Foods provides continual management service for the life of the franchise is such areas as bookkeeping, advertising, inventory control. Complete manuals of operations, forms, and directions are provided. Franchisors representatives work closely with franchisees and visit stores regularly to assist solving problems. For Goodness Sake Natural Foods sponsors meetings of franchisees and conducts marketing and product research to maintain high For Goodness Sake Natural Foods consumer acceptance.

GROVE FOODS, INC.
14100 East Jewell Avenue #8
Denver, Colorado 80014
Richard McCarty, Director of Franchising

Description of Operation: The Grove Kiosk operation offers a unique retail method for natural snack-food products. Each store is a self-contained booth merchandising 24 different natural snacks such as cashews, pineapple rings, carob malt balls or yogurt raisins.

Number of Franchisees: 20 in 12 States

In Business Since: 1978

Equity Capital Needed: $15,000 for first unit, $7,500 for additional units upon credit acceptance by Grove Foods, Inc.

Financial Assistance Available: A total investment of $20,000 is necessary for purchase of a The Grove franchise. The first unit requires a cash down payment of $15,000 with $5,000 financed by the company for two years. Additional units may be purchased for $7,500 cash and the balance financed for 5 years. The franchise fee pays a "turn-key" location including inventory, equipment, and kiosk.

Training Provided: Intensive 2 week training in Denver included in franchising fee. Travel, lodging and meals paid by franchisee.

Managerial Assistance Available: Complete procedures manual, accounting, purchasing forms and directions provided. Field Managers work closely and visit stores on an announced as well as unannounced bases. Grove Foods continually upgrade marketing and direct sales procedures as well as adding new products to its inventory.

HICKORY FARMS OF OHIO, INC.
300 Holland Road
Maumee, Ohio 43537
James Edwards, Vice President, Franchise Services

Description of Operation: Retail stores selling packages and bulk specialty food featuring the Hickory Farms BEEF STICK Summer Sausage, a variety of imported and domestic cheeses, candies and other related food products under the Hickory Farms label. Locations are usually situated in regional shopping center. The service and operation is under direct supervision of home office on a continuing basis.

Number of Franchisees: 530 in 47 States and Canada

In Business Since: 1951

Equity Capital Needed: Approximately $85,000 pluse leasehold improvements.

Financial Assistance Available: None, however, Associate Lease Agreement may be available in some situations. Capital requirements vary by location.

Training Provided: 2 weeks at home office in planning, purchasing, stocking and merchandising, advertising and business management. Two weeks prior to opening, a training counselor and store organizer take charge of the new store operation.

Managerial Assistance Available: Continuous communication by bulletins, correspondence, direct phone, in store visits by qualified home office personnel, Annual National Convention and interim regional meetings and training sessions are conducted.

HUNGRY BOY DELICATESSEN, INC.
6 Watson Place
Utica, New York 13502
Raymond Seakan, President

Description of Operation: Three sizes restaurant Deli Combination with a super large menu of a large variety.

Number of Franchisees: 3 in New York and Ohio

In Business Since: 1976

Equity Capital Needed: Style A - $25,000 Style B - $50,000 Style C - $90,000

Financial Assistance Available: Fifty percent financing with good credit references.

Training Provided: 1 month at our main unit, along with training, cooking, portion control and advertising, menu planning, managerial assistance available. We train the owners on all phases of the franchise and their appointed personnel. We offer monthly meetings to further train and teach them how to hire, plan, buy and arrange for catering and all types of promotions. We offer books, procedures on methods of training for cashiers, cooks, bus boys, preparation cooks, bookkeeper, etc.

Managerial Assistance Available: Continuous home office assistance.

ISCO, LTD.
INTERNATIONAL SERVICES COMPANY, LTD.
4760 Interstate Drive
Cincinnati, Ohio 45246
Carlton C. Perin, President

Description of Operation: Retail cheese, wine and gourmet shops featuring specialty foods and related products; and fast service deli-style sandwiches. Usually located in regional shopping centers, selected strip centers, and high density commercial retail plazas.

Number of Franchisees: 24 franchises in 14 States

In Business Since: 1975

Equity Capital Needed: $20,000 to $50,000 depending upon total cost of project and strength of your financial statement.

Financial Assistance Available: None, assistance can be provided in helping to obtain financing by presentations, relationships with SBA. Capital requirements vary by locations, depending upon size of proposed store and degree of leasehold improvements required.

Training Provided: 1 week of home study. 2 weeks of training in a Cheese Villa shop and planning initial inventory, stocking, merchandising, advertising and promotional programs. 1 week prior to opening a supervisor handles receipt of inventory, stocking of store, and grand opening preparations. Supervisory personnel on hand during first week of opening.

Managerial Assistance Available: Location evaluation, lease evaluation, custom architectural drawings for each store, full training, grand opening allowance, and continuing promotion assistance. Reduced cost on many resale items from major suppliers, inspection, financial and administration consultation and protected operating territory. Continuous communication by bulletin, newsletter, correspondence, telephone and visitation.

JITNEY-JUNGLE, INC.
440 North Mill Street
P. O. Box 3409
Jackson, Mississippi 39207
Howard V. Blair, President

Description of Operation: Convenience Food Store Franchisee Operation. Stores operated on a multi-store basis by franchisees under the registered name of Jitney Jr. or Jr. Food Marts and supermarkets under the name of Jitney-Jungle. Most stores are three dimensional; groceries, fast foods and self-service gasoline. Major concentration and future development geared to rural communities.

Number of Franchisees: 350 units in 13 States

In Business Since: 1919

Equity Capital Needed: $35,000 to secure inventory and to secure equipment financing, plus one time territory fee of $15,000. Requires investor with minimum $250,000 net worth.

Financial Assistance Available: None; company finds locations, secures leases, constructs building. Company can assist in preparing financial presentations for use with various lenders.

Training Provided: Operations consultants and food service personnel provide pre-opening assistance, in-store training, pre-opening merchandising, equipment set-up, store operations, vendor and distribution contracts and grand opening assistance. New franchisees attend 60 hour "working" session in a training unit prior to opening first unit, plus 24 hours of management information systems training.

Managerial Assistance Available: On-going contact and periodic visitations are made by operations consultants. Assistance is also provided on a continuing basis by food service, training and recruitment, real estate and accounting departments.

LI'L SHOPPER, INC.
811 East State Street
Sharon, Pennsylvania 16146
M. Roy Sexton, President

Description of Operation: Convenience grocery stores.

Number of Franchisees: 33 in Ohio and Pennsylvania

In Business Since: 1970

Equity Capital Needed: $22,000 to purchase inventory.

Financial Assistance Available: Company financing available to qualified parties with minimum $6,000 cash down payment. Balance can be paid out of operation over an extended period.

Training Provided: Store operations manual and intensive in-store training initially, with continuing counseling by field representatives.

Managerial Assistance Available: Continuous assistance in all phases of accounting, operations and merchandising is provided.

LITVA CORP.
2244 Crespi Lane
Westlake Village, California 91631
Littleton Strong, President

Description of Operation: Franchisor of Convenient Food Mart Stores in 5 counties. Stores are 3,000 square feet and are open from 7 a.m. to midnight, seven days a week and stock complete line of name brands.

Number of Franchisees: 8 in Southern California

In Business Since: 1971

Equity Capital Needed: $45,000

Financial Assistance Available: Owners must provide initial capital investment of $45,000 and LITVA can assist qualified individuals to obtain financing of equipment and inventory.

Training Provided: 6 week, in store training initially with periodic training in specific areas as needed.

Managerial Assistance Available: Stores are provided with management training, bookkeeping services, cash control, merchandising and inventory control, continuous training in all phases of Convenient Food Mart Store operation is provided.

MR. DUNDERBAK, INC.
P. O. Box 2708
Rocky Mount, North Carolina 27801
J. Robert Simpson, Director Business Development

Description of Operation: Mr. Dunderbak's Old World Deli & Cafe offers a combination of specialty merchandising elements that include a fast food sandwich and specialty restaurant, superior quality delicatessen, and unequaled cheese shop, a unique gourmet food shop, a noteworthy beer and wine shop, and an uncommon gift shop. The shop blends parts of all these elements into an old world atmosphere of fun, service, and quality.

Number of Franchisees: 30 in 15 States

In Business Since: 1962

Equity Capital Needed: Approximately $70,000 cash, plus $200,000 net worth.

Financial Assistance Available: Advice and counsel on local bank financing, with or without SBA Guarantee.

Training Provided: 5 week formal training in company school, 52 weeks of continued training after shop is opened. Two weeks on-site opening assistance by corporate operations staff.

Managerial Assistance Available: Operating manuals with continuous update and bulletins, visits by home office personnel to assist in general operations and specific problems.

NEW MORNING NATURAL FOODS
P. O. Box 4098
Waterbury, Connecticut 06714
Greg Nolan, Franchise Director

Description of Operation: Franchisor provides, complete turnkey store including furniture, fixtures, stock and equipment, site location, advertising for franchisee.

Number of Franchisees: 5 in Connecticut

In Business Since: 1975

Equity Capital Needed: $40,000

Financial Assistance Available: None
Training Provided: 3 week program conducted at existing stores and distribution center, and 1 week at franchisee's store.
Managerial Assistance Available: Complete training and managerial assistance for five years.

O.P.F.M. CORP.
3055 East 63rd Street
Cleveland, Ohio 44127

Description of Operation: O.P.F.M. Corp., is a national franchisor of "regional territories" for Open Pantry Food Marts. The regional franchisor licenses individual store owners within the territorial boundaries established by the regional licensing agreement. Open Pantry stores are highly stocked miniature supermarkets open from early morning to midnight every day of the year. The stores are limited to company specifications (2,000-2,500 square feet with parking) and are designed to facilitate fast, convenient purchase of daily grocery needs. Handle brand products, delicatessen sandwiches. Some with broasted chicken and self-service gasoline. Income is derived from a fee based on a percentage of total sales. Real Estate locations are selected by company real estate representatives.
Number of Franchisees: Over 200 in 15 States.
In Business Since: 1962
Equity Capital Needed: $15,000-individual store franchise, regional franchise depends on size of regional territory.
Financial Assistance Available: Regional franchisor arranges for financing of equipment fixtures and initial inventory. This financing is pre-arranged through the assistance of O.P.F.M. Corp.
Training Provided: Regional franchisors are provided complete headquarter training, plus continuous assistance throughout life of contract by expert field representatives. Store franchisees receive 3 week in-store training, plus continued assistance from regional field experts.
Managerial Assistance Available: Continued management service is furnished throughout the life of the franchise. In case of store franchise the services rendered include, but are not limited to, bookkeeping, merchandising, advertising, supervision, inventory, correct product mix and fiscal control.

QUICK SHOP MINIT MARTS, INC.
P. O. Box 1748
Vancouver, Washington 98668
William J. Ellis, President

Description of Operation: Convenience grocery stores approximately 1,800 square feet, open every day from 7 a.m. to midnight. Stores sell name brand groceries, some with self-serve gasoline, sandwiches, deli, etc. Quick Stop Minit Mart provides lease and assist franchisee to obtain financing for equipment and inventory. Do not solicit for franchisees outside of area where present stores are located. No franchises available!
Number of Franchisees: 52 in Washington (southwest part of the State only) and in Oregon (Portland area only).
In Business Since: 1965
Equity Capital Needed: Minimum $20,000
Financial Assistance Available: Franchisor assists franchisee to obtain financing for $43,000 of store equipment and fixtures and approximately $20,000 needed for balance of inventory - financing is usually obtained from local banks and/or wholesalers. Interest rate of about 3 percent above prime rate with length of loan at 60 months.
Training Provided: Prospective franchisee is trained for 2 week period in either a company operated store or trained by a current franchisee in an operating store.
Managerial Assistance Available: Continuing training by a store supervisor. Maintains at least one visit per week even after franchisee is qualified to operate store. No franchisee is presumed to be so well trained that no further help is needed. All bookkeeping done at central office for the franchisee.

QUIK STOP MARKETS, INC.
P. O. Box 1745
Fremont, California 94538
Gus Xepoleas, President
Larry Kranich, Vice President
Ken Boucher, Vice President

Description of Operation: Quik Stop will provide a fully equipped and completely stocked retail convenience grocery markets. Each market is approximately 2,000 square feet with adequate off-street parking. Markets are required to be open a minimum of 20 hours daily, seven days per week. Some locations are also equipped to sell gasoline on a self-service system. All markets are located in California.
Number of Franchisees: 90
In Business Since: 1965
Equity Capital Needed: Minimum of $13,000 to $22,000, (depending upon type of facilities offered) covers franchise fee, security deposits, change fund and a minimum $5,000 toward the purchase of merchandise inventory.
Financial Assistance Available: Financial assistance for the remaining cost of merchandise inventory ($20,000 to $30,000) may be arranged and paid from the profits of the business.
Training Provided: A complete manual of instructions is provided as well as in-store training under experienced supervision.
Managerial Assistance Available: Quik Stop provides continuing management services including accounting, advertising, marketing and pricing information, and quarterly financial statements. Field representatives visit markets regularly to offer assistance.

SNEAKY SWEETS INTERNATIONAL, INC.
840 North Fairfax Avenue
Los Angeles, California 90046
Bill Colligan, President

Description of Operation: Sneaky Sweets Desserteries offers a truly unique retail store operation. Sneaky Sweets, the World's First Dessertery, offers over 100 dessert items. Half are low calorie and the others are chosen from the best hi-cal items available. Seven days a week - 12 hours a day operation. Exclusive use of "Slim-Serve" lo-cal ice milk formula

Number of Franchisees: 4 in California
In Business Since: 1976
Equity Capital Needed: $40,000 to $95,000 - turn-key
Financial Assistance Available: None at this time.
Training Provided: Extensive 2 week training in soft-serve machine operation and general bookkeeping and full retail manager training for 2 individuals. Eight hours per-day for 10 days.
Managerial Assistance Available: A complete advertising kit and promotional material for specials supplied by International. On-going business advice and product development and testing of new recipes and formulas, all supplied to the franchisee on a continuing basis.

THE SOUTHLAND CORPORATION
2828 North Haskell Avenue
Dallas, Texas 75204
Joe C. Thompson, Jr., Executive Vice President - Retail

Description of Operation: Convenience grocery stores.
Number of Franchisees: 2,169 in 21 States plus District of Columbia.
In Business Since: 1956 (franchised operations)
Equity Capital Needed: Approximate average $23,560
Financial Assistance Available: The total investment required is from $12,500 to $20,000 dependent on geographic location (franchise fee $7,500 to $10,000 and investment $5,000 to $10,000). These minimum figures may increase dependent on the average weekly sales of each location. Minimum $12,500 cash down and balance paid out of operation over a reasonable time period. Financing available through company.
Training Provided: 2 weeks in local training store, 1 week in training center.
Managerial Assistance Available: Continuing advisory assistance through field representatives and other 7-Eleven personnel.

STEWART SANDWICHES INTERNATIONAL, INC.
P. O. Box 12120
5732 Curlew Drive
Norfolk, Virginia 23502
W. S. Henderson, Director, Franchise Relations

Description of Operation: Stewart Sandwiches International, Inc., offers production and wholesale distribution of frozen sandwiches for heating in in-fra-red or microwave ovens for consumption. Each production center is designed to meet area requirements for manufacture of approved sandwiches. Stewart Sandwiches International, Inc., provides the oven on renewable leases to agree with the terms of the franchise.
Number of Franchisees: 53 in all 50 States, including company-owned operations.
In Business Since: 1954
Equity Capital Needed: $50,000-$100,000 minimum
Financial Assistance Available: The total investment required including land, building, production equipment and inventory could exceed $250,000. Ovens are provided by franchisor on a lease basis. Franchisee will need to arrange own outside financing.
Training Provided: Intensive training in production, quality control, operations and systems at home office and on-site is scheduled for key personnel and sales training is available on a continuing basis.
Managerial Assistance Available: Franchisor in conjunction with National Franchise Association develops point of purchase advertising, and provides market research for new products. Coordination of sales efforts with national chain organizations is sponsored by the franchisor as is equipment design and testing.

SUNNYDALE FRANCHISE SYSTEM, INC.
400 Stanley Avenue
Brooklyn, New York 11207
George W. Cambell

Description of Operation: Sunnydale Franchise System, Inc., offers an ultra modern completely equipped retail convenience food store. Each is approximately 1,000 to 2,500 square feet. Our stores are open 7 days a week from 8 am to 10 pm.
Number of Franchisees: 21 in New York
In Business Since: 1963
Financial Assistance Available: The total cost of a Sunnydale Franchise store is approximately $55,000. $28,000 cash is required and $45,000 balance is payable over a 10 year period in equal installments. The company does its own financing if the operator has a good credit rating. The $28,000 includes a $15,000 inventory, and miscellaneous deposits of approximately $3,000.
Training Provided: A complete 4 week training program covering all phases of the store operation.
Managerial Assistance Available: Sunnydale provides constant supervision in regard to advertising, buying, inventory control, bookkeeping, cleanliness, etc. Complete manuals of operations and forms are provided.

SWISS COLONY STORES, INC.
1 Alpine Lane
Monroe, Wisconsin 53566
David N. Edwards, Vice President, Franchising
Kenneth A. Rittmueller, Franchise Development Director

Description of Operation: Retail stores offering popularly priced, high quality domestic and imported cheeses, sausage, European style pastries, candy, specialty foods, gifts, and a food service/sandwich program.
Number of Franchisees: 218 stores in 41 States
In Business Since: 1964
Equity Capital Needed: Approximately $100,000 plus leasehold improvements.
Financial Assistance Available: Equipment leasing available up to approximately $45,000.
Training Provided: 7 day mandatory, thorough training at home office in Monroe, Wisconsin, plus 2 weeks in-store training covering all phases of store operation, management and retailing.
Managerial Assistance Available: Continuous supervision in store at intervals by highly qualified company personnel. Constant high volume monthly merchandise program offered.

TELECAKE INTERNATIONAL
2265 East 4800 South
Salt Lake City, Utah 84117
Clarence L. Jolley, President

Description of Operation: National cake by phone service. Franchisee is usually a retail bakery.
Number of Franchisees: Over 3,000 locations in all States and Canada.
In Business Since: 1971
Equity Capital Needed: $250
Financial Assistance Available: None
Training Provided: None
Managerial Assistance Available: Continual direction of the operation of the Telecake system is provided.

TIFFANY'S BAKERIES, INC.
155 University Avenue
12th Floor
Toronto, Ontario
M5H 3B7
Canada
Ray L. Chipman, President
Charles B. Borash, Executive Vice President

Description of Operation: Tiffany's Bakeries, Inc., is America's largest chain of franchise exhibition bakeries specializing in fresh baked pastries and breads. Operational procedures and policies are standardize , as are the store design.
Number of Franchisees: Over 200 franchised operations in 43 States.
In Business Since: 1971
Equity Capital Needed: Approximately $50,000 cash.
Financial Assistance Available: Tiffany's Bakeries, Inc., does not provide direct financing to franchisees at the present time. However, it does provide assistance in obtaining financing such as, assisting the franchisee in preparing his proposal for bank financing, and meeting with potential lenders.
Training Provided: Tiffany's Bakeries, Inc., provides 3 weeks of formal classroom and store management training at its training school in Chicago. In addition, a 2 day orientation program is held at the Head Office. All stores are opened by qualified Tiffany's personnel with 10 days on premise training. Periodic visits during the year by our staff to assist in production and management.
Managerial Assistance Available: Franchisor supplies full operating manuals to all franchisees. In addition, provides continuous on-going assistance for the business including field crew visitations, costing analysis, new product formulation, technical updates on production and marketing assistance.

WESTGATE SYSTEMS, INC.
1708 Westgate Road
Eau Claire, Wisconsin 54701
William J. Cigan, President
Robert A. Purdy, General Manager

Description of Operation: The franchisor offers a Honor Shoppe franchise to market and distribute its product concept within a given area. Basically this concept is to provide snack foods to small to medium size offices and places of employment which provide a demand but which are often too small for vending machines. The unique aspect of this approach is that it relies on the honesty of the customers of the location rather than locks to protect its product and proceeds.
Number of Franchisees: 6 in Wisconsin and Minnesota
In Business Since: 1978
Equity Capital Needed: Minimum of $17,000
Financial Assistance Available: None
Training Provided: Westgate Systems, Inc., will train and guide the franchisee and all employees for an average of 3 to 4 weeks in all aspects of the business. Also, there is a periodic visit from the office of Westgate Systems, Inc., to supervise and aid in the running of the franchise.
Managerial Assistance Available: Westgate Systems, Inc., provides continual management service for the life of the franchise in such areas as bookkeeping, inventory control, delivery, and many other necessary services needed for the smooth operation of an Honor Shoppe franchise. Manuals are being prepared to guide the franchisee in all aspects of the business. Westgate Systems, Inc., is in close contact with, and does schedule periodic visits to, all franchisees. Westgate Systems, Inc., sponsors meetings of franchisees where all questions and problems can be discussed with the other franchisees and the management of Westgate Systems, Inc.

WHITE HEN PANTRY DIVISION
JEWEL COMPANIES, INC.
666 Industrial Drive
Elmhurst, Illinois 60126
Robert L. Swanson, Director of Franchising

Description of Operation: A White Hen Pantry is a convenience type food store of 2,500 square feet with up front parking for 10 to 15 cars. The store is open from 7 am to 12 pm, sometimes longer, 7 days a week. Product line includes delicatessen service, fresh bakery goods, fresh produce and a wide variety of the most popular staples. White Hen Pantries are franchised to local residents who become owner-operators of a "family business."
Number of Franchisees: 225 in Illinois, Indiana, Wisconsin and Massachusetts
In Business Since: 1965
Equity Capital Needed: $8,000
Financial Assistance Available: Total investment averages $20,000 to $22,000. Investment includes approximately $17,000 merchandise, $2,000 security deposit, $200 cash register fund, $400 supplies, $100 to 200 for licenses and $2,000 processing fee. A minimum investment of $8,000 is required. Financial assistance available.
Training Provided: Classroom and in-store training precede store opening. A special training facility is established for this purpose. Detailed operations manuals are provided.
Managerial Assistance Available: This is a highly organized program. Services provide all merchandising, accounting, promotion, and advertising (group health insurance optional). Store counselor visits are regular and frequent.

FOODS-ICE CREAM/YOGURT/CANDY/POPCORN/BEVERAGES

AUMAN EQUIPMENT COMPANY
Hiway 20 West
Galena, Illionis 61036
Norval L. Auman

Description of Operation: Ice cream making equipment for high quality old fashion ice cream, frozen yogurt machines, old style root beer barrels for keg style root beer. Other soft drink equipment, old fashion candy display, and pop corn machine. Limited sandwich menu using microwave oven. Old fashion soda fountain, with the old style soda fountain back bar.
Number of Franchisees: 5 in Iowa, Illinois and Wisconsin
In Business Since: Our company 38 years. This franchise only 3 years.
Equity Capital Needed: Total package for equipment (no building) $42,500 with one-third down balance bank financing to credit worthy party.
Financial Assistance Available: We participate with bank handling balance on a recourse basis. Equipment lease program also available.
Training Provided: On-the-job training for 2 weeks and continuous assistance when necessary. Bookkeeping and all phases of pricing as well as purchasing is included in training program.
Managerial Assistance Available: As long as franchisee is working under the franchise program, continual assistance is provided to franchisee. This includes all phases of the operation, introduction of new items and new methods, menu pricing, purchasing, advertising, bookkeeping, etc.

BARNHILL FRANCHISE CORPORATION
dba BARNHILL'S ICE CREAM PARLOR AND RESTAURANT
5 Berea Commons
Berea, Ohio 44017
John Minto, President

Description of Operation: Barnhill's Ice Cream Parlors and Restaurants are finished in the Gay 90 style featuring ice cream extravaganzas, soups, salads and sandwiches, with a large selection of candies and some gift items. Family oriented, with children's birthday parties a specialty.
Three sizes available: Barnhills I is a full table service operation with 150 plus seats in 4,000 square feet. Barnhills II is a fast service concept with 60 plus seats in 1,800 square feet, and Barnhills III is primarily carry out. Suggest locationing in strip centers.
Number of Franchisees: 3 franchisees and 2 company operations, all in Ohio
In Business Since: 1966
Equity Capital Needed: Barnhills I require $175,000-$200,000; Barnhills II require $95,000-$115,000; Barnhills III require $35,000-$50,000. Depending upon location, local costs etc.
Financial Assistance Available: None
Training Provided: At least 30 days on-the-job training of new managers in a designated Barnhills. Training must be completed prior to opening of new franchise. Policy is to train all key personnel that franchisee desires.
Managerial Assistance Available: Normal franchisor supervision of start-ups, accounting, advertising, purchasing, and operations.

BASKIN-ROBBINS, INC.
1201 South Victory Boulevard
Burbank, California 91506
Barney Brown, Director Franchising Services

Description of Operation: Retail ice cream store. Franchisor selects site for Baskin-Robbins store. Upon securing a satisfactory lease, the store is completely equipped, stocked with merchandise, and brought to a point where it is ready to open. This complete store is then sold to a qualified individual under a franchise after intensive training.
Number of Franchisees: Over 2,300 stores in 895 cities throughout the United States, Canada, Japan and Europe.
In Business Since: 1945
Equity Capital Needed: Approximately $25,000 to $50,000 depending on retail location.
Financial Assistance Available: Yes
Training Provided: A complete training program is provided plus on-the-job training in operating store under the guidance of experienced supervisors.
Managerial Assistance Available: Continuous merchandising program, accounting procedures, business counsel, and insurance program (source available).

BLUM'S OF SAN FRANCISCO, INC.
111 North 56th Street
Lincoln, Nebraska 68504
Clive Hilgert, President

Description of Operation: Candy stores, and candy and ice cream stores.
Number of Franchisees: 14 in Hawaii, Nebraska, Colorado and California.
In Business Since: 1890
Equity Capital Needed: $35,000 to $50,000
Financial Assistance Available: None
Training Provided: On-the-job training in store.
Managerial Assistance Available: Store planning, merchandising, inventory controls, operations manual and supervision.

BRESLER'S 33 FLAVORS, INC.
4010 West Belden Avenue
Chicago, Illinois 60639
Joseph Marley, Director of Franchising

Description of Operation: Multi-flavor specialty ice cream shops - featuring ice cream cones, hand-packed ice cream, yogurt, complete soda fountain and made-to-order ice cream specialty items.
Number of Franchisees: Approximately 360 in 33 States and Canada.
In Business Since: 1962
Equity Capital Needed: Approximately $35,000 plus working capital.
Financial Assistance Available: A present total investment of approximately $70,000 to $80,000 required plus working capital of which approximately 50 percent is in cash. Franchisee may obtain own financing, or at his request franchisor will attempt to obtain financing to the extent of 50 percent of the total required initial investment, repayable over a minimum 5 year period.
Training Provided: Classroom and in-store training comprising a minimum of 3 weeks duration.
Managerial Assistance Available: Franchisor assists franchisee in all aspects of shop operation, record-keeping, advertising and promotion and selling techniques. Manuals of operations and counseling are provided. Area licensees and home office field personnel are available to visit stores regularly.

CARTER'S NUTS, INC.
215 West 34th Street
New York, New York 10001
Robert Rogal, Marketing Director

Description of Operation: Retail nut outlets - containing a full variety of all the world's nuts and dried fruits—where all nuts are freshly roasted every day on the premises.
Number of Franchisees: 3 in New York
In Business Since: 1976
Equity Capital Needed: $35,000
Financial Assistance Available: 50 percent of equipment
Training Provided: 100 page operations manual is provided by franchisor to franchisee and an intensive in-store work program of two weeks is required. Two weeks assistance is provided upon opening of franchisee's store.
Managerial Assistance Available: Managerial assistance in purchasing and hiring.

CARVEL CORPORATION
201 Saw Mill River Road
Yonkers, New York 10701

Description of Operation: Retail ice cream shops, featuring both hard and soft ice cream, manufactured by the store owner in the shop for on and off premises consumption. Specializing in full line of ice cream (36 flavors, 60 varieties) for all occasions. Also cakes and dessert items. Locations include free standing, shopping center, and inner city types.
Number of Franchisees: Over 750 stores operating in 12 States
In Business Since: Carvel franchising ice cream stores since 1948. In business since 1934.
Equity Capital Needed: Approximately $40,000
Financial Assistance Available: Contacts and counsel in arranging needed finance.
Training Provided: 14 day training period covering all facets of store operation and complete standard operating procedure manual, plus 10 days assistance and training in opening store.
Managerial Assistance Available: Continuous in-field counseling covering merchandising, quality control, advertising, promotion, and annual area educational seminars.

THE COFFEE MERCHANT
THE WHOLE BEAN CORPORATION
5500 Grossmont Center Drive
La Mesa, California 92401
Richard D. Nye, Vice President

Description of Operation: The Coffee Merchant is a specialty retail store providing an exceptional variety of the worlds best coffees, fine teas and related accessories.
Number of Franchisees: 3 in California
In Business Since: 1979
Equity Capital Needed: $40,000 to $70,000 dependent on store size, location and construction need.
Financial Assistance Available: The franchisor will assist the franchisee in applying with local banks for financing.
Training Provided: The prospective franchisee is trained for a 2 week period in a company store with emphasis placed on merchandising and accounting skills.
Managerial Assistance Available: The franchisor provides on-going managerial assistance and has available accounting services for the franchisee.

DAIRY ISLE CORPORATION
P. O. Box 273
Utica, Michigan 48087
David K. Chapoton, Vice President

Description of Operation: Soft Ice Cream stores and fast food operation.
Number of Franchisees: 98 in 9 States
In Business Since: 1949
Equity Capital Needed: Minimum $20,000
Financial Assistance Available: Company assists qualified applicants in arranging financing.
Training Provided: 3 days or more depending on individuals being trained plus calls during the operating season.
Managerial Assistance Available: Operations of unit and follow up promotional ideas and equipment purchasing.

ERNIE'S WINE & LIQUOR CORP.
305 Littlefield Avenue
South San Francisco, California 94080
Ernie Van Asperen

Description of Operation: Retail liquor, beer and wine stores.
Number of Franchisees: 59 in California
In Business Since: 1938
Equity Capital Needed: $100,000
Financial Assistance Available: None
Training Provided: 40 hours on-the-job training.
Managerial Assistance Available: On weekly basis.

INTERCONTINENTAL COFFEE SERVICE, INC.
680 Fargo Avenue
Elk Grove Village, Illinois 60007
R. E. Howland, Executive Vice President

Description of Operation: A broad county area franchise with direct sales to businesses and institutions primarily involving office employees with 10 to 100 people. The nature of the business is to place free restaurant quality coffee making equipment in a place of business and supply coffee, cream, sugar, etc. and free service to the locations.
Number of Franchisees: 18 in 14 States
In Business Since: 1965
Equity Capital Needed: $5,000 and up.
Financial Assistance Available: Liberal monthly rental programs on all equipment are given. Initial $2,500 cash advance is paid and no franchisee fees are paid except on the basis of monthly sales.
Training Provided: Both home office training and in-the-field training of as much as 2 weeks are required and provided. Complete services and training in sales, accounting, purchasing, and mechanical service are covered.
Managerial Assistance Available: Continuous weekly and monthly technical and motivational assistance is part of the on-going relationship between a franchise distributor and I.C.S. Complete manuals of operations, sales and company policies are provided. Home office personnel continues to work closely with each franchisee distributor for the duration of the life of the franchise. Yearly distributor meetings are conducted at the home office at company's expense.

KARMELKORN SHOPPES, INC.
101 - 31st Avenue
Rock Island, Illinois 61201
Nick Caras, Vice President-Marketing

Description of Operation: Karmelkorn Shoppes make and sell Karmelkorn popcorn candy, popcorn, popcorn confections, a variety of kitchen style candies and related snack food items. New Shoppes range in size from 400 to 650 square feet and are mostly located in major shopping centers. Business hours are those established by the shopping center with minor variations. In most cases, the company accepts the primary lease liability and sublets to the owner-operator.
Number of Franchisees: 250 in 43 States
In Business Since: The original Karmelkorn Shoppe was established in 1929.
Equity Capital Needed: $30,000 to $40,000 when standard financing is available.
Financial Assistance Available: The total investment in a Karmelkorn franchised Shoppe varies according to construction costs. Most Shoppes in 1979 ranged $64,500 to $87,500. The company assists franchisee in applying for his original financing upon request.
Training Provided: A National Training Center at the Rock Island offices of Karmelkorn Shoppes, Inc., is built as a model Karmelkorn Shoppe to simulate working conditions during training. The 40 hour curriculum is designed for new and existing franchisees, as well as their Shoppe managers and key employees. Grand opening assistance is provided by a company representative.
Managerial Assistance Available: The franchisee receives and is instructed in the use of an operating manual, which is supplemented by special and monthly business newsletters, that provide updates and operational information. Management and supervisory services are provided for the life of the franchise, and include periodic supervision by training supervisors; annual conference with business, product and advisory seminars; assistance in obtaining sources of supply and equipment; promotional material, and assistance in planning promotion programs.

LONE STAR CANDY MANUFACTURING COMPANY
OF TEXAS, INC.
2227 North Main Street
Fort Worth, Texas 76106
Raymond Seakan, President

Description of Operation: Lone Star offers a distributorship on very unique lollipops to be distributed in any and all 50 States. These lollipops are banana pops, ice cream cone pops, spiral pops, twisty pops, dummy dib pops, pet pops, wacky pops, western pops, etc. We have four styles of distributorships - Super master - $14,975, Master - $11,975, Sub -$6,975, Mini - $3,975. Lone Star provides between 10 locations and 50 locations which they establish to start the distributor on a profit basis.
Number of Franchisees: 66 in 18 States
In Business Since: 1921
Equity Capital Needed: $7,000 and financing can be provided subject to franchisee's credit rating.
Financial Assistance Available: A total investment of the distributorship is necessary. Down payment when purchasing and balance in cash on delivery or financed if needed. Financial assistance is given to the franchisee on a 3 to 5 year basis. Franchisee has the option to arrange his own financing.
Training Provided: Lone Star will advertise and train people in the franchisee home location to expand the program to any degree that he desires giving these people a fair and designated commission.
Managerial Assistance Available: Lone Star provides continual management and training for the life of the franchise in such areas as bookkeeping, advertising, and inventory control. Training and retraining the distributor and his appointed people and assist them in getting more locations. The better trained franchisee is the more profit he gets and the more profit Lone Star gets.

HAZLETT ENTERPRISES, INC.
dba MAIN STREET ORIGINAL ICE CREAM PARLORS
P. O. Box 13396
St. Petersburg, Florida 33733
Dean L. Hazlett, President

Description of Operation: Old fashioned ice cream parlors serving real ice cream manufactured in-shop from over 200 recipes, gourmet sandwiches, salads, a complete fountain service, and a candy section. Franchisor selects the site, directs custom construction, and supplies inventory, in coordination with an approved franchisee.
Number of Franchisees: 12 in Florida and Hawaii
In Business Since: 1972
Equity Capital Needed: $50,000
Financial Assistance Available: Partial financing to qualified individuals.
Training Provided: Initial training program, approximately 2 weeks, is provided to not less than 3 employees of the franchisee, including the franchisee and the operator/manager, in store operation. Manufacturing training provided to designated in-shop ice cream maker.
Managerial Assistance Available: Continuous assistance available in stores operation, product manufacturing and control; advertising promotional guidance, and Annual Systems Conclave provided by franchisor.

MISTER SOFTEE, INC.
901 East Clements Bridge Road, P.O. Box D
Runnemede, New Jersey 08078
James F. Conway, Vice President and General Manager

Description of Operation: Retailing soft ice cream products from a mobile unit, a complete dairy bar on wheels. Dealer is given a franchised area to operate. Mister Softee, Inc. maintains a supply department plus a service and parts department. Franchisees are supported with a merchandising, promotional, and advertising program.
Number of Franchisees: 850 in 20 States
In Business Since: 1956
Equity Capital Needed: $12,000 minimum
Financial Assistance Available: Financing can be arranged for qualified individuals.
Training Provided: Franchisee is trained on his mobile unit in his franchised area for 1 week in merchandising, route planning, operation of the mobile unit, sanitation and maintenance.
Managerial Assistance Available: Area representative visits franchisee for continuing assistance periodically and suggesting improvements when needed. Standard operating procedure manaul, service manual, accounting ledgers. Inventory control forms are provided to each franchisee.

MOM'S DEVELOPMENT CORPORATION
445 Union Boulevard
Lakewood, Colorado 80228

Description of Operation: Old fashioned homemade-style ice cream parlors serving ice cream, speciality dessert items and related foods. Features on-premises preparation and self-serve sundae bars and other facilities. Located in neighborhood centers enjoying high walk-in traffic. Parlors require 640 - 1,200 square feet. Parlors typically open a minimum of 11 hours daily, 7 days a week. Franchise fee currently $15,000.
Number of Franchisees: 31 parlors open in 12 states; 7 presently under construction; 148 additional franchises pending subject to site selection, financing and construction.
In Business Since: 1975
Equity Capital Needed: Current total maximum investment is $100,000 including the $15,000 franchise fee.
Financial Assistance Available: Mom's does not itself provide direct business or equipment lease financing.
Training Provided: 1 week of comprehensive training at administrative offices, together with additional, pre-opening and continuing at-site training. Operating, training and products manuals provided with continuing update service.
Managerial Assistance Available: Mom's provides on-going parlor inspections, operations review, promotional campaigns and new products research and development with related recipe evaluation. Mom's supervises site selection, equipment acquisition, parlor construction, arranges for dairy and distributor supplies and provides business and accounting systems.

NATIONWIDE GOURMETS, INC.
Suite B35, Host Hotel Office Level
Tampa International Airport
Tampa, Florida 33607
Thomas Appleton, President

Description of Operation: Nationwide Gourmets, Inc., provides training, technical and other assistance plus an initial number of customers to launch the franchisee in the honor snack and office coffee service business. Nationwide Gourmets, Inc., provides exclusive use of roasted coffees processed in Nationwide's own roasting and packaging plants, along with Nationwide's own private brands of products allied to coffee such as non dairy creamer, hot cocoa, sugar, tea, etc.
Number of Franchisees: 11 in 10 States
In Business Since: 1978
Equity Capital Needed: $15,000 minimum
Financial Assistance Available: A total investment of $39,000 to $99,500, depending upon population of exclusive market area, is required to launch a Nationwide Gourmets franchise. Nationwide Gourmets, Inc., may assist the franchisee in arranging for financing of approximately 80 percent of the equipment package, which comprises between 20 - 30 percent of total investment.
Training Provided: A one week mandatory course at franchisor's headquarters, including classroom and field instruction. During the initial week of the launch of the new business, a Nationwide representative is on hand to assist in establishing and standardizing procedures and techniques and train local personnel.
Managerial Assistance Available: Nationwide Gourmets, Inc., provides continuing advisory service for the term of the franchise in promotional, business or operational problems. Representatives are available to visit franchisee's operation for consultations. Material is continually updated through monthly and other bulletins covering marketing developments, products, techniques, accounting and other systems, etc. Advertising, sales training aids and sales personnel are provided for continuous sales assistance. A vehicle and equipment leasing program is provided through Nationwide's leasing associations. Computer services are offered to franchisees along with financial analysis and legal assistance.

OLD UNCLE GAYLORD'S INC.
2435 Mission Street
San Francisco, California 94110
Gaylord W. Willis, Chairman

Description of Operation: Retail parlours sell a full line of company manufactured old-fashioned ice creams, frozen yogurts, pastries and espresso coffees, soups, salads and sandwiches. Licensing available for other areas.
Number of Franchisees: 13 in California
In Business Since: 1972, offering franchising since September 1976
Equity Capital Needed: $70,000 to $125,000 includes all franchise fees and a turn-key business.
Financial Assistance Available: None
Training Provided: Training includes all aspects of ice cream making, retailing and merchandising as well as finance and accounting for small business and personnel development. Normal pre-opening training is 2 weeks will follow-up on-site training after operation begins.
Managerial Assistance Available: On-site follow-up after opening for 40 hours. Weekly in-store and training sessions during formulative stages of the new business.

THE PEANUT SHACK OF AMERICA, INC.
P. O. Box 11025
Winston-Salem, North Carolina 27106
John A. Lindsay, Vice President

Description of Operation: Specialty nut and candy shops located within enclosed shopping malls.
Number of Franchisees: 65 in 15 States
In Business Since: 1974
Equity Capital Needed: $50,000 to $75,000
Financial Assistance Available: No financial assistance available. However, franchisor is available for consultation with lenders.
Training Provided: Initial training of staff (normally 1 to 2 weeks) and periodic visits thereafter.
Managerial Assistance Available: Initial training at same time staff training takes place. Periodic visits by operations staff thereafter.

POLAR BEAR ICE CREAM COMPANY
400 South Zang, Suite 1216
Dallas, Texas 75208
Larry Garrett, Director of Franchise Sales

Description of Operation: Polar Bear-Ashburn offers the complete old fashion all natural ice cream. Polar Bear-Ashburn has been manufacturing ice cream for over 35 years. Polar Bear-Ashburn has seating for 50 plus, a private party room, marble tables, Tiffany lights, glassware service, soda bar, unique sandwich menu. Emphasis on family dessert and luncheon meals.
Number of Franchisees: 50 locations in Texas and Louisiana
In Business Since: 1941
Equity Capital Needed: $18,000 to $25,000
Financial Assistance Available: Counsel and preparation of applications for financing only.
Training Provided: 2 weeks at home office training center at the expense of franchisee. Training includes complete menu preparation, development of specialty sale items, instruction in operations and management functions: daily reports, ordering, inventory, payroll, cash control, banking, scheduling, interviewing, hiring, advertising, special promotions, sale and cost forecasting, maintenance, and community public relations.
Managerial Assistance Available: Real estate selection, negotiation of lease or purchase of site, assistance in applying for financing, construction supervision. Operations Manual, Food Preparation Manual and employee handbooks, continuous visitation, analysts of operational cost, pre-opening supervision, employe interviewing and training, advertising plans.

REAL-RICH CORP.
5454 Wisconsin Avenue
Chevy Chase, Maryland 30015
Gerald I. Goldberg, President

Description of Operation: Retail ice cream stores and ice cream parlour restaurants. Real-Rich Corp., selects site, secures lease; designs, builds and equips store; trains franchisee prior to store opening; and continues to support franchisee after his purchase of the business.
Number of Franchisees: 14 in Maryland and Virginia
In Business Since: 1971
Equity Capital Needed: Approximately $35,000 to $60,000, depending on location and type of store.
Financial Assistance Available: Variable
Training Provided: On-site training at nearest store prior to franchisee opening own store. Continued training after opening.
Managerial Assistance Available: Continuous guidance relating to operational control, merchandising, inventory control, promotions, and personnel.

SEAKAN CANDY COMPANY
Division of SEAKAN ENTERPRISES, INC.
6 Watson Place
Utica, New York 13502
Raymond Seakan, President

Description of Operation: Four very different and unusual types of lollipops arranged on a revolving four tier carousel, consisting of banana pops, spiral pops, curley-Q pops and wacky pops selling for only 39 to 49 cents each. These candy carousels are placed at forty different type locations by our company for the franchisee. Ice cream stores, supermarkets, convenient stores, restaurants, delicatessens, etc., are some of the locations.

Number of Franchisees: 171 in 30 States
In Business Since: Seakan Candy Company 1946 - Seakan Enterprises, Inc., successor 1975
Equity Capital Needed: $3,975 - $6,975 - $11,975 - $14,975
Financial Assistance Available: None
Training Provided: Complete and thorough. Required time 1 week at the start. One week on your location and company assistance as needed. Fund raising training also given. Customer candy carousel routes are established by the sellers and it is in operation fifteen days after product arrives.
Managerial Assistance Available: We train you or your appointed personnel on how to buy, sell, promote, expand and train new personnel. Assistance available at all times for any and all reasons to insure success.

SWENSEN'S ICE CREAM COMPANY
915 Front Street
San Francisco, California 94111
Harry R. Kraatz, Vice President

Description of Operation: "Swensen's Ice Cream Factories" offer the complete range of ice cream operations from manufacture to sale. Each "factory" manufactures its own ice cream from secret formulas developed by the firm's founder, Earle Swensen, who has been in the ice cream business in San Francisco since 1948. Franchisees purchase their supplies from independent suppliers. Swensen's stores vary from 150 to 4,000 square feet and are complete turn-of-the-century ice cream parlors, featuring marble tables and soda fountain, tufted booths, tiffany-style lights and mahogany or oak woodwork and furnishings. Swensen's stores engage in the retail sale of ice cream, fountain products, and related items, light sandwiches and in newer units a limited hot food menu. "Swenson's Ice Cream Islands" are small units selling ice cream novelty items made to Swensen's specifications.
Number of Franchisees: 260 in 32 States, District of Columbia, Mexico, Canada, Japan, Singapore and Saudi Arabia.
In Business Since: 1963
Equity Capital Needed: $80,000 minimum; equity capital requirements may vary depending on size of the store.
Equity Capital Needed: Swensen's consults with franchisees regarding financing of project costs by independent financial institutions.
Training Provided: Training consists of a 4 week program in Swensen's training facility in Las Vegas, Nevada, where franchisees learn ice cream making, preparation of fountain items, ice cream specialty and other items, ice cream specialty and other items, food preparation store operation; accounting, store maintenance, inventory control and all other aspects of the operation of a Swensen's Ice Cream Factory.
Managerial Assistance Available: In addition to initial training, complete operations manuals and forms are provided. Franchisees are periodically provided with a new flavor recipes and related promotional material. Swensen's maintains full-time operations and product personnel who regularly visit stores to assist in managerial and product-related areas. These operations personnel are available at any time to assist franchisees upon request in addition to their regular visits. Franchisees submit monthly operating statements to Swensen's home office for analysis and comment.

SWIFT COMPANY
115 West Jackson Boulevard
Chicago, Illinois 60604
J. L. Anson, Manager, Franchising

Description of Operation: Dipper Dan retail ice cream shoppe - featuring ice cream cones, soda fountain items, hand packed ice cream, ice cream specialty items, food items, and a party room. The store is completely equipped, fixturized, stocked with new merchandise. It is then sold to a qualified individual.
Number of Franchisees: 350 in 15 States, and Japan
In Business Since: 1955 - franchising 1963
Equity Capital Needed: Approximately $45,000
Financial Assistance Available: Financial assistance is available from Company.
Training Provided: A complete program is provided which includes pre-opening training and on-the-job training.
Managerial Assistance Available: The shoppe owner is continuously assisted in all phases of merchandising and shoppe operations.

TOPSY'S SHOPPES, INC.
215 East 18th Street
Kansas City, Missouri 64108
Jack R. Jones, Vice President

Description of Operation: Topsy's Popcorn Shoppes are engaged in the sale, for off-premises confectionary items and soft drinks.
Number of Franchisees: 17 who have 21 Topsy's Shoppes in 8 States
In Business Since: 1966
Equity Capital Needed: $100,000
Financial Assistance Available: None
Training Provided: Topsy's offers a training program, 5-15 days in length, at its training center in Mission, Kansas. The training program includes all information necessary to operate a Topsy's Popcorn Shoppe, including food preparation, methods of maintaining cleanliness, quality standards, employee training, proper use of accounting forms and business practices.
Managerial Assistance Available: Topsy's customarily selects the franchise location and either arranges for construction, or provides complete plans and specifications, along with construction supervision, for a Topsy's Popcorn Shoppe. A complete operations manual, reporting methods and procedures for accounting, and advice with respect to purchasing and selection of suppliers are furnished. Topsy's also provides advice and consultation with respect to the operation of the Shoppe, administers the advertising fund and in general, materially assists the franchisee in all phases of operating the business.

ZACK'S FAMOUS FROZEN YOGURT
P. O. Box 4437
Biloxi, Mississippi 39531
Robert D. Hunt, Franchise Director

Description of Operation: Retail sale of multi-flavors of frozen yogurt, ice cream, and related items featuring distinctive special creations.
Number of Franchisees: 8 in Louisiana, Texas, and Mississippi
In Business Since: 1977
Equity Capital Needed: $25,000
Financial Assistance Available: Financial package preparation for lending institutions including SBA applications compiled and completed by the franchise company.
Training Provided: A comprehensive 2 week training program including; operations manual orientation, customer relations, reporting procedures, day to day operations, policies and procedures, a complete review of all major business functions and "trade secrets" of special recipes created by Zack's, and on-site training.
Managerial Assistance Available: Operations specialists to coordinate opening and refine staff operations, coordinated advertisements and promitons, consultation, employee training, product and inventory control, the Zack's experienced management/marketing team will always be available.

ZIP'Z
P. O. Box 5630
4470 Monroe Street
Toledo, Ohio 43613
D. K. Combs, Franchise Director

Description of Operation: Zip'z features soft ice cream - soft frozen yogurt with take-home items and the Zip'z "Make Your Own Sundae Bar." The average store is 1,000 square feet in strip shopping centers and malls.
Number of Franchisees: 250 in 20 States
In Business Since: 1972
Equity Capital Needed: $12,500 minimum cash
Financial Assistance Available: A total investment of $65,000 is necessary to open a Zip'z franchise. This amount varies, plus or minus 10 percent as per local code and amount of equipment. Zip'z charges $12,500 for franchise licenses and will supply equipment to operator if requested. Zip'z does not finance or lease equipment to operator. Franchisee must arrange own financing.
Training Provided: 7 day training school with complete bookkeeping, machine maintenance, operations, product, personnel training, etc., at the company training school. Also provided is audio visual training with an extensive operations manual. A Zip'z supervisor opens every store and trains personnel in the store at opening.
Managerial Assistance Available: Zip'z provides supervision of stores and outlets to purchase merchandise but does not sell food products directly to franchisees. The products must be bought from purveyors and must meet Zip'z standards. All printed materials must have Zip'z logo and other identification. Zip'z provides point of purchase materials for all stores and manual updates for new product developments on a continuing basis.

FOODS-PANCAKE/WAFFLE/PRETZEL

FLAPJACK CANYON
7600 Chevy Chase Drive, Suite 513
Austin, Texas 78752
Terry Negley, Vice President, Marketing and Public Relations

Description of Operation: Family style, full service menu specializing in flapjacks and breakfasts. A unique building, western decor, 152 seats. Franchise and area rights available for many States.
Number of Franchisees: 4 in 3 States.
In Business Since: 1974
Equity Capital Needed: $100,000 and ability to finance land and building.
Financial Assistance Available: No direct financial assistance. Will advise and assist based on financial statement of applicant.
Training Provided: 6 weeks - 2 at company center and 4 on-site for opening.
Managerial Assistance Available: Ongoing assistance in advertising, site selection, building plans, training, accounting and supervision.

GENERAL FRANCHISING CORPORATION
158 West 44th Street
2nd Floor
New York, New York 10036
Jean Louis Poncet, President

Description of Operation: French restaurants, specializing in the confection of crepes (French pancakes) served in a typical Brittany decor.
Number of Franchisees: 25 in 9 States
In Business Since: 1966
Equity Capital Needed: $85,000 which represents approximately one-half of total investment.
Financial Assistance Available: Up to 50 percent of total investment through General Contractors, provided potential franchisee shows financial stability. No assistance from franchisor.
Training Provided: 5 weeks - complete training in all phases and departments of the restaurant field.
Managerial Assistance Available: See above.

H. L. H. ENTERPRISES, INC.
P. O. Box 2964
Houston, Texas 77001
V. L. Brazil, Director of Franchise

Description of Operation: Kettle restaurant chain.
Number of Franchisees: 18 in 8 States
In Business Since: 1968
Equity Capital Needed: $60,000-$70,000
Financial Assistance Available: None
Training Provided: On-the-job training of from 4 to 16 weeks.
Managerial Assistance Available: Managerial instruction given during the normal on-the-job training. Technical assistance given by franchisor to key personnel prior to opening for business and after opening until the operation stabilizes. Periodic visits thereafter, approximately every quarter or more often if deemed necessary or requested.

INTERNATIONAL HOUSE OF PANCAKES RESTAURANTS
6837 Lankershim Boulevard
North Hollywood, California 91605
Bob R. Leonard, Vice President-Franchise Operations

Description of Operation: Full service family restaurant serving breakfast, lunch, dinner, snacks and desserts including a variety of pancake specialities and featuring cook's daily special. Wine and beer served in some locations.
Number of Franchisees: 400 in 40 states, Canada and Japan
In Business Since: 1958
Equity Capital Needed: $45,000 franchise fee plus financing of land, building and equipment.
Financial Assistance Available: None
Training Provided: 4 weeks classroom and on-the-job instruction
Managerial Assistance Available: Franchisor provides opening supervision, regular visits and assistance from field coordinators. Complete manual of operations specifies how each menu item is prepared and served, how the business is to be operated profitably.

MARY BELLE RESTAURANTS
P. O. Box 706
Orange, New Jersey 07051
George Livieratos, Acting Manager

Description of Operation: Mary Belle Restaurants are complete family-style restaurants with table service, uniquely styled; it combines all types of restaurants in one by featuring full menu-pancakes and waffle section with beautiful warm decor. 40 flavors ice cream made on premises. Stores are approximately 3,000 square feet. Complete construction or remodeling, equipment, seating provided by company.
Number of Franchisees: 28 in New Jersey, New York, Florida, Tennessee, and Pennsylvania
In Business Since: 1952
Equity Capital Needed: $30,000 to $60,000 depending on size.
Financial Assistance Available: Company will assist franchises with locating financing of balance, rate of interest and term of financing dependent of franchises' financial statement and ability.
Training Provided: Minimum 160 hours training period in operating store and company in-store trainer for as long as needed upon opening.
Managerial Assistance Available: Management and technical assistance included in training period, with continuing support from main company representatives and from area representatives. National and statewide advertising program will be developed by main company for implementation in franchisee's area as needed.

PERKINS CAKE & STEAK RESTAURANTS
4917 Eden Avenue
Edina, Minnesota 55424
McClelland Troost, President & Chief Executive Officer

Description of Operation: Family-style sit-down restaurant with full menu. Specializes in pancakes, waffles and steaks.
Number of Franchisees: 360 total restaurants (266 franchises and 94 company-owned) located in 30 staes.
In Business Since: 1957
Equity Capital Needed: Must be able to obtain financing for equipment, land and buildings, additional minimum cash required - $100,000.
Financial Assistance Available: Advice on financing or leasing for real estate and equipment.
Training Provided: Training programs available for all levels of restaurant employment.
Managerial Assistance Available: Provide assistance in advertising, training, building plans, site selection, accounting, and supervision.

UNCLE JOHNS FAMILY RESTAURANTS
ROXBURY OF AMERICA, INC.
9808 Wilshire Boulevard, Suite 300
Los Angeles, California 90212
Stan Levy, Vice President, Licensing

Description of Operation: A 184-seat family restaurant, decorated in the tradition of the 1890's, uniquely designed, delightful decor, featuring wide variety of pancakes, chicken, Belgian waffles and crepes, with do-it-yourself salad bar, lunch, dinner, desserts. Excellent food, fast, efficient service in good taste and moderately priced. Uncle John sells a license for up to 3 units within a reasonable mileage radius.
Number of Franchisees: 14 operating a total of 31 restaurants in 13 States
In Business Since: 1958
Equity Capital Needed: Must be able to obtain financing for land and buildings, additional minimum cash required $75,000.
Financial Assistance Available: None
Training Provided: A minimum of 4 weeks on-the-job training for both the owner/operator or his designee and an assistant manager.
Managerial Assistance Available: Uncle John provides specifications and plans for the building, for the sign and the equipment. Provides site selection approval, store opening supervision, an accounting system and operating system, advertising and marketing programs, purveyor orientation, product specifications, and guidance and counseling any time at the general offices of Roxbury of America, Inc. (parent company of Uncle John).

VAN'S BELGIAN CREPES AND WAFFLES INC.
540 North Francisca Avenue
Redondo Beach, California 90277
Col. Douglas J. Horlander

Description of Operation: The selling in America of the one, only and original Belgian waffles and crepes. Contracts are available for expanded areas only. This would in most cases mean an entire state, and several restaurants.
Number of Franchisees: 9 in 2 States
In Business Since: 1968
Equity Capital Needed: $800,000
Financial Assistance Available: None
Training Provided: 3 weeks recommended, training is an on-going and never ending program at no additional cost to contract holder. Two students per contract.
Managerial Assistance Available: On-going and never ending on "what and as" needed basis.

VILLAGE INN PANCAKE HOUSE, INC.
400 West 48th Avenue
Denver, Colorado 80216
Attention: William Felitti, Group Vice President, Market Development

Description of Operation: Full menu family restaurant that specializes in pancake, waffle and egg selections.
Number of Franchisees: 160 restaurants; 62 franchisees operating 117 restaurants in 28 States.
In Business Since: 1958
Equity Capital Needed: $93,000
Financial Assistance Available: Will, in certain instances, guarantee the land and building lease for the franchisee.
Training Provided: Minimum of 12 weeks pre-opening training plus ongoing program of instruction.
Managerial Assistance Available: Provide continuous consultation and supervision in all areas of marketing, operations and purchasing. Also, provide training staff for new restaurant openings, operating manuals and continuous industry updates.

WAFFLE KING OF AMERICA, INC.
P. O. Box 2687
Huntington, West Virginia 25726

Description of Operation: A complete breakfast menu specializing in waffles and pancakes. Coffee shop atmosphere with sandwiches and full course dinners also served.
Number of Franchisees: 4 in West Virginia, Virginia, and Kentucky
In Business Since: 1973
Equity Capital Needed: Approximately $25,000
Financial Assistance Available: No direct financial assistance, however company will assist in preparing all loan applications and assist franchisee with the presentation of the application. Equipment leases have been arranged through private sources.
Training Provided: 1 month training program for each franchisee prior to the opening of his store including classroom work and on-the-job training in an existing company store. Company personnel assist at each new location at time of opening.
Managerial Assistance Available: Never ending managerial and technical assistance is provided throughout the term of the franchise. Regular visits by company personnel are designed to keep each franchisee up to date with the latest ideas regarding his business and regular management meetings for both company and franchise managers are held.

FOODS-RESTAURANTS/DRIVE-INS/CARRY-OUTS

A & W RESTAURANTS, INC.
922 Broadway
Santa Monica, California 90406
Paul Hubert

Description of Operation: Drive-In-Walk-In Restaurants.
Number of Franchisees: 1,400 in 44 States
In Business Since: 1919
Equity Capital Needed: $50,000 and up
Financial Assistance Available: Equipment financing available.
Training Provided: 2 week training course - mandatory.
Managerial Assistance Available: Continuous assistance from field personnel.

ACROSS THE STREET RESTAURANTS OF AMERICA, INC.
620 United Founders Tower
Oklahoma City, Oklahoma 73112

Description of Operation: Family charcoal hamburger restaurant specializing in 1/4 pound hamburgers in 12 varieties, spaghetti, steaks, shrimp; telephone order system, Americana decor. Atmosphere above other fast food systems and just under a supper club theme.
Number of Franchisees: 8 in 3 States
In Business Since: 1964
Equity Capital Needed: $55,000 and up.
Financial Assistance Available: Franchisor will counsel franchisee in obtaining a loan.

Training Provided: Franchisor provides 14 days of training for franchisee's management at training center in Oklahoma City concerning all phases of operation; food preparation, cooking, make-up, procedures, etc. Franchisor's training personnel sent to franchisee's restaurant to assist for 10 days during restaurant opening.
Managerial Assistance Available: A.I.A. building plans & specifications provided to franchisee. Aid in site selection. Operations manual including policies, procedures, recipes, forms, etc.

THE ALL AMERICAN BURGER, INC.
1888 Century Park East,
Suite 214
Los Angeles, California 90067
Howard J. Kastle, Vice President

Description of Operation: Fast food restaurants, featuring The All American Burger, salad bars, Mexican food.
Number of Franchisees: Over 500 franchises sold throughout the United States and Europe
In Business Since: 1968
Equity Capital Needed: $40,000 and up
Financial Assistance Available: None at present time.
Training Provided: Franchisor provides up to 21 days of training in the "All American" methods of operation. In addition, on-location supervision for a period of 48 working hours prior to and after the opening of the restaurant.
Managerial Assistance Available: Standard plans and specifications for the franchised restaurant are provided to franchisee. Franchisor will administer advertising, public relation and promotional programs designed to promote and enhance the value of "All American Burger." Continuous supervision of operation at no cost to franchisee. Operations and policy manual plus bookkeeping system provided to the franchisee.

ANCHOR INN RESTAURANTS
5244 Valley Industrial Boulevard
Shakopee, Minnesota 55379

Description of Operation: Family-style, waitress served, "all-you-can-eat" restaurants (spirits available).
Number of Franchisees: 12 in Minnesota, Wisconsin, Michigan, and California
In Business Since: 1968
Equity Capital Needed: Approximately $150,000
Financial Assistance Available: None
Training Provided: Complete managerial program from time of inception to grand-opening. Actual on-the-job training of all phases of the individual restaurant.
Managerial Assistance Available: Managerial program - 3-6 weeks. Promotional package - duration of franchise agreement. Use of central purchasing - duration of franchise agreement. Training program - 3-6 weeks.

ANGELINA'S PIZZA INC.
RT #2 Box 658
Bonita Springs, Florida 33923

Description of Operation: A pizza business that is designed for a husband and wife to own and operate. Most of the business will be carry out. Our company sells the needed dry mix for the pizza dough and sauce.
Number of Franchisees: 4 in Ohio and Florida.
In Business Since: 1956
Equity Capital Needed: $5,000
Financial Assistance Available: Limited to the franchise fee.
Training Provided: 2 weeks at a company store and 1 week at franchisee's store.
Managerial Assistance Available: We furnish a operators manual, daily register sheets, assist in advertising and give start up assistance and continuous advice when needed to conduct a profitable business.

ANGELO'S ITALIAN RESTAURANTS OF ILLINOIS, INC.
3750 Winchester Road
Springfield, Illinois 62707
Angelo Yannone, President

Description of Operation: Angelo's offers Italian food and pizza for family dining in a unique way by combining fast food service with conventional waitress service in a "sit-down" eatery.
Number of Franchisees: 16 in Illinois and Missouri.
In Business Since: 1968
Equity Capital Needed: Total package excluding building and leasehold improvements approximately $40,000. Cash investment about $20,000.
Financial Assistance Available: Assistance in obtaining financing thru proper preparation of a loan request for presentation to local lending institutions.
Training Provided: Complete training is provided in a course of no less than 4 weeks in an established operating restaurant under supervision. Training includes food preparation, merchandising, inventory control, cost and equality control, selection and training of personnel and money management.
Managerial Assistance Available: Franchisor assistance and information are, in a large part, imparted and conveyed to a franchisee prior to and during the early months of his operation. Such assistance and information are furnished as a matter of company policy. Periodic inspections and assistance are provided by Angelo's management and staff on a continual basis for the life of the franchise.

ARBY'S, INC.
One Piedmont Center
3565 Piedmont Road, N.E.
Atlanta, Georgia 30305
Jefferson T. McMahon, President

Description of Operation: Fast food restaurant specializing in roast beef sandwiches.
Number of Franchisees: 121 in 41 States and the Virgin Islands. 925 stores open as of January 1, 1980.
In Business Since: 1969
Equity Capital Needed: $80,000 to $120,000 (Assuming land and building are leased) and ability to acquire financing.
Financial Assistance Available: None

Training Provided: 7 weeks training for designated owner/operator and manager in Corporate Headquarters Classroom and Company operated training unit in Youngstown, Ohio. Ten days of on-site, pre/post opening training.
Managerial Assistance Available: 10 days technical training at Corporate Headquarters. Two day management development seminars (optional).

ARMAN'S SYSTEMS, INC.
6165 Central Avenue
Portage, Indiana 46358
Carrol Sarkisian, President

Description of Operation: Fast food operation selling hot dogs, hamburgers, tacos and 53 flavors of ice cream, supplying: mixes for taco and chili and is most successful when owner operated.
Number of Franchisees: 13 in Indiana
In Business Since: 1967
Equity Capital Needed: $30,000 down $95,000 total
Financial Assistance Available: None, franchisee is to handle their own financing. Company builds and leases back.
Training Provided: Training on-the-job at our company owned store. Also 2 weeks after restaurant is open with company supervision.
Managerial Assistance Available: We will be available at all times, any time assistance is needed. We keep a monthly check on percentages to see that they don't get out of line.

ARTHUR TREACHER'S FISH & CHIPS, INC.
5830 Henry Avenue
Philadelphia, Pennsylvania 19128

Description of Operation: Arthur Treacher's Fish & Chips is a limited menu, quick service operation offering fish, chicken and other seafood products, produced by a patented process. All units are image building typical in interior and exterior design. Company furnishes site approval and guidance, brown-line prints and specifications. Licensee must lease or purchase site, build or cause to be built, building and purchase and install equipment. Licenses are sold on a unit basis only with availability of options for additional units, which require adherence to a performance schedule.
Number of Franchisees: 261 in 42 States, the District of Columbia and Canada with 610 franchise operated shops and 160 company operated shops.
In Business Since: 1969
Equity Capital Needed: Minimum equity $50,000 - minimum net worth $140,000.
Financial Assistance Available: None
Training Provided: 5 day training for licensee or his manager. Training of licensee personnel at licensee's restaurant prior to opening, supervision through opening period, retraining as deemed necessary.
Managerial Assistance Available: Full spectrum

AUNT CHILOTTA SYSTEMS, INC.
P. O. Box 1360
Aberdeen, South Dakota 57401
Don Briscoe, President

Description of Operation: Limited menu Mexican fast food, featuring carry-out, drive-thru and inside seating for approximately 30. The restaurant is 18' x 36' and it is built on-site. Also available are plans for malls or remodeling existing structures. The total charge, including the franchise fee, is $32,000, and it includes everything needed in the kitchen, from the freezer and refrigerator down to the pans and spoons. Total investment can range from $70,000 to $200,000.
Number of Franchisees: 15 in 7 States
In Business Since: 1976
Equity Capital Needed: It varies, but generally $25,001 to $50,000.
Financial Assistance Available: We give information and assistance that should help in securing your own local financing.
Training Provided: In a comprehensive 14-day training program you receive on-the-job training in a company-owned restaurant that includes food preparation, product knowledge, inventory, purchasing, portion control, shift scheduling, daily reports, cash register procedures, staff appearances and hygiene, public relations and success motivation.
Managerial Assistance Available: One of our operations directors will assist in the actual opening of your new business and on a continuing basis, we will supply monthly promotions and advertising materials, make periodic inspections, and continue our ongoing research and development to help increase profits.

BAGEL NOSH, INC.
110 East 73rd Street
New York, New York 10021
James McGuirk, Franchise Director

Description of Operation: Manufacturing of Bagels and sale of Delicatessen Meats, Salads, Smoked Fish on Bagels-no bread used-light hot meals-Health Salads-Cafeteria style with average unit seating 100.
Number of Franchisees: 50 in 14 States
In Business Since: 1973
Equity Capital Needed: $120,000 cash including $25,000 franchise fee
Financial Assistance Available: $275,000 needed to build and equip a Bagel Nosh. Equipment leasing available to qualified individuals - franchisee may select own bank or SBA.
Training Provided: 6 to 8 week mandatory in-store for training under supervision of company instructors for all owners, managers and personnel that franchisee wishes trained.
Managerial Assistance Available: Bagel Nosh provides continual management service for term of agreement in controls, quality controls. Company supervisors work closely with franchisees and visit all units on regional basis. Operational manuals are provided for all phases of Bagel Nosh operations and standards.

BARNABY'S FAMILY INNS, INC.
2832 West Touhy Avenue
Chicago, Illinois 60645
Charles Hackl

Description of Operation: Fast food; self-service. Menu includes pizza, large hamburgers and other hearty sandwiches, beer and soft drinks. Business is family oriented.
Number of Franchisees: 24 in Illinois, Indiana, Missouri, Florida, Virginia and Wisconsin.
In Business Since: 1968
Equity Capital Needed: $96,000 minimum
Financial Assistance Available: None, franchisee must arrange own financing with our assistance.
Training Provided: 4-6 weeks of classroom and on-the-job training.
Managerial Assistance Available: Assistance is provided for the duration of the contract in areas of operations, marketing, and accounting controls.

BARONE'S
1136 Maple Avenue
LaGrange Park, Illinois 60525
Nick Barone, President

Description of Operation: Italian/American family styled sit-down restaurant with carry-out and delivery service.
Number of Franchisees: 22 in suburban area of Chicago
In Business Since: 1968
Equity Capital Needed: $85,000 and a strong financial statement.
Financial Assistance Available: Yes
Training Provided: Thorough training is mandatory.
Managerial Assistance Available: Yes

BEEF & BREW FRANCHISE CO., INC.
10570 Southeast Washington Street
Portland, Oregon 97216
George Sabin, President
Don Dwyer, Operations Manager

Description of Operation: Beef & Brew is a full service dinner house restaurant with a cocktail lounge. Open for lunch at units where location merits. Open 7 days a week.
Number of Franchisees: 3 in Oregon
In Business Since: 1971
Equity Capital Needed: $120,000
Financial Assistance Available: Franchisor does not participate in financing in any way, but it can offer assistance in preparing a loan package or in negotiating leases.
Training Provided: Prior to the opening of the restaurant, franchisor will provide a mandatory on-the-job training program for the franchisee. The training program will be provided in an operating Beef & Brew where the franchisee will receive training for every job from dishwasher to manager. This will be followed by management training at franchisor's home office.
Managerial Assistance Available: Prior to and subsequent to the opening, franchisor will assist in hiring & training, ordering and stocking. Maintenance will test all equipment. Operations manual and recipe manual will be given and will be supplemented from time to time. During the operation, field counseling will be provided by operations manager. A monthly meeting in each unit will be attended by all franchisees.

BEEF CORRAL RESTAURANT, INC.
Park Centre-Tower A
Cleveland, Ohio 44114
Carl Whelpley

Description of Operation: Fast food.
Number of Franchisees: 11 in Ohio
In Business Since: 1966
Equity Capital Needed: $50,000
Financial Assistance Available: None
Training Provided: 6 weeks - all phases of operation.
Managerial Assistance Available: Continuous assistance during life of agreement.

BIG BENS INTERNATIONAL, INC.
Subsidiary of NORTH STAR ACCEPTANCE AND INVESTMENT CORPORATION
610 Park National Bank Building
5353 Wayzata Boulevard
Minneapolis, Minnesota 55416
John Campbell, Director of Franchise Development

Description of Operation: Big Ben Family Restaurants offer a food-from-scratch full menu concept served in an Olde English decor. Special features include a unique salad bar, freshly baked in-store pies for eat-in or take-home consumption, fresh breads, homemade Olde World soups and wine and beer served in elegant natural atmosphere.
Number of Franchisees: 5 in Minnesota
In Business Since: 1966
Equity Capital Needed: Approximately $100,000 not including land, building or equipment largely used as working capital and reserve.
Financial Assistance Available: None
Training Provided: 4 weeks comprehensive training at central training restaurant in Minnesota with minimum of 1 week on-the-site training at the time of opening.
Managerial Assistance Available: Site location help and advice, standard restaurant and equipment plans and specifications, buying sources, full operational manuals and continual servicing of restaurant through quality and operational control, personal visits by field personnel and updates on research and operational changes.

BIG DADDY'S RESTAURANTS
420 Lincoln Road Mall
Miami Beach, Florida 33139
Robert M. Napp, President

Description of Operation: Fast food restaurants - snack bars.
Number of Franchisees: 3 in New York and Florida
In Business Since: 1964
Equity Capital Needed: $100,000
Financial Assistance Available: Total cost of turnkey investment $100,000 - $200,000. Company will build unit and take back mortgage, above $100,000 down payment
Training Provided: 6 to 8 weeks, either in New York or Florida
Managerial Assistance Available: Constant supervision and assistance provided.

BIG T FAMILY RESTAURANT SYSTEMS
TASTEE FREEZ INTERNATIONAL, INC.
1515 South Mount Prospect Road
Des Plaines, Illinois 60018
George N. Mitros, President

Description of Operation: Year-round fast food services family restaurants featuring special designed inside seating decor packages. The menu includes a variety of foods, such as the Tastee Burger Family, Tastee Crisp Chicken Family, fish, salad bar, as well as provisions for local preferences. Also features the complete line of Tastee-Freez soft ice cream desserts. Seeking individuals or investor groups capable of multi-unit as well as single unit development in reserve market areas.
Number of Franchisees: Over 2,000 throughout 49 States and overseas.
In Business Since: 1950
Equity Capital Needed: Total investments for restaurant equipment and license run from $75,000 to $125,000, which does not include sales tax if applicable, or operating capital and food inventory.
Financial Assistance Available: None
Training Provided: Training course for all new licensees conducted at company training center and licensee's own store. Course covers managerial, accounting, promoitonal, food preparation and operational phases under actual operating conditions. Continuous in-field counseling thereafter, covering merchandising, quality control, advertising and promotion by company regional store-supervisors.
Managerial Assistance Available: Regional territorial franchisees and/or state supervisors continue to counsel licensee in cost controls, new operational methods, advertising, merchandising and quality control. Parent company assist with national and local advertising and promotion. In addition, company conducts national convention once each year for all licensees to exchange ideas on merchandising, advertising, management and new food preparation methods.

BIG TOP CORPORATION
dba BIG TOP DELIS
1120 Enterprise Court
Holly Hill, Florida 32017
Director of Franchising

Description of Operation: Big Top Delis offer a new style "Deli" operation serving Deli style sandwiches, hot dogs, salads, home party platters together with soft drinks. The stores average 1,200 to 1,500 square feet with seating for 40 to 60 in regional shopping malls. Skilled help nor food service background is not required.
Number of Franchisees: 54 stores in 22 States
In Business Since: 1974
Equity Capital Needed: An average of $25,000 to $30,000 in cash in required.
Financial Assistance Available: A total investment of between $80,000 to $110,000 is required.
Training Provided: The franchisee attends a mandatory 2 week training program at head office with travel and accommodations paid by the Company. Prior to the franchisees store opening at the Company's expense, the Company sends its store opening team to the location. This team assists in the hiring and training of employees and provides further on-site expertise prior, during, and after the store is opened.
Managerial Assistance Available: Complete operations manuals, forms, and systems are provided. Grand Opening promotion, publicity and advertising are arranged for by the Company. New product development and testing is carried on continuously at the home office and when proven passed on to the franchisee. Continued management service guidance and promotion such as monthly features with special point of sale materials are provided for the life of the franchise.

BLACK ANGUS SYSTEMS, INC.
13001 N.E. 14th Avenue
North Miami, Florida 33161
William Diamond, Executive Vice President

Description of Operation: Black Angus Restaurants feature moderately priced char-broiled steaks and other main dishes. A separate lounge area is usually provided. Kelly's Seafood Restaurants feature moderately priced fish and seafood with a major salad bar promotion.
Number of Franchisees: 7 in Florida and Louisiana.
In Business Since: 1958
Equity Capital Needed: $175,000 minimum or MESBIC. Contact company for disclosure statement.
Financial Assistance Available: None
Training Provided: Owner and/or his managerial staff are trained for a minimum of 2 weeks in an open and operating Black Angus. Additional supervision is given at the time of opening.
Managerial Assistance Available: Black Angus will provide instruction in bookkeeping and auditing services. Continuing inspection and assistance at the franchise level is available.

BLIMPIE INDUSTRIES, LTD.
370 7th Avenue
New York, New York 10001
Peter DeCarlo, President
Rene Alfani, Marketing Division

Description of Operation: Limited menu, non-cooking operation featuring "Blimpie"

style sandwiches, with taste and marketing concept, consisting of eat-in, take out cafeteria style units, with drive-thru systems when applicable.
Number of Franchisees: 114 in 17 States and Washington, D.C.
In Business Since: 1964
Equity Capital Needed: $40,000 - $45,000
Financial Assistance Available: Will assist in obtaining financing.
Training Provided: Comprehensive 2 week program with coverage during initial few weeks in business.
Managerial Assistance Available: Continual visits by area consultants.

BONANZA INTERNATIONAL, INC.
1000 Campbell Centre
8350 North Central Expressway
Dallas, Texas 75206
Edward Kosan, Vice President Franchise Development

Description of Operation: Franchisors of Bonanza Sirloin Pit Restaurants.
Number of Franchisees: Over 700 in 40 States and Canada
In Business Since: 1965
Equity Capital Needed: Amount varies. Contact company for full information.
Financial Assistance Available: Contact company
Training Provided: 30 days on-the-job training, plus 10 days of pre-opening training in company classrooms.
Managerial Assistance Available: Continuous guidance; field operations consultants call upon franchisee at least once per quarter.

BOWINCAL INTERNATIONAL, INC.
421 Virginia Street West
Charleston, West Virginia 25302
Buford Jividen, President

Description of Operation: Bowincal offers franchises for its family fast-food restaurants featuring "Simply Delicious" olde fashioned hot dogs and Bowincal soft-serve ice cream. Each store is free standing or store-front (most remodelled existing structures), with approximately 1,100 - 1,500 square feet. Bowincal provides a complete set of specs and drawings for the standardized equipment and decor.
Number of Franchisees: 14 in West Virginia, and South Carolina.
In Business Since: 1973
Equity Capital Needed: $25,000
Financial Assistance Available: A total investment of $55,000 to $75,000 is required to open a Bowincal franchise. The $25,000 cash required represents the franchise fee of $9,500, down payments on equipment and remodeling, security deposits, licenses and opening inventory. Bowincal provides no financing.
Training Provided: 10 day training program at the Company training center and Bowincal opening crew spends 2 weeks training franchisee's crew at franchisee's location.
Managerial Assistance Available: Bowincal offers franchisees its expertise in all phases of day to day operations; including employment, training, systems, advertising and sales promotion, inspection, retraining, uniforms and accounting systems.

BOY BLUE STORES, INC.
10919 West Janesville Road
Hales Corners, Wisconsin 53130

Description of Operation: Franchising of soft serve, frozen yogurt and limited menu stores.
Number of Franchisees: 47 in 3 States
In Business Since: 1963
Equity Capital Needed: Over $25,000
Financial Assistance Available: Boy Blue Stores, Inc., will assist the operator in finding sources of financing and will assist in the preparation of the necessary financial statements.
Training Provided: The operator is required to complete a 9 day training program at the National Headquarters training school and pass all the tests connected with the course.
Managerial Assistance Available: Semi-annual advertising meetings and profit seminars for the franchisees.

BOZ HOT DOGS
770 East 142nd Street
Dolton, Illinois 60419
Don Hart, President
Harry Banks, Secretary

Description of Operation: Fast food carry out - no grills or fryers. All steamtable operations. Limited menu.
Number of Franchisees: 10 in Indiana and Illinois
In Business Since: 1969
Equity Capital Needed: $25,000
Financial Assistance Available: None
Training Provided: New franchisee trained on location for 1 month, assistance from then on.
Managerial Assistance Available: Assistance from day one, stands are checked weekly for freshness, and cleanliness.

BQF STEAKHOUSES
7850 Market Street
Youngstown, Ohio 44512

Description of Operation: BQF Steakhouses are a fantastic family oriented steakhouse operation. We offer 9 types of steak dinners plus hamburgers, fish, shrimp and chicken. We have nicely paneled walls, carpet, and booths for customer convenience. The units seat approximately 170 with 4,136 square feet. The units utilize a red brick exterior developed with ease of maintenance in mind.
Number of Franchisees: 12 in Ohio, West Virginia and Pennsylvania
In Business Since: 1971
Equity Capital Needed: $40,000 minimum
Financial Assistance Available: We recommend sources we have had experience and influence with, but no direct financing ourselves.
Training Provided: Intensive 2 week on-the-job training for all new franchisees plus 2 weeks at franchisees outlet under the supervision of full time BQF employee.
Managerial Assistance Available: BQF provides continual management service for the life of the franchise in areas such as bookkeeping, advertising, inventory control, complete manuals of operations, forms and directions are printed. An area representative will work with franchisees and visit stores regularly to assist in solutions to any problems.

BROWNS CHICKEN
800 Enterprise Drive
Oak Brook, Illinois 60521
Phil Rohm

Description of Operation: Combination sit down/carry out restaurants. Speciality "chicken."
Number of Franchisees: 128 (including 19 company-owned) in Midwest and Florida.
In Business Since: 1965
Equity Capital Needed: $100,000 to $150,000 and ability to obtain financing on an additional $300,000 to $350,000.
Financial Assistance Available: Will assist in obtaining, but no direct financing ourselves.
Training Provided: 6 weeks training school plus continual training on an inspection basis or request from franchisee.
Managerial Assistance Available: Formal training school, monthly field inspections, special assistance upon request, annual franchise seminar and spring and fall advertising meeting.

BUN N BURGER INTERNATIONAL, INC.
41 East 42nd Street
New York, New York 10017

Description of Operation: Hamburger shops.
Number of Franchisees: 6 in New York
In Business Since: 1968
Equity Capital Needed: Over $50,000
Financial Assistance Available: None
Training Provided: As long as required.
Managerial Assistance Available: As much technical assistance as is needed for a long a period as is necessary.

BURGER CHEF SYSTEMS, INC.
College Park Pyramids, P. O. Box 927
Indianapolis, Indiana 46206
Joseph J. Kally, Director of Franchising

Description of Operation: Limited menu restaurants. Operation procedures and policies are standardized as are design and layout of building. Actively seeking new franchisees.
Number of Franchisees: Over 500 licensed restaurants in the United States.
In Business Since: 1958
Equity Capital Needed: $75,000 net worth of at least $150,000
Financial Assistance Available: None
Training Provided: Complete training program for franchisee-manager (up to 3) in all phases of restaurant operation and management.
Managerial Assistance Available: Managerial assistance on a ongoing basis through regular assigned field consultants.

BURGER INNS
1819 Peachtree Road, N.E.
Suite 308
Atlanta, Georgia 30309
Robert J. Shaw, President

Description of Operation: Fast food franchise offering both sit down and drive-thru service in a restaurant occupying from 850 to 1,200 square feet. Serving hamburgers, hot dogs, fish sandwiches, chicken sandwiches, french fried potatoes/onion rings/mushrooms, fried pies, shakes, assorted beverages and breakfast.
Number of Franchisees: 95 in 30 States; 1 in Washington, D.C. and 1 in Canada
In Business Since: 1977 (parent company, Garrett Equity, since 1973)
Equity Capital Needed: $30,000 minimum
Financial Assistance Available: None. Franchisee arranges for own financing but assistance is furnished to prepare loan package for submission to bank/SBA.
Training Provided: Company operated management training school provides extensive and detailed instruction in restaurant operations. In store training for managers under supervision of Director of Training. Pre-opening training for all personnel.
Managerial Assistance Available: Continuous supervision, management and technical assistance during franchise period covering site selection, building construction, equipment package, food preparation and control, accounting, and advertising. Regular store inspections to provide managerial support to franchisee.

BURGER KING CORPORATION
P. O. Box 520783
Miami, Florida 33152
Jeff Seeberger, Vice President, Franchise Development

Description of Operation: Limited menu restaurant specializing in hamburgers. Air-conditioned and heated. Seating of 50 to 130 people. Franchises available throughout most of the United States and abroad.
Number of Franchisees: More than 2,600 units located in all 50 States, the Bahama Islands, Puerto Rico, Canada, Spain, Guam, Germany, Sweden, Denmark, England and Australia.
In Business Since: 1954
Equity Capital Needed: $110,00 net worth $150,000
Financial Assistance Available: Franchisee arranges own financing, usually available in local banks and selected national finance or leasing companies.
Training Provided: Company operated regional training centers provide extensive and detailed instruction in restaurant operation, equipment, administration for franchisees and/or management.

Managerial Assistance Available: Operational assistance is provided on an on-going basis as needed through personnel located at regional and district offices operated by Burger King Corporation.

BURGER QUEEN ENTERPRISES, INC.
P. O. Box 6014 - 4000 DuPont Circle
Louisville, Kentucky 40206
George E. Clark, President

Description of Operation: Fast food restaurant.
Number of Franchisees: 164 in 7 States; 1 in Canada; 1 in London, England; 3 in Taipei, Taiwan.
In Business Since: 1963
Equity Capital Needed: $50,000 depending upon franchisee's financial capabilities.
Financial Assistance Available: Assistance in acquiring equipment loan or lease. Joint venturing opportunities for qualified candidates.
Training Provided: Development training program - 5 weeks - combined unit and classroom work at special training unit - follow up visits at franchisees unit by training director during next 25 weeks and continued visits by area supervisor.
Managerial Assistance Available: Continued assistance regarding operations and accounting through coordinators and correspondence from home office.

BURGER TRAIN SYSTEMS, INC.
6508 South Barnes
Oklahoma City, Oklahoma 73159
Mr. Edmond Hollie

Description of Operation: Burger Train Systems, Inc., offers a technical and expert assistance from accumulated knowledge and experience in the Fast Food Service; offering patented labor saving delivery equipment offered on arranged terms through banks, etc.
Number of Franchisees: 3 in Oklahoma and Texas.
In Business Since: 1968
Equity Capital Needed: $50,000 and up, depending upon operator's ability to finance.
Financial Assistance Available: We assist as a finder of finances for the franchisee; $120,000 is the total investment required, which does not include building or land. Finances required, depends on franchisee's credit, should have approximately $25,000 minimum for operating expenses.
Training Provided: 4 weeks mandatory training course for all new franchisees and their operating personnel, alternating from office to store as needed.
Managerial Assistance Available: Burger Train Systems, Inc., provides management service through the term of the franchise in all areas related to the operation, including, but not limited to, quality control, safety, public acceptance, advertising, innovation, counsel, etc., also conducting product and marketing research.

CAPTAIN D'S
P. O. Box 1260
1724 Elm Hill Pike
Nashville, Tennessee 37202
Attention: Franchise Director

Description of Operation: Seafood and hamburger restaurant with carry-out or self-service dining room. Menu features variety of seafood served in a pleasant, nautical theme atmosphere.
Number of Franchisees: 177 stores in 22 States
In Business Since: 1969
Equity Capital Needed: $50,000 and up depending on operator's ability to finance.
Financial Assistance Available: Franchisee is responsible for land, building and equipment.
Training Provided: 4 weeks formal and in-store training plus continuing on-the-job supervision.
Managerial Assistance Available: Captain D's is a division of a multi-state restaurant chain. This program first opened in 1969 and now have over 300 stores open. All operation and technical services of the parent company are available to the franchisee.

CASEY JONES JUNCTION, INC.
6235 West Kellogg
Wichita, Kansas 57200
M. Eugene Torline, President

Description of Operation: A family restaurant, catering to families with small children. Casey Jones Junction carries the railroad theme throughout its decor, menu, advertising, appearance, and atmosphere. A unique feature is the model train, which delivers "Tom Thumb" hamburgers, etc., to the children seated around the counter. Casey Jones Junction offers excellent food at reasonable prices. Breakfast, Lunch and Dinner are served.
Number of Franchisees: 8 in 6 States. Emphasis is currently in the mid-west and mountain states, however inquiries are welcome from all areas of the country, and overseas. The company welcomes inquiries from persons of all ethnic backgrounds.
In Business Since: 1968
Equity Capital Needed: From $8,000 to $40,000, plus building and land.
Financial Assistance Available: No direct financial assistance, however assistance is given to qualified applicants in finding sources of capital. Qualifications are based on applicants credit rating, judgment of ability, location of the proposed franchise, etc.
Training Provided: A comprehensive training program is provided for each franchisee, prior to opening of his franchise. The program is held at a location to be selected by the company, and includes intensive training in operations, accounting systems, inventory and quality control, personnel management, and other functions required for a successful operation. The franchisee participates in all phases of operations during this period. Cost of training is included in the franchise fee, however, travel, lodging, etc., are the responsibility of the franchisee. Franchisee is under the supervision of a company official for at least 1 week after unit is operational.
Managerial Assistance Available: Technical assistance is provided throughout the term of the franchise. Company provides accounting assistance, etc., at any time needed. Company monitors all purchases and approves all purveyors, and provides analysis of operations on a regular basis. Company has available construction plans, etc., for new construction, and will assist in layout and design of the unit if required. Company will also provide these services for franchisees wishing to utilize existing buildings. Periodic inspections by home office are required, and complete accounting statements must be submitted each month by franchisee. Immediate assistance is provided should problems arise. Assistance is also provided in advertising layout, if requested.

CASSANO'S INC.
1700 East Stroop Road
Dayton, Ohio 45429

Description of Operation: Cassano's Pizza & Seafood Restaurants specializing in the sale of pizza, seafood, pasta, sandwiches, desserts & miscellaneous beverages. Our free standing unit seat 60 to 95, however, many units are located in regional shopping centers. Over 99 units now in operation in nine States with several under construction. Cassano is actively seeking franchisees for all midwestern and eastern States.
Number of Franchisees: 20 in 8 States
In Business Since: 1953
Equity Capital Needed: Total package (excluding building and leasehold improvements) approximately $97,500. Minimum cash investment is approximately $40,000.
Financial Assistance Available: None
Training Provided: 4 weeks in-store and classroom instruction in home office facilities under the guidance of Cassano's training department.
Managerial Assistance Available: Marketing and advertising assistance, accounting system both daily and monthly records, engineering staff assistance. Regular visits and consultation from franchisors field representatives.

CHARLIE CHAN RESTAURANTS
50 Karago Avenue
Youngstown, Ohio 44512
Richard A. D'Onofrio, President

Description of Operation: Charlie Chan's purpose is the operation of a snack-bar or sit-down restaurant for the retail sale of Chinese and Chinese-American food products such as Egg Rolls, Chicken Chan, Shrimp Chan, Fish Tempora, Won-tons, Chanwich, Chan Fries, Chan Fritters, Fortune Cookies, Tea, Coffee, Soft Drinks and other Chan food and Chinese food products and related novelties with the Charlie Chan insignia printed thereon. All units are image building typical in interior and exterior design. Company presently concentrating on regional shopping centers and recreational areas. Company furnishes site approval and provides lease arrangements and guidance brown-line prints and specifications.
Number of Franchisees: 26 plus 2 company-owned in 12 States.
In Business Since: 1975
Equity Capital Needed: $35,000
Financial Assistance Available: Assistance in arranging financing provided on a regular individual basis.
Training Provided: Company-operated management training providing extensive detailed instruction in restaurant operation, equipment, administration for franchisees-management or both.
Managerial Assistance Available: Franchisor supplies full operating manuals to all franchisees. Also provides continuous on-going assistance for the business including field crew visitations, cost analysis, new product formulations, technical production updates and marketing assistance.

CHELSEA STREET PUB
c/o RANKEN INC.
8802 Shoal Creek
P. O. Box 9989
Austin, Texas 78766
Bert Bernstein, Vice President and Director of Franchising

Description of Operation: Chelsea Street offers a quick service seated food and drink operation in a English Pub atmosphere serving deli type sandwiches, salads, and a unique limited menu requiring no cooking. Also serving fancy alcoholic drinks of all types as well as beer and wine. Live entertainment nitely. Primarily located in major enclosed malls of high traffic, hours 11 am until 2 am six days a week.
Number of Franchisees: 4 plus 11 company-owned in Texas, New Mexico, Louisiana, Florida and Tennessee. Four under development.
In Business Since: 1973
Equity Capital Needed: $50,000 to $75,000
Financial Assistance Available: Total investment is approximately $250,000 the franchisee is required to arrange his own financing however Chelsea Street will assist in obtaining franchising by providing background information, projections, references etc., to the bank of franchisees choice.
Training Provided: Mandatory 45 day intensive training program including 15 days in Chelsea Street's home office school plus 30 days in on-the-job supervised training encompassing every phase of running a successful Chelsea Street Pub.
Managerial Assistance Available: Chelsea Street provides both technical and managerial assistance throughout the life of the franchise. Chelsea Street will supply site selection and build a complete pub as well as assist in opening the unit plus training all personnel. Continued assistance in advertising, supply, bookkeeping and entertainment and controls are provided in addition complete manuals of operations as well as forms and directions are provided and updated. 24 hour direct line consultation as well as periodic visits by Chelsea Street supervisors are provided to assist in maximizing income and quality.

CHICASEA, INC.
2004 Dabney Road
Richmond, Virginia 23230
Martin E. Bandas, Franchise Director

Description of Operation: Chicasea, Inc., operates and directs a chain of fast food restaurants serving fried chicken prepared from our secret recipe, plus shrimp, oysters, clams, fish & chips, seafood dinners, French fried potatoes, cold salads and drinks. Plans and specifications are available for both eat-in and take-home shops.
Number of Franchisees: 12 (including 5 company-owned) in North Carolina and Virginia
In Business Since: $30,000
Equity Capital Needed: $30,000 covers franchise fee, equipment, initial inventory and beginning operating capital. Franchisees with good credit ratings are usually able to obtain financing for a portion of the initial capital needed.

49

Training Provided: The franchisor provides training at a Chicasea location in Richmond, Virginia for the franchisee or his designee in the techniques and procedures of operating a Chicasea unit. Staff assistance is provided for shops opening and is available as needed.
Managerial Assistance Available: The Chicasea staff is available for assistance in site location, planning and construction, equipment purchasing and advertising. Trained personnel also advise on the use of the operation manual, which includes shop procedures, record keeping for the shop, forms and their use. The management staff is available at all times for counseling and guidance. Continuing inspections and supervisory training are provided throughout the term of the franchise agreement.

CHICKEN CHAMP
P. O. Box 52—North Hackensack Station
River Edge, New Jersey 07661
Irving Davidoff, Franchise Director

Description of Operation: Retail fast food take out stores featuring chicken, spare ribs, and seafood. Eat in accommodations also provided. Special provisions for parties, business meetings, civic events, and large gatherings. Chicken Champ will seek and establish a location in the general area of your choice if it does not infringe upon the trading area of an existing location.
Number of Franchisees: 5 in New Jersey and New York.
In Business Since: 1972
Equity Capital Needed: $20,000 minimum
Financial Assistance Available: Total investment for a complete turn-key operation including interior design and construction, equipment and installation is $34,900. $14,900 may be financed through Chicken Champs.
Training Provided: Franchisor provides a comprehensive training program to include preparation of food, ordering procedures, inventory control, bookkeeping, sales promotion, and store operations. In addition, Chicken Champ representatives work with the franchisee during the first two weeks of opening.
Managerial Assistance Available: Chicken Champ provides the franchisees with their exclusive recipes for sauces and breading. Continuous research is conducted in regard to product improvement and introduction of related new products for the benefit of the franchisees. Field representatives personally visit each location frequently to observe the operations and to recommend improvements to yield greater sales and higher profit for the franchisee.

CHICKEN DELIGHT
227 East Sunshine
Suite 119
Springfield, Missouri 65807
Wendell E. Lejeune, Vice President and General Manager

Description of Operation: Inside dining and/or carry out and delivery restaurant featuring chicken, shrimp, fish, BBQ ribs and pizza. Area franchises also available.
Number of Franchisees: 130 in 6 States and Canada
In Business Since: 1952
Equity Capital Needed: $50,000 to $150,000, depending on size of unit, and ability to acquire additional financing.
Financial Assistance Available: None
Training Provided: On-the-job training which includes all phases of operations.
Managerial Assistance Available: Continual assistance in all phases of operations is offered.

CHICKEN MARY'S SYSTEMS, INC.
Box 62489
Pittsburg, Kansas 66762
Larry Zerngast, President

Description of Operation: Family style sit-down restaurant specializing in fried chicken with other items on menu. Also interested in joint venture or merger with larger corporation for a large scale operation.
Number of Franchisees: 3 in Missouri and Kansas
In Business Since: 1930
Equity Capital Needed: $30,000 and up
Financial Assistance Available: Assistance in funding of land and building. Assistance in funding equipment.
Training Provided: Training program available for management. Duration of program depends on time required for individual.
Managerial Assistance Available: Continuous supervisory help.

CHICKEN UNLIMITED ENTERPRISE, INC.
105 West Adams Street
Suite 1070
Chicago, Illinois 60603

Description of Operation: Quick service dining featuring fried chicken. Menu consists of chicken sold by the individual part as well as dinners and boxes of large orders. Menu variety features fish and chips, shrimp dinners, hamburgers, apple puffs, french fries and cole slaw, as well as soft drinks. A typical restaurant is a free standing building featuring a 50 seat dining area and carry-out section.
Number of Franchisees: 65 locations in 2 States, plus Trinada and Bahamas
In Business Since: 1964
Equity Capital Needed: $99,000
Financial Assistance Available: None
Training Provided: Owner operator and/or manager receive 4 weeks training at company owned and operated training unit in Florida. During the first week of operation in franchisee's restaurant an operations specialist is present to work with the operator and most importantly, to assist in the training of the new personnel.
Managerial Assistance Available: Chicken Unlimited has a team field operations specialists who visit each restaurant frequently for continuing management guidance, training, and assistance with promotions.

CHIP'S HAMBURGERS
114 Grand Avenue
Wausau, Wisconsin 54476
B. H. Levine, President

Description of Operation: Carry-out fast food service with menu limited to hamburgers, fish, dessert tiems and soft drinks. Stores are located in large lots with ample auto parking and some inside seating. The company features the char broiled process of cooking. Stores are open 363 days a year from 10:30 am to 10:30 pm.
Number of Franchisees: 6 in Wisconsin, Michigan and Illinois
In Business Since: 1966
Equity Capital Needed: $25,000 minimum. Franchise and location fee of $7,500. The balance of $17,500 for down payment on equipment, lease deposits and operating capital.
Financial Assistance Available: The company will assist franchisee in securing necessary financing.
Training Provided: Intensive minimum of 30 days training course conducted at home office and training unit in city of home office.
Managerial Assistance Available: We provide continual management service for the life of each franchise in such areas as bookkeeping, advertising, inventory control. We provide complete manuals of operations, forms and directions for operation. Field managers are available in all regions to work closely with franchisees and managers and visit stores regularly to assist solving any problems. We arrange meetings of franchisees and conduct marketing and product research to maintain maximum consumer acceptance.

CHUCK CONNORS CHUCK WAGON DIVISION
TENDERFOOT INTERNATIONAL, INC.
500 North Harbor City Boulevard
Melbourne, Florida 32935
Thomas Moore, Director of Development

Description of Operation: Chuck Connors Chuck Wagon restaurants are limited menu, quick service food service facilities designed for regional shopping centers and malls. Each unit has a unique attention-getting store front with authentic Western decor throughout. The restaurant offers a limited breakfast, luncheon and dinner menu.
Number of Franchisees: 3 in Florida and Nevada plus 2 company-owned Tenderfoot Restaurants in Kentucky and Florida.
In Business Since: 1976
Equity Capital Needed: $10,000 required for inventory and operation capital.
Financial Assistance Available: A $10,000 cash investment is required and the Company does not recommend that any portion of this investment be financed. The Company negotiates and leases the premises and equipment. Each applicant must be willing to undergo a thorough personal screening evaluation. Upon approval he will receive a guaranteed salary when his restaurant opens, family hospitalization plan and a substantial life insurance program.
Training Provided: Applicant must be the active manager of the facility. An intensive program is conducted at the applicants facility for all of his personnel. Training may vary from one to two weeks depending upon applicant's capabilites. Each unit receives periodic visits and is monitored weekly by computer printouts.
Managerial Assistance Available: Company selects sites, negotiates lease, remodels the leased space to the Chuck Wagon concept, equips the facility with the latest food service equipment, including the exclusive Tenderfoot cooking unit. The majority of accounting, payroll, inventory and paperwork is provided by the home office so the restaurant's management can devote its efforts toward the continuing growth of the business.

CINDY'S INCORPORATED
P. O. Box 4718
Atlanta, Georgia 30302
A. L. Roberts, President

Description of Operation: Fast food restaurants, featuring Ole Time Hamburgers, Hot Dogs, Chick Ina Bun, Chili, French Fries and Desserts, with units for high volume locations and small towns, each with seated service and drive-thru windows. Cindy's, Inc., is a publicly held corporation traded over the counter as CNDY.
Number of Franchisees: 117 in 30 States
In Business Since: 1969; however the company entered the fast food industry in 1977
Equity Capital Needed: $50,000
Financial Assistance Available: Cindy's Franchise Division will assist in securing financing.
Training Provided: 2 weeks in training school located in Atlanta, Georgia.
Managerial Assistance Available: Assistance available in site selection, lease negotiations and arranging of financing on land, building and equipment. Our opening teams will be in each franchise outlet opened for a period of up to 10 days. They will see that all personnel are properly trained and that Cindy's procedures are being followed. Field supervisors will then be available in adequate numbers to help solve any problems that arise in day-to-day operations.

CIRCLES INTERNATIONAL NATURAL FOODS, INC.
310 Bay Ridge Avenue
Brooklyn, New York 11220
John Fahy, Franchise Manager

Description of Operation: Large menu with mixed ethnic specialities from all over the world and inexpensive gourmet fish and chicken dishes. Baked goods on premises and natural beverages.
Number of Franchisees: 3 in New York
In Business Since: 1976
Equity Capital Needed: $100,000
Financial Assistance Available: None
Training Provided: 2 weeks in home store and 2 weeks in franchisee's store.
Managerial Assistance Available: Daily checks on operations, five days. On-going development.

CLARK'S SUBMARINE SANDWICHES, INC.
417 University Avenue
St. Paul, Minnesota 55103
Clark Armstead, Franchise Director and President

Description of Operation: Clark's Submarine Sandwiches offers a unique fast food concept. We specialize in submarine sandwiches and offer the consumer a high food value at a reasonable price in an exciting package. Our stores are open 7 days a week from 10 am to 12 pm. We have been in business for over 18 years operating company owned stores. Our stores are free standing with convenient customer parking together with dining rooms, drive-up windows and take out facilities.
Number of Franchisees: 22 including company owned stores in Minnesota and Colorado.
In Business Since: 1959
Equity Capital Needed: $50,000
Financial Assistance Available: A total investment of up to $250,000 is necessary to open a Clark's Franchise. Clark's provides no financial assistance.
Training Provided: A mandatory training course is provided at company headquarters and on-site training at company stores in addition to additional training in franchisor's facility.
Managerial Assistance Available: Clark's provides continual management service for the life of the franchise in areas as bookkeeping, advertising, inventory control. Complete manuals of operations, forms and directions are provided—custom equipment, design, logos, building plans and site selection. District and Field persons are available and work closely with franchisees.

COLONEL LEE'S ENTERPRISES, INC.
17920 Ventura Boulevard
Encino, California 91316

Description of Operation: Specialty fast food restaurant: offering limited menu of individually prepared Mongolian Barbque of beef, lamb, pork and turkey meats and a variety of vegetables, and other complimentary items. Emphasis in on efficient service with inside seating service. Restaurant is operated under the trade name of Colonel Lee's IMongolian Bar-B-Q.
Number of Franchisees: 16 in California plus 2 company-owned.
In Business Since: 1967, franchise operation began in 1976.
Equity Capital Needed: $65,000 to $85,000 and ability to acquire financing.
Financial Assistance Available: Guarantee lease and equipment financing if necessary; if so, a 10 percent signing fee is required.
Training Provided: 4 weeks on-the-job training mandatory. Complete operational manuals and handbook provided.
Managerial Assistance Available: Regular visits by field supervisors. Advertising program, accounting system, management training provided by home office throughout the operations of the business. Advice and consultation with home office available on request.

COOKSHACK
724 Monument Road
Ponca City, Oklahoma 74601
Gene Ellis

Description of Operation: The Cookshack Co., is a manufacturing, supply and consulting service organization devoted specifically and entirely to the old time "Pit Barbecue" industry. Cookshack holds all modern patents on automatic barbecue equipment. Our automatic pits, supportive consultation services, recipes, condiments and native and imported cooking woods are marketed by franchised distributors per agreement attached.
Number of Franchisees: 8 in 8 States
In Business Since: 1963
Equity Capital Needed: One or more pickup or van type vehicles - 500 to 1,000 square feet of warehouse space.
Financial Assistance Available: Up to 80 percent of start up finance, namely inventory, for qualified people.
Training Provided: Service and operations manuals, descriptive literature and ongoing direct personal assistance in service and new techniques.
Managerial Assistance Available: Ongoing personal contact and transfer of ideas between franchised distributors.

COUNTRY BREADBOARD, INC.
441 Albany Post Road
Croton, New York 10520
A. Feicco, President

Description of Operation: Restaurant and retail bakery under one roof, Early American decor. Serves breakfast, lunch and dinner. Family oriented, modest priced menu. Retail bakery features bread, pies, cakes, cookies, cup cakes and pastries. Restaurant seats 100 to 150 patrons.
Number of Franchisees: 6 in New York, New Jersey and Pennsylvania.
In Business Since: 1976
Equity Capital Needed: $35,000 to $45,000. Total package $100,000 (does not include cost of land or building).
Financial Assistance Available: Provides assistance for lease purchase plan for equipment and furnishings. Provides complete plans for either free standing unit or renovated space.
Training Provided: All training conducted at company headquarters consists of 4-6 weeks of training, both classroom and on-the-job.
Managerial Assistance Available: A full support pre-opening program includes location search, lease negotiation, property purchase, etc. Continuous full support management assistance for the term of the franchise agreement, 20 years renewable.

COUNTRY KITCHEN INTERNATIONAL, INC.
7800 Metro Parkway
Minneapolis, Minnesota 55420
Otto B. Martinson, Jr., President and Chief and Chief Executive Officer

Description of Operation: Sit down service restaurant; family type, full-line menu offering home style cooked meals; modestly priced, 16-24 hour operation; high quality oriented; breakfast, lunch dinner, sandwiches, desserts and beverages.
Number of Franchisees: 336 in 29 States and 2 Provinces in Canada.
In Business Since: 1959
Equity Capital Needed: $50,000
Training Provided: Classroom and on-the-job training for up to 12 weeks, plus 2 weeks training during opening featuring complete manuals and audio visual training system.
Managerial Assistance Available: Supervision for the life of the contract, special menu service, programming advertising, purchasing programs, training up-dates, seminars, conventions, research and development, franchise committee meetings, and consulting service.

COZZOLI'S RESTAURANT - PIZZERIA
COZZOLI CORPORATION
1110 Brickell Avenue
Suite 606
Miami, Florida 33131
Merrill I. Lamb, President

Description of Operation: Full meal, sandwich shops, fast food take out units and pizza, fresh dough only. We now ship a complete equipment package for an individual to go into business anywhere in the world. Shopping centers and malls with major anchor, department stores preferred. Average seating is 70 and average annual volume is $350,000.
Number of Franchisees: 44 in New York, Florida, Texas and California.
In Business Since: 1951
Equity Capital Needed: $50,000 minimum
Financial Assistance Available: Complete financial assistance above the minimum amount.
Training Provided: 2 weeks in existing store and at least 1 week in his store under supervision. Training center is in Miami, Florida.
Managerial Assistance Available: We are available on any problem and as long as he wishes.

DAIRY CHEER STORES
2914 Forgey Street
Ashland, Kentucky 41101
W. H. Culbertson

Description of Operation: Fast food, sandwiches, chicken, fish, soup, beans, soft-serve and hard ice cream and serve yourself desserts, salad bar. Available for most states.
Number of Franchisees: 39
In Business Since: 1949
Financial Assistance Available: $5,000 franchise fee, building $70,000, equipment $55,000 and signs $16,000.
Financial Assistance Available: Local bankers are usually very helpful.
Training Provided: On-the-job training before and after opening.
Managerial Assistance Available: Instructions in technical operations, inspections, advertising, formulas and recipes.

DAIRY KING DISTRIBUTORS
1140 Yuma Street
Denver, Colorado 80204
Michael W. Kostic

Description of Operation: Fast food drive-in with carry-out, indoor seating, and drive-up window service. Featuring hamburgers, fries, specialty sandwiches, soft drinks, and a complete line of soft serve ice cream products with optional soft serve yogurt.
Number of Franchisees: 53 in 5 States. Operate in *Rocky Mountain Area* only.
In Business Since: 1948
Equity Capital Needed: Approximately $40,000 for equipment.
Financial Assistance Available: Up to 1/2 to qualified applicants on equipment. Nothing on land or buildings. Leasing also available. $2,000 service fee for feasibility study and complete layout and mechanical plans.
Training Provided: On-job and reinstallation training, advice on advertising, buying and accounting. Approximately 1 week.
Managerial Assistance Available: On-job-training only, 1-2 weeks.

DAIRY SWEET COMPANY
610 Southwest Des Moines Street
Ankeny, Iowa 50021
Virginia Klemm, President

Description of Operation: Fast food drive-in and carry-out restaurants featuring sandwiches, shrimp, chicken, soft drinks, and soft ice cream. Franchisee should have enough capital for down payment plus ground improvements, sewer, water and cement slab on which to set the building. We provide the building plans, and all the equipment. New 1980 phase includes eat-in area seating up to 75 people.
Number of Franchisees: 240 in 10 States
In Business Since: 1952
Equity Capital Needed: $25-$35,000 franchisee responsible for land and building financing.
Equity Capital Needed: Up to 75 percent financing to qualified applicant, or financing can be arranged for you.
Training Provided: On-the-job training at time of installation. Time depends on the individual and how much is necessary. Usually two days is sufficient.
Managerial Assistance Available: Continuous as long as franchisee is in business and wants assistance.

DANBI'S INC.
P. O. Box 4721
Shreveport, Louisiana 71104
Danny Faour, President

Description of Operation: Fast foods featuring pizza, Po-Boy's and salads.
Number of Franchisees: 15 in Louisiana, Texas, Kentucky, Alabama and New Mexico.
In Business Since: 1975
Equity Capital Needed: $50,000
Financial Assistance Available: None
Training Provided: 2 weeks at company-owned store.

Managerial Assistance Available: 2 days of managerial and technical assistance at opening with franchisee.

DANVER'S INTERNATIONAL, INC.
P. O. Box 41779
Memphis, Tennessee 38104
T. L. Berry, Director, Franchise Sales and Service

Description of Operation: Quality fast food restaurants featuring 1/3 pound hamburger; roast beef sandwiches, and 24 item salad bar.
Number of Franchisees: 33 in 10 States
In Business Since: 1973
Equity Capital Needed: $100,000
Equity Capital Needed: None
Financial Assistance Available: 12 week training program for owner and managers.
Managerial Assistance Available: Continuing support of franchise field team.

DER WIENERSCHNITZEL INTERNATIONAL, INC.
4440 Von Karman Avenue
Newport Beach, California 92660
Rick Donnelly, Franchise Director

Description of Operation: Fast food restaurant specializing in hot dogs and hamburgers. Drive thru service plus inside seating for 48 people.
Number of Franchisees: 350 in 22 States
In Business Since: 1961
Equity Capital Needed: $50,000-$150,000
Financial Assistance Available: None
Training Provided: 6 weeks of training provided.
Managerial Assistance Available: Continuous managerial assistance.

DINO'S PIZZA
2085 Inkster Road
Garden City, Michigan 48135
Michael Pacini, Franchise Director

Description of Operation: Restaurants, both carry-out and sit-down parolors, specializing in pizza, pasta and sandwiches.
Number of Franchisees: 140 units in Michigan, Florida, Ohio and Alabama.
In Business Since: 1961
Equity Capital Needed: Total investments depending upon unit between $50,000 and $90,000 with equity of one-third usually required, to range between $17,000 to $30,000.
Financial Assistance Available: Will assist in arranging financing.
Training Provided: Operations are required to attend the training program for a minimum of 300 hours which includes on-the-job training in designated units in Michigan and Florida. The training includes all phases of the business with continuing assistance to open the franchised unit.
Managerial Assistance Available: Franchise relations personnel are on call as needed and visit all locations on a regularly scheduled basis.

DOG N SUDS RESTAURANTS
Subsidiary of FROSTIE ENTERPRISES
1420 Crestmont Avenue
Camden, New Jersey 08101
Michael W. Fessler, Vice President

Description of Operation: Franchise company of drive-in and family sit-down restaurants, limited menu, specializing in a variety of hot dogs, hamburgers and special sandwiches.
Number of Franchisees: 130 in 14 States and Canada
In Business Since: 1953
Equity Capital Needed: $25,000 to $35,000. Franchisee responsible for land and building financing.
Financial Assistance Available: Direction for financial assistance is given.
Training Provided: Company training school called Rover College plus opening assistance by field service department.
Managerial Assistance Available: Continued assistance by field department.

DOMINO'S PIZZA, INC.
3853 Research Park Drive
Ann Arbor, Michigan 48104
Thomas S. Monaghan, Founder and President
David K. Kilby, Director of Franchising

Description of Operation: Domino's Pizza, Inc., is a rapidly expanding organization with pizza stores covering 28 states. Serving pizza and a cola beverage only, the stores, open 8½ hours daily, offer free delivery service, with emphasis on a 30-minute maximum delivery time. No inside seating, no alcoholic beverages. The building and general upkeep of the stores are inspected regularly by Domino's to insure its adherence to and maintenance of Domino's standards. Fifty percent growth is planned for 1980.
Number of Franchisees: 300 in 28 States
In Business Since: 1960
Equity Capital Needed: $9,500 franchise fee per unit. Total cost estimate, including franchise fee per unit. Total cost estimate, including franchise fee, falls in the range of $36,000-$64,300. Multiunit program available to investor groups. Exacting requirements including hands-on-management by one group member. $29,500 fee for five store package.
Financial Assistance Available: Suggestional consultation offered. Domino's provides no financing. Bank and lease sources available to qualified applicants.
Training Provided: Professional training school operates in Ann Arbor, Michigan which includes personal Assessment Interview, 70 hour Basic Management I/II classroom training, three week in-store training, and Advanced Management course. Trained personnel are provided for two weeks at opening of new unit in owner/operator units. Operations follow-up provided.
Managerial Assistance Available: Domino's keeps close ties with its franchisees and provides on-call assistance for the franchisee. Distributors, with jurisdiction over some large areas, keep communitcation lines open between the franchisees and the parent company through frequent correspondence, meetings, and a weekly newsletter.

Domino's respresentatives visit the shops regularly. In addition, Domino's offers assistance to its franchisees in the form of recommendations concerning personnel, equipment, and production activities. Commissary program is available in select markets which eliminates the "back room" food preparation.

DOUBLE DEE RESTAURANTS, INC.
14921 Ventura Boulevard
Suite 101
Sherman Oaks, California 91403
James W. Philbee, Secretary

Description of Operation: The Double Dee Restaurants, Inc. franchise system provides for the establishment of a fast food restaurant of approximately 1,650 square feet with adequate parking and access to premises. Normal operating hours vary from 10 to 14 hours per day. Seven days a week. Franchisee purchases equipment and franchise, but building and premises are provided under long term lease to owner/operator.
Number of Franchisees: 79 in 7 States
In Business Since: 1950
Equity Capital Needed: $15,000. Inventory, deposits, license, etc., would be additional, probably from $2,500 to $3,500.
Financial Assistance Available: The franchise and equipment investment will total from $35,500 to $39,500. Normal down payment of approximately 1/3 is applied to franchise and equipment. Financing for balance available from lending institutions if franchisees qualified.
Training Provided: Initial training of 1 to 2 weeks in presently operating Double Dee Restaurants store under qualified operator or area representative. Supervision of franchisee training at his own outlet of 1 week, with additional time for grand opening and its preparation, by qualified supervisor.
Managerial Assistance Available: Complete manual on store operation furnished. Supervisor assistance to establish bookkeeping records, provide advertising suggestions, store management and control.s Approximately once a month inspection and supervisory visits by area representative.

DRUMMER BOY FRIED CHICKEN
Division of VAN-ORR FOODS, INC.
2503 North Maple Avenue
Zanesville, Ohio 43701
R. T. Orr

Description of Operation: Fast food restaurants known as Drummer Boy Fried Chicken; to be constructed as either take home only units and/or inside dining units with seating for approximate 48 people. The menu consists primarily of fried chicken, served with various styles of potatoes, salads and selection of non-alcoholic beverages. Fish and sandwiches are also served.
Number of Franchisees: 5 in Ohio, West Virginia, Maryland, Delaware, and Florida.
In Business Since: 1969
Equity Capital Needed: Franchise fees, equipment and fixtures, land, building and lot preparation, inventory and working capital. Total approximately $235,000. Capital needs depend upon franchisee's financial position
Financial Assistance Available: None
Training Provided: Training mandatory to franchisee and all future management personnel. Currently a 2 week training course with in-depth curriculum covering operations manual, accounting procedures and in-store training.
Managerial Assistance Available: Site approval, construction blue prints and guidance, opening advertising package and continued advertising assistance, opening operation assistance and continued in unit support at least 4 times a year. Continued assistance from in house departments of operations, purchasing, advertising, construction, accounts, real estate and maintenance.

ETR, INC.
EL TACO RESTAURANTS
24001 Alicia Parkway Business Center
Suite 221
Mission Viejo, California 92675

Description of Operation: Mexican food drive thru restaurants - inside seating for 50 people. 20 percent of the business through the drive thru.
Number of Franchisees: 34 in 3 States
In Business Since: 1959
Equity Capital Needed: $64,000
Financial Assistance Available: None
Training Provided: 6 weeks in-store training.
Managerial Assistance Available: Supervision and weekly reports.

FAMOUS RECIPE FRIED CHICKEN, INC.
11315 Reed Hartman Highway
Suite 200
Cincinnati, Ohio 45241
Robert D. Acker, Director of Franchise Sales

Description of Operation: Famous Recipe Fried Chicken take-home and sit-down restaurants. Menu includes specially prepared fried chicken with hot butter tastin' biscuits, creamy mashed potatoes and gravy, fresh salads made daily in the units and other complementary items.
Number of Franchisees: 220 in 25 States and Trinidad, West Indies.
In Business Since: 1965
Equity Capital Needed: $60,000
Financial Assistance Available: The franchisor does not provide financial assistance. Franchisees with good credit ratings have been successful in obtaining financing for a substantial portion of the initial investment.
Training Provided: A 2 week formal training and management course is required for all new franchisees or their managers; and is conducted by qualified instructors at the franchisor's training facilities in Cincinnati, Ohio; plus 5 days of supervision and training at franchisee's location during initial start-up period.
Managerial Assistance Available: Famous Recipe provides standard building plans, advertising, operations and equipment manuals. Assistance in lease negotiations is also available. Quarterly visits by regional supervisors to assist in any problem areas. Advertising Division provides promotional and advertising materials and recommends

programs for local markets. Annual national convention is conducted for exchange of new ideas, food preparation methods, and promotional programs.

FARRELL'S ICE CREAM PARLOURS RESTAURANT
Division of MARRIOTT CORPORATION
Marriott Drive
Washington, D.C. 20058
James S. Brannan, Director of Franchise Development

Description of Operation: Farrell's is a Gay 90's style dining and ice cream parlour that also features candy and novelty items. Parlours may be located in malls or free standing buildings. Food and ice cream portions prepared for all size groups. Birthday parties encouraged and featured. Size of parlour is 4,700 square feet. Hours of operation are 11 am to 11 pm, Monday through Thursday and Sunday, 11 am to 1 am Friday and Saturday.
Number of Franchisees: 31 units located in 12 States - other areas are available.
In Business Since: 1963
Equity Capital Needed: $75,000 - $125,000
Equity Capital Needed: Franchisor will provide financing in the purchase of existing company-owned parlours; franchisor will not provide financing in developing new parlours.
Training Provided: A complete training program is provided - on-the-job training in an operating parlour, under the guidance of experienced supervisors.
Managerial Assistance Available: In addition to initial training, complete operations manuals and forms are provided. Staff and operations persons are available to assist franchisees.

FAST FOODS, INC.
JIFFY DRIVE-INS
P. O. Box 22054
Louisville, Kentucky 4022
Ralph W. Pettit, President

Description of Operation: Limited menu; sandwiches, seafood, breakfast a specialty. Open 7 days - 24 hours. Operation procedures and policy are standardized as are design and layout of building, counter stools and booths. A national franchise system styled Jiffy Drive-Ins, operation both company units and franchising to others.
Number of Franchisees: 4 in Kentucky and Wyoming.
In Business Since: 1953
Equity Capital Needed: $25,000
Financial Assistance Available: Financing available in local banks and selected national finance companies.
Training Provided: 2 week on-the-job intensive training in company stores and home office in all functions of operating the restaurant, inventory control, payroll procedure, and general accounting.
Managerial Assistance Available: The franchisee and/or manager must be under supervision of a company official throughout recruiting of restaurant employees, and 15 days after operations begins. Continued follow-up thereafter. Monthly S.O.P. inspections. Set up all food and paper suppliers. Negotiate and maintain price controls. Advertising and promotional guidance.

FAT BOY'S FRANCHISE SYSTEMS, INC.
1550 West King Street
Cocoa, Florida 32922
J. D. "Jay" Bradley, Public Relations Director

Description of Operation: Fat Boy's Bar-B-Q Franchise Systems offers franchisees the country's most successful barbeque restaurant business. The average restaurant serves breakfast, lunch and dinner based on a complete barbeque menu. Seating ranges from the 144 seat unit to the 196 seat restaurant.
Number of Franchisees: 59 in operation and 7 in construction in 6 Sates.
In Business Since: 1953
Equity Capital Needed: $50,000 minimum
Financial Assistance Available: Company will provide full bank and credit references to assist franchisee in obtaining his own outside financing.
Training Provided: Intensive "in-restaurant" training program. No prior restaurant experience necessary. Will completely train franchisee in operation of restaurant from cooking to purchasing to bookkeeping in an existing Fat Boy's. Training will continue until company and franchisee feel confident of franchisees readiness for success in opening his own restaurant.
Managerial Assistance Available: In addition to the complete program, company will send a start-up team to each grand opening to aid the franchisee in both the kitchen and floor areas. Bookkeeping service is provided if requested. Company continually assists in all aspects of operation from promotion thru menu pricing thru purchasing whenever franchisee experiences difficulty. All secret recipes and cooking knowledge is passed on to the franchisee. Quality control is maintained on a regular basis throughout the chain.

FORTY CARROTS, INC.
3961 MacArthur Boulevard
Newport Beach, California 92660
Joseph R. Bolker, President

Description of Operation: Healthy food restaurant with a warm natural setting, offering a menu of nutritious healthy salads, soups, sandwiches, carrot cake, fresh fruit juices, homemade cookies, muffins and quiche, as well as soft frozen yogurt with assorted toppings and smoothies. Also healthy hamburgers, dinners and brunch items. Plus healthy specialty squeezed alcoholic mixed drinks.
Number of Franchisees: 11 in New York, Virginia, Maryland, Colorado and California.
In Business Since: 1977
Equity Capital Needed: Depends on demographics of territory.
Financial Assistance Available: Franchisor does not provide finance program.
Training Provided: 2 weeks training at Carrot College plus 1 week in own store at opening.
Managerial Assistance Available: Initial - area feasibility study, site validation criteria. Marketing analysis, lease negotiations, architectural and design, contractors bid assistance. On-going - on-site analysis and evaluation of operation and personnel. Review and analysis of financial statements. Counseling as normally required.

FOSTERS FREEZE, INC.
1515 Chapala Street
Santa Barbara, California 93101
Sam Slater, Director of Marketing

Description of Operation: Franchisor of fast food and soft serve ice cream.
Number of Franchisees: 208 in California. Territorial or individual franchises available in California. Territorial franchises available elsewhere in the Continental United States.
In Business Since: 1947
Equity Capital Needed: Depending on demographics of territory.
Financial Assistance Available: None
Training Provided: Intensive training, both at the Home Office and on-the-job.
Managerial Assistance Available: Assistance in site selection and development. Continuing managerial and promotional assistance.

FRANCISCAN WEST INDUSTRIES
"LORD JIM'S PARLOUR"
2415 Annapolis Lane
Suite 111
Minneapolis, Minnesota 55441
Dale Erickson

Description of Operation: Franciscan West Industries offers a unique concept to the fast food industry "Lord Jim's Parlour." A European decor of an ice cream, pastry, pizza, omelets and sandwich shop. The sandwiches are gourmet world-wide sandwiches. The Parlour can be a free standing building or in-line in a shopping center. The units are located where there is heavy traffic and a large concentration of homes and apartments. Each location is 2,400 square feet plus, open 7 days a week. Franciscan West Industries will do site selection and negotiations of the ground, building or lease.
Number of Franchisees: 20 in 14 States
In Business Since: 1976
Equity Capital Needed: $35,000-$50,000
Financial Assistance Available: A total investment of $114,000 includes equipment and decor. The equipment package is approximately $39,000. Part financing available on equipment. Franchisee can arrange for outside financing.
Training Provided: Intensive 2 week mandatory training program. Additional training as needed.
Managerial Assistance Available: Computer accounting program available - Franciscan West Industries provides continued management and promotional service for duration of franchise control. Operations manual, business forms and instructions are provided. Continued marketing support.

FROSTOP CORPORATION
12 First Street
Pelham, New York 10803
J. J. Connolly, President

Description of Operation: Fast food drive-ins serving Frostop Root Beer and limited American fast food menu. Franchised Frostop Snack bars located in discount department stores. Remodeling kit available for remodeling of existing drive-ins or a free standing building such as a gasoline station.
Number of Franchisees: Over 250 contracts in 30 States.
In Business Since: 1926
Equity Capital Needed: Drive-ins $50,000 - Snack bars $25,000
Financial Assistance Available: Total investments vary according to land and building costs for drive-ins. Balances after down payments are financed by franchisee's local banks.
Training Provided: 2 weeks training in-store of franchisors selection. Operational manuals are provided.
Managerial Assistance Available: Frostop provides continual management service for the life of the franchise in such areas as menu, advertising, promotions. Complete manuals of operations, forms, and directions are provided. Frostop sponsors meetings of franchisees and conducts marketing and product research to maintain high Frostop consumer acceptance.

GEORGE WEBB CORPORATION
3540 North 126th Street
Brookfield, Wisconsin 53005
Betty Webb, President

Description of Operation: George Webb Restaurants—fast food counter and booth service. Occupies 1,600 square feet. Open 24 hours, 7 days. Serving breakfast, soups, sandwiches and quick lunches.
Number of Franchisees: 22 (52 units) in Wisconsin
In Business Since: 1948
Equity Capital Needed: $60,000 to $65,000
Financial Assistance Available: Total investment approximately $120,000. George Webb Corporation has financing available at franchisee's option, if credit references are satisfactory.
Training Provided: 14 days in a company unit plus 7 days in franchisee's unit.
Managerial Assistance Available: Daily for 30 days, weekly for 3 months, monthly for 6 months, bi-monthly for 3 months and 4 times a year for life. Emergency assistance whenever requested.

GOLDEN CHICKEN FRANCHISES
3810 West National Avenue
Milwaukee, Wisconsin 53215
Robert L. Bloom, President

Description of Operation: Fast food offering both carry outs and home delivery. Specializing in chicken, pizza and seafood. Open minimum of 6 days per week for 7 hours each day open. Each store requires approximately 800 square feet of space. Franchisee provides own space and equipment. Stores are located in store fronts and preferably strip shopping centers.
Number of Franchisees: 18 in Wisconsin and Minnesota.
In Business Since: 1959
Equity Capital Needed: $3,500 for franchise fee plus net cost for equipment and setup.

Financial Assistance Available: A total investment of approximately $20,000 is needed. Franchisor does no financing but will assist franchisee in securing sources. Primary source of financing has been leasing company. Franchisee puts up $5,000 for franchise fee, lease and security deposits and working capital. Balance usually financed over 60 month period.
Training Provided: Franchisee must spend 7 days at a company store. Franchisor spends 14 days with franchisee in his own unit after opening.
Managerial Assistance Available: Golden Chicken provides continual management service for the life of licensing agreement in such areas as bookkeeping, advertising and promotions. Franchisor visits stores a minimum of once a year, sponsors meetings of franchisees and keeps franchisee informed of new products and promotions via news letters.

GOLDEN SKILLET COMPANIES
2819 Parham Road
Richmond, Virginia 23229
Rob DelVerchio, Manager of Franchise Development

Description of Operation: Golden Skillet grants franchises for Golden Skillet Fried Chicken restaurants. Stores are free standing with modern design and victorian and country kitchen interior; 1,500 to 1,740 square foot building with a minimum of seating for 36 people; the majority of the business is carry out. Cooking process and Golden Skillet cooker is patented.
Number of Franchisees: Over 200 in 23 States, Canada, Japan and Puerto Rico.
In Business Since: 1963
Equity Capital Needed: Minimum cash including franchise fee if building, land, and equipment are leased - is approximately $27,000 plus a $10,000 franchise fee.
Financial Assistance Available: Equipment package including all signs, cash registers and seating is $61,000. Commercial Leasing Corporation, a Golden Skillet affiliate, can assist in arrangement of lease if licensee meets financial qualifications. Four percent royalties.
Training Provided: Golden Skillet franchise receive 9 days of intensive mandatory training in all aspects of the operation of a Golden Skillet franchise, including maintenance and accounting, additional back up training at the new store location.
Managerial Assistance Available: Golden Skillet provides a full range of support services to its franchisees. These include complete plans and specifications for buildings, signs, equipment, supplies, advertising materials, bookkeeping and record keeping systems, confidential operations manual and the ongoing attention of Golden Skillet supervisory and personnel.

THE GOODE TASTE CREPE SHOPPES, INC.
Box 2112
Steamboat Springs, Colorado 80477
John Keenan

Description of Operation: The Goode Taste Crepe Shoppes, Inc., is engaged in developing, licensing, and servicing a system of restaurants using the name "The Goode Taste Crepe Shoppe." The restaurants offer a varied breakfast, lunch, dinner and dessert menu, specializing in crepes and omelettes.
Number of Franchisees: 5 plus 1 company-owned in Colorado
In Business Since: 1974, franchising began in 1978
Equity Capital Needed: Franchise fee is $10,000. Minimum capital needed $50,000
Financial Assistance Available: Advice and counsel only.
Training Provided: The Goode Taste Crepe Shoppes, Inc., provides an intensive 2 week course to all new franchisees. The company also provides an opening staff to train franchisee employees at the franchised location.
Managerial Assistance Available: The Goode Taste Crepe Shoppes, Inc., continues with assistance in management and advertising, both at the franchisees location and through the home offices. The Goode Taste Crepe Shoppes, Inc., continues to help in upgrading product and marketing procedures.

GRANDMA LEE'S INTERNATIONAL HOLDINGS LIMITED
3258 Wharton Way
Mississauga, Ontario
L4X 2C4
Josef Meyer, President

Description of Operation: Grandma Lee's offers freshly baked quality bakery products, produced on-site, combined with an eating place, featuring soup and custom-made sandwiches. A store is ideally 2,000 square feet and is open 6 days a week from 7 until 7.
Number of Franchisees: 98 in New York, Montana, Canada and England
In Business Since: 1972
Equity Capital Needed: $50,000
Financial Assistance Available: None at this time.
Training Provided: Intensive mandatory 14 days training course is scheduled for all franchisees at company training store and school. On-site training of 5 days at franchise store under company employee supervision.
Managerial Assistance Available: Grandma Lee's provides continual management service for the life of the franchise in bakery, sandwich preparation, inventory control, accounting and advertising. Field staff are continuously supervising stores and company employees are available at all times to assist franchisees with their problems.

GREEK'S PIZZERIA, INC.
Box 189
7 North Jackson
Frankfort, Indiana 46041
A. C. Karamesines, President

Description of Operation: Old Tyme Tiffany decor with an open kitchen concept. Specialities are Neopolitan New York Style and Deep Dish Chicago Pan Pizzas, Calzone and Pastas. Carry out and delivery service available.
Number of Franchisees: 25 in Indiana and Texas
In Business Since: 1969
Equity Capital Needed: $15,000 minimum
Financial Assistance Available: An appropriate total investment of $77,500 is necessary to purchase a Greek's Pizzeria Turn-key operation. The down payment of $15,000 is usually the minimum amount required by local finance institutions.
Training Provided: Franchisee and 1 employee for a minimum period of 10 consecutive working days with an indepth, all inclusive mandatory course in the operation of a Greek's Pizzeria without cost except for travel and living expenses. This training will take place on the franchise premises or at a Greek's Pizzeria training center.
Managerial Assistance Available: Greek's Pizzeria offers professional assistance in marketing, real estate, construction, purchasing, advertising and accounting. Field consultants trained in restaurant operations continue valuable management assistance in advance training, restaurant operations cost control and other pertinent subjects as the need may arise. Corporate testing of new products and equipment in company stores by the Research, Development and Standards Department assure the highest quality throughout the system.

GREINERS SUBHOPS, INC.
9135 North Meridan Street
Suite A-1
C. Raymond Greiner, Sr., President
C. Raymond Greiner, Jr., Vice President

Description of Operation: Greiners Franchise Systems offers a unique retail eastern Sicilian style pizza. Each store approximately 1,500 square feet. Open 12 to 14 hours daily, 7-day week.
Number of Franchisees: 24 in Indiana
In Business Since: 1970
Equity Capital Needed: A total investment of $50,000-$80,000 is needed to open a franchised Greiners Submarine Sandwich Shop. Down payment of $17,000 is needed to cover franchise fee, security deposit and opening inventory. Balance can be handled through the banks and spread over a 5-year period.
Financial Assistance Available: Yes
Training Provided: 120 hours of an intensive mandatory training course is scheduled for all new franchisees and their personnel. The 120 hours training at the franchisees store under the supervision of an officer of the corporation.
Managerial Assistance Available: Greiners provides continual management service for the life of the franchise in such areas as bookkeeping, advertising and inventory control. Complete manuals of operations, forms, and directions are provided. Officers of the corporation are available and will work closely with franchisee. Regular visits to stores by officers will assist franchisee in solving problems.

GRIZZLY BEAR, INC.
P. O. Box 397
Ontario, Oregon 97914
Maureen Plaza, Franchise Director

Description of Operation: Grizzly Bear Pizza Parlors offer excellent food and friendly personal service in a unique early Western atmosphere. "Create your own" menus give an almost endless variety of pizzas and sandwiches. A self-service salad bar, as well as soups and assorted beverages complete the menu.
Number of Franchisees: 22 franchise and corporate stores in Oregon, Washington, Idaho and Utah. 3 units in Guatemala.
In Business Since: 1969
Equity Capital Needed: Minimum cash of $40,000 assuming land, building and equipment are leased. A net worth of $200,000 is recommended.
Financial Assistance Available: None, franchises are required to have an adequate net worth to obtain real estate and equipment financing on their own.
Training Provided: An in-depth training program for all new franchise owners and managers is mandatory. During a minimum 2 week training period, we cover such things as food, beverage, labor and overhead cost controls; planning and budgeting for your advertising and promotion programs; business management techniques, and daily operating procedures. All training is conducted at corporate headquarters and in a company owned Grizzly Bear, Inc. restaurant.
Managerial Assistance Available: Professional site location and customer profile research is conducted before a franchise sale is completed. Standard building and equipment spec are provided. Operational manuals are provided. Operational manuals are provided for all phases of Grizzly Bear, Inc., operations and standards, these are constantly up-dated. Audio-visual training aids for employee training as well as an opening team of highly qualified personnel and continued expert field supervision are some of the tools that are included in your franchise fee. Owners participate in constantly improving the Grizzly Bear concept through owner-management councils whose members are elected by the owners themselves. Quarterly owner meetings and the annual family convention further help you become acquainted and share ideas.

HAMBURGERS BY GOURMET LICENSE CORPORATION
2001 Kirby Drive
Houston, Texas 77019

Description of Operation: Hamburgers by Gourmet operates a regional chain of fast food restaurants specializing in char-broiled, quarter pound hamburgers. High quality and a unique variety of sandwiches are emphasized. The menu consists of 16 hamburger varieties made with assorted cheeses, sauces and condiments. The menu also includes chef salads, baked potatoes, home-made onion rings and beer. A breakfast menu is utilized in some locations.
Number of Franchisees: 6 in Texas, Oklahoma and Kansas
In Business Since: 1968
Equity Capital Needed: $45,000-$55,000 and financing ability.
Financial Assistance Available: None
Training Provided: Complete operational training provided at no cost to the licensee. Minimum of 2 weeks training required in all aspects of the operation including classroom and on-the-job instruction. Refresher training and improvement available upon request as needed.
Managerial Assistance Available: Licensor provides opening supervision and assistance, building plans, equipment layout, operational techniques, training, manual of operations, accounting procedures and formats, advertising materials and suggestions. Field personnel and home office personnel are available for assistance when needed. Frequent visits to the licensed units are made to assist and counsel.

HAPPY JOE'S PIZZA & ICE CREAM PARLORS
1875 Middle Road
Bettendorf, Iowa 52722
James K. Orr. President

Description of Operation: Happy Joe's Pizza & Ice Cream Parlors are decorated in an old fashioned turn of the century motif and feature superb pizza and premium quality ice cream creations. Family appeal is emphasized with birthday party celebrations a house specialty.
Number of Franchisees: 138 in 18 States
In Business Since: 1972
Equity Capital Needed: $80,000
Financial Assistance Available: None
Training Provided: Extensive on-the-job training including all facets of the operation lasting up to 30 days.
Managerial Assistance Available: Complete assistance and supervision in opening the business and an on-going program of managerial and operational training and assistance from field supervisors. Additional assistance in advertising and promotion is also available.

THE HAPPY STEAK, INC.
2246 East Date Avenue
Fresno, California 93706
H. T. Brooks, President
Description of Operation: Family-type steak house.
Number of Franchisees: 36 in California
In Business Since: 1969
Equity Capital Needed: Approximately $55,000
Financial Assistance Available: When required company guarantees are provided. Personal notes for franchise are accepted.
Training Provided: Complete in-company operated restaurants for approximately 3 weeks.
Managerial Assistance Available: Operations officer oversees the first 2 full weeks of operation under the franchisee.

HARBOR HOUSE, INC.
110 North Rochester Road
Clawson, Michigan 48017
James E. Williams, President
Description of Operation: Full service family restaurants, all-you-can-eat table service concept.
Number of Franchisees: 3 in Michigan and Ohio
In Business Since: 1978
Equity Capital Needed: $200,000
Financial Assistance Available: None
Training Provided: 4 week manager training in corporate restaurant. 2 week opening assistance including cadre staff.
Managerial Assistance Available: Inspection and advice during term of the franchise agreement. Cooperative purchasing available. Regular meetings with managers of other franchises and company stores. Forms, training, program available.

HARDEE'S FOOD SYSTEMS, INC.
P. O. Box 1619
1233 North Church Street
Rocky Mount, North Carolina 27801
Donald R. Mucci, Vice President-Franchise Development
Description of Operation: Fast Food limited menu restaurant.
Number of Franchisees: 1,250 in 35 States, Japan and Central America
In Business Since: 1962
Equity Capital Needed: $140,000 plus land and building
Financial Assistance Available: No financial assistance available. Require licensee to finance land, building, equipment, working capital and license fee.
Training Provided: 4 weeks training in field and one at home office. Recommended in restaurant training prior to school attendance. Ten days training and supervision at restaurant upon opening.
Managerial Assistance Available: Hardee's provides continued supervision on a scheduled basis and also provides bookkeeping methods, advertising direction, operating controls, complete operating manual, basic forms, continued advice and counseling.

HARTZ KRISPY CHICKEN
16630 Imperial Valley Drive
Suite 201
Houston, Texas 77060
W. L. Hartzog, President
Joel Jessee, Vice President
Description of Operation: Hartz Krispy Chicken is a fast food operation maintaining excellence of quality and providing the utmost in customer service. Krispy fried chicken and delicious chicken 'n dumplings are the main menu items. Side orders include potato salad, cole slaw, french fries, and corn on the cob. All food is served in an Early American atmosphere or may be taken out.
Number of Franchisees: 10 in Texas and Mississippi
In Business Since: 1972
Equity Capital Needed: $30,000, not including land and building. Acquisition of real estate is a franchisee responsibility.
Financial Assistance Available: Hartz Krispy Chicken provides guidelines for excellence and an atmosphere for performance, but it is not in the banking business. Hartz will assist in obtaining, but will not provide, financial assistance. Regardless, a prospective franchise should have cash or credit of about $75,000 for equipment.
Training Provided: Hartz requires at least 100 hours training at the franchisee's expense. Training facilities are provided by Hartz in Houston, Texas. Assistance and guidance, but not labor, is supplied during pre-opening stages.
Managerial Assistance Available: Hartz personnel continuously inspects and oversees franchise stores in order to maintain uniformity and quality. Discourse and correspondence is maintained with franchisees on a daily basis.

HOWARD JOHNSON COMPANY
220 Forbes Road
Braintree, Massachusetts 02184
Burton Sack, Group Vice President, Corporate Development and Real Estate
Description of Operation: Howard Johnson's Restaurants - full service restaurants; Ground Round - informal limited menu with a turn of the century atmosphere; Red Coach Grill - basically a high quality steak and seafood house.
Number of Franchisees: Howard Johnson's Restaurants (250), Ground Round (17) and Red Coach Grill (9) in 42 States, Puerto Rico and Canada.
In Business Since: 1925
Equity Capital Needed: Varies with franchise - cost of construction or lease, (minimum $200,00).
Financial Assistance Available: None
Training Provided: Opening staff - on-the-job training for service personnel. Supervisory personnel available at all times.
Managerial Assistance Available: Varies plus geographic training programs.

HUDDLE HOUSE, INC.
2947 East Ponce de Leon Avenue
Decatur, Georgia 30030
Charles Crowder, Vice President
Description of Operation: Twenty-four hour convenience restaurant serving breakfast, steaks, seafood items and sandwiches.
Number of Franchisees: 52 franchisees (72 units) in 6 States
In Business Since: 1964
Equity Capital Needed: $20,000 franchise licensing fee and $12,000 operating capital.
Financial Assistance Available: None
Training Provided: Orientation; 2 weeks at training units. Two weeks in-store training at their new unit.
Managerial Assistance Available: Training, continuous supervision, commissary food purchasing, restaurant equipment and supplies, operation manuals, daily accounting forms. District supervisors work closely with owner/operators to solve problems and promote profits.

HUNGRY HERO SYSTEMS, INC.
16 Church Street
Greenwich, Connecticut 06830
David G. Loeb, Vice President, Franchise Development
Description of Operation: Limited menu, fast food specializing in Hero sandwiches and hot plates, on premises services, delivery, take out service and catering. Area franchises also available.
Number of Franchisees: 6 in New York
In Business Since: 1976
Equity Capital Needed: $25,000
Equity Capital Needed: Total investment approximately $49,500. Cash required $25,000, balance may be financed for qualified applicants.
Training Provided: Full company training in all aspects of the operation. Turn key service provided by home office which includes site and lease assistance, equipment, construction, training, employee recruitment and grand opening promotion.
Managerial Assistance Available: Continuing management assistance in all phases of operation.

THE HUSH PUPPY CORPORATION
P. O. Box 1305
Texarkana, Arkansas 75501
David T. Smith, Executive Vice President
Description of Operation: The Hush Puppy is a full service fast food limited menu restaurant. We specialize in catfish dinners with all the trimmings.
Number of Franchisees: 18 in 8 States
In Business Since: 1972
Equity Capital Needed: Dependent on the requirements of the lending institution.
Financial Assistance Available: Franchisee must arrange own outside financing.
Training Provided: 60 days of on-the-job training at an existing Hush Puppy Restaurant.
Managerial Assistance Available: Continuous management and technical assistance for the life of the franchise in such areas as bookkeeping, menu pricing, cost of sales, inventory control. Operations manuals, forms and directions are provided.

INTERNATIONAL BLIMPIE CORPORATION
1414 Avenue of the Americas, 15th Floor
New York, New York 10019
Chuck Leaness, Franchise Director
Description of Operation: Limited menu operation featuring specialty sandwiches (Blimpie) with taste and marketing concepts. No cooking, eat-in, take-out and driving.
Number of Franchisees: 121 in 22 States
In Business Since: 1964
Equity Capital Needed: $35,000
Financial Assistance Available: Total investment ranges $80,000-$90,000 balance is financed over 5-years arranged by parent company
Training Provided: Comprehensive 2 week program training, coverage as needed during the first few weeks in business.
Managerial Assistance Available: Continual visits by area consultant.

INTERNATIONAL CHAR BROILER, INC.
875 Southeast Third Street
Bend, Oregon 97701
Garrett Rice, President
Description of Operation: International Char Broiler has put together a unique and appealing concept to the world of fast food restaurants. Incorporated in our image is the visual attraction of watching hamburgers sizzling over an open flame and a pleasing atmosphere of warmth and friendliness. The corporation has derived a successful system for satisfying the demands of the fast food customer while competing profitably in the fast food world. Also franchising a new concept called Cattlemen's Depot.

55

Number of Franchisees: 10 in California, Arizona and Oregon
In Business Since: 1978
Equity Capital Needed: $20,000 franchise fee
Financial Assistance Available: None
Training Provided: The franchisor shall make available a specialized mandatory training program of approximately 4 week's duration. The training program will include on-the-job training for all food preparation and service job functions, completion of administrative tasks and study of the operational manual. Franchisor will provide training personnel prior to and during the opening of the restaurant. The franchisor will assist in the "count-down" schedule to effect an orderly and efficient opening for business.
Managerial Assistance Available: The franchisor will assist the franchisee in the selection of the site location by giving counsel and advice relating to site selection and use. If the franchisee desires additional assistance in any management or operational problem, arrangements may be made with franchisor to furnish a qualified consultant. Also, in area seminars are conducted from time to time for restaurant managers.

INTERNATIONAL DAIRY QUEEN, INC.
P. O. Box 35286
Minneapolis, Minnesota 55435
B. V. Bloom, Director - New Store Development

Description of Operation: International Dairy Queen, Inc., is engaged in developing, licensing and servicing a system of franchised retail stores which offer a selected menu of soft dairy products, hamburgers and beverages marketed under "Dairy Queen," "Brazier" and "Mr. Misty" trademark.
Number of Franchisees: There are currently 4,844 "Dairy Queen" and "Dairy Queen/Brazier" stores located in all 50 States and eight foreign countries.
In Business Since: The soft serve dairy product was first offered to the public in 1938 with the first "Dairy Queen" store being opening in 1940. In 1962 certain territorial operators formed International Dairy Queen, Inc., by contributing their respective "Dairy Queen" territorial franchise rights.
Equity Capital Needed: The franchise fees are $20,000 for plan "A" and $13,000 for plan "B". All prospective franchisees must meet certain financial requirements.
Financial Assistance Available: International Dairy Queen, Inc., offers franchisees an opportunity to lease equipment from the company for a period of 5 to 7 years with a security deposit. Qualified franchisees may also purchase equipment on a conditional sales contract over a 5 year payment period with the required down payment.
Training Provided: International Dairy Queen, Inc.'s National Training Center in Minneapolis, Minnesota offers an intensive 2 week training course to all new and existing franchisees. The course covers sanitation, sales promotion, inventory control and basic functions of management. The company also offers new franchisees the services of a special opening team that assists operators in opening their new "Dairy Queen" or "Dairy Queen/Brazier" store.
Managerial Assistance Available: International Dairy Queen, Inc., maintains an operations specialty division in addition to regional and district managers, who provide continuing assistance involving store operation, product quality, customer convenience, product development, advertising, financial control, training, communication and incentives. A research and development department is engaged in developing new products, cooking methods and procedures. Sales promotion programs are conducted through newspapers, radio, television and billboards.

THE ITALIAN U-BOAT, INC.
679 West North Avenue
Elmhurst, Illinois 60126
Jeff Murphy, Director of Franchising

Description of Operation: The Italian U-Boat is a Deli-Sandwich Shop operation, specializing in submarines. There are 3 facets within the concept, a wide variety of sandwiches (eat in or take out), deli ("By the pound") and catering (party trays and 3', 4', 5', 6' submarines). Stores are open 7 days a week. The U-Boat carries a full line of top quality lunchmeats and cheeses (brands such as Dubuque, Eckrich, Norwestern, and Borden's), salads, chips, and various dessert items.
Number of Franchisees: 24 in Illinois
In Business Since: 1977
Equity Capital Needed: Begins at $15,000
Financial Assistance Available: An average total investment in a remodeled pre-existing structure is approximately $70,000. Financing assistance is available although not directly from the Italian U-Boat, Inc.
Training Provided: Complete 4 week training course. Two weeks in our training store and classroom for owners and/or managers, and two weeks in franchisee's unit after opening.
Managerial Assistance Available: The Italian U-Boat maintains an extensive field supervisory staff which is available to assist its franchisees in areas, such as inventory control, labor control, advertising, etc. An Operations Manual along with all forms are provided to the units. Monthly meetings with the franchisees are conducted to discuss any new products and/or procedures, along with guest speakers on a number of U-Boat related topics.

ITALO'S PIZZA SHOP, INC.
3560 Middlebranch Road, N.E.
Canton, Ohio 44705
Italo P. Ventura

Description of Operation: Italo's Pizza franchise is designed for the small investors or people who desire extra income besides their regular job. Any store over 900 square feet can be turned into a profit making operation.
Number of Franchisees: 15 in Ohio and California.
In Business Since: 1966, franchising since 1975
Equity Capital Needed: $9,000
Financial Assistance Available: A total investment of $45,000 for carry-out only and about $60,000 with dining room. Franchisee must provide outside financing.
Training Provided: Intensive 2 months on-the-job training in our main location, 2 cause weeks of assistance at the time of opening, and continuing assistance as needed.
Managerial Assistance Available: Italo's Pizza provides continual assistance and recommendations in any area. Forms and manuals are provided for the smooth performance of the business. Weekly or monthly visits by franchisor to help solve any problem and continued assistance by phone for any emergency.

JAKE'S INTERNATIONAL, INC.
1204 Carnegie Street
Rolling Meadows, Illinois 60008
David F. Denten, Executive Operations Manager

Description of Operation: Jake's International is a franchised pizza operation. Emphasis is on high quality food, cleanliness and efficient service in the carry out and delivery food industry. Pub type operations with full dining rooms and cocktail lounges are also available.
Number of Franchisees: 29 in Illinois
In Business Since: 1962
Equity Capital Needed: $25,000 minimum and the ability to acquire financing.
Financial Assistance Available: Equipment leasing if elected by the franchisee and if qualified.
Training Provided: Minimum of 200 hours in actual operations. Additional management training is provided on-the-job and throughout the duration of the franchise.
Managerial Assistance Available: Training, operations management, on-site field consulting and quality control assistance and makes available promotional advertising material. Access to central commissary, if desired.

JAPANESE STEAK HOUSES, INC.
The Maritimes C-22
2051 Northeast Ocean Boulevard
Stuart, Florida 33494
David H. Nelson, President

Description of Operation: Own, operate and franchise by licensee's of Japanese Steak House restaurants. The steak houses fit into a free standing building to suit or lease back situations, shopping centers, hotels and resorts.
Number of Franchisees: 24 in 8 States, South Africa and England.
In Business Since: 1962
Equity Capital Needed: Varies between $25,000 to $50,000 depending on marketing area.
Financial Assistance Available: Lease financing, available, if qualified.
Training Provided: Extensive training provided.
Managerial Assistance Available: Continuous training in managerial and technical assistance.

JERRY'S RESTAURANTS
JERRICO, INC.
P. O. Box 11988
Lexington, Kentucky 40579
Ernie Renaud, Executive Vice President

Description of Operation: Coffee shops and dining room operations. Family oriented, informal. Located in cities over 10,000. Interstate locations and in conjunction with motels. We will franchise on a selected basis and limited areas.
Number of Franchisees: 70 in Kentucky, Tennessee, Ohio, Indiana, and Florida
In Business Since: 1929
Equity Capital Needed: $100,000
Financial Assistance Available: None
Training Provided: Complete training course for management. Opening assistance in the form of traveling supervisory crew.
Managerial Assistance Available: Continued supervision program through field consultants.

JIFFY JOINTS, INC.
216 Capital National Bank Building
Austin, Texas 78701
Curtiss Ryan, President

Description of Operation: A specialty hot dog stand franchise featuring Jiffy Franks the "burpless" hot dog served in a special bun with a toasted hole in it to prevent the usual mess of eating a hot dog. Jiffy Franks were developed in 1971 and previously were sold only through theaters in the Southwest. The product leaves no after taste, does not cause indigestion or heartburn and does not shrink or shrivel when heated.
Number of Franchisees: 3 in Texas
In Business Since: 1978
Equity Capital Needed: $10,000-$25,000
Financial Assistance Available: Equipment package financing available. Also, $5,000 franchise fee financing available. Assistance in site selection.
Training Provided: 1 week supervised training. Inventory control, daily reports, and continuous operations assistance.
Managerial Assistance Available: Certified Public Accountant monthly profit and loss statements prepared at cost to franchisees. Continuous point of sale material and advertising promotions coordinated from the franchisor.

STANLEY FOODS AND EQUIPMENT COMPANY, INC.
dba JIFFY SHOPPES
8545 Ashwood Drive
Capitol Heights, Maryland 20027

Description of Operation: Jiffy Shoppes, offers a unique retail store operation. Each store is approximately 1,800 square feet with ample store front parking and open 12 to 14 hours daily, 7 days a week. Jiffy Shoppes offer a complete line of subs and pizzas, featuring 44 varieties. Convenient for dine in and carry out.
Number of Franchisees: 9 in Maryland
In Business Since: 1959
Equity Capital Needed: $45,000 to $50,000
Financial Assistance Available: Will assist each in all facets of financing and in some cases, will finance it ourselves.
Training Provided: 3 week intensive management training in one of company operated stores, 2 to 4 weeks training in franchisee's own store.
Managerial Assistance Available: Continued assistance throughout term of franchise with periodic inspections and meetings with franchisee on monthly basis and/or special retraining programs.

JRECK SUBS, INC.
531 Washington Street
Watertown, New York 13601
Charles Lehman, President

Description of Operation: Sit down and carry-out of submarine sandwiches in all stores. Stores vary in size depending on the area.
Number of Franchisees: 25 in New York and 3 in Ohio
In Business Since: 1967
Equity Capital Needed: $15,000
Financial Assistance Available: Securing outside financing in an advisory roll.
Training Provided: 3 weeks of intensive in-store training; including sandwich preparation, store management, bookkeeping, personnel, and operational procedures.
Managerial Assistance Available: Marketing, advertising assistance, operational, on a continuous assistance basis.

JUDY'S FOODS, INC.
6213 Charlotte Avenue
Nashville, Tennessee 37209
A. Thomas Mulle, Franchise Director

Description of Operation: Fast food restaurant, limited menu of hamburgers, shakes, chili, French fries and hot fruit pies, salads with dining room and drive-thru service window.
Number of Franchisees: 32 in 17 States
In Business Since: 1976
Equity Capital Needed: "Variable: $10,000 initial franchise fee, land, building and equipment must be financed by franchisee."
Financial Assistance Available: None
Training Provided: Up to 4 weeks in training school.
Managerial Assistance Available: 4 week training school. Continual assistance by our representatives to assist franchisee. Provide managerial assistance at opening. We provide a complete technical operations manual. We offer assistance in advertising, TV, radio and newspaper ads. Technical and operations bulletin issued monthly.

KENNEY'S FRANCHISE CORP.
1602 Midland Road
Salem, Virginia 24153
Eilliam Kenney, President

Description of Operation: Fast Food. Hamburgers, pressure fried chicken and other related food items.
Number of Franchisees: 4 in Virginia, West Virginia and Florida.
In Business Since: 1958
Equity Capital Needed: $10,000 franchise fee, $70,000 equipment and $10,000 working capital.
Financial Assistance Available: Not at this time
Training Provided: 2 week - total operation. Assistance by key personnel on opening.
Managerial Assistance Available: 2 week training at home office. Supervision for 1 week. Thereafter one visit per month or more often if required.

KEN'S PIZZA PARLORS, INC.
4441 South 72nd East Avenue
Tulsa, Oklahoma 74145
Michael E. Bartlett, Vice President

Description of Operation: The Ken's Pizza Parlor concept entails an integrated system utilizing an attractive free-standing building with a drive-thru window, a unique limited menu and a simplified operating concept. Taken all together, the system combines a profitable menu with comfortable table service format.
Number of Franchisees: 26 - A total of 166 locations (62 company-owned) in 14 States
In Business Since: 1961
Equity Capital Needed: Initial franchise fee -$10,000. Land, building and equipment must be financed by franchisee.
Financial Assistance Available: None
Training Provided: Training program provided in Tulsa, Oklahoma training store. Program is extensive and follows a formal "management training" manual. Time required varies between 4-12 weeks depending upon capabilities and previous experience of licensee.
Managerial Assistance Available: 3 full-time employees travel among franchise stores offering operational assistance, further training and inspections. Company regularly conducts new product and training seminars in its Tulsa facilities. All franchisees are invited to these seminars. Company also provides confidential training manual.

KFC CORPORATION
P. O. Box 32070
Louisville, Kentucky 40232
Rebecca Enders, Manager, Franchising Department

Description of Operation: Sale of Colonel Sanders' Kentucky Fried Chicken and related products.
Number of Franchisees: 720 in all States except Montana, Utah, and Florida.
In Business Since: March 1964 (purchase of Kentucky Fried Chicken, Inc., which was begun in 1952 by Colonel Harland Sanders.)
Equity Capital Needed: Variable, $4,000 initial franchise fee. Land, building and equipment must be financed by franchisee.
Financial Assistance Available: None
Training Provided: Required of all new franchisees and recommended for key employees - 12 day training seminar covering proper store operation including management, accounting, sales, advertising, catering and purchasing. Ongoing training provided in areas of customer service, general restaurant management and quality control. Also available - sales hostess instruction and seminars for instruction on specific KFC programs and equipment such as the automatic cooker. Franchisees are also provided with confidential operating manual.
Managerial Assistance Available: Engineering assistance regarding best suited building, blueprints, recommended floor plan lay-out, placement of selected equipment - field services assistance including store opening, periodic visits to assist in matters dealing with daily store operation, quality control standards - corporation offers regional and local seminars and workshops.

LAROSA'S INC.
2411 Boudinot
Cincinnati, Ohio 45238
Stewart A. Smetts, Franchise Director

Description of Operation: A full service, full menu. Italian style family restaurant especially known for pizzas. Most locations offer beer and wine.
Number of Franchisees: 40 in Ohio and Kentucky
In Business Since: 1954 - franchising began in 1967
Equity Capital Needed: $35,000
Financial Assistance Available: Prospective franchise owner must secure own financing.
Training Provided: Mandatory training for franchise owner in a corporate facility. Management and supervisory personnel to be trained in corporate facility at franchisees expense - duration of training depends on the experiences and capabilities of the personnel.
Managerial Assistance Available: An opening supervisory crew trains employees for 1 week prior to opening and stays approximately two weeks after opening. After the first 6 months, franchise operations personnel spend a day at all locations approximately once every 30 days.

LITTLE CAESAR ENTERPRISES, INC.
38700 Grand River Avenue
Farmington Hills, Michigan 48024
Robert Massey, Franchise Director

Description of Operation: Pizza carry-out stores, pizza parlors and a family restaurants. A fast food restaurant, featuring pizza and other Italian foods.
Number of Franchisees: 174 in Michigan, Ohio, Florida, North Carolina and Illinois.
In Business Since: 1959
Equity Capital Needed: $25,000 - $100,000 depending on type of operation
Financial Assistance Available: None
Training Provided: We have a management training center which encompasses on-the-job training.
Managerial Assistance Available: Operations, real estate/construction, accounting.

LIL' DUFFER OF AMERICA, INC.
2208 Hancock Street
Bellevue, Nebraska 68005

Description of Operation: Fast food drive-in restaurants.
Number of Franchisees: 18 in Iowa, Nebraska, South Dakota, Kansas and Missouri
In Business Since: 1966
Equity Capital Needed: Parent company assists franchisee in arranging needed financial assistance.
Training Provided: Franchisee is trained at his own expense for a minimum of 2 weeks in an existing Lil' Duffer store prior to opening his own new store. Company supervisors assist him in training his personnel prior to and during the opening of his store. Field supervisors give continuing assistance as long as a "License Agreement" is in effect.
Managerial Assistance Available: Regular visits by field supervisors. Advertising program, accounting system, management training provided by home office throughout the operations of the business. Advice and consultation with home office available on request.

LITTLE BIG MEN, INC.
2401 Montana Avenue
Suite 201
Billings, Montana 59101
Roger L. Howell, President

Description of Operation: Pizza restaurant chain emphasizing relaxed family dining. Units are approximately 3,500 square feet and seat 100-150 people.
Number of Franchisees: 11 operating 17 units in Montana, Wyoming, Idaho, South Dakota and Colorado.
In Business Since: 1972
Equity Capital Needed: $50,000 cash with a net worth of approximately $250,000
Financial Assistance Available: Financing presentation aid only.
Training Provided: An intensive 2 week training course if offered to each franchisee and/or their manager candidates prior to each unit's opening. In addition, a training group is provided at each opening to supervise the training of the unit's crew members. The training group is made up of the training director and at least one other qualified training assistant.
Managerial Assistance Available: Little Big Men provides continual management assistance in areas such as cost analysis and inventory control, menu mix, bookkeeping, advertising, and all related marketing areas including service and promotional analysis. Complete manuals are furnished for operations and accounting as well as support manuals for managers and employees, field consultants visit each unit every 60 days to determine problem areas and to assist in problem solving. Little Big Men also sponsors meetings of franchisees on semi-annual basis.

LITTLEFIELD'S RESTAURANT CORPORATION
301 East Cook Street
Suite E
Santa Maria, California 93454
William Lowe, Franchise Director

Description of Operation: Littlefield's Restaurant Corporation offers unique fast service restaurant operation featuring bar-b-que and deli foods. Each store is approximately 3,250 square feet with ample store-front park and open 12 to 14 hours daily 7 days a week.
Number of Franchisees: 20 in 7 States
In Business Since: 1971 (franchising since 1978)
Equity Capital Needed: $65,000 to $100,000 (franchise fee is $40,000).
Financial Assistance Available: Some assistance in securing build-to-suit property in some areas.
Training Provided: Extensive, 4 week program including 2 weeks in franchisees own outlet with experienced Littlefield's personnel. A 265 page training manual is included.
Managerial Assistance Available: Littlefield's Restaurant Corporation provides continual management service for the life of the franchise in such areas as bookkeeping,

advertising, inventory control. Complete manuals of operations, forms, and directions are provided. District and field managers are available in all regions to work closely with franchisees and visit stores regularly to assist solving problems. Littlefield's Restaurant Corporation sponsors meetings of franchisees and conducts marketing and product research to maintain high Littlefield's Restaurant Corporation consumer acceptance.

G-B-L CORPORATION
Franchisor of THE LITTLE KING
11811 "I" Street
Omaha, Nebraska 68137
Sid Wertheim, President
Description of Operation: G-B-L Corporation and The Little King of Omaha operate and direct a successful chain of submarine sandwich restaurants. Emphasis is on high quality food, freshly prepared in an atmosphere of efficient service and cleanliness.
Number of Franchisees: 10 in 6 States
In Business Since: 1968
Equity Capital Needed: Limited
Financial Assistance Available: 2 week course covering basic operational techniques, managerial methods, and business procedures conducted at headquarters in Omaha, Nebraska. Additional 2 week on-site training and supervision by field representative when location begins business.
Managerial Assistance Available: Regular field representative consultation and assistance. Company makes available promotional advertising material. Each facet of operation supported by detailed manuals.

LONDON FISH N' CHIPS, LTD.
306 South Maple Avenue
South San Francisco, California 94080
Description of Operation: Fast food service for both eat in and take out.
Number of Franchisees: 16 in California
In Business Since: 1967
Equity Capital Needed: $45,000 to $55,000
Financial Assistance Available: None
Training Provided: In shop training and in company shop training. Direct supervision in franchisee shop as needed.
Managerial Assistance Available: Help with bookkeeping. Advise on new methods and products and selling procedures for duration of franchise. Provide periodic inspection and instruction as needed.

LONG JOHN SILVER'S, INC.
JERRICO, INC.
P. O. Box 11988
Lexington, Kentucky 40579
Eugene O. Getchell, Vice President, Franchising
Description of Operation: Fast food restaurants-self-service-carry out or seating in a wharf-like atmosphere. Menu includes fish and fryes, shrimp, clams, oysters, chicken, hush puppies, cole slaw, dessert, a variety of hot and cold beverages, plus draft beer where legal and desired.
Number of Franchisees: 500 franchised plus 500 company-owned.
In Business Since: Founder started in 1929. Parent company, Jerrico, Inc., incorporated in 1946.
Equity Capital Needed: Varies. Contact company for full information.
Financial Assistance Available: None: Franchisees required to have adequate net worth to obtain real estate and equipment on their own.
Training Provided: 7 weeks formal training course for management.
Managerial Assistance Available: Continuous training and supervison program in all phases of management through training academy, field supervisors and home office personnel.

LORDBURGER SYSTEMS, INC.
3690 Orange Place
Suite 521
Beachwood, Ohio 44122
Louis A. Frangos, Executive Vice President
Description of Operation: Lordburger Systems, Inc., owns/operates and directs a successful chain of fast service family restaurants, serving a moderately priced menu. Emphasis is placed on quick, efficient service, high quality food and superior cleanliness standards. Menus consist of Lordburger's famous ground round hamburger. Hamburgers, cheeseburgers, fish sandwiches, ham & cheese sandwiches, French fries, shakes, ice cream sundaes, extended breakfast menu and assorted hot and cold beverages.
Number of Franchisees: 24 in Ohio.
In Business Since: 1971.
Equity Capital Needed: $85,000 to $95,000 and the ability to obtain financing for $110,000 minimum.
Training Provided: Lordburger provides a through comprehensive 300 hour, on-the-job, training program. This 300 hours is comprised of an orientation 2 week basic operations course, and 2 weeks of additional advanced management training course at the Lordburger Training Center, the balance of training is conducted in a Lordburger Restaurant.
Managerial Assistance Available: Lordburger Systems, Inc., provides operations, training, maintenance, and equipment manuals. Also provided are personnel management, quality control and purchasing programs. In addition, the company makes available promotional advertising and marketing materials, plus field operations representative for consultation and operational assistance.

LOSURDO FOODS, INC.
20 Owens Road
Hackensack, New Jersey 07601
Michael Losurdo, President
Description of Operation: Italian restaurant with accent on pizza.
Number of Franchisees: 10 in New York, New Jersey, Pennsylvania, North Carolina and Florida.
Equity Capital Needed: $25,000.

Financial Assistance Available: None.
Training Provided: 2 week training period plus regular monthly training session.
Managerial Assistance Available: Continual assistance in product preparation and advertising assistance.

LOVE'S WOOD PIT BARBEQUE RESTAURANTS
6837 Lankershim Boulevard
North Hollywood, California 91605
Bob R. Leonard, Vice President - Franchise Operations
Description of Operation: Complete full service barbeque restaurant featuring zesty barbequed ribs, beef, pork and chicken. Love's is a medium priced lunch and dinner house located in the Western United States. Love's restaurants are open for lunch, dinner and late evening suppers — most offering cocktail lounge service.
Number of Franchisees: 31 in Arizona, California, Colorado, Oregon, Washington (new units restricted to Southern California).
In Business Since: 1948.
Equity Capital Needed: $60,000 franchise fee plus financing of land, build and equipment.
Financial Assistance Available: None
Training Provided: 4 weeks classroom and on-the-job instruction.
Managerial Assistance Available: Franchisor provides opening supervision, assists in hiring of personnel plus regular visits and assistance from field coordinators. Complete manual of operations specifies how each menu item is prepared and served, how the business may be operated effectively.

LUM'S RESTAURANT CORPORATION
8410 Northwest 53rd Terrace
Suite 200
Miami, Florida 33166
Roy S. Lemaire, President
Description of Operation: Family restaurant with waitress, and carry-out service. Limited variety menu featuring steaks, and roast chicken, hamburgers, sandwiches and beer.
Number of Franchisees: 260 in 27 states.
In Business Since: 1954.
Equity Capital Needed: $60,000, if build-to-suit lease is arranged.
Financial Assistance Available: various.
Training Provided: 3 weeks of classroom and practical training at Lum's headquarters in Miami, Florida. Training covers all aspects of the business-operational procedures, bookkeeping, employee training, and management techniques. During the first 2 weeks of operation in the franchisee's restaurant, a representative is present to supervise the opening and assist in the training of any new personnel.
Managerial Assistance Avainable: Company representative visits franchisee's unit periodically for inspection and assistance. Home office personnel available to render assistance as required. Franchisee is issued a complete standard operating procedure manual which is constantly updated. Lum's sponsor meetings of franchisees and conducts marketing and product research. Bi-monthly newsletter sent to franchisee.

MAID RITE PRODUCTS, INC.
100 East Second Street
Muscatine, Iowa 52761
William F. Angell, President
Description of Operation: Fast food limited menu sandwich-type operation with various types of building and locations.
Number of Franchisees: 160 in most states.
In Business Since: 1928.
Equity Capital Needed: $3,000 average for franchisee fee.
Financial Assistance Available: None.
Training Provided: Complete on-job and classroom training.
Managerial Assistance Available: Home office personnel available at all times to offer advice and counsel on any and all aspects of the operation. Franchisee is provided with complete operating manuals and procedures.

MAMACITA'S INTERNATIONAL, INC.
388 East Willow Street
Long Beach, California 90803
Edward McNary, President
Description of Operation: Mamacita's offers a truly unique Mexican fast service, drive thru/sit down restaurant serving a broad menu of combination plates and a la carte items. The handsome building is modified Spanish design seating approximately 75 diners. The take out/drive thru offers families fast/hot and delicious Mexican food for take home eating. The interior design features natural woods, tile and greenery with a "South of the Border" ambience.
Number of Franchisees: 3 in California.
In Business Since: 1977 (first store and concept developed by El Torito Mexican Restaurants.)
Equity Capital Needed: Approximately $50,000 (Assuming land, building and equipment are leased.)
Financial Assistance Available: Total investment required to open a Mamacita's restaurant is a minimum of 22,000 square feet of land, plus approximately $250,000 (cash or credit) for building and equipment. Franchisees must arrange their own credit. In some cases Mamacita's may develop the entire package for lease to credit worthy franchisees. In all cases the Company will offer its' expertise and strength to assist franchisee in obtaining financing.
Training Provided: Intensive 3 week training at Mamacita's headquarters. Three months intensive indirect supervision at franchisee's location. Recall to headquarters for intensive 3 week management course conducted by professional management consultants. All training provided for operator and one assistant manager.

Managerial Assistance Available: Complete operations and equipment specifications manuals provided to each franchisee. Recipes, formulas, accounting and cost forms, management report forms covering all facets of operations provided each franchisee. District, field and headquarters management available at all times to visit with franchisees at their locations to assist in solving problems and improving operations.

MARTIN'S FRANCHISING SYSTEMS, INC.
6096 Gordon Road
Marbleton, Georgia 30059
Ray L. Martin, President
Description of Operation: Fast food restaurant with drive-thru, car service and inside seating facilities. We specialize in a chicken filet sandwich and other speciality items.
Number of Franchisees: 3 in Georgia.
In Business Since: 1962 — Martin's Franchising System since 1979.
Equity Capital Needed: $30,000 total. $10,000 working capital, $10,000 franchise fee and $10,000 equipment down payment.
Financial Assistance Available: Assistance in obtaining equipment financing (full package $80,000).
Training Provided: On-the-job training for 2 weeks prior to startup. 2 weeks after startup, plus any further assistance necessary for duration of contract.
Managerial Assistance Available: We provided the same as above for management personnel plus an operating manual along with periodic inspections and continuous monitoring of records for possible problems. We are involved in every aspect of the business.

MCDONALD'S CORPORATION
1 McDonald's Plaza
Oak Brook, Illinois 60521
Licensing Manager
Description of Operation: McDonald's Corporation operates and directs a successful nationwide chain of fast food restaurants serving moderately priced menu. Emphasis is on quick, efficient service, high quality food, and cleanliness. The standard menu consists of hamburgers, cheeseburgers, fish sandwiches, French fries, apple pie, shakes, breakfast menu, and assorted beverages.
Number of Franchisees: 4,859 in the United States, 890 internationally (including Canada).
In Business Since: 1955.
Equity Capital Needed: $125,000 minimum and ability to acquire outside financing $125,000 to $200,000.
Financial Assistance Available: None.
Training Provided: Minimum of 200 hours pre-registration and 300 plus post-registration, 11 days of basic operations training and 2 weeks managerial training at Hamburger University in Elk Grove, Illinois.
Managerial Assistance Available: Operations, training, maintenance, accounting and equipment manuals provided. Company makes available promotional advertising material plus field representative consultation and assistance.

METRO SANDWICH SHOPS OF AMERICA, INC.
Spence Station
P.O. Box 1117
Newport, Kentucky 41071
Carl M. Farmer, President
Description of Operation: Contemporary sandwich shops specifically designed to provide above-average food and service at affordable prices to office workers and sales people working in downtown metropolitan areas, large shopping malls and office buildings. Open from 7 am to 3 pm, Monday through Friday, Metro Shops feature fresh pastries, variety of regular and deli-type sandwiches, a self-service salad bar, soups and desserts. Carry-out, self-service and waitress service is provided. Individual and multi-unit franchises are available.
Number of Franchisees: 3 in Ohio, Kentucky and Indiana.
Equity Capital Needed: $15,000 to $25,000. Total investment is $60,000 to $90,000 depending upon location, size of the store and cost of renovations required.
Financial Assistance Available: Professionally prepared model loan applications and presentations are supplied. Other assistance, advice and counsel in obtaining financing is provided to the franchisee.
Training Provided: The Metro training program is tailored to the needs of the individual franchisee based on his expertise, education and experience in restaurant management. Franchisees with little or no relevant experience receive in-store and classroom training for up to 6 weeks in all aspects of restaurant operation and management.
Managerial Assistance Available: Field representatives provide assistance, advice and counsel during site selection, lease negotiations and renovation. They continue to work closely with the franchisee before, during and immediately after the store opens. Complete operations manuals and all necessary forms are provided. Field representatives contact franchisees periodically to review progress and to assist in instituting new policies and procedures to improve service, sales and profits. A national contracts program providing substantial savings on equipment, food, supplies and services is available to all franchisees. All Metro services are provided throughout the life of the franchise.

MINUTE MAN OF AMERICA, INC.
P.O. Box 828, 701 Collins
Little Rock, Arkansas 72203
Vernon L. Rodgers, Franchise Director
Description of Operation: Fast food speciality restaurant — free standing building (3,000 square feet) — carry-out and eat in featuring broiled hamburgers, 12 types of sandwiches and hot pies. At this time not interested in franchising any units over 450 miles from headquarters.
Number of Franchisees: 30 in 2 states.
In Business Since: 1965.

Equity Capital Needed: $75,000 turnkey-lease by franchisee on ground and building.
Financial Assistance Available: Advice and counsel only.
Training Provided: 6 weeks at home office at the expense of franchisee-required. Trainee will receive $200 weekly while training.
Managerial Assistance Available: Real estate selection based on computer test volume. Help in lease negotiation and equipment purchasing. Manager manual and on-the-job help in hiring and training first crew. Complete advertising programs through National Advertising Committee. Continuous visitation and invitational meetings.

MISTER S'GETTI RESTAURANT
2015 South Calhoun Street
Fort Wayne, Indiana 46804
Charles H. Sanderson
Description of Operation: Mister S'Getti offers a fast food system whereby a complete spaghetti dinner can be served steaming hot within 2 minutes at a price far below the average meal. All commisory items are available from the home office, but if the items can be purchased at a lesser price locally, the franchisee may buy from whoever he chooses, with the exception of the special Mister S'Getti Sauce Mix.
Number of Franchisees: 3 in Florida.
In Business Since: 1968.
Equity Capital Needed: $23,000.
Financial Assistance Available: A total investment of $45,000 is needed to open a Mister S'Getti Restaurant Carry-Out with a limited seating capacity of 18. An investment of $72,000 is needed for a restaurant with a seating capacity of 60. Mister S'Getti will secure financing for the franchisee with good credit references. A bookkeeping system and monthly profit and loss statements are furnished by Mister S'Getti to enable the franchisee to keep good records.
Training Provided: The franchisee is sent to the pilot restaurant for 2 weeks prior to the opening of his own to obtain intensive training of every phase of the operation. A representative of Mister S'Getti helps to open and works with the franchisee for 2 weeks and then checks and monitors his operation on a monthly basis.
Managerial Assistance Available: The franchisee has available to him a 24 hour, 7 days a week open phone line to answer any questions pertaining to the operation of his restaurant. Monthly inspections are made to assure sanitary measures are being used, and quality control of the food and service are at top levels. Records are kept and figured in percentages to Gross Sales to eliminate un-needed expenses and to discourage pilferage. Percentages are computed monthly and if any one item is out of line, it is drawn to the attention of the franchisee immediately.

MOM 'N' POP'S HAM HOUSE, INC.
Spring Street
P.O. Box 399
Claremont, North Carolina 28610
Marshall E. Digh, President
Charles F. Conner, Jr., Secretary
Richard S. Howard, Director of Franchise Development
Description of Operation: Mom 'n' Pop's Ham House, Inc., operates family style restaurants as well as fast service steak houses and fish restaurants. The company also franchises each type of restaurant. There are presently twelve company owned units and ten franchised units. The most popular franchise being the fast service steak houses operated under the tradename "Western Steer Family Steakhouse."
Number of Franchisees: 89 in 11 states.
In Business Since: 1970.
Equity Capital Needed: $60,000, if building and equipment are leased and franchisee credit sufficient.
Financial Assistance Available: Franchisor will offer trained assistance to franchisee to put together total franchise package. Franchisor does not offer direct financial assistance.
Training Provided: Franchisor will train managers, cooks, meat slicers and all other personnel necessary for staffing franchised unit.
Managerial Assistance Available: Mom 'n' Pop's provides extensive and continual assistance to franchisee in all areas of restaurant operation including, but not limited to, bookkeeping, inventory control, purchasing, operations manuals and constant field supervision.

MOM'S PIZZA, INC.
4457 Main Street
Philadelphia, Pennsylvania 19127
Nicholas Castellucci, President
Description of Operation: Fast food, new concept — Mom's Bake-At-Home Pizza.
Number of Franchisees: 10 in Pennsylvania, Maryland and New Jersey.
In Business Since: 1961.
Equity Capital Needed: $15,000 plus 20 percent outside Delaware Valley, 700 square feet needed.
Financial Assistance Available: Bank financing if needed.
Training Provided: 1 week.
Managerial Assistance Available: Continued help from main office.

MR. GATTI'S INC.
P.O. Box 34277
Louisville, Kentucky 40232
James E. Vogt, Vice President
Description of Operation: Mr. Gatti's is a pizza restaurant concentrating on quality products with fast service in a plushly decorated facility with an average of 125 seats. A unique pick-up window is also offered.
Number of Franchisees: 60 in 19 states.
In Business Since: 1964.
Equity Capital Needed: $30,000 to $50,000.
Financial Assistance Available: Franchisee is responsible for obtaining his own financing. Total investment is approximately $300,000.

Training Provided: 2 weeks at company operated school.
Managerial Assistance Available: Field consultation, purchasing methods, cost control procedures and operations manuals provided on a current basis.

MR. HERO SANDWICH SYSTEMS, INC.
6902 Pearl Road
Cleveland, Ohio 44130
Charles M. Feuer, Franchise Director
Description of Operation: Mr. Hero offers a unique and tasty product line, including several varieties of hot and cold sandwiches, featuring hot buttered steak sandwiches and fast food service.
Number of Franchisees: 72 units in Ohio, Pennsylvania and Florida.
In Business Since: 1965.
Equity Capital Needed: Minimum of $30,000 to $50,000.
Financial Assistance Available: Franchisee is responsible for obtaining his own financing with assistance from franchisor.
Training Provided: 5 weeks intensive program on-the-job in a training unit and in classroom sessions.
Managerial Assistance Available: Mr. Hero will provide assistance and advice in selection and securing of a location. Advisory services will be rendered relating to operations, preparation and development of recipes and food products, equipment needed and layout. Supporting services such as advertising, portion control systems and opening assistance will be provided. Supervisory staff will visit stores on a regular basis to assist in solving problems.

MR. PIZZA, INC.
560 Sylvan Avenue
Englewood Cliffs, New Jersey 07632
Richard Kurtz, President
Description of Operation: Franchise "turnkey," Mr. Pizza, family style restaurant. We furnish, equip, decorate and train franchisee.
Number of Franchisees: 24 in New York and New Jersey.
In Business Since: 1967
Equity Capital Needed: $20,000 minimum.
Financial Assistance Available: Total investment runs from $50,000 to $60,000, depending on size of store and type of equipment required. Balance payable to Company over period as short as 5 years to 9 years. Franchisee has option to obtain outside financing.
Training Provided: 2 weeks at training store.
Managerial Assistance Available: Assistance in site selection, lease negotiation, financing, accounting procedures, providing food suppliers plus periodic store visits.

MR. STEAK, INC.
International Headquarters
P.O. Box 5805 T.A.
5100 Race Court
Denver, Colorado 80217
Description of Operation: Mr. Steak, Inc., is a full service, sit down family type restaurant with seating facilities for up to 190 persons. The store hours are normally 11 a.m. to 9 p.m. We specialize in USDA Choice steaks, as well as seafood, chicken and sandwiches.
Number of Franchisees: 228 in 37 states and Canada.
In Business Since: 1962.
Equity Capital Needed: $55,000.
Financial Assistance Available: The total cash investment required is approximately $55,000 if the franchisee can secure own financing. Cost varies with lease deposits for local area. A purchase agreement for the franchise in the amount of $8,500 secures the area with the balance of $17,000 due when land and building lease is secured or site location purchased. Franchisee is responsible for securing land and building lease and equipment financing.
Training Provided: Comprehensive 7 weeks mandatory training is provided with the franchise fee for the restaurant manager. Travel, food and lodging is the responsibility of the trainee while in training.
Managerial Assistance Available: Opening and continuing assistance is provided by the company. Kinds and amount of assistance provided by the company is limited. The company provides operational assistance and new techniques developed by the company.

"MY APARTMENT" INTERNATIONAL, INC.
The Maritimes (C-22)
2051 Northeast Ocean Boulevard
Stuart, Florida 33494
David H. Nelson, President
Description of Operation: "My Apartment" is a quality Steak House featuring naturally aged USDA Prime Steaks, which are cooked at each guests' table by waitress chefs on specially designed cooking and eating tables.
Number of Franchisees: 15 (5 company-owned) in 5 states, Bahamas and Europe.
In Business Since: 1962.
Equity Capital Needed: $55,000.
Financial Assistance Available: Lease financing, available, if qualified.
Training Provided: Complete training is provided prior to the opening of the unit. Thereafter, continuous assistance is provided and supervision is offered each owner by the company.
Managerial Assistance Available: Continuous guidance.

MY PIE INTERNATIONAL, INC.
P.O. Box 33 - Hubbard Woods
Winnetka, Illinois 60093
Lawrence I. Aronson, President

Description of Operation: Operates a fine quality sit-down pizza and sandwich restaurant with soft beverages, beer, wine and in some cases hard liquor. This leisurely dining restaurant also has carry-out.
Number of Franchisees: 14 in 9 states.
In Business Since: 1971.
Equity Capital Needed: $300,000.
Financial Assistance Available: None.
Training Provided: 1 month at Chicago location.
Managerial Assistance Available: Franchisor aids and assists operator on an agreed continuing basis.

NATHAN'S FAMOUS, INC.
1515 Broadway
New York, New York 10036
Harold Norbitz, Vice President/Franchising, Real Estate
Description of Operation: Nathan's Famous Inc., franchised units offer a variety of foods, featuring the world famous all-beef frankfurter, in a nostalgic atmosphere, serviced to its stands, moderately priced. It is essentially a restaurant and fast food establishment. Nathan's Famous Inc., has variety of size of stores that fit various marketing areas.
Number of franchisees: 18 in New York, Florida, California, Ohio and New Jersey.
In Business Since: 1916.
Equity Capital Needed: Variable, depending upon size and location.
Financial Assistance Available: None.
Training Provided: Intensive, mandatory training for key personnel. Training could be up to 5 weeks at company's location. Training is under the direction of franchisor and is formalized in nature.
Managerial Assistance Available: Continual managment supervision. Specifications as to operations, food preparation, food specifications, accounting, advertising. Complete manual of operations is provided and field supervision is conducted by franchisor to assist franchisee. Nathan's continually does research and development.

NICKERSON FARMS FRANCHISING COMPANY
4135 South 89th Street
Omaha, Nebraska 68127
Robert L. Francis, Vice President
Description of Operation: Nickerson Farms is a combination restaurant, gift shop and gasoline retailer operating primarily on Interstate location.
Number of Franchisees: 4 in Indiana and Tennessee.
In Business Since: 1975.
Equity Capital Needed: $135,000 plus building and land.
Financial Assistance Available: None.
Training Provided: 8 weeks formal training including on-the-job training in a company operated unit.
Managerial Assistance Available: Periodic field inspections and special assistance upon request.

NOBLE ROMAN'S INC.
2909 Buick Cadillac Boulevard
Bloomington, Indiana 47401
Paul Mobley, Executive Vice President
Description of Operation: Noble Roman's is a restaurant business specializing in pizza and Italian foods for on premise and off premise consumption.
Number of Franchisees: 55 in Midwest, South and Southwest.
In Business Since: 1969 - Franchising since 1972
Equity Capital Needed: Franchise fee $12,500. Equipment package $50,000 to $75,000.
Financial Assistance Available: None
Training Provided: Training is provided at a company training center. The standard training period is approximately 4 weeks.
Managerial Assistance Available: Managerial and technical assistance is provided.

NUGGET RESTAURANTS INC.
4650 Brightmore Road
Bloomfield Hills, Michigan 48013
Gordon R. Eliassen, President
Description of Operation: Short order - full menu - portion controlled food and sandwich shop. Free standing building with required parking. Open 7 days a week. We construct 3,000 square foot store with lease.
Number of Franchisees: 20 in Michigan
Equity Capital Needed: $50,000
Financial Assistance Available: $50,000 down on total package of $135,000 with balance financed. Assistance in obtaining finances or optional for franchisee to secure. Building will have lease. Building costs approximately $240,000. Ownership of building is optional.
Training Provided: Consultation and training will be at company store for a month. Continuing for about another month when opening the new store, until franchisee is comfortable with his new business.
Managerial Assistance Available: A telephone call for assistance and information regarding new venture is always constant and a monthly CPA financial report keeps franchisor and franchisee fully aware at all times on trends of business.

THE ONION CROCK, INC.
P. O. Box 2088
Grand Rapids, Michigan 49501
William D. Kooistra, Vice President of Marketing
Description of Operation: Limited menu full service restaurant franchise specializing in soups, salads, and sandwiches.
Number of Franchisees: 5 in Michigan, 1 in Ohio and 1 in Wisconsin
In Business Since: 1974
Equity Capital Needed: $75,000 minimum; $400,000 minimum net worth

Financial Assistance Available: None
Training Provided: 2 weeks on-the-job training for franchisee and store manager in corporate stores and at corporate headquarters.
Managerial Assistance Available: On-site opening week assistance, periodic visits and continuous consultation availability by corporate staff or designates.

ORANGE JULIUS OF AMERICA
3219 Wilshire Boulevard
Santa Monica, California 90403

Description of Operation: Fast food operation, featuring the brand drink, "Orange Julius," made from freshly squeezed orange juice, and other flavors. Depending upon type of location, menu items may consist of hot dogs, hamburgers, french fries, and other snack type items. Primarily located in enclosed mall shopping centers.
Number of Franchisees: 523 in 16 States, Canada, Europe, Japan, the Philippines, and Australia
In Business Since: 1926
Equity Capital Needed: Approximately $30,000 to $50,000.
Financial Assistance Available: A total investment of approximately $80,000 to $110,000 is required. This amont is dependent upon the size of the store, menu selection, and the type of equipment required. The franchisee is required to arrange his own financing. Traditionally, franchisees have been able to contribute one-half in equity and finance one-half of the total investment, through their own financial sources. Franchises are sold on the basis of individual units. The franchisee pays for the cost of construction. The franchisor develops site location. Royalty of 6 percent of sales.
Training Provided: Approximately 10 days, including pre-opening training and training subsequent to the initial opening of the franchise.
Managerial Assistance Available: Managerial and technical assistance is provided for site selection, construction, equipment purchase, training of personnel and management. On-going supervision is provided.

PACIFIC TASTEE FREEZ, INC.
1101 South Cypress Street
La Habra, California 90631
N. W. Axene, President
Dick Granierie, General Manager

Description of Operation: Fast food drive-in restaurant featuring hamburger, Mexican food, ice cream and beverages.
Number of Franchisees: 65 in California and Oregon
In Business Since: 1955
Equity Capital Needed: Approximately $20,000-$30,000, including operating capital.
Financial Assistance Available: Equipment financing and or leasing assistance available.
Training Provided: 4 weeks in actual store.
Managerial Assistance Available: Duration of franchise, assistance through field representatives.

PAPPY'S ENTERPRISES, INC.
300 East Joppa Road
Towson, Maryland 21204
Robert B. Geller, Executive Vice President
Freeman Dixler, Vice President - Development

Description of Operation: Pappy's offers to franchise its unique plan of operation. Each restaurant is approximately 2,200 square feet and features sandwiches, pasta, pizza and beer in a family-oriented atmosphere. Stores run continuous promotions in order to induce families to patronize the restaurant.
Number of Franchisees: 36 plus 4 company-owned in 6 States
In Business Since: 1968
Equity Capital Needed: $7,500 franchise fee plus approximately 25 percent deposit on land, building and equipment package of $450,000 and ability to finance balance.
Financial Assistance Available: None
Training Provided: 3 week intensive training conducted at training store. Two week training in franchisee's store by representative of franchisor.
Managerial Assistance Available: Pappy's provides continuing advertising and promotions to franchisee. In addition, operations supervisor visits each store approximately every 6 weeks. Pappy's also provides an operations manual, forms, and bookkeeping systems.

PASQUALE FOOD COMPANY, INC.
19 West Oxmoor Road
Birmingham, Alabama 35209

Description of Operation: Prepare and serve to the public pizza, pasta, and a line of Italian-style sandwiches. Meat, bread and pizza doughs are manufactured and baked under strict quality control complete with chemist and laboratory.
Number of Franchisees: 190 plus 9 company-onwed outlets in 19 States
In Business Since: 1955
Equity Capital Needed: Approximately $25,000.
Financial Assistance Available: None
Training Provided: Initial 2 weeks training and periodically thereafter.
Managerial Assistance Available: Managerial and technical assistance provided.

PATSY'S PIZZA FRANCHISE INC.
20 Ohltown Road, Suite 210
Austintown, Ohio 44515
Donald J. Marshall

Description of Operation: Retail sales of pizza (whole or by the slice) and sandwiches. Restaurant featuring Italian food.
Number of Franchisees: 5 in 3 States
In Business Since: 1969
Equity Capital Needed: Package $75,000 to $90,000 (includes $15,000 for franchise fee). Package $150,000 to $175,000 (includes $15,000 for franchise fee).
Financial Assistance Available: None
Training Provided: 4 weeks of training
Managerial Assistance Available: 4 week training.

THE PEDDLER, INC.
P. O. Box 1361
Southern Pines, North Carolina 28387
J. P. Morgan, Jr., President

Description of Operation: The Peddler is a quality steak house featuring a unique salad bar and a fine steak which is cut at the guest's table then cooked over wood charcoal. Not fast food.
Number of Franchisees: 31 in 9 states
In Business Since: 1965
Equity Capital Needed: $80,000 to $100,000
Financial Assistance Available: None
Training Provided: 2 weeks of training in an operating restaurant is provided for the manager. Minimum of two days of assistance given during the opening.
Managerial Assistance Available: Managerial and technical assistance is provided for site selection, layout, equipment purchase, training of personnel, selection of supplies, and the opening. Assistance is continued through periodic inspection of operational procedure.

PEDRO'S FINE MEXICAN FOODS, INC.
Box 622
Columbus, Mississippi 39701
Robert Hartley, President
Webb Lowe, Chairman

Description of Operation: Pedro's combines the qualities of a fast food ala carte restaurant with the dine-in luxury of a full course dinner house. The result is a fast service quality product served in the relaxed atmosphere of real Mexico. Each store is approximately 2,400 square feet and is open seven days a week. All food is prepared fresh daily at each location which allows us to serve delicious food at a low cost.
Number of Franchisees: 28 in 11 states and Bermuda Islands
In Business Since: 1974 (a division of The All American Burger, Inc.)
Equity Capital Needed: $30,000
Financial Assistance Available: A total investment of $70,000 is necessary to open a Pedro's restaurant. The down payment of $30,000 pays for franchise fee ($12,500), opening inventory, security deposits, permits and licenses, training, and down payment on equipment package.
Training Provided: Pedro's provides an intensive 10 day training program encompassing every phase of running a successful Mexican restaurant. A complete operations manual is provided and additional training after restaurant is open.
Managerial Assistance Available: Pedro's staff assistants work closely with all franchisees to provide any assistance necessary to maintain quality food, good service, and proven profit.

PEPE'S, incorporated
1325 West 15th Street
Chicago, Illinois 60608
Mario Doualina, President
Robert Ptak, Secretary

Description of Operation: Pepe's, Incorporated franchises Pepe's Tacos Fast Food Mexican Restaurants. The restaurants are a combination carry-out and family dining. A full menu of Mexican meals is our specialty. Some restaurants offer beer and wine. Seating capacity is from 25 to 125 seats.
Number of Franchisees: 41 in Illinois, 10 in Indiana, and 1 in Florida.
In Business Since: 1967
Equity Capital Needed: $40,000
Financial Assistance Available: A total investment of from $50,000 to $125,000 is necessary to open a Pepe's Tacos Restaurant. This is for the cost of remodeling, purchasing equipment and signs, paying deposits for utilities and insurance, and payment of franchise fee. Pepe's, Incorporated helps to arrange for outside financing.
Training Provided: A new franchisee is required to train for a period of 2 weeks at one of our existing restaurants.
Managerial Assistance Available: Pepe's, Incorporated provides continuing management service during the entire franchise period in the area of quality control, advertising, inventory control, and new product development. A manual of operations and menu preparation is provided.

THE PEWTER MUG
207 Frankfort Avenue
Cleveland, Ohio 44113
Robert Wertheim

Description of Operation: English pub and restaurant, serving luncheon and dinner.
Number of Franchisees: 10 in Ohio
In Business Since: 1962
Equity Capital Needed: Approximately $150,000
Financial Assistance Available: None
Training Provided: Training of all personnel in parent restaurant in Cleveland and on premises by training staff.
Managerial Assistance Available: Assistance given in lease negotiations, general contracting, hiring of employees and coordination of kitchen and bar operation. We have our own man on premises 1 week before opening and 1 week after opening.

PEWTER POT MANAGEMENT CORPORATION OF MASSACHUSETTS
211 Middlesex Turnpike
Burlington, Massachusetts 01803
Kevin M. Hartigan, President

Description of Operation: Pewter Pot family restaurants, we believe, offer a more "total experience" than any similar chain in the country. Pewter Pot offers a warm, early American atmosphere with real wood, carpeting and hand painted murals; a varied menu of high quality foods including main courses, endless omelettes, hearty

breakfasts, all-American sandwiches, and bounteous desserts. Plus an extra measure of hospitality served up New England style.
Number of Franchisees: 27 in Massachusetts, 2 in Rhode Island and 1 in Connecticut
In Business Since: 1964
Equity Capital Needed: Approximately $100,000
Financial Assistance Available: A total investment of approximately $350,000 is needed to build and equip a Pewter Pot Family Restaurant. Pewter Pot does not finance any of the package.
Training Provided: Intensive 6 week mandatory training course is scheduled for all new franchisees and their manager. This course is conducted at the home office school and on-site company store under the supervision of a Pewter Pot supervisor.
Managerial Assistance Available: Pewter Pot Family Restaurants provide continual management services for the life of the franchise in such areas as operations, menu planning, advertising, inventory control, and food cost control.

PHILLY MIGNON
P.M.A. RESTAURANTS, INC.
2 Sylvan Way
Parsippany, New Jersey 07054
John Fiddes, President

Description of Operation: Fast food franchised restaurant trading as Philly Mignon featuring unique sliced steak sandwiches (cooked to order), hamburgers, Philly of Fish sandwiches, fried mushrooms, french fries and old fashioned hard ice cream and breakfast.
Number of Franchisees: 132 throughout the U.S., Puerto Rico and Canada
In Business Since: 1978
Equity Capital Needed: $25,000-$30,000
Training Provided: Intensive 2 week mandatory training course schedule for all new franchisees and/or their manager. Conducted at training school and on-site company store under supervision of training director. Covers operations, menu pricing, advertising, inventory control, food cost control.
Managerial Assistance Available: On-going operations assistance by field services group manager via periodic store visitation. Additional consultation provided on an as needed basis. Group manager on-site one week prior to opening. Assists in training store personnel. Standard basic specifications and plans, construction services, equipment package, furnishing, decor layout and signage. Grand opening and promotion assistance. Instruction manual relative to advertising/promotion, policies, operation merchandising, marketing. Advertising research assistance available, consultation and advice by company field supervisors. Standardized accounting cost control and promotion control system. Site selection and lease review.

PIETRO'S PIZZA PARLORS, INC.
407 Cernon Street
Vacaville, California 05688

Description of Operation: Family style restaurant - pizza, Italian/dinners, open 7 days a week 11 am to 12 pm.
Number of Franchisees: 6 in California
In Business Since: 1960
Equity Capital Needed: $75,000 to $150,000 depending on size of operation.
Financial Assistance Available: None
Training Provided: 8 weeks and then whatever is necessary
Managerial Assistance Available: Continuous service as needed.

PIONEER TAKE OUT CORPORATION
3663 West 6th Street
Los Angeles, California 90020
Paul Wilmoth, Vice President, Franchise Sales

Description of Operation: Pioneer offers a unique fast food service operation featuring eat-in and take-out fried chicken, fish and shrimp by the bucket or by the piece. Attractive signwork menu boards. Exterior and interior design offer efficient controls for franchise owner-operator and ease of operation to maximize profits.
Number of Franchisees: 250 in California, Nevada, Hawaii and Arizona
In Business Since: 1961
Equity Capital Needed: $70,000
Financial Assistance Available: Company may carry back part of the franchise fee for qualified individuals, with simple interest on balance. A total investment of $115,000 is all that is needed to establish a Pioneer Take Out unit including franchise fees, signs, lease, equipment and working capital.
Training Provided: 8 weeks: Intensive and complete training program; 4 weeks theory; 4 weeks on-the-job training under supervision of training director.
Managerial Assistance Available: Pioneer Take Out Corporation provides continuous management services for the life of the license in such areas as bookkeeping, advertising, quality, service, food preparation and control. Complete manuals of operations and food preparation are provided. Field coordinators work closely with licensees; visit stores regularly to assist solving problems. Pioneer regularly conducts licensee seminars and continuously performs market and product research to maintain high volume, profitable locations.

THE PIZZA INN, INC.
2930 Stemmons Freeway
P. O. Box 22247
Dallas, Texas 75222
R. P. Flack

Description of Operation: Operate and franchise pizza and allied Italian menu restaurants seating 150 people.
Number of Franchisees: 140 franchisees with 400 Inns (plus 340 company operated)
In Business Since: 1959
Equity Capital Needed: Minimum $75,000 (plus net worth of $150,000 for lease), depending on location.
Financial Assistance Available: Lease situation on equipment plus referral to developers who will develop for qualified franchisees.
Training Provided: Minimum 30 day training in training school plus opening assistance, with re-occuring training available at all times and periodic follow-up visits by specialized consultants.

Managerial Assistance Available: Complete operations manual furnished with franchise operations representative available at all times. Full range of marketing, operations and personnel development programs.

PIZZA MAN "HE DELIVERS"
5455 Wilshire Boulevard
Suite 1807
Los Angeles, California 90036
Wayne B. Jeppson, President

Description of Operation: Pizza Man offers a fast food home delivery operation. Each store is approximately 1,000 square feet, does 80 percent of its business in home delivery and is open 7 days a week 4 pm to midnight. Limited menu, low rent leases, turnkey operation.
Number of Franchisees: 36 in California
In Business Since: 1973
Equity Capital Needed: $20,000
Financial Assistance Available: Total investment of $60,000 is necssary. Down payment of $17,400. Pizza Man will assist in obtaining financing.
Training Provided: Complete training given. 2 weeks mandatory for Franchisee with 2 or more weeks available. All training at no charge to Franchisee. Training at Hollywood, California. Training for Franchisee's employees given at Franchisee's outlet.
Managerial Assistance Available: Pizza Man provides continual management assistance for the life of the franchise. Complete operation manuals, bookkeeping forms and direction are provided. Supervisor visits stores regularly to assist franchisee. Pizza Man provides advertising and promotional designs and research.

PIZZA TIME THEATRE, INC.
10060 Bubb Road
Supertino, California 95014
Donald K. Marks, Vice President

Description of Operation: Operate and franchise "family entertainment" pizza parlors offering varied menu with pizza, sandwiches, salads and sundaes. Animated characters, walk around costumed characters, family oriented amusements and large group parties are special features of Pizza Time Theatre.
Number of Franchisees: 8 units including company-owned units in California and Nevada
In Business Since: 1978
Equity Capital Needed: $250,000 plus operating capital
Financial Assistance Available: None
Training Provided: 3 weeks on-the-job in conjunction with "in class" instruction at Training School located in company-owned store.
Managerial Assistance Available: Pizza Time Theatre supplies franchisee operations manual, marketing manual and technical manuals, which are updated on a regular basis. Pizza Time Theatre maintains continual operational contact with each unit.

PLAYBOY CLUBS INTERNATIONAL, INC.
919 North Michigan Avenue
Chicago, Illinois 60611
C. Vincent Shortt, Senior Vice President
New Club Development

Description of Operation: A membership Club operating under the format name of "Playboy Clubs" featuring a unique decor setting for the service of luncheon, cocktails, dinner and evening entertainment. Service is performed by the world renown Playboy Bunnies.
Number of Franchisees: 10 locations in 10 States
In Business Since: 1960
Equity Capital Needed: Franchise equity would be necessary to finance an operation that would be capitalized in excess of one million dollars. Current franchise fee is $25,000.
Equity Capital Needed: We do *not* provide any kind or amount of financial assistance.
Training Provided: Training of management staff is orientation to the Playboy system of food service. Specific pre-opening training of Bunnies, bartenders and service personnel is done by Corporate trainers on site. After-opening training available at request of franchise holder.
Managerial Assistance Available: Continuous on-going assistance to franchise holder by Corporate and regional personnel. Franchise holder has total use of all Playboy Club International Corporate office resources. On site opening assistance, periodic inspections and consultation performed by field, regional and Corporate personnel.

POLOCK JOHNNY'S, INC.
111 West Lexington Street
Baltimore, Maryland 21201
John Kafka, President

Description of Operation: Fast food operation with a unique tasting sausage we produce in a glass enclosed USDA approved sausage company.
Number of Franchisees: 20 in Maryland
In Business Since: 1944
Equity Capital Needed: Approximately $75,000
Financial Assistance Available: Assistance in acquiring equipment loan.
Training Provided: 2 weeks on-the-job training at one of our company operated stores. We provide 2 weeks training by supervisor for start-up.
Managerial Assistance Available: Continuous assistance in areas such as advertising, inventory and quality control.

PONDEROSA SYSTEM INC.
P. O. Box 578
Dayton, Ohio 45401

Description of Operation: Cafeteria-style fast-food steak house featuring limited menu, moderate priced selection ranging from hamburger to T-Bone Steak.
Number of Franchisees: 231 units (plus 450 company-owned units) in 30 States and Canada
In Business Since: 1965
Equity Capital Needed: Over $100,000

Financial Assistance Available: No direct financial assistance is provided. Company may negotiate lease for the franchisee unit at option of franchisee.
Training Provided: 5 weeks of formal training in classroom in steak house with training instructor. Follow-on training in steak house as required to develop necessary skills.
Managerial Assistance Available: Complete operations manual detailing methods for scheduling labor, maintenance of equipment, training of employees, hiring practices, ordering supplies and recording and controlling expenses. Field Consultants provided on regular basis to help resolve operational problems. Seminars held to give advertising, promotional, and other managerial support to franchisee.

POPEYES FAMOUS FRIED CHICKEN, INC.
International Headquarters
One Popeyes Plaza
1333 South Clearview Parkway
Jefferson (New Orleans), Louisiana 70121
William A. Copeland, Executive Vice President
Franchise Division

Description of Operation: Fast food operations specializing in sale of specially seasoned products conducting business from single units with drive-thru and sit-down facilities.
Number of Franchisees: 220 in 25 States
In Business Since: 1972
Equity Capital Needed: Approximately $100,000 with sufficient net worth.
Financial Assistance Available: None
Training Provided: 6 weeks
Managerial Assistance Available: Accounting, operational, marketing, advertising and real estate.

PUDGIES PIZZA FRANCHISING, INC.
524 North Main Street
Elmira, New York 14901
Francis J. Cleary

Description of Operation: New York and Sicilian style pizza and a variety of hot and cold submarine sandwiches, burgers, french fries and standard soft drinks. 3,000 square feet free standing units with 72 and 82 seats and a drive-in window. Pudgies is presently considering expansion into other Northeastern States under multi-unit development agreements.
Number of Franchisees: 26 (33 units) in New York and Pennsylvania
In Business Since: 1973
Equity Capital Needed: $125,000, exluding building and leasehold improvements, minimum capital requirements - $50,000 approximately.
Financial Assistance Available: No direct financing available. Pudgies does, however, assist in the preparation of the financing application and the structuring of the bank presentation. Company also makes available, to qualified franchisees, a list of potential developers who have expressed interest in investing in leasehold improvements.
Training Provided: 6 week program of classroom and in-store instruction at the company's schooling facilities in Elmira, New York.
Managerial Assistance Available: Pudgies has an ongoing inspection program designed to evaluate the individual store and advise as to physical and technical aspects of the operation. Pudgies also has a continued product development program and test markets various related products for chain wide introduction to the menu.

RAX SYSTEMS, INC.
1169 Dublin Road
Columbus, Ohio 43216
Larry R. Ritter, Vice President, Franchising

Description of Operation: RAX Systems, Inc., is a new name for an established company, headquartered in Columbus, Ohio. We have been in the restaurant business since 1963, both as a franchisee of several major chains and as a developer of our own roast beef operation-RAX Roast Beef Restaurants. RAX Roast Beef restaurants serve a limited menu, specializing in roast beef. Service is fast and efficient and the dining area designed for our customer's comfort.
Number of Franchisees: 65 (including company-operated units) in 21 States. Units sold but not yet under construction in 18 other States.
In Business Since: 1978
Equity Capital Needed: $100,000 plus net worth for lease.
Financial Assistance Available: None
Training Provided: We have established a RAX Management Training Institute staffed by full-time instructors experienced in the successful operations of a RAX Roast Beef restaurant. The franchisee and 1 member from each of his units will be trained in all phases of operations. Prior to this 2 week training course, a schedule providing each attendee with 240 hours of training in a RAX Roast Beef restaurant is required.
Managerial Assistance Available: RAX provides initial standard specifications and plans for the building, equipment, furnishings, decor, layout and signs, together with advice and consultation concerning same; initial training in the RAX System, including the standards, methods, procedures and techniques utilized in implementing the RAX System; opening supervision and assistance from employees of RAX at the opening of each restaurant; RAX's confidential standard business policies and operations data instruction manuals; such merchandising, marketing and advertising research data and advice as developed by RAX; Area Supervisors available in all regions to work closely with franchisee and visit stores regularly to assist in solving problems.

REABAN'S, INC.
10726 Manchester Road
Kirkwood, Missouri 63122
John E. Reaban, Jr., Vice President

Description of Operation: Reaban's, Inc., franchises a fast food operation featuring hamburgers, chicken and other limited menu items. Its primary market is in small towns with a population of 1,000 to 20,000. Emphasis is placed on low franchisee investment and overhead.
Number of Franchisees: 28 in Illinois and Missouri
In Business Since: 1958
Equity Capital Needed: $10,000

Financial Assistance Available: A total investment of $25,000 is required for equipment, initial franchise fee and working capital. Normally $10,000 will cover down payment on equipment, franchisee fee and working capital with Reaban's, Inc., assisting in obtaining financing on the balance.
Training Provided: A minimum of 2 weeks on-site training at an existing restaurant.
Managerial Assistance Available: Reaban's, Inc., provides continuing assistance to the franchisee. Advertising programs are available on an optional basis. Regular visits are made to each operation.

ROAST BEEFERY RESTAURANTS INTERNATIONAL, INC.
761 North Lake Boulevard
P. O. Box 14657
North Palm Beach, Florida 33408
Emanual Segal, President, Chief Executive Officer

Description of Operation: Fast food restaurant. Each unit is about 2,400 square feet with parking in front and on both sides. Drive thru service. Inside seating of about 77. Open 7 days, 13 hours daily average. Serving USDA choice roast beef. Small selection of other deli type sandwiches, soup, and salad bar.
Number of Franchisees: 3 (plus 1 company-owned) in Florida
In Business Since: 1977 (original owner and concept since 1970)
Equity Capital Needed: License fee, $10,000. Ample funds and net worth needed.
Financial Assistance Available: Has varied with money market.
Training Provided: Intensive mandatory training is provided. Fourteen days minimum on-site at company unit; 14 day minimum under Roast Beefery supervision at franchisee's unit.
Managerial Assistance Available: Franchisor provides continual management service for the life of the franchise. This includes establishing controls for bookkeeping, inventory, purchasing. Complete forms and directions are provided. Field supervisors are available to work closely with franchisees.

RON'S KRISPY FRIED CHICKEN, INC.
10101 Fondren
Suite 300
Houston, Texas 77096
Steve Woodall, Executive Vice President

Description of Operation: Ron's Krispy Fried Chicken, Inc., is a fast food operation that specializes in fried chicken. Each store is between 1,681 and 2,400 square feet and is open 7 days a week. Ron's also sells many side orders to complement its chicken. A few of the side orders are mashed potatoes, gravy, potato salad, and cole slaw. About 75 percent of the business is take-out of which 30 percent uses the drive-thru window. The remainder is eat-in business.
Number of Franchisees: 15 in Texas and Alabama, New York, and New Mexico
In Business Since: 1971
Equity Capital Needed: $65,000
Financial Assistance Available: A total investment of at least $125,000 is needed to open a Ron's Krispy Fried Chicken, Inc., restaurant. This is providing that someone else builds the building for you. The ultimate responsibility is the franchise owner's to obtain the financing.
Training Provided: Ron's requires a minimum of 3 weeks training for its franchise owner/operators.
Managerial Assistance Available: Ron's provides an opening crew of two when needed. Ron's also provides a continuing management service for any need that may arise. Field supervisors are also available to help in unusual instances and will visit the franchise owner/operator once a month and more often, if necessary.

ROSATI FRANCHISE SYSTEMS, INC.
1000 Morse Avenue
Schaumburg, Illinois 60193
Rick Rosati, Franchise Director

Description of Operation: Rosati Franchise Systems, Inc., operates 10 carry-out and delivery pizzarias in the Chicagoland area. The stores are approximately 1,000 square feet and are located in small strip centers or convenience-type shopping centers. Store hours are 4:30 p.m. to midnight 7 days a week and carry a full line of pizzas and Italian foods.
Number of Franchisees: 12 including company-owned in Illinois
In Business Since: As Rosati Franchise Systems, 1978, as Rosatis Pizza, 16 years.
Equity Capital Needed: $45,000 total investment
Financial Assistance Available: None
Training Provided: Intensive 4 week training program is scheduled for all new franchisees. Two weeks in a company unit and 2 weeks in their own unit under the supervision of a full-time employee of Rosati Franchise Systems, Inc.
Managerial Assistance Available: Rosati Franchise Systems, Inc., provides managerial assistance for the life of the franchise. A complete operations manual is provided for all franchisees.

THE ROUND TABLE FRANCHISE CORPORATION
601 Montgomery Street
San Francisco, California 94111
Dick Dunke, President

Description of Operation: The Round Table Franchise Corporation franchises restaurants with a distinctive atmosphere offering pizza, sandwiches, hamburgers, salads and beverages. Appealing to a broad spectrum of the public, the restaurants are open 12 to 14 hours a day, 7 days a week.
Number of Franchisees: 185 in 7 States
In Business Since: 1962
Equity Capital Needed: Estimated capital (including initial franchise fee) $60,000.
Financial Assistance Available: Franchisee is required to provide sufficient funds to establish and open restaurant.
Training Provided: Franchisor offers mandatory on-site training course for new franchisees. Assistance and supervision in various other areas to open restaurant is also provided.
Managerial Assistance Available: The Round Table Franchise Corporation offers a variety of continuing managerial and technical advice including, but not limited to, advertising, store operations and bookkeeping techniques.

ROY ROGERS RESTAURANTS
#1 Marriott Drive
Washington, D.C. 20058
Norman P. Marraccini

Description of Operation: Fast food restaurant serving roast beef, chicken, burgers, shakes and fries.
Number of Franchisees: 17 franchisees with 79 units in 13 States
In Business Since: Marriott since 1927, Roy Rogers group since 1967
Equity Capital Needed: $80,000
Financial Assistance Available: None
Training Provided: 10 weeks hands-on training for owner/operator and 6 weeks training for each assistant manager.
Managerial Assistance Available: Assistance in site selection, assistance in opening unit, franchise consultant required to visit unit on a regular basis to advise franchisee and to assist in whatever way possible.

THE SALAD BAR CORPORATION
7575 East Main Street, Suite 204
P. O. Box 1845
Scottsdale, Arizona 85252
R. L. Drake, President

Description of Operation: Quick service restaurants featuring fresh, light, healthy foods (soups, salads, sandwiches) in a garden atmosphere.
Number of Franchisees: 50 in 14 States
In Business Since: 1974
Equity Capital Needed: $15,000 - Approximate total investment $85,000 - $135,000
Financial Assistance Available: Preparation of loan package for presentation to bank/SBA.
Training Provided: Complete intensive training provided in owner's store at time of opening.
Managerial Assistance Available: Assistance given in site location. Additional help and advice available whenever franchisee may have a sustaining need.

TALENT INVESTMENTS, INC.
dba SALAD SHOPPE
3601 Faraon
St. Joseph, Missouri 64506
Steve Poe, President, Director of Franchising

Description of Operation: Salad Shoppe offers a unique restaurant experience. We serve a variety of soups, salads and sandwiches. Each store is approximately 2,500 square feet in either downtown locations or retail shopping center near office space. Hours of operation are from 11 a.m. till 7 p.m. 6 days a week. Stores seat approximately 120 people and has full table service.
Number of Franchisees: 3 in Missouri and Kansas
In Business Since: 1978
Equity Capital Needed: $10,000 minimum
Financial Assistance Available: A total investment of $70,000 is needed to open a Salad Shoppe. Franchisee must arrange own outside financing. Franchisor will assist in locating financing.
Training Provided: Intensive 2 week, mandatory training course is scheduled for all new franchisees. Then 1 week training on location with full time franchisor employee.
Managerial Assistance Available: Salad Shoppe provides complete operations manual and continual management service for life. Managers are available to work closely with franchisees and visit stores on a regular basis. Company continues to research, market and develop Salad Shoppes for benefit of Company and franchisee.

SANDWICH GIANTS, INC.
954 Rice Street
St. Paul, Minnesota 55117
Raymond C. Augustine

Description of Operation: Fast food, submarine sandwiches, hamburgers, steak sandwiches etc. No cooking microwave oven operation.
Number of Franchisees: 3 in Minnesota
In Business Since: 1970
Equity Capital Needed: $10,000
Financial Assistance Available: All set up and ready to operate.
Training Provided: Training offered in our existing operations (no time limit)
Managerial Assistance Available: Continuous

SCHLOTZSKY'S INC.
B-423 Research
Austin, Texas 78758
Donald S. Dissman, President
Bob E. Lively, Vice President, Marketing

Description of Operation: Franchised sandwich shops with restricted menu limited specifically to Schlotzsky's unique sandwiches.
Number of Franchisees: 100 in 10 States
In Business Since: 1971—Schlotzsky's Inc. chartered on November 26, 1974
Equity Capital Needed: Approximately $70,000
Financial Assistance Available: Furnish background data and financial statements of Schlotzky's Inc. to funding sources of licensee.
Training Provided: Minimum of 2 days prior to opening, and 3 days following opening, with continuing on-site training as required.
Managerial Assistance Available: Supply complete and highly detailed operations manual covering every aspect of the Schlotzsky's System. Immediate response to all significant operational problems encountered by licensee. Inspections and quality controls subject to check or regular and consistent basis throughout life of agreement. Sponsor meetings. Issue monthly newsletter.

SCOTTO MANAGEMENT CORPORATION
8302 - 13th Avenue
Brooklyn, New York 11228
Dansby A. Council, Franchise Development

Description of Operation: Scotto Pizza Restaurants have a proven history of success in enclosed shopping malls, strip shopping centers, drive-ins, and business areas thru its unique limited menu and simplified operating concept. It is rapidly expanding nationwide with stores presently in 10 States.
Number of Franchisees: 30 stores with several company-owned.
In Business Since: 1972. Formerly operated as family-owned restaurants.
Equity Capital Needed: $40,000 to $60,000 depending on the size of store.
Financial Assistance Available: Bank financing for equipment.
Training Provided: 6 weeks on-the-job training at company-owned store.
Managerial Assistance Available: Complete operations manual furnished with operations, representative available at all times. Company gives assistance in site-location, lease negotiations, record control system, local advertising, management training, pre-opening and post-opening supervision.

SHAKEY'S INCORPORATED
3600 First International Building
1201 Elm Street
Dallas, Texas 75270
Michael G. Thompson, Director of Franchise Development

Description of Operation: Shakey's new look is a turn of the century motif featuring stained glass, tiffany lamps, hanging plants and natural woods. Customer dining areas have raised levels to create a comfortable atmosphere for the entire family. Menu features thick and thin crust pizza, sandwiches, the new "Market Street Fruit and Vegetable Stand" salad bar, domestic and imported beers, wine and an optional wine cocktail program along with soft drinks. Shakey's is currently developing free-standing restaurants as well as shopping center locations.
Number of Franchisees: 469 in 45 States, Canada, Mexico, Japan, Philippines, and Guam.
In Business Since: 1954
Equity Capital Needed: Varies
Financial Assistance Available: None, will assist in real estate negotiations upon request.
Training Provided: Complete training consisting of classroom and in-restaurant curriculum provided. Training at company facilities for a period of 3 weeks and grand opening assistance.
Managerial Assistance Available: Shakey's provides continual management service in such areas as marketing, quality control, and lease negotiations. Complete operating manuals are provided. Regional managers and dealer service consultants work closely with franchisees and visit restaurants to assist in any problem area. Franchisees meet generally 2-3 times a year to exchange views and opinions with Shakey's advisory staff.

SIR BEEF LTD., INC.
4300 Morgan Avenue
Evansville, Indiana 47715
Andrew Guagenti, President

Description of Operation: A fast food restaurant with a British atmosphere. Inside seating for 90, with a drive-up window. Very limited menu with a Roast Beef Sandwich as the feature item. (55 percent of sale in roast beef sandwich.) Fresh meat, not a processed loaf, roasted on-site continually. Company has been operating Farmer's Daughter Coffee Shops since 1954.
Number of Franchisees: 3 in Indiana and Kentucky
In Business Since: 1970
Equity Capital Needed: $30,000
Financial Assistance Available: None—will negotiate lease for franchise unit at option of franchisee.
Training Provided: Training provided at company-owned units and office in Evansville, Indiana. Six weeks training a necessity.
Managerial Assistance Available: Field Consultant works in unit with Management to insure that the Operation Manual, which details systems, procedures and controls are being followed.

SIR PIZZA INTERNATIONAL, INC.
700 South Madison Street
Muncie, Indiana 47302
R. W. Swartz

Description of Operation: Retail and commissary operations, selling pizza, sandwiches, etc., for both on-premise consumption and carry-out.
Number of Franchisees: 127 in 11 states
In Business Since: 1958
Equity Capital Needed: $50,000 to $100,000
Financial Assistance Available: None. Land acquisition is franchisee's responsibility.
Managerial Assistance Available: Regional managers continue to counsel franchisee in advertising, merchandising and quality control. Parent company assists with local advertising and promotion.

SIZZLER FAMILY STEAK HOUSES
12731 West Jefferson Boulevard
Los Angeles, California 90066
William R. Hobson, Director, Franchise Development

Description of Operation: Popular priced family steak house featuring a carefully planned menu, quality food, contemporary surroundings and customer participation format.
Number of Franchisees: 440 in 35 States
In Business Since: 1959
Equity Capital Needed: Must be able to obtain financing for land and building; additional minimum cash requirement of approximately $125,000.
Financial Assistance Available: None
Training Provided: 3 months "on-the-job" and classroom training at regional training stores (Los Angeles, California).
Managerial Assistance Available: Sizzler Family Steak Houses provides continued field and management services for life of the franchise in areas of marketing, advertising, and training of key personnel, accounting, purchasing, restaurant management and scheduled training schools and seminars. The Sizzler Restaurant Management Guide, a confidential plan for successful management, is provided each new licensee. Field representatives contact periodically to review progress and help institute new policies and procedures to improve service, sales and profits.

STEWART'S DRIVE-INS
Division of FROSTIE ENTERPRISES
1420 Crestmont Avenue
Camden, New Jersey 08103
Michael W. Fessler, Vice President, Sales

Description of Operation: Drive-in restaurants, with or without dining room with car-hop service.

Number of Franchisees: 70 in 5 States

In Business Since: 1924

Equity Capital Needed: $25,000 to $35,000

Financial Assistance Available: Land acquisition is franchisee's responsibility.

Training Provided: Complete on-the-job training program provided. Training covers all aspects of the business-operational procedures, bookkeeping, employee training, advertising and promotion and management techniques, menu selection.

Managerial Assistance Available: Regional managers continue to counsel franchisee in advertising, merchandising and quality control for the life of the franchise. Parent company helps with local advertising and promotion.

THE STRAW HAT RESTAURANT CORPORATION
6400 Village Parkway
Dublin, California 94566
John E. Shepanek, Vice President, Franchise Group

Description of Operation: The Straw Hat Restaurant system is a comprehensive pizza restaurant system for serving pizza, sandwiches (hot and cold), pasta, salad bar, beverages (including beer and win), emphasizing a clean and friendly atmosphere attractive to young adults, families and adults.

Number of Franchisees: 72 (105 franchise restaurants) in 6 States

In Business Since: 1969

Equity Capital Needed: $95,000 - minimum cash requirement/franchise fee: $15,000

Financial Assistance Available: None

Training Provided: 5-6 weeks and on-going seminars

Managerial Assistance Available: On-going marketing assistance; product research and development; on-going quality assurance; on-going operational supervision.

STUCKEY'S INC.
P. O. Box 370
Eastman, Georgia 31023
J. W. Spradley, President

Description of Operation: A one stop center for the traveler on the interstates and main U.S. highways. Specializing in unique pecan candies, a food service program featuring Stuckey's King of the Road hamburger, restaurant seating novelties, gifts and souvenirs, gasoline service and sparkling clean restrooms. Open 7 days per week, approximately 12-14 hours per day.

Number of Franchisees: 140 (plus 153 company-owned) in 38 States

In Business Since: 1931

Equity Capital Needed: Amount varies dependent upon individual situation. Determined during discussions.

Financial Assistance Available: Limited - dependent upon individual situation.

Training Provided: 3 week program in zone training stores. This includes business operation procedure, bookkeeping procedures, management techniques, on-the-job experience in our local shoppe and concepts and procedures of the administrative functions of the corporate office. Periodic region meetings for continuous updating on procedures and operations are held.

Managerial Assistance Available: Managerial and technical assistance is provided in site location, site preparation and building construction. Company representatives also visit units periodically for inspection and assistance in all phases of the business. Home office personnel are always available to assist the franchisee in all areas of the business. A complete accounting and retail auditing service is available at a nominal monthly fee. Stuckey's sponsors meetings of franchisees and meets with the Franchise Advisory Board. A newsletter is also sent to all franchisees.

SUBWAY
25 High Street
Milford, Connecticut 06460

Description of Operation: Preparation and sale of foot-long, specialty sandwiches (submarines). Present menu includes 18 varieties of hot and cold sandwiches. No cooking is involved other than in a microwave oven. All stores have a take-out service and many stores have eat-in facilities. Stores are open late 7 nights per week.

Number of Franchisees: 160 in 19 States

In Business Since: 1965

Equity Capital Needed: Approximately $15,000

Financial Assistance Available: Assistance available depending on analysis of financial and experience information.

Training Provided: Subway provides 2 weeks of comprehensive classroom and practical training at Subway headquarters for store owners and store managers. The classroom curriculum includes training in location selection, store construction, accounting procedures, management theory as well as instruction in business analysis, product formulas and control mechanisms specific to the Subway System. In addition to classroom study practical training is provided in one of the local Subway stores to develop skills in sandwich making along with the day to day operation and management of a successful Subway store. Upon successful completion of this two week training course, all owners are eligible to attend a Graduate Training course. This Graduate course is a week long seminar which deals more in depth with management theory and multiple unit operation. At any time during the life of the franchise any franchisee or designated manager may enroll in either of these training courses.

Managerial Assistance Available: During store construction, which takes between 25 to 60 days, managerial and technical assistance is provided for each franchisee by a field representative and an office coordinator assigned to handle their file. Areas covered in this assistance include site selection, store design and layout, interior construction, equipment purchasing, arrangement of suppliers and initial inventory ordering. When a store is scheduled to open, a field representative is available to help oversee the operation and provide back-up support for the store owner in areas of employee training and successful operational procedure. After store opening, periodic inspections and field visits are conducted in each unit by the assigned field representative to be certain all stores maintain company standards. Continual office support is made available to each franchisee through frequent contact with one's assigned coordinator. The coordinator-field representative system for service provides continual assistance and support for each franchisee through the life of the franchise (20 years). Periodically, a Newsletter, comprised of articles written by each department head is sent to all franchisees. With receipt of this Newsletter, all franchisees are kept continually apprised of new company policies and developments across the country. Also included in this publication are sections dealing with store management. Ongoing assistance in advertising is provided by the Franchise Advertising Fund which is directed by a Board of Directors comprised of 12 store owners elected by the franchisees.

TACO CASA INTERNATIONAL, LTD.
P. O. Box 4542
Topeka, Kansas 66604
James F. Reiter, Secretary-Treasurer
Alan Ward, President

Description of Operation: Taco Casa International, Ltd., is the operator and franchisor for Taco Casa restaurants. Taco Casa is a fast food Mexican restaurant featuring a limited menu and quick, courteous service in an attractive atmosphere. Taco Casa International, Ltd., operates both free standing and enclosed mall locations. Normal operating hours are from 11 a.m. to 12 midnight, 7 days a week.

Number of Franchisees: 15 in 6 States

In Business Since: 1963

Equity Capital Needed: The total franchise package is approximately $40,000 which includes equipment, inventory, start-up costs, starting capital.

Financial Assistance Available: May assist in methods for arranging financing.

Training Provided: An initial 2 week training school for new licensee's at our training school. One week opening assistance upon opening the new unit. Complete operations manual provided to unit. Continuous counseling and assistance with routine inspections by company representative. Monthly newsletter updating current events in Taco Casa and restaurant industry.

Managerial Assistance Available: Open line for licensee's inquiries and assistance. Pursual of weekly reports by Taco Casa headquarters and appraisal given. Routine inspections and assistance by company representatives. Bulletins concerning important legislation. Continuing research in products and procedures. Assistance in advertising. Regional or national advertising when minimum level of units make it possible.

TACO DEL SOL (T. d. S., Inc.)
1105 South 13th #206
Norfolk, Nebraska 68701
Richard E. Drummond

Description of Operation: Mexican fast food featuring extensive menu for both carry-out and semi-cafeteria sit down. All food prepared for dining room service is served on china silverware.

Number of Franchisees: 8 in Nebraska, Iowa and Washington.

In Business Since: 1978

Equity Capital Needed: $25,000

Financial Assistance Available: None

Training Provided: 2 weeks, in-store and classroom

Managerial Assistance Available: Continuing management and consulting services will be provided for the life of the franchise agreement. During construction, equipment installation and the first week of operation, home office personnel are available for assistance. A complete operations manual including forms, advertising formats, employee handbook and recipes is provided to each unit.

TACO HUT, INC.
3621 South 73rd East Avenue
Tulsa, Oklahoma 74145
David Jones, President

Description of Operation: Complete line of Mexican foods, convenient for either dine-in or carry-out operation. Unique system formulated around unusual decor and atmosphere.

Number of Franchisees: 70 in 13 States including Hawaii and Alaska.

In Business Since: 1965

Equity Capital Needed: $40,000 minimum

Financial Assistance Available: Consultation only

Training Provided: 2-3 weeks intensive management training on-site.

Managerial Assistance Available: On a continuing basis.

WOODSON-HOLMES ENTERPRISES, INC.
dba TACO JOHN'S
P. O. Box 1589
Cheyenne, Wyoming 82001
Harold Holmes and James F. Woodson

Description of Operation: Taco John's is a fast food, carry-out, limited menu, Mexican product offering. The 360 square foot Taco John's free standing building is constructed in Cheyenne and delivered to the franchisee's site complete with equipment and signs. Normal operating hours are 12 to 14 hours per day, 7 days a week. A large modular unit of 1,200 square foot which includes seating, carry-out and drive-thru is now being constructed in the Cheyenne plant for delivery in Spring of 1980. Prices on this unit will be available by contacting Woodson-Holmes Enterprises, Inc. Headquarters, P.O. Box 1589, Cheyenne, Wyoming 82001.

Number of Franchisees: 280 in 26 States in the West and Mid-West

In Business Since: 1969

Equity Capital Needed: $35,000 minimum

Financial Assistance Available: A total investment of $90,000 to $95,000 is necessary to open a Taco John's unit. The ideal method of financing is at a local bank, and Woodson-Holmes Enterprises is available to provide background information, projection, references, etc., to the bank to enable them to make a decision on the loan. A number of SBA loans have been obtained and a few units have been leased. If the franchisee desires to lease the building and equipment, Woodson-Holmes has sources available for them to contact.

65

Training Provided: An intensive 10 day mandatory training course is scheduled for all franchisees, or their managers, in Cheyenne, Wyoming. The training consists of a combination of classroom and actual production at an operating Taco John's unit.
Managerial Assistance Available: Woodson-Holmes Enterprises provides technical and managerial assistance through the life of the franchise. When the new Taco John's unit is open, we provide opening personnel for approximately 1 week thereafter periodical calls by Woodson-Holmes Enterprises field personnel, complete manuals of operation, forms, and directions are provided and are continually up-dated. In addition, advertising materials are provided periodically, a monthly newsletter gives operating tips and general information, and regional and national meetings are held throughout the year and provide additional assistance.

THE TACO MAKER, INC.
P. O. Box 9519
Ogden, Utah 84409
Gil L. Craig, President

Description of Operation: Mexican fast food, American style, franchising. Limited menu, semi-cafeteria, quick service, quality products.
Number of Franchisees: 45 in 9 States and Puerto Rico
In Business Since: 1977 (with 13 years in other Mexican fast food under different name).
Equity Capital Needed: $25,000 to $40,000
Financial Assistance Available: None
Training Provided: 30 day training school
Managerial Assistance Available: Continual ongoing follow-up in advertising, research and development, operational and other. Preopening and grand opening detail assistance.

TACO PLACE, INC.
843 North Cleveland-Massillon Road
Akron, Ohio 44313
J. Berentine, Vice President

Description of Operation: Taco Place offers a retail outlet designed for enclosed mall operations where high traffic is assured. Each store will be approximately 1,000 square feet open 6 days, 14 hours per day. "Total turn-key" operation available as owner manager or absentee. Concept, design, and foods for consumption among the fastest growing nationwide, namely Mexican American. Foods—limited menu for high traffic.
Number of Franchisees: 3 in Ohio
In Business Since: 1977
Equity Capital Needed: $30,000 minimum
Financial Assistance Available: A total liability of approximately $100,000 is required for each installation. Local banks and/or other financing available including SBA. Franchisor in selected cases will carry portions of franchise fees, training expenses and lease liability for mall space.
Training Provided: Intensive training in original free standing stores owned and operated by the founder in Northwest Ohio. Training manuals, etc., furnished.
Managerial Assistance Available: Continuing management consulting by the company and its consultants. Computer bookkeeping, technical data, and formulation of new products ongoing. Various periodic meetings of all concerned franchisee, owner operator, their personnel as well as C.P.A.'s, food service management experts, and other. Marketing research, management training, and expansion to free standing full service concepts as well, are in progress.

TACO PLAZA, INC.
235 Loop 820 Northeast
P. O. Box 18399
Fort Worth, Texas 76118
Craig M. Campbell, Executive Vice President

Description of Operation: Taco Plaza, Inc., a wholly owned subsidiary of ConAgra, Inc., operates and franchises fast-service restaurants featuring a limited menu of Mexican-style food and related items. Taco Plaza restaurants of approximately 2,000 square feet provide inside dining in an attractive atmosphere for 64 customers and feature a drive through window for take out customers. Normal operating hours are 12 to 14 hours, 7 days per week.
Number of Franchisees: 15 in Texas, Arkansas, South Carolina, Florida and Michigan.
In Business Since: 1971
Equity Capital Needed: A minimum of $40,000 with sufficient net worth to finance total investment of approximately $250,000 plus real estate of approximately 26,000 square feet.
Financial Assistance Available: None
Training Provided: Training is provided at company-owned facilities for 3-6 weeks depending upon prior experience, aptitudes and abilities of franchisee.
Managerial Assistance Available: A complete development manual and operations manual will be provided. In addition, Taco Plaza provides assistance in-site selection, real estate, supplier selection, hourly training and opening. Continuing advisory assistance is provided in all aspects of the operation of a Taco Plaza restaurant during the term of the franchise agreement.

TACO TICO, INC.
3305 East Douglas
Wichita, Kansas 67218
Jim Conley, Director of Franchise Operations

Description of Operation: A limited menu, Mexican-style fast food restaurant. The building is 2,160 square feet of a unique design providing dining room seating for 90, carry-out service, and possible drive-thru window service.
Number of Franchisees: 16 operating 70 outlets in 10 States
In Business Since: 1962 - offering franchises since 1966
Equity Capital Needed: $60,000 plus net worth of $250,000
Financial Assistance Available: None
Training Provided: 8 weeks of classroom and in-store training in Wichita, Kansas for managers, plus 7 days of training of all personnel in the outlet during opening week.
Managerial Assistance Available: All areas of the corporate structure are available to the Franchisee during the life of the relationship. Visits by company representatives to the franchised outlets are made quarterly to assist in all phases of operations.

TACO TIME INTERNATIONAL, INC.
P. O. Box 2056
3880 West 11th
Eugene, Oregon 97402
Donald Payne

Description of Operation: Mexican fast food restaurants.
Number of Franchisees: 210 in 13 States, including Alaska, Hawaii and Canada
In Business Since: 1960
Equity Capital Needed: $50,000 minimum
Financial Assistance Available: None
Training Provided: In-store and classroom - 6 to 8 weeks.
Managerial Assistance Available: Inspections, bulletins, research and development improvements.

QUICK FOODS, INC.
dba TACO VILLA
810 North Dixie
Odessa, Texas 79761
Roger A. Ellis

Description of Operation: Franchisor, Quick Foods, Inc., offers, sells, and grants franchises to others to operate quick service Mexican restaurants, in accordance with certain architectural designs, layouts, and interior decor specifications of franchisor, and to prepare and sell Mexican food using franchisor's methods of operation and certain secret recipes under the trade name "Taco Villa."
Number of Franchisees: 13 in New Mexico, Oklahoma and Texas
In Business Since: 1968
Equity Capital Needed: $70,000
Financial Assistance Available: None
Training Provided: Complete training in all phases of operation is provided in a company-owned Taco Villa outlet located in Odessa, Texas for a minimum of 2 weeks, and up to 12 weeks. Franchisor will also provide training for the franchisee's staff prior to opening of the Taco Villa restaurant.
Managerial Assistance Available: Continuing managerial supervision.

TERRY'S INTERSTATE, INC.
P. O. Box 6395
Tyler, Texas 75711
Terry J. Cooper, President

Description of Operation: Family style leisure dining restaurants located on interstate highways.
Number of Franchisees: 16 in New Mexico and Texas
In Business Since: 1968
Equity Capital Needed: $25,000
Financial Assistance Available: None
Training Provided: Comprehensive 6 week training in all aspects of the business.
Managerial Assistance Available: Continuous assistance in technical, sales and management areas.

TEXAS CATTLE COMPANY
4712 West Waco Drive
Waco, Texas 76710
Paul F. McClinton, President

Description of Operation: Theme fast food restaurants designed for locations in shopping centers, central business districts, or free standing buildings of approximately 2,000 square feet. Open 10-11 hours daily, 7 days a week. Renovation into TCC motif is provided, as well as inventory of TCC products (Barbeque sauces, meats, chili).
Number of Franchisees: 7 in Texas, franchises available nationwide.
In Business Since: 1960
Equity Capital Needed: $50,000
Financial Assistance Available: None
Training Provided: Management training for approximately 1 month in the prototype operation in Waco, Texas.
Managerial Assistance Available: Continuing service and managerial assistance by field managers for the life of the franchise.

TEXAS TOM'S INC.
P. O. Box 4592
Kansas City, Missouri 64124
Tom Nigro, President

Description of Operation: Offer a wide variety of food items on the menu and homemade recipes. Both sit down and carry out service is available and also Call-in service. We also feature several "Basket" combinations, unique to the fast food industry. Western decor.
Number of Franchisees: 17 in Missouri and Kansas
In Business Since: 1953
Equity Capital Needed: $50,000
Financial Assistance Available: Company assists qualified applicants in arranging financing. Assistance in obtaining equipment financing, equipment lease, sign lease and specifications.
Training Provided: 3 weeks of intensive management training at company school plus 3 weeks in-store training. Company also will send qualified representative after store opens for 2 weeks (minimum).
Managerial Assistance Available: Provide assistance in-site selection, building financing, lease negotiations, accounting referral, and continuous advisory assistance. Once a month company meetings plus newsletter sent out each month. Also, inspection of premises and advertising aids.

TIPPY'S TACO HOUSE, INC.
2853 West Illinois
Dallas, Texas 75233
W. L. Locklier, President

Description of Operation: Fast food to take home-using drive-thru and inside seating-Mexican food.

Number of Franchisees: 30 in 12 States
In Business Since: 1967
Equity Capital Needed: Cash and credit, approximately $45,000
Financial Assistance Available: None
Training Provided: Pre-opening training on location at operating unit and opening week training.
Managerial Assistance Available: Continuing assistance by personal visitations, letters, bulletins, telephone.

THE UPPER KRUST, INC.
11441 Chester Road
Cincinnati, Ohio 45246
Steven Keller, President

Description of Operation: The Upper Krust is a deli-style, fast food restaurant. Specialists in home made soups, salads and sandwiches. Franchised operations are housed in defunct restaurants keeping the initial cost of construction to a minimum. Proper operation of an Upper Krust can realize excellent net income from gross sales.
Number of Franchisees: 9 units in Ohio, Kentucky and Dubuque, Iowa
In Business Since: 1965
Equity Capital Needed: $75,000 to $150,000
Financial Assistance Available: None
Training Provided: Complete 30 day training course in home franchise in Cincinnati, Ohio. This training is most comprehensive in scope touching upon all facets of the operation such as cooling, serving, sanitation, ordering foods and other essentials, bookkeeping procedures and customer relations. Also, 3 days of on site training upon the opening of the new franchise.
Managerial Assistance Available: Every franchise is inspected monthly to insure the continued quality is maintained. All franchises are constantly informed on new products and techniques to improve their productivity and profitability.

WALT'S ROAST BEEF INTERNATIONAL, INC.
1635 Cranston Street
Cranston, Rhode Island 02920
Louis W. Spirite, President

Description of Operation: Restaurant specializing in Roast Beef sandwiches. Prototype range 2,000 to 3,000 square feet. Open 7 days a week, 11 a.m. to 11 p.m.
Number of Franchisees: 11 in New England States
In Business Since: 1967
Equity Capital Needed: $25,000
Financial Assistance Available: Investment of $90,000, minimum of $15,000 down payment pays for equipment, franchise fee and refurbishing of existing building. Walt's will help to get financing.
Training Provided: A training period of 4 weeks is required.
Managerial Assistance Available: Walt's provides continual management service for the existence of franchise.

WENDY'S OLD FASHIONED HAMBURGERS
c/o WENDY'S INTERNATIONAL, INC.
P. O. Box 256, 4288 West Dublin-Granville Road
Dublin, Ohio 43017
Director, Franchise Development

Description of Operation: Fast-service restaurant with quality food. Limited menu centered around fresh-cooked 1/4, 1/2, 3/4 pound hamburgers featuring plush dining rooms and a unique "pick-up" window.
Number of Franchisees: 1,815 units including company stores throughout the United States, Canada, Puerto Rico and Germany.
In Business Since: 1969
Equity Capital Needed: $500,000
Financial Assistance Available: None. Total investment $500,000 plus.
Training Provided: 2 to 11 weeks training for manager or operator in classroom and on-the-job at Wendy's Management Institute in Columbus, Ohio.
Managerial Assistance Available: Provide manuals and services to cover cost controls, personnel management, quality control, field consultation, operational efficiency and purchasing.

WHATABURGER, INC.
4600 Parkdale Drive
P. O. Box 6220
Corpus Christi, Texas 78411
Joseph A. Middendorf

Description of Operation: Operate and franchise fast food hamburger restaurants.
Number of Franchisees: More than 200 units operating in the U.S.
In Business Since: 1950
Equity Capital Needed: Minimum $80,000
Financial Assistance Available: Assistance in arranging financing with third party financial institution.
Training Provided: Company operated training school providing extensive and detailed instruction on all phases of restaurant operations.
Managerial Assistance Available: Ongoing operational and administrative assistance provided through field visits.

WIENNER KING CORPORATION
P. O. Box 4348
Charlotte, North Carolina 28207
George E. Kalinwosky, Franchise Development

Description of Operation: Fast food restaurants specializing in hot dogs and chili. Also features hamburgers. Seating capacity for 38 or 80 people depending on size of unit.
Number of Franchisees: 122 in 35 States; however, many franchisees have multiple units.
In Business Since: 1970
Equity Capital Needed: $25,000 to $40,000
Financial Assistance Available: Development based on individual's net worth.
Training Provided: It is mandatory that franchisee spend 2 weeks plus in training at company headquarters, both in operation of a unit and classroom lectures covering personnel, promotions, reporting and so forth. An annual franchise meeting is held to discuss latest chain-wide accomplishments and future goals.
Managerial Assistance Available: Continuous assistance provided throughout the term of franchise agreement. Each unit is visited periodically by a consultant to assist in maximizing income and by the quality department to assure maintenance of high uniform standards.

WIFE SAVER
2751 New Barton Chapel Road
Augusta, Georgia 30906
Chris A. Cunningham
George B. Cunningham

Description of Operation: Fast food restaurant featuring fried chicken and seafood. 100 percent disposable service used in dining room as well as carry-out. Earlier units were either 100 percent carry-out or with up to 40 seat dining room. New units seat approximately 100.
Number of Franchisees: 8 in Georgia and South Carolina.
In Business Since: 1965
Equity Capital Needed: $16,500 operating capital. 1979 unit cost - *land variable*, building $135,000 and equipment - $90,000.
Financial Assistance Available: None. We do not guarantee leases.
Training Provided: Minimum 4 weeks. Owner-operators only.
Managerial Assistance Available: Technical assistance provided throughout term of franchise. Prospective franchisee must know managements responsibility to manage and we offer additional training if needed on location.

WINKYS FAMILY RESTAURANTS
432 Green Street
Sweickley, Pennsylvania 15143

Description of Operation: Fast food/limited menu restaurants, featuring full breakfast menu, fresh-made donuts, hamburgers, roast beef sandwiches, fried chicken, fish & chips.
Number of Franchisees: 8 in Pennsylvania and West Virginia
In Business Since: 1962
Equity Capital Needed: $100,000
Financial Assistance Available: Franchisee must be able to secure own financing.
Training Provided: Minimum 6 weeks
Managerial Assistance Available: Continuous home-office assistance, field supervision and counsel.

WOODY'S LITTLE ITALY RESTAURANTS
5300 Walnut Street
McKeesport, Pennsylvania 15132
Gurino Antonelli, Secretary and Treasurer

Description of Operation: Restaurant with complete line of Italian food products. Food products prepared by the franchisor and finished at the franchisee's restaurant. Sit down, take out and delivery service.
Number of Franchisees: 14 locations in Pennsylvania.
In Business Since: 1968
Financial Assistance Available: $35,000
Financial Assistance Available: Assistance in obtaining financing.
Training Provided: 2 weeks at company location
Managerial Assistance Available: Complete training of all personnel. Assist opening with our own employees and managers.

THE WORLD'S WURST RESTAURANTS
6991 East Camelback Road
Scottsdale, Arizona 85251
Donald LeRoi Allison, President

Description of Operation: Contemporary fast food restaurants with a modern psuedo-bavarian interior featuring bratwurst, knockwurst, franks, beerwurst, german salami and roast beef with chili, german potato salad, sauerkraut, tater treats and draft beer, soda and coffee.
Number of Franchisees: 10 in 2 States
In Business Since: 1975
Equity Capital Needed: $31,000 and ability to acquire outside financing for an additional $32,500.
Financial Assistance Available: None
Training Provided: A full week at the franchise's restaurant, plus ongoing refresher guidance for the 20 year life of the license.
Managerial Assistance Available: Company representative visits franchisee's unit periodically for inspection and assistance. Home office personnel available to render assistance as required.

WUV'S INTERNATIONAL, INC.
Fort Lauderdale Executive Airport
5500-4 Northwest 21st Terrace
Fort Lauderdale, Florida 33309
Marshall Van Landingham, Director of Licensing

Description of Operation: WUV's International offers a unique restaurant concept with a combination of fresh product and a contemporary building design utilizing natural woods and greenery, producing a comfortable dining atmosphere for its customers. Product and equipment specifications along with WUV's building plans are supplied to all franchisees.
Number of Franchisees: 75 in 30 States; one franchised territory in Windsor, Ontario, Canada.
In Business Since: 1975
Equity Capital Needed: Approximately $50,000 minimum, assuming land, building, and equipment are leased.
Financial Assistance Available: Total investment required to open a WUV's Restaurant is a minimum of $400,000. This includes land, building, and equipment. Franchisees are provided with investment information on WUV's International, Inc., and its officers for presentation to banking institutions and investors. Franchisees must, at this time, arrange their own financing.

Training Provided: 3 day licensee orientation class for all franchisees to acquaint them with our advertising, real estate selection, construction, and operations. 200 hour management course conducted for management personnel. Covers all facets of operations. 5 day advanced operations course available to franchise management once they have been operating units for a minimum of 90 days.
Managerial Assistance Available: Complete operations and specifications manuals released to all franchisees. All forms and directions are provided. District and field managers are available to work closely with franchisees and visit stores on a periodic basis to assist in solving problems and improving operations. WUV's International conducts product research on a continual basis to maintain top quality.

YANKEE DOODLE DANDY
c/o YANKEE DOODLE HOUSE, INC.
188 Industrial Drive
Elmhurst, Illinois 60126
William Proyce, Vice President
Description of Operation: Fast food limited menu restaurants featuring hamburgers, hot dogs and roast beef sandwiches.
Number of Franchisees: 18 in Illinois
In Business Since: 1966
Equity Capital Needed: $35,000 and up, depending on location.
Financial Assistance Available: None
Training Provided: 4 week training in company-owned store.
Managerial Assistance Available: Continuing assistance provided by field consultant, to help franchisee achieve maximum profits and maintain uniform standards.

YOUR PIZZA SHOPS, INC.
207 - 7th Street Southeast
Canton, Ohio 44702
John Purney, Jr., President
Description of Operation: Carry-out, dining room operation with salad bar and or smorgasbord available.
Number of Franchisees: 13 in Ohio and Arizona
In Business Since: 1949
Equity Capital Needed: $15,000
Financial Assistance Available: We offer aid in obtaining financing.
Training Provided: 1 month training in one of our operating shops, then training in franchisee's own shop until we feel franchisee can handle their own operation.
Managerial Assistance Available: We are always available to our franchisees if they have any problems or questions of any kind, be it legal, accounting, managerial or operational, for as long as they remain a franchisee.

ZANTIGO AMERICA'S MEXICAN RESTAURANT
KFC CORPORATION
P. O. Box 32070
Louisville, Kentucky 40232
Ted Kurilec, Manager Franchise Sales and Administration
Description of Operation: A quick service restaurant offering a broad Mexican-American menu.
Number of Franchisees: Approximately 75 units
In Business Since: 1974 (merger of Zapata Foods, Inc., and Heublein, Inc.)
Equity Capital Needed: $75,000 minimum
Financial Assistance Available: None
Training Provided: 2 weeks mandatory training provided at a training center which includes in-store training. Additional training at the option of the franchisee or the company. In-store training system provided for hourly help.
Managerial Assistance Available: District managers provide assistance on store opening, marketing, product quality, service, store management, and operations. Seminars, meetings, operating manuals, and other publications keep the franchisee fully informed. Building plans and site location assistance is provided by the company.

GENERAL MERCHANDISING STORES

BEN FRANKLIN
DIVISION CITY PRODUCTS CORPORATION
1700 South Wolf Road
Des Plaines, Illinois 60018
L. V. Dambis, Vice President Franchise and Real Estate Development
Description of Operation: Ben Franklin Stores is a general merchandise operation. This Division of City Products Corporation provides both merchandise and retailing assistance to franchisees in all 50 States. The franchisee operates a private business with the advantages of chain-store buying, merchandising and promotional guidance, and a nationwide reputation for professional service to the public.
Number of Franchisees: 1,700 in 50 States
In Business Since: 1977
Equity Capital Needed: Minimun of $80,000
Financial Assistance Available: Financing is arranged through local and regional commercial institutions.
Training Provided: Training provided for franchisee and employees in selected stores by trained field personnel and store manager. Duration is flexible (usually 30 days) depending upon background, qualifications and needs of franchised owner.
Managerial Assistance Available: Assistance is available in finding locations, sales promotion and all phases of operation by periodic visits of field and headquarters personnel.

COAST TO COAST STORES
CENTRAL ORGANIZATION INCORPORATED
P. O. Box 80
Minneapolis, Minnesota 55440
J. Heino, Director of Franchise Retailing
Description of Operation: Retail "total hardware" store that features national brands plus private-label merchandise structured in 12 basic departments: hardware, electrical, plumbing, automotive, sporting goods, housewares/giftwares, paint and sundries, toys and wheel goods, home furnishings, appliances, building materials, and lawn/farm/garden supplies. Stores are designed to be dominant in their markets.
Number of Franchisees: More than 1,200 in 28 States
In Business Since: 1928
Equity Capital Needed: $30,000 to $150,000, depending on store size. Equity investment is secured by inventory and fixtures; there is not initial payment for the franchise. There is a monthly franchise fee of $45. Entire investment goes for inventory and store operations.
Financial Assistance Available: Franchisee normally furnishes half the initial capital needed; the company's division finance manager and district managers help negotiate additional term financing through local community sources.
Training Provided: New store owners attend a training school (with sessions, lodging and meals at company expense) that thoroughly covers all phases of store operations. Project and district managers help the new store owner with layout, display, set up and grand opening; thereafter, district manager makes continuing visits to give store owner additional training and counsel. This assistance is part of an ongoing program for the store owner.
Managerial Assistance Available: So that the store owner can devote his time to building his business, Coast to Coast offers a wide range of services that eliminate many tedious details. These services include complete bookkeeping and tax accounting; layout and display ideas to maximize inventory turnover, inventory control; pre-printed price tickets; electronic order entry system; group insurance program; sales circulars and merchandising helps; two merchandising meetings a year; training clincs; and continuing advice and assistance from the district manager and other store-operations personnel. Many of these are furnished without charge.

GAMBLE-SKOGMO, INC.
GAMBLE STORES DIVISION
5100 Gamble Drive
Minneapolis, Minnesota 55481
Description of Operation: Gamble Stores Division offers a complete retail store operation program. Merchandise lines are: hardware, automotive, sporting goods, major appliances, furniture, electrical, housewares, paints and supplies, lawn and garden, plumbing, electronics, carpet and floor covering.
Number of Franchisees: 865
In Business Since: 1925
Equity Capital Needed: $40,000 minimum
Financial Assistance Available: A minimum capitalization of $100,000 is recommended. Qualified applicants may borrow equity capital from (1) financial institutions or (2) local banks with Small Business Administration guarantees.
Deferred Dating on seasonal merchandise and sale orders as well as Floor Plan on major items and furniture is offered to provide short term financial assistance to dealers interest free.
Training Provided: An in-depth 2 week 105-hour program covering merchandising and operations is provided at no charge. Continuity in training is provided by field personnel on an on-going basis. In-store training programs are available on product knowledge and selling skills.
Managerial Assistance Available: Gambles provides a complete merchandising and store operations program with modern distribution centers. A centralized parts warehouse for fast delivery and service centers for repair of major appliances provide prompt service to consumers. Field personnel counsel and work with dealers on various store programs. Various services are also provided the dealer to assist in merchandising, operations, credit, finance and personnel—such as a complete accounting service, store operation manuals, pre-printed price tickets, electronic ordering units, circular-newspaper-radio advertising programs, store merchandise layout plan, monthly display packages, pre-printed order forms, inventory management report and on order report to improve merchandise turnover, consumer time payment credit program, complete insurance program and two merchandise markets each year for product knowledge and ordering.

MONTGOMERY WARD
One Montgomery Ward Plaza
Chicago, Illinois 60671
Donald C. Weibel, Catalog Sales Agency Manager
Description of Operation: Retail sales of all merchandise in Montgomery Ward catalogs.
Number of Franchisees: 1,400 in all States except Hawaii.
In Business Since: 1872
Equity Capital Needed: $15,000 minimum
Financial Assistance Available: Partial financing of fixtures, equipment, signs, display and seasonal merchandise. Sales Agent has option to secure his financing from other sources.
Training Provided: Formal 2 week management training - training school plus continued on-site training through self-training materials and personal contact, both on an individual and group basis.
Managerial Assistance Available: Many services available to Montgomery Ward's company-owned and operated Catalog Stores are made available, generally without charge and occasionally with a minimal charge to the Sales Agent. Periodic meetings are also conducted by Montgomery Ward personnel. An advisory council of Sales Agents meet semi-annually with Montgomery Ward Catalog House management team to discuss the business and to propose changes and new concepts or innovations for the consideration and action of Corporate management.

68

RASCO STORES
Division of GAMBLE-SKOGMO, INC.

2777 North Ontario Street
Burbank, California 91504
Franchise Personnel Manager

Description of Operation: Rasco Stores offer two types of franchises: Rasco Variety (a family store) and Toy World (toy specialty stores).
Number of Franchisees: 20 in 4 States
In Business Since: 1934

Equity Capital Needed: Minimum down payment: Rasco Variety $50,000. Toy World $5,000 to $80,000.
Financial Assistance Available: Franchisee, after initial down payment, may have the remainder of his indebtedness financed by Rasco Stores unless he prefers to arrange outside financing.
Training Provided: 2 to 3 days basic indoctrination in Burbank, California Office. Balance of training in the franchisee's store under the supervision of the district manager.
Managerial Assistance Available: Rasco Stores offer mass buying power, modern merchandising ideas, complete accounting services, store layout and opening assistance, advertising program. Store building rental plan, fixture rental plan and operating assistance by district managers and buyers.

HEALTH AIDS/SERVICES

ALPHA NURSES
909 Burnett Street
Wichita Falls, Texas 76301
J. D. Popejoy, Franchise Director

Description of Operation: Alpha Nurses is an *employer* of nursing and health care personnel and other para-medical personnel, which are made available to the growing market of geriatrics, post-operative, cardiacs, pediatrics and other convalescents in the privacy of their home, hospital and health related facilities.
Number of Franchisees: 3 in Texas and Arizona
In Business Since: 1978
Equity Capital Needed: From $20,000 to $30,000 depending on location.
Financial Assistance Available: Accounts receivable financing as needed.
Training Provided: Mandatory 3 week on-site training, plus 1 week on-site training as follow-up, as needed.
Managerial Assistance Available: Alpha provides continual management service for the life of the franchise in such areas as bookkeeping, advertising, inventory control. Complete manuals of operations, forms, and directions are provided. District and field managers are available in all regions to work closely with franchisees regularly to assist solving problems. Alpha sponsors meetings of franchisees and conducts marketing and service research to maintain high Alpha consumer acceptance.

DIET CONTROL CENTERS, INC.
1021 Stuyvesant Avenue
Union, New Jersey 07083
Ruth Landesberg, Secretary

Description of Operation: Conducts classes consisting of lecture motivation and exercises to obtain and maintain permanent weight loss.
Number of Franchisees: 18 in 6 States
In Business Since: 1968. A public company since 1971.
Equity Capital Needed: Mini franchise $3,500
Financial Assistance Available: Terms can be arranged.
Training Provided: Free training available at main office. Free training by mail where needed. Free on-the-job training.
Managerial Assistance Available: Training is extended on a continuing basis to franchises from the inception with unlimited duration. Nutritional and home economic department guidance. Periodic meetings available. Weekly telephone contact. Group and bookkeeping supplies are included.

ELAINE POWERS FIGURE SALONS, INC.
105 West Michigan Street
Milwaukee, Wisocnsin 53203
Elizabeth Browning, Vice President - Franchise Operations

Description of Operation: Elaine Powers Figure Salons is the world's largest figure control system of its kind. Elaine Powers offers women a short term, moderately priced program which is based on the proven principal that the only effective figure control method is one that combines sensible activity and eating habits. The salons are equipped with modern figure improvement equipment and are open 9 a.m. - 9 p.m. Monday thru Friday and Saturday 9 a.m. - 4 p.m.
Number of Franchisees: 91 in 35 States
In Business Since: 1964
Equity Capital Needed: $15,000 initial franchise fee; approximately $35,000 for equipment, leasehold improvements, and operating capital.
Financial Assistance Available: Partial financing may be available based on individual franchisees financial resources.
Training Provided: The franchisee is given a mandatory comprehensive 5 week training program which consists of 2 weeks in a company-owned salon and 3 weeks in their own salon.
Managerial Assistance Available: Franchisee receives complete manuals of operations, forms and directions. Elaine Powers also provides a continuing advisory service which includes consultation of marketing, business, or operational problems. The franchisee is provided on an on-going basis with materials and bulletins on advertising and promotion developments and techniques being used by Elaine Powers.

FAT FIGHTERS, INC.
3070 Lawrence Expressway
Santa Clara, California 95051

Description of Operation: Weight reduction centers operating under the name "The Weight Place." Program consists of a safe, nutritionally sound method of weight control for both men and women with use of vitamins and mineral supplementation. Program also includes special individually tailored dietary intake and daily counseling in behavior modification and nutritional control. Total positive approach to weight reduction.
Number of Franchisees: 29 in California, 1 out-of-state (Note: election for out-of-state only offered since Fall of 1979.)
In Business Since: 1975

Equity Capital Needed: $20,000 - Northern California (complete turn-key, with approximately $8,000 in resale products); $14,000 - Southern California (not turn-key, approximately same package as Northern California except for furniture and set-up); $8,000 - out-of-state (limited package).
Financial Assistance Available: Company capable of handling limited percentage of equity capital for maximum of 60 days at variable interest rate.
Training Provided: All franchise offerings include complete program training in all facets of business: nutrition, sales, behavior modification, vitamin and mineral supplementation, business management. Training from 2 to 6 weeks at main office in Santa Clara, California and at franchisees location, after opening. On-site training available if multiple units purchased.
Managerial Assistance Available: Complete operations manual describing all operations, including accounting and record keeping. On-going periodic seminars dealing with principals of nutrition and business management, new profit areas. Monthly newsletter covering nutritional information by M.D. and field assistance (each area stipulates different visiting times by professional personnel). Continuous investigation and research of new and improved methods and products. Full-time Staff Psycologist (Ph.D.) for behavior modification, and Nutritionist for any problems, at no additional charge. Co-op advertising in North California on national TV, TV Guide. Company ads included in packages for all areas.

GLORIA STEVENS FIGURE SALONS
10 Forbes Road
Braintree, Massachusetts 02184
William A. Butts, Director of Franchising

Description of Operation: Company operates a chain of franchised women's figure control salons. Membership programs are offered to women of all ages at modest prices, without the need for members to sign a written contract. The salons are designed to operate on a low overhead basis, and contain no costly 'frills' such as pools, saunas, etc. Our system, which we refer to as the M.E.D. method, consists of motivation — exercise, behavioral modification — diet; and each member is closely supervised by trained staff on the use of exercise equipment, dieting, nutrition, gymnastics, etc. The 'turn-key' franchise package presently being offered includes a completely equipped salon plus an exclusive territory in which to operate. Corporate plans call for expansion nationwide.
Number of Franchisees: 148.
In Business Since: 1969.
Financial Assistance Available: Individual turn-key franchises average $49,500 total price. After a 50 percent down payment, the balance may be financed.
Training Provided: Complete training course consisting of classroom and on-the-job training.
Managerial Assistance Available: Regular training meetings, seminars and conventions open for owners and staff members. Also, salon supervision and trouble-shooting available.

HEALTH CLUBS OF AMERICA
Box 4098
Waterville, Connecticut 06714
Gregg Nolan, Franchise Director

Description of Operation: Health and slenderizing salons with separate facilities for men and women.
Numbr of Franchisees: 18 in Connecticut, New York and New Jersey.
In Business Since: 1961.
Equity Capital Needed: Minimum of $10,000, depending on equipment.
Financial Assistance Available: Financing may be arranged through Horizons of America, Inc., parent company.
Training Provided: 1 week management training in main office in New York. At least 3 weeks of day-to-day operational training at own club.
Managerial Assistance Available: Company is always available for counseling.

HELPMATES NURSING SERVICES, INC.
1100 Connecticut Avenue, N.W.
Washington, D.C. 20036
Edward Crane, Executive Vice President

Description of Operation: National network of independently owned and operated nurses registries utilizing the Helpmates proprietary marks, systems and advertising. This unique health care franchise is ideal for doctors, nurses, and any other person concerned with offering quality home and institutional health care at reasonable prices through Registered Nurses, Licensed Practical Nurses, Nurses Aides and Home Health Care Aides.
Number of franchisees: 5 in New York, Maryland, Virginia and Florida.
In Business Since: 1970.

Equity Capital Needed: $2,500 to $25,000 for initial franchise fee depending on population, plus $5,000 to $15,000 for startup costs for first year of operations.
Financial Assistance Available: Franchisee must arrange own financing.
Training Provided: Training program including operation of registry, advice on establishment of clientele and marketing; maintenance of nursing personnel pool; coordination of health care services; staff utilization; maintenance of professional standards, and advice on becoming a community health information specialist.
Managerial Assistance Available: Complete operations manuals including forms, letterheads, and other documentation for immediate operation. Advice on accounting systems; inventory control; record keeping; business insurance; computer services and filing systems.

LEAN LINE, INC.
151 New World Way
South Plainfield, New Jersey 07080
Antonia S. Marotta, President

Description of Operation: A weight reduction organization. The people who join become members and they are expected to attend one meeting each week. The length of time of membership depends upon the amount of weight the individual needs to lose. A member may terminate his or her relationship at any time and not be penalized financially. The program teaches the member how to lose weight by utilizing a nutritionally sound diet and university tested behavioral techniques aimed at changing poor eating habits.
Number of Franchisees: 10 in 7 states.
In Business Since: 1968.
Financial Assistance Available: None.
Training Provided: Training takes franchises through all phases necessary to operate a successful business. Emphasis is placed upon class procedures and presentations which include the nutritional and psychological understanding necessary to indoctrinate the membership. Training manuals are also provided.
Managerial Assistance Available: The managerial and technical assistance is provided as part of the ongoing relationship. After their initial training, franchisees are at liberty to call upon us at any time for any assistance they may need. If there are any changes in policy or form, franchisees are thoroughly indoctrinated.

LYNN STEVENS, INC.
2080 North Boone School Road
Caledonia, Illinois 61011
James E. Littell, President

Description of Operation: Lynn Stevens Health Studio is a unique health studio system including a method of operation, customer service, technical knowledge, equipment and layout plan, health programs, and contract and accounting systems together with business techniques and practices.
Number of Franchisees: 11 in Illinois.
In Business Since: 1971.
Equity Capital Needed: Approximately $25,000 to $45,000 depending upon size of studio and population being serviced.
Financial Assistance Available: Terms can be arranged.
Training Provided: 6 week intensive training by corporate personnel; 3 weeks prior to opening, 3 weeks immediately following. Corporate representatives are available throughout the term of franchise to train new employees, conduct refresher courses, etc., as requested.
Managerial Assistance Available: Fully detailed operation and training manuals provided. Corporate representatives regularly visit studios for inspection and problem solving purposes. Seminars for franchisees and their staffs held annually.

MacLEVY PRODUCTS CORPORATION
92-21 Corona Avenue
Elmhurst, New York 11373
Monty MacLevy, President

Description of Operation: Health club and salon. Company collects no fees or royalties and only sells equipment to franchisee. Franchise operation available from associate companies and financing available from commercial credit organizations.
Number of Franchisees: 25
In Business Since: 1968.
Equity Capital Needed: $10,000 to $25,000.
Financial Assistance Available: No financial assistance provided by MacLevy. Financing available through commercial credit organizations. Company terms of purchase are 30 percent deposit with order balance cash on delivery.
Training Provided: 1 to 7 day training period available at various operating Health Clubs in different locations in the USA. Franchisor provides operations manuals "A Profitable Business," as well as instructional material and business systems to assist Health Club operator in initial operation. Franchisor also furnishes architectural advice, plans and layouts and suggests list of equipment.
Managerial Assistance Available: Managerial and technical assistance by telephone or through correspondence at no charge. Distributors for franchisor will make periodic visits to the franchisee.

MEDIPOWER
P.O. Box 613
Bellaire, Texas 77401
Floyd MacKenzie, President

Description of Operation: Computer-bookkeeping service to the medical profession. Selling products and services to physicians, hospitals, nursing homes, etc. Sale-rent-lease of patient's aid, hospital beds, wheelchairs, walkers, crutches, etc.
Nubmer of Franchisees: 3 in Texas.
In Business Since: 1969.
Equity Capital Needed: No franchise fee; investment limited to inventory; no minimum required.

Financial Assistance Available: None — on approved credit, 30 day open accounts.
Training Provided: Continuous sales training and on location aid for first 2 weeks.
Managerial Assistance Available: Continuous assistance on phases of operation.

NUTRI-SYSTEM WEIGHT LOSS MEDICAL CENTERS OF AMERICA, INC.
7425 Old York Road
Melrose Park, Pennsylvania 19026
Norman Amster, Marketing Director

Description of Operation: Nutri-System Weight Loss Medical Centers offers the consumer a comprehensive, medically supervised weight reduction program utilizing medical and professional treatment, individualized personal care and maintenance. Using Nutri/System 2,000, an exclusive pre-packaged natural food program, Nutri-System Weight Loss Medical Center provides rapid, safe weight loss without drugs, injections or diet pills.
Number of Franchisees: 230 in 29 states and Washington, D.C.
Equity Capital Needed: $45,000 minimum.
Financial Assistance Available: Franchisee has option to arrange own financing. Assistance in arranging financing is provided by franchisor.
Training Provided: Franchisor provides complete training for franchisees, medical personnel and entire office staff through training seminars, on-site instruction and training guides. Periodic training seminars and area coordinators provide continual follow-up supervision.
Managerial Assistance Available: Franchisor provides continued management and technical service in such areas as client treatment, bookkeeping, advertising, sales, inventory control and business management. Complete manuals of operations are provided along with printed and electronic instructional aids. National and district advisors work closely with franchisees to analyze and evaluate operations.

OUR WEIGH
3340 Poplar, Suite f330
Memphis, Tennessee 38111
Helen K. Seale, President

Description of Operation: A unique weight control group consisting of: thirty minute meetings, behavior modification, exercise, and most important a nutritional diet that allows members to eat what they like and not have to eat foods they don't like. First in the field to introduce "food rewards" and free weekly weigh in upon reaching desired weight.
Number of Franchisees: 5 in Arkansas, Tennessee, Mississippi, Georgia and Texas.
In Business Since: 1974.
Equity Capital Needed: Depending upon population in county cost of franchise can run from 1 to 10 percent of population — next 5 franchisees will get special price.
Training Provided: Seven to 10 working days training on the job at national headquarters plus visit from national headquarters executive opening week plus minimum of two visits a year from representative of national headquarters for promotional, publicity and and on the site training. Monthly letter sent to individual franchisees with latest nutritional, advertising, promotions, group leading, personal information.
Managerial Assistance Available: Twenty-four hours a day, 365 days a year open communication with national headquarters executives plus as mentioned above. Constant telephone calls, letters sent and visits to keep franchisees up to date on all aspects of their business.

PEOPLE CARE, INCORPORATED
29 West 34th Street
New York, New York 10001
Donald D. Jacobson, Chairman

Description of Operation: Placement of registered nurses, licensed practical nurses, nurses aides, homemakers, companions, therapists, etc., in the private home, hospital and nursing home. All are our direct employees.
Number of Franchisees: 10 in New York, New Jersey, Pennsylvania and Massachusetts.
In Business Since: 1976.
Equity Capital Needed: $17,500 franchise fee; $15,000 plus for working capital.
Financial Assistance Available: Payment terms re: franchise fee. Accounts receivable financing at cost (interim).
Training Provided: 2 weeks in home office (New York City). Three weeks at franchise location. Ongoing visits to franchisee.
Managerial Assistance Available: Provide constant marketing innovations and supervision of patient accounts and provided services to patients.

QUALITY CARE - USA, INC.
100 North Centre Avenue
Rockville Centre, New York 11570
Herman M. Schuster, President

Description of Operation: Quality Care - USA, Inc., is an **employer** of nursing and health care personnel and other paramedical personnel, which are made available to the growing market of geriatrics, post-operative, cardiacs, pediatrics and other convalescents in the privacy of their home, hospital and health related facilities.
Number of Franchisees: Offices — 121 in 38 states, operating in 48 states and Canada, total number of offices 192.
In Business Since: 1972.
Equity Capital Needed: $35,000.
Financial Assistance Available: A total franchise fee of $25,000 with $10,000 down, and a 24-month payout is available in most areas, dependent upon population.
Training Provided: Training on-site of franchise after a training course by Quality Care - USA, Inc., headquarters, is provided. Approximately 3-4 weeks of intensive training is necessary before approval as a qualified franchisee.
Managerial Assistance Available: Quality Care - USA, Inc., provides continuous, ongoing management service for the life of the franchise in the areas of personnel recruitment, advertising, bookkeeping, business getting, quality control, etc.

SPACE AGE FITNESS CENTERS
P.O. Box 266
Independence, Missouri 64050
Glen Henson, President

Description of Operation: A low profile health center featuring Isokinetic equipment. Can be family oriented or for women only. Only Space Age Fitness Centers may secure the Mini Gym Isokinetic exerciser. Call us toll free 1-800-821-3126.

Number of Franchisees: 15 in Missouri, Texas, Washington, D.C., Florida and Pennsylvania.

In Business Since: 1975.

Equity Capital Needed: $15,000.

Financial Assistance Available: None.

Training Provided: 2 weeks in franchisee's club, 3 days in manufacturers plant.

Managerial Assistance Available: Managerial and technical assistance provided in use of all equipment, office forms, bookkeeping, etc.

SPA DEVELOPMENT CORPORATION
(Licensor of JACK LA LANNE HEALTH SPAS)
2600 Flatbush Avenue
Brooklyn, New York 11234
Judy Scott, Vice President

Description of Operation: The company will operate and franchise others to operate Health Spas and Health and Fitness Centers offering a full range of regular supervised health and fitness programs. Facilities operate under the name of Jack La Lanne Health Spas or Jack La Lanne Health and Fitness Centers.

Number of Franchisees: 4 — additional franchises are being established in selected areas throughout the United States and overseas.

In Business Since: 1979.

Equity Capital Needed: $150,000.

Financial Assistance Available: The company does not offer financing.

Training Provided: Franchisees receive a minimum of 2 weeks training, covering all exercises, programming, spa procedure, touring, 10 points of sales and service procedure, calesthenics class, basic sales training, basic management procedures and office procedures.

Managerial Assistance Available: As it deems necessary the company will provide additional advisory services for such areas as advertising, business and operational problems, analysis of operational techniques, sales, marketing and financial data. Prior to opening the company provides assistance in such areas as site selection, location development, staffing and advertising.

STAFF BUILDERS MEDICAL SERVICES
122 East 42nd Street
New York, New York 10017
Walter E. Ritter, Vice President

Description of Operation: Supply medical services personnel to hospitals, nursing homes, institutions, doctors offices and for home care. Also provide temporary help services in office, industrial, data processing, marketing and technical for business and industry.

Number of franchisees: 16 in 12 states.

In Business Since: 1961 (Temporary Help).

Equity Capital Needed: $25,000.

Financial Assistance Available: Partial financing of franchise investment or financing of temporary payroll.

Training Provided: 2 weeks at New York headquarters, all expenses paid including manuals, procedures, systems for all phases of the business.

Managerial Assistance Available: Continuous communication with franchisee via telephone, mail (bulletins, supplies, materials, etc.) and visits. Promotional aids, sales programs, recruiting assistance and financial advice are all part of ongoing programs.

VENUS DE MILO, INC. OF CALIFORNIA
2111 Business Center Drive
Suite 240
Irvine, California 92715
Garland J. Fulcher, President

Description of Operation: Venus de Milo ladies reducing salons are unique among American exercise spas and salons. Venus emphasizes personal attention of the franchisee to the needs of the clientele of the salon. Many of Venus' franchisees have been members of our salons who have lost weight and were convinced the Venus program worked. In addition to the weight reduction service Venus salons offer Venus food supplements, exercise clothing and a soon-to-be introduced cosmetic line.

Number of Franchisees: 130 in 15 states.

In Business Since: 1975.

Equity Capital Needed: $35,000 to $38,500.

Financial Assistance Available: Franchisor does not provide any financial assistance.

Training Provided: The franchisee receives 3 to 5 days of intensive classroom instruction and testing. A franchise representative will assist the franchisee during a portion or all of the week before the salon opening and during a portion or all of the opening week. The franchise representative will instruct the franchisee on practical application of the material taught in the classroom.

Managerial Assistance Available: The franchisor provides the franchisee with information to establish simple and inexpensive bookkeeping system. Once every quarter the franchisor holds a meeting at which the ideas are discussed and questions answered. Every month a franchise representative will hold a meeting of her franchisees who discuss development and problems in their respective salons. Each franchisee is welcome to attend the training program as often as she believes necessary at no additional cost to her.

WEIGHT CONTROL INSTITUTE MARKETING CONCEPT, INC.
7444 Holabird Avenue
Baltimore, Maryland 21222
Irvin Mordes, President

Description of Operation: Weight Control Institute Marketing Concept, Inc., offers an effective way to lose weight and stop smoking through an original technique of subliminal hypnosis. Each professional operation consists of an office, waiting room and induction room fully equipped and furnished. Services are rendered in a classroom setting, but with greater physical comfort. Weight Control Institute provides a fully turn-key operation complete with operational, professional and business training.

Number of Franchisees: 5 in Maryland.

In Business Since: 1970.

Equity Capital Needed: $15,000 to $40,000 (depending on size of operation) buys turn-key operation complete with equipment, fixtures, furniture, 6 months operating supplies, technical and operative training.

Financial Assistance Available: Can be arranged.

Training Provided: Training in hypnosis and in the operation of the hypnosubliminal equipment for a period of 2 weeks or longer if necessary. Instructions in the bookkeeping involved in running the business, client relations, advertising programs and all record keeping procedures necessary for a smooth operation preliminary to the inception of the operation, so franchisee starts out totally prepared and confident.

Managerial Assistance Available: Periodic check-ups (especially at conception of the business) to ascertain the satisfactory progress being made and availability of Weight Control Institute for assistance whenever necessary regarding conducting the business, planning advertising, entertaining new ideas or solving any problems that may possibly arise.

HEARING AIDS

RCI, INC.
P.O. Box 397
Central Village, Connecticut 06332
Ralph Campagna

Description of Operation: Hearing aids in Montgomery Ward retail stores.

Number of Franchisees: 29 in 8 states.

In Business Since: 1961.

Equity Capital Needed: $5,000 to $10,000.

Financial Assistance Available: None.

Training Provided: Licensee must have State Hearing Aid Dispensing License. Two weeks indoctrination training. Follow-up training every month for 3 months operations. One "open house" promotion within first 6 months. Enrollment in NHAS home study course.

Managerial Assistance Available: Close business relationship maintained with licensee through sales meetings, publications, industry workshops and personal visits from licensor personnel.

HOME FURNISHINGS/FURNITURE-RETAIL/REPAIR/SERVICES

ABBEY CARPET COMPANY
6643 Franklin Boulevard
Sacramento, California 95823

Description of Operation: Specialty store-retail carpets. Franchisees are only available to people already in the retail carpet business.

Number of Franchisees: 62 in 13 states.

In Business Since: 1967.

Equity Capital Needed: $2,000.

Financial Assistance Available: None

Training Provided: None.

Managerial Assistance Available: None.

AMITY, INC.
410 Atlas Avenue
P.O. Box 7204
Madison, Wisconsin 53707
Jerry R. Cook

Description of Operation: Amity Inc., offers a unique "furniture stripping system" of equipment and chemicals for the stripping and restoration of antiques and furniture. The system to be located in purchasers rented or own shop. There are no contracts or restrictions.

Number of Franchisees: 500 in all states except Alaska.

In Business Since: 1971.

Equity Capital Needed: $4,000 minimum.

Financial Assistance Available: None.

Training Provided: Training provided at purchasers location for 1 day on use and application. Free consulting advice, conventions, seminars, newsletters.

Managerial Assistance Available: Technical advice provided on restoration, stripping and advertising.

BEST BROS., INC.
9 Kulick Street
Clifton, New Jersey 07011
David Raker or Harold Steinman
Description of Operation: Retail home decorator stores — featuring Best Bros., paint, wallcoverings, window shades, and sundries.
Number of Franchisees: 8 in New Jersey, New York, Pennsylvania and Florida.
In Business Since: 1940.
Equity Capital Needed: $70,000.
Financial Assistance Available: Up to $5,000 loan to qualified people.
Training Provided: Comprehensive in-store training — 4 to 6 weeks.
Managerial Assistance Available: Same as above.

CARPET COLOR SYSTEMS
1532 U.S. 19th South
Clearwater, Florida 33516
Donald A. Wagley, President
Description of Operation: Carpet Color Systems offers a complete carpet care program with a unique program of restoring carpet color and changing color of carpet in place.
Number of Franchisees: 32 in Florida and Kentucky.
In Business Since: 1975.
Equity Capital Needed: $4,995.50 minimum.
Financial Assistance Available: None.
Training Provided: An intensive 2 week training course is provided to all new franchisees at the company's home office at no charge to the franchisee. Classroom and on-the-job training is provided.
Managerial Assistance Available: A continual managerial and technical program is offered. Company provides assistance in advertising, accounting, inventory control and management. Field training in the franchisee's home area is also provided by home office personnel.

CARPETERIA, INC.
1122 North Vine Street
Hollywood, California 90038
Andrew Reid, Executive Vice President
Description of Operation: Franchising retail carpet outlets.
Number of Franchisees: 34 in California, Nevada, Washington, Texas and Oregon.
In Business Since: 1973.
Equity Capital Needed: $75,000 to $125,000.
Financial Assistance Available: None.
Training Provided: Complete 3 months training.
Managerial Asssitance Available: Managerial and technical assistance is provided for as much as needed.

CARPET-GENIE SYSTEMS, INC.
P.O. Box 1043
Boone, North Carolina 28607
D.E. Lasley, President
Description of Operation: Complete carpet maintenance program. Cleaning, repair, deodorizing, water damage, color-fast carpet dyeing on the floor. Emphasis on commercial accounts.
Number of Franchisees: 21 in 9 states.
In Business Since: 1974.
Equity Capital Needed: $10,000 to $12,000.
Financial Assistance Available: Franchise cost is $15,000. Equipment leasing available up to $7,000 to qualified buyer after credit check.
Training Provided: 1 week operations training, 1 week sales and office procedure training, follow-up training available on per diem basis, and regional meetings and 1 annual meeting optional.
Managerial Assistance Available: On-going technical and sales information by monthly newsletter, memos and bulletins. Phone assistance available at all times.

CASTRO CONVERTIBLES
1990 Jericho Turnpike
New Hyde Park, New York 11040
Robert J. Perdrizet, Executive Vice President
Description of Operation: Castro manufactures, sells and delivers its own exclusive line of convertible sleep sofas and other allied products in its own or franchised stores.
Number of Franchisees: 70 including company-owned stores.
In Business Since: 1931.
Equity Capital Needed: $50,000 to $100,000, depending on size of store and area.
Financial Assistance Available: Up to $10,000 in inventory to qualified franchisees.
Training Provided: Will set up complete showroom and train all personnel on-the-job or at our factory showroom in all phases of the operation followed up with continuing assistance and supervision as needed.
Managerial Assistance Available: Complete operating procedures including technical and managerial assistance on a continuing basis.

CHEM-CLEAN FURNITURE RESTORATION CENTER
Union, Maine 04862
George Koeck, Sales Manager
Description of Operation: Furniture stripping and refinishing.
Number of Franchisees: 80 in 16 states, Canada and Europe.
In Business Since: 1967.
Equity Capital Needed: $6,300 to $25,000.
Financial Assistance Available: Lease purchase plans available. No royalties, licensee owns all equipment outright. Equipment and solvents covered by U.S. and Canadian patents.
Training Provided: Up to 2 weeks of complete instruction in company-owned shop, plus follow-up.
Managerial Assistance Available: Complete operating procedures, including technical and managerial techniques. Annual meetings of franchisees.

CHEM-DRY CARPET CLEANING
8145-B Belvedere Avenue
Sacramento, California 95826
Robert Harris, President
Description of Operation: Chem-Dry offers a carpet cleaning business with innovative and scientific services and products so unique that legal counsel has indicated that a patent on the Chem-Dry process has been accepted by the United States Patent Office and its issuance is merely a matter of months. Chem-Dry is a Registered Trademark of Harris Research Inc. The soon to be patented Carbonated Cleaner™ has opened the door for a new and innovative approach to carpet cleaning and franchising. Included is an advertising package complete with professional radio jingles, animated television commercials and numerous creative, advertising ideas setting Chem-Dry apart as a distinctively new approach to carpet cleaning.
Number of Franchisees: 228 in 25 states and Canada.
In Business Since: 1977.
Equity Capital Needed: $4,300.
Financial Assistance Available: $4,300 down payment pays for equipment, supplies, advertising package, training and expenses. An additional $100 per month for 24 months at no interest brings the total investment to $6,700.
Training Provided: 2 days training includes on-the-job training with an established franchisee where business management as well as carpet cleaning skills will be taught.
Managerial Assistance Available: A franchisee, his managers or employees may obtain as much additional training as they desire at no charge.

CHROME CONCEPTS INC.
1255 South Kalamath
Denver, Colorado 80223
Gil Acheson, President
Description of Operation: Chrome Concepts is a unique modern furniture boutique featuring modular chrome and glass furniture, modern upholstered furniture, wall decor and lighting. Units are usually located in major shopping malls in approximately 800 square feet. Franchisee makes up chrome and glass furniture to customers specification on location using a modular system. Franchisee selects additional decorator items for display and sale from proven seller list provided by franchisor. Franchisee also sells retail fixtures, trade show exhibits, and office partitions from modular systems.
Number of Franchisees: 18 in 13 states.
In Business Since: 1973.
Equity Capital Needed: $25,000 minimum.
Financial Assistance Available: A total investment ranging from $35,000 to $75,000 is necessary to open a new Chrome Concepts operation. The large range allows for varied leasehold improvement costs. The franchisor aids in making loan proposal applications with the franchisee's local bank, and provides documentary data as requested by financial institutions.
Training Provided: A detailed 10 day training class is given to each franchisee and his key personnel. The training class is conducted in Denver in a classroom environment and actual home-owned stores. Additional training is given by field coordination staff during set-up phase of franchisee's operation. Training is further provided during the first few days of operation in franchisees newly opened facility. Review training is conducted on repetitive field visits.
Managerial Assistance Available: Continued consulting is provided by the Chrome Concepts staff for the life of the franchise. This consulting includes, but is not limited to the areas of merchandising. Inventory control, purchasing, sales techniques, bookkeeping, customer relations, assembly of furniture, logistics, time planning, budgeting, cost analysis, operational profit analysis and advertising. Complete operations manual, all forms, records and advertising material are available from franchisor. Chrome Concepts makes continued field trips to aid in franchise operation. Chrome Concepts further provides product analysis to assure best possible consumer acceptance and reduce purchasing errors.

CLEANMARK CORPORATION
49 Richmondville Avenue
Westport, Connecticut 06880
Helmuth W. Krause, President
Description of Operation: Cleanmark specialists provide Cleanmark brand commercial and residential cleaning service for carpets and furniture, drapes, walls. Smoke and flood restoration. Office cleaning. Carpet and furniture cleaning utilizes company-developed patented equipment and methods.
Number of Franchisees: 3 in Connecticut.
In Business Since: 1966, in franchising since 1979.
Equity Capital Needed: $5,000.
Financial Assistance Available: Company assists franchisee in obtaining local financing.
Training Provided: 5 day on-the-job and in-office training followed by 2-day setup visit by Company instructor. Continuous information service by bulletin, correspondence, and verbal communication.
Managerial Assistance Available: Cleanmark provides continued marketing, management, and technical assistance to franchisee.

CROSSLAND FURNITURE RESTORATION STUDIOS
5747 North Main Street
Sylvania, Ohio 43560
Hugh J. Crossland, President

Description of Operation: Full service furniture restoration services, including furniture stripping, furniture refinishing, repairing, upholstering, caning, etc., for household accounts, commercial and industrial accounts, institutions and antique dealers. Rust removal and prevention, buffing of brass, copper and bronze are services also offered.
Number of Franchisees: 104 throughout the Untied States and Canada, United Kingdom and Western Europe are to be opened in 1980.
In Business Since: Parent Company, Crossland Laboratories, Inc., 1944.
Equity Capital Needed: $22,500.
Financial Assistance Available: Company will finance $22,500 — 50 percent of total investment — for those who qualify. Company also has a Joint Venture Program that is available to qualified institutions etc.
Training Provided: Intensive and complete training in all phases of operation are provided prior to and following Grand Opening. Managerial and office training are included.
Managerial Assistance Available: Particular stress is placed on Managerial, Advertising, Sales Promotion and Marketing training in order to keep Crossland Studio owners familiar with new and sound ways to build and manage their businesses. The Veneer, a monthly newsletter in which owners are encouraged to exchange ideas and keep up with any improvements in techniques etc, is published.

DECORATING DEN SYSTEMS, INC.
P.O. Box 68165
5753 West 85th Street
Indianapolis, Indiana 46268
Steven C. Burston, President

Description of Operation: The retailing of custom-made draperies, carpeting, wallcovering, other related decorating items. All merchandise sold from samples. Business does not require inventory or retail store.
Number of Franchisees: 200 in 40 states.
In Business Since: 1970.
Equity Capital Needed: $5,000 to $10,000 depending on program selected.
Financial Assistance Available: Finance plan-one half down payment, balance financed over 18 month period at 12 percent per month.
Training Provided: In initial year, minimum of 2 weeks of classroom training, 1 week of on-the-job training, plus local and regional training. All training is on-going and continuously available.
Managerial Assistance Available: Grand opening preparation and attendance. Planning and sales projection meeting. American market evaluation. Post opening progress checks. On-going services in marketing, sales, business operations and business expansion as part of fee.

DELHI CHEMICALS, INC.
Delhi Building
Stamford, New York, 12167
George Bergleitner, President

Description of Operation: Franchise outlets provide a community service to commercial, industrial and family accounts in the removal of finishes from articles made of wood, metal, glass, marble, alabaster, tin, copper, brass, bronze, etc. Rust removal, tarnish removal, metal cleaning and rust prevention are included in the services offered. Work is accomplished by dipping or soaking the item treated in chemical solutions.
Number of Franchisees: 426 in 50 states.
In Business Since: 1966 — incorporated, 1968.
Equity Capital Needed: $25,000-$30,000 total cost of package.
Financial Assistance Available: $7,000-$10,000.
Training Provided: 4-½ days of classroom and shop training in all aspects of the business at the pilot shop in Atlanta, or 18 regional training centers in 16 states, Canada, Italy and Holland.
Managerial Assistance Available: Continual technical assistance upon request, usually in the form of resolving difficulties via letter or telegram. Additional training is available at all times in the pilot shop to keep franchisees current on broadening activities or for retraining in any aspect to augment this program. All programs are without charge to franchisees.

DIP 'N STRIP, INC.
2141 South Platte River Drive
Denver, Colorado 80223
E. Roger Schuyler, President

Description of Operation: Franchised and company-owned oeprations providing the household community, antique dealers, furniture refinishers, industrial and commercial accounts in the removal of finishes from wood and metal. Operation requires approximately 2,000 square feet of warehouse space with concrete floor, drain, cold water tap, 220 single-phase power, overhead door, and small office space. The removal is accomplished with a cold stripping formula in chemical solutions. Dip 'N Strip is a federally registered trademark since April 13, 1970. Dip 'N Strip trademark is registered in France, Germany, the Benelux Countries, and pending in the United Kingdom.
Number of Franchisees: 172 in 40 States, Canada and Europe.
In Business Since: 1970.
Equity Capital Needed: $7,200 — no franchise fee required.
Financial Assistance Available: $3,000 will be financed up to 3 years, simple 8 percent interest, and will be carried by the franchisor for those who qualify.
Training Provided: A complete training program is provided for 5 days of actual job and office training in all aspects of the business at the franchisee's own location prior to the grand opening. In Europe, the same training is provided at the Master Licensee pilot location.
Managerial Assistance Available: A complete operations manual and technical assitance is supplied during the training program, and in order to keep the franchisees current on the corporation and other franchisee's activities, a monthly newsletter Dip 'N Script, is published. All advertising mats, layouts, and slicks are provided without charge to the franchisees on request.

DRI-CAL'S ULTRA CARPET CARE SERVICE, INC.
100 Commerce Southwest
Grand Rapids, Michigan 49503
Robert A. Callanan, President

Description of Operation: Dri-Cal's Ultra Carpet Care Service, Inc., offers a unique carpet Drycleaning process. This patented process is known as Rotostatic; it enables a franchisee to dryclean carpeting and upholstery without using detergents or penetrating water resulting in a drying time of less than 45 minutes. Each franchisee is provided initially with sufficient quantities of equipment and supplies to enable full operation in two days.
Number of Franchisees: 18 in Michigan, dealerships in 7 other states, the Bahamas and Canada.
In Business Since: In Michigan since 1975; franchising since 1977.
Equity Capital Needed: $5,000 minimum.
Financial Assistance Available: A total investment of $5,000 provides sufficient training, equipment, and initial supplies with which to begin operations either part-time or full-time. Office type and location, transportation, administrative supplies are at the option of the dealer. Operating from a franchisee's home, it would take less than $500 for funding initial supportive requirements (excluding the cost of transportation). Additional requirements are acquired at 'cost' only, should franchisee so request.
Training Provided: Training manual is provided all new franchisees. Upon initial delviery of equipment and supplies, trained Dri-Cal technicians remain with new franchisee for a minimum of 2 days for on-site training experience. Workshops for all franchisees are held semi-annually. Operational concerns which are not manageable via written or verbal communications are dealth with via personal on-site visits of a Dri-Cal representative.
Managerial Assistance Available: Franchisees are free to operate their business in carpet and upholstery drycleaning in any manner they choose provided they maintain the high standards and quality reputation existing at the time of their investment. Dri-Cal officials are available for regular visits and problem solving projects. Communications through company newsletter, workshops, and regular voice and written communications help to maintain a 'family' and 'team work' atmosphere so that both franchisor and franchisee may find success.

DURACLEAN INTERNATIONAL
Duraclean Building
Deerfield, Illinois 60015
Stuart R. Smith, Marketing Vice President

Description of Operation: On-location cleaning of carpet and upholstery fabrics, plus soil-retarding, static removal, flame-retarding, spot removal, mothproofing and minor carpet repair.
Number of Franchisees: 1,200 in all 50 states, all provinces of Canada, and 28 other countries.
In Business Since: 1930.
Equity Capital Needed: $2,180 down payment.
Financial Assistance Available: Franchisor will finance balance of franchise cost after $2,188 down payment.
Training Provided: 5 day resident training school. One day training with experienced franchisee.
Managerial Assistance Available: Advertising, sales promotions, bookkeeping, laboratory services on cleaning and technical spotting. Regional meetings and international conventions bi-annually.

G. FRIED CARPETLAND, INCORPORATED
800 Old Country Road
Westbury, New York 11590
Al Fried, President

Description of Operation: Retail floor covering stores. Stores vary in size from 2,500 feet to 15,000 feet. Smaller stores are purely sample operations. Larger stores show samples and rolls.
Number of Franchisees: 27 in New York, New Jersey, Connecticut, Florida and Ohio.
In Business Since: Parent Corporation — 1889, Franchising Corporation — 1969.
Equity Capital Needed: Cash minimum $5,000 per individual. We suggest two partners in each franchise. In large stores cash requirements would be proportionately more.
Financial Assistance Available: We have been able to arrange loans, equal to amounts of cash put up by franchisee.
Training Provided: There is no definite training period required. We only want experienced floor covering professionals to apply.
Managerial Assistance Available: Franchisor constantly supervises franchisee's operation.

GUARANTEE CARPET CLEANING & DYE COMPANY
2953 Powers Avenue
Jacksonville, Florida 32207
Frank Woodruff, President

Description of Operation: The Guarantee system offers an excellent opportunity in the carpet and upholstery cleaning business. The ability to successfully dye and tint carpeting on location is a unique part of the process. Specially formulated

73

products have been thoroughly tested and proven. Regional warehouses are strategically located to ensure prompt service and minimize freight costs.
Number of Franchisees: 262 in 47 states and Washington, D.C.
Equity Capital Needed: $6,000 minimum excluding van-type truck.
Financial Assistance Available: Franchise fees are based on population. $4,000 per 100,000 population. Minimum franchise is $8,000 for 200,000 or less. We require ¼ down and balance payable weekly on non-interest bearing note retained in our office. Franchise fee may be paid in full at anytime without penalty. Complete equipment and initial expendable materials $3,500. Materials will produce $6,000 to $7,000 gross sales.
Training Provided: 2 weeks training in Jacksonville, both basic and advanced. Includes management, marketing and technical. Both classroom and field training.
Managerial Assistance Available: Guarantee provides continuous follow-up training for the duration of the franchise via nationwide toll free wats line, two regional meetings each year in all areas and annual national meeting and convention. Field assistance for specific problems at no charge to the franchisee. Marketing and technical manuals are provided and continually updated.

"JACK THE STRIPPER"
P.O. Box 16353
Memphis, Tennessee 38116
Mrs. Jack Aday, Jr.
Description of Operation: Stripping of paint and varnish from wood and metal.
Number of Franchisees: 4 in Tennessee, Alabama, Mississippi and New York.
In Business Since: Franchising since 1955.
Equity Capital Needed: About $10,000.
Financial Assistance Available: All franchises are outright sales, the franchisee owns the franchise and the equipment furnished with the initial purchase.
Training Provided: Extremely simple operation — we furnish 1 man, 1 day at the franchisee's location or more than that if they want to come to our place at their expense. This is all that is necessary.
Managerial Assistance Available: None — none needed.

JOHN SIMMONS, INC.
416 Grove Park Road
Memphis, Tennessee 38117
C. Paul Howse, Vice President
Description of Operation: Franchised retail gift operation specializing in home furnishings and unique gifts.
Number of Franchisees: 34 in 12 states.
In Business Since: 1960.
Financial Assistance Available: None.
Training Provided: Management training in Memphis 3 to 4 days — cover start to finish of 1 day out of operation. Operating manual is given and highlights are covered. When we supervise setting up of store, we will work with personnel in display, sales, and maintenance.
Managerial Assistance Available: We continue to work with franchise by sending a representative from the home office twice a year. We work with franchisee at 2 markets, talk with each by telephone when needed (as long as the franchise is in effect).

LEE'S PURCHASING INC.
dba LEE'S BARS, STOOLS 'N DINETTES
19562 Ventura Boulevard
Tarzana, California 91356
Leon J. Shapiro
Description of Operation: Retail stores specializing in sales of bars, barstools, dinettes and game sets.
Number of Franchisees: 6 in California.
In Business Since: 1962 — Franchising since 1973.
Equity Capital Needed: $75,000.
Financial Assistance Available: None.
Training Provided: Whatever is necessary and continual.
Managerial Assistance Available: Managerial and technical assistance provided in purchasing, advertising, sales aids, floor set up, floor display, criterias and maintaining sales books.

MAINTENANCE KING
89 West 43rd Street
Bayonne, New Jersey 07002
John J. Zuchowski
Description of Operation: Carpet cleaning and maintenance.
Number of Franchisees: 47 in New York, New Jersey, Connecticut, Pennsylvania and Florida.
In Business Since: 1978.
Equity Capital Needed: $18,000 full-time program. $14,000 part-time program.
Financial Assistance Available: Balance of $15,000 financed 5 years. 10 percent cash discount for full payments.
Training Provided: 1 week training program, 10 hours daily intensive.
Managerial Assistance Available: Continuous assistance available. The franchisee receives steady business accounts, continuous advertising, marketing and direct mail to keep your business growing. Our maintenance experts, business management, accounting and legal professionals are always available to answer questions and provide assistance.

NAKED FURNITURE, INC.
1012 Northpath
Wheaton, Illinois 60187
Lou Oates, President
Description of Operation: The Naked Furniture Store franchise is a retail establishment devoted to the retail sale of unfinished furniture, accessories and finishing materials. The inventory in each store contains approximately 30 percent of furniture and 90 percent of finishing materials prepared exclusively for Naked Furniture.
Number of Franchisees: 10 including company-owned in Illinois.
In Business Since: 1972.
Equity Capital Needed: $25,000 minimum cash requirement. An additional $25,000 to be obtained from bank loan.
Financial Assistance Available: No financing available. However, the company will assist with preparing a business package to present to bankers or financial outlets.
Training Provided: Intensified training program of 1-½ weeks. Both classroom and in-store instruction. Company personnel will assist before and after grand opening in franchisee's store.
Managerial Assistance Available: Company will provide assistance in lease negotiation, site approval, complete merchandise selection, ongoing advertising and promotion suggestions, forms and systems and continuous field supervision of retail operations.

NETTLE CREEK INDUSTRIES, INC.
Peacock Road
Richmond, Indiana 47374
Michael Ramsey, Director of Nettle Creek Shops
Description of Operation: Home furnishings retail stores specializing in fabrics and fabric products. These are located in high income shopping areas and cater to people that need advice and assistance in interior decorating. The stores are about 1,500 square feet and feature Nettle Creek products.
Number of Franchisees: 70 in 25 states.
In Business Since: 1950.
Equity Capital Needed: $60,000 — this is the entire cost of the franchise and physical set-up.
Financial Assistance Available: None.
Training Provided: Manuals and operating systems, on-site training of 1 week's duration, in factory training of 2 to 3 days duration and continuing support and advice after the franchise is opened.
Managerial Assistance Available: Nettle Creek provides bookkeeping systems, complete stationery supplies, advertising materials and operating manuals. Full time franchise coordinators assist in location research, store layout, shop owners after opening. If any assistance is requested by the franchisee in areas where we can help, our entire executive staff is available for consultation.

RIVIERA CONVERTIBLES, INC.
3876 South Santa Fe
Los Angeles, California 90058
W.E. Heuermann, President
Description of Operation: Riviera Convertibles manufactures sleeper-sofas known as convertibles, a phrase coined by this company. Retail outlets are franchised to individual owners who purchase merchandise from Riviera and are entitled to advertising material and coverage based on purchases.
Number of Franchisees: 32 in California and Nevada.
In Business Since: 1954 — present ownership, 1975.
Equity Capital Needed: Total investment required $100,000. Prospect must arrange own financing. Initial franchise fee: $10,000.
Financial Assistance Available: None, except credit terms on merchandise purchases.
Training Provided: Merchandising and display techniques, direct selling methods, product technical knowledge.
Managerial Assistance Available: On the site managerial advice is available as long as needed. Merchandising and advertising assistance is provided on continual basis throughout the life of franchise.

RUG CRAFTERS
3321 South Fairview Street
Santa Ana, California 92704
Russell C. Gates, Jr., Chairman of the Board
Description of Operation: Rug Crafters operates a system of retail stores specializing as the "do-it-yourself floor and wall decorating headquarters" using yarn art. The stores merchandise a wide variety of latch hook, speed tufting, and rya patterns, kits and supplies.
Number of Franchisees: 68 in 25 states.
In Business Since: 1970.
Equity Capital Needed: $15,000 to $20,000.
Financial Assistance Available: Total investment varies from $50,000 to $98,000 Company will assist in arranging financing.
Training Provided: The company provides a complete training program including product knowledge, store operation, selling techniques, inventory control and financial control. The program includes classroom and in-store training for approximately 2 weeks.
Managerial Assistance Available: Rug Crafters continually assists franchisee in all aspects of store operations including the introduction of new products, record keeping, selling methods, advertising and promotion. Rug Crafters provides an operations manual and the services of a field coordinator, in addition to the assistance available through the headquarters staff.

SIESTA SLEEP SHOP, INC.
386 Lindelof Avenue
Stoughton, Massachusetts 02072
Steven Glickman, President
Description of Operation: Retail specialty mattress outlets carrying brand name bedding.
Number of Franchisees: 5 in Massachusetts.
In Business Since: 1953.
Equity Capital Needed: $15,000 to $25,000.
Financial Assistance Available: Possible.
Training Provided: 6 to 8 weeks intensive training plus 3 months, as needed, extra supervision.
Managerial Assistance Available: Complete from stock room to management to sales and advertising. Program in effect for one year or less if not required.

SLUMBERLAND, INC.
2361 West Highway 36
Roseville, Minnesota 55113
Kenneth R. Larson
Description of Operation: Slumberland operates specialty stores within the home furnishing industry. Slumberland features name brand mattresses, sleep sofas and reclining chairs.
Number of Franchisees: 6 in Minnesota, Iowa and North Dakota.
In Business Since: 1967.
Equity Caital Needed: $20,000 to $50,000.
Financial Assistance Available: Limited.
Training Provided: Extensive training covering marketing, sales, advertising, and accounting.
Managerial Assistance Available: An ongoing relationship includes marketing, assistance, long range planning, site selection, delivery and warehousing.

SPRING CREST COMPANY
505 West Lambert Road
Brea, California 92621
Jack W. Long, Executive Vice President
Description of Operation: Spring Crest Drapery Centers, retail draperies, drapery hardware and accessories.
Number of Franchisees: 275 in 39 states, Canada, Japan, Australia and South Africa.
In Business Since: 1955, Franchising since 1968.
Equity Capital Needed: $18,000 to $30,000.
Financial Assistance Available: Up to 25 percent of total based on review of financial statement of franchisee.
Training Provided: Initial training at headquarters with additional training at franchise location.
Managerial Assistance Available: Operations manual. One area meeting and one national convention per year. Monthly newsletter. Consultation from regional managers or home office staff.

STANLEY STEEMER INTERNATIONAL, INC.
4654 Kenny Road
Columbus, Ohio 43220
Jack A. Bates, President
Wesley C. Bates, Executive Vice President
Betty B. Bailey, Vice President
Description of Operation: A complete franchise system for on-location carpet and furniture cleaning, water damage cleanup and odor removal services. Company manufactures patented intruck and portable equipment — maintains complete supplies to provide backup for franchises.
Number of Franchisees: Over 200 in 26 states, Canada and Australia.
In Business Since: 1947 carpet and furniture cleaning, 1972 manufacturing and franchise sales.
Equity Capital Needed: Variable, minimum $7,500.
Financial Assistance Available: 5 year lease program available on equipment and new truck.
Training Provided: 1 week or longer, depneding on need at company headquarters. Training conducted by training director with a great amount of on-the-job training with experienced cleaning crews. Periodic review and retraining provided when necessary. All manuals are provided.
Managerial Assistance Available: Bimonthly newsletter and periodic technical and service bulletins issued. Toll free wats lines for orders and technical help available. Specific department head help available on an individual basis. A complete advertising and marketing department is maintained for franchise support. Annual convention for franchisees. Major medical and hospitalization. Continuous research and development for improvement of cleaning methods and equipment, chemicals, etc. Testing of all new innovations.

STEAMATIC INCORPORATED
1601 109th Street
Grand Prairie, Texas 75050
Lindy Berry, General Manager
Description of Operation: Controlled-heat carpet cleaning service and portable in-home drycleaning service for upholstery and drapes.
Number of Franchisees: Over 175 in 37 states, Germany, Canada, Japan, Mexico, Ecuador, Labanon, Kwait and Jordan.
In Business Since: 1967.
Equity Capital Needed: $9,000 to $35,000.
Financial Assistance Available: If franchisee qualifies, one-third of franchisee fee can be financed through Fort Worth bank.
Training Provided: 2 weeks at headquarters at Grand Prairie, 1 week at franchisee's location.
Managerial Assistance Available: Continuous assistance in sales equipment service, advertising materials, research and development, computer management system.

STRIP-TECH, INC.
P.O. Box 179
136 Center Point Road, South
Hendersonville, Tennessee 37075
Leon Desmarais
Description of Operation: A furniture and in home stripping system with a complete line of paint remover solvents and equipment for use in cold solvent dip, flow or spray on dealer operations.
Number of Franchisees: Over 580 locations throughout the U.S.A.
In Business Since: New Parent Company, 1974 — Acquisition of dealers as late as 1960.
Equity Capital Needed: $2,000 to $20,000.
Financial Assistance Available: Bank planning.
Training Provided: On-site training upon installation depending on system 4 days to 3 weeks.
Managerial Assistance Available: Sales aids and marketing programs are complete plus monthly up-date and regional seminars. A full service program to keep dealers abreast of new developments at all times.

THE WOOD FACTORY, CORPORATION
3001 Wouth Croddy Way
Santa Ana, California 92704
Norman L. McGee, President
Description of Operation: Handcrafted Solid Wood Furniture and Wood Craft Items, stores located in regional mall locations. Operation includes retail store and local warehouse. Presently all stores are located in high volume malls.
Number of Franchisees: 6 Franchise — 6 Company — Total 12.
In Business Since: 1977.
Equity Capital Needed: $130,000 to $150,000.
Financial Assistance Available: None.
Training Provided: 5 days in Santa Ana, California at company headquarters and manufacturing plant. Retail training in the Westminster Mall Store location.
Managerial Assistance Available: Assistance provided by the Company in marketing and management.

LAUNDRIES, DRY CLEANING-SERVICES

A CLEANER WORLD
1213 Dorris Street
High Point, North Carolina 27262
S.S. McKarem, President
Description of Operation: "A Cleaner World" — the ultimate in total service in the drycleaning and shirt laundry industry. Each operation is housed in a standardized building, and features at-the-car service six days each. week. "A Cleaner World" lives up to its name in cleanliness with emphasis on fast, courteous service and quality workmanship.
Number of Franchisees: 48 in North Carolina, South Carolina, Virginia, Tennessee, and Georgia.
In Business Since: 1969.
Equity Capital Needed: $25,000.
Financial Assistance Available: None.
Training Provided: Training consists of 5 weeks of in-plant training following prescribed plan under supervision of a qualified training manager.
Managerial Assistance Available: Complete manual of operations, forms, and directions are provided. Continual assistance is also provided in such areas as bookkeeping, advertising, and inventory control.

ALDCLEAN ON PREMISE SYSTEMS, INC.
Division of ALD, Inc.
2002 Gaisford Street
Dallas, Texas 75226.

Description of Operation: Sales, servicing and operational training for On Premise Laundry Systems in industries using linens and/or uniforms in their daily operations, i.e. Nursing and health care centers, food service, lodging and industrial.

Number of Franchisees: 11 in 10 states.
In Business Since: Aldclean — 1974, ALD, Inc. — 1944.
Equity Capital Needed: $2,000.
Financial Assistance Available: None required.
Training Provided: Sales, service, and operational training provided on a continuing basis.
Managerial Assistance Available: Same as above plus all forms for internal processing of orders and service billings on a continuing basis. Training available in franchise office and at Dallas office.

BRUCK DISTRIBUTING COMPANY, INC.
9291 Arleta Avenue
Arleta, California 91331
Julius Bruck, President
Description of Operation: Eldon Drapery Drycleaning Franchisees: Servicing draperies for both commercial and residential building. Forty percent of business done under name of major department stores.
Number of Franchisees: 18 in California, Arizona, Washington, Utah, Hawaii and Oregon.
In Business Since: 1966.
Equity Capital Needed: $30,000 to $60,000.
Financial Assistance Available: None.
Training Provided: Complete production, installation, sales and office procedures. First portion in our training facility. Second portion in franchisees. We train for as long as franchisee feels is needed.
Managerial Assistance Available: Ongoing program.

COIT DRAPERY & CARPET CLEANERS, INC.
897 Hinckley Road
Burlingame, California 94010
L.L. Pressman, Franchise Director
Description of Operation: Supply and maintenance of draperies and other window furnishings.
Number of Franchisees: 60 in 35 states, Canada and Europe.
In Business Since: 1963.
Equity Capital Needed: Minimum $15,000 - $60,000.
Financial Assistance Available: Will extend credit to qualified individuals, but encourages outside financing.
Training Provided: Initial training at franchisor's plant in California or Monarch Headquarters in Chicago or at Cleanol Services, Toronto, Canada. Additional training at franchisee's plant.
Managerial Assistance Available: Refresher training at regional meetings, manual of operating instructions, continuous managerial and technical assistance, quality control and research and development programs. Regional meetings, bulletins, a house journal, and revisions to the franchise manual are used to disseminate information to franchisees.

COOK MACHINERY COMPANY
Division of ALD, INC.
4301 South Fitzhugh Avenue
Dallas, Texas 75226
Description of Operation: Country Clean laundry and drycleaning stores.
Number of Franchisees: 250 in all states.
In Business Since: 1946, Country Clean started 1970.
Equity Capital Needed: $15,000
Financial Assistance Available: Financing and leasing available for qualified applicants.
Training Provided: On-the-job training by local distributors. Service schools at the factory.
Managerial Assistance Available: Managerial and technical assistance provided by local distributors.

DUTCH GIRL CONTINENTAL CLEANERS
200 Frank Road
Hicksville, New York 11801
Michael U. Voelkel, President
Harvey S. Kleinman, Vice President, Sales
Description of Operation: On-the-premise boutique drycleaning store and pound cleaning.
Number of Franchisees: 200 in 20 states. Concept stores in Europe with same operation about 800.
In Business Since: 1964.
Equity Capital Needed: $25,000 to $30,000.

Financial Assistance Available: Financing up to 70 percent of equipment costs.
Training Provided: Initial training in operating school, followed by on-the-job training in franchisee's store. Training period is about 3 weeks.
Managerial Assistance Available: All phases of assistance are available in management advertising promotion, accounting and technical.

LONDON EQUIPMENT COMPANY
2243 Bryn Mawr Avenue
Philadelphia, Pennsylvania 19131
Ronald London, President
Description of Operation: Professional drycleaning, professional suede and leather cleaning, coin operated laundry and drycleaning.
Number of Franchisees: 254 in New Jersey, Pennsylvania and Delaware.
In Business Since: 1963.
Equity Capital Needed: $15,000.
Financial Assistance Available: 90 percent financing of equipment.
Training Provided: In-house training as required, suede and leather cleaning schools, service clinics.
Managerial Assistance Available: Field inspection and training.

MARTIN FRANCHISES, INC.
Franchise Department
2005 Ross Avenue
Cincinnati, Ohio 45212
Description of Operation: Fast service "Martinizing" drycleaning stores.
Number of Franchisees: 1,732 in 49 states.
In Business Since: 1950.
Equity Capital Needed: Minimum $25,000.
Financial Assistance Available: Must arrange own financing with assistance from local independent franchise representative.
Managerial Assistance Available: Supervision and guidance provided by local dealer and franchisor as requested by franchisee.

SPEED QUEEN COIN OPERATED LAUNDROMAT AND DRY CLEANER, INC.
801 Wager Street
Utica, New York 13502
Raymond Seakan, President.
Description of Operation: Speed Queen Coin Operated Laundromat and Dry Cleaner, Inc., offers to acquire a location, install the equipment, train the operator and assist with financing of a retail Coin Operated Laundromat and Dry Cleaning operation. We offer an unattended self service and also have added service sales shops selling plastic bags, soft drinks, candy and sandwiches. An optional service where we will do the laundry for the customer at 25 cents a pound. We do a marketing survey to help insure a profitability factor and we train the buyer in being able to service and manage this business.
Number of Franchisees: 130 in New York, 1 in Texas and 1 in Illinois.
In Business Since: 1959.
Equity Capital Needed: $7,500 and good credit.
Financial Assistance Available: A total investment is between $35,000 and $55,000 in order to own and operate this type store. The down payment of $7,500 is for inventory, security deposits, operating capital, licenses, permits and training. Speed Wash will finance the balance if the franchisee has good credit references and good character references. The franchisee has option to arrange his own financing.
Training Provided: 14 days of training, 16 hours per day as a mandatory training course is scheduled for all new franchisees and appointed personnel. Two days are conducted at their office and 12 days at the site.
Managerial Assistance Available: Speed wash provides continuous consulting management advice for the full duration of the store's operation in the field of bookkeeping, advertising, and inventory control. Interpretation of the manual of operations, all forms, and directions are provided. Franchisee has the option to place all of his products from Speed wash which will be at competitive prices.

LAWN AND GARDEN SUPPLIES/SERVICES

LAWN-A-MAT CHEMICAL AND EQUIPMENT CORPORATION
54 Kinkel Street
Westbury, New York 11590
Description of Operation: Lawn service and products for the home-owner, offering a wide range of products and services.
Number of Franchisees: 155 in 15 states.
In Business Since: 1961.
Equity Capital Needed: $3,500.
Financial Assistance Available: For qualified applicants.
Training Provided: Primary training at franchisor's centers.
Managerial Assistance Available: Agronomical, managerial, technical and sales training provided on a continuing basis at regular seminars and in the field. Personnel available to solve special problems.

LAWN DOCTOR INCORPORATED
P.O. Box 525, 142 Highway #34
Matawan, New Jersey 07747
Russell J. Frith, Vice President
Description of Operation: Professional automated lawn services.

Number of Franchisees: Over 260 in 27 states.
In Business Since: 1967.
Equity Capital Needed: Minimum of $12,500.
Training Provided: Extensive 1 week managerial, sales and technical training at the home office. One week technical training for each employee at the home office. Weekly workshops. Management seminars.
Managerial Assistance Available: All necessary initial bookkeeping, advertising, and sales promotional materials supplied. Close follow-up after initial training with service representatives available for both telephone and in the field assistance whenever required. Public relations consultation available. Extensive TV advertising campaigns in major markets.

LAWN KING, INC.
14 Spielman Road
Fairfield, New Jersey 07006
Joseph J. Sandler, President
Description of Operation: Automated lawn service.
Number of Franchises: Over 100 in 10 states.
In Business Since: 1970.
Equity Capital Needed: $60,000 for equipment and operating capital.

Financial Assistance Available: Limited financing may be arranged for qualified parties.
Training Provided: 2 weeks of intensive training at inception covering managerial, technical, sales, advertising and mechanical aspects. Continuing assistance provided.
Managerial Assistance Available: Bookkeeping/tax system, accounting service, contract forms, billing procedures, newspaper advertising layouts, direct mail program, television commericals, forms and tools for estimates and lawn analyses.

LAWN MEDIC INC.
1024 Sibley Tower Building
Rochester, New York 14604
Donald W. Burton, Chairman of the Board and President
Description of Operation: Automated lawn services.
Number of Franchisees: 163 in 27 states.
In Business Since: 1969.
Equity Capital Needed: $6,850 to $24,850; dependent upon level of involvement.
Financial Assistance Available: Franchisor will finance some franchisees.
Training Provided: 4 day classroom session plus 1 week in the field. Regular seminars and training meetings after franchisee is established.
Managerial Assistance Available: Assistance in bookkeeping, advertising, inventory control and tax advice. District and field managers render assistance. Continuous research in marketing, products and service.

LIQUI-GREEN LAWN CARE CORPORATION
6901 Pioneer Parkway
Peoria, Illinois 61614
B.C. Dailey, President
Description of Operation: Lawn spraying of fertilizer and weed control, plus many additives; each one is owner operated, consisting of a new Ford 2-ton truck, mounted with 1,200 gallon tank with injectors for special products.
Number of Franchisees: 28 in Illinois, Iowa, Pennsylvania, Indiana and Wisconsin.
In Business Since: 1953.
Equity Capital Needed: $35,000.
Financial Assistance Available: Must have one-half down, financial assistance available for the balance.
Training Provided: 2 weeks at the training base, plus continued assistance throughout the life of the contract. Regular 3 week visits.
managerial Assistance Available: Liqui-Green sponsors two seminars a year to introduce new ideas, products and advertising ideas. Liqui-Green is staffed with turf and tree experts for counsel to all its franchises.

SPRING-GREEN LAWN CARE CORP.
P.O. Box 908
Naperville, Illinois 60504
William R. Fischer, President
Description of Operation: Chemical application to commercial and residential lawns, trees and shrubs.
Number of Franchisees: 17 with 22 territories in Illinois and Indiana.
In Business Since: 1977.
Equity Capital Needed: $10,000 to $15,000.
Financial Assistance Available: No financial arrangements provided by franchisor. If franchisee so desires, one of the executive officers will assist the franchisee in obtaining a loan.
Training Provided: 1 week intensive training at beginning of franchise operation with on-going assistance as needed. Also, monthly instructional meetings as well as seminars at various times during the year.
Managerial Assistance Available: S-G provides managerial and technical assistance to the franchisees on an on-going basis. Training manuals as well as various publications are provided for each franchise. Field representatives visit each franchisee on a regular basis to provide assistance in an area where the franchisee may need help. 2 or 3 day seminars are also held during the year covering such items as Cash Flow Projections, Selling Skills and Technical Assistance. S-G also provides assistance in advertising and marketing and product research.

SUPERLAWNS, INC.
17032 Briardale Road
Rockville, Maryland 20855
Ron Miller, General Manager
Description of Operation: Superlawns offers a modern, realistic approach to the automated lawn care service business.
Number of Franchisees: 12 in Maryland, New Jersey and Virginia.
In Business Since: 1976.
Equity Capital Needed: From $12,500 plus operating capital.
Financial Assistance Available: Limited financing may be available to qualified persons.
Training Provided: Comprehensive training at the home office, in the field and on-the-job. This training includes advertising methods, business systems and accounting, office procedures, sales turf management and agronomy and general operations.
Managerial Assistance Available: Constant communication and cooperation by parent company to aid franchisee to become a better business person through understanding of advertising concepts, sales, customer relations, bookkeeping, general operations and service industry concepts, quality control, inventory controls, small business management and technical training for as long as required by franchisee. Assistance is only a phone call away.

MAINTENANCE/CLEANING/SANITATION-SERVICES/SUPPLIES

AMERICLEAN NATIONAL SERVICE CORPORATION
Hemlock Road
Boxford, Massachusetts 01921
Carl F. Whitaker, President
Description of Operation: Americlean is a registered trademark. The Corporation provides franchised professional cleaning services for homes, offices, apartment complexes, hospitals and institutions. Services include rugs, carpets, upholstery, floors walls, windows, furniture, fixtures,also residential fire restoration and housekeeping services.
Number of Franchisees: 6 in Massachusetts.
In Business Since: 1968.
Equity Capital Needed: $3,400 to $4,800 guaranteed repurchase agreement.
Financial Assistance Available: Corporate assigned regional managers assist franchisee with financing, machines, equipment and supplies through local or corporate sources.
Training Provided: Formal business training by established local Americlean associates when available until franchisee is capable of providing professional cleaning services to Americlean quality standards. Local business and training seminars held annually.
Managerial Assistance Available: Managerial assistance on a continuing basis from corporate officers and local regioal managers in business management including advertising development, sales promotion, training, bookkeeping, manuals, laboratory assistance, legal and financial help. Americlean offers additional benefits including life, medical and disability insurance also a retirement savings plan.

CHEMAN MANUFACTURING CORPORATION
5747 North Main Street
Sylvania, Ohio 43560
J. Morgan Crossland, President
Description of Operation: The name "CHEMAN" is a combination of two words, "CHEmical" and "MANufacturing." They describe the function of CHEMAN franchisees, which is to manufacture a line of nearly 50 of the most popular, fastest selling and highest profit maintenance and industrial products; which includes all types of detergents, waxes, floor and carpet cleaners, glass cleaners, degreasers, bowl cleaners, etc.
Number of Franchisees: 3 in 2 states and Puerto Rico.
In Business Since: 1978 (Parent company, Crossland Laboratories, Inc., in business since 1944).
Equity Capital Needed: $20,000 minimum.
Financial Assistance Available: A total investment of $40,000 and $50,000 is necessary to open a CHEMAN Manufacturing business. However, the parent company will finance 50 percent of the total investment on a Joint Venture arrangement for those who qualify. This permits qualified individuals to get started in this high profit business with an initial investment of only $20,000.
Training Provided: Complete and intensive training is provided in all phases of the business, including the compounding of all products, management, sales and marketing, hiring of personnel, bookkeeping etc. This training includes a manual of operations and is continuous during the life of the agreement in order to keep owners abreast of new developments etc., in order to assure continued success.
Managerial Assistance Available: CHEMAN provides continual assistance in every phase of the business; with advice and personal assistance in developing new business and adding new and/or improved products, together with the development of new or special products for customers. In short, everything is done to assist all CHEMAN operations to meet constantly changing conditions and develop successful, thriving business.

CHEMICAL FRANCHISING CORPORATION
P.O. Box 1064
Opa Locka, Florida 33054
John Hall, Jr., President
Description of Operation: Manufacture and sales of a line of commercial cleaning products. Extremely low cost and very high profit. Complete easily learned program includes total set up of small plant (20' x 30'); all initial equipment and supplies and total management system including accounting and sales.
Number of Franchisees: 4 in Florida and Kansas.
In Business Since: 1977.
Equity Capital Needed: Franchisee needs $15,000 as follows; $5,000 for his own operating capital, $4,000 for equipment and inventory and $6,000 franchise fee.
Financial Assistance Available: Some assistance.
Training Provided: 2 weeks initial in our plant, learn manufacture and sales. Thereafter six days the first quarter, six days in second quarter and one day per quarter thereafter.
Managerial Assistance Available: Complete management system provided. Help for recruiting and training sales personnel. New product development.

CHEM-MARK INTERNATIONAL, INC.
200 South Cypress Street
Orange, California 92666
Darol W. Carslon, President
Description of Operation: Market commercial dishwashing machines, glass washing equipment, cleaning and sanitation products for restaurants and institutions.
Number of Franchisees: 89 in 46 states.
In Business Since: 1959.
Equity Capital Needed: $18,000.
Financial Assistance Available: None.
Training Provided: 1 week in home office, plus 1 week on-the-job in own territory.
Managerial Assistance Available: Continued managerial and technical assistance.

MR. MAINTENANCE
7126 Van Nuys
Van Nuys, California 91405
Philip. A. Syphers, President

Description of Operation: ABC Maintenance Development Corporation has developed a complete system for providing commercial building maintenance services under the tradename of Mr. Maintenance. The company sales force develops as many customers as is desired by the franchisee. Customers are located in an area chosen by the franchisee. Area sub-franchising rights are available to qualified individuals who wish to see Mr. Maintenance franchises in selected regions of the country.
Number of Franchisees: 50 in California.
In Business Since: 1971.
Equity Capital Needed: $500 to $25,000 (proportional to the $ volume of customers provided).
Financial Assistance Available: Partial financing available.
Training Provided: Complete training is provided which lasts from 3 days to 2 weeks for the service franchisee to 1 month for area sub-franchisors. In either program the training consists of both classroom and field training.
Managerial Assistance Available: The company provides complete ongoing managerial services including computerized bookkeeping systems, billing, collecting, employee referrals, technical advice, sales assistance, company supervision and continuous management counciling.

MR. ROOTER CORPORATION
4220 Northwest 23rd
Oklahoma, City, Oklahoma 73107

Description of Operation: Mr. Rooter has developed improved equipment and marketing techniques in the sewer and drain cleaning business. Each licensee has access to the management skills and know-how of generations of master plumbers. The use of four U.S. patent office registered servicemarks and advertising aids designed to increase business. A step by step integrated business system and more. Dealers may operate from their home as husband and wife teams.
Number of Franchisees: 54 in 16 states.
In Business Since: 1968, Incorporated 1970.
Equity Capital Needed: Initial license fee $2,500 and up depending on population of territory. Equipment needed for one truck approximately $3,000. Dealers are also required to have a white van-type truck.
Financial Assistance Available: None by company. Applicants who qualify should be able to finance their equipment and truck at their local bank.
Training Provided: Complete training in sewer and drain cleaning and office procedures is available. This includes bookkeeping as well as on-the-job training. It takes approximately 5 days depending on prior experience of the new dealer.
Managerial Assistance Available: Mr. Rooter Corporation maintains a continuous home office advisory service for the lifetime of the agreement. This includes guidance in both managerial and technical aspects of the business. Dealers may take refresher training at any time at their convenience.

NATIONAL CHEMICALS AND SERVICES, INC.
506 Wrightwood Avenue
Elmhurst, Illinois 60126
Robert E. Knight, Secretary-Treasurer

Description of Operation: Route service doing commercial and industrial wash room cleaning and sanitation supplies.
In Business Since: 1964.
Equity Capital Needed: $7,500 minimum.
Financial Assistance Available: Limited financing to qualified individuals.
Training Provided: Intensive break-in training. 2 week period in service and sales.
Managerial Assistance Available: Continuing field and home office training as

NATIONAL MAINTENANCE CONTRACTORS, INC.
200 - 112th Avenue, N.E.
Bellevue, Washington 98004
Lyle R. Graddon, President

Description of Operation: National Maintenance Contractors is an association of independent janitorial contractors. These contractors purchase their accounts from "NMC" and are supported, for a fee, by "NMC's" administrative services. These services include a guarantee of lost account replacements, bonding, insurance, invoicing, collections, training, etc.
Number of Franchisees: 98 in Washington and Oregon.
In Business Since: 1973.
Financial Assistance Available: Total investment is dependent on the volume of accounts purchased. National Maintenance Contractors will carry one half of the total investment on a note for 1 year.
Training Provided: Initial on-the-job training is conducted in franchisee's accounts and optional additional training is handled in periodic classroom seminars.
Managerial Assistance Available: National Maintenance handles nearly all administrative services for life of the franchise. National also has additional staff for filling in for illness or vacations in all areas.

NATIONAL SURFACE CLEANING CORPORATION
4959 Commerce Parkway
Cleveland, Ohio 44128
David A. Sheridan, President

Description of Operation: National Surface Cleaning Corporation manufacturers specialized chemicals and equipment to clean exterior of masonry (stone or brick) buildings. This inexpensive process replaces the need for sandblasting to effectively clean brick or stone structures.
Number of Franchisees: 293 dealers in 41 states.
In Business Since: 1971.
Equity Capital Needed: $9,950.
Financial Assistance Available: Limited financing available.
Training Provided: Home office training for 1 week. Training in Dealer's area for 3 days. Additional in-field training available at no charge upon reasonable request.
Managerial Assistance Available: National Surface Cleaning Corporation provides continual management service in such areas as advertising, operations and sales. Complete manuals of operations, forms, and directories are provided. Field managers are available to work closely with dealers regularly to assist solving problems. The company sponsors meetings of dealers and conducts marketing and product research to maintain high National Surface Cleaning Corporation consumer acceptance.

POP-INS, INC.
Franchise Division
Parkhouse Centre
Suite #1
Columbiana, Ohio 44408

Description of Operation: Pop-Ins provides a "speed team" housekeeping service to suit the growing needs of today's society. Pop-Ins maids are uniformed and trained in unique cleaning procedures to cut time on-the-job to a fraction. Services offer an economical solution to housecleaning needs of working women, elderly or handicapped, singles, etc. Non seasonal highly professional and profitable business.
Number of Franchisees: Total of 114 Franchises.
In Business Since: 1977.
Equity Capital Needed: $10,000.
Financial Assistance Available: Pop-Ins, Inc., will finance up to 50 percent of the franchisee fee at current credit union rates (to qualified buyers).
Training Provided: Home office and field personnel are available at all times to train the franchisee and his employees in all phases of sales and business management. This continuous program helps to insure an efficient and successful operation. Films, seminars, self-training programs, on-the-job training programs, etc., are constantly being revised and up-dated to keep franchise informed on all aspects of his business.
Managerial Assistance Available: Pop-Ins provides continual management service for the life of the franchise. Home office staff trained to assist management in all phases of their business. If operation is to be absentee, manager may attend initial training in place of owner. Pop-Ins also has on its staff a highly qualified control department to enable franchisee to obtain maximum, successful results at minimum expense.

PORT-O-LET COMPANY, INC.
Subsidiary of THETFORD CORPORATION
2300 Larsen Road
Jacksonville, Florida 32207
James P. Smith, Vice President

Description of Operation: On-the-site temporary toilet facilities for construction sites, etc.
Number of Franchisees: 27 in 16 states; 9 company-owned operations in 6 states.
In Business Since: 1954.
Equity Capital Needed: $20,000 to $50,000.
Financial Assistance Available: Assistance in locating financing.
Training Provided: 1 week initial training at headquarters, 1 week in the field, 2 day return "refresher" course at end of 90 days.
Managerial Assistance Available: Franchisor furnishes equipment, all invoicing, record keeping, accounts receivable, collections, etc. In-field personnel available.

ROTO-ROOTER CORPORATION
300 Ashworth Road
West Des Moines, Iowa 50265
William F. Dau, Sales Manager

Description of Operation: Sewer and drain cleaning service.
Number of Franchisees: 720 in all 50 states.
In Business Since: 1935.
Equity Capital Needed: $5,000.
Financial Assistance Available: None.
Training Provided: Training available at home office, but most new franchisees prefer training at an operating franchise near their homes.
Managerial Assistance Available: Continued assistance in all phases of operation through field staff, manuals, bulletins, etc.

SERMAC
A Division of SERVICEMASTER INDUSTRIES, INC.
2300 Warrenville Road
Downers Grove, Illinois 60515
R. Thomas Gibson, General Manager

Description of Operation: SERMAC Licensees provide industrial pressure cleaning, vacuuming, exterior and interior brick, stone and metal cleaning, paint and graffiti removal, duct cleaning, and post-fire heavy duty cleaning or major surfaces. Franchisee delivers services on-location via fully-equipped cleaning vehicle with its own power source, water supply, chemicals, etc. Business designed to serve industrial-commercial markets.
Number of Franchisees: 49 in 24 states.
In Business Since: 1975.
Equity Capital Needed: $8,000 minimum.
Financial Assistance Available: The basic price for initial license fee is $8,000. Applicant then has a choice between an additional investment of $16,000 for trailer-mounted pressure cleaning equipment or $34,020 additional for the larger capacity truck-mounted equipment. Financing is available from the company for either equipment choice to qualified applicants. A minimum of $8,000 to $15,000 in additional working capital is required.
Training Provided: Initial 2 week on-the-job training divided between SERMAC headquarters and licensee's own location, followed by 2 day "set-up" training in licensee location under the supervision of full-time SERMAC executive. Self-study of manage-

ment, marketing and technical manuals also included. Initial 1 day local marketing training is provided before attending the 2 week training.
Managerial Assistance Available: SERMAC provides continual technical, management and marketing services to franchisee through personal visits, telephone contacts and regional and national workshops. Management and technical service representatives are available to work closely with franchisees. SERMAC research and development of existing and new services is provided on a continual basis.

SERVICEMASTER INDUSTRIES, INC.
2300 Warrenville Road
Downers Grove, Illinois 60515
Denis V. Horsfall, Vice President
Description of Operation: Professional cleaning of homes, offices, plants, public buildings and institutions, covering carpets, furniture, walls, floors, and fixtures.
Number of Franchisees: Over 2,300 in 50 states and 21 foreign countries.
In Business Since: 1947.
Equity Capital Needed: Home cleaning services offer — $8,700 and office cleaning services offer — $8,400.
Financial Assistance Available: Franchisor will finance qualified applicants.
Training Provided: Home study course, 2 weeks on-the-job with established franchisee, 1 day in the field with counselor, one week resident training school. Continuous training program provided for all licensees.
Managerial Assistance Available: Managerial assistance is available on a continuous basis, from the company and from the master franchise coordinator of franchisees in the field. The company makes available advertising, sales promotion, formal training, laboratory services, regional and international meetings.

SERVPRO INDUSTRIES, INC.
11357 Pyrites Way
Rancho Cordova, California 95670
Tal Denny, Chairman of the Board
Description of Operation: All types of cleaning, including carpets, furniture, walls, floors, drapes, deodorizing, flood and fire damage.
Number of Franchisees: Approximately 400 in 36 states.
In Business Since: 1967.
Equity Capital Needed: $12,500.
Financial Assistance Available: A total investment of $27,000 is necessary. We will finance 55 percent. Franchisee has option to arrange own financing.
Training Provided: On-the-job training, set up training, classroom training, and continuous training through National Convention and Regional Seminars.
Managerial Assistance Available: SERVPRO provides continual training, including bookkeeping, advertising, inventory control. Trainers are set up across the country to provide local training. Regional Seminars and National Conventions also provide continuous training.

SPARKLE WASH, INC.
177 East Washington Street
Chagrin Falls, Ohio 44022
Otto V. Jackson, President
Description of Operation: Sparkle Wash, Inc., operates and directs a successful national network of mobile power cleaning licensees. These individuals, partnerships, and corporations provide power cleaning for a diverse market, including: truck fleets, mobile and residential homes, commercial, governmental and industrial buildings, industrial and farm machinery, boats, etc. Power cleaning services are provided utilizing the company developed patent mobile cleaning units and marketing programs.
Number of Franchisees: 145 in 46 states and Canada.
In Business Since: 1965.
Equity Capital Needed: Plan A - $23,070 and Plan B - $41,350.
Financial Assistance Available: Plan A requires $23,000 initial capital outlay for qualified individuals; to include licensee fee and initial lease payment for the mobile power cleaning unit, 60-120 day chemical supply, marketing and business package. Plan B requires $41,350 obtained through local financing by the prospective licensee. Company provides support information necessary. Company also provides complete accounting system and spare parts requirements.
Training Provided: Initial training in equipment operation, maintenance, chemicals and marketing provided at Company headquarters. In the field training utilizes the licensees unit and operators.

Managerial Assistance Available: Company provides regularly a publication containing up-to-date marketing and technical information. Company also provides computer printouts of truck fleet operators, market surveys, advertising materials, sales and business consultation on general or specific needs. Company provides regional assistance program within licensee's home region.

SUNRISE MAINTENANCE SYSTEMS
1405 West Indian School Road
Phoenix, Arizona 85103
Robert A. Erickson, CBSE, President
Description of Operation: Sunrise Maintenace Company, Inc., has developed a complete system for providing commercial janitorial services under the name of Sunrise Maintenance Systems. The company develops sales to a level of approximately $100,000 per year, or will develop customers as is desired by the franchisee. Customers are located in a service area chosen by the franchisee.
Number of Franchisees: 3 in Arizona.
In Business Since: 1979.
Equity Capital Needed: $25,000 (proportional to the $ volume of customers provided).
Financial Assistance Available: Partial financing available to qualified buyers.
Training Provided: Complete training is provided in all facets of franchise operation including management, administrative, sales and service. Training includes classroom, films, manuals, on-the-job and on-going consulting assistance. Group training meetings are held periodically.
Managerial Assistance Available: Sunrise Maintenance Company, Inc., provides complete on-going managerial services including computerized bookkeeping systems, employee referrals, technical, sales and operations.

ULTRASONIC PREDICTABLE MAINTENANCE, INC.
Sales and Franchise Office
815 Sunrise Lane
Centralia, Washington 98531
Douglas Gribble, President
Description of Operation: Inspection of bearings — electrical systems, air systems, pressure and vacuum — steam systems (traps), gas sytems (leaks) propane and natural gas leaks, water system (leaks). Infrared scanning of electrical system — high resistance heating and loose or dirty electrical connections to prevent breakdowns and minimize downtime. Industry and homes.
Number of Franchisees: 3 in Washington, 4 in Oregon, and 2 in California.
In Business Since: 1968.
Equity Capital Needed: $25,000.
Financial Assistance Available: None by UPM, Inc.
Training Provided: 20 days on-the-job training — 2 days at home office on bookwork and forms (reporting), training is done by other successful franchisees.
Managerial Assistance Available: Franchisee can be a part of the company in that he or she may purchase stock, the company furnishes franchisee, equipment, training, followup sales assistance and some advertising. In most cases some established business is turned over to new franchisee in the area assigned unto them.

U.S. ROOTER CORPORATION
18 Remount Road
North Little Rock, Arkansas 72118
Troy L. Ratliff, President
Description of Operation: U.S. Rooter sewer and drain cleaning service franchise offers a set of patented sewer machines, accessories, a copyrighted name and service marks, a protected area, a 5 year contract with option to renew at the end of the 5 years.
Number of Franchisees: 10 in California, Louisiana and Arkansas.
In Business Since: 1968.
Equity Capital Needed: $3,000 minimum.
Financial Assistance Available: A minimum of $3,000 will buy the use of 1 set of machines and accessories. Small monthly payments (on a 5 year contract) both payments based on population or telephone book coverage.
Training Provided: Unless he is already experienced, a franchisee may at his option come to the home office for a minimum of 2 weeks training or more if desired, or to the nearest franchised area.
Managerial Assistance Available: U.S. Rooter Corporation will provide advice, verbal or written on different modes of advertising, how to solicit business; we provide a manual of operation and help in any media of his business that is possible for us to do.

MOTELS/HOTELS

ADMIRAL BENBOW INNS, INC.
Affiliate of MORRISON INCORPORATED
P.O. Box 160266
Mobile, Alabama 36625
E.F. Congdon, Vice President
Description of Operation: Chain of first class Motor Inns, offering outstanding accommodations to commercial and vacation travelers throughout the Southeastern U.S.
Number of Franchisees: 8 in 5 states.
In Business Since: 1969.
Equity Capital Needed: $200,000 to $300,000.
Financial Assistance Available: Assistance in locating sources of financing, along with overal construction, selection of F.F. & E.
Training Provided: Assistance in training of personnel to open and operate the property from original opening, throughout entire term of franchise.
Managerial Assistance Available: Assistance at all levels of management, as well as accounting, legal wage and salary, etc.

COACHLIGHT INNS
P.O. Box 6395
Tyler, Texas 75711
Terry J. Cooper, President
Description of Operation: Economy budget motels.
Number of Franchisees: 3 in Texas, Mississippi and New Mexico.
In Business Since: 1970.
Equity Capital Needed: $50,000.
Financial Assistance Available: None.
Training Provided: Comprehensive 6 week training in all aspects of the business.
Managerial Assistance Available: Continuous assistance in technical, sales and management areas.

DAYS INN OF AMERICA, INC.
2751 Buford Highway, Northeast

Atlanta, Georgia 30324
James T. Murphy, Sr., Vice President
Franchise Operations and Development
Description of Operation: Days Inns of America, Inc., is the operator and franchisor of 301 "Budget-Luxury" motels and restaurants linked by a toll-free computerized reservation system throughout 48 states and Canada. Profit centers include Inns, Lodges (family suites), restaurants, petroleum refueling stations and gift shops.
Number of Franchisees: 306 open in 27 states and Canada.
In Business Since: 1970.
Equity Capital Needed: Land (approximately three acres) over $300,000.
Financial Assistance Available: Will assist in preparation of loan application.
Training Provided: Management training — classroom as well as on-the-job training formalized program; also handbooks and manuals.
Managerial Assistance Available: Continual consulting privileges with franchisor's executives. Semi-annual franchise meetings. Franchisor will help franchise owners find qualified operating managers. Quarterly quality assurance visitations.

DOWNTOWNER/ROWNTOWNER - PASSPORT SYSTEM
P.O. Box 171807
Memphis, Tennessee 38117
Don T. Baker, Executive Vice President
Description of Operation: Diversified food service/lodging company.
Number of Franchisees: 65 in 23 states.
In Business Since: 1958.
Financial Assistance Available: Yes.
Training Provided: Training provided as long as franchise relation lasts.
Managerial Assistance Available: Continous guidance.

ECONO-TRAVEL MOTOR HOTEL CORP.
20 Koger Executive Center
P. O. Box 12188
Norfolk, Virginia 23502
Lloyd T. Tarbutton, Chairman of the Board
Robert N. Weller, President
Clarence L. Johnson, National Franchise Director
Description of Operation: National owner and/or management operator, international franchisor and supplier of Econo-Travel Motor Hotels and Econo Lodges. (Budget and full service budget hotels and motels.)
Number of Franchisees: Over 134 licensed or owned in 18 states (operational).
In Business Since: 1967
Equity Capital Needed: (a) New construction - one-fourth of total capital investment (could possibly be paid for or leased with subordinational land). (b) on conversion of an existing property the equity would be nothing.
Financial Assistance Available: None directly. Indirectly we help obtain mortgage financing. Also have savings to franchisee on furniture and supplies.
Training Provided: "Econo-Tech" - school that gives in-depth training to all management teams.
Managerial Assistance Available: Bookkeeping system, site selection, analyzation, economics of housekeeping and maintenance, motel inspection peridocially by regional operations directors; owner orientation, a two day seminar conducted several times yearly; advertising, marketing and public relations expertise. Will also furnish complete management package if desired.

FAMILY INNS OF AMERICA
P. O. Box 10
Pigeon Forge, Tennessee 37863
Kenneth M. Seaton, President
Description of Operation: Motels with food and beverage facilities.
Number of Franchisees: 34 in 10 states
In Business Since: 1971
Equity Capital Needed: Between $100,000 and $250,000 depending upon size desired.
Financial Assistance Available: Feasibility studies, plans, guidance and counseling with financial institutions, national contracts for lower construction cost. Investment opportunities thru limited partnerships.
Training Provided: Complete training; covering all phases of motel business, room renting, restaurant and lounge set up and planning as long as needed.
Managerial Assistance Available: Guidance and counseling on company policies, complete audit and accounting forms. Complete inspections by company, annual meetings and other help will be given at any time.

HAPPY INNS OF AMERICA, INC.
8849 Richmond Highway
Alexandria, Virginia 22309
Clark S. Morris, President
Description of Operation: Franchisor of motor inns.
Number of Franchisees: 20 in 7 states
In Business Since: 1970
Equity Capital Needed: Approximately 20 percent of construction cost.
Financial Assistance Available: Will assist in preparing the presenting mortgage package to financial institutions.
Training Provided: 30 days training for managers on-job - continued supervision throughout life of contract - operation manual, continually up-dated.
Managerial Assistance Available: Continual management assistance as needed.

HOLIDAY INNS, INC.
3796 Lamar Avenue
Memphis, Tennessee 38118
Laurence Parry, Vice President, Franchise Operations
Description of Operation: Hotels and restaurants.
Number of Franchisees: 1,510 franchises worldwide and 1,748 Holiday Inns worldwide.

In Business Since: 1954.
Equity Capital Needed: Varies depending on the size of the project.
Financial Assistance Available: None
Training Provided: 3 week course at Holiday Inn University.
Managerial Assistance Available: Continuing guidance as needed.

HOMETELS OF AMERICA, INC.
c/o THE FRANCHISE GROUP, INC.
3644 East McDowell
Phoenix, Arizona 85008
Henward Banks, President
Description of Operation: Hotels and motor hotels. Each guest rental unit is a suite, with kitchenette. Features include free breakfast and complimentary cocktail hour. Restaurant facilities are not required in most locations.
Number of Franchisees: 28 plus 11 company-owned locations in 6 states
In Business Since: 1969
Equity Capital Needed: Approximately 25 percent of total capital investment.
Financial Assistance Available: Company will lend its expertise in short and long term financing as well as equity gap techniques.
Training Provided: Formal training school and on-the-job training, in company properties and in franchisee's property.
Managerial Assistance Available: Management manuals, advertising manuals, seminars, advertising, marketing and public relations, reservation systems design and architectural assistance and continuing guidance as needed.

HOWARD JOHNSON'S MOTOR LODGE
220 Forbes Road
Braintree, Massachusetts 02184
Burton Sack, Group Vice President - Corporate Development & Real Estate
Description of Operation: Motor hotels and hotels with food.
Number of Franchisees: 400 licensed properties in 42 states, Puerto Rico and Canada. Plus 130 company operations.
In Business Since: 1925
Equity Capital Needed: Varies with franchise - cost of construction or lease. (Minimum - $300,000).
Financial Assistance Available: None
Training Provided: Opening staff - on-the-job training for service personnel. Supervisory personnel available at all times.
Managerial Assistance Available: Varies plus geographic training programs.

QUALITY INNS INTERNATIONAL, INC.
10750 Columbia Pike
Silver Spring, Maryland 20901
Jerry R. Manion, Senior Vice President
Description of Operation: Motor Inns with food and beverage facilities.
Number of Franchisees: 330 in the U.S., Canada, Europe and Mexico
Equity Capital Needed: 1941
Financial Assistance Available: $275,000 to $325,000 plus land and financing.
Financial Assistance Available: Assistance in preparing and presenting mortgage application.
Training Provided: Orientation program for owners or managers prior to motel opening. Continuing seminar programs. Complete operations manual available.
Managerial Assistance Available: Guidance on company policies, procedures, accounting forms and methods included in training course. Franchisor will help owners find qualified executives. Complete management capability.

RAMADA INNS, INC.
3838 East Van Buren Street
Phoenix, Arizona 85008
Attention: Executive Vice President, Ramada Inn System
Description of Operation: Hotels and Motels, and computer services.
Number of Franchisees: 650 in the United States and worldwide.
In Business Since: 1959
Equity Capital Needed: A minimum 25 percent of total gross investment.
Equity Capital Needed: Market surveys, guidance, and counseling.
Training Provided: Continuous year-round training in the field, the Creative Ramada program, and in the Ramada Inn Management Development Center. Special on-the-job training available when requested by franchisee.
Managerial Assistance Available: Continual counseling, privileges with franchisees and corporate executives. Assistance in marketing and in local level sales, as well as guidance in regional sales and promotion effort.

RED CARPET INNS OF AMERICA, INC.
MASTER HOSTS INNS
444 Seabreeze Boulevard
P. O. Box 2510
Daytona Beach, Florida 32015
William A. Harwood, Executive Vice President
Description of Operation: Franchising and operation of motels.
Number of Franchisees: 115 in United States, Canada and Mexico.
In Business Since: 1969 (Red Carpet); 1953 (Master Hosts)
Equity Capital Needed: 30 percent of total cost.
Financial Assistance Available: Assistance is rendered in preparation of mortgage package and introduction to financial institutions.
Training Provided: On-the-job training given at company-owned operations during planning stages.
Managerial Assistance Available: Management company for the purpose of managing franchised motels.

RODEWAY INNS INTERNATIONAL, INC.
2525 Stemmons Freeway
Suite 800
Dallas, Texas 75207
Robert V. Walker, President

Description of Operation: The Rodeway Inns system is unique in that it is a total franchise program designed to provide the individual owner/operator brand name recognition, a toll free one number reservation network, national advertising and marketing capabilities and free operational support without having the inherent conflict of company-owned or managed properties operating within the same system.
Number of Franchisees: 150 in 30 states, Mexico and Canada
In Business Since: 1962
Equity Capital Needed: Approximately 20 percent of total cost.
Financial Assistance Available: Will assist in preparation of mortgage presentation.
Training Provided: Seminars in the various operational areas of concern. Training facility being established.
Managerial Assistance Available: Continuing management assistance through inspection, evaluation and consultation.

SHERATON INNS, INC.
Sixty State Street
Boston, Massachusetts 02109
Joseph A. McInerney, President
Description of Operation: Franchising subsidiary of The Sheraton Corporation, a system of hotels and inns worldwide.
Number of Franchisees: 325 in operation in 44 states and 15 other countries.
In Business Since: 1962
Equity Capital Needed: Approximately 20 percent of total cost.
Financial Assistance Available: Will assist in preparing mortgage presentation.
Training Provided: Seminars are periodically scheduled around the country and are open to both new and existing franchisees.
Managerial Assistance Available: Professional management assistance by Regional Directors of Operation and various manuals, sales, advertising and marketing guidance, inspections, regional and national meetings.

SUPER 8 MOTELS, INC.
224 Sixth Avenue, S.E.
Aberdeen, South Dakota 57401
Joann LaBay, Director of Franchise Relations
Description of Operation: Super 8 Motels, Inc., is a franchisor of "Budget Motels" which offer a full sized room with free color TV, Direct Dial phones and attractive decor, and which have room rates beginning at $14.88 singles.
Number of Franchisees: 75 in 15 states
In Business Since: 1972
Equity Capital Needed: Up to $100,000 depending upon size of motel and arrangements with lender.
Financial Assistance Available: Will assist franchisee in seeking mortgage financing.
Training Provided: Complete management training program is provided, including on-the-job training, films, classroom study, examinations.
Managerial Assistance Available: Day-to-day managerial, advertising and accounting services provided. Complete front office procedures and accounting systems are included.

THRIFTY SCOT MOTELS, INC.
P. O. Box 399
St. Cloud, Minnesota 56301
Jerry W. Severson
Description of Operation: Thrifty Scot Motels, Inc., offer a high quality, economy motel operation. Each motel offers 24-hour front desk and phone service, color TV, adjustable heating and air conditioning, complimentary Continental breakfast and ample parking.
Number of Franchisees: 21 in 7 states
In Business Since: 1973
Equity Capital Needed: None - No initial franchise fee.
Financial Assistance Available: Franchisor does not offer any financing arrangements
Training Provided: New motel personnel receive a week's training in all phases of motel operations at an existing Thrifty Scot under the supervision of a full-time manager.
Managerial Assistance Available: Franchisor provides assistance in areas of bookkeeping, advertising, etc. Personnel from the home office are available to work with franchisees and visit motels on a regular basis to assist in solving problems. Franchisor sponsors seminars for franchisees regarding marketing, advertising, housekeeping, employee training, group purchasing, etc.

TRAVELODGE INTERNATIONAL, INC.
250 Travelodge Drive
El Cajon, California 92090
Jere M. Hooper, Vice President
Description of Operation: Motor motels with full facilities and motels.
Number of Franchisees: 233 in 45 states and worldwide.
In Business Since: 1947.
Equity Capital Needed: $100,000 to $400,000.
Financial Assistance Available: Will assist franchisee in finding funds.
Training Provided: 1 week training at home office.
Managerial Assistance Available: Area meetings and seminars are held periodically. Quarterly inspections are standard procedure.

TREADWAY INNS CORPORATION
140 Market Street
Paterson, New Jersey 07505
James F. Horrigan, Director of Franchise Development
Description of Operation: Motor inns with full facilities.
Number of Franchisees: 12 in 6 states.
In Business Since: 1912.
Equity Capital Needed: $500,000
Financial Assistance Available: Will assist franchisee in locating financing.
Training Provided: Treadway assists franchisee in selection of manager and department heads, who may attend on-the-job training for up to 6 weeks at one or more Treadway Inns.
Managerial Assistance Available: Franchisor makes available to franchisee operating manuals, consultation so that franchisee may have the benefit of Treadway's experience relating to the creation and operation of the Inn.

PAINT AND DECORATING SUPPLIES

DAVIS PAINT COMPANY
1311 Iron Street
North Kansas City, Missouri 64116
Jesse E. Bagby, General Sales Manager
Description of Operation: Retail paint and wallpaper stores. Also handle drapes, picture framing, unfinished furniture, floor coverings and decorative gifts.
Number of Franchisees: 110 in 9 states. Only Midwestern states served.
In Business Since: 1944.
Equity Capital Needed: $25,000 to $30,000.
Financial Assistance Available: Partial financing available to qualified individuals.
Training Provided: Training at franchisor's plant. Field training by factory personnel and regional sales manager.
Managerial Assistance Available: Complete assistance in-site location, lease arrangements, store layout, advertising, sales promotion, bookkeeping, insurance, and management techniques. Franchisor personnel and field representatives make regular calls.

PET SHOPS

DOCKTOR PET CENTERS, INC.
Dundee Park
Andover, Massachusetts 01810
Leslie Charm, President
Eugene H. Kohn, Vice President
Description of Operation: Retail pets, supplies and pet accessories.
Number of Franchisees: 72 franchisees operating in 142 stores in 31 states.
In Business Since: 1966.
Equity Capital Needed: Approximately $60,000 to $75,000.
Financial Assistance Available: Yes, in certain cases.
Training Provided: 3 weeks at franchisor's headquarters. Subjects covered include store operations, care and maintenance of pets, accounting, management, inventory, maintenance and personnel selection, merchandising, etc.
Managerial Assistance Available: Advice on stocking, fixture arrangement, receipt of livestock, maintenance procedures, and profit control, etc. On-the-site advisor guides franchisee during first 2 weeks of operations. Advertising materials, accounting forms and season signs furnished. Counselors make frequent visits to stores to assist franchises.

FLYING FUR PET TRAVEL SERVICE
310 South Michigan Avenue
Chicago, Illinois 60604
R.I. Fredriksen, National Manager
Description of Operation: Animal shipping — U.S.A. — Overseas with pickup and delivery service, vaccination certificates, animal boarding on stopovers or delay in-transit program. Coast-to-coast network includes and provides veterinarian, animal hospital and clinic, grooming. Includes documentation and moving-storage coordination. Traveling kennels available.
Number of Franchisees: 15 in 10 states.
In Business Since: 1970.
Equity Capital Needed: $500.
Financial Assistance Available: None.
Training Provided: 2 to 3 initial meetings and follow-up as needed.
Managerial Assistance Available: As needed.

PEDIGREE PET CENTERS, DIV. OF PEDIGREE INDUSTRIES, INC.
11 Goldthwait Road
Marblehead, Massachusetts 01945
Milton Docktor, President
Description of Operation: Retail pets, supplies, accessories and grooming services.
Number of Franchisees: 4 in Maine, Massachusetts, Florida and New Jersey.
In Business Since: Predecessor in business since 1927.
Equity Capital Needed: Approximately $40,000.
Financial Assistance Needed: Franchisor may assist in obtaining financing.
Training Provided: 4 weeks at franchisor's headquarters. Covers store operation, care of pets, accounting, management, inventory, maintenance and personnel selection.
Managerial Assistance Available: Advice on stocking, fixture arrangement, receipt of livestock, and maintenance procedures. On-the-site advisor guides franchisee during first week of operations. Advertising materials and standardized accounting and report forms furnished. Counselors make visits to stores to assist franchisees.

PETLAND, INC.
195 North Hickory Street
P.O. Box 1606
Chillicothe, Ohio 45601
Edward R. Kunzelman, President

Description of Operation: Retail pets, pet supplies, and pet related items; grooming services.
Number of Franchisees: 38 plus 5 company-owned stores in 10 states and Canada.
In Business Since: 1967.
Equity Capital Needed: $15,000 to $30,000, depending on store size and location.
Financial Assistance Available: Franchisor may finance a portion of the cost and will also assist in preparation of financial presentation package.
Training Period: 4 weeks in operating stores as assigned and classroom at Ohio main office or Florida office. Additional assistance in-store after opening.
Managerial Assistance Available: Assistance in merchandising, livestock management, and maintenance procedures. On-the-site advisor guides franchisee during first week of operations. Advertising materials and standardized accounting and report forms furnished. Area field supervisors make periodic visits and inspections and will give assistance in problem areas. Advertising manual, operations manual, counter reference book, and all forms and guarantees for operations are provided.

PET MASTER, INC.
4161 Southwest 6th Street
Ft. Lauderdale, Florida 33317
Jack Vander Plate, President
Description of Operation: Pet Master, Inc., is a mobile pet grooming service. The franchise includes an air conditioned step van fully equipped to bathe, dip and groom all dog breeds in its fully contained mobile unit in the customer's driveway Also carried is a full supply of pet needs and grooming supplies.
Number of Franchisees: 6 in Florida.
In Business Since: 1973.
Equity Capital Needed: $7,000 to $10,000.
Financial Assistance Available: Mobile van can be financed on a 5 year lease or 5 year bank loan.
Training Provided: 5 weeks of training at company's training center Ft. Lauderdale, Florida. Courses include breed identification, dog handling, art of grooming, bookkeeping and customer relations. 5 weeks training with experienced groomer in your mobile van in your own franchise territory. Continuous assistance In every phase of business.
Managerial Assistance Available: Pet Master provides continual management service for the life of the franchise in such areas as advertising, public relations, and new ideas and products in the industry.

PRINTING

ALPHAGRAPHICS, INC.
Department Y
845 East Broadway
Tucson, Arizona 85719
Rodger G. Ford, President
Description of Operation: An AlphaGraphics Rapid Print Center is the printshop of the future. By taking advantage of technological advances, we can provide quality printing rapidly for every profession and business, regardless of its size.
Number of Franchisees: 11 including company-owned stores.
In Business Since: 1970.
Financial Assistance Available: Total investment is $75,000 to $108,000 approximately 70 percent financiable through several sources.
Training Provided: 2 weeks of intensive training is provided at company headquarters in Tucson, Arizona. There is an additional week of on-site training prior to opening. The curriculum includes: customer relations, employee relations, equipment operation, planning and budgeting, accounting, marketing and computer estimating.
Managerial Assistance Available: On-going assistance is provided to all franchisees through regularly scheduled visits from headquarters, as well as troubleshooting over the phone or in person by company executives. National accounts buying plan, monthly merchandising and advertising programs, equipment reviews, up-dated procedures and annual planning and budgeting are all part of the AlphaGraphics' support package.

BIG RED Q QUICKPRINT CENTERS
7300 International Drive
Holland, Ohio 43528
C.D. Baxstresser, National Franchise Director
Description of Operation: Big Red Q Quickprint Centers specialize in high quality, low cost instant printing to primarily small to medium-sized businesses and organizations. Each unit is modeled to a highly visual and unique format featuring a divided lobby area. Package includes equipment necessary to provide complete printing, copying and bindery (finishing) services.
Number of Franchisees: Over 285 in 30 states and Canada.
In Business Since: 1967.
Equity Capital Needed: Approximately $15,000.
Financial Assistance Available: Equipment package can be provided on a 7-year lease of 5-year bank loan.
Training Provided: 2 weeks of intensive instruction at our International Training Center. The Center is designed to stimulate actual store conditions. The curriculum includes equipment operation, advertising and sales promotion and business management.
Self-instructional materials provided. Franchisees also receive 2 full weeks of opening assistance from a field service representative fully trained in store operation.
Managerial Assistance Available: On-going owner assistance includes computerized bookkeeping and reporting system, owner's hotline, advertising and sales promotion kits, research and development bulletins, and a monthly newsletter. Other assistance includes regional 1-day seminars, counseling by corporate staff specialists, store visits and an annual convention.

INSTY-PRINTS, INC.
417 North Fifth Street
Minneapolis, Minnesota 55401
John O. Prater, Marketing Manager
Description of Operation: Franchised Instant Litho Printing Centers, offering high-quality printing, cutting, folding, stapling, collating, drilling and padding.
Number of Franchisees: 205 locations in 30 states, plus Washington, D.C., Puerto Rico, Israel and Thailand.
In Business Since: 1935; franchising since 1965.
Equity Capital Needed: $25,000 minimum cash payment. Financing available to qualified applicants on remainder of $50,000 total investment.
Financial Assistance Available: Up to $25,000 of total $50,000 investment may be financed through Insty-Prints, Inc., by qualified applicants. $25,000 minimum cash requirement covers (a) equipment down payment, (b) opening paper and supplies inventory, (c) $5,000 business working capital retained by franchisee, and (d) franchisee fee.
Training Provided: 4 weeks at Minneapolis headquarters, covering use of equipment, advertising, estimating, paper, freight, bookkeeping, counter procedures, inventory and cost control, and general unit management. Fifth week in franchisee's own unit, under home office field supervision. Additional personnel training in Minneapolis headquarters at no additional charge throughout term of agreement.
Managerial Assistance Available: Annual regional workshops, continuing management and technical advice, instant in WATS telephone communication, continuing advertising and promotion programs, complete operations and sales manuals, periodic bulletins, National Advertising Fund.

KWIK-KOPY CORPORATION
5225 Hollister
Houston, Texas 77040
Thomas F. Malone, Marketing Director
Description of Operation: A Kwik-Kopy Center franchise offers a system for production and sale of high quality printing, duplicating, copying, bindery and attendant services on rapid time schedules tailored to meet the customers' desire. The franchise includes volume buying discounts on the purchase of equipment, furniture, fixtures and supplies, market research, site selection, negotiation of real estate leases, selection, installation and arrangement of equipment, furniture and fixtures, complete training in management systems, procedures and equipment operation, public relations, sales and advertising programs with proven rapid sales building results, start-up assitance, continued support services in all phases of technical and business management problems over the entire 25-year term of the franchise agreement.
Number of Franchisees: 492 in 37 states, Canada and Great Britain.
In Business Since: 1967.
Equity Capital Needed: $19,500.
Financial Assistance Available: A total investment of $58,500 is necessary to open a Kwik-Kopy Center. Approximately two-thirds of this amount can be financed for credit worthy applicants.
Training Provided: Completion of an intensive 3-week training course is provided by Kwik-Kopy Corporation at its management training center and is required prior to opening a Kwik-Kopy Center. Additional on-the-job training in the franchisee's place of business during and after start-up is also provided. Training includes equipment operation, accounting, advertising, sales and business methods proven successful in Kwik-Kopy Center operations.
Managerial Assistance Available: The company provides continued support services to its franchisees for the full life of the franchise agreement, including management and legal counsel, advertising, training of new employees and retraining through field representatives who provide on-site assistance as required. Top management is available for assistance and counseling by telephone at all times, through nationwide toll-free WATS lines available to all franchisees.

MINUTEMAN PRESS INTERNATIONAL, INC.
1640 New Highway
Farmingdale, New York 11735
Roy W. Titus, President
Description of Operation: A Minuteman Press franchise offers a unique approach to retail printing. Not only the ability to produce high quality instant printing, but because of the versatility of the equipment used in our centers, we have the additional ability to do multicolor printing, make photostats, make overhead visuals and screen half tones. Our package contains all the necessary equipment for printing, cutting, folding, padding, collating, stapling, plus initial supply of ink, film, paper inventory, stationery and sales aids. Also included, is the research of the area, securing of an acceptable location and overseeing the complete renovation of the location, including the installation of fixtures, furniture, and all accessories needed to operate a successful Minuteman Press Full Service Printing Center.

82

Number of Franchisees: Over 350 in over 30 states and Canada.
In Business Since: 1973.
Equity Capital Needed: Approximately $21,500 (plus $5,000 to $6,000 working capital).
Financial Assistance Available: $50,000 to $59,000 total investment, with approximately 60 percent financing available through Minnesco (a division of the 3M Company).
Training Provided: Minutemen Press requires completion of a 2 week training program in the Minuteman's National Training Center, plus minimum of 1 week continued training at the franchisees own location under home office field supervision. Training covers use of all equipment, advertising, estimating, bookkeeping, marketing and sales promotion, counter procedures, inventory, cost control and general management.
Mangerial Assistance Available: The company has regional offices in Atlanta, Baltimore, Boston, Chicago, Cleveland, Dallas, Denver, Los Angeles, Fort Lauderdale, Philadelphia, Pittsburgh, Portland, Oregon, San Francisco, Seattle and Toronto, Canada as well as Long Island, to provided continued support services and guidance to its franchisees for the full term of the franchise agreement, including management marketing, advertising, training of new employees. Franchisees are kept current with results of research and new equipment through periodic meetings and seminars and visits by field representatives who provide assistance as required. Continued counseling and assistance is available at all times by calling either the regional or home office.

(PIP) POSTAL INSTANT PRESS
8201 Beverly Boulevard
Los Angeles, California 90048
Bill LeVine, President
Description of Operation: World's largest while-you-wait printing operation. Pioneers in the instant printing field — one of the country's fastest growing industries — PIP serves the requirements of professionals, businesses, industry, religious organizations, civic groups and individuals for quality, low-cost printing. In addition to printing, PIP locations offer photocopying service as well as padding, stapling, folding, cutting, drilling and collating. Package includes equipment, initial supplies and sales promotion material necessary for the successful operation of a while-you-wait printing business. A PIP printing location is approximately 1,000 square feet.
Number of Franchisees: Over 560 in 41 states, Washington, D.C. and Canada. (40 company locations).
In Business Since: Parent Company (commercial printing firm) organized in 1943. Postal Instant Press, 1964.
Equity Capital Needed: $15,000 ($12,000 operating capital). Total $56,000 (exclusive of operating capital).
Financial Assistance Available: Franchisor will finance up to $41,000 to qualified individuals.
Training Provided: 2 weeks of intensive training at PIP headquarters, national training center is given by highly skilled, experienced, professional printing instructors. Training covers the use of all machines and equipment used, advertising, promotional aids, marketing, estimating, record keeping, inventory and cost control, counter procedures, sales, all phases of business management and procedures, in addition to communcations, employee relations and communications skills. On-going training is given at Conclaves and Regional Seminars.
Managerial Assistance Available: Regularly scheduled visits from field Coordinators. Collect phone calls to headquarters are authorized for immediate response in answer to questions or problems. Technical, advertising, promotional and operations manuals are provided. Accounting guidance on request. Publicity, public relations and advertising assistance given. Legal counsel and management consultation when requested. On-going research and development bulletins covering equipment, materials and supplies used in the printing industry. National Advertising Program on CBS, ABC and NBC radio networks plus regional advertising programs. Extensive video film program for on-going training and education. Additional on-going communication PIP-Line Newsletter and Advisory Committee.

THE PRINTING PLACE, INC.
P. O. Box 1040
Easton, Pennsylvania 18042
Arthur Alan Leaver, President
Description of Operation: A Printing Place Center is a "convenience printing" center where printing and related services for large and small businessmen, professionals and service organizations can be obtained in a minimum of time at modest prices. Equipment used is modern and simple to operate, yet advanced enough to be found in many leading commercial printing plants.
Number of Franchisees: 4 in Pennsylvania, West Virginia and Texas.
In Business Since: 1973
Equity Capital Needed: $15,000 down payment plus $5-$6,000 working capital. Owner should be able to support self for 3-6 months while building up sales.
Financial Assistance Available: Total price, exclusive of working capital $40,000. Because this price includes full capability such as professional camera, financing of $25,000 can be secured from various sources on basis of substantial "hardware" equity in package.
Training Provided: About 2 or 3 weeks is provided, usually in the new owner's Printing Place Center in a regional Operating Training Center. Special instruction in sales, merchandising and general business practices are also given "on-site" to meet local conditions.
Managerial Assistance Available: Management accepts its responsibility to maintain up-to-date liaison regarding latest equipment, supplies, techniques and marketing practices. Management is on call for trouble-shooting; specialized advertising and promotion campaigns; and business operational requirements. Periodic visits by Company Representatives are made to operating Centers. Heavy emphasis is on top-quality, low-cost supplies to Centers at large discounts to encourage Center owners to operate profitably with attractive, competitive prices to their customers

THE PRINTING SUPERMART, INC.
532 Bloomfield Avenue
Verona, New Jersey 07044
Robert N. Seidman, President
Description of Operation: Complete printing, cutting, typesetting and word processing facility in an average 1,200 square foot facility.
Number of Franchisees: 3 in New Jersey
In Business Since: 1979
Equity Capital Needed: $13,500
Financial Assistance Available: Assistance in financing balance of purchase price ($28,500) which includes the most complete equipment, inventory and supply package offered in the industry.
Financial Assistance Available: 3 week initial training, continuing updating in all aspects of the business thereafter.
Managerial Assistance Available: Continuous in all areas of business.

PRINTMASTERS, INC.
120 South Sepulveda Boulevard
Manhattan Beach, California 90266
Robert C. Dudley, National Sales Manager
Description of Operation: Printmasters, Inc., offers an opportunity for enthusiastic and motivated people to achieve their management and promotional potential in the field of high volume quality instant printing. The Printmaster package includes a complete line of equipment, material and supplies, plus the major items of office furniture required to operate an effective instant printing center.
Number of Franchisees: 8 in California
In Business Since: 1977
Equity Capital Needed: Cost of franchise package $49,500. Minimum cash investment $17,500. Working capital $8,000.
Financial Assistance Available: Financing available $32,000 (to qualified individuals).
Training Provided: Technical, managerial and promotional training provided. Minimum of 1 week at the franchise training center. Minimum of 1 week at the franchisee's location. Managerial and promotional input continues, as well as technical assistance, through quality control visits and direct contact with franchisee. All aspects of owning and operating an instant printing center are covered in detail.
Managerial Assistance Available: Each franchisee undergoes a CPA consultation for the purpose of setting up the center's books and record keeping system. The franchisee receives continued management, marketing and promotional guidance and support for the duration of the franchise license agreement. Supply sources, pricing techniques and group purchasing discounts are provided on a constant basis. Periodic quality control visits review current and introduce new technical, managerial and marketing skills and products. Printmasters emphasizes the need for ongoing interaction between the franchisee and the company headquarters. Direct lines of communication are always open to assist, guide and offer support.

QUIK PRINT, INC.
100 North Main, Suite 300
Wichita, Kansas 67202
Wayne Jenkins, President
Description of Operation: Quick copying of letterheads, envelopes, price sheets and other copy.
Number of Franchisees: 55 in 21 states plus 55 company-owned units.
In Business Since: 1963
Equity Capital Needed: $52,500
Financial Assistance Available: Will assist in securing financing.
Training Provided: 4 to 6 weeks at franchisor's headquarters, plus 2 weeks on-the-job at franchisee's new location.
Managerial Assistance Available: Management services in the area of bookkeeping, advertising, equipment and production techniques.

SIR SPEEDY, INC.
P. O. Box 1790
892 West Sixteenth Street
Newport Beach, California 92663
Harold C. Lloyd, Vice President, Franchise Sales
Description of Operation: Franchise of Instant Printing Centers
Number of Franchisees: 300 in 27 states
In Business Since: 1968
Equity Capital Needed: $56,000 total investment, $38,000 of which may be financed, plus approximately $15,000 for working capital and living expenses.
Financial Assistance Available: Financing is available for up to $32,000 of the initial $52,000.
Training Provided: 4 weeks with continued up-dating by field support.
Managerial Assistance Available: Lease Negotiations, Site Analysis, Administrative advice and service, *Complete Turnkey Operation*, Marketing and Advertising support, Accounting system, *Royalty Rebate Program*, National Contract Purchasing Power.

SPEEDY PRINTING CENTERS, INC.
Corporate Offices
30700 Telegraph Road, Suite 4530
Birmingham, Michigan 48010
Vernon G. Buchanan, President
James W. McDonald, Vice President
Description of Operation: Speedy Printing Centers, Inc., offers franchises having an outstanding profit potential in the fast growing instant printing industry. A center is set up with all the necessary equipment for printing, folding, cutting, padding, copying, drilling as well as all other accessories needed to operate a successful instant printing center.
Number of Franchisees: 65 in Michigan, Illinois, Alabama and South Carolina.
In Business Since: 1972
Equity Capital Needed: $22,500 plus $12,500 working capital.
Financial Assistance Available: Franchisor will assist the franchisee in financing equipment package either through a 5-year lease purchase or a 5-year bank loan.

Training Provided: Completion of an extensive 4-week training course which includes bookkeeping and reporting system, equipment operation and maintenance, marketing, pricing, work scheduling and management of employees. Franchisor's representative also assists franchisee in his or her location during his or her first week of operation plus returning visits at least every 60 days.

Managerial Assistance Available: Speedy Printing Centers provides the continuing support system to all of its franchisees for the life of the franchise agreement. This includes advertising, management consultation; employment services; negotiate national contracts for supply and equipment discounts; equipment, maintenance and repair seminars; sales seminars; press and camera services; technical and supply bulletins; monthly newsletter; and continuing research of new equipment and supplies. The corporate offices are available for personal assistance and counseling by telephone or in person.

REAL ESTATE

ACTION BROKERS CORPORATION
5001 West 80th Street
Bloomington, Minnesota 55437
Richard O. Watland, President

Description of Operation: Real estate sales.
Number of Franchisees: 10 in Minnesota
In Business Since: 1975
Equity Capital Needed: $5,000
Financial Assistance Available: Local financing
Training Provided: Pre-license classes and training classes and management.
Managerial Assistance Available: All experienced brokers and licensed with the State prior to obtaining a franchise.

BETHOM CORPORATION
dba BETTER HOMES REALTY
675 Ygnacio Valley Road, Suite A202
Walnut Creek, California 94596
Ernest H. Ewan, President

Description of Operation: Bethom Corporation, dba Better Homes Realty is principally engaged in the business of franchising real estate sales offices.
Number of Franchisees: 300 in California
In Business Since: 1969
Equity Capital Needed: $6,500
Financial Assistance Available: None
Training Provided: Total management and salesman orientation; continued management assistance; on-going educational seminars.
Managerial Assistance Available: Total management and salesman orientation; continued management assistance; on-going educational seminars.

CENTURY 21 REAL ESTATE CORPORATION
18872 MacArthur Boulevard
Irvine, California 92715
Sam Bruenio, Vice President

Description of Operation: Must be qualified Real Estate Broker with good track record in the industry. In effect, he or she must be able to run a Real Estate Brokerage operation.
Number of Franchisees: Over 7,000 in 50 states
In Business Since: 1972
Equity Capital Needed: Net worth of approximately $10,000 for each franchise.
Financial Assistance Available: Local financing where applicable.
Training Provided: Constant training for Broker and Sales Associates. (Not including outlying areas of metroplex.)
Managerial Assistance Available: Management workshops where applicable.

EARL KEIM REALTY, INC.
26250 Northwestern Highway
Southfield, Michigan 48076
Thomas Ervin, President

Description of Operation: Real estate franchise, with complete range of services and unique protected area concept.
Number of Franchisees: 84 in Michigan
In Business Since: 1958
Equity Capital Needed: Franchise agreement fee $7,000.
Financial Assistance Available: Possible
Training Provided: Earl Keim Realty, Inc. (sold under the name of The Keim Group outside Michigan) provides post-license training. This unique post-license program combines classroom and in-office programs, and is designed to make the new salesperson productive as soon as possible. Bi-weekly newsletters, special seminars, and periodic sales rallies round out the sales-person training program.
Managerial Assistance Available: Beginning with a realistic budget and sales forecast, the managerial assistance gives specific guidance in recruiting, interviewing, training, goal-setting, motivating, and equipping a salesperson, so as to obtain a highly profitable business. Other services provided include a national referral service, home warranty program, corporate relocation division, and in-house advertising agency.

ELECTRONIC REALTY ASSOCIATES, INC.
4900 College Boulevard
Shawnee Mission, Kansas 66201
J. Michael Jackson

Description of Operation: Electronic Realty Associates, Inc. (ERA), is a membership organization for licensed real estate brokerage firms offering its services and programs for use of its members. ERA grants the use of its registered marks to its members to promote identification with ERA's marketing services and to permit coordination of advertising programs. ERA members participate in a national referral program and in a home warranty program. ERA services also include advertising materials, training programs, technical assistance for member's real estate brokerage operations.
Number of Franchisees: 2,500 in 50 states
In Business Since: 1971
Equity Capital Needed: Approximately $9,000 maximum.
Financial Assistance Available: ERA does have a financial assistance program for new members. The initial fee is $7,000 plus $500 for each branch office, all of which must accompany the application for membership, our alternate payment plan is $2,300 accompanying the application for membership, $2,400 in 30 days and $2,400 in 60 days. The remaining amount required for the initial investment can range from $50 to $1,475 depending on the members option under the Membership Agreement.
Training Provided: A new member must participate in a 3 day training program to familiarize the broker with the ERA services available. A further training program for sales associates is scheduled for the member's offices under ERA employee's full-time supervision. Finally, ERA offers a Sales Training Program. All training is provided on a tuition free basis for real estate brokers who become members.
Managerial Assistance Available: ERA procides continuing management service to member brokers in areas of training, advertising, insurance, and home warranty administration. Complete manuals of operations forms and directions are provided. Regional Managers and Service Representatives are available in all regions to work closely with members and visit their offices to visit and assist in problem solving. ERA sponsors Broker Councils in each locality and conducts marketing and product research to maintain high ERA consumer acceptance.

EMBASSY RENTAL AGENCY
P. O. Box 706
Orange, New Jersey 07051
George Livieratos, President

Description of Operation: Embassy Rental Agency is a full real estate service specializing in the apartment and home rentals.
Number of Franchisees: 3 in New Jersey
In Business Since: 1963
Equity Capital Needed: $10,000 minimum
Financial Assistance Available: As long as party is qualified, franchisor will help financing.
Training Provided: Full training in our home office as long as is necessary for franchisee to succeed.
Managerial Assistance Available: Constant support while in training, with continuing support from main company.

EXECU-SYSTEMS, INC.
727 East Maryland
Phoenix, Arizona 85014
Mark Lestikow, National Marketing Manager

Description of Operation: National franchisor for the original 100 percent concept. Execu-Systems is designed to assist individuals and entities in the development of strong, multi-office companies operating general real estate brokerages using the Execu-Systems 100 percent concept as the foundation.
Number of Franchisees: 67 offices in 23 states
In Business Since: 1965
Equity Capital Needed: $7,500 licensing fee. Will need minimum of $15,000-$20,000.
Financial Assistance Available: None
Training Provided: Intensive 2 day workshop, given by national staff, instructing new member how to own and operate the Execu-Systems 100 percent concept using methods with 15 years of proven success. A 300 page operations manual, coupled with accessibility of a national staff, who also administer company-owned offices, provide on-going assistance. A regional consultant program is also provided where applicable. Program assists new member in early phases of operation.
Managerial Assistance Available: Unlimited consultation is proven successful accounting process, recruiting, secretarial hiring, and advertising methods is provided. National and regional meetings over topics of vital interest to members. Operation of national referral service and volume purchasing available to member brokers and their associates.

50 STATES REAL ESTATE, INC.
9850 Metro Parkway West
Phoenix, Arizona 85021
Richard L. Behner, President

Description of Operation: Real Estate franchise for independent brokers. Consists of training methods, marketing tools, created advertising format, client follow-up systems, referral network and a systems and procedure guide.
Number of Franchisees: 18 in Arizona, 1 in Ohio and 1 in Colorado
In Business Since: 1978
Equity Capital Needed: $2,500 for initial franchise fee.
Financial Assistance Available: There is no financial fee.
Training Provided: Training for the franchisee is recommended and guidance in this area is provided but strictly at the expense of the franchisee. Regional directors will be available for consultation and advice in areas of experience and expertise. Training methods and tools are provided for salespeople by the regional directors.
Managerial Assistance Available: Managerial assistance is very important and we believe professionals, in training technical experience, should be teaching the prospective franchisees. There are several technical companies we would recommend. We have a guidelines & procedure manual which we provide for every franchisee.

GALLERY OF HOMES, INC.
1001 International Boulevard
Suite 900
Atlanta, Georgia 30354
Michael J. Ramatowski, National Marketing Director

Description of Operation: Gallery of Homes, Inc., franchises existing experienced real estate brokers of good reputation and proven ability and provides common image, referral services, advertising, education, and staff assistance in return for fees as specified in the agreement. Preference is given to brokers with membership in professional real estate organizations. Standards are high. Applicants should contact existing franchisees or headquarter's office for information.
Number of Franchisees: 800 operating approximately 1,500 locations in all states except Hawaii, plus Provences of Canada.
In Business Since: 1950
Equity Capital Needed: An existing business plus $7,000.
Financial Assistance Available: None
Training Provided: A 6 day orientation program and staff assistance and participation of new franchisees in local councils of franchisees. Additional professional courses (sales, management, fiscal control) available. Complete video tape training available (52 tapes). National Advertising Program.
Managerial Assistance Available: In addition to the above, continuous personal assistance upon request by telephone. Manuals are provided that cover general Gallery of Homes techniques, office layout, referrals and corporate business leads, supplies catalogs, image program, advertising format guide, and other material upon request as available, there are no additional charges for this material and assistance.

GOVERNMENT EMPLOYEES REAL ESTATE OF AMERICA, INC.
711 Executive Place, Suite 300
P. O. Box 53647
Fayetteville, North Carolina 28305
Guy A. Ciampa, President

Description of Operation: Government Employees Real Estate is a Real Estate Franchise for Firms of Realtors. It is exclusive in that one franchise is awarded in one area Board of Realtors on a Dollar Volume Basis. It is designed to specialize in Real Estate for the Military, Veterans and Civil Service active and retired. A network of "GERE" member firms is contemplated to cover each installation from Coast to Coast, Alaska and Hawaii and overseas relocations centers in England, Germany, Spain and Italy. The "GERE" logo and name ties in with the service offered and is an asset to firms located near Military/Civil Service installation, State Capitols, and Retiree areas. A Lifetime Membership program for Special Benefits to qualified personnel is in process.
Number of Franchisees: 30 in 19 states
In Business Since: 1978
Equity Capital Needed: $4,000 (initial franchise fee) for franchise, for region; price is determined by area, installations and real estate market. "GERE" Mid-Atlantic Region was formed in November 1979, comprising of Washington, D.C., Maryland, New Jersey, Delaware, Pennsylvania and Virginia. "GERE" is in the process of selling other regions.
Financial Assistance Available: None
Training Provided: Since all franchisees are members of the Local and National Association of Realtors, whose sales training programs are the best available, Government Employees Real Estate does not offer this training. However, each firm is oriented on policies and procedures and trained on the use and benefits of the franchise. Seminars and conventions are contemplated in the future for orientation purposes.
Managerial Assistance Available: Managerial assistance only in "GERE" policies, advertising and general assistance is given through the "GERE" Headquarters.

HELP-U-SELL, INC.
1400 East Katella
Anaheim, California 92805
Cathy Vallevieni, Vice President

Description of Operation: Help-U-Sell helps sellers of real estate property sell their property "by owner" for a low fixed fee $950 to $1,450 at most offices.
Number of Franchisees: 15 in California as of this moment, however we do expect to go nationwide in the very near future.
In Business Since: 1976
Equity Capital Needed: 25 in California as of this moment, however we are going nationwide this year.
Financial Assistance Available: None
Training Provided: Up to 10 days at corporate headquarters (or other mutually agreed location) in the Help-U-Sell method.
Managerial Assistance Available: Full training in the Help-U-Sell method and continued assistance for the term of the franchise.

HERBERT HAWKINS REALTORS, INC.
5770 North Rosemead Boulevard
Temple City, California 91780
Mark S. Cassell, Director of Franchise Sales

Description of Operation: Herbert Hawkins Realtors is a general real estate brokerage firm consisting of franchised and company-owned locations servicing client's home buying and listing needs. Franchise members are provided with a full range of financial, training, advertising, and support services. Close continuing support is provided through regional staff on an ongoing basis. Assistance in site selection and feasibility studies on each location is available upon request.
Number of Franchisees: 125 in California
In Business Since: 1947
Equity Capital Needed: $4,500 for franchise plus office equipment and fixtures.
Financial Assistance Available: Franchise can be purchased on terms.
Training Provided: Complete and continuous real estate training provided. A licensing school is opened and operated in each region of market penetration by the Herbert Hawkins Company. Real estate "Sales Training" is provided to agents of franchised locations at no cost by franchisor. Approved "Continuing Education" programs and credits are given to all agents on a regular basis, and programs qualify agents for renewal of licenses in states where continuing education units are required. Management training for franchisees and their managers and qualified agents are provided at no cost. Investment training is available. An initial training course is provided to all new franchisees. All classes are presented on a live lecture basis.
Managerial Assistance Available: Complete management assistance is provided on an on-going basis by local regional directors. Programs are provided for financial, advertising, and training assistance. Funds are made available by the Herbert Hawkins Company to franchisees to offer clients equity loans and guaranteed sales. Institutional advertising is placed and coordinated by the headquarters office. Escrow services, mortgage services, relocation service, client follow-up programs, home warranty service, printing services, insurance services, and termite services are available and provided by the Herbert Hawkins Company.

HOME SELLERS CENTER, INC.
1800 Century Boulevard
Suite 1600
Atlanta, Georgia 30345
Hal Firestone, President
Peter J. Fellicetta, Vice President

Description of Operation: Franchising of independent real estate offices into a national network of local offices operating under a common name whose services help the home owner sell his home for a small flat fee rather than a large commission.
Number of Franchisees: 135 in 36 states
In Business Since: 1977
Equity Capital Needed: $25,000 in cash and/or credit for franchising fee set up costs and day to day operations.
Financial Assistance Available: Local financing where applicable.
Training Provided: Complete training of owners and managers at the corporate headquarters in Atlanta, Georgia and complete training of secretaries and sales people in local areas.
Managerial Assistance Available: Continual training sessions and sales rallies and ongoing educational seminars.

THE HOME TEAM, INC.
1233 South Commercial Street
Neenah, Wisconsin 54956
Norman DeBroux, National Marketing Manager

Description of Operation: The Home Team, Inc., is a membership organization for licensed, reputable real estate brokerage firms offering its services and programs for use of its members. Members are granted the use of registered marks and a variety of marketing services and programs.
Number of Franchisees: 10 in Wisconsin
In Business Since: 1978
Equity Capital Needed: $500 minimum
Financial Assistance Available: None
Training Provided: Training is available in all phases of real estate sales and office management.
Managerial Assistance Available: Management workshops where applicable.

INTERNATIONAL REAL ESTATE NETWORK, INC.
16133 Ventura Boulevard, Suite 880
Encino, California 91436
C. J. Seibert, Jr., President

Description of Operation: Full service real estate franchise with heavy emphasis on television advertising. Low fee structure with majority of fee spent on broker advertising. Extensive referral system, full compliment of broker aids, etc.
Number of Franchisees: Over 1,000 throughout the United States and Canada.
In Business Since: 1974
Equity Capital Needed: Franchises are normally sold to established operating real estate companies. No start up capital required. Franchise membership fees range from $4,250 to $7,000 depending on state development stage.
Financial Assistance Available: Will finance part of initial fee on occasion.
Managerial Assistance Available: Available - Audio video training program. Plus company sponsored seminars, annual conventions, state and regional advisory boards.

LAND MART OF AMERICA, INC.
300 Spring Building
Little Rock, Arkansas 72203
Edward H. Held, President

Description of Operation: A national real estate franchise company offering master franchises and individual franchises across America.
Number of Franchisees: 23 in 6 states
In Business Since: 1976
Equity Capital Needed: $3,000
Financial Assistance Available: A total investment of $3,000 is necessary to secure franchise. With good credit references Land Mart will take a down payment of $1,500 and $500 per month for 3 months. A percentage of all sales made by franchisee is paid to franchisor.
Training Provided: Intensive training courses are offered continually under the supervision of a full-time Land Mart representative.
Managerial Assistance Available: Land Mart provides continual management service for the life of the franchise in such areas as advertising, catalogs, area folders, listing folders, supplies and stationery at cost, referral network, confidential lists and a home office Wats line for referrals and service.

NEW WORLD REAL-ESTATE INC.
755 West Big Beaver
Suite 133
Troy, Michigan 48084

Description of Operation: New World Real-Estate Inc., is a full service network, principally engaged in the business of franchising real-estate sales offices in addition to granting area rights in other states, will assist local firms in other states to set up franchise firms of their own or assist franchise firms in expansion.

85

Number of Franchisees: 35 in Michigan
In Business Since: 1975
Equity Capital Needed: $25,000 for regional rights for out of state organizations for a limited period. $2,950 initial franchise fee plus sufficient working capital for equipment and fixed expenses.
Financial Assistance Available: New World Real-Estate will negotiate and assist in financing the franchise fee.
Training Provided: Franchisee receives management and continued sales and attitude training for its sales personnel. Exclusive New World training program and audio video program designed by one of the leading sales and management trainers in the country.
Managerial Assistance Available: Training providing franchisee receives management, and continued sales and attitude training to its sales personnel.

PARTNERS REAL ESTATE, INC.
1101 Connecticut Avenue, N.W.
Suite 1002
Washington, D.C. 20036
James S. Bugg, President
Description of Operation: Franchisor of real estate brokers.
Number of Franchisees: Approximately 200 in 17 states
In Business Since: 1976
Equity Capital Needed: $3,300
Financial Assistance Available: None
Training Provided: Sales associate training, management development, office secretary.
Managerial Assistance Available: Very in-depth during start-up and continuous through operation.

RAM, INC., REALTORS
12901 Saratoga Avenue
Saratoga, California 95070
Clare P. Rooney, President
Description of Operation: "Full-service" real estate operation.
Number of Franchisees: 3 in California
Equity Capital Needed: 1966
Financial Assistance Available: None
Training Provided: Assist in set-up procedures, accounting, training new sales personnel.
Managerial Assistance Available: Assistance provided at request of franchisee.

REAL ESTATE ONE LICENSING COMPANY
29630 Orchard Lake Road
Farmington Hills, Michigan 48018
Daniel J. Stevens, President
Description of Operation: Real Estate One Licensing Company, franchises real estate brokers into a network using Real Estate One trademark properties, systems, training methods, and referral programs.
Number of Franchisees: 50 in 2 states
In Business Since: 1972
Equity Capital Needed: Franchisee fee is $3,900
Financial Assistance Available: Real Estate One will finance the franchise fee.
Training Provided: Real Estate One provides management seminars, and 4 day training courses for both brokers and sales associates.
Managerial Assistance Available: In addition to training courses, Real Estate One provides management consultation by telephone, franchise manuals, advertising aids, supplies and forms.

REALTY COMPANY OF AMERICA
National Office
550 West Colfax Avenue
Denver, Colorado 80204
Richard Chaves, Franchise Director
Description of Operation: Franchise real estate companies under the name of Realty Company of America.
Number of Franchisees: 12 in Colorado and New Mexico
In Business Since: 1973
Equity Capital Needed: $700 for main office. $350 for branch office and 1 percent gross commissions.
Financial Assistance Available: $50,000 line of credit to qualified franchisess.
Training Provided: Standard operation manual.
Managerial Assistance Available: Realty Company of America provides continual management services for the life of the franchise in the area of bookkeeping and advertising. State Master Franchisee provides supervisor of compliance of operations manual. A vote of 51 percent of the active franchise of any given state can change any part of operating manual.

REALTY 1, INC.
2425 Stevenson Drive
Springfield, Illinois 62703
Michael L. Clarke, Executive Vice President
Description of Operation: Franchising reputable, experienced, existing real estate brokerage businesses, providing a common or multi market image, national referral service, training and education, sales promotion material, discount purchasing advertising planning regional market listings, insurance benefit programs and staff assistance in return for service fee as provided in the exclusive territory franchise agreement. A three level approval is required for membership.
Number of Franchisees: 65 in Illinois, Missouri and Iowa
In Business Since: 1974
Financial Assistance Available: $5,000 initial fee and an established operating real estate business.
Financial Assistance Available: None
Training Provided: A 4-part, 112-hour cycle training program; on sight sales associate post license training. Provided at no cost to franchisee; plus continuous workshops, conference and clinics offering information on pertinent subject matter in the real estate industry.

Managerial Assistance Available: An on sight "Operations Improvement Program" 20-40 hours in length to include business planning, personnel and recruiting, advertising and fiscal control. An "operations handbook" to include referral program, regional market listing, identify, ad kit, supply catalog and insurance benefit programs. In addition an on sight once a month service visit and on call consultation on any operation situation, plus special interest conferences. All no charge to franchisee.

REALTY USA/INTERSTATE REFERRAL SERVICE, INC.
P. O. Box 402, Route 9
Clifton Park, New York 10206
Chris Schmid, President
Description of Operation: Realty USA franchise is offered only to licensed and operating residential real estate brokerage firms, to provide uniform means of identification and assistance in advertising, promotion and marketing. Includes membership in Interstate Referral Service referral and marketing network of 210 offices in 40 states.
Number of Franchisees: 66 in 25 states
In Business Since: 1972 - Franchising 1975
Equity Capital Needed: No requirement. Initial franchise fee $4,990. Service fee, 1-1/2 percent of gross commissions to firms.
Financial Assistance Available: None
Training Provided: 12 week tape and workbook training program for licensed salespeople; one day indoctrination meeting at franchisee's office and periodic review meetings for management and staff. Additional programs and assistance are available.
Managerial Assistance Available: Realty USA furnishes a policies and procedures manual, forms, and other materials; also assistance in advertising and personnel recruitment, evaluation and training. Company representatives and in some areas field personnel provide consultation and assistance. Interstate Referral Service sponsors periodic meetings of Realty USA franchisees and Interstate members.

REALTY WORLD CORPORATION
7700 Little River Turnpike
Annandale, Virginia 22003
William L. Janeski, President
Description of Operation: Full service network - for the independent real estate broker including broad educational programs and courses for agents, brokers, and management; supplying international name and logo, referral system, and mass advertising programs, etc. There are two types of franchises available - one a master license for a large territory (such as a whole state) and the master licensee intern franchises for the local real estate broker, (full explanation upon request).
Number of Franchisees: Over 2,700 in 49 states, District of Columbia and Canada
In Business Since: 1974 in United States
Equity Capital Needed: The master franchise: $50,000, the local franchisee: no specific amount.
Financial Assistance Available: None
Training Provided: Master franchisee receives approximately 30 days of training and instruction. For the local franchisee, training is ongoing. A course known as Program IV was written and instructed initially by Dr. John C. Lang and is a 4 phase management training program involving all phases of management training such as: Introduction to Management, Behavioral Science approach, Functions and Duties of Management, Administration in Management, Human Relations, Supervision and Evaluation, Communications, Procedures and Techniques, Interviewing Techniques, Problem Solving, Counseling, etc.
Managerial Assistance Available: Same as above. All manuals for management courses and services are provided by Realty World licensees. The regional staff is trained in franchising for at least 3 weeks prior to marketing.

RED CARPET CORPORATION OF AMERICA
1111 Civic Drive, Suite 300
Walnut Creek, California 94596
William A. Kokorelis, Vice President of Marketing/Sales
William H. Thompson, National Director of Franchise Development
Description of Operation: Red Carpet Corporation of America is principally engaged in providing a full-service real estate franchise to independent real estate brokerage firms by making available research, marketing programs, education systems for management and sales associates, full range advertising techniques for all media, sales aids, publicity systems, referral programs, home protection programs, national sales award programs, errors and ommisions insurance programs, and complete audio-visual broker and associate education programs. The Red Carpet system is unique in fostering franchise participation in design and implementation of these and expanding programs, as well as participation in implementation of useful programs on a community level.
There are two types of franchises available: 1. Master Franchise: available in selected large areas (states or larger). 2. Real Estate Office Franchise: available from the Master franchisee or Red Carpet Corporation, depending on the area in which the franchise will be operated.
Number of Franchisees: Over 1,400 in 25 states and District of Columbia.
In Business Since: 1966
Equity Capital Needed: The equity capital required is not specific, since the franchisee is generally already in the real estate business. The overall financial position of each applicant for the franchise is reviewed upon application to ensure adequate capitalization and operating funds.
The initial investment for the *first* office purchased, including estimated changeover costs and start-up materials is approximately $10,500. Such costs for franchisees purchasing additional franchises, initially or later, will be lower due to a reduced initial franchise fee on such "multiple franchises."
Financial Assistance Available: Red Carpet Corporation of America does not directly provide financial assistance for new franchisees, but will assist the franchisee to locate sources of financial assistance.
Training Provided: *Professional Real Estate Management:* management development course for brokers and/or their managers, designed to improve skills in planning, recruiting, interpersonal communication and broker council operations. *Professional Communications Skills:* available for the development of an individual's interpersonal communication skills. This 3 day program is based on "benefit selling." Audio cassette

and programmed learning are featured. A 1-day refresher course adds impact, skill retention, and refinement. *Professional Recruiting Skills:* this course teaches how brokers and managers can recruit and retain the best people, and also to assess the individual's strengths, making interviewing and screening much more effective. Audio-cassette and programmed learning guides are parts of the training. A special recruiting film for use in career seminars is also available. *Local Publicity Made Simple:* a unique, step-by-step guide for generating publicity in local suburban newspapers to support local marketing and advertising efforts while building an image of Red Carpet as a vital part of the community. *Professional Sales Training Program:* a complete audio-visual professional sales training program incorporating Red Carpet programs such as the marketing communications manual, the sales presentation manual, professional communications skills, and others. It is designed to be used with or without an instructor, can be used as a basic and on-going training program for sales associates, and is a full-service program, not just addressing selling and listing. The manner in which this program is designed will allow updates and additions in the future.
Managerial Assistance Available: The franchisee or his designated manager is provided with a management development course to improve skills in planning, recruiting, interpersonal communication, and other topics. Additional assistance is available via broker council programs and trained corporate or master franchise support personnel.

RE/MAX OF AMERICA, INC.
7935 East Prentice Avenue
Englewood, Colorado 80111
Daryl Vesperson, Vice President, Operation
Description of Operation: RE/MAX of American, Inc., is a national network of independent real estate brokers operating under the RE/MAX 100 percent Commission Concept. This method of operation was designed to help solve many of the problems facing today's real estate broker. An association is created of sales people who retain 100 percent of every commission dollar they earn and in return, the sales agents are responsible and share in the expenses of the operation. Member brokers are allowed the use of all registered marks to develop national identity as well as continuity in advertising and public relations programs. Sales aids, a national referral program, volume purchasing discounts, associated manuals, brochures, and recruiting aids are provided to all licensee brokers along with management consulting and technical assistance to assist the franchisee in development. RE/MAX will add the RE/MAX Home Protection Plan and Group Errors and Omissions Insurance coverage to its services in January 1980.
Number of Franchisees: 550 in 40 states and Canada.
In Business Since: 1973.
Equity Capital Needed: An average of $7,500.
Financial Assistance Available: RE/MAX of America provides financial assistance for new member-brokers in the form of financing initial franchise fees.
Training Provided: A new Broker-Owner must attend a 4 day RE/MAX management development course conducted at the national headquarters in Denver, Colorado. This course covers the program required to insure success on the broker's part and includes recruiting, secretarial procedures, bookkeeping principals, initial office development, advertising, national referral and overall management training. Additionally, seminars are held for both Broker-Owners and associates semi-annually in various cities across the country. There are no charges for the initial Broker-Owners training, however, there is a minimal charge to help defray expenses for the semi-annual training programs.
Managerial Assistance Available: On-going consulting services and managerial guidance are provided on a regular basis to all individuals within the system. Each Broker-Owner is contacted individually to discuss his development and any encountered problems. Twenty-four regional directors are strategically located throughout the United States and along with their staffs provide on-site assistance needed by the franchisees. Broker-Owners Councils and Sales Advisory Councils are developed within each area and provide continuity of effort and consistency in operation throughout the organization.

SECURITY PACIFIC REAL ESTATE, INC.
587 Ygnacio Valley Road
Walnut Creek, California 94596
Clifford Fick, General Manager
Description of Operation: Security Pacific is offering franchises for real estate brokerage offices.
Number of Franchisees: 3 in California.
In Business Since: 1971.
Equity Capital Needed: $5,000.
Financial Assistance Available: None.
Training Provided: Security Pacific from time to time will provide training seminars for franchisees at a nominal cost.
Managerial Assistance Available: Franchisee will be provided with an operations manual; which will contain operations guidelines, office commission structures, recruiting and retention of sales personnel as part of his franchise agreement. Franchisee will receive a Broker Orientation when the office is open. Management training seminars will be made available from time to time at a nominal cost.

SKI & SHORE PROPERTIES, INC.
1231 U.S. 31 North
Petoskey, Michigan 49770
John M. Georgi, President
Description of Operation: A recreational oriented real estate franchise assisting real estate offices in resort areas. The basis of the franchisor is continuing assistance to insure individual office growth.
Number of Franchisees: 20 in Michigan.
In Business Since: 1969.
Equity Capital Needed: $10,000.
Financial Assistance Available: None.
Training Provided: Continuing Sales and Management training program.
Managerial Assistance Available: The company supplies a complete set of secretarial, policy and operations manuals plus has an on-going improvement program offering new products, techniques and information to insure the individual offices stay in the forefront of the real estate industry.

STATE FARM REALTY, INC.
21450-A, Golden Springs Drive
Walnut, California 91789
Earl H. Jorgensen, Jr., Director of Licensing
Description of Operation: Development of a nationwide system of general real estate brokerage offices, available to qualified real estate brokers.
Number of Franchisees: 8 in California. Marketing is in its initial phase and nationwide expansion is underway. With regional administrators in Florida, Illinois, Texas and New York.
In Business Since: 1976.
Equity Capital Needed: Only a small monthly fee.
Financial Assistance Available: Some.
Training Period: Periodic sales training, and motivational seminars.
Managerial Assistance Available: Management consultation, public relation assistance and motivational ideas.

STATE WIDE REAL ESTATE
2209 Ludington Street
Escanaba, Michigan 49829
Hugh. D. Harris
Description of Operation: Real estate brokerage franchising.
Number of Franchisees: 65 in Michigan and Wisconsin.
In Business Since: 1945.
Equity Capital Needed: $10,000 to $20,000.
Financial Assistance Available: None.
Training Provided: Accounting and trust bookkeeping.
Managerial Assistance Available: 1 week sales associates and broker training.

THE STERLING THOMPSON GROUP
1250 Highway 35
Middletown, New Jersey 07748
Stan Ellberger, Executive Vice President
Description of Operation: The Sterling Thompson Group offers a complete and continuing program for operating a real estate brokerage office. The uniqueness lies with the fact that we are a real estate company offering franchises — not a franchise company.
Number of Franchisees: Over 60 plus 18 company-owned in New Jersey. In process of getting approval in other states.
In Business Since: 1979.
Equity Capital Needed: Initial franchise fee $3,900.
Financial Assistance Available: Limited financing for initial fee.
Training Provided: Training for sales associates and broker/management provided continuously, salesmanship training for associates consists of 6 ½-day sessions. Technical skills for associates for an additional 6½ sessions. Broker/manager seminars and workshops presented twice monthly.
Managerial Assistance Available: Continuous assistance from headquarters and in the field covering every aspect of running a real estate brokerage operation from recruiting salespeople (the Sterling Thompson School of Real Estate) to preparing advertising budgets.

3% REALTY, INC.
1123 North Third Street
Marquette, Michigan 49855
J. Barry Cook
Description of Operation: Discount real estate brokerage 3 percent commission for selling homes.
Number of Franchisees: 4 in Wisconsin.
In Business Since: Real estate sales since 1974, franchising 1979.
Equity Capital Needed: $3,000 franchise fee.
Financial Assistance Available: None.
Training Provided: Up to 1 week, training in methods of operating a 3% Realty Office.
Managerial Assistance Available: Operations manual and advertising.

UNITED SECURITY ASSOCIATES REALTY, INC.
Also U.S.A REALTY
2216 Sepulveda Boulevard
Torrance, California 90501
Roger Adams, President
Description of Operation: Small, local real estate franchise for the small office that wants a larger image and sales training for salespeople.
Number of Franchisees: 6 in California.
In Business Since: 1972 as a franchise.
Equity Capital Needed: $1,500 plus cost, approximately $400 plus 3 percent of gross commissions.
Financial Assistance Available: May offer terms for franchise.
Training Provided: Sales training for salespeople and any help broker may need. We also have a real estate licensing program.
Managerial Assistance Available: Same as above.

RECREATION/ENTERTAINMENT/TRAVEL/SUPPLIES

AMERICAN SAFARI CORPORATION
7000 S.W. 62nd Avenue PTH "A"
Miami, Florida 33143
Attention: R.M. Deutman
Description of Operation: Recreation vehicle rental franchise specializing in motor home rental.
Number of Franchisees: 30 in 28 states.
In Business Since: 1976.
Equity Capital Needed: $15,000 plus excellent financial statement.
Financial Assistance Available: Motor home financing is available to qualified applicants.
Training Provided: 1 week initial training program and continuing thereafter.
Managerial Assistance Available: Continuous counseling in all aspects of the business.

BATTING RANGE PRO
5954 Brainerd Road
Chattanooga, Tennessee 47421
E.K. Magrath, Jr.
Jay M. Grant
Description of Operation: 6 to 9 JUGS Coin Operated Pneumatic Tire, Variable Speed, Baseball and Softball Pitching Machines. A ball is pitched every 6 seconds at a charge of 50 cents for 12 to 18 baseballs. Baseballs are automatically reloaded to the hopper.
Number of Franchisees: 15 in 5 states.
In Business Since: 1979.
Equity Capital Needed: $20,000 to $50,000, depending on the number of baseball pitching machines installed.
Financial Assistance Available: Limited.
Training Provided: Complete operational kit is provided to instruct operators that will cover most questions asked.
Managerial Assistance Available: Site selection advice, complete batting range plans available, assistance in construction planning. Complete lock and key construction available if desired.

CAPTRAN FRANCHISE CORPORATION
1619 Periwinkle Way
Sanibel, Florida 33957
John F. Sweeney, President
Description of Operation: Franchises for the development of Interval Ownership Resorts. Providing assistance in the development and sales of fee simple interests in condominium units.
Number of Franchisees: 3 in Florida.
In Business Since: Parent in business since 1975. Franchise operations since 1979.
Equity Capital Needed: $250,000 to $500,000.
Financial Assistance Available: Franchisor can provide assistance in obtaining construction and installment loan financing through affiliated companies and subsidiaries.
Training Provided: Intensive initial sales and resort management training provided by franchisor. Continuing training of sales personnel throughout the term of franchise, seven years.
Managerial Assistance Available: Covered in above description.

CHANCE MANUFACTURING COMPANY, INC.
801 Wager Street
Utica, New York 13502
Raymond Seakan, President
Description of Operation: We manufacture and sell franchises on sit down pin ball machines and a 1-2-4 Play Player TV Video games that has 10 functions and 6 different games. We place these games on locations for our franchisee, with his assistance, in his area of operation. We install these games in restaurants, pizza parlors, hotels, motels, home bar rooms, recreation center, resort areas, bowling alleys, etc.
Number of Franchisees: 96 in 34 states.
In Business Since: 1975.
Equity Capital Needed: $2,995 to $25,000.
Financial Assistance Available: None.
Training Provided: We place TV Video games on location and train the franchisee to do the same. We also train him on promoting and servicing and installing the equipment.
Managerial Assistance Available: Complete manual of operation, list of locations, style to work with; assist with brochures, literature and bi-monthly seminars. Special promotions and contests are taught to owners and their appointed employees.

CORNER POCKETS OF AMERICA, INC.
1445 Broadwater Avenue
P.O. Box 20878
Billings, Montana 59104
George Frank, President
Description of Operation: National franchisor of Corner Pocket billiard lounges featuring beverages, specialized foods, pocket billiard tables, football tables and other amusement games.
Number of franchisees: 44 in 10 states.
In Business Since: 1973.
Equity Capital Needed: $75,000 with satisfactory financial background.
Financial Assistance Available: None.
Training Provided: Approximately 2 weeks: — formal training at corporate office and on-the-job training in field opening.
Managerial Assistance Available: Managerial and technical assistance is provided on a continuing basis. Intermittent pocket billiard promotions, leagues, tournaments, and exhibitions. Predesigned plans and specifications for standard building, assistance in site selection, construction, opening and grand opening.

COURT MANAGEMENT COMPANY, INC.
10460 Miamisburg-Springboro Pike
Miamisburg, Ohio 45342
William P. Henderson, Executive Vice President
Description of Operation: Court Management Company, Inc., offers the opportunity for independent business people to own and operate their own racquetball club. Clubs vary in size, number of courts, and extent of amenities depending on size of community and extent of existing competition.
Number of Franchisees: 5 in Ohio, North Carolina and New York.
In Business Since: 1976.
Equity Capital Needed: Minimum of $15,000.
Financial Assistance Available: Typical club is set up as a limtied partnership with franchisee acting as the general partner. Total project costs range from $650,000 up. Typical financing is 60 percent mortgage (Court Management will help obtain mortgage) and 40 percent equity (most from limited partners secured by the franchisee).
Training Provided: Extensive 2 week marketing and management training provided prior to opening. On-going management consulting for first 2 years on a monthly basis.
Managerial Assistance Available: Complete operations manual and systems provided. Complete forms package available. Contact established for franchisee with all appropriate industry vendors. Initial purchasing assistance provided in all areas.

DISCO FACTORY
6901 Jerricho Turnpike
Syossett, New York 11791
Burt Tenser, President
Description of Operation: Licensed individuals to operate a mobile discoteque called Murray the K's Disco on Wheels — can be active or absentee management. Licensee rents portable discoteque and disco entertainment to bars, restaurants and private social functions.
Number of Franchisees: 24 in 5 states and Canada.
In Business Since: 1975.
Equity Capital Needed: $10,000.
Financial Assistance Available: We do not finance their investment, however, we supply them with many things at no charge.
Training Provided: Continuous training of the licensee's disc jockeys. Also training in marketing.
Managerial Assistance Available: Constant supervision in both marketing and technical areas.

EMPRESS TRAVEL FRANCHISE CORPORATION
293 Madison Avenue
New York, New York 10017
Jack Cygielman, President
Description of Operation: Empress Travel offers a unique retail travel agency operation, in an exciting, stimulating, year round business, which gives its participants great pleasure and financial reward. An Empress Travel franchise has full support and assistance at all times, from management.
Number of Franchisees: 50 in New York, New Jersey, Connecticut, Pennsylvania, and Washington, D.C.
In Business Since: 1958.
Equity Capital Needed: $35,000 including working capital.
Financial Assistance Available: Yes.
Training Provided: Intensive training course for all new franchisees and their personnel at the home office and on site at company offices, also at franchisees outlet.
Managerial Assistance Available: Empress Travel provides continual management service with advertising, complete manuals of operations, forms, and directions, etc. Management works closely with franchisees, and assist solving all problems. Empress Travel sponsors meetings of franchisees and conducts marketing research to maintain high Empress Travel consumer acceptance.

FUGAZY TRAVEL FRANCHISES, LTD.
645 Madison Avenue
New York, New York 10022
Louis Victor Fugazy, Vice President
Description of Operation: Full service travel agency.
Number of Franchisees: 12 in 6 states.
In Business Since: 1970.
Equity Capital Needed: $30,000 franchise fee plus $35-$40,000 working capital.
Financial Assistance Available: None.
Training Provided: Fugazy will aid licensee in leasing and furnishing of a travel office, secure necessary approvals form IATA & ATC, provide trained account executives to establish factors necessary in opening a fully appointed travel agency for 20 days.
Managerial Assistance Available: Fugazy will assist licensee in recruitment of staff and to provide a training program for two of the personnel of licensee which encompasses 45 hours over 15 sessions. It will also provide continuing training of personnel of licensee as Fugazy may determine to be necessary.

FUNNY FUN FUN GOLF
6 Watson Place
Utica, New York 13502
Raymond Seakan, President

Description of Operation: Funny Fun Fun Golf offers the most enjoyable and profitable happy concept of enjoying miniature golf for the young and the young at heart and all those in between. This computerized talking golf course causes a happy feeling during the whole time of play. It is open 7 days a week from 8 a.m. to 11 p.m. weekdays, and Friday and Saturday until 1 a.m. All products needed, parts, inventory, manuals, instructions and training are supplied to the franchisee by Funny Fun Fun Golf.

Number of Franchisees: 3 in Texas, 1 in Ohio and 1 in California

In Business Since: 1978

Equity Capital Needed: $25,000 minimum

Financial Assistance Available: A total investment of $100,000 to $125,000 is necessary to own and operate a Funny Fun Fun Golf franchise. The down payment of $20,000 pays for a down payment, inventory, security deposits, licenses, permits, and training. Funny Fun Fun will assist in financing the balance on an 8 year program and franchisee has the option to do his own financing.

Training Provided: A trained management executive will supply a mandatory training period of 30 days starting with the first day of opening the franchise. The training will consist of fund raising, direct radio, television and newspaper advertising, school clubs and senior citizen groups to play during slow play periods. Finalizations on bookkeeping, cash flow, how to operate the food concessions, how to do preventative maintenance and electrical maintenance.

Managerial Assistance Available: Funny Fun Fun will stand behind the product for 1 year free service and 1 year free parts warranty. The management of Funny Fun Fun will stand by to answer any questions for the duration of the operation. Any new and improved ideas will be on a no charge basis and the franchisee may attend any and all seminars that are held in the future so as to keep him informed and increase his profit potential.

FUN SERVICES, INC.
321 East Cullerton Street
Chicago, Illinois 60616
Don Zimmerman, General Manager

Description of Operation: Fun Services franchisees provide a service of professional Fun Fairs for the leisure time and recreational industries. The primary market in fund raising organizations, such as elementary school P.T.A.'s, churches, youth and fraternal organizations. Entertainment is also provided to industrial picnics and Christmas parties, as well as conventions and shopping center openings. The service provided includes booths, games and prizes which are all professionally programmed to insure profits for the organization and fun to the participants. All equipment and supplies needed to perform multiple events simultaneously are provided as part of the franchisee package, as well as a cargo van for delivery and warehousing. In addition, programs have been developed in the fund raising service field involving candy sales, door to door merchandise sales and gift programs through the schools.

Number of Franchisees: 105 in 38 states

In Business Since: 1966

Equity Capital Needed: $3,950 (total franchise cost $19,950).

Financial Assistance Available: Fun Services, Inc., finances up to $16,000 of initial franchise cost over a 5-year contract. No payments are required during the first 2 months of operation.

Training Provided: 4 day formal school at Fun Services headquarters. Room, board and local transportation provided as part of training school. Field assistance provided as needed.

Managerial Assistance Available: Complete manuals of operation, forms and directions are provided. Complete promotional program with brochures, letters mail folders, enclosures and stamps provided. Continual top management support, newsletters, regional and national meetings of franchisees. Continual research and periodic introduction of new items, programs, games and fund raising concepts.

GO-KART TRACK SYSTEMS
5954 Brainerd Road
Chattanooga, Tennessee 37421
Jay M. Grant, President

Description of Operation: 12 to 15 concession type go carts which are rented for a 5-minute ride on approximately 800' curved tract at a speed of 18-20 mph.

Number of Franchisees: 26 in 10 states

In Business Since: 1972

Equity Capital Needed: $30,000

Financial Assistance Available: Limited

Training Provided: Training on-the-job until operator is completely satisfied he can handle the job. Manager's manual will cover most questions that come up.

Managerial Assistance Available: Site selection, complete track and building layout, and construction planning. Complete lock and key construction available, if desired.

GOLF PLAYERS, INC.
5954 Brainerd Road
Chattanooga, Tennessee 37421
Earl Magrath, President

Description of Operation: Miniature golf courses with very large, colorful, and distinctive figures and caricatures - some animated. Operation under the name "Sir Goony Golf."

Number of Franchisees: 48 in 11 states

In Business Since: 1964

Equity Capital Needed: $28,600 for franchise.

Financial Assistance Available: Franchisor is able to furnish only limited help on financing. Most financing must be provided by franchisee.

Training Provided: Training at home office and on-the-job. Continuing help by personal visits, newsletters and phone calls. A complete operational manager's manual is provided.

Managerial Assistance Available: Engineering design and construction planning; continuing management service and advice.

LOMMA ENTERPRISES, INC.
1120 South Washington Avenue
Scranton, Pennsylvania 18505
J. C. Rogari, Executive Vice President

Description of Operation: Prefabricated miniature golf courses that can be used indoors or outdoors with limited space. It is a one-person, non-commodity business.

Number of Franchisees: 1,470 in all 50 states

In Business Since: 1960

Equity Capital Needed: $5,000

Financial Assistance Available: A minimum down payment is needed, and the balance can be payable up to a 2 year period. Complete and concise free franchise program with no franchise or royalty fees to pay.

Training Provided: A complete operational and promotional kit is provided to franchisees.

Managerial Assistance Available: A concise manager's guide and periodic training seminars, along with national festivities and an international miniature golf tournament.

LST TRAVEL, INC.
P. O. Box 52 - North Hackensack Station
River Edge, New Jersey 07661
Irving Davidoff, Franchise Director

Description of Operation: Travel agency franchise featuring total travel services and special package programs.

Number of Franchisees: 5 in New Jersey

In Business Since: 1973

Equity Capital Needed: Total turnkey investment - $13,900

Financial Assistance Available: None

Training Provided: Company provides comprehensive training program, managerial assistance.

Managerial Assistance Available: Field representatives personally visit each location frequently to observe the operations and to recommend improvements to yield greater sales and higher profit for the franchisee.

MISS AMERICAN TEEN-AGER INC.
P. O. Box 221
New Milford, New Jersey 07646
Sol Abrams, President

Description of Operation: Pageant for girls between the ages of 13 through 17, with national winner designated as "Miss American Teen-Ager." Franchisees for local contests are awarded to business firms, individuals and organizations throughout the United States on a year to year basis. Pageants are to promote increased sales, traffic attendance, profits, publicity and prestige.

Number of Franchisees: Franchises are awarded for one year periods. Franchise holders are given first option for renewing in their areas for following year. Approximately 50 state franchises are awarded each year.

In Business Since: 1960

Equity Capital Needed: $750 to $2,000 depending upon size of state desired. Little or no money needed for operation.

Financial Assistance Available: None

Training Provided: Complete operation manual and press kit provided. 1-1/2 hour TV tape is also available. Personal consultation of national management available at all times.

Managerial Assistance Available: Company provides counseling and managerial services to meet all needs.

PUTT-PUTT GOLF COURSES OF AMERICA, INC.
P. O. Box 35237
Fayetteville, North Carolina 28303
Don S. Clayton, President

Description of Operation: Franchised miniature golf facilities with standardization of color scheme, construction, and putting surface.

Number of Franchisees: Over 400 in 40 states, and 5 foreign countries.

In Business Since: 1954

Equity Capital Needed: $25,000 to $125,000

Financial Assistance Available: No financing provided by company, however, assistance in obtaining financing through banks and SBA is available.

Training Provided: 1 week annually at international convention. Six regional, two-day seminars each year from March 1st thru July 1st.

Managerial Assistance Available: Complete computer accounting. Complete manager's manual. Complete promotional program provided including radio, TV, and newspaper advertising, etc., for the duration of the length of the contract.

PUTT-R-GOLF INC.
3914 West Market Street
Akron, Ohio 44313
Donald C. Nelson

Description of Operation: Supply plans and equipment for family fun centers concentrating on miniature golf, baseball batting ranges, slo-pitch softball batting ranges.

Number of Franchisees: 19 in 10 states and Canada

In Business Since: 1952

Equity Capital Needed: $29,500

Financial Assistance Available: Plans, material lists and consulting

Training Provided: Informal

Managerial Assistance Available: As needed basis.

SLO POKE INC.
3914 West Market Street
Akron, Ohio 44313
Donald C. Nelson, President

Description of Operation: Slo Poke is a unique (patent applied for) under-hand

throwing, slo pitch softball pitching machine, licensed for protected territories.
Number of Franchisees: 13 in 9 states
In Business Since: 1978
Equity Capital Needed: $35,000 plus land.
Financial Assistance Available: None
Training Provided: Construction plans and assistance available during construction.
Managerial Assistance Available: As needed basis.

TOUR MATES ORGANIZATION, LTD.
11 Grace Avenue
Great Neck, New York 11021
Gene J. Finz, President

Description of Operation: A retail travel agency chain which relies heavily on its "European-Sidewalk Cafe" motif and its enlistment of several dozen straight commission "Tour Masters" and "Tour Mates" in each location which act as its sales force. The marketing concepts employed by the company have won it fame in its industry and place it amongst the top 4 percent in its marketing area.
Number of Franchisees: 12 in 7 states
In Business Since: 1973
Equity Capital Needed: $29,500 (plus some $20,000 in working capital). There are no residuals or royalties.
Financial Assistance Available: Limited financing available.
Training Provided: A comprehensive 4 week training program is provided the franchisee, his designated manager, and his staff of travel agents. Additionally, a 40 hour management course is provided the franchisee and his designated manager. Regular industry research and development - a perpetual education - is provided.
Managerial Assistance Available: Franchisor performs location analysis and site acquisition; constructs store in company image and motif; provides all necessary opening inventories and supplies; provides all accounting and bookkeeping systems; coordinates all advertising activity amongst all company-owned and franchise locations; selects and hires manager and staff of agency; provides comprehensive 4 week training program to franchisee, manager, and sales staff; provides additional 40 hour management training program to franchisee and manager; performs periodic inspections of the operation; provides industry research and development; offers thorough aid in day-to-day operation of the agency. There are no royalties nor residuals paid to the franchisor by the franchisee.

TRAVEL NETWORK CORPORATION
825 Seventh Avenue
New York, New York 10019

Description of Operation: Franchisor of retail travel agencies, offering start-up assistance, training, operational support, coordinated advertising and public relations programs, and exclusive products and programs.

Number of Franchisees: 140 throughout United States and Canada
In Business Since: May 1979
Equity Capital Needed: Total investment of $70,000
Financial Assistance Available: Partial financing of initial franchise fee available.
Training Provided: Complete initial training, a minimum of ten weeks, provided as part of franchise fee. On-going training available.
Managerial Assistance Available: Start-up and operational assistance included in franchise fee. Operational support comes from national headquarters as well as a network of regional field offices.

2001 CLUBS OF AMERICA, INC.
Great Southern Center
Bridgeville, Pennsylvania 15017
James Kowalczyk, Vice President

Description of Operation: Franchising and operation management of complexes trading as 2001 Entertainment Complexes, V.I.P. Entertainment Complexes, Chesterfields, and LaClique Clubs.
Number of Franchisees: 15 in Pennsylvania, New York, Florida, Georgia, Louisiana and Tennessee.
In Business Since: 1974
Equity Capital Needed: $500,000
Financial Assistance Available: Available to qualified applicants.
Training Provided: Franchisee receives intensive training at headquarters offices. Franchisee's manager receives up to 16 weeks training at operating facility other key personnel (bar managers, D.J.'s Assistant Managers) 3 weeks training.
Managerial Assistance Available: Continuous assistance in operational controls, personnel management, facility management, advertising, public relations, music programming, visual programming.

YOGI BEAR'S MINI GOLF AND SNAK SHOPPE
Division of LEISURE SYSTEMS INC.
30 North 18th Avenue, Unit 9
Sturgeon Bay, Wisconsin 54235
J. E. Webb, Executive Vice President

Description of Operation: Franchising and development of miniature golf courses using the cartoon character Yogi Bear as its promotional vehicle. Snack shops, and gift shops can be operated incidental to the miniature golf course operation.
Number of Franchisees: 6 in Midwest
In Business Since: 1969 franchising campground resorts. Started franchising mini golf courses in fall of 1977.
Equity Capital Needed: $20,000 to $75,000
Financial Assistance Available: Financing package assistance.
Training Provided: On-site training at operating unit.
Managerial Assistance Available: Ongoing operational support through merchandise and promotional programs.

RETAILING - NOT CLASSIFIED ELSEWHERE

ALUMA ART DESIGNS
Division of SEAKAN ENTERPRISES, INC.
801 Wager Street
Utica, New York 13502
Raymond Seakan, President

Description of Operation: We import aluminum foil imprinted pictures from England and distribute to distributors all over the United States. These are sold through gift shops, furniture stores, boutique shops, etc.
Number of Franchisees: 31 in 6 states
In Business Since: 1977
Equity Capital Needed: $2,995 to $9,975
Financial Assistance Available: 50 percent down - balance on delivery of product.
Training Provided: A training course at our factory on hiring labor, common business management, operating routes and information on how to train your people in locating and fund raising.
Managerial Assistance Available: We offer assistance in advertising, promotion and training. All new ideas will be sent along on a no charge basis.

AMERICAN HANDICRAFTS-MERRIBEE NEEDLEARTS
2617 West Seventh Street
Fort Worth, Texas 76107
Ty Whorton, Director, Special Sales

Description of Operation: Retail craft and needleart dealership. Company makes available its warehouse product line to dealers and supports them with sales promotional flyers mailed to current customers. Dealers may purchase from outside sources also.
Number of Franchisees: 410 in all states but Connecticut, Hawaii and Vermont.
In Business Since: Merribee - 1930. American Handicrafts - 1932
Equity Capital Needed: $4,000 *minimum* for American Handicrafts-Merribee. $10,000-$15,000 range preferred.
Financial Assistance Available: None
Training Provided: None
Managerial Assistance Available: Telephone contact.

AMERICAN VISION CENTERS, INC.
40 Horton Avenue
Lynbrook, New York 11563
Paul Supovitz, Director of Franchising

Description of Operation: The Company franchises and operates "American Vision Center" retail stores specializing in the sale of eyeglasses, contact lenses and related optical items. They offer a unique operational system as well as related merchandising and advertising programs. The Company also owns and operates National Contact Lens Plan, Inc., offering the customer additional or replacement contact lenses at reduced rates; and National Contact Lens Distributors, Inc., a wholesale supplier of optical products.
Number of Franchisees: 9 in 6 states
In Business Since: 1977
Equity Capital Needed: $25,000
Financial Assistance Available: The total investment in an American Vision Center will run from $75,000 to in excess of $100,000 depending upon store size and physical store improvements required. This investment includes a franchise fee of $10,000; approximately $23,000 in optical and lab equipment; approximately $20,000 in inventory with the balance for fixtures and improvements. Company will assist in obtaining outside financing.
Training Provided: An intensive training program is provided by the Company for all of its franchisees and their personnel. Training in sales, internal procedures, management, product knowledge and financial analysis is conducted at its home office and at a Company operated training store. There is no charge for the training program, however all travel and living expenses are paid by the franchisee.
Managerial Assistance Available: The American Vision Center system provides the support, buying power and merchandising expertise of a major optical chain and provides continuing operational assistance and supervision to its franchised stores. A detailed operations manual is provided and full supervision is available in all areas to work closely with franchisees to solve problems and improve store operations.

ATHLETIC ATTIC MARKETING, INC.
P. O. Box 14503
Gainesville, Florida 32604
W. Hardee McAlhaney, Executive Vice President

Description of Operation: Athletic Attic offers a specialty sporting goods concept to the ever increasing physical fitness conscious consumer. Product mix includes a heavy concentration in athletic footwear, running and tennis apparel, tennis and recquetball equipment and other exercise equipment. Stores are primarily in heavy-traffic malls and are constructed with an attractive cedar motif.
Number of Franchisees: 183 in 36 states, District of Columbia, Puerto Rico, New Zealand and Japan
In Business Since: 1972
Equity Capital Needed: Total capitalization varies from $60,000 to $182,000 depending on size and location of store. A minimum of 25 percent equity from franchisee is required.
Financial Assistance Available: No financial assistance is provided by the franchisor. However, all necessary information for loan applications is available.
Training Provided: Training program includes 2 days of classroom instruction in all aspects of store operations and 3 days of in-store instruction at franchisor's training store.

Managerial Assistance Available: Assistance includes, but not limited to the following: site selection, lease negotiations, store design, basic construction drawings, product mix assistance, opening suppliers accounts, accounting systems, inventory systems, on-site opening assistance, complete operations manual, advertising manual, local advertising materials, national advertising and publicity support, monthly management and newsletters, field representative visits, annual sales meetings.

BATHTIQUE INTERNATIONAL LTD.
161 Norris Drive
Rochester, New York 14610
Don A. Seipel, President
Description of Operation: A retail bath and bed specialty shop offering bath and bed products and accessories.
Number of Franchisees: 50 in 25 states (10 additional company-owned shops)
In Business Since: 1969
Equity Capital Needed: $35,000 to $60,000
Financial Assistance Available: Bank financing up to approximately 50 percent of above.
Training Provided: A concentrated 1 week training period is conducted for all new franchisees. Two individuals for each franchise participate in a 1 week manager training program. This program includes a classroom and on-the-job training under experienced managers. An additional 2 weeks of on-site location assistance is provided by the home office staff at the time the franchisees' shop opens.
Managerial Assistance Available: Bathique International provides continuing review and feedback concerning shop operations in areas such as sales, purchasing, advertising, and labor schedule. Merchandising is recommended to franchisees after testing in company shop. Merchandise is bought directly from recommended suppliers, quantity discounts available. A continuous personnel training program is strongly emphasized. Advertising materials are provided regularly including direct mail books. Annual and regional conferences are conducted.

THE BOOK RACK - THOUSANDS OF USED PAPERBACK BOOKS
2703 East Commercial Boulevard
Fort Lauderdale, Florida 33308
Virginia R. Darnell, President
Description of Operation: A used book shop franchise service involving the supplying of initial stock, training for franchisees, including the two-for-one book trading format, use of the franchise name, continuous consultation for franchisees, and the publication of a monthly newsletter.
Number of Franchisees: 143 in 27 states
In Business Since: 1963
Equity Capital Needed: $6,000 plus living expenses for the first year.
Financial Assistance Available: None
Training Provided: 1 week or as long as necessary.
Managerial Assistance Available: Constant consultation plus monthly newsletter.

BUDGET TAPES & RECORDS, INC.
10625 East 47th Avenue
Denver, Colorado 80239
Evan Lasky
Description of Operation: Retail tapes and records.
Number of Franchisees: 95 in 18 states
In Business Since: 1970
Equity Capital Needed: $30,000 to $35,000
Financial Assistance Available: Assist in loan proposal preparation.
Training Provided: 2 to 3 weeks retail and warehouse training.
Managerial Assistance Available: To assist owner in selecting a location for owner's Budget Tapes & Records business; to assist owner in the selection of owner's initial inventory and owner's furniture, fixtures and equipment to be installed in owner's store; to assist in the selection of such signs, decals and other identifying insignia as are specified by Budget; to develop advertising and promotional materials to be made available to owner from time to time in quantities to be specified by Budget, the cost of which shall be reimbursed by owner to Budget, and to generally assist owner in the operation and management of owner's Budget Tapes and Records business.

BUNING THE FLORIST, INC.
144 East Las Olas Boulvard
Fort Lauderdale, Florida 33301
Description of Operation; Buning the Florist, Inc., offers unique retail florist shops throughout the United States. Store size depends on program. Franchise package includes inventory, site selection, and design plus full accounting services and training. Company operates 20 wholly owned units in addition to franchise locations.
Number of Franchisees: 20 in Florida.
In Business Since: 1925.
Equity Capital Needed: Total investment varies from $39,900 and up depending on package.
Financial Assistance Available: Will finance portion of fee to qualified applicant.
Training Provided: 4 weeks of classroom training and 2 weeks on-the-job training.
Managerial Assistance Available: Buning provides continual management services, along with providing all accounting functions, advertising and regular monthly profit and loss statements. Field supervisors work closely with all locations.

BYTE INDUSTRIES INCORPORATED
2501 Arden Road
Hayward, California 94545
Dave Pava
Description of Operation: Retail Micro computer store, selling personal computers and small business systems, related peripherals, supplies, services and software to the end user.
Number of Franchisees: 75 existing dealers coast to coast.
In Business Since: 1975.
Equity Capital Needed: $50,000 to $100,000.
Financial Assistance Available: Assistance in the development of a comprehensive business plan and loan proposal.
Training Provided: 3 to 4 weeks technical and operations.
Managerial Assistance Available: Continued Management Guideline Services, National Advertising Program, Wholesale Supply Relationship and Product evaluation.

CANDLE-LITE INC.
770 South Adams Road, Suite 112
Birmingham, Michigan 48011
Jack L. Cloud, President
Description of Operation: Candle-Lite Shoppes carry a complete line of candles, candle accessories, and home decor items.
Number of Franchisees: 4 in Michigan, Ohio and Kentucky.
In Business Since: 1978.
Financial Assistance Available: None.
Training Provided: Necessary training given depending upon qualification of franchisee.
Managerial Assistance Available: Purchasing assistance and management assistance given for duration of franchise period. Complete manuals of operations, forms and directions are provided. Candle-Lite sponsors meetings of franchisees and conducts marketing and product research to maintain high consumer acceptance. Merchandising director works closely with franchisees and visit shoppes regularly to assist solving problems.

COMPUTERLAND CORPORATION
P.O. Box 2177
14400 Catalina Street
San Leandro, California 94577
Description of Operation: Franchisor offers an opportunity to operate a retail store dealing in computers, computer systems and related items, in a protected location, supported by marketing and purchasing services, under the name, Computerland.
Number of Franchisees: 114 in 35 states and 9 foreign countries.
In Business Since: 1976.
Equity Capital Needed: An estimated $50,000 is needed to secure financing for a total investment of $120,000 to $155,000.
Financial Assistance Available: No direct financing available, however, franchisor will assist franchisee in preparing a loan proposal package to present to a bank or other loaning institutions.
Training Provided: The initial training program for franchisees is a 60-hour course. Subjects covered are product knowledge, sales training and management, accounting and merchandising. Up-dating and refresher courses will be offered as the need arises.
Managerial Assistance Available: Upon opening of the store, franchisor offers in-store aid for the first 45 days of business and also supplies and keeps up-dated, an operations manual which includes bookkeeping direction, develops advertising aids for the franchisee, makes available its inventory for purchase by franchisee at cost and protects the Computerland name. It is the policy of the franchisor to give all possible aid to the franchisee, as franchisees' success is our success.

CONROY'S, INC.
10524 West Pico Boulevard
Los Angeles, California 90064
C.M. Conroy, President
Description of Operation: Conroy's Inc., provides the license to operate under the Conroy's name, and the Conroy's system of flower and plant stores. Services of the franchisor include site location and acquisition; minimum two months training at full pay at a franchised unit (and an operations manual); and coordination and management of regional advertising. Once a unit is in operation, Conroy's provides full accounting services (profit and loss statements, balance sheets, comparative analysis, percentage rations, etc.) including the processing of payroll and accounts receivable billings. Extensive management assistance available during training, and while in operation, as needed. Licensee may contract with Conroy's to assist in the construction of their unit.
Number of franchisees: There are a total of 24 stores in operation as of January 31, 1980 with five additional stores in construction and other sites in various stages of acquisition.
In Business Since: 1960, franchising since 1974.
Equity Capital Needed: Minimum $50,000 in cash, additional collateral required.
Financial Assistance Available: Florists' Capital Corporation (FCC) an affiliate of Conroy's Inc., may provide long-term (15 years, the first 5 years are interest only) loans to qualified applicants with which to finance a portion of the licensees' building improvements (licensees own their own leasehold improvements). FCC is a Federal Licensee under the Small Business Investment Act of 1958.
Training Provided: Minimum 2 months training in a licensed unit. In addition, classroom training will be provided. Training will encompass all phases of the retail flower and plant industry, personnel management, holiday management and all phases of operations. Conroy's assists in training until licensee opens unit and after as needed within licensee's unit. Licensee may request and receive assistance as needed within their unit.
Managerial Assistance Available: Conroy's handles advertising and accounting as described above and provides opportunities for mass buying for licensees to obtain products at lowest prices. There is no obligation to purchase from franchisor.

CONSUMER PRODUCTS OF AMERICA
Division of MATTAWAY SHOE COMPANY
10450 Southwest 187th Terrace
Miami, Florida 33157
M. Mattaway, President
Description of Operation: Rack merchandising footwear and general merchandise in supermarkets, super drug stores and variety stores.
Number of Franchisees: 4 in Florida, Texas, Louisiana and New Jersey.
In Business Since: 1944.
Equity Capital Needed: $25,000 to $60,000.
Financial Assistance Available: None.
Training Provided: 2 weeks to 30 days as required.
Managerial Assistance Available: Continuing.

THE ELECTRONICS BOUTIQUE
811 Church Road
Suite 110
Cherry Hill, New Jersey 08002
Description of Operation: Retail stores located in enclosed shopping malls, merchandising electronic oriented consumer products.
Number of Franchisees: 15 in 5 states.
In Business Since: 1977.
Equity Capital Needed: $40,000.
Financial Assistance Available: Will provide franchisee with assistance and guidance to obtain financing.
Training Provided: 1 week training in home office and 1 week in franchise location.
Managerial Assistance Available: Continuous guidance and buying assistance.

THE ENERGY SHED, INC.
1639 Terrace Drive
St. Paul, Minnesota 55113
Francis E. O'Neil, President
Description of Operation: Retail stores featuring wood burning, insulation, ventilation, weather proofing, solar products and systems.
Number of Franchisees: 16 in 5 upper Midwest states.
In Business Since: 1977.
Equity Capital Needed: $48,000-$62,000.
Financial Assistance Available: Franchisee arranges outside financing if necessary.
Training Provided: Intensive 6 day formal training at home office, followed by field training, annual conference, in store clinics.
Managerial Assistance Available: Management and technical aid provided by home office staff specialists on and off site. Management and technical manuals provided.

FAUX PAS, INCORPORATED
P.O. Box 51273
Jacksonville Beach, Florida 32250
Joseph Le Clair
Description of Operation: We establish jewelry fashion centers in boutiques, drug stores, beauty salons, schools, car shops, gift shops, hospitals, hotels, specialty stores, malls, mass merchandisers, chains, etc. Our program offers guaranteed sales to the distributor as well as to the retailer. We specialize in "Ear Piercing" using the original patented "Steri-Quik" system. Training is available for those who wish to promote ear piercing clinics along with $500,000 liability policy at no charge.
Number of Franchisees: 215 in 30 states.
In Business Since: 1976.
Equity Capital Needed: $9,800 and up depending on how many accounts one wishes to service.
Financial Assistance Available: None.
Training Provided: Field training is provided in the city by the distributor for at least 1 week and arrangements can be made for more if needed.
Managerial Assistance Available: Managerial and technical assistance is provided on a continuing basis.

FLOWERAMA OF AMERICA, INC.
3165 West Airline Highway
Waterloo, Iowa 50701
Bryan Patzkowski, Franchise Director
Description of Operation: Flowerama of America, Inc., franchise offers a unique innovative and dynamic specialty retail store operation. Two types of stores (kiosk-350 square feet and in-line-1,000 square feet) located in prime locations in enclosed mall shopping centers only, offer fresh cut flowers, floral arrangements, potted plants, and other horticultural related products, plus related floral accessories and gifts, to the consumer public at popular prices. Flowerama provides a turnkey shop, from site selection to store design and construction under long-term leases to its franchisees.
Number of Franchisees: 87 in 24 states.
In Business Since: 1966.
Equity Capital Needed: $10,000 to $30,000.
Financial Assistance Available: Assists franchisee in obtaining financing from local bank. Supplies merchandise for resale on 30-day account basis.
Training Provided: 5 days at home office and 3 days at shop location.
Managerial Assistance Available: Flowerama provides continual management service for the life of the franchise in such areas as bookkeeping, advertising, inventory control. Complete manuals of operations, forms, and other directions are provided. Managers are available to work closely with franchisees and visit stores regularly to assist solving problems.

FLOWER WORLD OF AMERICA, INC.
1655 Imperial Way
Mid-Atlantic Park
West Deptford, New Jersey 08086
Robert Sheets, President
Description of Operation: Retail flowers, gifts and related items. Shops are located in strip shopping centers, shopping malls and downtown locations.
Number of Franchisees: Over 100 in U.S. and Canada.
In Business Since: 1959.
Equity Capital Needed: $15,000
Financial Assistance Available: Assistance to franchisee in obtaining financing from banks or lending institutions.
Training Provided: 3 weeks for more training consisting of bookkeeping, sales and floral designing.
Managerial Assistance Available: Management assistance provided during the duration of the agreement both in sales, accounting, designing, advertising and inventory. Managers are available to work closely and make periodic visits.

FRAME AND SAVE
3126 Dixie Highway
Erlanger, Kentucky 41018
Charles Karlosky, President
Description of Operation: Frame and Save offers to the public a "Do-It-Yourself Shop." Each store is approximately 2,000 square feet with a set up of 8 individual working booths. Frame and Save has a line of quality mouldings and mats.
Number of Franchisees: 19 in 6 states.
In Business Since: 1973.
Equity Capital Needed: $30,000.
Financial Assistance Available: None.
Training Provided: Intensive 2 weeks, mandatory training course is scheduled for all new franchisee's at one of our locations. This training, involves learning the techniques of cutting and assembling moulding, mats, glass and conservation of valuable art work. Also, Frame and Save gives the franchisee one week of professional supervision at your location.
Managerial Assistance Available: Frame and Save provides continual contact with each individual franchisee with all update pricing and new techniques of the framing industry. District managers are available in all regions to work closely with the franchisees and visit the stores regularly to assist solving problems.

FRAMEKING CORPORATION
Formerly CAMROSE ART CORPORATION
385 Oser Avenue
Hauppauge, New York 11787
Jerry Camina, President
Description of Operation: Quality discount framing, art and wall decor center. All manufacturing done in central plant that services all franchisees on weekly basis. Frameking center is a retail (non-manufacturing) sales facility.
Number of Franchisees: 21 operating units in New York, Connecticut, Massachusetts, Pennsylvania and New Jersey.
In Business Since: 1967.
Equity Capital Needed: $29,500.
Financial Assistance Available: Company provides financing of up to $12,500.
Training Provided: Complete pre-opening training program and continuous on-site retraining on an ongoing basis.
Managerial Assistance Available: Company provides complete operational manual, all necessary inventory controls, all operational forms and day to day assistance on all phases of operation.

GALLERY OF MINIATURES, INC.
1350 Galloping Hill Road
Union, New Jersey 07083
Stuart Randolph, Vice President
Description of Operation: Miniature houses and complete furnishings, commonly called Doll Houses. Built on a scale of 1" to 1'. Each Gallery specializes in these miniature items and provides a full selection for the hobbyist and the serious collector. In addition, a full line of lower priced merchandise for children.
Number of Franchisees: 4 in Colorado, New York and New Jersey.
In Business Since: 1976.
Equity Capital Needed: Turnkey — total investment including franchise fee, inventory, fixtures, decor, training, site selection and working capital for lease is approximately $38,000 (depends on location).
Financial Assistance Available: None.
Training Provided: 1 week classroom and on-the-job training plus 2 weeks of training on the franchisees premises plus complete manual of operations.
Managerial Assistance Available: Franchisor provides complete source of supply purchased at the franchisees option plus continuous advertising and management assistance for the term of the contract and renewal.

THE GRATE FIREPLACE SHOPPE
450 Country Club Drive
Bensenville, Illinois 60106
William C. Benson, President
Description of Operation: Specialty shop, selling fireplaces, fireplace equipment and accessories, gas grills and patio supplies and home decorative items.
Number of Franchisees: 26 in Texas, Illinois, Wisconsin, New Jersey and Indiana.
In Business Since: 1965.
Financial Assistance Available: Total investment of between $72,000 to $136,000, depending on the cost of construction and fixturing the store and the amount of initial inventory. The Grate Fireplace will assist franchisee in securing his own bank loan.

Training Provided: Intensive, 2 week, mandatory training course plus actual in store experience with an existing store owner. A representative of the company will attend store opening and work with store owner for first week. Continued assistance programs and seminars provided.

Managerial Assistance Available: The Grate Fireplace provides continual marketing and management assistance for the life of the franchise. Complete manuals of operations, forms and directions are provided. Product source lists and promotional materials are supplied and continuously updated.

THE GREAT FRAME UP SYSTEMS, INC.
3915 Commercial Avenue
Northbrook, Illinois 60062
Steven Bellew, Marketing Director

Description of Operations: Great Frame Up Centers are completely inventoried and equipped retail stores specializing in high volume sales of quality do-it-yourself picture frames. All necessary materials and equipment are provided for the complete fulfillment of each customer's framing needs at an absolute minimum price.

Number of Franchisees: 35 in 9 states.
In Business Since: 1975.
Equity Capital Needed: Approximately $60,000.
Financial Assistance Available: Currently the licensor provides no direct financing of licensee locations. The Great Frame Up Systems, Inc., does provide Pro Forma statements and detailed financial statements for examination by lending institutions and will assist a licensee in preparing his own bank package.

Training Provided: An intensive 7 week training period provides licensee with complete working knowledge of The Great Frame Up System of operation. Both "Hands On" classroom situations and on-the-job training are part of the comprehensive program.

Managerial Assistance Available: The Great Frame Up Systems, Inc., is in constant touch with each of its licensees. It provides a flow of customer response to each store, field reports on each store operation, review of financial data, updating of operations and management manuals, a flow of advertising and public relations materials, and top level management review of operational problems. Managerial consultants available to licensees are senior staff members who have operated the busiest stores in the system. Affiliates of the home company provide a complete line of inventory and equipment to all licensees at prices extremely competitive in the marketplace.

HABERSHAM PLANTATION CORPORATION
Lot #5, Collier Road, Industrial Park
Toccoa, Georgia 30577
H. Dean Carroll, Director of Franchising

Description of Operation: Habersham Plantation Corporation offers the right to engage in a business for the retail sale of handcrafted, colonial primitive American furniture, furniture accessories and gifts in a substantially standardized retail store under the Service Mark and Trade Name "Habersham Plantation Country Store." Each store is approximately 3,000 square feet, located in sophisticated upper-middle to upper-upper regional malls. The store is furnished with extensive inventory of HPC products as well as with over 400 manufacturers and/or distributors of accessories and gifts, creating a total concept look.

Number of Franchisees: 35 concept stores nationally.
In Business Since: 1972.
Equity Capital Needed: Approximately 25 percent of total investment.
Financial Assistance Available: An approximate investment of $130,000 to $240,000 No formal financial program exists, however, commercial banking institutions, venture capital sources, financial holding companies, and the United States Small Business Administration and highly receptive to the program. In addition, the franchisee has the option of arranging outside financing.

Training Provided: A comprehensive, formal 1 week training seminar is available at the corporate headquarters. In addition, other available outlets for training are local training by regional managers and Habersham Plantation Corporation Store Planning and Interior Design Departments, semi-annual Market Place training, regional interior design and concept training, and regular visits by regional managers and other corporate executives and staff.

Managerial Assistance Available: Habersham Plantation Corporation provides experienced regional managers and corporate executives and staff to assist new and established Habersham Plantation Country Store owners in all phases of the operation. At the corporate headquarters the executives and various staff offer their services to dealers in assisting them in any and all activities by giving continuous advice, guidance and assistance through national and regional meetings, seminars, correspondence, telephone, and personal conversation. Additional assistance is available in in-store training in such areas as in-store on-line computer systems, advertising (locally and nationally), personnel, inventory control, bookkeeping, interior design, merchandising, retailing, and total concept operations. HPC furnishes the franchisees with a detailed operations manual containing complete information and procedures for the day-to-day operation of the business. HPC also provides each store with a resource directory listing over 400 manufacturers and/or distributors of accessories and gifts that blend to the concept. Financial analysis, trend projections, and continuous product knowledge are available to increase current and long range profitability.

HANDY HARDWARE CENTERS, INC.
2515 Metropolitan Drive
Trevose, Pennsylvania 19047
Dave Lawrence, Director of Marketing

Description of Operation: Distribute hardware, housewares, variety and toy products through network of independent dealers who service displays placed in drug stores, food stores, convenience stores throughout American.

Number of Franchisees: 475 throughout the Untied States.
In Business Since: 1975.
Equity Capital Needed: $8,950.
Financial Assistance Available: None.

Training Provided: Dealer is trained by a field marketing representative who secures the retail locations for the dealer and then provides on-the-job training. There is ongoing training provided by home office: newsletters, etc.

Managerial Assistance Available: Handy Hardware Centers provide an operations manual, necessary forms and assistance from our professional staff.

HEROES WORLD CENTERS, INC.
66 Morris Street
Morristown, New Jersey 07460
Ivan Snyder

Description of Operation: Retail store catering to items relating to fictional and real to life super heroes and super stars. Featuring toys, electronic games, books, T-shirts and wearing apparel, new and collector comic books. Super Heroes is a trademark of the Marvel Comics Group and DC Comics, Inc. used under license.

Number of Franchisees: 10 in 8 states.
In Business Since: 1976.
Equity Capital Needed: Minimum of $12,200 plus additional credit of $25,000.
Financial Assistance Available: No financial assistance is provided. Franchisor will finance one half of the initial inventory to qualified franchisees.

Training Provided: Both classroom and on-the-job training required at company headquarters; plus on-the-job training in the franchisee's store.

Managerial Assistance Available: Continuous managerial assistance from field personnel. Membership in Heroes World buying cooperative.

INSTANT REPLAY, INC.
Suite 803
American City Building
Columbia, Maryland 21044
Dennis R. Black, President

Description of Operation: Instant Replay offers an athletic specialty concept. Product mix includes a heavy concentration in athletic footwear, running, swimwear and related athletic apparel. Major lines include Nike, Adidas, Brooks, Etonic, etc., plus related soft good items such as T-shirts, warm-up suits, athletic bags, etc.

Number of Franchisees: 17 in Pennsylvania, Maryland, Virginia and Florida.
Equity Capital Needed: $7,000 up front for franchise fee, plus approximately $70,000 for inventory investment and construction.
Financial Assistance Available: No financial assistance is provided, but does furnish franchisee with complete loan information packet for lending institution.

Training Provided: 1 week training in franchisor's office, 1 week training in an existing store, (optional), and 1 week training in franchisee's new store.

Managerial Assistance Available: On-going, all budgeting and open to buy programming, recommended merchandise action, seasonal display changes, and financial advice and assistance with regard to supplier. General advice on day-to-day business problems. Total negotiation of lease and site selection and evaluation.

KITS CAMERAS, INC.
1051 Industry Drive
Seattle, Washington 98188
Franchise Director

Description of Operation: A Kits Camera franchise system offers a unique opportunity in the operation of a specialty photographic equipment and supplies store. Most stores are located in enclosed shopping centers. The store carries an extensive line of brand name and private label merchandise.

Number of Franchisees: 65 in Washington, Idaho and Canada.
In Business Since: 1961 (Canada) 1975, (USA).
Equity Capital Needed: Total investment of approximately $62,500 of which $30,000 has to be cash.
Financial Assistance Available: Franchisor will assist franchisee in arranging the balance from a commercial bank.

Training Provided: 4 to 6 weeks course at the head office and company stores. Successful completion of training course a pre-requisite to obtaining a franchise.

Managerial Assistance Available: Kits Cameras provide continuous management service for the life of the franchise in areas of bookkeeping, advertising, merchandising, and store operations. Coordinators visit stores regularly to provide assistance. Semi-annual conventions are sponsored by Kits Cameras.

LAFAYETTE ELECTRONICS SALES, INC.
P.O. Box L
Syosset, New York 11791

Description of Operation: Retailing consumer electronics.
Number of Franchisees: 100.
In Business Since: 1921.
Equity Capital Needed: $35,000-$50,000.
Financial Assistance Available: None.

Training Provided: On-the-job training in another franchisee-owned stores is available, but firm prefers that prospective franchisees have retail electronics background.

Managerial Assistance Available: Uniform accounting system. On-going advertising program.

LELLY'S DRIVE IN PHOTOS, INC.
4641 State Road 84
Ft. Lauderdale, Florida 33314
Kenneth H. Lelly

Description of Operation: Retail photo store.
Number of Franchisees: 11 in Florida.
In Business Since: 1968.
Equity Capital Needed: $15,000 to $24,000.
Financial Assistance Available: Bank and Small Business Administration.
Training Provided: Intensive 15 days on-the-job training in one of the operating stores.
Managerial Assistance Available: Franchisor furnishes continuing management and technical assistance to franchisee.

LITTLE PROFESSOR BOOK CENTERS, INC.
33200 Capital
Livonia, Michigan 45150
Jon Wisotzkey, Franchise Director

Description of Operation: Little Professor Book Centers are service-oriented family reading centers carrying a full selection of hardcover, papercover and magazine titles. Each store, of approximately 1,800 square feet is provided with fixtures, inventory and inventory management systems to help simplify store operations.
Number of Franchisees: 130 stores in over 30 states.
In Business Since: 1969.
Equity Capital Needed: Approximately $40,000 of a total investment of $65,000.
Financial Assistance Available: Little Professor Book Centers, Inc., will assist in obtaining personal outside financing, if so desired.
Training Provided: Little Professor Book Centers franchisees participate in an established training program to learn the important aspects of retailing including: promotion, inventory and financial control, customer satisfaction and merchandising. The training program is conducted for 7 to 10 days in an operating store and in the new location.
Managerial Assistance Available: Little Professor Book Centers, Inc., provides continuous assistance and counsel in bookstore operation throughout the length of the franchise. Periodic visits are made by representatives of Little Professor Book Centers, Inc. Performance and results are evaluated and recommendations are offered on improving sales and profit. Experienced personnel are always available to assist in the solution of any problems. Comprehensive advertising and inventory management programs are provided.

MIDWEST INDUSTRIES, INC.
200 Walnut
Yankton, South Dakota 57078
Chris Christopherson, Franchise Director

Description of Operation: Franchise is an operation for the sale of kitchen and bathroom cabinets plus countertops. Each franchise also offers window and door package for homes.
Number of Franchisees: 14 in South Dakota, Nebraska, Iowa and Minnesota.
In Business Since: Franchise program started June, 1978.
Equity Capital Needed: Approximately $25,000.
Financial Assistance Available: Financial assistance is handled by the franchisee through his financial institution.
Training Provided: Initial training for 1 week, then continued training until franchisee is capable of doing everything for themselves.
Managerial Assistance Available: Same as above.

MISS BOJANGLES, INC.
P.O. Box 14589
Baton Rouge, Louisiana 70808
Mike Stokes, President

Description of Operation: Retail fashion jewelry operation locating exclusively in enclosed malls. Merchandise in the $3 to $75 range. Complete turnkey operation to franchisee: franchisor develops location and lease, supplies blueprints, assists in construction, merchandising and stocking stores, etc.
Number of Franchisees: 51 in 19 states.
Equity Capital Needed: $17,500 to $65,000 depending on size and type of location and financial arrangements.
Financial Assistance Available: Financing is available.
Training Provided: Complete on sight training in all aspects of running a busienss: advertising, bookkeeping, buying, merchandising, personnel, etc.
Managerial Assistance Available: Bi-weekly merchandising bulletins, periodic memos from home office, visits by district managers and home office exeuctives, telephone contact with home office, advertising promotions. Franchisor sponsors monthly sales contest with cash prizes. Annual convention and more.

MISTER CLARK'S
5851 East 34th Street
Indianapolis, Indiana 46222
Robert A. Lutey, President

Description of Operation: Retail servicing applicance dealers banded together to benefit from the combined purchasing power of the whole. Also by mutual contribution the total dollar packages can achieve wider range and maximum exposure for advertising and promotional programs. Franchising only in Indiana.
Number of Franchisees: 13 in Indiana.
In Business Since: 1968.
Equity Capital Needed: Open.
Financial Assistance Available: Mister Clark's is a non-profit corporation.
Training Provided: No formal training, but the group as a whole combines for the assistance, training and well being of the individuals.
Managerial Assistance Available: Group discussions and individual consultations.

NELSON'S PHOTOGRAPHY STUDIOS, INC.
41 Colonial Arcade
Cleveland, Ohio 44115
Joseph G. Ballard, General Manager

Description of Operation: Candid wedding photography specialist and volume portrait photography. Nelson's Franchise System offers a unique retail photo studio operation. 750 to 1,200 square feet needed. Open five days a week, eight hours per day. An inventory of frames, samples, manuals, supplies, floor plans and decorating schemes provided. Nelson's provides all photo equipment needed and the services of our modern electronic finishing laboratory. All art work and finishing of old photos available at competitive prices.
Number of Franchisees: 9 in Ohio.
In Business Since: 1961.
Equity Capital Needed: $15,000.
Financial Assistance Available: A total investment of $25,000 is necessary to open a Nelson's franchise. The down payment of $15,000 pays for inventory equipment and training. All equipment needed is included. Nelson's will finance the balance if franchisee has good credit references (4 years). Franchisee has option to arrange own outside financing.
Training Provided: Intensive 3 weeks mandatory training course is scheduled for all new franchisees and their personnel. Two weeks conducted at the home office school and on-site at company training store; 1 week at franchisee's outlet under the supervision of full time Nelson's supervisor.
Managerial Assistance Available: Nelson's provides continual management service for the life of the franchise in such areas as bookkeeping, advertising, etc. Complete manuals of operations, forms and directions are provided. District managers are available to all regions to work closely with franchisees and visit stores regularly to assist solving problems. Nelson's sponsors meetings of franchisees and conducts marketing and product research to maintain high Nelson's consumer acceptance, and supplies constant new promotions to secure additional business. Nelson's will provide franchisee its finishing lab services at rates lower than he can obtain elsewhere, if desired.

OPEN BOOK MARKETING CORPORATION
2966 Biddle
Wyandotte, Michigan 48192
David Sucher, Vice President

Description of Operation: The Open Book is a family oriented mass market book store with a complete selection of hardcovers, paperbacks, and magazines.
Number of Franchisees: 20 in Michigan and Ohio.
In Business Since: 1971.
Equity Capital Needed: $20,000.
Financial Assistance Available: Franchisor will assist in obtaining local bank financing. Total investment will be $30,000 to $40,000.
Training Provided: 2 weeks in-store trianing program covers all aspects of book store operation. One week is offered before store opening in an existing location. The second week is in the franchisor's location.
Managerial Assistance Available: Open Book Marketing will do site selection, lease negotiation, store layout, and stocking of the store. Company representatives provide continuous assistance for the life of the contract.

THE PEARL FACTORY
Division of CRATER ENTERPRISES
2270 Kalakaua Avenue
Suite 1401
Honolulu, Hawaii 96815
Berry Pickering, Franchise Manager

Description of Operation: The Pearl Factory is a unique merchandising concept which capitalizes on people's curiosity, love of excitement and the increasing demand for jewelry. At the Pearl Factory, customers pick out an oyster, which is guaranteed to contain at least one pearl. The oyster is opened before their eyes, the pearl is removed and then the customer can make a selection from among a wide variety of jewelry settings. In a matter of moments the pearl is set permanently onto the jewelry while the customer waits.
Number of Franchisees: 7 in Maine, Hawaii, Louisiana and Florida.
In Business Since: 1972.
Equity Capital Needed: $10,000-$30,000.
Financial Assistance Available: None.
Training Provided: The franchise package includes an initial 5 day training session for two in Hawaii. Additional training is available each year, for brush-up or training new personnel. For all training seminars, the franchisee only pays for personal expenses and transportation.
Managerial Assistance Available: The Pearl Factory franchise includes an ongoing program designed to insure maximum success for franchisees through our unique merchandising and marketing skills. You will be kept current on the latest merchandise and sales tools through a regular franchise bulletin. Our staff is available to you for consultation throughout the year to assist you in all phases of operation.

PHONE WORLD INTERNATIONAL, INC.
General Office: 4239 Transit Road
Buffalo, New York 14221
Albert Hurwitz, Director of Marketing
S. Ginsberg, President

Description of Operation: The franchise will authorize the franchisee to own and operate a Phone World Communications Center Retail Store. the stores will have a similar decor to establish national identity. The products sold will consist of decorative residential, business telephones of all types, telephone accessories, such as jacks, plugs and cords, etc., and peripheral business telecommunications equipment, such as auto dialers, call diverters, speakerphones, answering devices and home or personal computers.
Number of Franchisees: 6 including company-owned in Minnesota and New York.
In Business Since: 1974.
Equity Capital Needed: Approximately $25,000, total cost of franchise is $69,500.
Financial Assistance Available: The franchisor will cooperate and assist the franchisee in obtaining financing.
Training Provided: The franchisor provides an initial training program for the franchisee or the franchisee's designated manager approved by the franchisor, prior to the opening of the store, consisting of training in basic techniques of store management, cost control, sales methods, merchandise ordering, basic accounting and cash control procedures, and basic familiarity with the products and product service requirements and procedures. The training will be carried on at the franchisee's store prior to opening, and if the franchisor deems it necessary, the initial training may continue for a short period after opening of the store. Training program will require at least 10 business days.
Managerial Assistance Available: Phone World International shall provide marketing, technical and management assistance by a member of the Phone World operating team. The franchisee will also be provided with newsletter bulletins describing new marketing techniques, advertising programs and new products.

PHOTO DRIVE THRU, INC.
1003 Market Street
Palmyra, New Jersey 08065
Robert Ricci
Description of Operation: Film sales and processing. Kiosk operation. Agent: Marketing Consulting Services, Robert E. Sax, President, 218 North Church Street, Moorestown, New Jersey 08057.
Number of Franchisees: 22 in Pennsylvania, New Jersey, New York and Delaware.
In Business Since: 1973.
Equity Capital Needed: $25,000.
Financial Assistance Available: Up to 50 percent to qualified buyer.
Training Provided: Minimum, 2 weeks (with continued supervision).
Managerial Assistance Available: Continuous for length of agreement.

PHOTO PLAZA
P.O. Box 52, North Hackensack Station
River Edge, New Jersey 07661
I. Davidoff, Franchise Director
Description of Operation: Drive-up Kiosk units providing photo developing service including sales of cameras and related equipment and supplies.
Number of Franchisees: 24 in New York, New Jersey and Connecticut.
In Business Since: 1956.
Equity Capital Needed: $17,400.
Financial Assistance Available: Franchisor will finance $7,500 of the total amount due.
Training Provided: Complete plant indoctrination as well as on-site training both before opening and for at least 1 week after opening.
Managerial Assistance Available: Franchisor has their own photo finishing plant to guarantee franchisee of superior workmanship with over 20 years in the photo finishing business. Continuous merchandising and advertising assisting to obtain the maximum in sales and profit.

PHOTOQUICK OF AMERICA, INC.
27 Pacella Park Drive
Randolph, Massachusetts 02368
William Lawson, Marketing Manager
Description of Operation: PhotoQuick of America provides the only complete photo lab franchise available. Every store contains film developing equipment where customer's pictures, reprints and enlargements are made in just 6 hours. Picture taking supplies, including film, flash, batteries, albums and frames are also sold.
Number of Franchisees: 19 with 23 locations in 8 states.
In Business Since: 1977.
Equity Capital Needed: $45,000-$50,000.
Financial Assistance Available: Approximately $85,000 financing must be obtained by franchisee.
Training Provided: Mandatory 6-7 week program covers operating equipment, accounting, retailing, advertising, and all facets of business. First 2 weeks at Quincy, Massachusetts training facility, rest at franchisee's location.
Managerial Assistance Available: Prior to opening, PhotoQuick provides assistance in site selection, leasing, construction, obtaining financing and purchasing. Continual assistance is available in advertising, marketing, employee training, quality control, bookkeeping, and all aspects of the operation. Individual lab visits are made by Photo-Quick personnel, who also conduct refersher seminars at convenient locations in each marketing area.

PIER 1 IMPORTS, INC.
2520 West Freeway
Fort Worth, Texas 76102
Jerold D. Schultz, Director Associate Store Department
Description of Operation: A specialty retailer offering a wide assortment of home furnishings, decorative and gift items from foreign and domestic sources.
Number of Franchisees: 60 in 26 states.
In Business Since: 1966.
Equity Capital Needed: $50,000 to $75,000.
Financial Assistance Available: None.
Training Provided: 7 to 10 days in-store training.
Managerial Assistance Available: Continuing assistance provided in merchandising, products, suppliers and advertising.

RADIO SHACK DIVISION
TANDY CORPORATION
1600 One Tandy Center
Fort Worth, Texas 76102
Robert R. Lynch, Vice President, Dealer Division
Description of Operation: September 1971, Radio Shack withdrew its offer to franchise. All previous commitments are being honored. Radio Shack presently offers a licensing program to established retailers in towns of 18,500 or less in population. The dealerships are called Authorized Sales Centers.
Number of Franchisees: 2,900 in all states, West Indies, Central America, Canada, Western Europe, South America, Africa, Near East, Guam, American Samoa, Saudi Arabia, Lebanon, New Zealand and Scandanavia.
In Business Since: 1971.
Equity Capital Needed: $10,000 to $30,000.
Financial Assistance Available: Assist with bank presentation. No direct financial aid provided by franchisors.
Training Provided: Since dealerships are granted only to existing retailers, no formal training is provided. Procedures manual, display guide and miscellaneous instructional materials supplied upon approval of applicant.
Managerial Assistance Available: Weekly scheduled phone consultation, periodic visits (usually twice a year) for review of performance. Free ad mat service to introduce new lines and explain advertising and promotional plans. Provide technical manuals covering operational and servicing of consumer electronics merchandise.

THE RINGGOLD CORPORATION
9513 Dalecrest
Houston, Texas 77080
Thomas J. Devine, President
Description of Operation: The "Frame Factory" and "Framin' Place" shops are retail picture framing and art shops. Each shop is designed to allow the customer to choose how their "picture" is to be framed and then do all the work themselves in the shop. The shop personnel cut or prepare all materials exactly as the customer chooses and then assists the customer in any way necessary to guarantee a professional job.
Number of Franchisees: 132 in 24 states.
In Business Since: 1971.
Equity Capital Needed: Very flexible.
Financial Assistance Available: Assistance in arranging financing.
Training Provided: Not less than 2 weeks initially. One week immediately after the shop is opened. Regular seminars of shop owners are held for continuing education. Trade associations have regular local meetings and monthly periodicals.
Managerial Assistance Available: Managerial assistance is on a regular monthly basis. Technical assistance is provided on a group basis or when requested.

ROYALE SPORTING GOODS, INC.
P.O. Box 52-North Hackensack Station
River Edge, New Jersey 07661
Irving Davidoff, Franchise Director
Description of Operation: Sporting goods franchise featuring the retail sale of a wide variety of name brand sporting goods and related items.
Number of Franchisees: 4 in New York.
In Business Since: 1968.
Equity Capital Needed: Total turnkey investment — $48,000 ($30,000 is inventory).
Financial Assistance Available: None.
Training Provided: Company provides comprehensive 2 week training in company-owned store and 2 weeks in franchisee's store.
Managerial Assistance Available: Royale makes available special "buys" which are offered to the Royale management first by manufacturers because of the rapport established over the years. In addition, field representatives personally visit the locations to observe operations and recommend improvements to yield greater sales and higher profit for the franchisee. Royale also arranges for famous sports personalities to participate in special promotions at the store from time to time.

SKATE STREET INC.
410 Atlas Avenue
P.O. Box 8232
Madison, Wisconsin 53707
Rose Schensky, President
Description of Operation: Skate Street Inc., offers a complete shop for renting outdoor roller skates, selling outdoor and indoor rink skates, parts, gear and repair service.
Number of Franchisees: 3 in Wisconsin and Illinois.
In Business Since: 1979.
Equity Capital Needed: $7,000 to $15,000.
Financial Assistance Available: None, investment secured by inventory.
Training Provided: 1 week training provided plus training and manuals for all store operations.
Managerial Assistance Available: Advertising, general business, and free consulting advice available.

SOUND WEST
2701 Brooks Street
Missoula, Montana 59801
James L. Rhines
Description of Operation: Retail electronics stores featuring national brands and private label merchandise. The franchisee operates a private business with the advantages of volume buying, merchandising and promotional guidance.
Number of Franchisees: 15 in Montana, Washington, Oregon and Idaho.
In Business Since: 1973.
Equity Capital Needed: $75,000 ($25,000 down).
Financial Assistance Available: Company wil counsel with franchisee and after determining need and ability, will assist in preparing the financial package to aid in securing necessary funds.
Training Provided: 2 week training course, consisting of 2 weeks at parent company classroms and actual retail store work, plus 1 week in franchisee's own operation.
Managerial Assistance Available: A divisional field consultant works with each franchisee to promote success with updated marketing formulas, technical information, and sales training.

SPEEDY WAGON SALES CORPORATION
2440 Central Avenue
St. Petersburg, Florida 33712
L.W. Freeman, President
Description of Operation: Marketing of handicapped products with emphasis on transportation and wheelchair driving of van type vehicles with electric wheelchair lifting equipment.
Number of Franchisees: 34 plus marketing retail outlets in 25 states and Washington, D.C.

In Business Since: 1972.
Equity Capital Needed: $5,000.
Financial Assistance Available: Buy-back guarantee on products. Product discounts and financing of government paper.
Training Provided: Factory training — 3 to 5 days — depending on operating.
Managerial Assistance Available: Marketing guide plus training. Business training on accounting procedures unique to business. Guidelines on business procedures for expansion and territorial development.

SPORT-ABOUT, INC.
7691 Central Avenue Northeast
Fridley, Minnesota 55432
Ron C. Eastman, President
Description of Operation: Sport-About — a network of retail sporting goods businesses operating under the name of Sport-About. All types of sporting goods available for either a general or a specialized sporting good business. Franchisee may begin as a part-time home operated business before going into a retail store. Franchisor provides access to suppliers of sporting goods, offers volume discounts, centralized ordering, billing services, limited credit, catalogs and operational manual.
Number of Franchisees: 180 in 27 states.
In Business Since: 1978.
Equity Capital Needed: $1,000 minimum.
Financial Assistance Available: Limited.
Training Provided: Limited.
Managerial Assistance Available: Limited.

SPORT SHACKS, INC.
Birch Lake Professional Building
1310 East Highway 96
White Bear Lake, Minnesota 55110
Roger L. Adair, President
Description of Operation: Services to retail sporting goods stores and dealers, using a franchise system for co-op buying and training, and general retail assistance.
Number of Franchisees: 700 in the United States.
In Business Since: 1974.
Equity Capital Needed: Miniumu of $6,500.
Financial Assistance Available: None.
Training Provided: 5 day home office orientation program covering product knowledge, general merchandising, inventory, supplier analysis, etc. Two day on-site training before opening retail outlet.
Managerial Assistance Available: Management assitance provided in the form of management and merchandising bulletins, by quarterly newsletter, and franchise operations manual. There is an annual convention and trade show and in-office assistance from home office personnel.

TEAM CENTRAL, INCORPORATED
720 - 29th Avenue Southeast
Minneapolis, Minnesota 55414
James P. Johnson, Vice President, Franchise Development
Description of Operation: Retail electronics stores specializing in consumer-oriented entertainment products such as component stereo, television, portable electronics, communication equipment, and computers.
Number of Franchisees: 64 (107 stores) in 19 states.
In Business Since: 1946.
Equity Capital Needed: Total investment of $70,000-$160,000. Franchisees must have a substantial personal net worth.
Financial Assistance Available: TEAM Central, Incorporated will assist with bank presentation and lease negotiation.
Training Provided: Operating procedures, warranty and sales training manuals provided upon approval of applicant. Continued in-store training, management seminars, and sales training aids from TEAM Central library available to all owners.
Managerial Assistance Available: Store set up including plans, drawings, and counseling, on fixturing and inventory provided. TEAM representatives available to set up and open store and to conduct in-store operational training. Two yearly conferences — one of which is a merchandising/trade show, the other a management seminar dealing with store operations. Continued assistance provided through updated manuals, bulletins and in-store counseling.

THE TINDER BOX INTERNATIONAL, LTD.
P.O. Box 830
Santa Monica, California 90406
Laurence Simpson, President
Description of Operation: Retail pipes, tobacco, cigarettes, cigars and gifts, primarily in regional shopping centers.
Number of Franchisees: 184 in 37 states.
In Business Since: 1928.
Equity Capital Needed: $25,000 to $45,000.
Financial Assistance Available: Will introduce franchisees to bankers or provide directly.
Training Provided: 10 day product familiarization training for franchisee and wife at franchisor's headquarters. Personal guidance by specialists during first 2 weeks of operation at franchisee's own store.
Managerial Assistance Available: Advertising, retailing product counseling by phone, mail. Regular couselor — salesman visits to franchisee's operation. Franchisee may, but is not required to, buy his stock from franchisor.

T-SHIRTS PLUS, INC.
P.O. Box 1049
3630 I-35 South
Waco, Texas 76703
Kenneth E. Johnson, Sr., President
Description of Operation: Family oriented specialty stores selling t-shirts and associated garments individualized according to the wishes of each buyer; personalization done while buyer waits. Also make up special orders for businesses, teams, clubs and similar groups with whatever design they desire.
Number of Franchisees: 200 in 41 states, coast to coast.
In Business Since: 1975.
Equity Capital Needed: $40,000-$70,000.
Financial Assistance Available: None.
Training Provided: Attendance of 1 week at T-Shirt College before store opens. Company personnel assist in setting up and opening store; then make monthly visits to assist as needed. Company provides WATS service to enable store operators to obtain answers to specific questions. Monthly newsletter to all stores includes merchandising plans, helpful ideas and other information.
Managerial Assistance Available: Company provides field representatives who visit stores monthly. Company provides WATS services, makes home office personnel constantly available to store operators and managers to assist as needed as well as for fast handling of shirt orders. Company's monthly publication and annual meetings also keep all franchisees abreast of developments. Regularly updated operators manuals are furnished all operators for continuing use.

UNITED CONSUMERS CLUB
833 West Lincoln Highway
Schererville, Indiana 46375
Richard M. Teibel
Description of Operation: United Consumers Club offers a unique new private buying service allowing merchandise to be shipped directly from manufacturers and distributors directly to a local address. Thus avoiding the costly expense of the "middleman." Each catalog center is approximately 2,400 square feet and is open 5 days a week. An extensive inventory of brand name merchandise and catalogs are available to the membership. For easy ordering of furniture, carpeting and appliances.
Number of Franchisees: 40 in 12 states.
In Business Since: 1972.
Equity Capital Needed: $15,000.
Financial Assistance Available: A minimum investment of $25,000 is necessary to open a UCC franchise. The $15,000 pays for inventory, catalogs, carpet samples, fabric swatches, forms and training. UCC will finance the balance if the franchisee has good credit references; however, franchisee may elect to secure local financing.
Training Provided: An intensive 20 day mandatory training course is scheduled for all new franchisees. A 3 day school is conducted at the home office covering bookkeeping, sales presentations, and recruiting personnel. The balance of the 7 days are spent at an on-the-job program as a designated operational location.
Managerial Assistance Available: UCC provides continual management service for the life of the franchise in the areas of accounting, sales and recruiting personnel. Complete manuals of operations, forms and directives are provided. Field supervision is also available to work closely with franchisees and conduct marketing and product information seminars.

G & B CONCEPTS
dba UP AGAINST THE WALL
304 Delaware
Kansas City, Missouri 64105
Ed Groves, President
Description of Operation: Retail life style store. Picture framing, furnishings, and contemporary housewares.
Number of Franchisees: 7 in Missouri, Oklahoma and Kansas.
In Business Since: 1974.
Equity Capital Needed: $40,000 to $60,000.
Financial Assistance Available: Assistance for SBA and conventional loans.
Training Provided: 10 to 14 days training for key personnel.
Managerial Assistance Available: All phases of managerial assistance.

VIDEO CONCEPTS
7700 East Iliff
Suite C
Denver, Colorado 80231
Robert Koontz, Director of Store Development
Description of Operation: Video Concepts offers a unique home video and consumer electronics retail store. A turnkey operation, a Video Concepts store is generally located in shopping malls with good traffic counts. Large screen televisions, video recorders, cameras, video games and computers all make up the product mix in the exciting new retail store.
Number of Franchisees: 3 in Colorado and Texas.
In Business Since: 1978.
Equity Capital Needed: $100,000 and approximately $50,000 capital loan.
Financial Assistance Available: An approximate investment of $150,000 is necessary to properly open and operate a Video Concepts store. Franchisor will assist franchisee with a capital loan based on an equity investment of $100,000.
Training Provided: Prior to store opening, franchisee must complete a 2 week training program at franchisors main office in Denver, Colorado.
Managerial Assistance Available: Video Concepts offers continuing managerial support through field visitations and a complete manual of operations. Franchisee is given the opportunity to participate in volume buying efforts with the Video Concepts main office to procure video equipment at a better cost.

WHIRLIGIG STORES INCORPORATED
2700 Saturn Street
Brea, California 92621
Gerald A. Bly, Director of Franchising
Description of Operation: Retail "one-stop" party and paper supply stores.
Number of Franchisees: 11 in California, Arizona and Texas.
In Business Since: 1971.
Equity Capital Needed: $135,000 total investment.
Financial Assistance Available: Distribute and aid in preparation of bank loan package for application for financial assistance.
Training Provided: 12 working days. Subjects covered include: history of Whirligig, industry background, store fixture layout strategy, merchandise display, party consultant training, customer relations, community relations, store policies, cash register training, accounting and reporting procedures and advertising.
Managerial Assistance Available: Regular quarterly visits by field service representatives.

WICKS 'N' STICKS, INC.
P.O. Box 40307
Houston, Texas 77040
Harold R. Otto, Chairman of the Board
Description of Operation: Wicks 'N' Sticks offers our franchisees a unique and charming retail candle and related candle accessory gift store operation. Each franchisee is provided with a complete "turnkey" operation which includes all inventory, supplies, leasehold improvements, display fixtures, and all necessary equipment. Wicks 'N' Sticks has complete candle manufacturing facilities in Houston to supply our 156 stores in 35 states with the highest quality candles available.
Number of Franchisees: 126 in 34 states.
In Business Since: 1968.
Equity Capital Needed: The total cost of our franchise is approximately $113,500 for a new store.
Financial Assistance Available: Financial assistance may be provided by Wicks 'N' Sticks, Inc.
Training Provided: 1 full week in Houston at company expense, where every phase of the store's operation is covered in an in-depth training program. An operations manual, a simplified bookkeeping system, a price book which lists all of our vendors (their product lines, terms, etc.), all personnel and payroll related forms, procedures and applicable state and federal procedures are supplied. Once the franchisee has taken possession of the store, our district manager for that area will train him for a period of 2 weeks in that store. Continuous corporate support is provided.
Managerial Assistance Available: Wicks 'N' Sticks, Inc., follows the philosophy that our mutual success is contingent upon cooperation and communication with our franchisees. Wicks 'N' Sticks, Inc., schedules franchisee meetings, normally in conjunction with major gift shows throughout the country, and has also provided franchise financial seminars. We are in constant communication with our franchisees, both by telephone and by letters, to inform them of new merchandising techniques and new products that have been introduced to us here at corporate headquarters. Our district managers and corporate headquarters personnel are readily available to provide our franchisees with the support. District managers call on assigned franchised locations approximately once a month to assist these stores with any operational questions, color coordination, displays and to present new lines of merchandise.

WORLD OF LAMINATING
Division of MECHANCIAL MAN CAR WASH FACTORY, INC.
801 Wager Street
Utica, New York 13502
Raymond Seakan, President
Description of Operation: A complete laminating service. A retail operation servicing people in their homes and businesses such as copy centers. Printer, graphic art stores, photo shops, schools, churches, etc. This is operated in franchisee's home with low overhead.
Number of Franchisees: 32 in 8 states
In Business Since: 1975
Equity Capital Needed: $7,500
Financial Assistance Available: $3,750 or a lease or bank loan backed by good credit references.
Training Provided: 1 week to set-up machine and train each franchisee which includes setting up your local accounts and newspaper advertising. Also training your appointed employees when you expand.
Managerial Assistance Available: Full merchandise program and company assistance and training available as needed and requested. We assist in hiring and training of managers on an absentee basis operation.

SECURITY SYSTEMS

COUNTERFORCE PROTECTION SYSTEMS, INC.
1331 West Central Boulevard
Orlando, Florida 32805
Troy Deal, President
Frank Shaffield, Executive Vice President
Description of Operation: Complete line of automatic, wireless, burglar, fire, hold-up, medical and security devices for residential and commercial applications. Nation-wide alarm monitoring with UL approved station. Complete and highly successful marketing program. Parent company assists the franchisee in all phases of operating their business.
Number of Franchisees: 4 in Florida
In Business Since: 1978
Equity Capital Needed: $15,000 to $50,000 depending upon territory.
Financial Assistance Available: The initial investment includes the total start-up cost and training, sales aids, demonstration units, literature, forms, installation equipment, and initial retail stock.
Training Provided: Intensive 5 day training program at company training center covering all aspects of marketing, service, planning and business management. Follow-up training and field training when necessary and is always available.
Managerial Assistance Available: Operation manual, sales presentation, and full management training program including flow of authority and responsibilities. Field assistance by executive personnel to assist in sales recruiting and training. Complete legal and accounting methods. Train for easy "turnkey" operation start-up.

DICTOGRAPH SECURITY SYSTEMS
P. O. Box 96
Florham Park, New Jersey 07932
Myles C. Goldberg, Vice President
Description of Operation: Vast line of automatic burglar, fire and smoke, hold-up and security devices for residential, commercial, institutional and industrial application as well as closed circuit TV and camera surveillance equipment for deterrants against shoplifting, pilferage and theft. Company specializes in (optional) set-up of central station and off-premises monitoring facilities enabling distributor to produce a continuing monthly income.
Number of Franchisees: 171 in most every state; several Canadian; 27 European.
In Business Since: Parent company since 1902
Equity Capital Needed: Territorial variations. Minimum $10,500. Inventory refundable on 1 year money back guarantee.
Financial Assistance Available: Equipment financing available on Sentinel 4 leasing. Portion of lease incomes assigned to local distributors through national accounts departments of Sentinel 4 Division.
Training Provided: 2 weeks on national academy training at company's international headquarters building. Training includes class and field instruction for proper guidance and assistance in sales, administration, installation and service maintenance; a series of periodic Regional Seminars in various areas of the U.S., etc.
Managerial Assistance Available: The corporation is constantly developing new materials, manuals, and sales presentation literature for its distributors, as well as conducting Regional Seminars and International Conventions following through with ongoing assistance as provided by account executives. Account executives are assigned to each distributorship to give help and guidance on a continuing basis. Field assistance by executive personnel to assist in sales help and recruiting of additional sales and technical personnel. National Public Relations Department staff will assist as needed locally to help develop distributors' activities through use of most media, including audio/visual presentations.

HONOR GUARD SECURITY SERVICE
1725 Eye Street, N.W., Suite 304
Washington, D.C. 20006
William L. Devries, President
Description of Operation: Honor Guard provides uniformed, armed security officers, guards, watchmen, crowd control specialists on a temporary or contract basis. Residential and commercial alarms.
Number of Franchisees: 3 in Wisconsin, Texas and Georgia.
In Business Since: 1973
Equity Capital Needed: $7,500 and up.
Financial Assistance Available: Accounts receivable and payroll financing, payment of taxes, all record keeping and monthly P & L and balance sheet.
Training Provided: 1 week initial training. One day per 6 months on-site plus unlimited telephone and correspondence training. Annual seminar.
Managerial Assistance Available: Coninuing surveillance and management consulting guidance in most facets of business.

RAMPART INDUSTRIES, INC.
One Oxford Valley
Langhorne, Pennsylvania 19047
Thomas Fleisher, Vice President
Description of Operation: Rampart Industries, Inc., has developed a complete and highly successful dealer program for the residential/small commercial security alarm market. Both the equipment, and the marketing program have been specifically designed for this rapidly growing marketplace. Their systems are sold and installed only by authorized Rampart Dealers and all promotion is done under the Rampart name to foster and reinforce a National Consumer Brand-Name awareness in this relatively new mass market. The parent company assists the Dealer in all aspects of operating the business and has introduced a very successful nationwide central station monitoring facility.
Number of Franchisees: 46 in 19 states and Washington, D.C.
In Business Since: 1974
Equity Capital Needed: $4,000 to $15,000
Financial Assistance Available: The initial investment represents the total start-up cost and includes training, sales aids, demonstration kits, literature forms, installation supplies, etc. In extreme cases, Rampart has internally financed part of the inventory portion of the initial investment, but these instances are rare due to the minimal amounts involved.
Training Provided: Comprehensive, intensive 3-5 day Dealer training programs are held at the Company Training Center covering all aspects of the business such as marketing, service, planning and business management. This training and subsequent follow-up assistance is the core of the program and accounts for the dealers' excellent success

record. Additional field training is also arranged when necessary and always available.
Managerial Assistance Available: Rampart provides extensive follow-up assistance for the life of the franchise in the sales, technical and business management areas. A staff of specialists in these areas deals directly with the Dealer on specific problems. Full factory support is provided for equipment testing, repair, research and new product development. The home office advertising department and outside agency continually develop and field test new marketing programs and techniques and the field sales staff implements these with the Dealers. Dealer Newsletter and manual updates further keep the field abreast of all developments. Contests and motivational programs are continually run. Dealers are organized into regions with regional managers, regional meetings and seminars and regional coordination of local marketing.

SOFT DRINK/WATER BOTTLING

BUBBLE-UP COMPANY
2800 North Talman Avenue
Chicago, Illinois 60618
Roy Gurvey, Director of Marketing
Description of Operation: Issued to soft drink bottlers who are in operation in various areas of the world. No fee is required; no royalty, or percentage of sales required. We sell only one item to franchisees, and that is Bubble-Up concentrate, from which is produced a lemon lime soft drink.
Number of Franchisees: 155 in all 50 states
In Business Since: 1939
Equity Capital Needed: Must be in the bottling business.
Financial Assistance Available: Credit extended occasionally on the purchase of Bubble-Up concentrate; also financing available for the purchase of Bubble-Up returnable bottles to be used in the precise marketing area.
Training Provided: Training unnecessary due to the fact that franchisee is in the bottling business of soft drinks; training is provided by our personnel relative to the sale, distribution of merchandise and advertising of Bubble-Up, in particular all during the term of the franchise agreement.
Managerial Assistance Available: Assistance rendered to franchisee concerning his entire operation relative to Bubble-Up which would include accounting, production, sales and advertising and technical assistance relative to laboratory techniques used in production. These services are provided regularly and at any other times that franchisee requests.

COCK 'N BULL, LIMITED
5664 West Raymond Street
Indianapolis, Indiana 46241
Harold A. Bateman, President
Description of Operation: Manufactures soft drinks and soft drink extracts. Franchises are issued to interested bottlers.
Number of Franchisees: 8 in 5 states and Guam
In Business Since: 1945
Equity Capital Needed: Must be in bottling business
Financial Assistance Available: Cooperative advertising.
Training Provided: Sales and technical training on a continuing basis.
Managerial Assistance Available: Ongoing assistance provided for length of franchise.

COTT CORPORATION
197 Chatham Street
New Haven, Connecticut 06513
James E. Oravetz, Vice President
Description of Operation: Franchise brands include: Cott, Mission, Clicquot Club, Big Giant Cola, Quiky, Energade. Manufactures soft drink extracts, dairy flavor bases, fountain syrup. Franchises (or private label extract) are available to established bottlers, canners who desire mixers, flavors or sugar free beverages.
Number of Franchisees: 185 in all 50 states and international
In Business Since: 1926
Equity Capital Needed: Sufficient to buy raw materials, packaging supplies and limited introductory expense.
Financial Assistance Available: Provides limited assistance in some instances, and will share market introductory cost.
Training Provided: Sales and technical assistance and training on continuing basis.
Managerial Assistance Available: In marketing, sales, financial and technical areas.

DAD'S ROOT BEER COMPANY
2800 North Talman Avenue
Chicago, Illinois 60518
Roy Gurvey, Director of Marketing
Description of Operation: Issued to soft drink bottlers who are in operation in various areas of the world. No fee is required; no royalty, or percentage of sales required. We sell only one item to franchisees, and that is DAD's concentrate, from which is produced DAD's Root Beer finished product.
Number of Franchisees: 155 in all 50 states
In Business Since: 1939
Equity Capital Needed: Must be in the bottling business.
Financial Assistance Available: Credit extended occasionally on the purchase of DAD's Concentrate; also financing available for the pruchase of DAD's returnable bottles to be used in the precise marketing area.
Training Provided: Training unnecessary due to the fact that franchisee is in the bottling business of soft drinks; training is provided by our personnel relative to the sale, distribution of merchandise and advertising of DAD's Root Beer, in particular all during the term of the franchise agreement.
Managerial Assistance Available: Assistance rendered to franchisee concerning his entire operation relative to DAD's Root Beer, which would include accounting, production, sales and advertising and technical assistance relative to laboratory techniques used in production. These services are provided regularly and at any other times that franchisee requests.

DOUBLE-COLA COMPANY
3350 Broad Street
Chattanooga, Tennessee 37402
Wayne R. Downey, President
Description of Operation: Manufacture and sale of soft drinks.
Number of Franchisees: 150 throughout the United States.
In Business Since: 1922
Equity Capital Needed: $20,000 up
Financial Assistance Available: Promotional allowances
Training Provided: Field help given by our regional managers in sales, marketing, advertising, production, etc.
Managerial Assistance Available: Continuous

MOUNTAIN VALLEY SPRING COMPANY
150 Central Avenue
Hot Springs, Arkansas 71901
John G. Scott, President
Description of Operation: Distributing Mountain Valley Water from Hot Springs, Arkansas and twelve imported bottled waters from Europe.
Number of Franchisees: 118 in 43 states
In Business Since: 1871
Equity Capital Needed: No investment for franchise rights. Capital needed for truck, warehouse, etc., or to purchase existing operation from current franchisee.
Financial Assistance Available: Advertising assistance for local identify.
Training Provided: On-the-scene training, or at a convenient Mountain Valley operation. Annual 3 day training refresher course at convention.
Managerial Assistance Available: Products arrived packaged, no technical assistance needed for them; managerial assistance given on training noted above.

SWIMMING POOLS

CALIFORNIA POOLS, INC.
4600 Santa Anita Avenue
El Monte, California 91731
David G. Morrill, Vice President
Description of Operation: Swimming pool contracting, selling and installation.
Number of Franchisees: 25 in California.
In Business Since: 1952.
Equity Capital Needed: $20,000.
Financial Assistance Available: Financing available, to qualified franchises.
Training Provided: 1 week extensive. One day each month thereafter. Experience is normally required.
Managerial Assistance Available: Franchisor is in constant contact with franchisee. All bookkeeping and accounting is done by centralized computer.

CASCADE INDUSTRIES INCORPORATED
Talmadge Road
Edison, New Jersey 08817
Ernest B. Zencker, Vice President
Description of Operation: Sell and install Buster Crabbe Pools, accessories and supplies. These pools, manufactured by the inventors of in-ground vinyl lined pools are available in over 50 sizes and shapes and incorporated many exclusive patented features that contribute to long lasting beauty, continuing service with extremely low maintenance, and low energy consumption.
Number of Franchisees: 250 in 40 states.
In Business Since: 1954.
Equity Capital Needed: Advance deposit on initial pool orders plus approximately $250 for selected sales aids.
Financial Assistance Available: None.
Training Provided: Continued guidance available. Frequent sales and installation seminars. Field service representatives and retail marketing managers help dealers locally as needed.
Managerial Assistance Available: As above.

LA FLEUR POOL SYSTEMS, INC.
447 Vista Avenue
Addison, Illinois 60101
Robert L. LaFleur, President
Description of Operation: Service, maintenance, repair and supply swimming pools.
Number of Franchisees: 14 in 5 states.
In Business Since: 1975.
Equity Capital Needed: $8,000.
Financial Assistance Available: None.
Training Provided: Service training school with examinations and field experience — 2 week session.
Managerial Assistance Available: Continuous.

LIFETIME POOLS, INC.
1819 H Street, N.W.
Washington, D.C. 20006
Richard Micheel

Description of Operation: Sales and installation of swimming pools.
Number of Franchisees: 3 in Virginia, District of Columbia and Maryland.
In Business Since: 1966.
Equity Capital Needed: $5,000.
Financial Assistance Available: None.
Training Provided: 1 week training in Washington, D.C. on the installation of a pool, and sales methods.
Managerial Assistance Available: Franchisee is given 1 week training at Washington, D.C. and assistance is given, when and as needed in the field.

SAN JUAN PRODUCTS, INC.
P.O. Box 652
Hemet, California 92343
George Sullivan, President

Description of Operation: San Juan Products, Inc., offers a tried and proven one-piece fiberglass swimming pool, in various sizes, to installing dealers who have construction experience either in the swimming pool industry or general construction.
Number of Franchisees: 52 in 12 states.
In Business Since: 1960.
Equity Capital Needed: $10,000 to $20,000.
Financial Assistance Available: Training, sales aids, special tools, custom trailer, etc., worth approximately $4,300.
Training Provided: 1 to 3 weeks provided by San Juan to all licensees.
Managerial Assistance Available: Perpetual observation and systems provided by San Juan.

TOOLS/HARDWARE

IMPERIAL HAMMER, INC.
9226 North Second Street
Rockford, Illinois 61111
John R. Sassaman, President

Description of Operation: Manufacturer of industrial hammers and vise jaws. Light non-ferrous metal foundry, selling and servicing industry and maintenance plants of all types.
Number of Franchisees: 7 in 7 states.
In Business Since: 1957.
Equity Capital Needed: $35,000 depending on size of territory.
Financial Assistance Available: Financial assistance is available to qualified individuals.
Training Provided: 2 weeks in franchisor's plant and office to learn complete operation.
Managerial Assistance Available: Assistance always available to help find location, assist, advise and counsel at all times.

MAC TOOLS, INC.
P.O. Box 370
South Fayette Street
Washington Court House, Ohio 43160
Tom Sizer and/or F.J. Kibbey

Description of Operation: Distributors carrying complete inventory of over 8,000 tools, calling directly on mechanics and light industry. These tools consist of a complete assortment of all small hand tools, sockets, wrenches, punches, chisels, screwdrivers, tool boxes, penumatic tools, as well as special tools designed for the automotive market.
Number of Franchisees: 1,000 throughout the United States and Canada.
In Business Since: 1938.
Equity Capital Needed: Over $20,000.
Financial Assistance Available: The $20,000 starting amount includes a basic starting inventory, initial deposit on a lease truck, business supplies, and backup capital. All financing is arranged on a local level by the persepctive distributor. There are no franchisee fees and the original investment is protected by a buy-back agreement.
Training Provided: Each distributor is assigned to a district manager who lives in the local area and does all necessary training, will aid in displaying the trucks, establishing bookkeeping systems, and technical knowledge. They spend approximately 3 weeks with any new distributor and then maintain a monthly contact. Also will continue to work with the distributor as he deems necessary.
Managerial Assistance Available: Same as above.

SNAP-ON TOOLS CORPORATION
2801 - 80th Street
Kenosha, Wisconsin 53140
General Sales Manager

Description of Operation: Independent dealer concept for the distribution of hand tools and equipment to the professional mechanic, independent garage, car dealership, service stations, and related businesses. The dealer purchases his inventory, maintains his own stock, and calls directly on his customers, selling and delivering the product from a van or walk-in truck.
Number of Franchisees: Over 2,700 dealers in all 50 states.
In Business Since: 1920.
Equity Capital Needed: $15,000 to $45,000.
Financial Assistance Available: Several types of financing plans are available which would include consignment of merchandise, financing for open accounts, and a contract program for long-term financing of equipment items, etc. The dealer purchases all tools at a discount and no other fees are involved. Product return privileges and protection against price reductions are provided.
Training Provided: The free training program includes business fundamentals, product knowledge, and sales assistance on a continuing basis. A field sales manager provides guidance in selecting and securing a display van and provides personal assistance on early trips through the area and offers other assistance on a continuing basis where needed.
Managerial Assistance Available: In addition to the field sales manager, assistance is afforded by branch managers and branch sales managers who are sales administrators. Finance division managers give advice on credit.

VULCAN TOOLS
United-Greenfield Division of TRW, INC.
2300 Kenmore Avenue
Buffalo, New York 14207
Douglas H. Burdick, General Manager

Description of Operation: Independent franchised dealers and warehouse owners purchase mechanics' hand tools, shop supplies and equipment from the company at a very favorable discount. They in turn, market these items from a van or panel-type truck directly to the user at a suggested resale price. Territories are assigned based on the number of potential customers rather than by geographic size. Customers include garages, truck and bus fleets, new and used car dealers, service stations, constractors, marinas, airports, appliance shops and all mechanics therein employed.
Number of Franchisees: Over 100 throughout the U.S., Puerto Rico and Canada.
In Business Since: 1960.
Equity Capital Needed: Dealers: $2,000 minimum. Warehouse: $8,000 minimum.
Financial Assistance Available: Dealer financing: Dealer must own suitable vehicle and have cash investment of not less than $2,000 for inventory. Company will finance inventory up to $6,000 on long-term, no interest repayment plan for a qualified man. Thirty day financing for any sales made to established business houses. Warehouse financing: None available.
Training Provided: Training 3 days on use of catalog, sales book, reporting forms, truck display and tool selection. One week's initial field training in dealer's own territory. Continuing sales and demonstration assistance offered on regular basis. Standard procedure manual furnished. Instruction booklets furnished on all equipment items.
Managerial Assistance Available: Complete training in all forms necessary for conduct of business. Counseling on inventory and accounts receivable turnover. No handling charge on dealer return of inventory. Assistance in taking physical inventory and computation at no charge. Regularly scheduled sales meeting and technical clinics. Technical bulletins furnished free of charge.

VENDING

FORD GUM & MACHINE CO., INC.
Division of AUTOMATIC SERVICE COMPANY
Newton & Hoag Streets
Akron, New York 14001
John H. Fry, Executive Vice President

Description of Operation: Manufacturer and distributor of chewing gum, candy and candy coated confections for sale through self-service vending machines, also manufactured and distributed to franchisees by the company.
Number of Franchisees: 166 in all states, Canada and Puerto Rico.
Equity Capital Needed: $18,000 to $25,000.
Financial Assistance Available: Extended credit to new franchisees for: (a) expansion of franchised territory, (b) purchase of existing franchise from retiring franchisee, and (c) purchase of equipment and supplies.
Training Provided: Home office, plant visit 3 to 5 days, for orientation and product manufacture, merchandising, record keeping, accounting, machine assembly, and vending route supervision. On-the-job training in machine and service operation in franchisee's area with complete supervision — 2 to 4 weeks.
Managerial Assistance Available: Permanent field staff for emergency assistance and/or recurring assistance when needed or desired.

WATER CONDITIONING

CHEMICAL ENGINEERING CORPORATION
P.O. Box 246
Churubusco, Indiana 46723
L.D. Gordon, Executive Vice President

Description of Operation: Sales, rentals and servicing of water conditioning equipment. customers include residence, business (commercial and industrial) and institutions.
Number of franchisees: 20 in Indiana, Ohio, Illinois and Michigan.
In Business Since: 1956.
Equity Capital Needed: $10,000.
Financial Assistance Available: None.
Training Provided: Training includes all phases of business including sales, accounting and technical.
Managerial Assistance Available: Complete manuals of operations, all forms and literature are provided. Periodic seminars are held covering both technical and selling activities. In-field assistance is available whenever required. Assistance in preparation of quotations for commercial and industrial water treatment equipment is also provided.

CULLIGAN INTERNATIONAL COMPANY
One Culligan Parkway
Northbrook, Illinois 60062

Description of Operation: Parent company is supplier to franchisee for water conditioning equipment. Franchisee sells, leases, maintains, and repairs water conditioning equipment for domestic, commercial and industrial consumers.
Number of Franchisees: 931 in U.S. and Canada.
In Business Since: 1938.
Equity Capital Needed: $20,000 and up.
Financial Assistance Available: Franchisor has various credit arrangements available for qualified franchisees with reference to the purchase of equipment from franchisor.
Training Provided: Franchisor provides 1 week training at established dealership and 1 week training at Northbrook, Illinois headquarters. Franchisor also provides management training, sales training, and technical training through frequent visits to franchisee's dealership by company personnel.
Managerial Assistance Available: Franchisor has continuing managerial and technical assistance to franchisee through traveling field managers, technical service engineers, district sales managers and industrial managers. This assistance is available to all franchisees as needed.

RAINSOFT WATER CONDITIONING COMPANY
121 East Mason Street
P.O. Box 90
Santa Barbara, California 93102
Ivan W. Carter, Vice President, Franchise Management

Description of Operation: Sell, lease and rent home, commercial and industrial water treatment equipment.
Number of Franchisees: 250 in most states (excluding Hawaii).
In Business Since: 1953.
Equity Capital Needed: Varies from $15,000 minimum.
Financial Assistance Available: Assist in establishing retail financing. Rental financing to qualified dealers on selective basis.
Training Provided: In plant and field training in sales, service and operation.
Managerial Assistance Available: Continuing contract for training and assistance through national and regional seminars, plus regular, person to person contact from regional field representatives.

RAYNE CORPORATION
121 East Mason Street
P.O. Box 90
Santa Barbara, California 93102
Ivan W. Carter, Vice President, Franchise Management

Description of Operation: A franchise system for the installation of water systems on either a sale or rental basis. These systems include soft water, drinking water (filters and reverse osmosis units), commercial water coolers, commercial and light commercial water conditioning equipment, as well as the ancillary support materials.
Number of Franchisees: 74 in 8 states.
In Business Since: 1954.
Equity Capital Needed: $40,000 to $100,000 depending upon the scope of the operation. Purchases of existing franchises require approximately 25 percent down payment ($25,000 to $150,000).
Financial Assistance Available: Various leasing and conditional contract purchasing programs are available for the acquisition of capital equipment.
Training Provided: Initial training from 1 week to 1 month depending upon the scope of the operation, with continued direct assistance in areas of marketing, merchandising, selling and technical proficiency.
Managerial Assistance Available: Ongoing managerial up-grading by means of RITE (Rayne Information, Training and Education) meetings in addition to individual counseling and assistance on a day to day basis, and annual conventions.

SCIENTIFIC WATER SYSTEMS, INC.
132 Demanade Boulevard
P.O. Box 52886
Lafayette, Louisiana 70505
O.A. Ranstead, General Manager

Description of Operation: Non-chemical water conditioning services for commercial institutional and industrial accounts.
Number of Franchisees: 8 in Louisiana and 2 in Texas.
In Business Since: 1975.
Equity Capital Needed: $10,000.
Financial Assistance Available: None.
Training Provided: 5 day concentrated training program conducted in our headquarters at Lafayette, Louisiana.
Managerial Assistance Available: Continuous marketing and managerial assistance with all technical services provided by franchisor's staff.

SUPERIOR WATER CONDITIONERS
2015 South Calhoun Street
P.O. Box 545
Fort Wayne, Indiana 46801
Charles H. Sanderson, President

Description of Operation: Superior Water Conditioners, Division of Superior M-TOW, Inc., offers a unique and very lucrative product that can be used by every building that has a need for water. The Superior Water Conditioner's primary function is to prevent and eliminate hard water scale in boilers, air conditioners, hot water heaters, or any other water using vessels where lime or corosion is a problem. factory training is provided.
Number of Franchisees: 205 in 50 states and 12 in foreign countries.
In Business Since: 1967.
Financial Assistance Available: Total investment of $25,000 for inventory and needed supplies. Superior Water Conditioners will finance $15,000 provided franchisee has a good credit rating and has good managing ability.
Training Provided: Factory training is provided covering the different types of installation that are applicable. In-depth studies and case histories of previous users of the Superior Water Conditioner are used to familiarize the franchisee with different types of equipment. Field-training is provided 30 days after the franchisee has had his basic instructions.
Managerial Assistance Available: Technical information is constantly being provided for the franchisee and a special telex line is answered 24 hours, 7 days a week that is available for anyone having a question concerning installation of the Superior Water Conditioner or the equipment being used in conjunction with it. An initial supply of Sales, Service and Installation manuals are furnished at no charge to the franchisee.

WATERCARE CORPORATION
1520 North 24th Street
Manitowoc, Wisconsin 54220
William W. Granger, President

Description of Operation: Water conditioning sales and service, domestic, industrial, institutional and commercial. Method of service and sales is portable exchange water conditioners, permanently installed water conditioners on a rental basis and outright sales.
Number of Franchisees: 101 dealers in 27 states, 1 dealer in Canada
In Business Since: 1948
Equity Capital Needed: $5,000
Financial Assistance Available: After initial financing WaterCare provides dealer growth money on plant equipment and rental water conditioners.
Training Provided: Includes techniques of water conditioning, water analysis, sales and service of equipment, office procedures, management, all of which is done at our home office and plant in Manitowoc, Wisconsin and our "Dealer-Lab" company-owned retail operation at Green Bay, Wisconsin. Time is approximately 1 week in Wisconsin and 1 week by dealer counselor at the franchisee's place of operation. In addition, monthly call on franchisee by dealer counselor and semi-annual area work seminars.
Managerial Assistance Available: Same as above

WATER PURIFICATION SYSTEMS, INC.
1465 Southwest 21 Avenue
Ft. Lauderdale, Florida 33312
Fred Mussler, President

Description of Operation: Water Purification Systems offers a unique direct and builder sales opportunity. System 1 is a U.S. Government (EPA) approved water processor (EPA #35920.1), which is an excellent substitute for bottle water. System 1 also removes volatile organic compounds from drinking water like chloroform. New EPA minimum standards for chloroform in city water are making the public very aware of the hazards of drinking city water.
Number of Franchisees: 34 in 16 states
In Business Since: 1972
Equity Capital Needed: $5,000 and up
Financial Assistance Available: No charge for training and marketing programs, only the inventory purchased.
Training Provided: 4 days initially at the home office-periodic field training as required by distributor.
Managerial Assistance Available: WPS provides continual technical assistance with materials, new products, Government coordinator. Complete manuals for instruction, advertising, and sales presentations are available. WPS sponsors meetings in distributors areas, and backs their product with research to maintain high customer acceptance.

WATER REFINING COMPANY
500 North Verity Parkway
Middletown, Ohio 45052

Description of Operation: Water conditioning sales - rentals - service.
Number of Franchisees: Approximately 853 in 46 states
In Business Since: 1956
Equity Capital Needed: $5,000 and up
Financial Assistance Available: Total sales (marketing), business, service, etc.
Training Provided: Continuing
Managerial Assistance Available: Continuing

MISCELLANEOUS WHOLESALE AND SERVICE BUSINESSES

ALMOST HEAVEN HOT TUBS
Route 1-F
Renick, West Virginia 24966

Description of Operation: Manufacture of Redwood Hot Tubs and Jacuzzi Baths.
Number of Franchisees: 63 in 50 states, Puerto Rico, Virgin Islands and Canada
In Business Since: 1968
Equity Capital Needed: Approximately $5,000 - no franchise fee
Financial Assistance Available: Helping in arranging financing through local banks.
Training Provided: 1 week training at manufacturing facility in Renick, West Virginia.
Managerial Assistance Available: Continual seminars, monthly bulletins etc. 24-hour emergency assistance, sales leads provided at no charge. Cooperative advertising program. Dealer territory protection.

AMERICAN HERITAGE AGENCY, INC.
Heritage Building
104 Park Road
West Hartford, Connecticut 06119
Rita Ann Gelinas, Director

Description of Operation: Wedding consulting business furnishes services tailored to the needs of the bride-to-be.
Number of Franchisees: 6 in Connecticut, Massachusetts and New York
In Business Since: 1925
Equity Capital Needed: $10,000
Financial Assistance Available: Financing of up to 50 percent of the franchise fee provided credit standards can be met.
Training Provided: 12 days of formal classroom training and on-the-job training at established office; up to 30 days training at franchisee's own office; periodic briefings and meetings.
Managerial Assistance Available: Liaison officer available to help in solving problems, expanding operations and suggesting improvements.

THE ARMOLOY CORPORATION
118 Simonds Avenue
DeKalb, Illinois 60115
Jerome F. Hejbl, President

Description of Operation: Metal coating, that is electrodeposited chromium, for wear and corrosion precision parts.
Number of Franchisees: 10 in 9 states
In Business Since: 1955
Equity Capital Needed: $110,000
Financial Assistance Available: None
Training Provided: Complete training period at corporate headquarters for key personnel. Continuing assistance in any phase of the business.
Managerial Assistance Available: Technical assistance is run by our quality control laboratory, and Corporate provides any managerial help that is needed. We have advertising, administrative and sales help available.

ARMSTRONG PEST CONTROL
Division of Armstrong Building Maintenance
P. O. Box 8306
Albuquerque, New Mexico 87198

Description of Operation: Provides Pest Control services to homes, offices, buildings, schools and industrial plants on annual contracts. Franchisees receive training, equipment, sales promotions, protected territory, and access to company's national accounts.
Number of Franchisees: 3 in 2 states
In Business Since: 1946 Franchising since 1979
Equity Capital Needed: $4,800
Financial Assistance Available: Partial financial assistance available.
Training Provided: 2 weeks training at home office and 2 weeks training in the field. Training for State Examination provided.
Managerial Assistance Available: Continuous management assistance, technical bulletins, training meetings and periodic staff visits. Training films for employees. TV and Radio Commercials, also co-op advertising from Company.

ASI SIGN SYSTEMS INC.
13344 Beach Avenue
Marina del Rey, California 90291
W. Andrew Dodenhoff, Vice President

Description of Operation: ASI Sign Systems Inc., offers franchises which give franchisees the license and right to operate a sign business using the ASI Sign System. The ASI Sign System consists of various components. Together, they offer to franchisees the techniques, know-how, information, equipment, materials, supplies and business and marketing formats which enable the franchisee: to manufacture subsurface imaged signs; to obtain from qualified sources other kinds of finished signs and other products, materials and consumable supplies; and, to efficiently conduct a sign business.
Number of Franchisees: 20 in 14 states
In Business Since: 1977
Equity Capital Needed: $23,700
Financial Assistance Available: A total investment of approximately $40,000 is needed to cover additional equipment, supplies, rental space and operating capital. The franchisor offers no financial assistance.
Training Provided: An intensive 5 day training course is held for all new franchises at the home office. An additional 3 days of training and opening assistance is held at the franchisee's location.
Managerial Assistance Available: ASI Sign Systems provides on-going assistance in sales, marketing, manufacturing and administration. Comprehensive operations manuals are provided. ASI has field personnel who regularly visit and work with the franchisees in all phases of the business.

BADGE MAN INTERNATIONAL LTD.
2740 South Harbor Boulevard
Suite E
Santa Ana, California 92704
Dennis D. Hunt, President

Description of Operation: Badge Man franchisees sell and manufacture quality identification name badges. Each franchisee, after completion of training, will provide local service to hotels, restaurants, real estate agencies, banks, title insurance companies, hospitals, social clubs, organizations, etc., in their area. National advertising and customer referrals, back up the franchisees local efforts in developing badge identification programs.
Franchisees operate a low overhead facility from their homes. Badge Man is the world's largest system of badge making operations with more than 7 years experience. Manufacture badges for such people as Hilton Hotels, Century 21 Real Estate, Baskin Robbins, Denny's Restaurants, Dunkin' Donuts, Telephone Company, Rotary, Elks Lodge, etc.
Number of Franchisees: 53 in 20 states and a Master Licensee in Canada and the United Kingdom.
In Business Since: 1974 (founder began Badge Manufacturing in 1972)
Equity Capital Needed: $10,500 (includes all equipment and start-up materials and supplies)
Financial Assistance Available: None
Training Provided: A 1 week comprehensive training program is conducted in Santa Ana, California by a professional instructor and staff. All equipment is included in the franchisee fee and complete instruction is given in-depth in all areas including: badge production, machine operation, badge design, layout, bookkeeping, customer service, marketing, sales, and advertising.
Managerial Assistance Available: Badge Man International, Ltd., provides continual franchise development program headed by a director of franchise services, who is available by telephone at any time. New accounts and referrals are stimulated through national advertising and trade show exhibits. A monthly newsletter serves as a constant communications tool to introduce new opportunities, product lines, production tips, share ideas, etc. Personal visits from home office, as well as meetings help to keep all franchisees informed and aware of the developing markets.

BAR-MASTER, INTERNATIONAL
2206 Beverly Boulevard
Los Angeles, California 90057
J. H. McMillen, President

Description of Operation: Manufacture soft drink and liquor dispensers and market them through local distributors. Units approved by Pepsi-Cola and successfully tested by Coca-Cola. Approved by 7-Up.
Number of Franchisees: 90 in 40 states
In Business Since: 1952
Equity Capital Needed: $3,000 to $10,000
Financial Assistance Available: None
Training Provided: 2 weeks. Engineering support in the field.
Managerial Assistance Available: Ongoing assistance as long as relationships last. Literature, advertising.

CHEM-TEX HOT TANK PRODUCTS CORPORATION
P. O. Box 171, Highway 301 South
Wilson, North Carolina 27893
R. H. Williams, President

Description of Operation: Manufacturer of the Hot Tank (patented) and related cleaning solutions for ferrous and non-ferrous materials to be used in the industrial, manufacturing and institutional markets. The company has a line of some 25 cleaning products that are available to the distributor.
Number of Franchisees: 3 in North Carolina and South Carolina
In Business Since: 1977
Equity Capital Needed: $10,000
Financial Assistance Available: None
Training Provided: A thorough and extensive training course is scheduled for all new franchisees. Time: 2 weeks at the home office. On sight training if needed. Complete office manual is available for use by franchisee and kept current by the home office during the life of the franchise.
Managerial Assistance Available: CHEM-TEX will provide continual service for the life of the franchise in all areas of the operations. Direct managers will continue to assist in problem solving. The company will continue new market concept product research and products improvement and make available at new additional franchise charge. Charges only for new and improved products and equipment.

COMMERCIAL MOBILE SERVICES INC.
851 Hinckley Road
Burlingame, California 94010
Daniel E. Kelliner, President

Description of Operation: Commercial Mobile Services, Inc., is a California based corporation operating specially designed mobile vans under the name of MoTech. Franchisees operate appliance repair service in both the domestic and commercial field.
Number of Franchisees: 14 in California.
In Business Since: 1977.
Equity Capital Needed: $38,000.
Financial Assistance Available: Minimum cash investment — $25,000 includes parts, inventory, tools and equipment, technical and administrative training, accounting system and franchise fee. Additional $2,500 is to be retained by franchisee as working capital. Total investment $38,000.

Training Provided: Comprehensive 6 weeks training course is provided at company school. Field training is provided at the opening of the operation to insure licensees' success.
Managerial Assistance Available: MoTech provides continual management service for the life of the franchise in such areas as bookkeeping, regional and national advertising, and inventory control. Complete manuals of operation and forms are provided. Home office personnel are available to assist in problem solving. Ongoing training is provided to constantly up-grade dealer's skills.

DIVERSIFIED ARTS
15 Palmer Road
Waterford, Connecticut 06385
Joseph Abrahms, Owner

Description of Operation: Part-time distributor — required 8 to 10 hours per week to service accounts to whom paintings are consigned. Also will aid in setting up of full time galleries.
Number of Franchisees: 9 in 7 states.
In Business Since: 1971.
Equity Capital Needed: $4,500 — part-time — requires 4 days a month after area is set up.
Financial Assistance Available: None.
Training Provided: Part-time. Supply original oil paintings and all replacement and exchange paintings at no cost to distributor. One week field training to establish outlets who display and sell the paintings.
Managerial Assistance Available: Continual assistance both in field and through newsletters in which all ideas are dessiminated to all.

KEY KORNER SYSTEMS, INC.
3233 -½ Midway Drive
San Diego, California 92110
Paul Gross, President

Description of Operation: Key shops and convenience centers. Complete business includes all phases of key cutting, lock repairing, engraving, rubber stamps. All shops located at the entrance of major retail shopping centers. Operator does not need previous experience.
In Business Since: 1969.
Equity Capital Needed: Approximately $5,000 to $15,000.
Financial Assistance Available: Financing available for equipment and inventory.
Training Provided: 2 weeks at headquarters, plus 1 to 2 weeks at dealer's shop. Training covers accounting, customer relations, marketing, management and all technical aspects of key cutting and lock repair.
Managerial Assistance Available: Continuing ongoing program of technical and management assistance.

MACHINERY WHOLESALERS CORP.
3510 Biscayne Boulevard
Miami, Florida 33137
Mark Fields, President

Description of Operation: Machinery Wholesalers is a totally unique used machinery brokerage network providing a computerized seller-to-buyer service through our IBM computer with a data bank of more than 25,000 buyers and offices coast to coast.
Number of Franchisees: Over 20 multiple territories in 20 states.
In Business Since: 1974.
Equity Capital Needed: Territories $19,000-$50,000.
Financial Assistance Available: Up to 50 percent, depending on amount of territories purchased by franchisee.
Training Provided: 5 working days of training from 8 a.m. to 7 p.m.
Managerial Assistance Available: Continuous supply of information, we are part of every sale.

MEISTERGRAM
310 Lakeside Avenue, West
Cleveland, Ohio 44113
L.D. Katz, President

Description of Operation: Meistergram is the originator and largest source of monogram embroidery equipment and supplies and has been in business since 1931. Much or our equipment is sold to department stores and manufacturers. Several hundred of our accounts are individuals who acquire equipment to set up their own monogram service.
Number of Franchisees: 700 in 48 states.
In Business Since: 1931.
Equity Capital Needed: $4,000 - $10,000.
Financial Assistance Available: None.
Training Provided: Training available on premises.
Managerial Assistance Provided: Factory trained instructor installs machine on premises and teaches franchisee how to operate and maintain equipment, work with different materials and garments. Complete supplies and services available.

MY NAILS, INC.
5354 North High Street
Columbus, Ohio 43214
Bonnie A. MacAllister, President

Description of Operation: Franchising of Permanent Artificial Fingernail Salons and Total Hand and Body Care Centers featuring European influenced aesthetic services. Over 50 percent of nail business concentrated on biters by medical referral or otherwise. Manufacture of all necessary and related supplies and retail products. Distributorships available in certain states.
Number of Franchisees: 54 in 17 states.
In Business Since: 1973.

Equity Capital Needed: $20,000 to $25,000 (Franchisee fee $15,000 plus additional $5-$10,000 start up capital).
Financial Assistance Available: Limited.
Training Provided: Intensive 2 week initial training period with on-going assistance and training at no charge.
Managerial Assistance Available: On-going managerial and promotional assistance.

NATIONWIDE EXTERMINATING
A Division of NATIONWIDE CHEMICAL
P. O. Box 3027
Hamilton, Ohio 45013
David M. Valentine, President

Description of Operation: Nationwide Exterminating offers a chemical and equipment distributorship of U-Do-It pest control products. Nationwide has registered the most complete line of professional products for sale to the general public.
Number of Franchisees: 43 in 7 states, 4 in Israel and 1 in England
In Business Since: 1968
Equity Capital Needed: Distributorship $4,000
Financial Assistance Available: Outside only.
Training Provided: Intensive 14 day training course immaterial of any previous training is suggested.
Managerial Assistance Available: Continuous assistance and direction.

NORTH AMERICAN CARBIDE CORP.
4800 Nome Street
Denver, Colorado 80239
Peter Scognamillo, Executive Vice President

Description of Operation: North American Carbide offers equipment and technology for the recycling and regrinding for carbide metals used in the metalworking, oil and gas and mining industry.
Number of Franchisees: 40 in 23 states and Canada
In Business Since: 1977
Equity Capital Needed: $137,500, represents cost of Equipment and Manufacturing License.
Financial Assistance Available: None
Training Provided: Comprehensive 2 week training program in marketing and sales, engineering and equipment operation.
Managerial Assistance Available: 30 year contract provides engineering and technical service.

PARKING COMPANY OF AMERICA
National Office
550 West Colfax Avenue
Denver, Colorado 80204
Richard Chaves, President

Description of Operation: Self-service parking lots and garages.
Number of Franchisees: 18 in 12 states
In Business Since: 1963
Equity Capital Needed: $10,000
Financial Assistance Available: None
Training Provided: 6 months in Denver
Managerial Assistance Available: Annual convention and seminars in Denver

REDD PEST CONTROL COMPANY, INC.
4114 Northview Drive
Jackson, Mississippi 39206
Marvin Jordan

Description of Operation: Pest and termite control.
Number of Franchisees: 5 in Tennessee, Louisiana, Mississippi and Florida
In Business Since: 1946
Equity Capital Needed: $15,000 minimum
Financial Assistance Available: Franchisee will be able to factor his accounts receivable and furnish financing for equipment and vehicles.
Training Provided: 3 to 6 months depending on background.
Managerial Assistance Available: Extensive assistance for the first year; additional assistance therafter, as required.

SELECTRA-DATE CORPORATION
2175 Lemoine Avenue
Ft. Lee, New Jersey 07024
Robert Friedman, President

Description of Operation: Computer-dating has been around since Art Linkletter started playing matching games with a Univac Computer in the late fifties. But that was just for laughs. Today its for love and money, with a score of computer-dating firms throughout the country reporting brisk business. Selectra-Date, one of the pioneers, now offers a complete turnkey package that makes it possible for any reputable individual with a sound business or professional background to enter this fascinating work. Since all computer processing is handled entirely by the company, no technical knowledge is required.
Number of Franchisees: 9 in 10 states
In Business Since: 1966
Equity Capital Needed: $4,500
Financial Assistance Available: The total required investment for promotional material, initial advertising, franchise fee, and for forms and stationery is $9,000, of which Selectra-Date will finance $4,500 for qualified franchisees. In addition the franchisee should have sufficient capital to adequately equip his office and to see him through the first 30 days of operation.
Training Provided: A full time Selectra-Date executive thoroughly trains each franchisee in all phases of the business during the first week he is in operation.
Managerial Assistance Available: Selectra-Date furnishes continuing individual guidance and support in all phases of the franchisee's operation.

STRETCH & SEW, INC.
P. O. Box 185
Eugene, Oregon 97401
Ann Person, President and Chief Executive Officer

Description of Operation: Stretch & Sew Fabric Centers specialize in quality knit fabrics. The Centers teach a unique technique in sewing knit fabrics using Stretch & Sew Patterns and Books.
Number of Franchisees: 196 franchised stores; 11 company-owned stores
In Business Since: 1969
Equity Capital Needed: $60,000 - $100,000 total investment with acceptable financing.
Financial Assistance Available: In the form of guidance in preparing the appropriate loan documents and proposal to present to lending institutions.
Training Provided: Retail management training held in Eugene, Oregon for a 3-6 week period. Instructor training, 3 day program, held in Eugene, Oregon; Florence, Kentucky, and certified Stretch & Sew Fabric Centers.
Managerial Assistance Available: Stretch & Sew provides continual management service for the life of the franchise agreement. The field support department is available to assist each Center. Conventions and workshops are also available.

MARKETING CONSULTANTS OF AMERICA
c/o SUM-TAN DIVISION
474 Perkins Extended
Memphis, Tennessee 38117
W. C. (Bill) Richey

Description of Operation: The use of a booth enclosing ultra-violet lights to produce a tan, upon exposure to the human skin.
Number of Franchisees: 300 plus in 22 states
In Business Since: 1978
Equity Capital Needed: Total investment under $10,000
Financial Assistance Available: Equipment leasing plan - or finance plan available.
Training Provided: An initial training school plus field training.
Managerial Assistance Available: Accounting, advertising, legal help, marketing, insurance, administration, research, site selection, supervision throughout the term of the agreement.

SUNTIQUE TANNING SALONS
510 North Kings Highway
Cherry Hill, New Jersey 08034
Don Chanslor, Franchise Director

Description of Operation: Suntique offers a fully constructed turnkey tanning salon business. Each location is thoroughly researched by our Real Estate Department. Salons derive income from the sale of tanning service, in addition to high quality skin care products, high fashion sun glasses and other sun related products.
Number of Franchisees: 11 in New Jersey, New York, Pennsylvania and Washington, D.C.
In Business Since: 1979
Equity Capital Needed: $19,900
Financial Assistance Available: None
Training Provided: Intensive 2 day training course at a company operated salon which includes: skin analysis, record keeping, sales, retailing, purchasing and operations.
Managerial Assistance Available: Suntique provides continuous managerial and promotional assistance throughout the term of the agreement, particular emphasis is placed on a powerful advertising campaign and co-op advertising is coordinated monthly. A complete, updated operations manual is provided to all franchisees.

TEMPACO, INC.
1701 Alden Road
P. O. Box 7667
Orlando, Florida 32804
David L. McDuffie, President
A. A. Voges, Vice President
Joseph Peters, Marketing Manager

Description of Operation: Wholesale heating, air conditioning, refrigeration supplies, parts and controls.
Number of Franchisees: 5 in Florida
In Business Since: 1946
Equity Capital Needed: Approximately $7,000 to $60,000
Financial Assistance Available: Assistance on inventory, accounts receivable and fixture financing available on individually-constituted basis.
Training Provided: 2 weeks - introductory training, supplemental and retraining on a non-scheduled basis.
Managerial Assistance Available: Continuous management counsel in areas of bookkeeping, inventory control, accounts receivable, operational procedures, training, advertising and publicity, purchasing control, sales in accordance with the need of the franchise.

TEPCO, INC.
3609 Marquis Drive
Garland, Texas 75042
John Michell, General Manager
R. J. Sineni, Vice President, Marketing

Description of Operation: Manufactures of electronic air cleaning and air pollution control equipment.
Number of Franchisees: 70 in 50 states
In Business Since: 1969
Equity Capital Needed: $15,000
Training Provided: 3-4 day sessions on-the-job training during the first year. Field training during the first 120 days. Training as required thereafter.
Managerial Assistance Available: Continuous managerial and technical assistance in sales, marketing, advertising, engineering, service and maintenance.

TERMINIX INTERNATIONAL, INC.
855 Ridge Lake Boulevard
P. O. Box 17167
Memphis, Tennessee 38117
Lee R. Olmstead, Manager, Franchise Relations

Description of Operation: Terminix International is a nationwide company that offers termite and pest control services to commercial and residential customers. It is made up of approximately 115 franchised offices and 80 company-owned offices as well as 50 Sears Termite and Pest Control offices. It provides a wide range of services to include technical assistance and training, makes available for purchase chemicals and marketing materials as well as many other benefits.
Number of Franchisees: 70 in 46 states
In Business Since: 1927
Equity Capital Needed: $10,000 to $20,000 (contingent upon size of market and operating requirements)
Financial Assistance Available: None; franchisee must arrange own outside financing.
Training Provided: Comprehensive training programs, both written and classroom style, are conducted and made available. However, due to the technical nature of the business, candidates must have on-the-job practical experience to be considered for a franchise.
Managerial Assistance Available: Terminix provides both managerial and technical assistance consultation. Operating manuals are made available to ensure quality control. Seminars and clinics are also conducted with management conferences being scheduled at least once annually.

UNITED AIR SPECIALISTS, INC.
4440 Creek Road
Cincinnati, Ohio 45242
Jeff Miller, Distribution Development Manager

Description of Operation: Sales and service of Smokeeter electronic air cleaners.
Number of Franchisees: 65 in all 50 states
In Business Since: 1966
Equity Capital Needed: $10,000 initial inventory with additional $25,000 working capital available.
Financial Assistance Available: None
Training Provided: Comprehensive 3 day factor seminar, field training, regional and national meetings.
Managerial Assistance Available: Factory and field training, support and managerial consultation. Marketing and advertising support program available.

UNITED WORTH HYDROCHEM CORPORATION
P. O. Box 366
Fort Worth, Texas 76101
Roy Coleman, President

Description of Operation: Chemical water treating and chemical cleaning service for cooling towers, boilers, closed systems and heat exchangers. Program built around personal service. Start as one person operation and grow from there. Territory is fully protected.
Number of Franchisees: 13 in 8 states
In Business Since: 1959
Equity Capital Needed: $1,500
Financial Assistance Available: Franchisee must have personal capital or income to support his family needs during first year.
Training Provided: Training school of 2 weeks at home office for theory. Close training in the field during first few months. Close technical support from there on.
Managerial Assistance Available: Worth provides continuous management, sales and technical service to all franchisees. Laboratory support is available on a no charge basis. Technical seminars are held on a semi annual basis. Worth conducts continuous product reserach.

U.S. FIREWORKS OF AMERICA, INC.
Route 1
Waxahachie, Texas 75165
Thomas E. Manley, President

Description of Operation: Manufacture, direct importers, wholesalers, and retailing of Department of Transportation class C pyrotechnic (fireworks).
Number of Franchisees: Less than 100.
In Business Since: 1969
Equity Capital Needed: $150,000 cash, or a net worth of $400,000.
Financial Assistance Available: Franchisor will prepare finance package at a cost to franchisee.
Training Provided: 1 week at our home office located 22 miles South of downtown Dallas, Texas; plus 1 week of training in the field.
Managerial Assistance Available: Continuous assistance is available upon request.

MISCELLANEOUS

ALLIED BUSINESS BROKERS, INC.
100 Northcreek Office Park, Suite 108
Atlanta, Georgia 30327
John L. Harrigan, President

Description of Operation: Assist in the sale and merger of mid-sized businesses.
Number of Franchisees: 19 in 13 states
In Business Since: 1971
Equity Capital Needed: $18,000
Financial Assistance Available: None
Training Provided: 1 week training session in Atlanta.
Managerial Assistance Available: Allied agrees to provide franchisees training which includes guidance towards finding potential sellers, listing businesses for sale, preparing profiles on businesses listed, development of advertising programs and techniques for consummating sales to prospective purchaser's acquisition criteria

BARTER SYSTEMS, INC.
4848 North MacArthur
Oklahoma City, Oklahoma 73122
Larry M. Inks, President

Description of Operation: Barter Systems, Inc., authorizes others to operate local trade exchanges which utilize barter principles. The franchisees are trained in the manner of operation which would be most efficient in the coordination of barter exchanges between members. The franchisees sell members in these trade exchanges to businesses and individuals in the area of the franchise. Each local trade exchange acts as clearinghouse arranging for the barter of goods and services between members. The local trade exchange keeps records of the barter credits accumulated and other credits spent by each member. The local trade exchange receives income from the sale of membership and renewals of memberships and from a 10 percent fee on all transactions. Barter exchanges between members of different local trade exchanges may be consummated through an independent organization known as Trade Network International, Inc., which facilitates the transfer of trade units between exchanges.
Number of Franchisees: 30 in 15 states
In Business Since: 1978
Equity Capital Needed: $5,000 minimum
Financial Assistance Available: There is no provision in the franchise agreement or in the practice of the franchisor for any financing of either the franchise fee or royalty payments or material purchases by the franchisee. In the event that the franchisee seeks financing for such money, it is done independently of Barter Systems, Inc., which receives no rebates, finders fees or other consideration from any person or institution arranging such financing.
Managerial Assistance Available: Barter Systems, Inc., conducts a complete training program for the franchisee. Personalized instruction is given in every aspect of the operation of a trade exchange which could concern the operation of a trade exchange on a day-to-day basis. Minimum length of this initial training is 6 days. Periodic sales seminars and trade department workshops are conducted to train the personnel of the franchisee. In addition, in-field training during the opening period of the new franchise is provided.
Managerial Assistance Available: Continuous

CATHEDRALITE DOMES
820 Bay Avenue
Suite 302
Capitola, California 95010
Tate Miller, President

Description of Operation: Cathedralite Domes is the largest geodesic dome manufacturer in the United States and products carry local and national building code approvals. Franchisees market the dome shell framing package for residential homes or commercial buildings. The framed dome shell is easily assembled on-the-job site in one to two days by an owner-builder or building contractor. (The finished interior and exterior is completed for the client by the franchisee or a local building contractor or the home owner, using local building suppliers.)
Number of Franchisees: 45 in the United States
In Business Since: 1968
Equity Capital Needed: Estimated capital including initial franchise fee of $60,000 to $100,000.
Financial Assistance Available: None
Training Provided: Comprehensive administrative, technical and marketing training seminars are conducted on a regular basis after the completion of the initial training program.
Managerial Assistance Available: Cathedralite Domes provides continued corporate services by area development management staff to assist franchisee in the areas of marketing, advertising and daily support functions. The Cathedralite Dome confidential operational and technical manuals are provided each new licensee at the initial training seminar. Corporate regional area development managers maintain daily contact to provide support and conduct scheduled training seminars.

COFFEE, TEA & THEE, INC.
P. O. Box 11025
Winston-Salem, North Carolina 27106

Description of Operation: Gourmet coffee and tea specialty shops located within enclosed shopping malls.
Number of Franchisees: 5 in 4 states
In Business Since: 1979
Equity Capital Needed: $50,000 to $75,000
Financial Assistance Available: No financial assistance available. However, franchisor is available for consultation with lenders.
Training Provided: Initial training of staff (normally 1 to 2 weeks) and periodic visits thereafter.
Managerial Assistance Available: Initial training at same time staff training takes place. Periodic visits by operations staff thereafter.

THE DETROIT II CORPORATION, INC.
AUTO DEALERSHIPS
255 South Orange Avenue
P. O. Box 2200
Orlando, Florida 32802

Description of Operation: A national network of retail used car dealers independently owned and operated under the umbrella of a corporated program and image with the assistance of a national advertising and promotion program to supplement regional and local market; warranty programs including 12-month or 12,000 mile limited warranties for vehicles under five years old and six months or 6,000 miles warranties for six year old cars; finance and insurance programs; full bookkeeping systems; management seminars; sales incentive programs and sales seminars; microfiche inventory system and quality controlled vehicle inspection program through authorized Detroit II Service Centers.
Number of Franchisees: 4
In Business Since: In research and development since 1977, incorporated in 1978 and first franchise sold in 1979.
Equity Capital Needed: Depending on planning potential which means the estimated number of vehicles sold in a given period which dictates size of real estate lot, financing for vehicles (floor planning) taxes, etc., which in turn dictates capitalization needed.
Financial Assistance Available: None
Training Provided: Sales training seminars on local and regional levels made available initially and mandatory in due course.
Managerial Assistance Available: Continual assistance available in every area of operation including regional and corporate office assistance in mangement, finance and administration, local, regional and national advertising and promotion and local and regional sales seminars.

THE DETROIT II CORPORATION, INC.
AUTO SERVICE CENTERS
255 South Orange Avenue
Orlando, Florida 32802

Description of Operation: A national network of automotive service centers, operating in tandem with Detroit II retail used car dealers to provide inspection controls and repair or reconditioning work which will lead to vehicle certification as a Detroit II warrantied automobile Service Center also has the opportunity of doing all warranty work on Detroit II vehicles. Centers operate independently but under a corporate umbrella that provides national advertising and promotion.
Number of Franchisees: 4
In Business Since: In research and development since 1977; incorporated in 1978 and first franchise sold in 1979.
Equity Capital Needed: Dependent on size of the business estimated on number of vehicles to be inspected in a given period, which dictates size of facility, number of bays and stalls, size of parts inventory taxes and assessments, all of which in turn dictates necessary capitalization.
Financial Assistance Available: None
Training Provided: Training provided in operation of automotive industry most sophisticated mechanical, electrical and electronic analyzer systems, exhaust and emission analyzers as well as public relation and sales procedure for both front office and mechanics.
Managerial Assistance Available: Continual assistance available in every area of operation from Detroit II dealerships to regional and corporate assistance in management, finance and administration, national advertising and in regular technical seminars and mechanical, analyzer and vehicle inspection meetings.

GASTON'S INC.
3277 Sacramento Street
San Francisco, California 94115
Douglas D. Gaston, President

Description of Operation: Gaston's Ice Cream of San Francisco offers a wide selection of ice cream delicacies and fountain items for take out. There are over 100 flavors of ice cream all developed by its founder Doug Gaston. The ice cream is made fresh daily on the premises.
Number of Franchisees: 30 in California
In Business Since: 1976
Equity Capital Needed: Approximately $40,000 to $60,000 depending on location and type of store.
Financial Assistance Available: The Company will assist the franchisee in applying for financing. The Company will not make direct loans to franchisee.
Training Provided: Gaston's training program will consist of a 2 week training period. The franchisee will be trained in manufacturing, preparing all ice cream delicacies and fountain items, in accounting, inventory control, store management, employee management, customer relations, and other additional areas.
Managerial Assistance Available: Gaston's franchisees are given a Confidential Manual which gives in detail the complete operations of a Gaston's Ice Cream Shop. Gaston's available at all times to the franchisee to offer assistance in any problems the franchisee may have.

THE HEADQUARTERS COMPANIES
120 Montgomery Street
San Francisco, California 94104
Michael D. London, President

Description of Operation: Leases Executive Offices with complete support services. Offices and support services available to both full time users and occasional users. Each client receives, in addition to use of office, a receptionist, telephone answering, secretarial, word processing, office supplies and an array of other support services such as radio paging, facsimile transmission, electronic document distribution, telex, conference rooms, furniture rental, printing, direct mail and more. The various services are made available to the business community in general, not only those using the office space, so that the office center functions as a business support service bureau for the entire city in which it is located. Company officials stress that the array of support services will continue to change as the new office technology unfolds in the future. The overall concept envisions franchised locations in both major and minor business cities across the country linked together in a communications network of office centers providing support services to the business community.
Number of Franchisees: 24 in 7 states
In Business Since: 1967, franchising since October 1978
Equity Capital Needed: An initial investment of approximately $50,000 in cash to open (which includes $12,500 franchise fee and $4,000 opening training and education fee). In addition franchisees are required to have access to at least $30,000 in working capital. Also required is the financial capacity to finance between $60,000 and $120,000 for furniture, fixtures, equipment and leasehold improvements.
Financial Assistance Available: Assistance is available only in arranging financing.
Training Provided: 3 weeks in classroom environment at training and development center in San Francisco corporate offices to teach business methods, systems, policies and procedures, sales and management techniques using state of the art systems and technology. Pre-opening guide, sales and marketing manuals, forms manuals, operations manual and accounting system are included. In addition subsequent periodic training is provided in new product developments, new marketing techniques and developing technology.

Managerial Assistance Available: Site selection, lease negotiation, pre-opening planning to include architectural assistance in design and space planning, equipment, furniture, fixtures, and supplies ordering and coordination of leasehold buildout. After training, and prior to opening, marketing and administrative advisor teams assist in training staff on site and establishing marketing strategies tailored to the specific business community. After becoming operational the marketing and administrative advisors assist in developing profitable strategies for the ongoing development of the center by regularly scheduled visits in the field. In addition, national advertising programs are supplemented by regional and local advertising and public relations programs developed and maintained by the franchisor working with each franchisee for the local market. Additionally, accounting support and management reports such as Business Evaluation Analysis are provided monthly through use of the franchisors data processing capability. Field advisors and national staff provide on-site assistance to solve problems and assist the center owner in moving forward in a profitable direction. Franchisee advisory committees, monthly newsletters, bi-weekly updates, corporate identity program, and national meetings round out the communications and management assistance provided for by The Headquarters Companies.

LABOR WORLD, INC.
2814 North Kedzie Avenue
Chicago, Illinois 60618
Alan E. Schubert, President

Description of Operation: Supply temporary labor to industry.
Number of Franchisees: 3 in Illinois
Equity Capital Needed: 1974
Financial Assistance Available: $75,000
Financial Assistance Available: None
Training Provided: At least 2 weeks at home office and 2 weeks in franchisee's city.
Managerial Assistance Available: Furnish sales aids and management assistance for as long as franchise contract exists.

TROPICAL RENT-A-CAR
4131 North 24th Street, Suite 101
Phoenix, Arizona 85016
M. P. Brown, Vice President

Description of Operation: Based on Honolulu, Hawaii. Started in 1969 with 4 cars, and peaked at more than 3,000 cars ten years later. Now expanding nationally.
Number of Franchisees: 5, including company-owned in Hawaii, Washington and Arizona
In Business Since: 1969
Equity Capital Needed: Varied according to size of operation. Offering franchises to *new car dealers, existing rental operators,* and (*inventors . . . only* if they buy out a profitable existing operation). A potential licensee should compare the Tropical program with all others, before signing with any system.
Financial Assistance Available: None
Training Provided: Continuous consultation and advice to assist in running all aspects of a car rental business.
Managerial Assistance Available: No charge for assistance, though licensee pays for telephone calls to seek advice in operating his location. No charge for mailed information. We advise in all operational, sales and marketing areas in detail.

MASTER-KLEEN
DYNAMIC MACHINERY CORPORATION
12350 South Belcher Road
Largo, Florida 33543
Jon D. Willeke, Vice President

Description of Operation: Dynamic Machinery Corporation designs and manufactures nationally advertised M/K MASTER-KLEEN high pressure washing systems. MASTER-KLEEN systems provide low maintenance and high performance to clean exterior of homes, building, truck fleets, etc., to include residential, commercial and industrial cleaning needs.

Number of Franchisees: 237 in 18 states
In Business Since: 1972
Equity Capital Needed: $4,000
Financial Assistance Available: Limited
Training Provided: Comprehensive 3-day training consisting of field training in cleaning, marketing of services, and equipment maintenance, and repair.
Managerial Assistance Available: Dynamic Machinery Corp., provides assistance on a continual basis through telephone communication with dealers; periodic bulletins regarding new products and problem solving. Periodic visits to franchise locations. Optional additional training is handled in classroom every 2 weeks. In some cases established business is turned over to new franchisee in areas assigned to them.

CARMEN'S INC.
17580 Frazho Street
Roseville, Michigan 48066
Frank Sgroi, Vice President

Description of Operation: Carmen's is in the business of operating and franchising restaurants featuring Carmen's Italian style foods and Carmen's Pizza using the name Carmen's, Carmen's Restaurant, Carmen's Party Store, etc.
Number of Franchisees: 22 in Michigan and Tennessee
In Business Since: 1959 and began franchising in 1969
Equity Capital Needed: $10,700 initial franchise fee for a Party Store and $15,000 initial franchise fee for a Family Restaurant Disco.
Training Provided: Carmen's Inc. will assist franchisee in arranging needed financial assistance.
Managerial Assistance Available: Carmen's will provide 4 weeks on-the-job training that will cover every phase of operation. Plus 2 weeks in franchisee's own outlet with experienced Carmen's personnel.
Managerial Assistance Available: Carmen's Inc., provides continual supervision for the life of the franchise. Manuals of operation, and directions are provided. Company makes available promotional advertising material plus field representation, consultation and assistance.

S & D INC.
PHOTOGRAPHIC INVENTORY
P. O. Box 4046
Morgantown, West Virginia 26505
James Earl Smith, President

Description of Operation: Photographic Inventory specializes in providing photo-documentation of personal and industrial inventory and commercial and legal photographic documentation. This service is being provided nationally by a system of independent franchisees supported by the corporate headquarters.
Number of Franchisees: 49 in 22 states
In Business Since: 1977
Equity Capital Needed: $2,000 plus cost of camera equipment.
Financial Assistance Available: None
Training Provided: Continuous; in the form of Work Books, verbal counseling, and training seminars.
Managerial Assistance Available: Continuous; same as above.

SUNBURST INTERNATIONAL, INC.
1977 Section Road
Cincinnati, Ohio 45237

Description of Operation: Sunburst offers exciting opportunities for the establishment of sun tan centers utilizing unique tanning equipment, products and promotion methods. Can be operated by absentee owner.
Number of Franchisees: 85 in 17 states
In Business Since: 1979
Equity Capital Needed: $18,000 and up depending on outlet.
Financial Assistance Available: None
Training Provided: Initial on site training of manager, operational and sales persons.
Managerial Assistance Available: On-going assistance provided.

INDEX OF FRANCHISING COMPANIES

BY CATEGORY

Automotive Products/Services

AAMCO Transmissions, Inc. 1
ABC Mobile Brake 1
ABT Service Centers 1
Acc-U-Tune 1
Aid Auto Stores, Inc. 1
ATV-Auto, Truck and Van, Inc. 1
Auto Oil Changers 1
Bernardi Bros., Inc. 1
Bou-Faro Company 2
Brake & Alignment Supply Corp., Inc. 2
Car Doctor Int'l. Marketing, Inc. 2
Car-Matic Systems, Inc. 2
Car-X Service Systems, Inc. 2
Cook Machinery Company 2
Cottman Transmission Systems, Inc. 2
Delk Transmission Franchise, Inc. 2
Detroit II Auto Dealership 104
Detroit II Auto Service Centers 104
Diamond Quality Transmissions Centers of America, Inc. 2
Drive Line Service, Inc. 2
Dr. Nick's Transmissions, Inc. 3
East Coast Radiator Franchises, Inc. 3
Econo Lube N'Tune, Inc. 3
Endrust 3
E.P.I. Inc. 3
The Firestone Tire & Rubber Company 3
5 Minute Oil Change, Inc. 3
Frank's Muffler Shops 3
General Rust Proofing Inc. 4
Gibraltar Transmissions 4
B. F. Goodrich Company 4
The Goodyear Tire & Rubber Company 4
Grease Lighting, Inc. 4
Grease Monkey International, Inc. 4
Great Bear Automotive Centers, Inc. 4
Hercules Car/Truck Rustproofing 4
Insta-Tune, Inc. 4
Interstate Automatic Transmissions Co., Inc. 4
Jiffiwash, Inc. 5
Jiffy Lube International, Inc. 5
Kinetic Energy Manufacturing Company 5
King Bear Enterprises, Inc. 5
Lee Myles Associates Corporation 5
MAACO Enterprises, Inc. 5
MacCleen's Car Wash 5
Mad Hatter Mufflers of Florida, Inc. 5
Malco Products, Inc. 6
Mechanical Man Car Wash Factory, Inc. 6
Meineke Discount Muffler Shops, Inc. 6
Midas International Corp. 6
Minit-Lube 6
Miracle Auto Painting 6
Mr. Transmission, Inc. 6
Nagcoglass 6
National Automotive Services Associates 6
National Auto Service Centers, Inc. 7
NTW, Inc. 7
OTASCO 7
Parts, Inc. 7
Penn Jersey Auto Stores, Inc. 7
Perma-Shine Inc. 7
Poly-Oleum Corporation 7
Power Vac Incorporated 7
Power Wash, Inc. 8
Precision Transmission, Inc. 8
Precision Tune, Inc. 8
Rochemco 8
Scotti Muffler Centers, Inc. 8
Seasonall Automotive, Inc. 8
Service Center 8
Sir Waxer, Incorporated 8
Speedi-Lube, Inc. 8
Speedy Transmission Centers, Inc. 9
Stop A Flat-Chalfont Industries 9
Thrift-Way Auto Centers, Inc. 9
Tidy Car Inc. 9
Tuff-Kote Dinol, Inc. 9
Tuffy Service Centers, Inc. 9
Tune-Up Clinic, Inc. 9
The Tune-Up Man, Inc. 9
Tunex, Inc. 10
Ultra Tune, Inc. 10

Valley Forge Products Company 10
Western Auto 10
Whites Home and Auto Stores 10
Xpert Tune Franchise Group, Inc. 10
Ziebart Rustproofing Company 10

Auto/Trailer Rentals

Ajax Rent A Car Company 10
American International Rent-A-Car 10
Budget Rent A Car Corporation 11
Compacts Only Rent A Car System, Inc. 11
Dollar Rent A Car Systems, Inc. 11
Econo-Car International, Inc. 11
Hertz System, Inc. 11
Holiday Rent-A-Car System 11
National Car Rental System, Inc. 11
Payless Car Rental System, Inc. 11
Thrifty Rent-A-Car System 11
Tropical Rent-A-Car 105

Beauty Salons/Supplies

Edie Adams Cut & Curl 12
The Barbers, Hairstyling for Men and Women, Inc. 12
Command Performance 12
Great Expectations Precision Haircutters 12
Hair Performers 12
Kenneth of London, Ltd. 12
Magic Mirror, Inc. 12
Roffler Industries, Inc. 12
S.M.R. Enterprises, Inc. 12

Business Aids/Services

Allied Business Brokers, Inc. 103
American Advertising Distributors, Inc. 13
American Dynamics Corp. 13
American Facilities Inspection, Inc. 13
Associated Tax Consultants of America 13
Audit Controls, Inc. 13
Barter Systems, Inc. 104
Best Resume Service 13
Binex-Automated Business Systems, Inc. 13
H & R Block, Inc. 13
Business Brokerage Group 14
Business Consultants of America 14
Business Data Services, Inc. 14
Business Exchange, Inc. 14
Commercial Services Company 14
Comprehensive Accounting Services Corporation 14
Comprehensive Business Services Corp. 14
Computer Servicecenters, Inc. 15
Contacts Influential 15
Corporate Finance Associates 15
Creative Prospects, Inc. 15
Credit Service Company 15
Critical Factor Systems, Incorporated 15
Dixon Commercial Investigators, Inc. 15
J. P. Dolan Associates & Company 15
EconoTax, Inc. 15
The Epicurean Dinner Club 15
General Business Services, Inc. 16
Getting To Know You International, Ltd. 16
The Headquarters Companies 104
Housemaster of America, Inc. 16
Incotax Systems, Inc. 16
Marcoin, Inc. 16
Medi-Fax, Inc. 16
Muzak Corporation 16
NADW Marketing, Inc. 16
National Computerized Control, Inc. 17
National Diversified Brokers 17
National Fire Repair, Inc. 17

106

INDEX OF FRANCHISING COMPANIES, "By Category"

National Homeowners Service Association, Inc. 17
National Housing Inspections 17
Nationwide Income Tax Service Co. 17
Newcomers Service International, Inc. 17
OnTop Division (Seaman Nuclear Corporation) 18
Profitpower International 18
Reliable Business Systems, Inc. 18
RFG, Inc. 18
S & D Inc., Photographic Inventory 105
Safeguard Business Systems 18
Sandy Hook Scientific Inc. 18
Simplified Business Services, Inc. 18
SMI International, Inc. 18
Southwest Promotional Corporation 18
Systemedics, Inc. 18
Tax Man, Inc. 19
Tax Offices of America 19
Telecheck Services, Inc. 19
Tel-Life Stations of America 19
TV Facts 19
T.V. Tempo, Inc. 19
VR Business Brokers, Inc. 19
Whitehill Systems 20
Edwin K. Williams & Co. 20

Campgrounds
Jellystone Campgrounds 20
Kamp Dakota, Inc. 20
Kampgrounds of America, Inc. 20
Safari Campgrounds 20

Children's Stores/Furniture/Products
Baby-Tenda Corporation 20

Clothing/Shoes
Athlete's Foot Marketing Associates, Inc. 21
Fleet Feet 21
Formal Wear Service 21
Forty Love Tennis Shoppe, Inc. 21
Gingiss International, Inc. 21
Heel 'N Toe, Inc. 21
Jilene, Inc. 21
Just Pants 21
Knapp Shoe Company 22
Lady Madonna Management Corp. 22
Mode O'Day Company 22
Modern Bridal Shoppes, Inc. 22
Pauline's Sportswear, Inc. 22
Sally Wallace Brides Shope, Inc. 22
Shirt Tales, Ltd. 22
Wild Tops Franchising, Inc. 22
Wrangler Wranch Franchising Systems, Inc. 22

Construction/Remodeling-Materials/Services
Cathedralite Domes 104
Davis Caves, Inc. 23
Dicker Stack-Sack International 23
Duradek Permanent Sundecks 23
Easi-Set Industries 23
Eldorado Stone Corporation 23
General Energy Devices, Inc. 23
K-Krete, Inc. 23
Lavastone International, Inc. 23
Marble-Crete Products, Inc. 23
Marble-Flow Industries, Inc. 23
Masonry Systems International, Inc. 24
Mill-Craft Housing Corporation 24
New England Log Homes, Inc. 24
Paul W. Davis Systems, Inc. 24
Perma-Jack Co. 24
Perma-Stone Company 24
The Permentry Company 24
Poraflor, Inc. 24
Porcelain Patch & Glaze Company of America 24
Porcelite International, Inc. 24
Pour Man Systems 24
Rapid Economical Construction Systems Corp. (R.E.C.S.) 25
Redi-Strip Co., Inc. 25
Speed Fab-Crete Corporation International 25
Zell-Aire Corporation 25

Cosmetics/Toiletries
Christine Valmy, Inc. 25
Color Me Beautiful Cosmetics 25
Fashion Two Twenty, Inc. 25
i Natural Cosmetics 25
Judith Sans International, Inc. 26
Lady Burd Exclusive Cosmetics, Inc. 26
Syd Simons Cosmetics, Inc. 26

Drug Stores
Le$-On Retail Systems, Inc. 26
Medicine Shoppes International, Inc. 26

Educational Products/Services
Allstate Contractors Schools 26
Allstate Real Estate License School 26
Anthony Schools 26
Audio Visual Educational Systems 26
Barbizon Schools of Modeling 27
Butler Learning Systems 27
Child Enrichment Centers 27
Dootson Driving Schools 27
Evelyn Wood Reading Dynamics 27
Image Improvement, Inc. 27
Institute of Reading Development 27
International Travel Training Courses, Inc. 27
John Robert Powers Finishing & Modeling School 28
Leisure Learning Centers, Inc. 28
Management Institute 28
Mary Moppets Day Care School, Inc. 28
Masters' Driving Academy, Inc. 28
Mind Power, Inc. 28
Music Dynamics 28
Nadeau Looms, Inc. 28
Patricia Stevens International, Inc. 28
R.E.A.D.S., Inc. 28
Robert Fiance Systems, Inc. 29
Teller Training Institutes, Inc. 29
Up-Grade Educational Services, Inc. 29

Employment Services
AAA Employment Franchise, Inc. 29
Acme Personnel Service 29
Adia Temporary Services, Inc. 29
Bailey Employment System, Inc. 30
Baker & Baker Employment Service, Inc. 30
Bryant Bureau 30
Business & Professional Consultants, Inc. 30
Career Concepts, Inc. 30
Delta Group, Inc. 30
Dr. Personnel, Inc. 30
Dunhill Personnel System, Inc. 30
Ells Personnel Systems, Inc. 31
Employers Overload Company 31
Engineering Corporation of America 31
F-O-R-T-U-N-E Franchise Corporation 31
Gerotoga Industries, Inc. 31
Gilbert Lane Personnel Service 31
Harper Associates, Inc. 31
Hartman Temporary Personnel 31
Hazel & Jarvis 32
Heritage Personnel Systems, Inc. 32
Kogen Personnel, Inc. 32
Labor World, Inc. 105
Management Recruiters International, Inc. 32
Management Search, Inc. 32

INDEX OF FRANCHISING COMPANIES, "By Category"

Manpower, Inc. 32
Marsetta Lane Temp-Services 32
Norrell Temporary Services, Inc. 33
The Olsten Corporation 33
Parker Page Associates, Inc. 33
Personnel Pool of America, Inc. 33
Place Mart Franchising Corporation 33
Remedy Temporary Services, Inc. 33
Retail Recruiters International, Inc. 33
Ritta Personnel System of North America, Inc. 33
Romac and Associates, Inc. 33
Roth Young Personnel Service, Inc. 34
Sales Consultants International 34
Sanford Rose Associates, Inc. 34
SARCO, Inc. 34
S-H-S International 34
Snelling and Snelling, Inc. 34
Staff Builders Int'l., Inc. 34
Temporaries, Incorporated 34
Temporarily Yours of America 35
Uniforce Temporary Personnel, Inc. 35
VIP Personnel Systems 35

Equipment/Rentals
Apparelmaster, Inc. 35
Nation-Wide General Rental Centers, Inc. 35
Showertel Systems Corporation, Inc. 35
Taylor Rental Corporation 36
Typing Tigers 36
United Rent-All, Inc. 36

Foods—Donuts
Bite Size Meals, Inc. 36
Country Style Donuts, Incorporated 36
Donutland, Inc. 36
Dunkin' Donuts of America, Inc. 36
Mister Donut of America, Inc. 37
Southern Maid Donut Flour Company, Inc. 37
Spudnuts, Inc. 37
Tastee Donuts, Inc. 37

Foods—
Grocery/Specialty/Stores
Augie's Inc. 37
The Big Cheese, Inc. 37
Cheese Shop International, Inc. 37
Chipper Cookie Shops, Inc. 37
The Circle K Corporation 38
Convenient Food Mart, Inc. 38
Cookie Factory of America 38
Edgemar Farms 38
Eurobake Cie, Inc. 38
For Goodness Sake Franchise 38
The Glass Oven Baking Company, Inc. 38
Grove Foods, Inc. 39
Hickory Farms of Ohio, Inc. 39
Hungry Boy Delicatessen, Inc. 39
ISCO Ltd. 39
Jitney-Jungle, Inc. 39
Li'L Shopper, Inc. 39
Litva Corp. 39
Mr. Dunderbak, Inc. 39
New Morning Natural Foods 39
O.P.F.M. Corp. 40
Quick Shop Minit Marts, Inc. 40
Quik Stop Markets, Inc. 40
Sneaky Sweets International, Inc. 40
The Southland Corporation 40
Stewart Sandwiches International, Inc. 40
Sunnydale Franchise System, Inc. 40
Swiss Colony Stores, Inc. 40
Telecake International 40
Tiffany's Bakeries, Inc. 41
Westgate Systems, Inc. 41
White Hen Pantry Division 41

Foods—
Ice Cream/Yogurt/Candy/Popcorn/Beverages
Auman Equipment Company 41
Barnhill Franchise Corporation 41
Baskin-Robbins, Inc. 41
Blum's of San Francisco, Inc. 41
Bresler's 33 Flavors, Inc. 42
Carter's Nuts, Inc. 42
Carvel Corporation 42
The Coffee Merchant 42
Coffee, Tea & Thee, Inc. 104
Dairy Isle Corporation 42
Ernie's Wine & Liquor Corp. 42
Gaston's Inc. 104
Intercontinental Coffee Service, Inc. 42
Karmelkorn Shoppes, Inc. 42
Lone Star Candy Mfg. Co. of Texas, Inc. 42
Main Street Original Ice Cream Parlors 43
Mister Softee, Inc. 43
Mom's Development Corporation 43
Nationwide Gourmets, Inc. 43
Old Uncle Gaylord's, Inc. 43
The Peanut Shack of America, Inc. 43
Polar Bear Ice Cream Co. 43
Real Rich Corp. 43
Seakan Candy Company 43
Swensen's Ice Cream Company 44
Swift Company 44
Topsy Shoppes, Inc. 44
Zack's Famous Frozen Yogurt 44
Zip'Z 44

Foods—
Pancake/Waffle/Pretzel
Flapjack Canyon 44
General Franchising Corporation 44
H.L.H. Enterprises, Inc. 45
International House of Pancakes 45
Mary Belle Restaurants 45
Perkins Cake & Steak Restaurants 45
Uncle John's Family Restaurants 45
Van's Belgian Crepes and Waffles, Inc. 45
Village Inn Pancake House, Inc. 45
Waffle King of America, Inc. 45

Foods—
Restaurants/Drive-Ins/Carry-Outs
A & W Restaurants, Inc. 45
Across The Street Restaurants of America, Inc. 45
The All America Burger, Inc. 46
Anchor Inn Restaurants 46
Angelina's Pizza, Inc. 46
Angelo's Italian Restaurants of Illinois, Inc. 46
Arby's, Inc. 46
Arman's Systems, Inc. 46
Arthur Treacher's Fish & Chips, Inc. 46
Aunt Chilotta Systems, Inc. 46
Bagel Nosh, Inc. 46
Barnaby's Family Inns, Inc. 47
Barone's 47
Beef & Brew Franchise Co., Inc. 47
Beef Corral Rest., Inc. 47
Big Ben's International Inc. 47
Big Daddy's Restaurants 47
Big T Family Restaurant Systems 47
Big Top Delis 47
Black Angus Systems, Inc. 47
Blimpie Industries, Ltd. 47
Bonanza International, Inc. 48
Bowincal International, Inc. 48
Boy Blue Stores, Inc. 48
Boz Hot Dogs 48
BQF Steakhouses 48
Browns Chicken 48
Bun N Burger International, Inc. 48
Burger Chef Systems, Inc. 48
Burger Inns 48
Burger King Corporation 48

INDEX OF FRANCHISING COMPANIES, "By Category"

Burger Queen Enterprises, Inc. 49
Burger Train System, Inc. 49
Captain D's 49
Carmen's Inc. 105
Casey Jones Junction, Inc. 49
Cassano's Inc. 49
Charlie Chan Restaurants 49
Chelsea Street Pub 49
Chicasea, Inc. 49
Chicken Champ 50
Chicken Delight 50
Chicken Mary's System, Inc. 50
Chicken Unlimited Enterprise, Inc. 50
Chip's Hamburgers 50
Chuck Connors Chuck Wagon Division 50
Cindy's, Inc. 50
Circles International Natural Foods, Inc. 50
Clark's Submarine Sandwiches, Inc. 51
Colonel Lee's Enterprises, Inc. 51
Cookshack 51
Country Breadboard, Inc. 51
Country Kitchen International, Inc. 51
Cozzoli's Restaurant-Pizzeria 51
Dairy Cheer Stores 51
Dairy King Distributors 51
Dairy Sweet Company 51
Danbi's Inc. 51
Danver's International, Inc. 52
Der Wienerschnitzel International, Inc. 52
Dino's Pizza 52
Dog N Suds Restaurants 52
Domino's Pizza, Inc. 52
Double Dee Restaurants, Inc. 52
Drummer Boy Fried Chicken 52
El Taco Restaurants, Inc. 52
Famous Recipe Fried Chicken, Inc. 52
Farrell's Ice Cream Parlours Restaurant 53
Fast Foods, Inc. 53
Fat Boy's Franchise Systems, Inc. 53
Forty Carrots, Inc. 53
Fosters Freeze, Inc. 53
Franciscan West Industries 53
Frostop Corporation 53
George Webb Corporation 53
Golden Chicken Franchises 53
Golden Skillet Companies 54
The Goode Taste Crepe Shoppes, Inc. 54
Grandma Lee's International Holdings Limited 54
Greek's Pizzeria, Inc. 54
Greiners Subhops, Inc. 54
Grizzly Bear, Inc. 54
Hamburgers By Gourmet Licensing Corporation 54
Happy Joe's Pizza & Ice Cream Parlors 54
The Happy Steak, Inc. 55
Harbor House, Inc. 55
Hardee's Food Systems, Inc. 55
Hartz Krispy Chicken 55
Howard Johnson Company 55
Huddle House, Inc. 55
Hungry Hero Systems, Inc. 55
The Hush Puppy Corporation 55
International Blimpie Corporation 55
International Char Broiler, Inc. 55
International Dairy Queen, Inc. 56
The Italian U-Boat, Inc. 56
Italo's Pizza Shop, Inc. 56
Jake's International, Inc. 56
Japanese Steak Houses, Inc. 56
Jerry's Restaurants 56
Jiffy Joints, Inc. 56
Jiffy Shoppes 56
Jreck Subs, Inc. 57
Judy's Foods, Inc. 57
Kenney's Franchise Corp. 57
Ken's Pizza Parlors, Inc. 57
KFC Corporation 57
LaRosa's, Inc. 57
Lil' Duffer of America, Inc. 57
Little Big Men, Inc. 57
Little Caesar Enterprises, Inc. 57
Littlefield's Restaurant Corp. 57
The Little King 58
London Fish N' Chips, Ltd. 58
Long John Silver's Inc. 58
Lordburger Systems, Inc. 58
Losurdo Foods, Inc. 58
Love's Wood Pit Barbeque Restaurants 58
Lum's Restaurant Corporation 58
Maid Rite Products, Inc. 58
Mamacita's International, Inc. 58
Martin's Franchising Systems, Inc. 59
McDonald's Corporation 59
Metro Sandwich Shops of America, Inc. 59
Minute Man of America, Inc. 59
Mister S'Getti Restaurant 59
Mom 'N' Pop's Ham House, Inc. 59
Mom's Pizza, Inc. 59
Mr. Gatti's, Inc. 59
Mr. Hero Sandwich Systems, Inc. 60
Mr. Pizza, Inc. 60
Mr. Steak, Inc. 60
"My Apartment" International, Inc. 60
My Pie International, Inc. 60
Nathan's Famous, Inc. 60
Nickerson Farms Franchising Company 60
Noble Roman's Inc. 60
Nugget Restaurants, Inc. 60
The Onion Crock, Inc. 60
Orange Julius of America 61
Pacific Tastee Freez, Inc. 61
Pappy's Enterpises, Inc. 61
Pasquale Food Company, Inc. 61
Patsy's Pizza Franchise, Inc. 61
The Peddler, Inc. 61
Pedro's Fine Mexican Foods, Inc. 61
Pepe's Incorporated 61
The Pewter Mug 61
Pewter Pot Management Corporation of Massachusetts 61
Philly Mignon 61
Pietro's Pizza Parlors, Inc. 62
Pioneer Take Out Corporation 62
The Pizza Inn, Inc. 62
Pizza Man "He Delivers" 62
Pizza Time Theatre, Inc. 62
Playboy Clubs International, Inc. 62
Polock Johnny's, Inc. 62
Ponderosa System, Inc. 62
Popeyes Famous Fried Chicken, Inc. 63
Pudgies Pizza Franchising, Inc. 63
Rax Systems, Inc. 63
Reaban's Inc. 63
Roast Beefery Restaurants International, Inc. 63
Ron's Krispy Fried Chicken 63
Rosati Franchise Systems, Inc. 63
The Round Table Franchise Corporation 63
Roy Rogers Restaurants 64
The Salad Bar Corporation 64
Salad Shoppe 64
Sandwich Giants, Inc. 64
Schlotzsky's, Inc. 64
Scotto Pizza Management Corp. 64
Shakey's Incorporated 64
Sir Beef Ltd., Inc. 64
Sir Pizza International, Inc. 64
Sizzler Family Steak Houses 64
Stewart's Drive-Ins 65
The Straw Hat Restaurant Corporation 65
Stuckey's Inc. 65
Subway 65
Taco Casa International, Ltd. 65
Taco Del Sol 65
Taco Hut, Inc. 65
Taco John's 65
The Taco Maker, Inc. 66
Taco Place, Inc. 66
Taco Plaza, Inc. 66
Taco Time International, Inc. 66
Taco Villa 66
Terry's Interstate, Inc. 66
Texas Cattle Company 66
Texas Tom's Inc. 66
Tippy's Taco House, Inc. 66
The Upper Krust, Inc. 67
Walt's Roast Beef International 67
Wendy's Old Fashioned Hamburgers 67
Whataburger, Inc. 67
Wiener King Corporation 67
Wife Saver 67
Winkys Family Restaurant 67
Woody's Little Italy Restaurants 67
The World's Wurst Restaurants 67
WUV's International, Inc. 67
Yankee Doodle Dandy 68
Your Pizza Shops, Inc. 68
Zantiago Mexican-American Restaurants 68

109

INDEX OF FRANCHISING COMPANIES, "By Category"

General Merchandising Stores
Ben Franklin 68
Coast to Coast Stores 68
Gamble-Skogmo, Inc. 68
Montgomery Ward 68
Rasco Stores 69

Health Aids/Services
Alpha Nurses 69
Diet Control Centers, Inc. 69
Elaine Powers Figure Salons, Inc. 69
Fat Fighters, Inc. 69
Gloria Stevens Franchise Division 69
Health Clubs of America 69
Helpmates Nursing Serices, Inc. 69
Lean Line, Inc. 70
Lynn Stevens, Inc. 70
MacLevy Products Corporation 70
Medipower 70
Nutri-System 70
Our Weigh 70
People Care Incorporated 70
Quality Care USA, Inc. 70
Space Age Fitness Centers 71
SPA Development Corporation 71
Staff Builders Medical Services 71
Venus de Milo, Inc. of California 71
Weight Control Institute 71

Hearing Aids
RCI, Inc. 71

Home Furnishings/Furniture-Retail/Repair/Services
Abbey Carpet Company 71
Amity, Inc. 71
Best Bros., Inc. 72
Carpet Color Systems 72
Carpeteria, Inc. 72
Carpet-Genie Systems, Inc. 72
Castro Convertibles 72
Chem-Clean Furniture Restoration Center 72
Chem-Dry Carpet Cleaning 72
Chrome Concepts, Inc. 72
Cleanmark Corporation 72
Crossland Furniture Restoration Studios 73
Decorating Den Systems, Inc. 73
Delhi Chemicals, Inc. 73
Dip 'N Strip, Inc. 73
Dri-Cal's Ultra Carpet Care Service, Inc. 73
Duraclean International 73
G. Fried Carpetland, Incorporated 73
Guarantee Carpet Cleaning & Dye Co. 73
"Jack The Stripper" 74
John Simmons, Inc. 74
Lee's Bars, Stools 'N Dinettes 74
Maintenance King 74
Naked Furniture, Inc. 74
Nettle Creek Industries, Inc. 74
Riviera Convertibles, Inc. 74
Rug Crafters 74
Siesta Sleep Shop, Inc. 75
Slumberland, Inc. 75
Spring Crest Company 75
Stanley Steemer International, Inc. 75
Steamatic Incorporated 75
Strip-Tech, Inc. 75
The Wood Factory Corporation 75

Laundries, Dry Cleaning-Services
A Cleaner World 75
Aldclean On Premise Systems, Inc. 75

Bruck Distributing Co., Inc. 76
Coit Drapery & Carpet Cleaners, Inc. 76
Cook Machinery Company 76
Dutch Girl Continental Cleaners 76
London Equipment Company 76
Martin Franchises Inc. 76
Speed Queen Coin Operated Laundromat and Dry Cleaner, Inc. 76

Lawn and Garden Supplies/Services
Lawn-A-Mat Chemical and Equipment Corporation 76
Lawn Doctor Incorporated 76
Lawn King, Inc. 76
Lawn Medic Inc. 77
Liqui-Green Lawn Care Corporation 77
Spring-Green Lawn Care Corp. 77
Superlawns, Inc. 77

Maintenance/Cleaning/Sanitation-Services/Supplies
Americlean National Service Corporation 77
Cheman Manufacturing Corp. 77
Chemical Franchising Corporation 77
Chem-Mark International, Inc. 77
Master Kleen 105
Mr. Maintenance 78
Mr. Rooter Corporation 78
National Chemicals and Services, Inc. 78
National Maintenance Contractors, Inc. 78
Pop-Ins, Inc. 78
Port-O-Let Company, Inc. 78
Roto-Rooter Corporation 78
Sermac 78
Servicemaster Industries, Inc. 79
Servpro Industries, Inc. 79
Sparkle Wash, Inc. 79
Sunrise Maintenance Systems 79
Ultrasonic Predictable Maintenance, Inc. 79
U.S. Rooter Corporation 79

Motels, Hotels
Admiral Benbow Inns, Inc. 79
Coachlight Inns 79
Days Inns of America, Inc. 79
The Downtowner/Rowntowner-Passport System 80
Econo-Travel Motor Hotel Corp. 80
Family Inns of America, Inc. 80
Happy Inns of America, Inc. 80
Holiday Inns, Inc. 80
HomeTels of America, Inc. 80
Howard Johnson's Motor Lodge 80
Quality Inns International, Inc. 80
Ramada Inns, Inc. 80
Red Carpet Inns of America, Inc. 80
Rodeway Inns International, Inc. 80
Sheraton Inns, Inc. 81
Super 8 Motels 81
Thrifty Scot Motels, Inc. 81
Travelodge International, Inc. 81
Treadway Inns Corporation 81

Paint and Decorating Supplies
Davis Paint Company 81

Pet Shops
Docktor Pet Center, Inc. 81
Flying Fur Pet Travel Service 81
Pedigree Pet Centers 81
Petland, Inc. 81
Pet Master, Inc. 81

INDEX OF FRANCHISING COMPANIES, "By Category"

Printing
Alpha Graphics Inc.	82
Big Red Q Quickprint Centers	82
Insty-Prints, Inc.	82
Kwik-Kopy Corporation	82
Minuteman Press International, Inc.	82
(PIP) Postal Instant Press	83
The Printing Place, Inc.	83
The Printing Supermart, Inc.	83
Printmasters, Inc.	83
Quik Print, Inc.	83
Sir Speedy, Inc.	83
Speedy Printing Centers, Inc.	83

Real Estate
Action Brokers Corporation	84
Better Homes Realty	84
Century 21 Real Estate Corporation	84
Earl Keim Realty, Inc.	84
Electronic Realty Associates, Inc.	84
Embassy Rental Agency	84
Execu-System	84
50 States Real Estate, Inc.	84
Gallery of Homes, Incorporated	85
Government Employees Real Estate of America, Inc.	85
Help-U-Sell, Inc.	85
Herbert Hawkins Realtors, Inc.	85
Home Sellers Center, Inc.	85
The Home Team, Inc.	85
International Real Estate Network, Inc.	85
Land Mart of America, Inc.	85
New World Real-Estate Inc.	85
Partners Real Estate, Inc.	86
Ram, Inc., Realtors	86
Real Estate One Licensing Company	86
Realty Company of America	86
Realty 1, Inc.	86
Realty USA/Interstate Referral Service, Inc.	86
Realty World Corporation	86
Red Carpet Corporation of America	86
Re/Max of America, Inc.	87
Security Pacific Real Estate, Inc.	87
Ski & Shore Properties, Inc.	87
State Farm Realty, Inc.	87
State Wide Real Estate	87
The Sterling Thompson Group	87
3% Realty, Inc.	87
United Security Associates Realty, Inc.	87

Recreation/Entertainment/Travel-Services/Supplies
American Safari Corporation	88
Batting Range Pro	88
Captran Franchise Corp.	88
Chance Manufacturing Co., Inc.	88
Corner Pockets of America, Inc.	88
Court Management Company, Inc.	88
Disco Factory	88
Empress Travel Franchise Corporation	88
Fugazy Travel Franchises, Ltd.	88
Funny Fun Fun Golf	89
Fun Services, Inc.	89
Go-Kart Track Systems	89
Golf Players, Inc.	89
Lomma Enterprises, Inc.	89
LST Travel, Inc.	89
Miss American Teen-Ager, Inc.	89
Putt-Putt Golf Courses of America, Inc.	89
Putt-R-Golf, Inc.	89
Slo Poke, Inc.	89
Tour Mates Organization, Ltd.	90
Travel Network Corporation	90
2001 Clubs of America, Inc.	90
Yogi Bear's Mini Golf and Snack Shoppe	90

Retailing—Not Elsewhere Classified
Aluma Art Designs	90
American Handicrafts-Merribee Needlearts	90
American Vision Centers, Inc.	90
Athletic Attic Marketing, Inc.	90
Bathtique International Ltd.	91
The Book Rack-Thousands	91
Budget Tapes & Records, Inc.	91
Buning The Florist, Inc.	91
Byte Industries, Inc.	91
Candle-Lite Inc.	91
Computerland Corp.	91
Conroy's Inc.	91
Consumer Products of America, Inc.	92
The Electronics Boutique	92
The Energy Shed, Inc.	92
Faux Pas, Inc.	92
Flowerama of America, Inc.	92
Flower World of America, Inc.	92
Frame and Save	92
Frameking Corporation	92
Gallery of Miniatures, Inc.	92
The Grate Fireplace Shoppe	92
The Great Frame Up Systems, Inc.	93
Habersham Plantation Corp.	93
Handy Hardware Centers, Inc.	93
Heroes World Center Inc.	93
Instant Replay, Inc.	93
Kits Cameras Inc.	93
Lafayette Electronics Sales, Inc.	93
Lelly's Drive In Photos, Inc.	93
Little Professor Book Centers, Inc.	94
Midwest Industries, Inc.	94
Miss Bojangles, Inc.	94
Mister Clark's	94
Nelson's Photography Studios	94
Open Book Marketing Corp.	94
The Pearl Fctory	94
Phone World International, Inc.	94
Photo Drive Thru, Inc.	95
Photo Plaza	95
PhotoQuick of America, Inc.	95
Pier 1 Imports, Inc.	95
Radio Shack	95
The Ringgold Corporation	95
Royale Sporting Goods, Inc.	95
Skate Street, Inc.	95
Sound West	95
Speedy Wagon Sale Corporation	95
Sport About, Inc.	96
Sport Shacks, Inc.	96
Team Central Incorporated	96
The Tinder Box International Ltd.	96
T-Shirt Plus, Inc.	96
United Consumers Club	96
Up Against the Wall	96
Video Concepts	96
Whirligig Stores Incorporated	97
Wicks 'N' Sticks, Inc.	97
World of Laminating	97

Security Systems
Counterforce Protection Systems, Inc.	97
Dictograph Security Systems	97
Honor Guard Security Service	97
Rampart Industries, Inc.	97

Soft Drinks/Water-Bottling
Bubble-Up Company	98
Cock 'N Bull, Limited	98
COTT Corporation	98
Dad's Root Beer Company	98
Double-Cola Company	98
Mountain Valley Spring Company	98

111

INDEX OF FRANCHISING COMPANIES, "By Category"

Swimming Pools
California Pools, Inc. ...98
Cascade Industries, Inc. ...98
La Fleur Pool Systems, Inc. ...98
Lifetime Pools, Inc. ...99
San Juan Products, Inc. ...99

Tools, Hardware
Imperial Hammer, Inc. ...99
Mac Tools, Inc. ...99
Snap-On Tools Corporation ...99
Vulcan Tools ...99

Vending
Ford Gum & Machine Co., Inc. ...99

Water Conditioning
Chemical Engineering Corporation ...99
Culligan International Company ...100
Rainsoft Water Conditioning Company ...100
Rayne Corporation ...100
Scientific Water Systems, Inc. ...100
Superior Water Systems, Inc. ...100
Watercare Corporation ...100
Water Purification Systems, Inc. ...100
Water Refining Company ...100

Miscellaneous Wholesale/Service Business
Almost Heaven Hot Tubs ...101
American Heritage Agency, Inc. ...101
The Armology Company ...101
Armstrong Pest Control ...101
Asi Sign Systems Inc. ...101
Badge Man International Ltd. ...101
Bar-Master International ...101
Chem-Tex Hot Tank Products Corporation ...101
Commercial Mobile Services, Inc. ...101
Diversified Arts ...102
Key Korner Systems, Inc. ...102
Machinery Wholesalers Corp. ...102
Meistergram ...102
My Nails, Inc. ...102
Nationwide Exterminating, Inc. ...102
North American Carbide Corp. ...102
Parking Company of America ...102
Redd Pest Control Company, Inc. ...102
Selectra-Date Corporation ...102
Stretch & Sew, Inc. ...103
Sum-Tan Division ...103
Sunburst International Inc. ...105
Suntique Tanning Salons ...103
Tempaco, Inc. ...103
Tepco, Inc. ...103
Terminix International, Inc. ...103
United Air Specialists, Inc. ...103
United Worth Hydrochem Corporation ...103
U.S. Fireworks of America, Inc. ...103

INDEX OF FRANCHISING COMPANIES

ALPHABETICAL LISTING

A

A Cleaner World 75
A & W Restaurants, Inc. 45
AAA Employment Franchise, Inc. 29
AAMCO Transmissions, Inc. 1
Abbey Carpet Company 71
ABC Mobile Brake 1
ABT Service Centers 1
ACC-U-Tune 1
Acme Personnel Service 29
Across The Street Restaurants of America, Inc. 45
Action Brokers Corporation 84
Edie Adams Cut & Curl 12
Adia Temporary Services, Inc. 29
Admiral Benbow Inns, Inc. 79
Aid Auto Stores, Inc. 1
Ajax Rent A Car Company 10
Aldclean On Premise Systems, Inc. 75
The All American Burger, Inc. 46
Allied Business Brokers, Inc. 46
Allstate Contractors Schools 26
Allstate Real Estate License School 26
Almost Heaven Hot Tubs 101
Alpha Graphics, Inc. 82
Alpha Nurses 69
Aluma Art Design 90
American Advertising Distributors, Inc. 13
American Dynamics Corp. 13
American Facilities Inspection, Inc. 13
American Handicrafts-Merribee Needlearts 90
American Heritage Agency, Inc. 101
American International Rent-A-Car 10
American Safari Corporation 88
American Vision Center, Inc. 90
Americlean National Service Company 77
Amity, Inc. 71
Anchor Inn Restaurants 46
Angelina's Pizza, Inc. 46
Angelo's Italian Restaurants of Illinois, Inc. 46
Anthony Schools 26
Apparelmaster, Inc. 35
Arby's, Inc. 46
Arman's Systems, Inc. 46
The Armology Company 101
Armstrong Pest Conttol 101
Arthur Treacher's Fish & Chips, Inc. 46
Asi Sign Systems Inc. 101
Associated Tax Consultants of America 13
Athlete's Foot Marketing Associates, Inc. 21
Athletic Attic Marketing, Inc. 90
ATV-Auto, Truck and Vans, Inc. 1
Audio Visual Educational Systems 26
Audit Controls, Inc. 13
Augie's Inc. 37
Auman Equipment Company 41
Aunt Chilotta Systems, Inc. 46
Auto Oil Changers 1

B

Baby Tenda Corporation 20
The Badge Man International, Ltd. 101
Bagel Nosh, Inc. 46
Bailey Employment System, Inc. 30
Baker & Baker Employment Service, Inc. 30
The Barbers, Hairstyling for Men and Women, Inc. 12
Barbizon Schools of Modeling 27
Bar-Master International 101
Barnaby's Family Inns, Inc. 47

Barnhill Franchise Corporation 41
Barone's 47
Barter Systems, Inc. 104
Baskin-Robbins, Inc. 41
Bathtique International, Inc. 91
Batting Range, Pro 88
Beef & Brew Franchise Co., Inc. 47
Beef Corral Rest., Inc. 47
Ben Franklin 68
Bernardi Bros., Inc. 1
Best Bros. Inc. 72
Best Resume Service 13
Better Homes Realty 84
Big Ben's International, Inc. 47
The Big Cheese, Inc. 37
Big Daddy's Restaurants 47
Big Red Q Quickprint Centers 82
Big T Family Restaurant Systems 47
Big Top Delis 47
Binex-Automated Business Systems, Inc. 13
Bite Size Meals, Inc. 36
Black Angus Systems, Inc. 47
Blimpie Industries, Ltd. 47
H & R Block, Inc. 13
Blum's of San Francisco, Inc. 41
Bonanza International 48
The Book Rack-Thousands 91
Bou-Faro Company 2
Bowincal International, Inc. 48
Boy Blue Stores, Inc. 48
Boz Hot Dogs 48
BQF Steakhouses 48
Brake & Alignment Supply Corp. Inc. 2
Bresler's 33 Flavors, Inc. 42
Browns Chicken 48
Bruck Distributing Co., Inc. 76
Bryant Bureau 30
Bubble-Up Company 98
Budget Rent A Car Corporation 11
Budget Tapes & Records, Inc. 91
Buning The Florist, Inc. 91
Bun N Burger International, Inc. 48
Burger Chef Systems, Inc. 48
Burger Inns 48
Burger King Corporation 48
Burger Queen Enterprises, Inc. 49
Burger Train Systems, Inc. 49
Business Brokerage Group 14
Business Consultants of America 14
Business Data Services, Inc. 14
Business Exchange, Inc. 14
Business & Professional Consultants, Inc. 30
Butler Learning Systems 27
Byte Industries, Inc. 91

C

California Pools, Inc. 98
Candle-Lite Inc. 91
Captain D's 49
Captran Franchise Corp. 88
Car Doctor Int'l. Marketing, Inc. 2
Career Concepts, Inc. 30
Car-Matic Systems, Inc. 2
Carmen's Inc. 105
Carpet Color Systems 72
Carpeteria, Inc. 72
Carpet-Genie Systems, Inc. 72
Carter's Nuts, Inc. 42

113

INDEX OF FRANCHISING COMPANIES, "Alphabetical"

Carvel Corporation 42
Car-X Service Systems, Inc. 2
Cascade Industries, Inc. 98
Casey Jones Junction, Inc. 49
Cassano's Inc. 49
Castro Convertibles 72
Cathedralite Domes 104
Century 21 Real Estate Corporation 84
Chance Manufacturing Co., Inc. 88
Charlie Chan Restaurants 49
Cheese Shop International, Inc. 37
Chelsea Street Pub 49
Cheman Manufacturing Corp. 77
Chem-Clean Furniture Restoration Center 72
Chem-Dry Carpet Cleaning 72
Chemical Engineering Corporation 99
Chemical Franchising Corporation 77
Chem-Mark International 77
Chem-Tex Hot Tank Products Corporation 101
Chicasea, Inc. 49
Chicken Champ 50
Chicken Delight 50
Chicken Mary's System, Inc. 50
Chicken Unlimited Family Restaurant 50
Child Enrichment Centers 27
Chipper Cookies Shops, Inc. 37
Chip's Hamburgers 50
Christine Valmy, Inc. 25
Chrome Concepts Inc. 72
Chuck Connors Chuck Wagon Division 50
Cindy's, Inc. 50
The Circle K Corporation 38
Circles International Natural Foods, Inc. 50
Clark's Submarine Sandwiches, Inc. 51
Cleanmark Corporation 72
Coachlight Inns 79
Coast to Coast Stores 68
Cock 'N Bull, Limited 98
The Coffee Merchant 42
Coffee, Tea & Thee, Inc. 104
Coit Drapery & Carpet Cleaners, Inc. 76
Colonel Lee's Enterprises, Inc. 51
Color Me Beautiful Cosmetics 25
Command Performance Systems 12
Commercial Mobile Services, Inc. 101
Commercial Services Company 14
Compacts Only Rent A Car System, Inc. 11
Comprehensive Accounting Services Corporation 14
Comprehensive Business Service Corporation 14
Computerland Corp. 91
Computer Servicecenters, Inc. 15
Conroy's, Inc. 91
Consumer Products of America, Inc. 92
Contacts Influential 15
Convenient Food Mart, Inc. 38
Cook Machinery Company (Country Clean Laundry) 76
Cook Machinery Company (Sofspar Car Wash) 2
Cookie Factory of America 38
Cookshack 51
Corner Pockets of America, Inc. 88
Corporate Finance Association 15
COTT Corporation 98
Cottman Transmission Systems, Inc. 2
Counterforce Protection System, Inc. 97
Country Breadboard, Inc. 51
Country Kitchen International, Inc. 51
Country Style Donuts, Inc. 36
Court Management Company, Inc. 88
Cozzoli's Restaurant Pizzeria 51
Creative Prospects, Inc. 15
Credit Service Company 15
Critical Factor Systems Company, Inc. 15
Crossland Furniture Restoration Studios 73
Culligan International Company 100

D

Dad's Root Beer Company 98
Dairy Cheer Stores 51
Dairy Isle Corporation 42
Dairy King Distributors 51
Dairy Sweet Company 51
Danbi's Inc. 51
Danver's International, Inc. 52
Davis Caves, Inc. 23
Davis Paint Company 81
Days Inns of America, Inc. 79
Decorating Den Systems, Inc. 73
Delhi Chemicals, Inc. 73
Delk Transmission Franchise, Inc. 2
Delta Group, Inc. 30
Der Wienerschnitzel International, Inc. 52
Detroit II Auto Dealerships 104
Detroit II Auto Service Centers 104
Diamond Quality Transmissions Centers of America, Inc. 2
Dicker Stack-Sack International 23
Dictograph Security Systems 97
Diet Control Centers, Inc. 69
Dino's Pizza 52
Dip 'N Strip, Inc. 73
Disco Factory 88
Diversified Arts 102
Dixon Commercial Investigators, Inc. 15
Dockter Pet Centers, Inc. 81
Dog N Suds Restaurants 52
J. P. Dolan Associates & Company 15
Dollar Rent A Car Systems, Inc. 11
Domino's Pizza, Inc. 52
Donutland, Inc. 36
Dootson Driving Schools 27
Double-Cola Company 98
Double Dee Restaurants, Inc. 52
The Downtowner/Rowntowner-Passport System 80
Dri-Cal's Ultra Carpet Care Service, Inc. 73
Drive Line Service, Inc. 2
Dr. Nick's Transmissions 3
Dr. Personnel System, Inc. 30
Drummer Boy Fried Chicken 52
Dunhill Personnel System, Inc. 30
Dunkin Donuts of America, Inc. 36
Duraclean International 73
Duradek Permanent Sundecks 23
Dutch Girl Continental Cleaners 76

E

Earl Keim Realty, Inc. 84
Easi-Set Industries 23
East Coast Radiator Franchises, Inc. 3
Econo-Car International, Inc. 11
Econo Lube N'Tube, Inc. 3
EconoTax, Inc. 15
Econo-Travel Motor Hotel Corp. 80
Edgemar Farms 38
Elaine Powers Figure Salons, Inc. 69
Eldorado Stone Corporation 23
Electronic Realty Associates, Inc. 84
The Electronics Boutique 92
Ells Personnel Systems, Inc. 31
El Taco Restaurants, Inc. 52
Embassy Rental Agency 84
Employers Overload Company 31
Empress Travel Franchise Corp. 88
Endrust 3
The Energy Shed, Inc. 92
Engineering Corporation of America 31
E.P.I., Inc. 3
The Epicurean Dinner Club 15
Ernie's Wine & Liquor Corp. 42
Eurobake Cie, Inc. 38
Evelyn Wood Reading Dynamics 27
Execu-Systems 84

INDEX OF FRANCHISING COMPANIES, "Alphabetical"

F

Family Inns of America, Inc.	80
Famous Recipe Fried Chicken, Inc.	52
Farrell's Ice Cream Parlours Restaurant	53
Fashion Two Twenty, Inc.	25
Fast Foods, Inc.	53
Fat Boy's Franchise Systems, Inc.	53
Fat Fighters, Inc.	69
Faux Pas, Inc.	92
50 States Real Estate, Inc.	84
The Firestone Tire & Rubber Company	3
5 Minute Oil Change, Inc.	3
Flapjack Canyon	44
Fleet Feet	21
Flowerama of America, Inc.	92
Flower World of America, Inc.	92
Flying Fur Pet Travel Service	81
Ford Gum & Machine Co., Inc.	99
For Goodness Sake Franchise	38
Formal Wear Service	21
F-O-R-T-U-N-E Franchise Corporation	31
Forty Carrots, Inc.	53
Forty Love Tennis Shoppe, Inc.	21
Fosters Freeze, Inc.	53
Frame and Save	92
Frameking Corporation	92
Franciscan West Industries	53
Frank's Muffler Shops	3
Frostop Corporation	53
Fugazy Travel Franchises, Ltd.	88
Funny Fun Fun Golf	89
Fun Services, Inc.	89

Hair Performers	12
Hamburgers By Gourmet Licensing Corp.	54
Handy Hardware Centers, Inc.	93
Happy Inns of America, Inc.	80
Happy Joe's Pizza & Ice Cream Parlors	54
The Happy Steak, Inc.	55
Harbor House, Inc.	55
Hardee's Food System, Inc.	55
Harper Associates, Inc.	31
Hartman Temporary Personnel	31
Hartz Krispy Chicken	55
Hazel & Jarvis	32
The Headquarters Companies	104
Health Clubs of America	69
Heel 'N Toe, Inc.	21
Helpmates Nursing Services, Inc.	69
Help-U-Sell, Inc.	85
Herbert Hawkins Realtors, Inc.	85
Hercules Car/Truck Rustproofing	4
Heritage Personnel Systems, Inc.	32
Heroes World Centers, Inc.	93
Hertz Systems, Inc.	11
Hickory Farms of Ohio, Inc.	39
H. L. H. Enterprises, Inc.	45
Holiday Inns, Inc.	80
Holiday Rent-A-Car System	11
Home Sellers Center, Inc.	85
The Home Team, Inc.	85
HomeTels of America, Inc.	80
Honor Guard Security Service	97
Housemaster of America, Inc.	16
Howard Johnson Company	55
Howard Johnson's Motor Lodge	80
Huddle House, Inc.	55
Hungry Boy Delicatessen, Inc.	39
Hungry Hero Systems	55
The Hush Puppy Corporation	55

G

G. Fried Carpetland, Incorporated	73
Gallery of Homes, Incorporated	85
Gallery of Miniatures, Inc.	92
Gamble-Skogmo, Inc.	68
Gaston's, Inc.	104
General Business Services, Inc.	16
General Energy Devices, Inc.	23
General Franchising Corporation	44
General Rust Proofing Inc.	4
George Webb Corporation	53
Getting To Know You International, Ltd.	16
Gerotoga Industries, Inc.	31
Gibraltar Transmissions	4
Gilbert Lane Personnel Service	31
Gingiss International, Inc.	21
The Glass Oven Baking Company, Inc.	38
Gloria Stevens Franchise Division	69
Go-Kart Track Systems	89
Golden Chicken Franchises	53
Golden Skillet Corporation	54
Golf Players, Inc.	89
The Goode Taste Crepe Shoppes, Inc.	54
B. F. Goodrich Tire Company	4
The Goodyear Tire & Rubber Company	4
Government Employees Real Estate of America, Inc.	85
Grandma Lee's International Holdings Limited	54
The Grate Fireplace Shoppe	92
Grease Lighting, Inc.	4
Grease Monkey International, Inc.	4
Great Bear Automotive Centers, Inc.	4
Great Expectations Precision Haircutters	12
The Great Frame Up Systems, Inc.	93
Greek's Pizzeria, Inc.	54
Greiners Subhops, Inc.	54
Grizzly Bear, Inc.	54
Grove Foods, Inc.	39
Guarantee Carpet Cleaning & Dye Co.	73

I

i Natural Cosmetics	25
Image Improvement	27
Imperial Hammer, Inc.	99
IncoTax Systems, Inc.	16
Instant Replay, Inc.	93
Insta Tune, Inc.	4
Institute of Reading Development	27
Insty-Prints, Inc.	82
Intercontinental Coffee Service, Inc.	42
International Blimpie Corporation	55
International Char Broiler, Inc.	55
International Dairy Queen, Inc.	56
International House of Pancakes	45
International Real Estate Network, Inc.	85
International Travel Training Courses, Inc.	27
Interstate Automatic Transmissions, Co., Inc.	4
ISCO Ltd.	39
Italian U-Boat, Inc.	56
Italo's Pizza Shop, Inc.	56

H

Habersham Plantation Corp.	93

J

"Jack The Stripper"	74
Jake's International, Inc.	56
Japanese Steak Houses, Inc.	56
Jellystone Campgrounds, Ltd.	20
Jerry's Restaurants	56
Jiffiwash, Inc.	5
Jiffy Joints, Inc.	56
Jiffy Lube International, Inc.	5
Jiffy Shoppes	56
Jilene, Inc.	21
Jitney-Jungle, Inc.	39
John Robert Powers Finishing & Modeling School	28

INDEX OF FRANCHISING COMPANIES, "Alphabetical"

John Simmons, Inc. 74
Jreck Subs, Inc. 57
Judith Sans International Inc. 26
Judy's Foods, Inc. 57
Just Pants 21

K

Kamp Dakota, Inc. 20
Kampgrounds of America, Inc. 20
Karmelkorn Shoppes, Inc. 42
Kenneth of London, Ltd. 12
Kenny's Franchise Corp. 57
Ken's Pizza Parlors, Inc. 57
Key Korner Systems, Inc. 102
KFC Corporation 57
Kinetic Energy Manufacturing Company 5
King Bear Enterprises, Inc. 5
Kits Cameras Inc. 93
K-Krete, Inc. 23
Knapp Shoe Co. 22
Kogen Personnel, Inc. 32
Kwick-Kopy Corporation 82

L

Labor World, Inc. 105
Lady Burd Exclusive Cosmetics, Inc. 26
Lady Madonna Management Corp. 22
Lafayette Electronics Sales, Inc. 93
La Fleur Pool Systems, Inc. 98
Land Mart of America, Inc. 85
LaRosa's Inc. 57
Lavastone International, Inc. 23
Lawn-A-Mat Chemical and Equipment Corporation ... 76
Lawn Doctor Incorporated 76
Lawn King, Inc. 76
Lawn Medic, Inc. 77
Lean Line, Inc. 70
Lee Myles Associates Corporation 5
Lee's Bars, Stools 'N Dinettes 74
Leisure Learning Centers, Inc. 28
Lelly's Drive In Photos, Inc. 93
Le$-On Retail Systems, Inc. 26
Lifetime Pools, Inc. 99
LiL' Duffer of America, Inc. 57
Li'L Shopper, Inc. 39
Liqui-Green Lawn Care Corporation 77
Little Big Men, Inc. 57
Little Caesar Enterprises, Inc. 57
Littlefield's Restaurant Corp. 57
The Little King 58
Little Professor Book Centers, Inc. 94
Litva Corp. 39
Lomma Enterprises, Inc. 89
London Equipment Company 76
London Fish n' Chips, Ltd. 58
Lone Star Candy Mfg. Co. of Texas, Inc. 42
Long John Silver's Inc. 58
Lordburger Systems, Inc. 58
Losurdo Foods, Inc. 58
Love's Wood Pit Barbeque Restaurants 58
LST Travel, Inc. 89
Lum's Restaurant Corporation 58
Lynn Stevens, Inc. 70

M

MAACO Enterprises, Inc. 5

MacClean's, Inc. 5
Machinery Wholesalers Corp. 102
MacLevy Products Corporation 70
Mac Tools, Inc. 99
Mad Hatter Mufflers of Florida, Inc. 5
Magic Mirror, Inc. 12
Maid Rite Products, Inc. 58
Main Street Original Ice Cream Parlors 43
Maintenance King 74
Malco Products, Inc. 6
Mamacita's International, Inc. 58
Management Institute 28
Management Recruiters International, Inc. 32
Management Search, Inc. 32
Manpower, Inc. 32
Marble-Crete Products, Inc. 23
Marble-Flow Industries, Inc. 23
Marcoin, Inc. 16
Marsetta Lane Temp-Services 32
Martin Franchises Inc. 76
Martin's Franchising Systems, Inc. 59
Mary Belle Restaurants 45
Mary Moppets Day Care School, Inc. 28
Masonry Systems International, Inc. 24
Master Kleen 105
Masters' Driving Academy, Inc. 28
McDonald's Corporation 59
Mechanical Man Car Wash Factory, Inc. 6
Medicine Shops International, Inc. 26
Medi-Fax, Inc. 16
Medipower 70
Meineke Discount Muffler Shops, Inc. 6
Meistergram 102
Metro Sandwich Shops of America, Inc. 59
Midas International Corp. 6
Midwest Industries, Inc. 94
Mill-Craft Housing Corporation 24
Mind Power, Inc. 28
Minit-Lube 6
Minute Man of America, Inc. 59
Minuteman Press International, Inc. 28
Miracle Auto Painting 6
Miss American Teen-Ager, Inc. 89
Miss Bojangles, Inc. 94
Mister Clark's 94
Mister Donut of America, Inc. 37
Mister S'Getti Restaurant 59
Mister Softee, Inc. 43
Mode O'Day Company 22
Modern Bridal Shoppes, Inc. 22
Mom 'N' Pop's Ham House, Inc. 59
Mom's Development Corporation 43
Mom's Pizza, Inc. 59
Montgomery Ward 68
Mountain Valley Spring Company 98
Mr. Dunderbak International, Inc. 39
Mr. Gatti's, Inc. 59
Mr. Hero Sandwich Systems, Inc. 60
Mr. Maintenance 78
Mr. Pizza, Inc. 60
Mr. Rooter Corporation 78
Mr. Steak, Inc. 60
Mr. Transmission, Inc. 6
Music Dynamics 28
Muzak Corporation 16
"My Apartment" International, Inc. 60
My Nails, Inc. 102
My Pie International, Inc. 60

N

NADW Marketing, Inc. 16
Nadeau Looms, Inc. 28
Nagcoglass 6
Naked Furniture, Inc. 74
Nathan's Famous, Inc. 60
National Automotive Services Associates 6
National Auto Service Centers, Inc. 7
National Car Rental System, Inc. 11
National Chemicals and Services, Inc. 78

INDEX OF FRANCHISING COMPANIES, "Alphabetical"

National Computerized Control, Inc. 17
National Diversified Brokers 17
National Fire Repair, Inc. 17
National Homeowners Service Association, Incorporated 17
National Housing Inspections 17
National Maintenance Contractors, Inc. 78
National Surface Cleaning Corporations 78
Nationwide Exterminating, Inc. 102
Nation-Wide General Rental Centers, Inc. 35
Nationwide Gourmets, Inc. 43
Nationwide Income Tax Service Company 17
Nelson's Photography Studios 94
Nettle Creek Industries, Inc. 74
Newcomers Service International, Inc. 17
New England Log Homes, Inc. 24
New Morning Natural Foods 39
New World Real-Estate, Inc. 85
Nickerson Farms Franchising Co. 60
Noble Roman's Inc. 60
Norrell Temporary Services Inc. 33
North American Carbide Corp. 102
NTW, Inc. 7
Nugget Restaurants Inc. 60
Nutri-System 70

O

Old Uncle Gaylord's, Inc. 43
The Olsten Corporation 33
The Onion Crock, Inc. 60
On Top Division (Seaman Nuclear Corp.) 18
Open Book Marketing Corp. 94
O.P.F.M. Corp. 40
Orange Julius of America 61
OTASCO 7
Our Weigh 70

P

Pacific Tastee Freez, Inc. 61
Pappy's Enterprises, Inc. 61
Parker Page Associates, Inc. 33
Parking Company of America 102
Partners Real Estate, Inc. 86
Parts, Inc. 7
Pasquale Food Company, Inc. 61
Patricia Stevens International, Inc. 28
Patsy's Pizza Franchise, Inc. 61
Paul W. Davis Systems, Inc. 24
Pauline's Sportswear, Inc. 22
Payless Car Rental System, Inc. 11
The Peanut Shack of America, Inc. 43
The Pearl Factory 94
The Peddler, Inc. 61
Pedigree Pet Centers 81
Pedro's Fine Mexican Foods, Inc. 61
Penn Jersey Auto Stores, Inc. 7
People Care Incorporated 70
Pepe's Incorporated 61
Perkins Cake & Steak Restaurants 45
Perma-Jack Co. 24
Perma-Shine Inc. 7
Perma-Stone Company 24
The Permentry Company 24
Personnel Pool of America, Inc. 33
Petland, Inc. 81
Pet Master, Inc. 81
The Pewter Mug 61
Pewter Pot Management Corporation of Massachusetts 61
Philly Mignon 62
Phone World International, Inc. 94
Photo Drive Thru, Inc. 95

Photo Plaza 95
Photoquick of America, Inc. 95
Pier 1 Imports, Inc. 95
Pietro's Pizza Parlors, Inc. 62
Pioneer Take Out Corporation 62
Pizza Inn, Inc. 62
Pizza Man "He Delivers" 62
Pizza Time Theatre, Inc. 62
Place Mart Franchising Corporation 33
Playboy Clubs International, Inc. 62
Polar Bear Ice Cream Co. 43
Polock Johnny's, Inc. 62
Poly-Oleum Corporation 7
Ponderosa System, Inc. 62
Popeyes Famous Fried Chicken 63
Pop-Ins, Inc. 78
Poraflor, Inc. 24
Porcelain Patch & Glaze Company of America 24
Porcelite International 24
Port-O-Let Company, Inc. 78
(PIP) Postal Instant Press 83
Pour Man Systems 24
Power Vac Incorporated 7
Power Wash, Inc. 8
Precision Transmission, Inc. 8
Precision Tune, Inc. 8
The Printing Place, Inc. 83
The Printing Supermart, Inc. 83
Printmasters, Inc. 83
Profit Power International 18
Pudgies Pizza Franchising Inc. 63
Putt-Putt Golf Courses of America, Inc. 89
Putt-R-Golf, Inc. 89

Q

Quality Care USA, Inc. 70
Quality Inns International, Inc. 80
Quick Shop Minit Marts, Inc. 40
Quik Print, Inc. 83
Quik Stop Markets, Inc. 40

R

Radio Shack 95
Rainsoft Water Conditioning Company 100
Ram, Inc., Realtors 86
Ramada Inns, Inc. 80
Rampart Industries, Inc. 97
Rapid Economical Construction Systems Corp. (R.E.C.S.) 25
Rasco Stores 69
Rayne Corporation 100
Rax Systems, Inc. 63
RCI, Inc. 71
Reaban's Inc. 63
R.E.A.D.S., Inc. 28
Real Estate One Licensing Company 86
Real Rich Corp. 43
Realty Company of America 86
Realty 1, Inc. 86
Realty USA/Interstate Referral Service Inc. 86
Realty World Corporation 86
Red Carpet Corporation of America 86
Red Carpet Inns of America, Inc. 80
Redd Pest Control Company, Inc. 102
Redi-Strip Co., Inc. 25
Reliable Business Systems, Inc. 18
Re/Max of America, Inc. 87
Remedy Temporary Services, Inc. 33
Retail Recruiters International, Inc. 33
RFG, Inc. 18

117

INDEX OF FRANCHISING COMPANIES, "Alphabetical"

The Ringgold Corporation 95
Ritta Personnel System of North America, Inc. 33
Riviera Convertibles, Inc. 74
Roast Beefery Restaurants International, Inc. 63
Robert Fiance System, Inc. 29
Rochemco 8
Rodeway Inns International 80
Roffler Industries, Inc. 12
Romac and Associates 33
Ron's Krispy Fried Chicken 63
Rosati Franchise Systems, Inc. 63
Roth Young Personnel Service, Inc. 34
Roto-Rooter Corporation 78
The Round Table Franchise Corporation 63
Royale Sporting Goods, Inc. 95
Roy Rogers Restaurants 64
Rug Crafters 74

S

S & D Inc., Photographic Inventory 105
Safari Campgrounds 20
Safeguard Business Systems 18
The Salad Bar Corporation 64
Salad Shoppe 64
Sales Consultants International 34
Sally Wallace Brides Shops, Inc. 22
Sandy Hook Scientific Inc. 18
Sandwich Giants, Inc. 64
Sanford Rose Associates, Inc. 34
San Juan Products, Inc. 99
SARCO Inc. 34
Schlotzsky's, Inc. 64
Scientific Water Systems, Inc. 100
Scotti Muffler Centers, Inc. 8
Scotto Pizza Management Corp. 64
Seakan Candy Company 43
Seasonall Automotive, Inc. 8
Security Pacific Real Estate, Inc. 87
Selectra-Data Corporation 102
Sermac 78
Service Center 8
ServiceMaster International, Ltd. 79
Servpro Industries, Inc. 79
Shakey's Incorporated 64
Sheraton Inns, Inc. 81
Shirt Tails, Inc. 22
Showertel Systems Corp., Inc. 35
S-H-S International 34
Siesta Sleep Shops, Inc. 75
Simplified Business Services, Inc. 18
Sir Beef Ltd., Inc. 64
Sir Pizza International, Inc. 64
Sir Speedy, Inc. 83
Sir Waxer, Incorporated 8
Sizzler Family Steak Houses 64
Skate Street, Inc. 95
Ski & Shore Properties, Inc. 87
Slo Poke, Inc. 89
Slumberland, Inc. 75
SMI, International, Inc. 18
S.M.R. Enterprises, Inc. 12
Snap-On-Tools Corporation 99
Sneaky Sweets International, Inc. 40
Snelling and Snelling, Inc. 34
Sound West 95
Southern Main Donut Flour Company, Inc. 37
The Southland Corporation 40
Southwest Promotional Corporation 18
SPA Development Corporation 71
Space Age Fitness Centers 71
Sparkle Wash, Inc. 79
Speed Fab-Crete Corporation International 25
Speedi-Lube 8
Speed Queen Coin Operated Laundromat and Dry Cleaner, Inc. 76
Speedy Printing Centers, Inc. 83
Speedy Transmission Centers, Inc. 9
Speedy Wagon Sales Corporation 95
Sport About, Inc. 96
Sport Shacks, Inc. 96

Spring Crest Company 75
Spring-Green Lawn Care Corp. 77
Spudnuts, Inc. 37
Staff Builders International, Inc. 34
Staff Builders Medical Services 71
Stanley Steemer International, Inc. 75
State Farm Realty, Inc. 87
State Wide Real Estate 87
Steamatic Incorporated 75
The Sterling Thompson Group 87
Stewart Sandwiches International Inc. 40
Stewart's Drive-Ins 65
Stop A Flat - Chalfont Industries 9
The Straw Hat Restaurant Corporation 65
Stretch & Sew, Inc. 103
Strip-Tech, Inc. 75
Stuckey's Inc. 65
Subway 65
Sum-Tan Division 103
Sunburst International, Inc. 105
Sunnydale Franchise System 40
Sunrise Maintenance Systems 79
Suntique Tanning Salons 103
Super 8 Motels 81
Superior Water Conditioners 100
Superlawns, Inc. 77
Swensen's Ice Cream Company 44
Swift Company 44
Swiss Colony Stores, Inc. 40
Syd Simons Cosmetics, Inc. 26
Systemedics, Inc. 18

T

Taco Casa International, Inc. 65
Taco Del Sol 65
Taco Hut, Inc. 65
Taco John's 65
The Taco Maker, Inc. 66
Taco Place, Inc. 66
Taco Plaza, Inc. 66
Taco Tico, Inc. 66
Taco Time International, Inc. 66
Taco Villa 66
Tastee Donuts, Inc. 37
Tax Man, Inc. 19
Tax Offices of America 19
Taylor Rental Corporation 36
Team Central Incorporated 96
Telecake International 41
Telecheck Services, Inc. 19
Teller Training Institute, Inc. 29
Tel-Life Stations of America 19
Tempaco, Inc. 103
Temporaries, Incorporated 34
Temporarily Yours of America 35
Tepco, Inc. 103
Terminix International, Inc. 103
Terry's Interstate, Inc. 66
Texas Cattle Company 66
Texas Tom's Inc. 66
3% Realty, Inc. 87
Thrift-Way Auto Centers, Inc. 9
Thrifty Rent-A-Car System 11
Thrifty Scot Motels, Inc. 81
Tidy Car Inc. 9
Tiffany's Bakeries, Inc. 41
The Tinder Box International, Ltd. 96
Tippy's Taco House, Inc. 66
Topsy's Shoppes, Inc. 44
Tour Mates Organization, Ltd. 90
Travelodge International 81
Travel Network Corporation 90
Treadway Inns Corporation 81
Tropical Rent-A-Car 105
T-Shirts Plus, Inc. 96
Tuff-Kote Dinol, Inc. 9
Tuffy Service Centers, Inc. 9
Tune-Up Clinic, Inc. 9

118

INDEX OF FRANCHISING COMPANIES, "Alphabetical"

The Tune-Up Man, Inc. 9
Tunex, Inc. 10
TV Facts 19
T.V. Tempo, Inc. 19
2001 Clubs of America, Inc. 90
Typing Tigers 36

U

Ultrasonic Predictable Maintenance, Inc. 79
Ultra Tune, Inc. 10
Uncle John's Family Restaurants 45
Uniforce Temporary Personnel, Inc. 35
United Air Specialists, Inc. 103
United Consumers Club 96
United Rent-All, Inc. 36
United Security Associates Realty, Inc. 87
United Worth Hydrochem Corporation 103
Up Against the Wall 96
Up-Grade Educational Services, Inc. 29
The Upper Krust, Inc. 67
U.S. Fireworks of America, Inc. 103
U.S. Rooter Corporation 79

V

Valley Forge Products Company 10
Van's Belgian Crepes and Waffles, Inc. 45
Venus de Milo, Inc. of California 71
Video Concepts 96
Village Inn Pancake House, Inc. 45
VIP Personnel Systems, Corp. 35
VR Business Brokers, Inc. 19
Vulcan Tools 99

W

Waffle King of America, Inc. 45
Walt's Roast Beef International 67
WaterCare Corporation 100
Water Purification Systems, Inc. 100
Water Refining Company 100
Weight Control Institute 71
Wendy's Old Fashioned Hamburgers 67
Western Auto 10
Westgate Systems, Inc. 41
Whataburger, Inc. 67
Whirligig Stores Incorporatied 97
White Hen Pantry Division 41
Whitehill Systems, Inc. 20
Whites Home and Auto Stores 10
Wicks 'N' Sticks, Inc. 97
Wiener King Corporation 67
Wife Saver 67
Wild Tops Franchising, Inc. 22
Edwin K. Williams & Company 20
Winky's Family Restaurants 67
The Wood Factory Corporation 75
Woody's Little Italy Restaurants 67
World of Laminating 97
The World's Wurst Restaurants 67
Wrangler Wranch Franchising Systems, Inc. 22
WUV's International, Inc. 67

X

Xpert Tune Franchise Group, Inc. 10

Y

Yankee Doodle Dandy 68
Yogi Bear's Mini Golf and Snack Shoppe 90
Your Pizza Shops, Inc. 68

Z

Zack's Famous Frozen Yogurt 44
Zantiago Mexican-American Restaurants 68
Zell-Aire Corporation 25
Ziebart Rustproofing Company 10
Zip'z 44

The Franchise Handbook dmr